CHURCHILL AND HITLER

CHURCHILL

AND

HITLER

In Victory and Defeat

John Strawson

Constable · London

First published in Great Britain 1997
by Constable and Company Ltd
3 The Lanchesters, 162 Fulham Palace Road
London W6 9ER
Copyright © 1997 John Strawson
The right of John Strawson to be identified
as the author of this work has been asserted
by him in accordance with the Copyright,
Designs and Patents Act, 1988
ISBN 0 09 475840 9
Set in Monophoto Garamond 11½pt by
Servis Filmsetting Ltd, Manchester
Printed in Great Britain by
St Edmundsbury Press Ltd
Bury St Edmunds, Suffolk

A CIP catalogue record for this book
is available from the British Library

Contents

Illustrations

Preface and Acknowledgements

The second time I met Winston Churchill was in Italy in August 1944. The Prime Minister had managed to squeeze in among his many other duties a visit to his old regiment, the 4th Hussars, then bivouacked not far from Ancona and about to move north to take part in the Gothic Line battles. I, as a troop leader, was one of those on parade to welcome the most illustrious Colonel that the regiment has ever had. We were paraded with our tanks on a huge grass airfield and shortly after Mr Churchill's aircraft had landed, and he, together with the Commander-in-Chief in Italy, Field Marshal Sir Harold Alexander, had been greeted by our commanding officer, a bizarre occurrence interrupted, although only temporarily, the planned programme. Despite efforts to guide him to the saluting base by another route, the great man, dressed as Colonel, 4th Hussars, stepped out purposefully in a direct line from the aircraft towards the position where the regiment was paraded, only to be confronted soon afterwards by an anti-tank ditch, part of the airfield's defences. Nothing daunted, he plunged down into it to the obvious distaste of Field Marshal Alexander, who was, as always, elegantly attired. Nevertheless Alexander, our Commanding Officer and various aides-de-camp followed. It was just as well, for when the Prime Minister attempted to climb *out* of the anti-tank ditch, he found it beyond his powers and only combined heaving at his not inconsiderable posterior by the Commander-in-Chief and other lesser military mortals succeeded in extricating him. The inspection and parade then proceeded, and were brought to a close by Churchill's indicating that all ranks should close round him while he stood on a jeep to address us. There followed one of those fine extempore declarations about the state of the game, which ended with an expression of his pride that his old regiment would shortly be giving the Hun another knock. Finally, he had tea with us in a tent, during which all the officers were presented to him.

I should perhaps add that I had met him for the first time in Egypt in 1943, while Churchill was attending the Cairo Conference. On this occasion, too, he was inspecting his old regiment, again dressed as our Colonel, and found everything to his satisfaction (especially as one of our tanks was named *Churchill* and as it passed the saluting base, he gave not a conventional salute but the V-sign) – except that we were not yet wearing the ribbon of the Africa Star, which had been authorized months before. A few words were spoken and that evening a team of Egyptian seamstresses arrived at our camp to sew the ribbon on to our battledress tunics. I recall too that at subsequent 4th Hussars dinners in London after the war, which Churchill frequently attended, he would some-times seem to be a little grumpy at the start of the evening, but after a few glasses of champagne, would brighten considerably, and by the end would be in glowing form. How honoured we were! How greatly we loved it all, and him!

The number of books about Churchill and about Hitler is so great that to be guilty of adding to it must call for some explanation. All I can offer here is that – having had the good fortune to serve in Churchill's regiment, the 4th Queen's Own Hussars; to have been presented to him both in the field during the war and at regimental affairs after it; to have commanded his regiment (by then amalgamated with the 8th King's Royal Irish Hussars to form the Queen's Royal Irish Hussars); like Churchill himself, to have had the honour of serving as Colonel of the Regiment; and to have had a part to play at Churchill's funeral – I have often felt that I would like to do so. It is clear that even if Churchill had never become Prime Minister, he would still have gone down as one of this country's great men, one who made world history. That he did become Prime Minister to inspire and lead the nation in its finest hour was, of course, brought about by the machinations of Hitler, so that Churchill's story cannot ade-quately be told without also dwelling on that of Hitler.

In spite of there being an imbalance in their two careers, for Churchill was a world-famous figure before Hitler had been heard of, it seemed possible to examine their lives together, for each of them affected the other so pro-foundly. I am grateful therefore to Constable & Company for the opportunity to do so. This opportunity produced a special dividend for me, as it was neces-sary carefully to study the majestic and monumental biography of Winston Churchill, begun by his son, Randolph, and then completed – the bulk of it written – by Sir Martin Gilbert. As I did so, it became clear that although I thought I already knew a lot about Churchill's life and achievements, the more I read, the more I learned and the more I admired him. I am most grateful to Sir Martin Gilbert, for permission to quote from his books (see page xii), on which I have frequently drawn both for facts in the narrative and for the sayings, letters and papers of the numerous characters portrayed. Apart from this official biography, there are, of course, many other works, which it was both a duty and a pleasure to examine – among them the recollections of men like Sir John Colville and Anthony Montague Browne, who served Churchill so loyally and well; and not overlooking revisionist works, such as those by John Charmley and Andrew Roberts. Of all books *about* Churchill, the one I still turn to with the greatest sympathy, although it is probably the shortest, is Sir Isaiah Berlin's portrait of *Mr Churchill in 1940*. Above all, perhaps, in content, range, language and sheer capacity are the books of which Churchill was himself the author; notably *The Second World War*, but not overlooking *The River War*, *My Early Life*, *The World Crisis*, and *Great Contemporaries*. There are in the text some references to Sir Michael Howard's views on both the Mediterranean and overall strategy favoured by Churchill, and these references are taken from his *The Mediterranean Strategy in the Second World War*; similarly the opinions of A.J.P. Taylor are from his *English History 1914–1945*; those of Lord Bullock from *Hitler: A Study in Tyranny*; and those of H.R. Trevor-Roper (Lord Dacre of Glanton) from *The Last Days of Hitler*. The author and publisher are most grateful for permission to quote from these works. No study of Hitler can be made, of course, without reference to *Mein Kampf* and *Hitler's War Directives*.

I have drawn on many other works in this presentation of Churchill and Hitler (the reader will find them listed in the Bibliography), and of these I owe a particular debt to: Sir Arthur Bryant's *The Lion and the Unicorn*; Alan Clark's *Barbarossa* and *The Donkeys*; John Charmley's *Churchill: The End of Glory*; Sir Robert Ensor's *England 1870–1914*; David Fraser's *Alanbrooke*; Heinz Guderian's *Panzer Leader*; David Irving's *Hitler's War*; John Keegan's *The Battle for History* and *The Face of Battle*, as well as his 'Churchill's Strategy' (the latter essay appears in *Churchill*, edited by Robert Blake and Wm Roger Louis); Fred Majdalany's *Cassino: Portrait of a Battle*; James (Jan) Morris's *Farewell the Trumpets*; Harold Nicolson's *Diaries and Letters* (three volumes edited by Nigel Nicolson); Albert Speer's *Inside the Third Reich*; Chester Wilmot's *The Struggle for Europe*.

I wish to thank my wife for her invaluable assistance in the preparation and production of this book. I am indebted to Richard Lamb for drawing my attention to, and indeed lending me, a book by Reinhard Spitzy, *So haben wir das Reich verspielt*, in which Spitzy describes his life as a member of the German Diplomatic Corps and, later, the Intelligence Service, during which he had many encounters with Hitler. I am also most grateful to Mr Toby Buchan for his invaluable advice and assistance in editing the text.

I have made some use of passages from previous works of mine, where the events described coincided with those in this book, and for permission to do so I am grateful to B.T. Batsford Ltd (*The Battle for North Africa*; *Hitler as Military Commander*; *The Battle of the Ardennes*; *The Battle for Berlin*) and Secker & Warburg (Reed Books) (*The Italian Campaign*; *Gentlemen in Khaki*). I would like to thank the photocopying staff of Coates & Parker, Warminster, for their cheerful and courteous help in making copies of my typescript.

Extracts from Winston S. Churchill's letters, speeches and articles reproduced with permission of Curtis Brown Group Ltd on behalf of the Estate of Sir Winston S. Churchill. Copyright Winston S. Churchill.

Extracts from the official biography of Sir Winston S. Churchill by Randolph S. Churchill and Sir Martin Gilbert reproduced with permission of Curtis Brown Group Ltd on behalf of C&T Publications Ltd. Copyright © C&T Publications Ltd.

Dramatis Personae

Aitken, *see* **Beaverbrook**

Alexander, General (Field Marshal) the Hon. Sir Harold (Rupert Leofric George), 1st Earl Alexander of Tunis (1891–1969). Distinguished himself at Dunkirk, May 1940; GOC Burma, directing skilful evacuation of British, Commonwealth and Imperial; succeeded Auchinleck as C-in-C, Middle East, August 1942. Deputy C-in-C of all Allied ground forces in Africa, February 1943; succeeded Eisenhower as Supreme Allied Commander, Mediterranean Theatre, 1944; promoted field marshal, November 1944; commanded Allied offensive in Italy; Governor-General of Canada, 1946–52; Defence Minister, 1952–4.

Allenby, General (Field Marshal) Sir Edmund (Henry Hynman), 1st Viscount Allenby of Megiddo (1861–1936). Commanded 1st Cavalry Division, then Third Army, on Western Front, 1915–17. C-in-C Egyptian Expeditionary Force, 1917–18; entered Jerusalem, 1917. Routed Turks at Megiddo, September 1918, captured Damascus and Aleppo, October. High Commissioner to Egypt, 1919–25.

Amery, Leo (Leopold Charles Maurice Stennett) (1873–1955). Correspondent during South African War; Conservative MP 1911–45; First Lord of the Admiralty, 1922–4; Colonial Secretary, 1924–9; Colonial and Dominions Secretary, 1925–9; Secretary of State for India, 1940–5; wrote a number of books. Friend and champion of WSC. His eldest son, John, recruited by Nazis in 1940, hanged for treason, 1945.

Anderson, Sir John (later 1st Viscount Waverley) (1882–1958). Independent Nationalist MP, 1938–50; Lord Privy Seal, 1938; Home Secretary and Minister of Home Security, 1939 (Anderson air-raid shelter, designed for people's homes, named after him); Lord President of the Council, 1940–3; Chancellor of the Exchequer, 1943–5; Chairman, Atomic Energy Advisory Committee, 1945–8.

Arnim, General Jürgen, Baron von (1891–1971). Served in Great War, then became a tank specialist. Commanded a panzer division in Barbarossa, then Fifth Panzer Army in Tunisia, 1943, succeeding Rommel as C-in-C Africa. Surrendered Axis forces in Tunisia to Allies, May 1943; interned for rest of war in Britain, then USA.

Arnold-Forster, Hugh (Oakeley) (1855–1909). Unionist MP for West Belfast, 1892–1906, and Croydon, 1906–9; Secretary to the Admiralty, 1901; Secretary of State for War, 1903–5; advocate of reforms to the army and War Office; wrote a number of books.

Asquith, Herbert Henry, 1st Earl of Oxford and Asquith (1852–1928). Liberal MP 1886–1916; Home Secretary/ 1892–5; Chancellor of the Exchequer, 1905–8; Prime Minister 1906–16. Took Britain into war, 1914; his Liberal government brought to an end, 1915, after which he led Coalition government; criticized for conduct of war and for urging

Home Rule for Ireland; resigned, 1916, in favour of Lloyd George; resigned Liberal leadership, 1926.

Attlee, Clement (Richard), 1st Earl (1883–1967). Labour MP, 1922–50; Chancellor, Duchy of Lancaster, 1930; Postmaster-General, 1931; deputy leader, Labour Party, 1931–5; leader, 1935; Lord Privy Seal, 1940–2; deputy Prime Minister, 1942; Lord President of the Council, 1943; Prime Minister, 1945–51; retired as Labour leader, 1955.

Auchinleck, Field Marshal Sir Claude (John Eyre) (1884–1981). GOC-in-C, Northern Norway, 1940; C-in-C India, 1941; C-in-C Middle East, 1941–2; drove Rommel out of Egypt, November 1941– early 1942; his forces then driven back to El Alamein, with loss of Tobruk; took personal command of army and defeated Axis forces at 1st Battle of Alamein, July 1942; replaced by Alexander, August 1942; C-in-C India again, 1943–7; field marshal, 1946; Supreme Commander, Armed Forces of India and Pakistan during transitional period to inde- pendence, 1947; refused a peerage; retired to Morocco, 1967.

Badoglio, Marshal Pietro (1871–1956). Governor-General of Libya, 1928–33; conquered Abyssinia, 1935–6; C-in-C Italian Army, May 1940; resigned after Italian reverses in Albania, October 1940. When Mussolini ousted, July 1943, formed and headed non-Fascist govern- ment; negotiated armistice with Allies and declared war on Germany, 1943; resigned when unable to form govern- ment, 1944.

Baldwin, Stanley, 1st Earl Baldwin of Bewdley (1867–1947). Conservative MP, 1908–37; Chancellor of the Ex- chequer, 1922–3; Prime Minister 1923–4 and 1924–9; attacked by WSC and others for supporting Dominion status for India; Lord President of the Council in National government, 1931–5; Prime Minister, 1935–7; slow to admit the threat from Germany in the 1930s, but intro-

duced measure of rearmament from 1936; highly critical of appeasement; praised for handling of Abdication crisis, 1936; retired May 1937.

Balfour, Arthur James, 1st Earl of Balfour (1848–1930). Nephew of Lord Salisbury; Conservative MP 1874–85; 1885–1905; 1906–22; First Lord of the Treasury, 1891–2 and 1895–1902; Prime Minister, 1902–6, succeeding Salisbury; resigned as Conservative leader, 1911. First Lord of the Admiralty, 1915; Foreign Secretary, 1916–19; Lord Presi- dent of the Council, 1925–9. Responsi- ble, 1917, for Balfour Declaration, which gave British support for a Zionist home- land in Palestine provided rights of non- Jews there safeguarded, this formed basis for League of Nations mandate, 1920.

Baring, *see* **Cromer**

Beatty, David, 1st Earl (1871–1936). Naval Secretary to WSC during his first term as First Lord of the Admiralty, 1912–13; commanded Battle Cruiser Squadron of the Grand Fleet, 1913–16; won Heligoland Bight action, August 1914; won Battle of the Dogger Bank, January 1915; com- manded Battle Cruiser Squadron and 5th Battle Squadron at Jutland, 1916; C-in-C Grand Fleet, 1916–19; took surrender of German Imperial High Seas Fleet, November 1918; admiral of the fleet, 1919; First Sea Lord, 1919–27.

Beaverbrook, Sir Max (William Maxwell Aitken), 1st Baron (1879–1964). Canadian born; made fortune by age thirty; emigrated to Britain, 1910; Con- servative MP, 1910; Chancellor of Duchy of Lancaster, 1917; Minister of Infor- mation, 1918. Resigned offices, 1918, to build up newspaper empire; joined Churchill's War Cabinet, August 1940; Minister of Aircraft Production, 1940–1; Minister of Supply, 1941–2; led first Anglo-American mission to Moscow, 1941; head of British lend-lease admin- istration in USA, 1942; Lord Privy Seal, 1943–5. One of the closest, as well as one of the most influential, of WSC's friends.

Beck, General Ludwig (18??–1944). Chief of the Army General Staff, 1933; opposed Hitler's expansionist plans; resigned before Munich, August 1938; recalled as C-in-C First Army, September 1938; figurehead for German resistance to Hitler from 1938; chief military leader in anti-Hitler conspiracy; to have been head of state if coup had succeeded; captured, 20 July 1944, was allowed to commit suicide, but failed twice; finished off by a sergeant.

Bernadotte, Count Folke (1885–1948). Diplomat (and nephew of King Gustav V of Sweden); President of Swedish Red Cross; acted as a mediator in both world wars; conveyed Himmler's surrender offer to British and US Governments, April 1945. Appointed UN mediator in Palestine, 1948; assassinated by Zionist Stern Gang.

Bevin, Ernest (1881–1951). Trade unionist; built National Transport and General Workers' Union out of smaller organizations, and was its General Secretary; 1921–40. Chairman, TUC, 1936–7; Labour MP, 1940–51; Minister of Labour and National Service, 1936–7; within Labour Party opposed appeasement and championed rearmament; Foreign Secretary, 1945–51; Lord Privy Seal, 1951.

Blomberg, Field Marshal Werner von (1878–1943). By 1930 was second-in-command of German Army; that year removed from post by machinations of Schleicher. War Minister, 1933; C-in-C of Wehrmacht, 1935. Forced to resign, 1936 (although promoted field marshal that year, when he married a prostitute, Hitler claiming this brought officer corps into disrepute. In fact, Nazis used this as excuse to replace several senior officers with Führer's own nominees.

Blood, General Sir Bindon (1842–1940). Commanded Malakand and Buner Field Forces, 1896–8, in which he commended WSC; commanded in Eastern Transvaal, 1901; in Punjab, 1901–7; Chief Royal Engineer, 1936–40.

Blumentritt, General Günther (1892–1967). With Rundstedt and Manstein produced plan for conquest of Poland; Chief of Operations to Rundstedt in Polish (1939) and French (1940) campaigns; Chief of Staff, Fourth Army, in Russia, 1941; helped plan counter-invasion defences, France, 1942. Chief of Staff to Rundstedt, June 1944, then to Kluge on Rundstedt's dismissal; Chief of Staff to Rundstedt again on latter's appointment as C-in-C West, September 1944; his *Von Rundstedt: The Soldier and the Man* published in English, 1952.

Bock, Field Marshal Fedor von (1885–1945). Commanded German forces in Anschluss, 1938; commanded army group in German invasions of Poland (1939) and Low Countries and France (1940; field marshal, July 1940), and in Russia, 1941. Dismissed by Hitler after failure to take Moscow, 1941, then appointed to command army group in the Caucasus, 1942. Dismissed again, July 1942, after disagreements with Hitler; killed with wife and daughter in air raid.

Bonham Carter, Lady Violet (born Helen Violet *Asquith*), Baroness Asquith of Yarnbury (1887–1969). Only daughter of H. H. Asquith; close friend of WSC; President, Liberal Party, 1945–7; stood unsuccessfully for Parliament, 1945 and 1951. Published *Winston Churchill As I Knew Him*, 1965.

Bormann, Martin (1900–45). Early member of Nazi Party; took part in Munich Putsch, 1923. Deputy Party Leader, May 1941, on Hess's flight; Hitler's Personal Secretary, 1943, wielding enormous influence with Führer; promoted Reich Minister (Party Chancellor), 1945. Thought to have escaped Berlin; sentenced to death in his absence, Nuremberg, 1946. In 1972 a body uncovered during excavation work in Berlin formally recognized as his by forensic experts, although rumours that he survived persist.

Brabazon of Tara, 1st Baron (John Theodore Cuthbert *Moore-Brabazon*)

(1884–1964). First Englishman to pilot a powered aircraft, 1909; Conservative MP, 1918–29, 1931–42; PPS to WSC, 1919, when latter Minister for War and Air; Minister of Transport, 1940, Minister of Aircraft Production, 1941–2.

Bracken, Brendan Rendall, Viscount Bracken (1901–58). Irish born; arrived in England from Australia, 1919; admirer, and became a friend, of WSC; founded *Banker* and acquired *Financial News* and *Investor's Chronicle*, among other journals; joint owner of *The Economist*, 1929; Conservative MP, 1929–45 and 1945–51; PPS to WSC, 1939–41; Minister of Information, 1941–5; First Lord of the Admiralty, 1945; Chairman, *Financial Times*.

Bradley, General (General of the Army) Omar (Nelson) (1893–1981) Commanded US II Corps in Tunisia and invasion of Sicily, then US ground forces in invasion of Normandy, June 1944; after breakout advanced rapidly into heart of France. Took command of US Twelfth Army Group, August 1944; crossed Rhine, March 1945; linked up with Red Army on Elbe, 25 April 1945; his successes, like Patton's, marred by disagreements with British, especially Montgomery. General of the Army, 1950; memoirs, *A Soldier's Life* and *General's Life*, published 1951, 1983.

Brauchitsch, Field Marshal (Heinrich Alfred Hermann) Walther von (1881–1948). C-in-C of German Army and member of Hitler's secret 'inner cabinet', 1938; directed invasions of Poland, 1939, and Norway, Denmark, Low Countries and France, 1940; field marshal, July 1940; opposed Barbarossa, but directed initial operations, June-December 1941; resigned after heart attack and failure to take Moscow, December 1941; succeeded as Army C-in-C by Hitler; sent for trial at Nuremberg; died in prison before case heard.

Braun, Eva (1910–45). Became Hitler's mistress probably *c.* 1933; he kept her in background, mostly at Berghof. Determined to share his fate, arrived Berlin, 15 April 1945; married Hitler in Führerbunker, 29 April; on following day committed suicide with him, she by poison. Her body, like his, burned in Chancellery garden.

Brodrick, (William) St John (Fremantle), 9th Viscount Midleton and 1st Earl of Midleton (1856–1942). Conservative MP, 1880–5, 1885–1906; Secretary of State for War, 1900–3, and for India, 1903–5; leader of Unionists in Southern Ireland; helped to negotiate truce between Irish republicans and British, 1921.

Brooke, Field Marshal Sir Alan Francis, 1st Viscount Alanbrooke (1883–1963). Commanded II Corps in France, 1939–40, and distinguished himself in Dunkirk evacuation; CIGS, 1941–6; Chairman, Chiefs of Staff Committee, 1941–5; field marshal, 1944. Friend, comforter and adviser to – and occasional target of – WSC, as well as one of the few who could dampen or divert some of his wilder flights of strategic fancy. With WSC, was to a considerable extent responsible for strategy that eventually defeated Hitler. His controversial wartime diaries (*The Turn of the Tide*, 1957; *Triumph in the West*, 1959) offended WSC, who never forgave him.

Brüning, Heinrich (1885–1970). Elected to Reichstag, 1924, became leader of Catholic Centre Party. Chancellor, 1930, but forced to govern by presidential decree. Ousted, 1932, under Nazi pressure exacerbated by economic and social crisis. Fled Germany, 1934; Professor of Government, Harvard, 1339–52; Professor of Political Science, Cologne, 1951–5. The last determined political opponent of Nazism in the Weimar Republic.

Buller, General Sir Redvers (Henry), VC (1839–1908). Saw action Canada, 1870, West Africa, 1873, three wars in South Africa (1878–9 [VC, 1879]; 1879; 1881), and Egypt and the Sudan (1882–5); GOC Army Corps, South Africa, 1899; defeated at Colenso, December 1899; and Spion Kop, January 1900; after other reverses eventually relieved Ladysmith; severely criticized in Britain; replaced in overall command by Lord Roberts; cleared Natal of enemy forces, winning decisive victory at Bergendal, August 1900. Returned to England, 1901; after further criticism and a row with Roberts was dismissed in October.

Cadogan, Sir Alexander (George Montagu) (1884–1968). Permanent Under-Secretary, Foreign Office, 1938–46; British delegate to the UN, 1946–50; Chairman, BBC, 1952–7. His diaries from 1938–45 published 1971.

Campbell-Bannerman, Sir Henry (1836–1908). Liberal MP, 1868–1908; Secretary for War, 1886 and 1892–5; leader of Liberal Party in House of Commons, 1899; Prime Minister (the first ever officially to hold that title), December 1905; resigned due to ill health, April 1908; died within weeks.

Canaris, Admiral Wilhelm (1887–1945). Joined Imperial German Navy, 1905; commanded U-boats during Great War; became intelligence expert; retired from navy, 1934. Promoted admiral and appointed by Hitler to head Abwehr. Implicated, probably unjustly, in July 1944 plot; sent to Flossenburg concentration camp and hanged there, April 1944.

Carson, Sir Edward (Henry), Baron Carson (1854–1935). Barrister; Unionist MP for Dublin University, 1892–1918; defended Lord Queensberry in libel action brought by Oscar Wilde, 1895; Solicitor-General for England, 1900–5; leader of Irish Unionists in House of Commons, 1910; led movement for a separate government in Ulster, 1911; established private army, Ulster Volunteers, to resist Home Rule, 1912; Attorney-General, 1915–16; First Lord of the Admiralty, 1916–1917; member of

War Cabinet, 1917–18; resigned over intention to apply Home Rule Bill to all Ireland; MP for Belfast constituency, 1918–21; resigned as leader of Ulster Unionists when appointed a Lord of Appeal in Ordinary, 1921–9.

Casey, Richard Gardiner, Baron Casey (1890–1976). Served with ANZAC during Great War (DSO, MC); MP, Australian Parliament, 1931; Minister of Supply and Development, Australian Government, 1939; his country's first Minister to USA, 1940; appointed by WSC as Minister Resident, Middle East, and as member of War Cabinet, 1942; Governor of Bengal, 1944–6; Minister for External Affairs, Australian Government, 1951–6; retired, 1960; Governor-General of Australia, 1965–9.

Cecil, Lord Hugh (Richard Heathcote Gascoyne-), Baron Quickswood (1869–1956). Youngest son of Lord Salisbury; Conservative MP, 1895–1906; 1910–37; in 1900 was leader of group of young Conservatives whose aim was to enliven a government they felt lacked purpose; became a close friend of WSC; Provost of Eton, 1936–44.

Cecil, Robert (Arthur Talbot Gascoyne-), 3rd Marquess of Salisbury, *see* **Salisbury**

Chamberlain, Sir (Joseph) Austen (1863–1937). Eldest son of Joseph and half-brother of Neville; Liberal Unionist MP, 1892–1914, 1914–37; Chancellor of the Exchequer, 1903–5; Secretary of State for India, 1915–17; member, War Cabinet, 1918; Chancellor again, 1919–21; leader of Conservative Party, 1921; Lord Privy Seal, 1921–2; Foreign Secretary, 1924–9; awarded 1925 Nobel Peace Prize for part in Locarno Treaties; First Lord of the Admiralty in National government, 1931; thereafter refused further office.

Chamberlain, Joseph (1836–1914). Father of Austen and Neville; Liberal MP, 1877; President of the Board of Trade, 1880–5; leader of Liberal Unionists, 1891–5; Colonial Secretary, 1895–1903; resigned office and campaigned for Tariff Reform, 1903–5; crippled by paralysing illness, 1906; took no further part in politics.

Chamberlain, (Arthur) Neville (1896–1940). Son of Joseph and half-brother of Austen; Prime Minister, May 1937; during crisis over Czechoslovakia, September 1938, flew to Germany for talks with Hitler, believing that in ensuing Munich Agreement he had secured 'peace in our time'. Abandoned appeasement, March 1939, after Nazis occupied Prague; offered support to Poland, which pledge was honoured, September 1939, when Britain declared war on Germany. Criticized in Parliament and press, resigned in favour of WSC, May 1940 after Nazi invasions of Denmark and Norway, especially criticism of British failures in Norway. WSC appointed him Lord President of the Council, with a seat in War Cabinet; terminally ill, resigned all offices, 1 October 1940; died shortly afterwards, having refused all titular honours.

Cherwell, Viscount (Frederick Alexander Lindemann) (1886–1957). German born scientist; Director, RFC Experimental Physics Station, Farnborough, 1914; tested and proved theory of recovery from aircraft spin in courageous and, as it seemed, suicidal flight. Professor of Experimental Philosophy, Oxford, 1919–56, and Director Clarendon Laboratory, which he revived. Close friend of WSC, became his personal scientific adviser, 1940; Paymaster-General, 1942–5 and 1951–3, also advising Government on science, particularly nuclear physics. Resumed professorship, 1953. His partnership with WSC was both valuable and fruitful.

Churchill, Lord Randolph (Henry Spencer) (1849–95). Father of WSC; third son of 7th Duke of Marlborough; Conservative MP, 1874, 1880, 1885–95; married American beauty, Jeanette

(Jennie) Jerome. Secretary of State for India, 1885–6; Chancellor of the Exchequer and Leader of House of Commons, 1886 (then the youngest to hold either office); resigned on a point of principle and from increasing ill health, December 1886; died of 'general paralysis'. Disapproved of his elder son, who nevertheless hero-worshipped him.

Ciano, Galeazzo, Count of Cortellazzo (1903–44). Married Mussolini's daughter, Edda, 1930; rose rapidly in Fascist hierarchy, becoming a member of the Supreme Council; Foreign Minister, 1936–43; dismissed by Mussolini, February 1943; in turn, voted for Mussolini's dismissal, ending of Fascist regime and, ultimately, Italian surrender, July 1943. Tried by neo-Fascist court; shot, 11 January. An often ridiculous figure, Ciano was nevertheless an astute and intelligent observer of Fascist and Nazi affairs, and a mordant critic of Nazi pretensions. His widow died in 1997.

Clark Kerr, Sir Archibald (John Kerr), Baron Inverchapel (1882–1951). Australia born; joined British Diplomatic Service, 1905; Ambassador to Iraq, 1935; to Russia, 1942–6; attended inter-Allied conferences in Moscow, Tehran (November–December 1943), Yalta (February 1945), and Potesdam (July–August 1945); had close contact with WSC during Tehran and Yalta Conferences; also earned Stalin's trust. Special Ambassador to Netherlands East Indies, 1945; Ambassador to USA, 1946–8.

Clark, General Mark (Wayne) (1896–1984). Commanded US Fifth Army (with British X Corps under command) in Salerno landings, September 1943, and in subsequent breakout; criticized for liberating Rome rather than destroying German forces before they could withdraw and reorganize. Commanded Fifth Army throughout Italian campaign, advancing into Austria, 1945; C-in-C, US Occupation Forces, Austria; firmly resisted Soviet hectoring. Wrote *Calculated Risk*

(1950) and *From the Danube to the Yalu* (1954).

Clemenceau, Georges (1841–1929). French Prime Minister, November 1917 to January 1920. His courage and fire united France during Ludendorff Offensive, March–April 1918, and inspired drive for final victory. Presided over Paris Peace Conference; sought to impose harshest terms upon Germany; even so, many French felt he had been overly lenient; resigned, January 1920. From retirement, constantly warned against the dangers of a reborn Germany.

Colville, Sir John (Rupert) (1915–198?). Joined Diplomatic Service, 1937; Assistant Private Secretary to Neville Chamberlain, 1939, then to WSC, May 1940–October 1941, when he joined RAF as a pilot. Recalled, late 1943, to his post in Churchill's private office, stayed on as Assistant Private Secretary to Attlee; Principal Private Secretary to WSC, 1951–5. Played leading role in establishment of Churchill College, Cambridge. His books include a memoir, *Footprints in Time* (1976), and *The Churchillians* (1992)

Cooper, (Sir) Alfred Duff, 1st Viscount Norwich (1890–1954). Conservative MP 1924–9, 1931–45; Secretary for War, 1935–7; First Lord of the Admiralty, 1937; resigned over Munich Agreement and appeasement policy, September 1938. Minister of Information in WSC's Cabinet, 1940; Chancellor of the Duchy of Lancaster, 1941–3; Resident Cabinet Minister, Singapore (which fell to Japanese, February 1942), 1941–2; Ambassador to France, 1944–7. Published, among other works, *Old Men Forget* (1953). Married society beauty and wit Lady Diana Manners; WSC greatly enjoyed the company of both.

Crewe, Marquess of (Robert Offley Ashburton *Crewe-Milnes*, 2nd Baron Houghton) (1858–1948). Lord President of the Council, 1905–8, 1915–16; Lord Privy Seal twice, 1908–11, 1912–15;

Colonial Secretary, 1908–10; Secretary of State for India, 1910–15; resigned with Asquith, December 1916. Ambassador to France, 1922–8; Secretary for War again, 1931; Leader of Independent Liberals in House of Lords, 1936–44; married daughter of Lord Rosebery. It was at Crewe House in London that WSC first met Clementine Hozier.

Cripps, (Sir Richard) Stafford (1889–1952). Labour MP; expelled from Labour Party, 1939, for opposition to appeasement; Ambassador to Russia, 1940–2; Lord Privy Seal and Leader of the Commons, 1942; went to India with 'Cripps offer' of Dominion status; Minister of Aircraft Production till 1945; readmitted to Labour Party; Chancellor of the Exchequer, 1947–50.

Cromer, 1st Earl of (Sir Evelyn Baring) (1841–1917). British Agent and Consul-General to Egypt, and thus effectively Governor, 1883–1907. Handled crisis over the Mahdist rebellion in the Sudan, which culminated in the Battle of Omdurman, during which WSC took part in charge of 21st Lancers. President of Dardanelles Commission, 1916, which examined causes and conduct of the Gallipoli campaign, and before which WSC was called. With Curzon, Cromer was among the greatest of British imperial administrators.

Cunliffe-Lister, Sir Philip, 1st Earl of Swinton (1884–1972). Conservative MP, 1918–35; President, Board of Trade, 1922; Colonial Secretary, 1931–5; Air Minister, 1935; resigned, 1938; Resident Minister, West Africa, 1942; various ministries post-war; retired, 1955.

Cunningham, Lieutenant-General (General) Sir Alan (Gordon) (1887–1983). GOC East Africa, 1940; reconquered Abyssinia, 1940–1; commanded Eighth Army in Western Desert, 1941, but dismissed by Auchinleck during Crusader battles for being too defensive; High Commissioner for Palestine, 1945–8.

Cunningham, Admiral (Admiral of the

Fleet) Sir Andrew, Viscount Cunningham of Hyndhope (1883–1963). C-in-C Mediterranean, 1939; launched torpedo aircraft attack on Italian fleet at Taranto, 1940; defeated Italians at Battle of Cape Matapan, 1941; Allied Naval Commander, Mediterranean, 1942; commanded naval operations in invasions of North Africa, Sicily and Italy, 1943; First Sea Lord, 1943–6.

Curzon, George Nathaniel, Marquess Curzon of Kedleston (1859–1925). Conservative MP, 1886–98; Viceroy of India, 1898–1905; Lord Privy Seal, 1915; opposed ending of Gallipoli operation; member, War Cabinet, from December 1916; Foreign Secretary, 1919–24. Probably the greatest of all British proconsuls, though his haughty and patrician manner made him enemies.

Daladier, Édouard (1884–1970). French Prime Minister (for a third term), 1938–40; signed Munich Agreement, September 1938; declared war on Germany 1939. Replaced by Reynaud, March 1940, was first War Minister and then Foreign Minister. Arrested after Fall of France by Vichy authorities; tried in 1942, but verdict suspended; from March 1943–April 1945 interned in France and then Germany.

Dalton, (Edward) Hugh (John Neale), Baron Dalton of Forest and Frith (1887–1962). Labour MP, 1924–9, 1929–31, 1935–59; Minister for Economic Warfare, 1940–2; President, Board of Trade, 1942–5; Chancellor of the Exchequer, 1945–7, but resigned after leaking Budget details to newspaper. Held other ministerial posts subsequently. WSC 'much disliked' him.

Darlan, Admiral Jean (Louis Xavier Francois) (1881–1942). French Naval C-in-C, 1939; his mistrust of Britain confirmed by Royal Navy's attack on French fleet at Mers-el-Kebir; joined Pétain's Vichy government. Was by chance in Algiers when Allies invaded, and agreed to collaborate with them;

much disliked, was assassinated in Algiers by French anti-Vichy fanatic.

Deakin, Sir William (b. 1913). First in Modern History at Oxford; worked with WSC on *Marlborough* and, later, *The History of the English-Speaking Peoples*; Fellow and Tutor, Wadham College, Oxford, 1936–19; led first British Mission to Tito's partisans, Yugoslavia, 1943 (DSO); Warden of St Anthony's College, Oxford, 1950–68. Author of a number of books; greatly liked by WSC.

Denikin, General Anton Ivanovich (1872–1947). Took command of the White forces in southern Russia, April 1918. Gained control of northern Caucasus; in May 1919 launched major offensive through Ukraine towards Moscow. Defeated by Red Army at Orel, October 1919; handed over command to Wrangel, April 1920, and fled to Paris. Emigrated to the USA, 1945.

Dill, General (Field Marshal) Sir John (Greer) (1881–1944). CIGS, May 1940; discouraged WSC from early offensive operations, being thought over-cautious as a result; opposed sending troops from Middle East to Greece; resigned as CIGS, 1941; travelled to USA with WSC, December, and remained there as senior British representative on Chiefs of Staff Committee. Died in office; admired by American political and military leaders, was buried in Arlington National Cemetery, Virginia.

Dönitz, Grand Admiral Karl (1891–1980). Commanded U-boat fleet, 1939–43, sinking 15 million tons of Allied shipping; C-in-C Kriegsmarine, 1943; named Reich President in Hitler's will; formed 'Acting Reich Government', whose only act was to negotiate the German surrender; sentenced at Nuremberg to ten years in Spandau.

Dowding, Air Chief Marshal Sir Hugh (Caswall Tremenheere) 1st Baron Dowding (1882–1970). C-in-C RAF Fighter Command, 1936–40, had overall command in both Battle of France and Battle of Britain. Was held in high esteem by WSC, something Dowding failed to realize; his refusal to let WSC – who was being pressurized by French – send more fighters to France undoubtedly contributed to victory in Battle of Britain.

Ebert, Friedrich (1871–1925). Chairman of Social Democratic Party, 1913; appointed Chancellor, November 1918; elected first President of Weimar Republic, February 1919, and remained so until his death; dealt firmly with extremists of right and left.

Eden, (Robert) Anthony, 1st Earl of Avon (1897–1977). Foreign Secretary, 1937–8 (when he resigned over Munich), 1940–5, 1951–5; Prime Minister, 1955–7; having succeeded WSC when he retired from politics; WSC was not altogether certain Eden was a suitable successor.

Eisenhower, General (General of the Army) Dwight David (1890–1969). Graduated West Point, 1915; commanded allied forces in invasions of North Africa, Sicily and Italy; Supreme Commander, Allied Forces Europe, 1943–5, and overall commander of Allied invasion of Normandy, June 1944; President of the United States, 1953–61. Although criticized as having no experience of commanding troops in battle, his especial skill lay in keeping together a vast army of disparate allies, and driving them on to victory, which often absorbed all his considerable diplomatic talents.

Falkenhayn, General Erich von (1861–1922). Succeeded Moltke as Chief of the Army General Staff after defeat on the Marne, September 1914; planned and commanded Verdun offensive, February 1916, but relieved of command, August, when it became clear that operation was failing after appalling casualties. A better strategist than field commander.

Fisher, Admiral of the Fleet Sir John (Arbuthnot), 1st Baron Fisher (1841–1920) Champion of *Dreadnought* class of battleships; although retired, recalled as First Sea Lord by WSC, then First Lord of the Admiralty, on outbreak of war, 1914; planned naval victory off Falkland Islands, 1914; disapproved of naval attempt to force Dardanelles and, having quarrelled with WSC, resigned. WSC recognized his genius, but found he 'alternately loved and hated him'.

Foch, Marshal Ferdinand (1851–1929). Contributed to victory at the Marne, 1914; commanded Army Group of the North, 1915–16; Chief of the Army General Staff, 1917; appointed Supreme Commander of all Allied armies in France, March 1918, the need for a single unified command having been driven home by German successes in Ludendorff Offensive. Marshal, 1918; elected to Academie Francaise.

Freyberg, Lieutenant-General Sir Bernard (Cyril), VC, 1st Baron Freyberg (1889–1963) English born, but parents emigrated to New Zealand; won VC on the Somme, 1916; also won DSO and two Bars, and was wounded six times. Recalled to command 2nd New Zealand Expeditionary Force, 1939; commanded in Crete, 1941; fought in North Africa and Italy, winning third Bar to DSO; Governor-General of New Zealand, 1945–52; long-standing friend of WSC.

Fritsch, General Werner, Fretiherr von (1880–1939). C-in-C of German Army, 1934; opposed introduction of Nazi ideology into armed forces, which infuriated Hitler; forced into retirement on a trumped-up charge of homosexuality, 1938. Accompanied his old artillery regiment in Polish campaign, 1939; killed by sniper outside Warsaw.

Gamelin, General Maurice (Georges) (1872–1958). C-in-C of Anglo-French forces, 1940, his antiquated defensive policy of 'solid fronts' proved disastrous, and he was hurriedly replaced by Weygand. Tried by a Vichy court and imprisoned in Germany and Italy, 1943–5.

Gaulle, General Charles (André Joseph Marie) de (1890–1970). Commanded armoured division with some success on north-western front during German invasion, May 1940; recalled to be Under-Secretary of Defence in Reynaud's Cabinet. With fall of France fled to England to rally Free French (later Fighting French). In May 1943 became joint Chairman, with Giraud, of the French Committee of National Liberation, ousting Giraud in October to become sole leader. Triumphantly entered Paris with Fighting French forces, August 1944. Elected Prime Minister, then first President, of Fifth Republic, December 1958; re-elected 1965, 1968. Resigned April 1969, after heavy defeat of his policies; died suddenly at his home. A difficult ally, nevertheless did more than any other to restore France to the position that WSC, among others, felt she should occupy in world affairs.

Georges, General Joseph (1875–1951). Seriously wounded during assassination of King Alexander of Yugoslavia and French Foreign Minister, Marseilles, October 1934. C-in-C North-East Front in May 1940, which included Gort's BEF and the RAF's Air Component. Many senior British officers thought him France's best general. Brought out of France to Algiers by Allies, 1943; joined Giraud, but was soon retired.

Giraud, General Henri (Honoré) (1879–1949). Commanded French Seventh Army under Georges, May 1940; captured, 19 May, but escaped to Unoccupied France, April 1942; made his way to Algiers after Allied invasion of North Africa; with US backing became joint President of CFLN with de Gaulle, June 1943; C-in-C all Fighting French forces, July. Ousted by de Gaulle, November 1943; relinquished military command, April 1944.

Goebbels, Reich Minister (Paul) Josef (1897–1945). Early member of Nazi Party; Propaganda Minister on Hitler's accession to power, 1933; Special Plenipotentiary for Total War, August 1944;

played important part in prolonging war beyond point at which Germany had any hope of winning. Fanatical Nazis and devotees of Hitler, he and his wife had their six children killed by lethal injection, then themselves shot by an SS officer, 1 May 1944.

Göring, Reich Marshal Hermann (Wilhelm) (1893–1946). One of Hitler's earliest supporters; commanded storm troops; prime mover in 'Night of the Long Knives' purge of SA; founded Gestapo; set up first concentration camps. As Air Minister, built up the Luftwaffe, which he commanded throughout war, but lost his standing after series of failures, notably Luftwaffe's defeat in the Battle of Britain and growing British bombing campaign. Principal defendant at Nuremberg; took poison just before he was to be hanged, 15 October 1946.

Gort, General (Field Marshal) Lord, VC (John Standish Surtees Prendergast *Vereker*), 6th Viscount (1886–1946). CIGS, 1938; C-in-C BEF in France, 1939–40; Governor of Gibraltar, 1941–2; of Malta, 1942–4; field marshal, 1943; High Commissioner for Palestine and Transjordan, 1944–5.

Gott, Lieutenant-General William (Henry Ewart) (1897–1942). Commanding XIII in Western Desert, 1942, was chosen by WSC to command Eighth Army when Alexander replaced Auchinleck, but killed when his aircraft was shot down while on his way to Cairo for discussions with WSC. Regarded as an outstanding commander.

Graziani, Marshal Rodolfo, Marchese di Neghelli (1882–1955). As Governor and C-in-C, Libya, advanced into Egypt, 1940, but was comprehensively defeated by Wavell, 1940–1, losing hundreds of thousands of men as prisoners and vast masses of material. Resigned his command, 1941; on collapse of Fascist regime in Italy, 1943, joined Mussolini in northern Italy. Sentenced for war crimes, 1950, but released same year because of ill health. Remained active in Italian neo-Fascist movement.

Greenwood, Arthur (1880–1954). Labour MP 1922–31 and 1932–54; member, without portfolio, of War Cabinet, 1940–2; responsible for economic affairs, 1940, and for reconstruction, 1941–2; Lord Privy Seal, 1945–7; Paymaster-General, 1946–7; Minister Without Portfolio, 1947. An outspoken opponent of appeasement and a tireless member of WSC's War Cabinet.

Grey, Sir Edward, Bt, 1st Viscount Grey of Fallodon (1862–1933). Liberal MP, 1885–1916; Parliamentary Under-Secretary, Foreign Office, 1882–5; Foreign Secretary, 1905–16; President, League of Nations, from 1918; Ambassador to USA, 1919–20.

Gröner, General Wilhelm (1867–1939). Succeeded Ludendorff as Chief of Staff to the Imperial German Army in 1918; one of the few to oppose the rise of the Nazis in government; Defence Minister and Minister of Interior, 1928; forced to resign, May 1932, after he and Brüning had banned the SA.

Guderian, Colonel-General Heinz (1888–1954). Tank expert, architect of blitzkrieg, created the panzer divisions that overran Poland in 1939 and France and the Low Countries in 1940. Commanded XIX Panzer Corps in France, with dazzling success; commanded Second Panzer Group, Army Group Centre, in Barbarossa, 1941, but dismissed after failure to take Moscow. Reinstated as Inspector-General of Armoured Forces by Hitler in 1943; appointed Chief of Army Staff, July 1944; given command of the Eastern Front, but dismissed again, March 1945. One of the few senior officers to stand up to Hitler; his *Panzer Leader* published in English, 1952.

Halder, Colonel-General Franz (1884–1971). Chief of Army Staff, September 1938; was from an early date opposed to Hitler, but his caution – and ambition –

prevented him joining 'resistance' within Wehrmacht. Like Guderian, was prepared to argue with Hitler; sacked for advocating withdrawal from Russia, late 1942; held no other command. Implicated in July 1944 plot; eventually sent to Dachau; gave evidence for prosecution at Nuremberg war trials. His 3–volume *War Diary* published 1962–4.

Halifax, 1st Earl of (Edward Frederick Lindley *Wood*) (1881–1959). Viceroy of India, 1926–31; as Foreign Secretary, 1938–40, implemented Chamberlain's appeasement policy; Ambassador to USA, 1941–6.

Hankey, Sir Maurice (Pascal Alers), 1st Baron (1877–1963). Secretary to the Imperial War Cabinet, 1914–18; concurrently Secretary to the Cabinet, to the Committee of Imperial Defence, and Clerk of the Privy Council, until his retirement in 1938. Appointed a member of War Cabinet in 1939; Chancellor of the Duchy of Lancaster, 1940; Paymaster-General, 1941–2.

Himmler, Reichsfuhrer-SS Heinrich (1900–45). Reich Minister of the Interior; head of Gestapo and SS; C-in-C of Replacement Army and Chief of Army Equipment, 1945; attempted to negotiate surrender before Hitler's death via Count Bernadotte; committed suicide while a prisoner of war after being recognized, 23 May 1945. Hitler, wrongly, thought him the most loyal of his inner circle.

Ironside, General (Field Marshal) Sir (William) Edmund, 1st Baron (1880–1959). Commanded the Allied expedition to Archangel in support of White Russian forces against Bolsheviks, 1918–19; CIGS September 1939–May 1940; C-in-C Home Forces, May-July 1940, with responsibility for defences against invasion; field marshal, 1940.

Ismay, General Sir Hastings (Lionel Ismay), 1st Baron (1887–1965) Served as Assistant Secretary to Committee of Imperial Defence from 1926; this led to his service as Chief of Staff to WSC from

1940, during which time he became both a great friend and a most trusted adviser. Secretary for Commonwealth Relations, 1951–2; Secretary-General, NATO, 1952–7.

Jodl, Colonel-General Alfred (1890–1946). Head of Operations Staff at OKW; injured by bomb blast in attempt on Hitler's life, July 1944; signed German surrender on Dönitz's behalf, at Rheims, 7 May 1945; sentenced to death at Nuremberg; hanged, 16 October 1946.

Keitel, Field Marshal Wilhelm (1882–1946). Head of OKW, 1938–45; sentenced to death at Nuremberg; hanged, 16 October 1946. Maintained his long reign at OKW by combination of treachery towards his fellows, and sycophancy towards Hitler.

King, Admiral (Fleet Admiral) Ernest (Joseph) (1878–1956). Of British parentage; C-in-C, US Atlantic Fleet, January–December 1941; C-in-C US Fleet, December 1941; Chief of Naval Operations, March 1942–December 1945; masterminded carrier-based operations against Japanese; Fleet Admiral, 1944

Koniev, Marshal Ivan Stepanovich (1897–1973). Combined military and political careers; elected to Central Committee of Communist Party, 1939; commanded forces that broke first German offensive 1941; helped to prevent relief of German Sixth Army, Stalingrad, 1942; took command of Second Ukrainian Front, 1943; smashed German offensive in south, reconquering Ukraine and crossing Dnieper; marshal, 1944; commanded First Ukrainian Front, 1944; liberated Crimea; occupied Prague, 1945; his troops first to enter Berlin, April 1945. Succeeded Zhukov as C-in-C Red Army, 1946; later First Deputy Defence Minister and Inspector-General of Ministry of Defence.

Krosigk, Count Lutz, Schwerin von (1887–1977). Finance Minister, 1932–45; confirmed in that post and appointed Acting Head of Reich Government in Hitler's will, 1945; sentenced to ten years' imprisonment, but released, 1951; senior officer of Bonn Institute of Finance and Taxation, 1951–71.

Leeb, Field Marshal Wilhelm, Ritter von. One of sixteen generals sacked for lack of enthusiasm for Nazism, January 1938; reinstated, 1939; commanded Army Group C, France, 1940; field marshal, July 1940; commanded Army Group North in Barbarossa, 1941; relieved of command after setbacks in Russia, January 1942.

Lindemann, Professor Frederick, *see* Cherwell, 1st Viscount

Mannerheim, Carl-Gustav Emil, Freiherr von (1867–1951). Finnish C-in-C in Russo-Finnish War, 1939–40; led Finns in Russia from June 1941 after Finland sided with Germany; arranged armistice with Russia and switched Finland to Allied side, 1944; President of Finland, 1944–6.

Manstein, Field Marshal Erich von (1887–1973). Chief of Staff to Rundstedt in Polish campaign; commanded panzer corps in Russia, 1941–3; staged successful counter-attack at Kharkov, 1942, but failed to relieve Sixth Army at Stalingrad. Sentenced for war crimes, 1946, but realeased, 1953. His *Lost Victories* published in English, 1959.

Manteuffel, General Hasso, Freiherr von. Commanded Fifth Panzer Army in Ardennes offensive, December 1944–January 1945; commanded Third Panzer Army on Eastern Front, 1945; member of the Bundestag (west German parliament), 1953–7.

Margesson, (Henry) David (Reginald), 1st Viscount (1890–1965). Conservative MP, 1922–3, 1924–42; Secretary for War, 1940–2; WSC replaced him as War Secretary with Sir James Grigg, 1942.

Marsh, Sir Edward (Howard) (1872–1953). Patron and champion of contemporary British art and literature; editor and publisher of the five volumes of

Georgian Poetry (1912–22); friend, patron and literary executor of Rupert Brooke. Joined Colonial Office, 1896, and worked for WSC there, 1906–8; between 1910 and 1929 worked for him at Home Office, Admiralty, Ministry of Munitions, War Office, Colonial Office again, and Treasury. Helped WSC with *Marlborough*.

Molotov, Vyacheslav Mikhailovich (1890–1986; born V. M. Skriabin). Chairman of the Council of People's Commissars (i.e. Prime minister), 1930–41; Foreign Minister, 1939–49 and 1953–6. Concluded Nazi-Soviet Non-Aggression Pact with Ribbentrop, August 1939. Expelled from Party posts for 'Stalinist activities', 1956; periodically denounced by Khrushchev. Apparently retired, *c.* 1962.

Montague Browne, Anthony Arthur Duncan (born 1923). Pilot in RAF, 1941–5 (DFC, 1945); in 1952 seconded from Diplomatic Service as Private Secretary to WSC, and stayed on in that capacity until latter's death, 1965. His account of his years with WSC, *Long Sunset*, published 1995.

Montgomery, General (Field Marshal) Sir Bernard, 1st Viscount Montgomery of Alamein (1887–1976). Earned reputation commanding division in retreat to and evacuation from Dunkirk; appointed by WSC to command Eighth Army, August 1942; defeated Rommel at El Alamein, October 1942; criticized for lack of drive during his command of Eighth Army in Sicily and Italy, 1943; commanded Allied ground forces in D-Day landings, June 1944, and for some weeks afterward; again criticized for slowness of advance; field marshal, September; commanded Twenty-First Army Group from France to Northern Germany; took surrender of all German forces in North-West Europe on Lüneburg Heath, 4 May 1945. C-in-C British Occupation Forces, Germany, 1945–6; thereafter held many senior posts, including CIGS and Deputy Supreme Commander (under Eisenhower again), NATO Forces Europe; retired 1958. Published a number of books, including his controversial *Memoirs*. His skill as a commander sometimes marred by arrogance and an almost pathological inability to get on with his American colleagues; admired by WSC who, even so, was not blind to Montgomery's faults; for his part, Montgomery resisted WSC's attempts to hustle him into attacking before he felt ready.

Morgenthau, Henry, Jr (1891–1967). US Secretary to the Treasury, 1934–45; formulated 'Morgenthau Plan', 1944, once defeated, whereby, among other policies, Germany, after defeat, would be prevented for all time from having means to make war. Publication of the plan in Germany, however, provided Hitler and Goebbels with a propaganda windfall, not least because Morgenthau was a Jew.

Morley, John, 1st Viscount Morley of Blackburn (1838–1923). Journalist, latterly on *Saturday Review*, 1860–7; editor, *Fortnightly Review*, 1867–82, making it the most influential Liberal journal of its day; edited *Pall Mall Gazette*, 1880–83; Liberal MP, 1883–95, 1896–1908; Secretary of State for India, 1905–10; Lord President of the Council, 1910–14. Apart from his journalism, wrote many books, including a famous life of Gladstone.

Mountbatten, Admiral (Admiral of the Fleet) Lord Louis, 1st Earl Mountbatten of Burma (1900–79). Son of Prince Louis of Battenberg; a great-grandson of Queen Victoria; commanded destroyer flotilla, 1939–41; saw action in Mediterranean; Chief of Combined Operations, 1941–3; Supreme Allied Commander, South-East Asia, 1943–6; last Viceroy of India, 1946–7; Governor-General, 1947–8. Murdered by IRA.

Neurath, Baron Konstantin von (1873–1956). German Ambassador to Italy, 1921; to Britain, 1930; Foreign Minister, 1932–8; 'Reich Protector of Bohemia and

Moravia' (i.e. Czech provinces annexed by Germany in March 1939), 1939–43; sentenced at Nuremberg to fifteen years' imprisonment, but released from Spandau in 1954.

Papen, Franz von (1879–1969). Catholic Centre Party member of Prussian Diet, 1921–32; Chancellor, May 1932, but forced to resign, November; appointed Vice-Chancellor when Hitler became Chancellor, January 1933; was fortunate to survive 'Night of the Long Knives', but later reconciled with Nazis; played key role in Anschluss, 1938; Ambassador to Turkey, 1939–44. Acquitted at Nuremberg for lack of evidence; sentenced to eight years' imprisonment by a German court, February 1947, but released, 1949. His *Memoirs* published in English, 1953.

Patton, General George (Smith) (1885–1945). Commanded US Seventh Army in invasion of Sicily, 1943, then US Third Army during and after invasion of Normandy; spearheaded Bradley's drive through France and closed the Rhine, often pushing forces so hard they outstripped supply lines and came close to running out of fuel. Crossed the Rhine and swept on into Bavaria. Killed in a road accident, Germany, December 1945. Nicknamed 'Old Blood and Guts'; flamboyant, outspoken to point of rudeness, had little time for his British fellow commanders.

Paulus, Field Marshal Friedrich von (1890–1957). Commanded Sixth Army in Russia, undertaking siege of Stalingrad, September 1942; his army eventually isolated and unable to be resupplied, January 1943; appointed field marshal by Hitler a few days before he surrendered on 31 January – against the Führer's express orders. Gave evidence for the prosecution at Nuremberg, 1946; released from Soviet captivity, 1953; settled in East Germany.

Pétain, General (Marshal) Henri (Philippe Omer) (1856–1951). Took command of French Second Army at Verdun, 1916, and by his tenacity ensured defence held, becoming national hero; Marshal of France, 1918. Appointed Prime Minister, June 1940, almost immediately negotiated armistice with Germans, 22 June; in July established government for Unoccupied France at Vichy. When Germans occupied all France, November 1942, Pétain effectively became German puppet; taken to Germany after Allied invasion, 1944; tried for treason in Paris, July 1946, received sentence of death, commuted to life imprisonment; died in prison on the Ile de Yeu, Bay of Biscay; his request to be reburied at Verdun consistently refused.

Raeder, Grand Admiral Erich (1876–1960). C-in-C of what became the Kriegsmarine, 1928; in 1930s successfully evaded terms of the Treaty of Versailles and expanded the navy. Resigned, 1943, after strategic disagreements with Hitler. Sentenced at Nuremberg to life imprisonment, but released from Spandau on grounds of ill health, 1955.

Ribbentrop, Joachim von (1893–1946). Joined Nazi Party c. 1921; made fortune as wine merchant; Ambassador to Britain, 1936–8; Foreign Minister, 1938–45; negotiated alliance with Italy and Japan (Rome-Berlin-Tokyo Axis) from 1936, culminating in Tripartite Pact September 1940; concluded secret Nazi-Soviet Non-Aggression Pact with Molotov, August 1939; one of the architects of German expansion. Sentenced to death at Nuremberg; hanged, 16 October 1946.

Rokossovsky, Marshal Konstantin (1896–1968). Commanded Soviet Sixteenth Army in defence of Moscow, 1941; played important role in defence of Stalingrad, 1943; commanded First Byelorussian Front, 1944; halted outside Warsaw while SS quashed Warsaw Uprising of General Tadeusz ('Bór') Komorowski; captured Warsaw, January 1945; took Danzig and cut off German forces in Courland; linked up with British forces at Wismar, May 1945.

Rommel, Field Marshal Erwin (1891–1944). Served with distinction in Great War; given command of the Afrika Korps in North Africa, February 1941; drove British out of Libya and cut off Tobruk, reversing all Wavell's victories over Italians, April 1941; in turn pushed back in Crusader battles, November 1941–January 1942; counter-attacked, 21 January 1942; British forced to retire to Egyptian frontier; captured Tobruk, 21 June; promoted field marshal; drove British back to El Alamein; checked, then counter-attacked and driven back by Auchinleck at 1st Battle of Alamein, 1–27 July; defeated by Montgomery at Alam Halfa, 30 August–1 September; decisively defeated and driven westwards at 2nd Alamein, 23 October–4 November; summoned back to Germany, March 1943; appointed by Hitler to command Channel defences in France; severely wounded by British aircraft, 17 July 1944; while convalescing in Germany, implicated in July attempt on Hitler's life; formally offered choice between suicide or court martial, public disgrace and execution; took poison in order to protect his family from reprisal, 14 October 1944; given state funeral with full military honours. Earned his enemies' respect, to whom he was, and remains, the 'Desert Fox'.

Rundstedt, Field Marshal (Karl Rudolf) Gerd von (1875–1953). Commanded occupation forces in the Sudetenland, 1938, but relieved of command in February when Hitler purged army of officers insufficiently enthusiastic for Nazism; recalled, 1939, and commanded army groups in invasions of Poland and France, May–June 1940; field marshal, 16 July; commanded Army Group South in Barbarossa, June 1941, but relieved of command, November; C-in-C West, February 1942; again dismissed, July 1944, after successful Allied invasion; had overall command of Ardennes offensive, December 1944–January 1945; relieved of command for fourth and final time, March 1945; charged with war crimes, but case dropped on grounds of ill health.

Salisbury, 3rd Marquess of (Robert Arthur Talbot Gascoynne-Cecil) (1830–1903). Conservative MP, 1853–68; Secretary of State for India, 1866–7 and 1874–8; Prime Minister and Foreign Secretary, 1885; resigned, February 1886, but again Prime Minister (and First Lord of the Treasury), July 1886–1892; formed, 1895, Coalition government in which he was again Prime Minister and Foreign Secretary; resigned Foreign Secretaryship and became Lord Privy Seal, 1900; resigned in favour of his nephew, Balfour, July 1902. Last Prime Minister to govern from the House of Lords.

Sassoon, Siegfried (1886–1967). Served gallantly on Western Front (MC; unsuccessful recommendation for VC); eventually wounded, 1917, sent to psychiatric hospital; his statement denouncing war's prolongation read out in House of Commons, July; despite this, returned to active service, until wounded in head, July 1918 and returned to England. Editions of his war poems published 1917, 1918, and 1919 (with later collections); after the war embarked upon his trilogy of war novels, collectively known as *The Complete Memoirs of Georcre Sherston*.

Schleicher, General Kurt von (1882–1934). Played an important part in helping Seeckt sceretly rebuild Reichewehr; head of Ministry Bureau, Ministry of Defence, 1928; instrumental in sacking of Blomberg, 1930; Chancellor, December 1932; failed to secure dictatorial powers, thus paving the way for Hitler's succession; Locarno treaties, 1925; obtained Germany's admission to the League of Nations, 1926. Awarded Nobel Peace Prize, 1926.

Schörner, Field Marshal Ferdinand (1892–1973). Commanded army group facing Soviet forces in Czechoslovakia, 1945; it was hoped he would relieve Berlin and rescue Führer; Hitler's last appointed field marshal, 5 April; named Army C-in-C in Hitler's will, 29 April; held out to the last; imprisoned by the Russians until 1955; arguably the most Nazi of all senior German generals.

Schuschnigg, Dr Kurt von (1897–1977). Became Chancellor of Austria when Dollfuss murdered during attempted coup by Austrian Nazis, July 1934; resisted Hitler's plans for union of Austria with Germany, but his proposed referendum provoked Nazi invasion of Austria, and thus the Anschluss; imprisoned by Nazis; emigrated to USA; Professor of Political Science; University of St Louis, 1948–67; returned to Austria, 1968.

Seeckt, Colonel-General Hans von (1886–1936). Chief of Staff of the Army (i.e. C-in-C), 1919, until 1926 was driving force behind rebuilding of the German armed forces while circumventing the terms of the Treaty of Versailles; his greatest legacy, however, lay in principles he instilled into the new Reichswehr. Hindenburg, jealous of his standing, forced his retirement, October 1926. Seeckt's well-trained, well-armed and highly disciplined Reichswehr formed basis for vastly expanded conscript armies with which Hitler conquered most of Europe.

Seyss-Inquart, Dr Artur von (1892–1946). Austrian pro-Nazi (though not a member of the Party); provided respectable facade for Austrian Nazis; Minister of Security, February 1938; conspired with Papen and Goring in Anschluss, March; appointed Austrian Chancellor; appointed Governor of Holland, 1940; ruthlessly exploited population for slave labour, among much other brutality; named Foreign Minister in Hitler's will, 1945; sentenced to death at Nuremberg; hanged, 16 October 1946.

Sikorski, General Wladyslaw (1881–1943). Head of Polish Government-in-Exile, London, June 1940. Signed treaty with Soviet Union after start of Barbarossa, 1941, but relations worsened with discovery of Soviet treatment of Polish prisoners, and particularly when details of Katyn massacre of Polish officers became known, April 1943; diplomatic relations between Soviet Union and Polish Government-in-Exile severed by Russians, 25 April; only strong intervention by WSC prevented full-scale rift. Killed in air crash near Gibraltar, 4 July 1943.

Speer, Albert (1905–81). Appointed Hitler's architect, 1934; Reich Minister for Armaments and War Economy, 1942; opposed Hitler in last months of the war, even admitting this to Führer himself; tried at Nuremberg, 1946, where he was only Nazi leader to admit responsibility for his actions; sentenced to twenty years' imprisonment, which he served in Spandau. His *Inside the Third Reich* and *Spandau: The Secret Diaries* published in English 1970 and 1976.

Speidel, General Dr Hans (1897–1984). Served on Western Front in Great War; gained doctorate in philosophy, 1925; Chief of Staff to Rommel, Army Group B, on Western Front, 1944; refused to carry out Hitler's order to destroy all bridges in Paris; subsequently refused order to destroy Allied-occupied city with heavy artillery and Vls; leading conspirator in July 1944 plot; arrested by Gestapo, 7 September 1944; admitted nothing and betrayed no one; escaped and hidden by priest until US forces arrived. Latterly Commander Allied Land Forces, Central Europe, 1957–63, a NATO appointment that aroused widespread controversy when announced.

Strasser, Gregor (1892–1934). Early member of Nazi Party; took part in

Munich putsch, 1923; competed with Hitler for leadership; resigned from Party, 1932; murdered during 'Night of the Long Knives', 1934.

Stresemann, Gustav (1878–1929). German Chancellor, August–November 1923, then Foreign Minister until his death. Believed that Germany should adhere to terms of Treaty of Versailles; negotiated reduction in German war reparations payments; an architects of the resigned, January 1933; murdered, with wife, during 'Night of the Long Knives', 30 June 1934, a victim of his own devious machinations.

Student, Colonel-General Kurt. Pioneer of airborne forces; commanded airborne troops that took frontier fortresses during Nazi invasion of Low Countries and France, 1940; led same in successful conquest of Crete, 1941; held no operational command for three years, Hitler, appalled by very heavy losses in Crete, having lost faith in airborne forces; formed and commanded German First Parachute Army, September 1944; significantly contributed to defeat of British 1st Airborne Division at Arnhem; commanded his army in infantry role during defence of Western Front, 1944–5.

Swinton, 1st Earl of, *see* **Cunliffe-Lister.**

Westphal, General Siegfried (1884–1972). Chief of Staff to Kesselring, Army Group C, in Italian campaign, 1943–5. His *The German Army in the West* published in English, 1951.

Weygand, General Louis Maxime (1867–1965). Recalled from retirement as French C-in-C during Battle of France; recommended armistice with Germans; arrested Gestapo and imprisoned in Germany, 1942. Tried in France as a collaborator, but released, 1946; in 1948 his sentence of 'national infamy' quashed. Wrote *The Role of General Weygand* and *Recalled to Service* (English editions 1948, 1952).

Wingate, Major-General Orde Charles

(1903–1944). Organized successful resistance to Italians in Abyssinia, 1940–1; formed, trained and led 'long-range penetration groups' ('Chindits') in India; first Chindit operation behind Japanese lines in Burma, February 1943; second, larger, operation, March 1944; killed in air crash while flying in, 24 March. The kind of soldier who most appealed to WSC, who took Wingate with him on one of his trips to USA.

Witzleben, Field Marshal Erwin von (1881–1944). C-in-C West, May 1941; retired due to ill health, 1942; involved with anti-Hitler plotters, was to succeed as C-in-C of Wehrmacht once Führer had been assassinated; arrested after failure of July 1944 plot; tortured by Gestapo and 'tried' before a People's Court; hanged, 8 August 1944.

Wood, Sir (Howard) Kingsley (1881–1943). Conservative MP, 1918–43; Secretary of State for Air, 1938–40; Lord Privy Seal, 1940; Chancellor of the Exchequer, 1940–3. Did valuable work in increasing RAF's fighting strength before war broke out.

Yudenich, General Nikolai Nikolaevich (1862–1933). Commanded Russian forces against Turks during Great War. After 'October' Revolution, 1917 and the armistice between Russia and the Central Powers, fought on White Russian side. From Finland, commanded armies in assault against Bolshevik-held Petrograd, but was defeated; withdrew from conflict that same year.

Zhukov, Marshal Georgi Konstantinovich (1896–1974). Chief of Staff to Red Army, 1941; assisted in defences of Leningrad and Moscow, 1941; launched first Soviet counter-offensive, December 1941; trapped German attackers at Stalingrad, November 1942; heavily defeated Germans at Kursk, 5–15 July 1943, notably by deployment of Soviet armour; marshal, 1943; commanded breakthrough in Byelorussia, 1944, and final offensive on Oder, April 1945, which led to capture of Berlin, 2 May; headed Allied delegation at final German surrender, 7 May. C-in-C, Soviet Occupation Zone, Germany, 1945–6, but on return to Moscow was demoted, largely through Stalin's jealousy. Defence Minister, 1956, but in October 1957 relieved of his duties and denounced; restored to Soviet and Party favour, 1965. His *Memoirs* published in English, 1971.

I was conscious of a profound sense of relief. At last I had the authority to give directions over the whole scene. I felt as if I were walking with destiny, and that all my past life had been but a preparation for this hour and for this trial.

WINSTON CHURCHILL, 10 May 1940

I can only be grateful to Providence that it entrusted me with the leadership in this historic struggle which, for the next five hundred or a thousand years, will be described as decisive, not only for the history of Germany, but for the whole of Europe and indeed the whole world.

ADOLF HITLER, 11 December 1941

> Give me my scallop-shell of quiet,
> My staff of Faith to walk upon;
> My scrip of joy, immortal diet,
> My bottle of salvation,
> My gown of glory (Hope's true gage),
> And thus I'll take my Pilgrimage.
> SIR WALTER RALEGH, 'The Passionate Man's Pilgrimage'

CHAPTER 1

Victory and Defeat

Whatever you may do, we shall fight on for ever and
ever and ever.

WINSTON CHURCHILL

If we wished to select one area of military activity for which Britain has shown
a singular aptitude, it would be that of avoiding defeat. Practice makes perfect,
they say, and herein perhaps lies the explanation for the nation's consistent
success in this respect. Such reiteration may in turn be explained by a second
example of running true to form. On each occasion that the British have
entered into a prolonged conflict with some well-armed European power, they
have done so, as far as their army was concerned, in a state of notorious unpreparedness. It was fortunate therefore – indeed Britain's survival depended on it
– that their rulers did not make a habit of wholly neglecting the strength and
efficiency of the Royal Navy. Not all Elizabeth I's brave words at Tilbury nor
the courage of her yeomen could have prevailed against the finest infantry in
the world had not Drake, Hawkins and the other captains prevented the
Spanish Armada from ferrying Parma's troops to these shores. And no man
can suppose, had Nelson and his band of brothers not been there to engage
the enemy, and had Napoleon's veteran soldiers actually landed in Sussex and
Kent to find themselves faced by local Volunteers and Militia with no training
or discipline, or even proper weapons, that the result of such an encounter
could have been anything but unfavourable to this country.

In these and other cases, once the British grasped the severity of their
danger and that only their navy stood between themselves and defeat by a
foreign power, they pulled themselves together, mustered armies, showed that
their own horse, foot and guns could in the end prove themselves the match of
any others, and so at length by courtesy of the Royal Navy's supremacy at sea,
took war to the lands and capitals of their enemies. Yet no sooner were their
efforts rewarded with well-earned, though costly, victory than the government
of the day would set about the business of dismantling the very military

organization which had preserved both the country's integrity and her reputation.

At no time was the danger of defeat, nor the almost sublime indifference to
its likelihood, more marked than in 1940. There were but few powerful cards in
this country's hands when the Battle of France was over, despite the 'miracle'
of Dunkirk. What mattered, however, was that these inadequate cards were
held by 'a man larger than life . . . a man superhumanly bold, strong and imaginative . . . an orator of prodigious powers . . . a mythical hero who belongs to
legend as much as to reality'[1] – in short, by Winston Churchill. Such was his
ability to inspire – the word is not too extravagant – the nation; such were the
consequent industry and resolution of the British people; such the integrity
and vigilance of the Royal Navy and the nation's merchant fleet; such the gallantry, skill and endurance – in the face of a pressure which came close to
breaking it – of the Royal Air Force; and such the support received from
Britain's Colonies and the Dominions – that the enemy's design to invade and
overwhelm these islands was thwarted. Sir Isaiah Berlin has maintained that the
way in which Churchill spoke to the British people in the summer of 1940 was
such that 'they conceived a new idea of themselves . . . they went forward into
battle transformed by his words . . . He created a heroic mood . . . So hypnotic
was the force of his words, so strong his faith, that by the sheer intensity of his
eloquence he bound his spell upon them . . .'[2]

He was, however, not the only leader to have this gift. The arch-enemy, the
very source of the danger which threatened Britain in 1940 as she had never
been threatened before, was himself what Alan Bullock has called the greatest
demagogue in history. What had brought Churchill to the leadership of his
country was the person and purposes of Adolf Hitler. It was he who, in *Mein
Kampf*, had called for one last decisive battle with France. He may then have
been speaking as an adventurer, but it was his very gift of oratory, combined
with uncanny political acumen, infinite reserves of resolution, nerves of steel,
an indomitable will and sheer perseverance that had brought him to power in
the first place. His eloquence was such that he cast a spell on his audiences,
perhaps as no military leader before or since has ever done. He himself said of
the orator that 'from the living emotion of his hearers the apt word which he
needs will be suggested to him and in its turn this will go straight to the hearts
of his hearers'. He was, of course, referring to himself, and he could hardly
have summed up better his own unique facility.

Adventurer or not, once the war had started and after the initial German
success in Poland, Hitler began to urge the General Staff to steel themselves for

---

[1] Isaiah Berlin, *Mr Churchill in 1940*.
[2] Ibid.

an attack on the Western Allies, and in November 1939 had declared with extra-ordinary foresight that he placed a low value on the French Army, which, he believed, was but a mirror of its people and would swiftly crack up after initial setbacks. How totally he was to be vindicated was soon apparent when in May 1940, as Supreme Commander-in-Chief of the Wehrmacht (the German armed forces), he launched his troops against the French, British, Dutch and Belgian armies. We will follow later the progress of this campaign and the manner in which its conduct was crucially influenced by Hitler himself. It is enough to say here that even Hitler was surprised by the rapidity and complete-ness of his success. The French defeat was absolute.

When Hitler realized the extent of his triumph, he gave appropriate thanks to Providence, talked about the greatest battle in world history – there were to be many more of these – and praised the army and its leaders. He boasted of the peace arrangements he would impose on France which would compensate for all the injustices inflicted on the German people since the Thirty Years War. He would in turn humiliate the French nation by conducting the armistice arrangements in the same railway carriage at the same place in the Forest of Compiègne as the French had done twenty-two years earlier at the end of the First World War. Rudyard Kipling suggested in a celebrated poem that if we could meet with Triumph and Disaster and treat those two impostors just the same, we would have the Earth and all that is in it. On 21 June 1940 we see Hitler savouring triumph with all the meanness, vindictiveness, arrogance and contempt that were such prominent features of his character. In that Compiègne clearing, where stood the monument recording the German Reich's submission on 11 November 1918, the Führer is observed by an American correspondent:

> He steps off the monument and contrives to make even this gesture a mas-terpiece of contempt . . . He glances slowly round the clearing . . . Suddenly, as though his face were not giving quite complete expression to his feelings, he throws his whole body into harmony with his mood. He swiftly snaps his hands on his hips, arches his shoulders, plants his feet wide apart. It is a magnificent gesture of defiance, of burning contempt for the place and all that it has stood for in the twenty-two years since it witnessed the humbling of the German Empire.[1]

So much for France. As for the British – they could have peace as soon as Germany's colonies, taken over after her defeat in 1918, were returned. Hitler came up against an unforeseen snag, however. The British were not interested

[1] William L. Shirer, *Berlin Diary*.

in peace. Before the Battle of France was over, Churchill had made it plain to the demoralized French ministers that whatever they might do, 'we are resolved to fight on for ever and ever and ever'. Indeed, he had already declared his – and thus his country's – resolution three days after becoming Prime Minister, in succession to Neville Chamberlain, who resigned after the disastrous Allied defeat in Norway. It was a curious chance that on the very same day during which the Wehrmacht began to cut down the Allied armies in France and Belgium, 10 May 1940, Churchill assumed the great burden of leading the British people and Empire towards their own finest hour, an hour, not of victory, but of defiance against seemingly insuperable odds. Three days later, on 13 May, he spoke these immortal words in the House of Commons:

I would say to the House, as I said to those who have joined this Government: 'I have nothing to offer but blood, toil, tears and sweat'.[1]

We have before us an ordeal of the most grievous kind. We have before us many, many long months of struggle and of suffering. You ask, what is our policy? I will say: It is to wage war, by sea, land and air, with all our might and with all the strength that God can give us; to wage war against a monstrous tyranny, never surpassed in the dark, lamentable catalogue of human crime. That is our policy.

You ask, what is our aim? I can answer in one word! It is victory, victory at all costs, victory in spite of all terror, victory, however long and hard the road may be; for without victory, there is no survival. Let that be realized; no survival for the British Empire, no survival for all that the British Empire has stood for . . .

At all costs! The cost was indeed to be heavy – the decline of the very British Empire Churchill was so determined and anxious to preserve, the hegemony of the United States, the huge expansion of the Soviet Union, the bankruptcy of Britain. That the aim was victory, few doubted. Yet even Churchill himself confessed to his colleagues that although the British people might trust him, he could give them nothing but disaster for a long time. As for the policy, how was war to be waged? It seemed that Hitler's panzers and Stukas were sweeping all before them. How were they to be stopped?

On the day Churchill became Prime Minister, Hitler was in his headquarters at Münstereiffel, and was soon to hear that the Wehrmacht's strategy of feinting in the north to lure the French and British armies into Belgium, so that the

---

[1] 'When Mr Churchill offered his people tears, he spoke a word which might have been uttered by Lincoln or Mazzini or Cromwell . . .' Berlin, op. cit. 'Blood, toil, tears and sweat' is in fact a quotation from Garibaldi.

main German thrust in the centre at Sedan would meet little resistance, was working even better than had been hoped. A year later he recalled that he could have wept with joy as he saw the Allies falling into the trap set for them. On 13 May, while Churchill is making his memorable declaration to the House of Commons, the spearhead of Rundstedt's Army Group A, Guderian's XIX Panzer Corps, is crossing the Meuse, expanding the hole thus made in the French line and rushing the panzers on towards the Channel, which they would reach a week later, cutting the Allied armies in half. The French Army's plight was admirably summed up by Vercors: 'The wholesale retreat towards Dunkirk turned into an epic, but it was a sombre epic. The disaster was immeasurable. The French Army was smashed to pieces, cut to shreds by the tanks, nailed to the ground by the enemy's Stukas. A hundred miles from the front dazed soldiers were still streaming back.'[1]

While Churchill is talking of victory as an aim, Hitler is savouring victory as a fact. By mid-June it is all over. Why had the German Army triumphed so rapidly? We will trace later how it came about that Hitler established a powerful, well-equipped army and a proper tactical doctrine to go with it, the two indispensable ingredients for winning victories and which together overcame the Reich's enemies as though they had been summer clouds. In the battle for France the German superiority – not in numbers, where they were slightly inferior, but in leadership, training, tactics and morale – was overwhelming. Allied forces, strung out along the front, with no depth, no proper reserves, no means of rapid movement, concentration or co-ordination, were no match for, indeed, simply had no chance against, fast, integrated armoured columns, supported by the Luftwaffe, which struck hard and deep into Allied territory.[2] On 5 June Hitler issued an order of the day: 'Dunkirk has fallen . . . with it has ended the greatest battle of world history. Soldiers! My confidence in you knew no bounds. You have not disappointed me.'

Hitler had every reason for confidence. Churchill had perhaps rather less reason, yet with the bulk of the British Expeditionary Force and many Allied soldiers successfully evacuated from Dunkirk, he showed no sign of lacking it when he addressed the House of Commons on the day before Hitler issued his triumphant message. Never was his resolution and stirring oratory put to more effective use. He told the House that he, himself, had full confidence that if all were to do their duty, nothing were neglected, proper arrangements made, as they were being made, they would once more prove they were able to defend

---

[1] Jean Bruller, *La Bataille du Silence.*
[2] When Churchill was in Paris on 16 May and asked General Gamelin, the French Commander-in-Chief, who had just outlined the German breakthrough: 'Ou est la masse de manoeuvre?' the reply, delivered with a shrug and shake of the head was: 'Aucune.'

their island home, to ride out the storm of war and outlive tyranny's menace 'if necessary for years, if necessary alone'. It might be that large parts of Europe, old and famous states, would fall into the Gestapo's grip and under Nazi rule. But 'we shall not flag or fail. We shall go on to the end.' They would fight in France, on the seas and oceans, they would fight with growing strength and confidence in the air, they would defend their island no matter what the cost. They would fight on the beaches, the landing grounds, in the fields, in the hills. 'We shall never surrender'. Even if parts of Britain were 'subjugated and starving' (although he did not for one moment believe that such a possibility existed), still the Empire, protected by the British fleet, would fight on until 'in God's good time, the New World, with all its power and might, steps forth to the rescue and liberation of the old'.

Despite some claims to the contrary,[1] Churchill accurately depicted the course of events. Britain did go on to the end; her troops did fight in France and on the seas and oceans; within a few months of his pronouncement the Battle of Britain was fought and won; there was plenty of fighting on beaches – North Africa, Sicily, Italy and France, as well as in the Far East; fields, streets and hills became the scenes of numerous battles. Surrender was never on the cards, and the New World did at length step forward and lend its necessary weight to the liberation of Europe – and of South-East Asia. Those who heard Churchill's words at the time never forgot their impact. As Martin Gilbert has reminded us, the writer Vita Sackville-West was stirred by the 'massive backing and resolve' behind the words; her husband, Harold Nicolson, wrote that the spirit of the Prime Minister's speech made him feel that he could face a 'world of enemies'. They were echoing the feelings of thousands.

'It fell to me in these coming days and months,' wrote Churchill himself, 'to express their [the people's] sentiments on suitable occasions. This I was able to do because they were mine also. There was a white glow, overpowering, sublime, which ran through our island from end to end.' In commenting on this, Sir Isaiah Berlin emphasizes that Churchill is not giving himself sufficient credit for his own part in inducing these sentiments in the British people. It was because Churchill himself seemed, and indeed *was*, so sure, so unyielding, so indomitable that his people responded to, welcomed and reinforced his mood. 'He idealized them with such intensity that in the end they approached his ideal and began to see themselves as he saw them: "the buoyant and imperturbable temper of Britain which I had the honour to express" – it was indeed, but he had a lion's share in creating it.'

---

[1] Dr Charmley – there has of late been a great vogue for revisionism – in his *Churchill: The End of Glory*, calls this great speech of Churchill's 'sublime nonsense', but he is, of course, profoundly mistaken.

Shortly after Churchill made his great speech, I was in Stratford-upon-Avon, on leave, and enjoying a performance of Shakespeare's *King John*. As I recall, the part of Philip Faulconbridge, bastard son of Richard Coeur de Lion, was played by Basil Holloway, and when he spoke the play's final words, clad in armour, he turned to face the audience and raised his sword high:

> This England never did, nor never shall,
> Lie at the proud foot of a conqueror . . .
> Now these our princes are come home again,
> Come the three corners of the world in arms,
> And we shall shock them. Naught shall make us rue,
> If England to itself do rest but true.

Shakespeare usually has a phrase or verse to suit every circumstance or sentiment. Never could this have been borne out with more fidelity. The effect on the audience was electric. A silence abnormally long was followed by prolonged and tumultuous applause. There could have been few dry eyes or unmoved hearts amongst those who filed out of the theatre.

Churchill himself was another Coeur de Lion. And there was no doubt in the minds of his countrymen as to the rightness and necessity of defiance in defeat. England's princes, in the form of the Expeditionary Force evacuated from Dunkirk, had indeed come home again. But as the Prime Minister made clear, wars are not won by evacuations, and if the three corners of the world in arms did *not* come against us, how were we to shock them? How, in short, were we to wage war? It could, of course, be done, was being done, at sea, and before many months had passed, the Royal Air Force was to shock the Luftwaffe. But how was the war to be waged *on land*? The miracle of Dunkirk might have saved the British Army. But where and with what was it now to fight?

The dilemma of what to do next was not Churchill's alone; it was also Hitler's. Indeed, on 19 July 1940 the Führer saw no reason why the war should continue! He had been disappointed that German overtures for peace with Britain, made through neutral capitals in the previous month, had produced no response. His thinking was realistic in every respect except with regard to the character of the British people and their leader. To Hitler, the very extent of his victory in the West made it not less but more likely that the British would come to terms. He had never wished to interfere with the integrity of the British Empire or the independence of the British nation. The return of German colonies, and a free hand in Eastern Europe, these he sought. What could the British now hope to achieve? Their army had been driven from the Continent and their former allies, Poland, France and Belgium had been defeated.

Norway, Denmark and Holland had also been overrun and occupied. Why therefore was it not possible for Germany and Britain to come to some agreement? So reasoned the Führer.

He should have paid more attention to what Churchill had told the House of Commons on 18 June, the anniversary of the Battle of Waterloo, when he warned his countrymen of the imminent likelihood of a German attack, both from the air and by invasion. The Battle of France was over, he declared, and he expected that the Battle of Britain was about to begin. On this battle would depend the survival of Christian civilization. He predicted that the enemy's entire military weight would soon be turned on this country. Hitler knew that he had to break Britain or lose the war. If, therefore, the British people could stand up to him, all Europe might be free; if not, the entire world and all that mattered in it might be lost. 'Let us therefore brace ourselves to our duty and so bear ourselves that if the British Empire and its Commonwealth lasts for a thousand years men still will say: This was their finest hour.' It was thus, as even some of Churchill's critics have conceded, that his will and purpose imprinted themselves on the British people. Translating this purpose into practical military measures was not to be so simple a matter, however.

Despite the British Prime Minister's splendid words and resolutions, we find Hitler in his speech to the Reichstag of 19 July actually making a direct appeal for peace, and couching this appeal in characteristically egotistic and bombastic language. It caused him pain, he declared, that Fate should have selected him to deal the final blow to an empire which he had never intended to harm, let alone destroy. He therefore felt it his duty to make an appeal – not begging favours from a position of defeat, but rather as a conqueror seeking a reasonable compromise – that common sense should prevail in order to end a war which now need not be pursued.

Yet three days *before* making this appeal Hitler had issued his War Directive No 16 for the invasion of England, which was codenamed Operation Sea Lion. It cannot be said that the Führer felt much enthusiasm for the idea. Apart from the fact that an invasion would put an end to his unrealistic dream of an alliance with Britain, he was fully aware that such an undertaking would be 'exceptionally daring'. He might have added 'exceptionally dangerous', and to some extent this danger was acknowledged in the directive, which noted that Britain's air force would need to be neutralized, both in material and morale, to the point at which it would no longer be in a position to interfere with the proposed German crossing.

Hitler's dilemma as to what to do after the fall of France revealed the fatal flaw in blitzkrieg. It was not so much that there were no specific plans and preparations for the invasion of England, which Hitler had never envisaged while he had been planning to overthrow France; rather, it was a failure to provide the resources and strategic flexibility for a long war, involving the close co-operation of all three elements of military power – air, sea and land. At the time of the Sea Lion directive, the Germany Navy was keenly opposed to the plan of concentrating 1,000 large barges (essential for industrial waterway traffic, from which they would be requisitioned to carry the invasion force) and other shipping on the Channel coast, while the Luftwaffe, however conscious its leaders may have been of the need to gain air superiority over the Channel and beyond, did little or nothing to bring about this prerequisite of invasion. Hitler himself declared that if preparations for the invasion could not be completed by the beginning of September, the Wehrmacht would have to consider alternative plans.

There was, of course, an element of self-deception in all Hitler's deliberations about whether or not to invade England. As early as July 1940 he had expounded to his commanders-in-chief his ideas as to one of these alternatives for the Wehrmacht. If Operation Sea Lion did not take place, he argued, Germany must by some other means eliminate any hope that the British might have of succour from elsewhere. Britain's only possible allies, he said, were Russia and America. If Russia were conquered, therefore, Japan's consequently increased power in the Far East would so concern the United States of America that she too would drop out of the European picture. Thus the destruction of the Soviet Union must become part of Germany's struggle, and the sooner this was done the better. Moreover, such an attack would have to be of such weight and swiftness that the Russian state would be shattered by a single blow. 'If we start in May 1941, we will have five months in which to finish the job' – *Also sprach Hitler*. In this exposition he was simply justifying what had all along been his intention – the destruction of the Soviet Union. His *Weltanschauung* (world philosophy) – indeed, his mission – was to ensure that the Nazi racist ideology of the élite would save Europe from the Jewish-Bolshevik ideology of the masses. *Mein Kampf* was explicit on this point: 'We National Socialists . . . turn our gaze towards the land of the East . . . Russia and her vassal border states . . . This colossal Empire in the East is ripe for dissolution.'

By turning the arguments upside-down in this manner, Hitler was ignoring the two great rules of strategy. The first of these, the master rule, is correctly to select the primary objective. The second rule is to concentrate and deploy forces in such a way as to achieve the object. In 1940 – at a time when Russia was still, if not Germany's ally, certainly not an enemy (indeed was still actually supplying Germany with strategic material) – there was but one enemy, Great Britain. Yet Hitler could not or would not see that the subjection of Britain was not subsidiary, not a preliminary, to an attack on Russia. It was an indispensable condition of victory, as Churchill himself had made plain.

Besides, there were more ways of savaging the United Kingdom than solely by direct invasion. When it became clear during the Battle of Britain that Sea Lion's prerequisite of air mastery by the Luftwaffe was not going to be achieved; when Göring committed the two fundamental errors of not concentrating on destroying RAF Fighter Command's radar stations and of switching his attacks from fighter airfields to London; when finally the Royal Air Force won its great victory of 15 September (Churchill described it all as 'a time when it was equally good to live or die') and thus put paid to the feasibility of Sea Lion, Hitler had no hesitation in cancelling the operation two days later. But all this did not mean that the Wehrmacht could no longer concentrate its efforts against Britain.

In this regard, Hitler's naval Commander-in-Chief, Admiral Raeder, had a far sounder strategic instinct than did his master. Raeder tried to persuade the Führer that Germany should concentrate on war against Britain, more especially in the Mediterranean which he described as 'the pivot of the British Empire'. As everyone knew, Germany's ally, Italy, was weak. Britain would therefore try to knock Italy out of the war first, and in order to make this easier would aim to get control of the whole of North Africa (Italy at the time controlled Libya, as well as Abyssinia – now Ethiopia – and Italian Eritrea). Thus Germany must act to prevent this happening. In co-operation with Spain and Vichy France,[1] they must seize Gibraltar and secure French North Africa. After that German forces together with the Italians should capture Egypt and the Suez Canal, then by advancing through Palestine and Syria, threaten Turkey. There was, of course, nothing new in the idea. It was after all Napoleon who had maintained that 'in order to destroy England utterly, we must get possession of Egypt'. What is more Napoleon did not merely say it, he attempted it, although Nelson and Sidney Smith, together with events in France, robbed him of the immense promise of strategic prizes. Raeder concluded that if German forces were to advance that far, Turkey would be in Germany's power, and then the problem of Russia would show up in a very different light; indeed, an advance on the Soviet Union from the north might then be unnecessary. It has to be allowed that Raeder knew he was talking sound strategic sense.

But leaving aside the Russian problem – and a part of Raeder's persuasiveness lay in the fact that he presented his Mediterranean ideas as a solution to this very problem – what sort of plight would a successful execution of Raeder's plan have landed Britain in? For the British the Middle East was all important. It was not merely that its defence and continued possession was vital to British strategic interests. Since, as Sir Michael Howard has pointed out,

---

[1] When France surrendered in June 1940, the Germans occupied roughly one-half of the country, and set up a puppet French government, which had its headquarters at Vichy.

it was recognized that there might be no prospect in 1940 of Britain's mounting a direct attack on Germany with ground troops, the Middle East nevertheless represented an alternative theatre of operations where British forces could not only harass the enemy, but could severely damage them. Italy's entry into the war in June had turned this theatre into an active military area. 'As a centre of gravity of British forces it was second only to the United Kingdom.' Churchill, who was never in doubt about the strategic importance of North Africa and the Middle East saw in this theatre a means of not just avoiding defeat, but of inflicting it upon the enemy, and it was here that his yearning to take the initiative and mount offensives could be satisfied.

Given, however, that in the early stages it would be the Axis powers which would enjoy the initiative, and given too that whereas Germany would seek to dominate eastern and south-eastern Europe, Italy would try to do the same in North Africa and the Mediterranean, British strategy became clear. That strategy would be, first, to guarantee the integrity of Egypt and other Middle Eastern countries, and their resources; and second, to take the offensive as soon as possible in order to gain control of the Mediterranean, and then mount attacks against the Axis powers in Europe itself. It was from this broad concept that the so-called 'Mediterranean strategy' emerged. And Churchill's vision and boldness were well illustrated by his determination to reinforce the Middle East even at a time when the integrity of the British Isles was by no means guaranteed. Accepting that the British could not challenge Germany's position on the Continent this method of waging war was not only sound, but apart from maritime and air operations, there was no alternative. In essence, the intention was to wrest the initiative from the Axis powers, to check their advances and gains, and to tighten the ring around enemy-controlled Europe and thus enable blows by land, sea and air to be struck at them.

We shall examine later how this broad idea developed specific objectives – in the end nothing short of conquering all North Africa so that the Mediterranean could be opened to Allied shipping and offensives staged against the Italian mainland. Churchill went further and subsequently spoke of the possibility, once North Africa was in Allied hands, of flexible manoeuvres by which Hitler's Europe could be assaulted both from the Atlantic and the Mediterranean. Then it would be feasible 'to push either right-handed, left-handed or both-handed as our resources and circumstances permit'. Churchill was perhaps allowing his fertile imagination to run away with itself, and Sir Michael Howard brings us down to earth when he states that the concept was not one of manoeuvre at all, but of attrition. For Germany the Mediterranean would become an obligation which would gradually wear down Axis strength. It was to be a huge distraction – a distraction moreover of incalculable importance when Germany's titanic struggle in Russia was in the balance; and it would be an enforced dissipation of effort which would prevent Germany's adherence to the prime axioms of strategy – singleness of aim and concentration of force. Yet given Churchill's overriding concern with inflicting rather than avoiding defeat, this policy of attrition, while not yielding dividends quickly, was the best choice among an option of difficulties.

And so we see our two world historical figures as early as 1940 coming to decisions which determined the course and outcome of a war which was to last for another five years. Once Churchill had declared for victory even, as A.J.P. Taylor put it, 'if this meant placing the British Empire in pawn to the United States, even if it meant Soviet domination of Europe'; once the newly appointed Prime Minister had thus expressed the resolution of his own people, his words had – as Taylor again states – 'charted the history of England for the next five years'. In a similar way, once Hitler's decision to attack the Soviet Union was made, a decision he had long pondered and finally spelled out to his generals in July 1940, and later turned into a War Directive beginning with the ominous words: 'The German Armed Forces must be prepared, even before the conclusion of the war against England, to crush the Soviet Union in a rapid campaign' – once this decision had been taken and the directive signed and issued, the die was cast. Charles XII of Sweden had tried to dethrone the Tsar; Napoleon had determined to call Alexander I to account; now Hitler was to kick in the door of the Soviet state in order to bring the whole rotten structure crashing down. About structures being brought crashing down there was to be no doubt – but not as had been planned.

How did these two men of destiny, these two makers of world history, set about conducting their grand strategic affairs? Let us take a brief look at them, before turning back the pages to trace their paths to greatness, at this time in the autumn of 1940, when they both were wrestling with the problem of how to win the war. First, Winston Churchill, presiding over a meeting of the Defence Committee. It must, of course, be remembered that Churchill, Minister of Defence as well as Prime Minister, regarded himself as an expert on war. A.J.P. Taylor has described in his inimitable way the unique position and prestige that he enjoyed. Having been a regular soldier, seen action in India, the Sudan, South Africa and on the Western Front, served as a minister in the Great War, twice been First Lord of the Admiralty, loving uniforms and frequently wearing them, with row upon row of campaign medals, 'His mind teemed with original, often dangerous ideas, and he could sustain them with technical arguments.' To the public at large Churchill was the man who bore the whole weight of the war. He may have been an amateur strategist, yet he was one of genius. In all his dealings with his subordinates, whether military men, ministers or civil servants, he retained a Puck-like sense of fun. He would talk of the need to shoot a few generals. He would harangue the War Cabinet, rather than hold consultations. All he wanted, as he himself would explain, was compliance with his wishes after reasonable discussion. Yet he would in the end defer to the professional views of service chiefs when they ran counter to his own. Churchill did not merely provide inspiring leadership. He determined strategy.

There he sits, then, at a Defence Committee meeting on 31 October 1940. It was an especially important one in that it would consider the war's future conduct. Present at it, apart from ministers and the Chiefs of Staff, were senior officers of all three services. In reviewing the situation, aggravated by Italy's invasion of Greece, Churchill drew comfort from Britain's ability actually to continue the war, but deplored her incapacity to mount any major offensive before 1942. In acknowledging that Germany was master of Europe and could do what she liked there, he foresaw the likelihood of a German confrontation with Russia, and again stressed the need, now that the danger of invasion was 'relatively remote' further to reinforce the Middle East. Yet, he told the Defence Committee:

> The question might be asked 'How are we to win the war? . . . For the moment all that we could do was to bank on the pressure of the blockade accompanied by the remorseless bombing of Germany and Italy. By 1941, however, we would be in a position to take on medium operations of an amphibious nature; and by 1942, we should be able to deliver very heavy overseas attacks . . .

Meanwhile survival depended on maintaining the life of Britain, which meant that air defence and sea communications must be looked to.

If Churchill were uncertain as to how to proceed with winning the war, the same may be said of Hitler who, as Supreme Commander of the Wehrmacht, and apart from conducting War Councils at the Berghof or in the Berlin Chancellery, issued his general instructions by means of War Directives from his headquarters. OKW (Oberkommando der Wehrmacht) was staffed by such men as Field Marshal Keitel, who regarded the Führer as the greatest strategic genius of all time, and General Jodl, the Operations Chief, who, even when things were going badly in the latter stages of the war, asked Guderian whether he knew of a better Supreme Commander than Adolf Hitler. Yet War Directive No 18, issued in November 1940, both intimated doubts about what to do and, in effect, hinted at the potential dissipation of the Wehrmacht. The directive ranged wide. Apart from keeping alive the possibility of reverting to Operation Sea Lion, commanders-in-chief were to consider a number of operational options. There were in fact few parts of Europe which did not figure in Hitler's broad strategic survey. France was to be persuaded to secure her African possessions against the British and against General Charles de Gaulle's Free French forces, then being formed in Britain, *and* to begin to participate in the war on Germany's side. Spain, too, was to be brought into the war in order to help drive the British from the western Mediterranean. Gibraltar was to be captured and the Straits closed. In order to assist the Italians in their offensive against Egypt, the Wehrmacht would alert a panzer division for service in North Africa. German shipping would be made ready to transport troops and equipment, and the Luftwaffe would plan attacks on Alexandria and the Suez Canal. The occupation of the Greek mainland would also be planned. Yet perhaps the most significant part of the entire directive lay in references to continuing preparations for possible operations against Russia. Hitler, as was customary with him, ended his directive by calling for reports from commanders-in-chief on these broad guidelines, so that he could issue orders as to the manner and timing of each operation. At this stage of the war, he was still willing to listen to advice and proposals from his subordinates. Had he followed their advice, the war's outcome might have been very different. But, as we shall see, the forthcoming Russian campaign gave rise to such events that the Führer took into his own hands the detailed and day-to-day direction of operations, and by doing so began to give orders which were arbitrary, unrelated to facts and in the end, fatal. It is true, of course, that Hitler's grasp of military and technical detail amazed all who came into contact with it, and his memory was astonishing. But the education which counted in a military commander – experience of command in the field at all levels – he totally lacked. Thus while he did have both an extraordinary grip of military detail and an unrivalled capacity for strategic generalization, nearly all decisions on the field of battle are dictated by considerations between these two, and here he was deficient.

In examining, therefore, these respective directions about how the war was to be prosecuted, we see that at this time, November 1940, there was a similarity in the uncertainty of each leader's concept of how things would go. No such similarity existed between the two persons concerned. There could have been no greater contrast in breeding, upbringing, character, disposition, taste or experience. Churchill was genial, warm-hearted, generous, emotional, witty, open, overflowing with life and appreciative of all its pleasures, chivalrous and honourable. Hitler was secretive, cold-hearted, ignoble, vindictive, close, venomous, narrow, petty and dishonourable. Yet they had certain accomplishments and interests in common: both were accomplished amateur strategists, both loved to dabble in and commanded remarkable grasp of military detail, both loved dressing up in military uniforms, both were prodigious orators, both had strong historical imaginations, both painted, both were for ever fighting, neither could give up. Each would have found comfort in Milton's lines:

What though the field be lost?
All is not lost; th'unconquerable will . . .
And courage never to submit or yield.

But whereas Hitler would enthusiastically have endorsed the line omitted
above – 'And study of revenge, immortal hate' (the words after all are spoken
by Satan) – Churchill would have had nothing to do with revenge or hate. He
fought to save Britain's freedom and honour. Hitler fought for German hegemony, for revenge and conquest and the enslavement or the annihilation of
others. That Britain did not succumb was because of Churchill; that Germany
did was because of Hitler. The Führer was always wanting to make world
history, and in this he succeeded. Churchill was not so concerned with *making* it
as with taking part in it – and then writing about it both for posterity *and* for
profit.

We have seen already Hitler mafficking in victory, and have yet to see how
malignant he could be in defeat. We have seen also how dauntless Churchill
could be in defeat, and have yet to see how magnanimous he could be in
victory. Here is perhaps the essential difference between the two men. One,
Führer of the Third Reich, Supreme Commander of the Wehrmacht and later
Commander-in-Chief of the German Army too, exercised absolute control
over one of the most professional, skilful, courageous, fanatically devoted and
powerful groups of armed forces the world had yet seen, and in his capricious
use of them, drawn by an unrelenting will, he brought his country down into
total and ignominious defeat. The other, while bursting with strategic ideas,
some brilliant, some bizarre, exercised restrained, persistent and inspiring
control over a heterogeneous bunch of brave, spirited, yet at times artlessly
amateurish soldiers, sailors and airmen who, slowly but surely, and with the
indispensable aid of powerful allies, turned defeat into victory, albeit at a price
so heavy that revisionist historians have censured his conduct of the war as
ruinous to his country's subsequent welfare.

Here is a curious and diverse pair to juggle with, as we follow their political
and military fortunes and misfortunes. Alike in being warlords, Hitler and
Churchill could hardly have been less alike in origins.

CHAPTER 2

The Lure of Politics

Youth is a blunder; Manhood a struggle; Old Age a regret.

BENJAMIN DISRAELI

I

In 1889 there took place two events of great moment: Winston Churchill decided he wanted to be a soldier, and Adolf Hitler was born. Churchill's predilection for soldiering was aroused within a matter of weeks after arriving at his public school, Harrow. It seems that his interest was caught by a letter in the school magazine deploring the poor drill, slovenliness and weakness in numbers of Harrow's Rifle Corps, which was derided by the rest of the school. More 'smart and influential fellows' were needed. However deficient in these qualities Winston Churchill might have been at the time, he joined the corps and greatly enjoyed its activities, writing enthusiastically to his mother about manoeuvres carried out at Rickmansworth in May 1888. Even at the age of thirteen (he had been born on 30 November 1874) he displayed in his letters home a remarkable fluency and turn of phrase, together with confidence on his own future paramountcy. 'I am going to write you a proper epistle,' he tells his mother, 'hoping that you will forgive my former negligence', or 'I hope to come out top . . . I feel in working trim & expect many rises in my position.'

In March 1889 he gives his father an account of another sham battle with the Rifle Corps at Aldershot. 'It was great fun. The noise was tremendous . . . We were defeated because we were inferior in numbers & not from any want of courage.' He goes on to say that he has bought a book on drill and intends to go in for the Corporal Examinations next term. He has been to the range and fired twenty rounds. All this zeal for the Rifle Corps on his son's part, together with the boy's splendid collection of model soldiers, clearly had their effect on his father, Lord Randolph Churchill. Winston's own account of it in *My Early Life* explains what happened when his father paid a formal visit of inspection. After twenty minutes of studying 'with a keen eye and captivating smile' an impressive parade of fifteen hundred soldiers – horse, foot and guns – Lord Randolph asked his son if he would like to go into the army. Having in mind how splendid it would be to command an army – not just to be part of it, mind you, but to command it – a decided affirmative was returned. Thus Churchill joined the

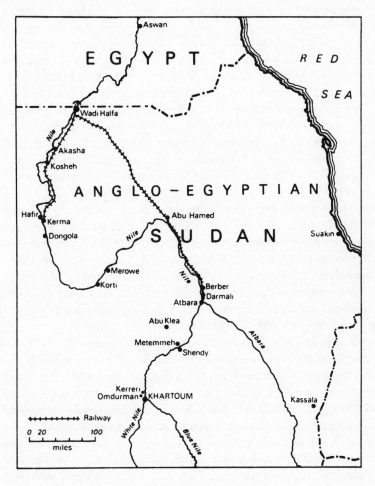

Army Class at Harrow in September 1889. His first steps on life's path were now clear, and thus far this life had been an easy, privileged one. Nephew of the eighth Duke of Marlborough, son of an American heiress and a former Chancellor of the Exchequer and Leader of the House of Commons, he had been born with a ducal spoon in his mouth. What is more, he had been born at

Blenheim Palace in Oxfordshire, the magnificent house, designed by Sir John Vanbrugh, which a greatful nation had presented to John Churchill, first Duke of Marlborough.

About five months before Churchill joined the Army Class at Harrow, a very different creature had made his appearance in the world. On 20 April 1889, in a small inn at Braunau in Upper Austria, on the border with Bavaria, a son was born to the wife of a customs officer in the service of the Imperial Habsburg dynasty, the rulers of what was then the Austro-Hungarian Empire. In his days of power Adolf Hitler was fond of reflecting on the circumstances of his rise from a humble background of obscure poverty and lack of academic or social opportunity to become head of a powerful state, suggesting, among other things, that such a change in fortune and position must be unique in history. He would, too, frequently meditate on his own uniqueness – and in this he was surely not mistaken. Yet emphasis on his lowly origins and poverty was, like so many things about him, a product of his own imagination rather than a reflection of the facts.

That Hitler's early days were so unsatisfactory was largely due to his own inclination. In 1900, when he was eleven years old, he was sent to a perfectly adequate secondary school in Linz, the Realschule, which prepared its pupils for a career in commerce. He left it five years later, simply because his performance there had been so poor – there was no question of his mother, who had been widowed in 1902, being unable to afford the fees. At this time in his life Hitler was disinclined to take advantage of opportunity, a deficiency to be more than compensated for later. His lack of, indeed rejection of, formal education was often to find expression during his years of power in his contempt for both the academic profession and for what it tried to do: 'to turn us into erudite apes like themselves'. It may be said, too, that the example of his father's career can scarcely have been a source of inspiration, for Adolf Hitler harboured a great ambition to become an artist. In *Mein Kampf* he recalled the endless disagreements which he had with his father on this point. The more his father sought to persuade his son to follow his own profession, the more stubborn Hitler became in rejecting it. At the same time, the more he insisted that he should study painting, the more vigorously his father opposed him. Nor was this the only reason for his father's dissatisfaction, for the boy's school reports were consistently bad. Even at school, however, Hitler had displayed two characteristics that were to persist throughout his astonishing career: first, he cast himself in the part of a leader, requiring other boys to acknowledge his right to their subordination; second, he was moved, inspired even, by history's lesson of German nationalism.

As one of his schoolmasters recalled, however, he was also cantankerous, wilful, arrogant and bad-tempered. Moreover he was notoriously lazy and lacking in self-discipline, the discipline either to apply himself properly to his studies or to fit into the social group around him. Already he was revealing those tendencies to become what he did indeed later become – a drop-out. His formal schooling ended in 1905. His widowed mother had moved to Linz, and there Hitler idled away the next two years, refusing to get a job, but instead dreaming frivolously of becoming an architect or artist, going to the theatre, enjoying in particular the historically romantic grandeur of Wagner, and otherwise frittering his time away. 'He lived in a world of his own,' writes Alan Bullock, 'content to let his mother provide for his needs, scornfully refusing to concern himself with such petty mundane affairs as money or a job.'

A powerful influence then exerted itself on his way of life – Vienna, which Hitler visited in 1906. What he saw and heard there, the imperial city's great state buildings, its solemn temples and gorgeous palaces, the paintings in its galleries, the music in its Opera House, its theatres, its libraries, all these inspired in him an ambition to enter Vienna's Academy of Fine Arts. In the following year he had his first shot at gaining a place there as a student of art. He was to be disappointed, for the Academy's examiners pronounced his test drawings to be unsatisfactory, offering instead the unpalatable advice that he should study architecture, advice he did not heed. Yet the lure of Vienna persisted. After his mother's death at the end of 1907, he returned to Vienna with enough money to live on, and his desire to enter the Academy unquenched. He did not try to do so again, however, until September 1908, and meanwhile led a lonely life, except for the companionship of one friend from Linz, August Kubizeck. Work and women seemed not to interest him. Hours spent in meditation, wandering about, resentful pondering, were more to his taste. He had, observed Alan Bullock, 'the artist's temperament without either talent, training or creative energy'. Yet he later described his time in Vienna as an 'exacting school' which hardened him and made him capable of further hardness – he was to present the world with unequivocal evidence of the latter. Having again failed to get into the Academy of Fine Arts, and being ineligible for the School of Architecture, he took refuge in obscurity.

Occasional casual work, painting and selling postcards, living in dosshouses, idling the days away – this was the pattern of Hitler's life. Meagre, frustrating, purposeless, utterly undistinguished, it must indeed have been weary, stale, flat and unprofitable. There was but one thing for which he seemed to show enthusiasm – talking. And it was what he talked about, and the manner in which he did so, that revealed something of what was to come: German nationalism; contempt for the working classes; hatred of the Jews; the overriding need for struggle (*Mein Kampf* is properly translated as *My Struggle*). Many years later, in 1928, one of Hitler's speeches contained a passage in which he glorified the idea of struggle. It was struggle, as old as life itself, which would determine events. Those with strength and ability would always win; those who were weak and incompetent were doomed to lose. Humanity was not the solution to man's problems, but brutality. You had to fight for life in order to win it. What mattered above all was the possession of willpower; with it, a man could achieve anything. It would not be long before Hitler was to show his fellow creatures that he meant what he said.

If one form of willpower is the will to succeed, then it was possessed in full measure by Churchill, too. Whereas Hitler's youth was a sorry tale of idleness, resentment, rejection and disillusion, Churchill's was one of opportunity, ambition, adventure and industry. We may perhaps take as an early instance of his self-confidence the occasion in November 1890 when he sat the Preliminary Examination for the Royal Military College (as it was then called), Sandhurst. Some of this confidence was evident in a letter to his mother before the examination, in which he tells of schoolmasters who take great interest in him and who report well on his work. He is sure he has a fair chance and is determined to have a good try at it. He concedes that arithmetic and algebra are dangerous areas, but is sure of English – 'I am working my very best . . . I cannot do anything more than try.' He writes again after one examination and this time confides that he has had a piece of good fortune. In deciding which particular map might come up for examination, he chooses New Zealand at random, which then turns out to be the first question. His letter to 'Darling Mama' considers that this is luck, goes on to say that he has had a successful day, and adds a material point – 'A Remittance would not be altogether misplaced.' His confidence was not misplaced either, for he passed the examination in every subject, greatly to the delight of his mother.

It was at this time that Churchill first came in touch with a sporting interest which was subsequently to give him both further pleasure and fame – the world of racing, for his father had rented Banstead Manor, near Newmarket, and had for some years owned or part-owned a number of racehorses. There Winston and his younger brother, Jack, derived much joy from building a hut, with moat and drawbridge, which they named 'the Den'. Graduating from toy soldiers to live beings, the potential Sandhurst cadet would drill his brother and cousins and any others he could muster to take part. He revelled, too, in country life – hunting rabbits, skating, riding, keeping chickens. Back at Harrow in 1891, while his father was away in South Africa, Churchill wrote regularly to his mother. In July he is seriously alarmed that he may not be able both to attend the annual cricket match against Eton at Lord's, or to enjoy the mid-term holiday that went with it. He is, however, rewarded, and he goes with Count Kinsky (an admirer of his mother) to the Crystal Palace, where there was a great review of the Country Fire Brigades performed in the presence of the German Emperor, Kaiser Wilhelm II. The uniform worn by His Imperial

Majesty profoundly impresses Churchill and in letters to both his brother, Jack, and his father, he describes the splendid helmet surmounted by a white eagle, the white tunic and steel cuirass. Shortly afterwards Churchill has a serious disagreement with his mother about the advisability of his spending some weeks in France, a course recommended by Harrow's headmaster in order to improve the boy's likely marks in the forthcoming French examination. Winston violently opposes the idea – 'I beg and Pray that you will not send me to a vile, nasty, fusty, beastly French "Family".' Rather surprisingly, in another letter he also cools towards a military career – 'I feel less keen about the Army every day', and even thinks the Church would suit him better!

His mother knows better, however, writing to her husband that although Winston is at present 'slouchy and tiresome', he will be all right when he gets to Sandhurst. Moreover he does go to France, and from there writes to his mother on Christmas Eve 1891 that he is enjoying riding at Versailles – 'Les chevaux ne sont pas mal. Ils sont veritablement rosses [sorry beasts]. Mme Monsieur M's mère ne dit rien que "Son progrès est merveilleux". "N'est-ce pas extraordinaire etc etc".' But he is longing to return, and back at Harrow he shows his application and pugnacity by winning the school fencing championship in March 1892, going on to become the Public Schools Fencing Champion. His academic achievements, however, did not match this combative success. Taking the Entrance Examination to Sandhurst for the first time in July 1892, he heard the following month that he had failed. His father was not pleased, but noted that there would be another chance to take it in November. The headmaster of Harrow, the Reverend J.E.C. Welldon, in a letter to Lord Randolph, considers that Winston is well up to the standard needed to pass into Sandhurst, if not that November then certainly in the following summer. This is precisely what happened – he did pass in the summer of 1893, aged eighteen.

Winston Churchill's son, Randolph, in his comprehensive portrait of his father's *Youth, 1874–1900*, provides a most penetrating comment on the young man at this stage of his remarkable career, pointing out that the legend of the stupid schoolboy is quite false. Winston may have been wilful and mutinous, and was indeed unhappy at school, partly because his parents kept him at a distance, but these things 'compelled him to stand on his own feet and to make his way in the world by his own exertions and by his own methods. He had to fight every inch of his road through life' (here we may perhaps detect a similarity between his struggle, although under very different conditions, and Hitler's); 'nothing came easily to him, not even oratory and writing, in which he was later to excel. To achieve success he had to develop that intense power of concentration which, as it grew, was to serve him and his countrymen so well.'

Lady Randolph might have thought that all would be well once Churchill got to Sandhurst. It was far from being so. In the first place although he wrote enthusiastically to his father about passing the examination, this enthusiasm was not shared by Lord Randolph, who replied witheringly that it was one thing to pass an examination creditably, but quite another to do so only barely. His marks were such that he would not be eligible for an infantry cadetship, but only for the cavalry. Lord Randolph lamented that with all his advantages, with all the abilities that he, Winston, thought he had and that others spoke of, with all the efforts made to ease his life and encourage his work, yet the best that could be achieved was that 'you come up among the 2nd rate and 3rd rate class who are only good for commissions in a cavalry regiment'. There was also the additional grievance that having failed to get into the 60th Rifles, 'one of the finest regiments in the army', his going to the cavalry would cost Lord Randolph a further £200 a year. In any event, he added, he would not allow Winston to remain in the cavalry, but would later seek an exchange to an infantry regiment. By a further twist of circumstances, when Winston actually got to Sandhurst, there *was* an infantry vacancy, although in the end he did join the cavalry. From Sandhurst he writes to his father that he is contented there, despite the discomfort, the discipline and the food – although dinner is grandly conducted with a menu in French, this is the only French thing about it – and he has 'My Servant' who blacks boots, clears up and does odd jobs, if tipped! 'Altogether, I like the life. I am interested in the drill and in the military education I shall receive.' After all, the army *was* to be his career, he feels keen on it, the course will make him mentally, morally and physically better. He ends his letter by hoping that his father will write and send him some money.

As Churchill subsequently recorded: 'Horses were the greatest of my pleasures at Sandhurst', and in one of his most universally acclaimed books, *My Early Life*, he offers to parents the advice that they should give their sons horses rather than money, for no one ever came to grief, other than honourable grief, from riding horses. Time spent in the saddle was never wasted. Ruin might come to young men through owning or betting on horses, but not by riding them, unless of course they broke their necks at the gallop – 'a very good death to die'.

Winston was to face death both at the gallop with the cavalry and, less glamorously, as the commanding officer of an infantry battalion, and in each case he did so fearlessly. His father at this time – 1893 – had little more than a year to live (his last years were tragic, as a general paralysis slowly overtook him), and one of the saddest features of his approaching death was that at last he and his son were drawing closer together. In October of that year Lord Randolph writes to his mother that Sandhurst has done wonders for Winston – he is steadier, has smartened up, is upright and well-mannered. Winston's own account of this time makes it clear that 'he had acquired a new status in my father's eyes', and he greatly enjoyed being taken about by Lord Randolph to meet both political colleagues and racing friends. The Sandhurst cadet found such company and such conversation that ensued infinitely entertaining. Moreover, it seemed to him that his father held the key to all that mattered, and he laments that just as their relationship was beginning to hold out the prospect of a most rewarding alliance, Lord Randolph quitted the scene for ever. Before he died, however, there was further disagreement between them as to which regiment Winston should join. His father was still anxious that it should be the 6oth Rifles, but by this time his son had met the commanding officer of the 4th Hussars and had been profoundly impressed both by the personality of Colonel Brabazon and by the dazzling attraction of hussar uniform. Early in 1894 he writes to his mother, listing the numerous advantages of his joining the cavalry. Promotion is much quicker, you are commissioned earlier, the 4th Hussars are going to India, where the cavalry always get good stations and where keeping horses is cheaper, riding is much better than walking, there is the special interest of life with horses, and he has friends in the regiment. In the end, and despite further attempts by his father to get him into the 6oth Rifles, Churchill was commissioned into the 4th Hussars in February 1895. Before Lord Randolph had died in the previous month, he had given his son some priceless advice about soldiering: 'The Army is the finest profession in the world if you work at it and the worst if you loaf at it.'

It was not only horses and the cavalry which captured Churchill's interest at this time. While at Blenheim in December 1893 he establishes a firm friendship with his cousin Sunny Blandford, eldest son of the Duke of Marlborough, refers to the 'beautiful Polly Hackett', and does well at Sandhurst, both academically and in riding school. Nor was this all. During his long life Churchill made countless speeches and wrote innumerable articles for news-papers, and the first signs of this other career became evident in November 1894, during his last term at Sandhurst. Being always something of a hedonist, despite an absolute devotion to duty, it was fitting that this first essay into social controversy should see him opposing a campaign waged by the London County Council and led by a woman called Mrs Ormiston Chant, 'to separate the bars of the Empire Theatre in Leicester Square from the adjoining prome-nade where attractive and good-natured ladies of the town used to parade themselves'. Churchill allied himself firmly with a virtually memberless organization called the Entertainments Protection League, said that he was prepared to make a speech if need be, and sent a letter to the *Westminster Gazette*, which was published over the initials WLSC[1] and which gives us an example of his style, which some critics later condemned as artificial, declama-tory and falsely eloquent, yet which the more discerning saw as 'a formal mode

[1] He had been christened Winston Leonard Spencer Churchill.

of English utterance' expressing the author's 'heroic, highly coloured, sometimes over-simple and even naïve, but always genuine, vision of life'. We may
perhaps permit ourselves a taste of this language (and its surprising relevance
to today's world), written, we must recall, when Churchill was still a Sandhurst
cadet and only nineteen years old:

> The improvement in the standard of public decency is due rather to
> improved social conditions and to the spread of education than to the
> prowling of the prudes . . . Now, Sir, I submit that the only method of
> reforming human nature and of obtaining a higher standard of morality is
> by educating the mind of the individual and improving the social conditions
> under which he lives. This is a long and gradual process, the result of which
> is not to be obtained in our generation. It is slow, but it is sure . . .

In deploring obedience to prudish voices (indeed, it brings to mind puritan
efforts to close the Elizabethan and Jacobean theatres), Churchill placed the
obligation to counter moral evil firmly with the Government. He did more
than just write an article, however. After partitions had actually been erected to
effect this supposedly desirable separation, he even took part in tearing down
the barricades and then addressed the mob of some hundreds who were engaging enthusiastically in this destruction. Although, as he later recorded, there
was no report of what he said, his words were evidently listened to, and ended
with a distinctly political appeal to those present that, having pulled down the
barricades, they should at the next municipal election pull down also those
responsible for having them erected. Churchill was highly pleased with all this,
writing to his mother that he had made 'an essay in journalism', and referring to
another letter he had sent to the *Daily Telegraph* (but which in fact arrived after
that newspaper had ended its correspondence on this particular subject).

While these events were in progress, Lord and Lady Randolph were sailing
round the world, and it was only now that Churchill began to understand how
very seriously ill his father was. He writes in great concern to his mother,
begging her to give him all news of his father without reserve, and cajoling her
to look on the bright side and try to obtain enjoyment from all the places she is
visiting. But for Lord Randolph the end was near. So unwell was he in India that
their world tour was cut short and they returned to England, arriving in
London on Christmas Eve 1894. Within a month Lord Randolph was dead.
Now Winston Churchill, twenty years old and about to be commissioned into
the 4th Hussars, was head of the family, responsible for his brother, Jack, and
his mother. His own son, Randolph, sums up the prospect before him as he is
about to embark on his military career. He was at least his own master. 'He had
a stout heart, an audacious spirit, colossal ambition, a late-maturing but

[24]

massive brain from which elements of genius cannot be excluded, a sharp sword; and he was soon to fashion himself a valuable and rewarding pen, which was in the next few years, combined with his thirst for adventure, to liberate him from the thraldom of penury and open all doors during the seventy years that lay ahead.' In other words, the world lay before him, ripe for conquest, and with sword and pen he was to conquer it as completely as man ever did.

Churchill's life with the 4th Hussars provided him with what he most needed – opportunity. There was opportunity to enjoy all that horses had to offer, including steeplechasing and polo, at which he excelled; there was opportunity to educate himself by extensive reading; there was opportunity, even while liking the soldier's life, to contemplate playing the much more fascinating game of politics, and thereby follow in his father's footsteps; there was opportunity for active service, to seek 'the bubble reputation, even in the cannon's mouth', and seek also recognition in the form of campaign medals and gallantry awards; there was opportunity to write about his adventures and so gain, not merely a wider audience than mere soldiering would yield, but a substantial income too. We may perhaps glance at some early instances of his balancing equitation and contemplation. In August 1895 he writes to his mother from Aldershot, where the 4th Hussars are stationed, that every day eight or nine hours are spent in the saddle, some of these playing polo, yet 'mental stagnation' is in danger of becoming a state of mind into which soldiers fall because the power of thought is subjected to routine and discipline. But he tries to counter this effect by 'reading & re-reading Papa's speeches'. What is more, he sets himself the task of tackling Gibbon's *Decline and Fall of the Roman Empire*, whose rich and stately prose was to have such a profound and beneficial effect on his own style of composition. That same summer the 4th Hussars moved from Aldershot to Hounslow in order to prepare for posting to India in the following year. Although most cavalry officers spent the winter hunting, this was a pursuit somewhat beyond Churchill's pocket, and he looked about instead for some adventurous pursuit, one which would cost less but which would be even more exciting. It was hardly surprising that he chose to set sail for a 'seat of war'.

This particular seat was Cuba, then still a colony of Spain, where in 1895 the Spanish were attempting to suppress the latest in a long series of risings against them. Churchill had not only obtained permission from his commanding officer, Colonel Brabazon, that he and a friend from the 4th Hussars, Reginald Barnes, should visit the Cuban battlefields and see what intelligence about new weapons could be picked up, but also that he should send letters from the front to the *Daily Graphic* and be paid five guineas a time for them. On his way to Cuba Churchill saw something of the United States and its people, and these first impressions had a profound influence on him; indeed, his subsequent reverence for that country and its institutions owed much to these first contacts. He writes to his brother, Jack, that it is 'a very great country . . . Not pretty or romantic but great and utilitarian.' There might be little tradition, but everything was essentially practical and matter-of-fact. In other letters he is deeply struck by the immense influence of 'business enterprise' and concludes that 'the first class men of America are in the counting house and the less brilliant ones in the government'. He recognizes the country's 'vulgarity', but sees in it a sign of strength, and pictures the American people 'as a great lusty youth – who treads on all your sensibilities, perpetrates every possible horror of ill manners – whom neither age nor just tradition inspire with reverence – but who moves about his affairs with a good hearted freshness which may well be the envy of older nations of the earth.'

Once Churchill arrived in Cuba he had enough excitement to satisfy both himself and the readers of his dispatches to the *Daily Graphic*. Attached to the staff of General Valdez, he and Barnes take part in the General's pursuit of insurgents and, fittingly enough, Churchill hears his first shots fired in anger on 30 November 1895, his twenty-first birthday. The events were duly recorded both for his own gratification and for that of his readers. During this pursuit of the enemy, Churchill and his companions decide to bathe in a nearby river, are fired at by the rebels, and hurriedly collect fifty men who then engage the advancing enemy and drive them off. That night they are again under fire in camp, and next day take part in an advance over open ground under General Valdez's command. In his account of the action to his mother, Churchill praises the General for his bravery. Valdez, conspicuous in a white uniform and mounted on a grey horse, had attracted many bullets; since Barnes and Churchill were with him, they were in a dangerous enough place, and Churchill 'heard enough bullets whistle and hum past to satisfy me for some time to come'. As a result he was awarded a Spanish decoration, the Red Cross (not, however, worn by him), but also came in for a good deal of criticism on both sides of the Atlantic for having taken part in the operation at all. There is, of course, nothing unusual about chairborne grudges against adventurous spirits. One of his own most telling comments on what he had seen of the campaign, however, concerned how many bullets were expended to kill one soldier. Two hundred might have been regarded as an average; in Cuba, he said, it was nearer two hundred thousand.

During the time he had spent in New York before going to Cuba, Churchill had met and acquired the friendship of Mr Bourke Cockran, a lawyer and a Democrat member of Congress. Back at home, with still many months to go before the 4th Hussars set sail for India, Churchill wrote to Cockran on the question of what was the duty of government. Above all, he declared, it should be practical. Principle must give way to what was expedient, but the chief aim should be to try to make people both happier and better looked after. In particular, he was concerned by Cockran's condemnation of English rule in what was then a united Ireland – an issue which was to be dominant during many years of Churchill's political career. He pointed out to the American that what was needed in Ireland was 'firm generous government', not the maintenance of resentment and anger. The English had lost their patience with proposals for a Home Rule Bill,[1] and although the question was bound to be revived, it would eventually be solved by 'a wider measure of Imperial Federation'. These were weighty matters for a young cavalry officer of twenty-one to be addressing, yet the result of such correspondence – for Cockran, unlike most of Churchill's contemporaries, recognized latent genius when he encountered it – was eminently valuable. The Congressman's reply to Churchill urged him to embark on a study of 'sociology and political economy', and he pointed out that the young man's gift for expressing himself so clearly and winningly should be employed so as 'to take a commanding position in public life'. True ability, he added, would always be rewarded with opportunity, and Churchill's combination of comprehensive opinions and lively eloquence pointed to the likelihood of a great career. In the first volume of the enthralling portrait of his father, Randolph Churchill points out that Cockran's confident judgement of, and subsequent influence on, Churchill were profoundly and enduringly important. For his part, Churchill later described Cockran as his model – 'I learned from him how to hold thousands in thrall'.

On 11 September 1896 Churchill sailed with his regiment for India aboard the *SS Britannia*. Before doing so he had continued his practice of mixing with and getting to know 'top people', for most doors were open to the son of Lord and Lady Randolph. Among those he met and talked with were the Liberal politican Herbert Asquith and the Conservative Arthur Balfour – both future Prime Ministers – Joseph Chamberlain, the Colonial Secretary in the Conservative Government, and Field Marshal Lord Wolseley, Commander-in-Chief of the British Army. He never hesitated to make use of important people in support of his own career, and even before leaving for India had occasion to do so, for he now viewed the prospect of nine years in that distant station, so far away from the hub of political activity, England, with dismay. Moreover, the magnet of further active service – whether in South Africa, Rhodesia or the Sudan – was exerting its powerful attraction. But his pleas, despite their urgency – 'A few months in South Africa would earn me the S.A. medal [and

[1] The principle underlying Home Rule was the establishment of a parliament in Dublin to deal with internal affairs in Ireland. The movement was launched in 1870, and was to be a divisive issue in British politics until the partition of Ireland in 1921, when Northern Ireland gained Home Rule in the form of the parliament at Stormont, and Southern Ireland was granted dominion status.

other awards] . . . Thence hot foot to Egypt – to return with two more decorations in a year or two – and beat my sword into an iron despatch box' (as he wrote to his mother) – were in vain. It would not be long, however, before he was winning further fame, and providing himself with further literary opportunity, in India, the Sudan and South Africa.

Even before getting to India, and then while soldiering there, Churchill's thoughts turned frequently to politics; not only dwelling on how to be elected to the House of Commons, but also on how to support himself in a political career, for in those days Members of Parliament received no pay. Nevertheless he found agreeable diversions on the voyage – playing piquet and chess, and practising speech-making, in defiance of the slight impediment which was to stay with him throughout his life. Life at Bangalore, where the 4th Hussars were stationed, was pleasant enough. He cultivates his bungalow garden, collects butterflies, and falls in love with Pamela Plowden, but does not greatly care for Anglo-Indian society with all its formalities and niceties. Also he is impatient with the restrictions of military life in India, although greatly enjoying the polo (although he was obliged to play with his upper arm strapped to his body because he had dislocated his right shoulder when disembarking at Bombay). There is also the lure of further active service in Egypt, and he writes to his mother in February 1897 to tell her that if he can get there, it would be worth soldiering on for a few years, unless an opportunity to get into Parliament should come up. His decided views on the political matters of the day are expressed in numerous letters to Lady Randolph, and he tells her that these views spring from differentiating between right and wrong, whereas the motives of the Tory Government, headed by Lord Salisbury are determined by material profit. In one letter, while conceding the Prime Minister's strength and cleverness, he roundly condemns him for his policy of maintaining the Ottoman (Turkish) Empire's integrity, even at the cost of helping to crush a rebellion against Turkish rule in Crete, both with British troops and by naval blockade of Greece to prevent Greek aid to those insurgents. And why, he asks, is Salisbury so set on helping Turkey? Why, to keep the Russians from having Constantinople. Not that Churchill trusts Russia either. Even though he sees the arguments for Russia's having access to a warm-water port, she does not act in good faith, and it is inconceivable that she is disinterested. He goes on to tell his mother that were he in the House of Commons, he would go to any lengths to oppose Russian aims. He would even try to enter Parliament as a Liberal, were it not for his implacable hostility to Home Rule for Ireland. As things were, he would side himself with 'Tory Democracy'. He finishes his letter with a remarkable statement of the 'creed of Tory Democracy' whose results would be 'Peace & Power abroad – Prosperity & Progress at home'. Given the extraordinary consistency of Churchill's long parliamentary and ministerial career, it is fitting to note in detail what it was he wrote down while still only a twenty-two-year-old, and junior, cavalry officer, stationed thousands of miles from home:

1. Reform at home.
Extension of the Franchise to every male. Universal Education. Equal Establishment of all religions. Wide measures of local self-government. Eight hours [in the working day]. Payment of members [of Parliament] (on request). A progressive Income Tax. I will vote for them all.

2. Imperialism abroad.
East of Suez Democratic reins are impossible. India must be governed on old principles. The colonies must be federated and a system of Imperial Defence arranged. Also we must combine for Tariff & Commerce.

3. European Politics.
Non Intervention. Keep absolutely unembroiled – Isolated if you like.

4. Defence.
The Colonies must contribute and hence a council must be formed. A mighty navy must keep the seas. The army may be reduced to a training depot for India with one army corps for petty expeditions.

5. To maintain the present constitution of Queen – Lords – Commons – and the Legislative union as at present established.

As we examine his progress from Member of Parliament to junior Minister, to high ministerial office, and at length Prime Minister, we will see how this creed was maintained or modified.

It was not merely writing, however, which occupied so much of Churchill's time at Bangalore. There was much reading to be done as well. Apart from Gibbon, he reads Macaulay's *History of England* and his numerous essays (many of which, of course, are brilliant expositions of the world's great men), Adam Smith's *Wealth of Nations*, and innumerable volumes of the *Annual Register*.[1] Macaulay he finds 'crisp and forcible', Gibbon 'stately and impressive' – and all four epithets admirably fit Churchill's own incomparable use of the English language. The recommendations of Gibbon and Macaulay persuade him to read both Saint-Simon's *Memoirs* and Pascal's *Provincial Letters*. He devours, too, Plato's *Republic* and Rochefort's *Memoirs*, and cannot get enough of the *Annual Register*, explaining in a letter to his mother that whereas this latter source is invaluable for absorbing facts, it is the power of expression which he learns by

[1] On English politics.

studying the works of Macaulay, Gibbon and Plato which will enable him to make use of his knowledge to the greatest effect. His son, Randolph, summarized all this prodigious and disciplined study by saying that Churchill 'became his own university'.

At home on leave in the summer of 1897 he is intent on pursuing both his political and his military aspirations. A rally of the Primrose League, a Conservative political organization, gives him the opportunity to make his first public speech, and he makes full use of it. Already we see his extraordinary command of language and his skilful contrasts of the grandiloquent and the matter-of-fact. In reminding his audience of the broken state of the Tory Party at the end of Disraeli's second administration in 1880, he maintains that

> its principles were unpopular; its numbers were few; and it appeared on the verge of extinction. Observe it now. That struggling remnant of Toryism has swollen into the strongest Government of modern times. And the great Liberal party which in 1882 was vigorous, united, supreme, is shrunk to a few discordant factions of discredited faddists, without numbers, without policy, without concord, without cohesion, around whose necks is bound the millstone of Home Rule.

What was more, it was the Primrose League which had so influenced this change in fortune by 'pegging away' and convincing the public that Tory principles would bring about a proper reward. On the whole the newspapers reported in Churchill's favour, one weekly referring to 'an auspicious debut' which 'delighted his audience by the force and mental agility' of his speech, adding that he was but twenty-three (still twenty-two, in fact), was serving with the 4th Hussars, yet was hoping for a seat in Parliament. Another newspaper warned against the spoiling effects of too much notoriety and flattery, pointing out that many a young MP entered the House with a reputation, which they quickly forfeited once there. No such fate was to overtake Churchill.

Meanwhile, still in England, Churchill had heard that trouble on the North-West Frontier of India, stirred up by Pathan tribesmen, meant that an expedition was to be sent to pacify the area, under the command of General Blood, an old friend from whom Churchill had received an undertaking that in such an event, he, Churchill, might accompany the expedition. Such news made Churchill cut short his leave and hurry back to India, meanwhile bombarding General Blood with telegrams reminding him of his promise. Not for the first time, what some critics of Churchill called 'medal-hunting' and being 'pushy' paid off. By September 1897 he found himself part of the Malakand Field Force, attached to a brigade which was about to mount a punitive raid into the Mamund Valley, and so for the first time *in action* with British forces. What is more, his mother had succeeded in getting the *Daily Telegraph* to agree to publish – and pay for – a number of Churchill's 'letters' from the front. The action itself was all that he might have hoped for, as a letter to his mother, dated 19 September, shows:

> I must give you some account of my personal experiences on the 16th. I started with the Cavalry and saw the first shots fired. After half an hour's skirmishing I rode forward with the 35th Sikhs [infantry] until firing got so hot that my grey pony was unsafe. I proceeded on foot. When the retirement began I remained till the last and here I was perhaps very near my end . . . this retirement was an awful rout in which the wounded were left to be cut up horribly by these wild beasts . . . A subaltern . . . and I carried a wounded Sepoy [native infantryman] for some distance and might perhaps, had there been any gallery, have received some notice. My pants are still stained with the man's blood. We also remained till the enemy came to within 40 yards firing our revolvers . . . I felt no excitement and very little fear. All the excitement went out when things became really deadly . . . Altogether I was shot at from 7.30 [a.m.] till 8 [p.m.] on this day and now begin to consider myself a veteran. Sir Bindon has made me his orderly officer, so that I shall get a medal and perhaps a couple of clasps . . .[1]

Churchill goes on to tell his mother that this day's affair has been a major action, but he believes the worst is over and is relieved that the Empire has suffered no great loss. Two weeks later he takes part in another serious battle, is under fire for five hours while attached to the 31st Punjab Infantry, quite a change, as he comments, from the British cavalry, and has at the time of writing an awful headache. But strange as the life is, it is an amusing game and he will stay at it, reflecting in his uncomfortable trench that 'food and a philosophical temperament are man's only necessities . . .' General Blood is well pleased with Churchill's performance and grants him a Mention in Dispatches – the citation making it plain that his brigade commander 'has praised the courage and resolution of Lieutenant W.L.S. Churchill, 4th Hussars . . . who made himself useful at a critical moment'. It was not only by distinguishing himself in the field, however, that Churchill gained from his first taste of battle. There was also the material for his first book, and on returning to Bangalore he began to write *The Story of the Malakand Field Force*.

He worked hard at the book, sending the manuscript to his mother on the last day of 1897, asking her to arrange everything for its publication, including

---

[1] That is, a campaign medal, on the ribbon of which are worn clasps bearing the names of individual actions in that campaign.

the proof-reading. With the help of Balfour Lady Randolph finds a publisher, Longmans, and the book duly appears. In spite of innumerable printing errors and thoroughly reprehensible proof-reading, the book is well received and more than 8,000 copies are published between March 1898 and the end of that year. But Churchill is appalled by the slovenly work which has gone into its production – 'there are about 200 misprints, blunders & mistakes'. He calls the book 'an eyesore and I scream with disappointment and shame when I contemplate the hideous blunders that deface it'. However, reviews were favourable, and one magazine, the *Athenaeum*, went so far as to find evidence of the genius of his immediate forebears and of the first Duke of Marlborough, wishing that this new literary wonder might be as great a military man as the Duke – and more honest a politician. The reviewer detects in Churchill's style the influence of Edmund Burke, Disraeli and Napier (author of a huge and majestic history of the Peninsular War), but calls the work a model of military history, adding that it needs but proper correction for a second edition to become a classic. One great benefit of this literary success was that Churchill found himself sought after by magazine editors and book publishers who wanted him to write more, an idea which naturally appealed to him greatly. He was, however, still hankering after further campaigning, and although he failed in his attempt to take part in further skirmishing on the North-West Frontier, he succeeded in winning a far greater prize – by his customary method of pulling every high-powered string in sight – that of joining General Kitchener's army in its breath-taking adventure of reconquering the Sudan. Here he would find not only the thrilling excitement of cavalry action, but just the sort of material he could revel in for the writing of another book.

Kitchener (with whom Churchill was to have much to do in the Great War) was one of the most ambitious, opinionated, unscrupulous – and successful – soldiers in the British Army. Having been appointed Sirdar (Commander-in-Chief) of the Egyptian Army in 1892, he was able to set about the task on which he had long set his heart – reconquest of the Sudan. In this he could be sure of the Prime Minister's support, for Lord Salisbury, who had formed his third administration in 1895, was essentially an imperialist. And indeed it was to Lord Salisbury himself that Churchill appealed in July 1898, explaining that he wanted to join the expedition because 'the recapture of Khartoum will be a historic event' and – there was nothing like being straightforward – because he could write a book about it that would be useful, not least from a 'monetary point of view'. Salisbury had enjoyed reading Churchill's Malakand book, and asked Lord Cromer, the Consul-General and virtual ruler of Egypt as the British 'Agent', to ask Kitchener to find a place for Churchill. There is little doubt that had it been left to Kitchener, he would have refused, but happily other influences were at work through General Sir Evelyn Wood, Adjutant-

General at the War Office, and Churchill to his great delight found himself posted to the 21st Lancers and ordered to report forthwith to that regiment at Abbasiya Barracks, Cairo.[1] Ever mindful of the political career he was striving for, he made his second public speech at Bradford. It was enthusiastically received, something which reinforced further his determination to leave the army once he had won further fame and honour in the field.

Before we follow his adventures at Omdurman, we may note what his son, Randolph, has to say about his father's character and position at this time. He observes that already Churchill was deeply conscious of a 'sense of destiny, of power and of greatness'. This absolute certainty and self-confidence did not always endear him to his fellows. Of course, he made use of whatever influence his name, his connections, his father's reputation could command. Who would not have done so? Yet there were those who regarded Churchill's undoubted courage and ambitious determination as being not quite congruent with their ideas of what was appropriate to a Victorian gentleman. Nevertheless, being without money, 'he had nothing to lose' by thrusting himself forward at every opportunity and making use of those great people who were prepared to help him. 'He was a soldier of fortune. He had to make his way, he had to make his name . . . it was his own daemon which led him on to fame, prosperity and honour.' His activities in the Sudan and, later, in South Africa did much to set him on this path to fortune.

It cannot be said that General Kitchener was greatly enchanted on learning that the 21st Lancers (which for the last thirty-four years had served in India and Ireland without seeing a shot fired in anger, and thereby earned themselves the mock motto 'Thou shalt not kill') had been reinforced by the arrival of Lieutenant W.L.S. Churchill, 4th Hussars. Nevertheless, on 2 September 1898 Kitchener ordered the regiment to reconnoitre southward towards Omdurman, as he intended to occupy the town before the Khalifa's forces could do so, and thus avoid the dangers and difficulties of street fighting, where his superior firepower would be least effective. So it was that the celebrated charge of the 21st Lancers, in which Churchill participated, took place. The reconnaissance turned out to be a charge through a *khor*, or dry watercourse, in which several thousand of the Khalifa's men were concealed. In his account of the battle Churchill recalls that suddenly in front of them hundreds of men and some scores of horsemen appeared to rise up out of the ground to confront the galloping lancers, whose reaction was merely to increase the pace and so, by sheer momentum, get through. In a subsequent letter to Colonel Ian Hamilton, Churchill explained that as he and his troop closed with them, the enemy seemed to be about four deep:

[1] Where the author found himself as a young officer of the 4th Hussars in 1942.

But they all fell knocked A.O.T. [arse over tip] and we passed through without any sort of shock. One man in my troop fell. He was cut to pieces. Five or six horses were wounded by back handers etc. But otherwise unscathed. Then we emerged into a region of scattered men and personal combats. The troop broke up and disappeared. I pulled into a trot and rode up to individuals firing my pistol [because of his injured shoulder, Churchill was armed with a Mauser automatic pistol, rather than a sabre] in their faces and killing several – three for certain – two doubtful – one very doubtful. Then I looked round and saw the Dervish mass reforming . . . I realized that this mass was about twenty yards away, and I looked at them stupidly for what may have been two seconds. Then I saw two men get down on their knees and take aim with rifles – and for the first time the danger and peril came home to me. I turned and galloped. The squadron was reforming nearly 150 yards away. As I turned both shots were fired and at that close range I was grievously anxious. But I heard none of their bullets – which went Heaven knows where. So I pulled into a canter and rejoined my troop – having fired exactly ten shots and emptied my pistol – but without a hair of my horse or a stitch of my clothing being touched. Very few can say the same.

The whole affair had lasted perhaps two minutes, during which the 21st Lancers had achieved almost nothing except some death and a lot of glory. Some twenty of the enemy were killed. The regiment had lost seventy killed or wounded and more than a hundred horses. Worst of all, they had failed utterly in the one task of real value which they might have carried out – discovering that the bulk of the Khalifa's huge reserve, hidden behind a hill, was about to emerge and fall on the rear of Kitchener's now advancing army. But a brigade of Egyptian and Sudanese regiments commanded by Colonel Macdonald behaved magnificently in repelling the Dervish hordes, and when those hordes, after suffering appalling losses, saw that Macdonald's men were being reinforced, they drew off. By a coalition of relentless organization, perseverance, the steadiness of both British and local troops, and a goodly portion of luck, Kitchener had won. The Mahdist army was as good as destroyed, with some 10,000 of them killed for the loss of only 28 British soldiers.

In his letter to Hamilton two weeks after the action, Churchill writes that he is glad to have added the experience of a cavalry charge to his other military exploits, and that although dangerous enough he had not found it especially exciting. He adds that he himself is now in great disfavour with the high command and that Kitchener is furious that Sir Evelyn Wood had sent him out to take part in the affair. He then concedes that Kitchener is a great general, but has 'yet to be accused of being a great gentleman', and ends by saying that

Kitchener was backing a certainty from the outset, and 'has had the devil's luck to help him beside'. It might be added that Churchill too had the devil's luck, first, in having the pull with those in high places to get him to the battle; second, in coming through it without a scratch; and third, because the campaign provided him with the material for his second book, a highly acclaimed account of the whole affair published as *The River War*.

Although Churchill returned to England in October, he was determined to continue his personal battle for distinction and position on a variety of fronts – back to India and the 4th Hussars for the Inter-Regimental Polo Tournament; making speeches to keep his name to the fore in politics; working on his account of the Sudanese campaign, as well as completing a novel, *Savrola*, which he had started some time earlier; and being ever ready to hurry to the scene of military action, which was soon to offer further adventures in South Africa. Sir Isaiah Berlin has pointed out that Churchill built his life 'on the supreme value of action', and it was this foundation which in the end also made him such a supreme character in politics.

In between his military doings and darings in the Sudan and South Africa, he made a remarkable speech to the Conservative Association of Southsea in October 1898:

> To keep the Empire you must have the Imperial spark. Where is the glory of an armed sluggard living on the terror he has excited in the past? That is the debauched Imperialism of ancient Rome. Where is the glory of the starving peasant arrayed in purple and in cloth of gold? That is the Imperialism of modern Russia . . .
>
> To keep our Empire we must have a free people, an educated and well fed people . . . We would have an Empire and make all share the glory. '*Imperium et Libertas*' is the motto of the Primrose League, and it may also be the motto of Progressive Toryism. You have two duties to perform – the support of the Empire abroad and the support of liberty at home . . . We want young men who do not mind danger, and we want older and perhaps wiser men who do not fear responsibility . . . So the great game goes on, and, gentlemen, it is for you to say that it shall go on – that it shall not be interrupted until we are come through all the peril and trial, and rule in majesty and tranquillity by merit as well as by strength over the fairest and happiest regions of the world in which we live.

Churchill in his own person combined the young man who did not mind danger and the older man who did not fear responsibility as perhaps no one before or since has done. No one played the Great Game against peril and trial with such courage and such vigour.

II

A different sort of triumph awaited Winston Churchill on his return to India and his regiment. In February 1899 the 4th Hussars played the 4th Dragoon Guards in the final of the Inter-Regimental Polo Tournament at Meerut, and won. There was some controversy about who actually hit the 4th Hussars goals – they won by four goals to three, Churchill claiming three of his side's – but none about the indispensable part played by Churchill. Apart from polo, writing occupied much of his time, as he continued to work on *The River War*. He gave advice to his mother about her magazine, the *Anglo-Saxon*, which appeared in June 1899 and survived for more than two years; he also resumed work on his novel, *Savrola*. In March of that year he finally left India, spending some weeks in Cairo, where he received much help from Lord Cromer in learning more of Egyptian political matters and in meeting leading people in Cairo, including the Khedive himself. While in Egypt Churchill took the decisive step of sending in his papers to the Horse Guards, thus resigning from the Regular Army. His son, Randolph, comments that this decision was audacious, for he had no formal training for any other profession. Of course, he was determined to enter Parliament, but there was still the little matter of earning enough money to support himself. No doubt he would be able to make money with his pen, but nothing was settled there. Randolph Churchill concludes this particular reflection on his father's hopes and ideas by emphasizing that running risks came naturally to him, and would result in many changes of fortune during his life. At this time, however, fortune was with him.

No sooner had Churchill arrived home than he was presented with his first chance of entering the House of Commons. In June 1899 the Oldham Conservation Association, because of one Tory member's death and another's resignation, asked him to fight the seat and to find a second candidate (Oldham was a two-member constituency) as running mate. The man chosen was James Mawdsley, a trade unionist. Their Radical opponents were Alfred Emmott, a mill-owner, and Walter Runciman, who came from a shipping family; both were not only wealthy but also outstandingly able. Churchill's wry reflection was that whereas these rich Radicals could champion needy causes with huge sums of money, he and Mawdsley could hardly find £500 between them. He still cherished tender feelings for Pamela Plowden, and tried to persuade both her and his mother to aid him in his election efforts, but to no effect. In a letter to Lady Randolph he says he is troubled by a sore throat, but philosophically consoles himself by commenting that if polo tournaments can be won with a dislocated shoulder, then so can seats in Parliament with a sore throat. He was, however, defeated, but narrowly enough to be able to take a composed view of it all. In any event, more stirring affairs were shortly to occupy him.

The immediate cause of the Boer War of 1899–1902 was the resentment of the Boers – the descendants of the original Dutch settlers in South Africa – at British colonial policy which, they felt, would deprive the Transvaal of its independence. Certainly Britain, and in particular the Colonial Secretary, Joseph Chamberlian, had an eye on annexing the Transvaal, not least for its immensely rich mineral deposits.

The spark that lit the flame of war between Britain and the two 'Boer' states, the Transvaal and the Orange Free State, sprang from the dissatisfaction of Johannesburg's 'Uitlanders' ('foreigners'; that is white inhabitants of the Transvaal not of Boer stock, many of them British, who had done much to develop the Rand's gold industry) because, denied the right to vote, they had no voice in the conduct of Transvaal's government. Things came to a head when, late in 1898, a British worker was shot and killed by a Boer policeman. To the Uitlanders it looked like murder. The Boer jury and judge took a different view, and the policeman was not merely acquitted, but commended. The Rand's British subjects thereupon sent a petition to Queen Victoria, which some 22,000 of them had signed. It reached Lord Salisbury, the Prime Minister, in March 1899, and was taken seriously by him and his government, leading to negotiation between the British High Commissioner in South Africa, Sir Alfred Milner, and President Kruger of the Transvaal. First one side, then the other, would make offers to resolve their differences. Jan Christian Smuts (who was to figure so largely in the Boer War itself, the Great War and the Second World War, and was to become a great ally of Churchill's) made proposals which seemed to reconcile these differences, but Kruger, who seemed bent on conflict, scuppered them, and later rejected Chamberlain's conciliatory counter-proposals.

When Winston Churchill heard of this rejection in September 1899, he was certain that it would mean war. He was right. On 11 October Kruger's ultimatum expired, and Britain went to war against the two Boer states. After receiving an offer from the *Daily Mail* to go to South Africa as their war correspondent, he contacted the *Morning Post*, for which he had written previously, and concluded a lucrative agreement with that newspaper. Before leaving for South Africa, Churchill played his customary game of making sure he would have access to all the people there that mattered by persuading the Colonial Secretary, Chamberlain, to write to Milner. He also made sure that everything to make his task there both easier and more agreeble should be available by buying or ordering telescopes, field glasses, compasses and large quantities of wine, spirits and lime juice to accompany him on the sea voyage to Cape Town. He sailed from Southampton in the *Dunottar Castle* on 14 October, finding himself in the company of General Sir Redvers Buller, who was to take command of the British forces in South Africa.

While he was still at sea, Churchill's book about the Sudan campaign, *The River War*, was being printed, and appeared soon after his arrival at Cape Town.

Most of the reviews were favourable, although the *Saturday Review* criticized the book's 'ponderous and pretentious' style, finding fault with the author's 'egoism' and 'airs of infallibility'. The *Daily Mail* was more generous:

> Mr Winston Spencer Churchill is an astonishing young man, and his *River War* (Longmans) is an astonishing triumph. It is well-written, it is impartial, it is conclusive, and we do not think that any other living man could have produced it.

This was high praise indeed, although the reviewer went on to say that the book was too long, and also pointed out that it was really two books, one dealing with the British record in the Sudan before Kitchener's campaign, 'written in the severe style of Gibbon', the other describing the campaign itself, including the author's own part in it, and this was the 'work of a war correspondent' admirable in its 'movement and energy'. The book reveals Churchill's special feeling for General Gordon and his mission in Khartoum, and indeed the author's own summing up of Kitchener's defeat of the Dervish armies displays this feeling: 'The diplomatist said: "It is to please the Triple Alliance" [a secret treaty between Germany, Austria-Hungary and Italy]. The politician said: "It is to triumph over the Radicals". The polite person said: "It is to restore the Khedive's rule in the Soudan". But the man in the street said: "It is to avenge General Gordon".' All in all, the *Daily Mail*'s reviewer concluded it was an excellent book. Events in South Africa, however, robbed Churchill of an opportunity to read these reviews until many weeks after they appeared.

Churchill's adventures in South Africa were numerous, varied, thrilling, and made of just the stuff to engender general applause. He started out as a war correspondent, was captured and became a prisoner of war, escaped and became a popular hero, then finally served as a soldier once more, this time as a lieutenant in the South African Light Horse, taking part in the shambles of Spion Kop and the triumphant relief of Ladysmith. There was nothing unusual about his being in the thick of things. On 24 January 1900, Churchill, required by General Warren's headquarters to take a message to Lieutenant-Colonel Alec Thorneycroft, commanding the embattled troops on Spion Kop (all officers on the hill senior to him having been killed or wounded), climbed the mountain in the darkness, picked his way through the dead and wounded, with occsional bullets flying past, found Thorneycroft and handed him his new orders. But Thorneycroft had already decided to retire from Spion Kop and declined to accept his instructions to await reinforcements and dig in to hold the plateau for another day. Nothing that Churchill could say moved him from his determination to abandon the position, and on encountering the reinforcing infantry and sappers, he simply ordered them to counter-march. Churchill's view was that Thorneycroft was mistaken. The real fault lay with lack of clear orders, for there was no doubting the exceptional personal courage of Thorneycroft and his gallant soldiers. But they were left too long without support or direction, and had taken savage casualties. 'A young active divisional general, having made all plans for the relief, would have joined him [Thorneycroft] on the summit at nightfall and settled everything in person.'

The capture of the Spion Kop feature would not in itself have brought about the relief of Ladysmith, although it would have hastened it. The beleaguered town was not finally relieved until the end of February 1900. Churchill was there with the South African Light Horse, and described how they crossed a river, moved across hills which bore the scars of battle, came out on a plain which led to Ladysmith and saw the Boers in full retreat. Although he and his fellow cavalrymen were longing to pursue the retiring enemy, Buller decided against it and the British simply moved on to the town itself:

All day we chafed and fumed, and it was not until evening that two squadrons of the S.A.L.H. were allowed to brush through the crumbling rearguards and ride into Ladysmith. I rode with these two squadrons, and galloped across the scrub-dotted plain, fired at only by a couple of Boer guns. Suddenly from the brushwood up rose gaunt figures waving hands of welcome. On we pressed, and at the head of a battered street of tin-roofed houses met Sir George White [the general commanding the Ladysmith garrison] on horseback, faultlessly attired. Then we rode together into the long-beleaguered, almost starved-out, Ladysmith. It was a thrilling moment.

After further adventures during Field Marshal Lord Roberts's advance to and capture of Johannesburg and Pretoria, Churchill went home and at the so-called 'Khaki' election of October 1900 – arranged by Chamberlain to exploit the government's popularity in the light of Roberts's victories – was elected to represent Oldham in the House of Commons as a Conservative. His life as a politician was to be even more spectacular than his career as a soldier, although as we shall see, he had not done with soldiering yet. Before we highlight some of the events between Churchill's South African adventures and his election at Oldham, it is necessary to recall that the Boer War dragged on until May 1902, and that although the British terms were generous, the conflict had engendered bitterness that would never die, and as James (now Jan) Morris pointed out, 'the Boers were to win the Boer War in the end'. It was perhaps Kipling's pronouncement on the whole affair that stuck in the mind of the British public most starkly:

Let us admit it fairly, as a business people should,
We have had no end of a lesson: it will do us no end of good . . .

It was our fault, and our very great fault – and now we must turn it to use.
We have forty million reasons for failure, but not a single excuse.
So the more we work and the less we talk, the better results we shall get –
We have had an Imperial lesson; it may make us an Empire yet!

Before the Boer War, Churchill had been known only to a relatively narrow public. During it he became a national hero and a world-famous figure, for, even before Spion Kop and the relief of Ladysmith, other adventures had brought him to public notice. After disembarking at Cape Town at the very end of October 1899, anxious to reach the battlefields as quickly as possible, he and some fellow war correspondents moved by rail and ship to Durban, then hired a train to take them northwards to the front in Natal. They got as far as Estcourt, and from there Churchill decided to travel on in an armoured train commanded by an old comrade from his days on the North-West Frontier, Captain Aylmer Haldane. It was a decision that led to one of his most celebrated adventures, for it was this train which, on 15 November 1899, was ambushed by the Boers between Frere and Chieveley, north of Estcourt, and during the action which followed Churchill once more showed his coolness, courage and initiative under fire. The Boers had blocked the railway line, and as Captain Haldane later reported:

> Mr Winston Churchill, special correspondent of the *Morning Post* who was with me in the truck next the gun-truck offered me his services, and knowing how thoroughly I could rely on him, I gladly accepted them, and undertook to keep down the enemy's fire while he endeavoured to clear the line ... The Boers maintained a hot fire with rifles, 3–15 pr Creusot guns and a Maxim shell fire ... For an hour efforts to clear the line were unsuccessful ... but Mr Churchill with indomitable perseverance continued his difficult task, and about 8.30 a.m. the engine forced its way past the obstructing truck ...

Haldane goes on to explain the circumstances under which he was obliged to submit to capture by the Boers, and reiterates his praise for Churchill's conduct in attempting to save the engine, even though he was frequently under the enemy's direct fire. Churchill's gallant conduct was also reported by Captain Wylie, who was wounded in the action. Wylie speaks of him as 'as brave a man as could be found', while the railwaymen who were present 'are loud in their praises of Mr Churchill'. Churchill's servant, Thomas Walden, writes to Lady Randolph that he has heard all about it from the train driver, who tells Walden 'there is not a braver gentleman in the Army ... Every officer in Estcourt thinks Mr C. and the engine-driver will get the V.C. .... The engine, with Mr C. on it, got back to Frere station safe, and then Mr C. would get off and go back to look after Captain Haldane.' It was then, while Churchill was back at the scene of the fight to attend the wounded, that he encountered first two dismounted Boers, who fired at him as he attempted to evade them, and then 'a horseman galloping furiously, a tall, dark figure, holding his rifle in his right hand. He pulled up his horse almost in its own length and shaking the rifle at me shouted a loud command.' Churchill's first thought was to reach for his Mauser pistol, forgetting that he had earlier taken it off and left it in the engine while engaged in clearing the line. Unarmed, with the Boer horseman (who was subsequently alleged to be the commander of the ambush and a future general, Louis Botha) only forty yards distant and covering him with his rifle, Churchill had no alternative but to surrender himself as a prisoner of war.

The destruction of the armoured train and the capture of most of its occupants, including the *Morning Post*'s correspondent, were dramatic enough in themselves, and the news passed rapidly round the world. His subsequent escape created a sensation. On the grounds that he was a war correspondent and thus a non-combatant, Churchill, from his cantonment on the racecourse at Pretoria, applied repeatedly to the Boer authorities to be released from captivity and returned to British lines. The Boers, however, mindful of the part their prisoner had played in the ambush, took a different view; a note from Commandant-General Piet Joubert, Commander-in-Chief of the Boer forces, to the State Secretary of the Transvaal, Francis Reitz, dated 28 November 1899, made it plain that Churchill had been captured while engaged in hampering Boer operations, and therefore should not merely be treated like other prisoners of war, but guarded even more closely. Two days afterwards, on 30 November, Churchill had his twenty-fifth birthday, and in a letter to his old American friend, Cockran, reflected on how terrible it was that so little time remained to him. He had also realized that his efforts to obtain his liberty by appealing to the Boers were not going to succeed, and therefore turned his mind to alternative methods of escape.

Winston Churchill left his own detailed account of how he got away from his Pretoria prison. He and two others, Captain Haldane and a man called Brockie, planned to climb out of a latrine at the back of the buildings, and made their first bid on 11 December, only to be thwarted by the presence of a sentry. Next night they tried again. Again the sentry was there, but when Churchill went back again by himself, he found the sentry's back was turned and was able to jump over a wall into the garden beyond.[1] Attempts by Haldane

---

[1] An article in the *Sunday Times* dated 27 April 1997 suggests that Churchill let down Haldane and Brockie by escaping alone. But Churchill was first and always one to seize opportunity when it was presented to him, and here is an example of this. Haldane escaped later and rose to high command.

and Brockie to join him were, however, not successful as the sentry was again alert, so Churchill went on alone. He walked through the streets of Pretoria, came across the railway line to Portuguese East Africa (now Mozambique), climbed on to a train, disembarked before it was light, walked on and at length had the astonishing luck to knock on the door of the only man within twenty miles who was likely to be of help to him. John Howard proved to be a friend in need and in deed. He hid Churchill in a mine for three nights and days, and then, with the aid of Charles Burnham, a storekeeper, arranged for him to be concealed in a load of wool bales going by train to Lourenço Marques, the capital and main port of neutral Portuguese East Africa (now Maputo). On the night of 19 December his journey to freedom began. The plan worked; Burnham met Churchill at Lourenço Marques goods station, and conducted him to the British Consul, who arranged for a passage to Durban aboard the steamer *Induna*. He arrived there on the afternoon of 23 December 1899.

For all those sympathetic to the British cause the news was greeted with jubilation. It was high time there was something to celebrate, for in that month of December everything was going wrong for the British, and the so-called 'Black Week' saw General Gatacre defeated at Stormberg on 10 December, General Lord Methuen trounced by General Cronje at Magersfontein on the following day, and Buller himself, trying to relieve Ladysmith, was driven back by Botha at Colenso on the 15th, with severe losses. No wonder that Churchill's escape was hailed with such fervour. 'The headlines of the world's press screamed the news,' wrote his son. 'Telegrams poured upon him: he was hailed in Durban as a popular hero.' He did not stay there long, however, but travelled by train to Pietermaritzburg in Natal and then on to Buller's headquarters. Buller described him as a fine fellow and wished that he were in command of regular soldiers, rather than writing 'for a rotten paper'. Although Churchill was not to command regular troops, he did serve with the South African Light Horse, and as we have seen, had further adventures under fire. While in Natal he continued to send letters to his mother and to Pamela Plowden. Moreover he was joined by his brother, Jack, for whom he had obtained a commission in the same regiment. Jack was to be lightly wounded in a skirmish in February 1900, but Winston seemed to bear a charmed life.

Apart from undertaking to write another book and further magazine articles, Churchill was able to look at reviews of his novel, *Savrola*, which had been published in February 1900. These reviews reached him while he was still in Ladysmith, and were varied. Although there was some criticism of its immaturity and lack of convincing characterization, the book received praise for its wit and excitement, its command of language and its revelation of the author himself. The writing of political novels by young men aspiring to political power inevitably brought about references to Disraeli, and just as the young

Disraeli had told Lord Melbourne that he wanted to be Prime Minister, so before the lifting of the siege of Ladysmith Churchill had confided to a somewhat sceptical group of refugees at Estcourt that 'I shall be Prime Minister of England before I'm finished.' Some months later he was told by Captain Percy Scott, RN, commanding HMS *Terrible*, that one day he, Scott, would shake hands with Churchill as Prime Minister. If one consistency of Churchill's beliefs and character stands out from others, it is this certainty that his own star would rise, and that his innumerable escapes from death on the battlefield meant that he was to be spared in order that he might achieve great things.

Ever keen to get back into action, Churchill now pulled all available strings to be attached to Field Marshal Lord Roberts's[1] army which was to invade the Transvaal, the heart of Boer-held territory. Once again he was in luck, and in April 1900 received a note from Roberts's private secretary that the Field Marshal – for Churchill's father's sake – was agreeable to his accompanying the force as a correspondent. It led to another hair-raising adventure, when on patrol with a scouting sortie, Churchill had dismounted at a kopje near Dewetsdorp, only to encounter a dozen Boers. On trying to remount, he suffered a slipped saddle and a bolting animal, leaving him only a hundred yards from the enemy with no cover and no means of escape. His luck held, however, for a scout, Trooper Roberts, rode across his path, stopped, told him to mount up behind and away they went from the Boer bullets, although not before one had hit the trooper's horse. Roberts bemoaned his poor animal's wound, and was hardly consoled by Churchill's pointing out that he had saved his life – it was the horse that concerned the trooper. Seven years later, as a result of Churchill's intervention, Roberts was awarded the Distinguished Conduct Medal. Churchill's final escapades in South Africa were first to take part with his cousin, the Duke of Marlborough, in his friend Lieutenant-General (as he had become) Ian Hamilton's capture of Pretoria itself, on 5 June, and second, to distinguish himself at Diamond Hill five days later. In this latter engagement Churchill, seeing that the key to the battle was the occupation of the summit of Diamond Hill, succeeded in climbing to a position on the mountain from which he was able to signal to Hamilton that the rushing of the summit with mounted infantry would win the battle. So it did, and Hamilton recorded later that 'Winston gave the embattled hosts at Diamond Hill an exhibition of conspicuous gallantry [the phrase often used in recommendations for the VC] for which he has never received full credit.' Then, at the beginning of July 1900, Churchill sailed for home. 'In eight months,' writes his son,

---

[1] After the early British reverses, Roberts was sent out to take over as Commander-in-Chief. Buller continued to command his army corps, but no longer had overall command of all British and Imperial forces in the campaign.

he had managed to make a name for himself both at home and abroad. He had established that reputation for courage to which he so ardently aspired: he had made friends as well as enemies in high places: he had confirmed that he could earn his living with his pen: he had learned to think for himself and – that most blessed of all gifts of the statesman – to form independent views: he had matured and developed and now felt fully qualified to mount a more important stage.

New triumphs awaited him at home – the success of two books he wrote about the Boer War, both published in 1900, lecture tours, and most important of all, his selection as a Conservative candidate for Oldham in the forthcoming general election that autumn. This time he won a seat, and so in February 1901 began his new career in the House of Commons. It cannot be said that for Winston Churchill youth was a blunder, as Disraeli had it. Yet manhood would certainly be a struggle (and not only for him, but for Hitler too). The first volume of Randolph Churchill's portrait of his father has as its theme – described in rather grand terms – 'How an under-esteemed boy of genius, of noble character and daring spirit seized and created a hundred opportunities to rise in the world and add glory by his own merit and audacity to a name already famous.' There may have been some blunders along the way, but at the age of twenty-six, Churchill, already renowned as a soldier and a writer, enjoying world fame, had followed *his* father into the House of Commons and was about to make his mark as a statesman. In 1915, at the same age, Adolf Hitler, of whom no one had then ever heard, was to find himself serving as a private soldier in the Imperial German Army. Yet it was his experiences both in the Great War and its immediate aftermath which were to present Hitler with the opportunity to rival even Churchill in the attainment and wielding of political power.

Winston Churchill's life as a statesman, as a military leader, as a writer and orator, as a family man and sportsman, as a painter and gardener, as one of the most clubbable of men – this life is so lengthy, so varied, so controversial, so distinguished and so full of ups and downs that we must pick and choose between events and activities in order to understand how his character determined incident, and how incident illustrated his character. It was hardly surprising that the new young Member of Parliament, so sure of himself and his future destiny, 'with incomparably more experience of life and of the world than many of his parliamentary colleagues ten or twenty years older than himself', should on the occasion of his maiden speech in the House of Commons have been listened to by a crowded House and have earned praise from the press. The date was 18 February 1901, the occasion a response to a powerful attack by the Liberal David Lloyd George on the way in which war

[44]

was being waged in South Africa. It had been expected that Lloyd George would move an amendment to the Address on the King's Speech – Edward VII's first, his mother, Queen Victoria, having died on 22 January – but in the event he did not do so. Although this change meant that Churchill was obliged to adjust his introductory remarks, he was able to do so, aided by a suggestion from a fellow Conservative who was seated beside him, with style and wit, effectively contrasting the moderation in which an admentment to the Address

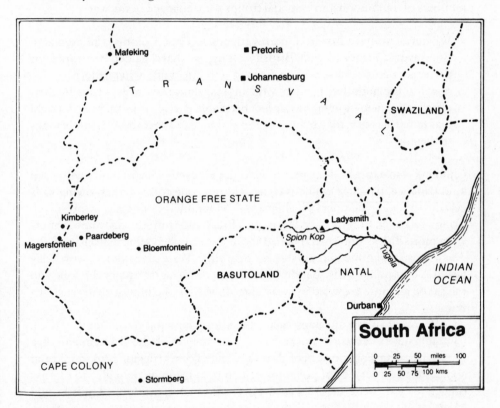

might have been couched with the violence of Lloyd George's actual attack on the conduct of military affairs in South Africa. There was perhaps no member more likely to be listened to with regard to these affairs than Churchill, who demolished Lloyd George's suggestions, and went on to illustrate his belief – a belief that was to endure through many future conflicts – in magnanimity towards an enemy, once that enemy had been defeated. He 'appealed for leniency towards the rebels [Boers] and called for a promise to those willing to surrender that their security, their religion, their rights and the honours of war

[45]

should be guaranteed'. We may note here that the final terms for ending the Boer War, under the Treaty of Vereeniging of May 1902, *were* generous.

During his speech Churchill showed his skill in debate, his generosity in paying tribute to his friends and supporters, his ability to hit hard at rancorous critics and to rise to great heights of patriotic eloquence. In trying to comfort members who harboured grave doubts about the South African War, he referred them to its effect on certain other parts of the British Empire (large numbers of Dominion and Imperial troops were engaged in the war):

> Whatever we have lost in doubtful friends in Cape Colony [a reference to Boer sympathizers in that British colony] we have gained ten times, or perhaps twenty times, over in Canada and Australia, where the people – down to the humblest farmer in the most distant provinces – have by their effective participation in the conflict been able to realize, as they never could realize before, that they belong to the Empire, and that the Empire belongs to them.

Churchill also expressed his gratitude to the House for hearing him with such kind patience, patience which was, he felt, referring to his father, owing to 'a certain splendid memory which many honourable members still preserve'. Congratulations from both sides of the House and from the daily newspapers were more or less universal. He had more than fulfilled expectations, and the *Daily Telegraph* summed up his success by saying: 'Perfectly at home, with lively gestures that pointed his sparkling sentences, he instantly caught the tone and the ear of a House crowded in every part.' It was but the first of many such triumphs.

Not content with speaking again twice on the subject of South Africa, Churchill next intervened most effectively in support of the Government on a question concerning the right of the War Office alone to decide who should and should not be selected for positions of command, and its right also to dismiss officers found to be incompetent. Forty years later, as Prime Minister and Minister of Defence, he had no hesitation in appointing or sacking those general officers whom he deemed deserving of the one or the other. But for now, in March 1901, Churchill made it plain to the House that experience of war was, to say the least of it, an aid to understanding the issues involved. In this particular case, which concerned the dismissal of Major-General Sir Henry Colvile for his mistakes in command during the Boer War, Churchill made some telling points which are as relevant today as they were then (as anyone who has served in the modern British Army can confirm). 'I have noticed', he observed, referring to recent wars in which the country – and he himself – had been engaged, 'a tendency . . . to hush everything up, to make everything look as fair as possible

. . . ugly facts are smoothed and varnished over, rotten reputations are propped up, and officers known as incapable are allowed to hang on and linger in their commands . . .' By intervening so effectively in the debate, Churchill earned the gratitude of the Secretary of State for War, St John Brodrick, and even received a congratulatory letter from Lord Curzon, Viceroy of India.

Yet when it came to Brodrick's plan for reforming the army, which meant in effect expanding it and thus spending more money on it, Churchill found himself unable to lend his support. Not for the last time, he put his faith, and thus wanted to put the country's money, in the Royal Navy. A *better* army, of course, he supported, but this did not necessarily mean a bigger one. 'Any danger that comes to Britain would not be on land; it would come on the sea. With regard to our military system we must be prepared to deal with all the little wars which occur occasionally on the frontiers of the Empire. We cannot expect to meet great wars . . . our game essentially is to be a naval and commercial power. I cannot look upon the army as anything but an adjunct to the navy . . .' Thus Churchill gave his views in a speech to the Liverpool Conservative Association, and he reinforced his plea when it came to the debate on the army scheme which took place in the House of Commons on 13 May 1901. While deprecating the need for three army corps, he showed remarkable foresight in predicting what would be the effect of a European war, a war which could not 'be anything but a cruel, heart-rending struggle, which, if we are ever to enjoy the bitter fruits of victory, must demand, perhaps for several years, the whole manhood of the nation, the entire suspension of peaceful industries, and the concentration to one end of every vital energy in the community'. For a young man of twenty-six, whose life up to this time had been spent largely risking his neck in Queen Victoria's little wars in pursuit of Britain's great, romantic, imperial dream, reading widely the classical works of literature and history, writing innumerable letters as well as books about his campaigns, cultivating the friendship and support of the day's outstanding personalities, and playing polo, a young man who had been in the House of Commons for a mere three months, this picture of what was indeed to come little more than a dozen years later showed an imaginative grasp of no mean order.

There was another aspect of Churchill's disagreement with government policy which was profoundly important. 'It marked', he himself wrote later, 'a definite divergence of thought and sympathy from nearly all those who thronged the benches around me.' One illustration of this divergence was the formation of a kind of dining club composed of Tory 'rebels'. Apart from Churchill himself there were the Duke of Northumberland's heir, Lord Percy; the Prime Minister's youngest son, Lord Hugh Cecil; the Hon. Arthur Stanley, a younger son of the Earl of Derby; and Ian Malcolm. They were known as the Hughligans or Hooligans.

Lord Rosebery, who had not only been the Liberal Prime Minister from 1894 to 1895, but had also published a masterly study of Napoleon on St Helena, as well as biographies of Cromwell, Pitt the Elder, Pitt the Younger, and Peel, had been a friend of Lord Randolph's (among many shared interests, Rosebery's horses had won the Derby three times) and was now a friend of his son. At this time, January 1902, Rosebery, a staunch Imperialist, was at odds with his party in this respect, and had in the previous month made a speech at Chesterfield on which Churchill commented in an address of his own delivered at Blackpool, scene of one of his father's great platform triumphs. Churchill welcomed what Rosebery had to say because it 'breathes the spirit of patriotism' and 'because he is the only man amongst the opposition who has a patrotic mind . . . Lord Rosebery possesses the three requirements an English Prime Minister should have. He must have a great position in Parliament, popularity in the country, he must have rank and prestige.' Had he added the heart of a lion, an insatiable relish for action, a profound sense of history and incalculable powers of oratory, Churchill might have been describing himself as he assumed that great office thirty-eight years later.

Churchill's drift away from the Conservative Party was further illustrated during a debate in the House of Commons concerning another South African affair. This particular case was about a newspaper editor who had been imprisoned in South Africa for libelling Kitchener (General Lord Kitchener of Khartoum, as he had become, had succeeded Roberts as C-in-C in November 1900), and who after his release had been refused permission to visit this country because it would not do to have anti-British views bandied about in Britain. This seemed so absurd to the Liberals and the Hooligans that at the subsequent division the latter voted with the former – to no effect as it transpired, although Chamberlain, in answer to criticism of the Government's ineptness, complained that what the Government required was support from its party members when in trouble, not just when it was in the right. The comment brings to mind the rejoinder of Lord Melbourne, when Prime Minister, to a troublesome colleague who promised his support when Melbourne was in the right. 'That is no use at all,' said Melbourne, 'what I want is men who will support me when I am in the wrong.' It was an idea taken to its furthest extreme in a remark attributed to Disraeli: 'Damn your principles! Stick to your party.'

Apart from continuing to promote his own position in Parliament and in the country, Churchill was to find himself at odds with Chamberlain over tariff reform, Chamberlain being in favour of Imperial preference (indeed, he resigned from the Government over this in 1903), Churchill a firm advocate of free trade. So strongly did Churchill feel about it that he wrote to the Prime Minister, Balfour (Salisbury having retired from public life in July 1902), on 25

May 1903. By reminding ourselves of part of his letter we are able to savour both his conviction and the measured eloquence with which he expressed himself:

> You have shown me so much kindness in the past that I am encouraged to write to you frankly now about Mr Chamberlain's recent statements; & indeed the matter seems to me so important that it is my duty to do so.
>
> At Birmingham he advocated Preferential Tariffs with the Colonies; in his letter of Monday to a Mr Loveday he revealed plain Protectionist intentions; & in the House on Friday last he showed himself prepared to use Old Age Pensions as a lever to attain these ends. Now I see it stated by Mr Bonar Law that you are agreed with him in all this.
>
> I earnestly hope that this is not true & that you have not taken an irrevocable decision. Hence this letter.

Churchill then goes on to state his absolute opposition to an alteration in the country's free trade policy. Moreover, he maintains, this whole matter was of overriding importance – A policy of protection would lead to commercial ruin. He then put two points to Balfour, first, that nationally there was no need for any great fiscal amendment; second, that from the Conservative Party's present strong standing and record, there was no justification in taking great risks by implementing major changes in policy. Churchill assures the Prime Minister that 'an attempt on your part to preserve the Free Trade policy and character of the Tory party would command my absolute loyalty'; failing that, though, 'I must reconsider my position in politics.' It was, however, not until a year later, in May 1904, that Churchill actually crossed the floor of the House of Commons and seated himself on the Liberal benches. In that year he had decided that his future lay with the Liberal Party, had incurred the displeasure of the Oldham Conservatives (who, not unnaturally, did not accept his offer to stand for re-election), had confided his views to his friends, and had made a profound impression on many who now, for the first time, came into contact with his forceful character and remarkable gifts of conversation. Wilfrid Scawen Blunt, the poet and traveller, noted his 'wit, intelligence, and originality', and admired, too, his literary powers. Churchill's assurance reminded Blunt of Lord Randolph, although he judged the son to have more ability. He also remarked Churchill's 'engaging plain-spokenness and readiness to understand', and said that he expected the young MP to enjoy great success in politics.

One diarist observed of Churchill's defection to the Liberals that as far as this would affect his future career, it was held by other members of the House that he had made a mistake, for he had not yet established a firm position, was 'still a skirmisher in the political field,' although he might be 'counted on to make himself quite as disagreeable on the Liberal side as he did on the Unionist'. He was to do much more than that. It was indeed a bold step to have taken, but then Churchill never lacked courage, and it was moreover a step which led quite soon to what he most longed for – *office*.

III

Many years later, when Churchill had become Prime Minister and Hitler was at the height of his military triumphs, the Führer was mistaken enough to dismiss his enemy as a superannuated drunkard supported by Jewish gold. Never having met the British leader nor those who knew him well, Hitler completely failed to realize that like himself, Churchill was one of the toughest men to have held power in centuries (despite his own admission that he 'blubbed a lot' when emotionally moved), infinitely better acquainted with the world, far more experienced in military affairs, and apart from having what Hitler so absolutely lacked – humour, humanity and a zest for all that was good in life – had also a quick grasp of technological invention and an unrivalled talent for grappling with wide strategic issues. Yet there was just a gleam of truth in the reference to Jewish gold, for having crossed the floor to the Liberal side, Churchill was conscious of the need to find a constituency which he could contest for the Liberals. He found it in Manchester. 'Manchester,' writes Randolph Churchill,

> was the perfect staging-post for him and he was the perfect candidate for a Manchester seat. Manchester was the citadel of doctrinaire free trade and Churchill had proved his credentials by intimating that he was about to break with the Tories on this very issue and by his capacity for expounding the free trade argument in the liveliest and most up-to-date fashion. He was now to make himself highly acceptable to the powerful Jewish community in Manchester.

When the general election came in January 1906, Churchill was to win a triumphant success, as was the Liberal Party as a whole.

Although it had been predicted that Churchill would make himself disagreeable from the Opposition benches, it was not especially evident that this was so when he took up the cudgels on behalf of the Army once again. Hugh Arnold-Forster had replaced Brodrick at the War Office and had introduced a new scheme for the army. Churchill did not think much of it and, in an article for the *Daily Mail* dated December 1904, put his finger firmly on a point which many non-military men who try to tinker with the army's structure consistently fail to understand. He reminded his readers that the army was not to be compared with some trading company which could constantly be changed in size and shape according to the market, nor was it to be thought of as a building which could be pulled about or rebuilt according to a whim. It was essentially a living organism. 'If it is bullied, it sulks; if it is unhappy, it pines; if it is harried, it gets feverish; if it is sufficiently disturbed, it will wither and dwindle and almost die.' It was indeed fortunate for the army that there would before long be a Liberal administration which would appoint the brilliant R.B. Haldane as Secretary of State for War. Haldane it was who asked the vital question: 'What is the army for?' and having determined the answer, so acted to put things in order that when, in 1914, the army was to face its greatest challenge and danger, it was able to do so with confidence, superhuman perseverance and ultimate mastery. Ironically, Haldane had left the War Office two years earlier, but among his reforms and innovations was the establishment of the Territorial Force, which was to play a crucial part in the coming war.

In the House of Commons itself, Churchill continued his lively per-formances, on one occasion in the summer of 1904 even teasing the Prime Minister himself about the Government's failure to get its business done within the parliamentary term, which produced the almost unheard of need to prolong the session until 15 August – three days after the Glorious Twelfth! Churchill's gibes extended to congratulating Balfour on still being there:

> The procedure of the House of Commons has been mutilated. Never mind! A great quantity of money has been expended! Never mind! No legislation of any value has been passed! Never mind! But here is the Prime Minister, at the end of the session, a great deal more than many people could have expected or hoped for. I offer to the right honourable gentleman, most sin-cerely, my most humble congratulations on his achievement.

Churchill was in similarly sardonic form soon after the opening of Parliament in February 1905. Speaking in the House about Supplementary Army Estimates, he surpassed even his own grandiloquence in his criticism of the army's overindulgence in high-ranking officers whose sole function seemed to be the donning of splendid trappings. His words would have been echoed by many a critic of the practice, but perhaps only he could have classified these officers as 'those gorgeous & gilded functionaries with brass hats and orna-mental duties who multiply so luxuriously on the plains of Aldershot & Salisbury'.

In the summer of 1905 a duel which had been waged between Lord Curzon, the Viceroy of India, and Kitchener, by now the Commander-in-Chief there, came to a head. Their disagreement arose from the question of who was to exercise control of the Indian Army's administration, Kitchener maintaining that it was he who should do so, Curzon insisting that the Viceroy's powers in this matter should be upheld. The campaign ended in Kitchener's triumph and Curzon's resignation. Churchill, who was later to work closely with both men, predictably supported Curzon, for he had always regarded military power as being subordinate to constitutional authority. 'I should be greatly disconcerted,' he wrote to this mother, 'if I thought the Liberal party were prepared to acquiesce in the handing over of the Indian Empire to an ambitious and indocile soldier.'

It is not unusual in British politics for the administration in power to regard the Opposition party as being quite unfit for government, and such was certainly Balfour's view in the early part of 1905. By then his own administration had been irreparably split by the tariff reform controversy, and his support in the House had been reduced to a small remnant. To those who accuse him of clinging to office, however, the plea must be made that during this year the Prime Minister not only set on a sound foundation the Committee of Imperial Defence, but also did much to strengthen the Entente Cordiale (the Anglo-French Entente of 1904 had ended a long period of friction between the two countries) – both of which were to play so crucial a part in the coming world crisis. At length, in December 1905 Balfour did resign and the King sent for the Liberal leader, Sir Henry Campbell-Bannerman, who therefore formed a government before the formality of a general election.

Now at last was to come the opportunity for which Churchill's energy, experience, patriotism, industry, eloquence and sheer commitment so wholly qualified him. It was at once clear that Campbell-Bannerman wished to include Churchill in his government, and after some discussion he was offered the post of Under-Secretary for the Colonies, which he ardently accepted. Churchill was particularly attracted by the circumstance that as the Colonial Secretary, the Earl of Elgin, sat in the Lords, all business in the House of Commons would be handled by himself. He received numerous congratulatory letters, including one from his predecessor in office, his cousin, the Duke of Marlborough, who generously declared how formidable Churchill would be in maintaining the new Government's colonial policy – 'Your speeches will be read throughout the Colonies.' It is worth recalling that Churchill was still only thirty-one.

One of the first things that Churchill did on taking up his office was to appoint Edward Marsh as his private secretary. It was an unerring choice, for they suited each other so well that they became great friends, and Marsh was to serve as Churchill's in all the ministerial offices he held, until Marsh himself retired two years before the Second World War began. Randolph Churchill reminds us that in his memoirs, Eddie Marsh (as he was always known) recalls that at a time when he was still uncertain whether they would get on well together, he confided in Churchill's former love, Pamela Plowden (by then

Countess of Lytton) as to his misgivings. 'Her answer,' Marsh wrote, 'was one of the nicest things that can ever have been said about anybody', and was to the effect that the first time you met Winston you saw all his faults and you spent the rest of your life discovering his virtues – 'And so it proved.' In order to enjoy the fruits of office, however, Churchill had first to win another election, for in January 1906 the King had dissolved Parliament. To Manchester, therefore, Churchill and Marsh went to fight the seat of North-West Manchester, for which the former had been adopted as a Liberal candidate.

As was to be expected Churchill made several speeches during the election campaign; and as was also to be expected his main theme was free trade. His election address itself had made plain his absolute opposition to any forms of preferential or protective tariffs, and his clear support both for this country's freedom to buy what it wanted in the world's markets, and for the freedom of the world's markets to compete with home industries. This line of argument was heard sympathetically not only by Liberal supporters, but also by Tory businessmen who were equally committed to free trade. Indeed, one of the leading cotton manufacturers, Mr Broadhurst, in a remarkable declaration three days before the election, went so far as to expect all free trade Unionists (the Tory party was generally known as the 'Conservative and Unionist Party until the settlement of Ireland in 1922) to vote according to their principles and so ensure the election of Churchill. They might not agree with Churchill on all points, but even though some sacrifice might have to be made 'I hope no Free Trade Unionist will allow any personal feeling on such points to prevent him from supporting in this election the great cause of Free Trade, of which Mr Churchill is a most able and courageous champion.'

Although Disraeli is said to have remarked to Bulwer Lytton, 'Damn your principles! Stick to your party,' in Manchester in 1906 Churchill was eloquent in explaining that there may be circumstances when action which amounted to a change of party may be not merely justifiable, but becomes an absolute duty. Conscious no doubt of his own change and of the support which he is receiving from Unionists, he declares himself 'proud to stand on this platform tonight with gentlemen of position and influence in Manchester who have chosen rather to face the obloquy of leaving their former party than abandon the principle which they hold dear'. He went on to point out that by acting in this way 'they would be among the supporters of the Government they helped to bring into being; and further, in the end it would be open to them to *go back and rejoin the party*[1] from which for the time being they had severed themselves.'

Free trade was not the only issue, although the main one, that figured in the various addresses which Churchill gave. There was also the question of

---

[1] Author's italics. Winston Churchill did go back and rejoin the Conservative Party in 1924.

Chinese labour in South Africa,[1] and such was Churchill's reasoning and clarity on the matter that it excited the admiration of a *Daily Mail* correspondent, who praised the Liberal candidate for doing what no other politician had done – explaining the problem in simple, convincing terms and persuading his audience to listen to him. What is more, he made it plain that the new government's policy would be to prevent any extension of the Chinese labour system (there was, in any case, deep hostility among South African whites to Chinese immigration). Further opportunity for Churchill's readiness of response to interruption or disturbance occurred during a suffragette demonstration. When, at a meeting a few days before the election, a woman bearing a flag with 'Votes for Women' on it interrupted Churchill's replies to questions, he brought her on to the platform and persuaded the audience to hear what she had to say. Asked whether he would support giving the vote to women, Churchill, making it clear that fairness and chivalry must be shown to women even if they asked to be treated like men, and that the weaker sex dependent on men must receive courtesy, admitted that in the House of Commons he had voted in favour of woman's suffrage, but that at meetings such as this, subject to constant disturbance, he would not give any undertaking.

On the evening of 13 January after the votes had been counted. Churchill found himself a triumphant victor. And it was not only he who had triumphed. The Liberal Party as a whole had done so too, and now enjoyed an overall majority in the House of Commons. Campbell-Bannerman's government was thus confirmed in office, and Churchill resumed his work as Under-Secretary for the Colonies. Not that ministerial office in itself was sufficient for him. It is perhaps an illustration of his versatility and industry, and of the almost unlimited compass of his talent and sheer capacity for work, that at the time of the election campaign, the literary task at which he had been toiling for nearly four years, his biography of his father, *Lord Randolph Churchill*, was published. On the whole, the book received most flattering reviews. In particular, the *Times Literary Supplement* spoke of the pleasure in finding that a life so well worth writing of had been so well written. Churchill's portrait of his father, the *TLS* opined, was done in the best of taste, and

as for self-restraint, who could have believed that Mr Winston Churchill could write a book that is full of Mr Chamberlain, and not altogether empty

[1] The use of imported indentured Chinese labourers, prepared to work for the same low wages as black miners in the deep-level mines of the Rand, caused something of a political scandal. The Chinese were treated abysmally, many being flogged despite a promise that they would not be. Milner, by then Governor of the two former Boer states and of the Cape, as well as High Commissioner, was censured in the House of Commons in 1905, and resigned. The issue of 'Chinese slavery' helped to bring the Liberals to power.

of Mr Balfour, and yet write it like an historian, and not at all like a man on a party platform? But he has ... The book is, on the whole, a serious and fair-minded record of Lord Randolph's career. But its interest never flags for a moment. No-one who cares for politics will willingly put it down when it is once in his hands.

Lord Rosebery, himself a biographer of extraordinary power and lucidity, also found it difficult to put down. It was 'good-humoured, impartial, vivid, sympathetic and written in an admirable style, with little refreshing ironies to flavour the whole composition'. The book deserved to do well, and it did.

The Colonial Office suited Churchill. Apart from his responsibilities to conduct House of Commons business, the issues at stake were themselves of enormous importance, and none more so than the question of South Africa's future. Much of the credit for the conciliatory agreement reached there must go to Churchill. He knew the country, he knew the people, he knew above all that only generosity and trust could lead to a lasting settlement. As was customary with him, when it came to putting the interests of the country and the Empire before those of party, he was at his most persuasive when arguing in the House of Commons, as he did on 31 July 1906, for the granting of a free constitution to the Transvaal.[1] He appealed to the Opposition to give their support to the measure so that it could be invested

> with something of a national function. With all our majority we can only make it the gift of a Party; they can make it the gift of England. And if that were so, I am quite sure that all those inestimable blessings which we confidently hope will flow from this decision will be gained more surely and much more speedily; and the first real step taken to withdraw South African affairs from the arena of British Party Politics, in which they have inflicted injury on both political Parties and in which they have suffered grievous injury themselves.

Ian Hamilton, with whom Churchill had served both in India and in South Africa, wrote to say with what pleasure he had witnessed his friend's handling of this difficult matter, and declared himself to be 'a staunch upholder of your genius'. There were to be many more exchanges between them – most particularly in 1915 during the ill-fated Dardanelles campaign. A further note of

[1] The two defeated Boer states, the Transvaal and the Orange Free State (which the British had renamed the Orange River Colony) had become Crown Colonies under the terms of the Treaty of Vereeniging. However, Boer voters outnumbered British voters in both colonies, which meant that both, again according to the terms of the treaty, would with British agreement be reconstituted as self-governing colonies.

approval came from King Edward VII himself, who added in his own hand-writing (on a letter from his Assistant Private Secretary acknowledging one of Churchill's to the King) how glad he was to see that Churchill was becoming a 'reliable Minister and above all a serious politician', something which required country to be put before party. During his discussions of the Chinese labour question, Churchill had used the expression 'terminological inexactitude' to dismiss the notion that Chinese labourers in the Rand were subjected to slavery. Not everyone regarded his use of the phrase as serious, for it was characteristic of his enjoyment in employing a kind of polysyllabic lightheartedness in debate. To some, of course, the expression was a mere euphemism for 'lie', and we are at once reminded of Stanley Baldwin's comment that Churchill 'cannot really tell lies. That is what makes him so bad a conspirator.' We may pause here to observe what a contrast there was between Churchill and Hitler in this regard. Hitler was addicted to lying, and admitted as much in *Mein Kampf*, whose language displays all the meanness and ignobility of its author:

> In the big lie there is always a certain force of credibility; because the broad masses of a nation are always more easily corrupted in the deeper strata of their emotional nature than consciously or voluntarily, and thus in the primitive simplicity of their minds they more readily fall victims to the big lie than the small lie, since they themselves often tell small lies in little matters, but would be ashamed to resort to large-scale falsehoods. It would never come into their heads to fabricate colossal untruths and they would not believe that others could have the impudence to distort the truth so infamously ... The grossly impudent lie always leaves traces behind it, even after it has been nailed down.

Hitler was to show that this was not merely a demonstration of his contempt for the very people to whom he was to have so great an appeal. It was a recipe for propaganda; propaganda which, in time, would become so penetrating, so powerful, so ruthless and so effective that it would win him battle after battle without so much as a shot being fired. In 1906, however, Hitler was only seventeen, toying with the idea of studying art, mooching about in Vienna, wholly unknown, without work, without friends, and with little prospect of bettering himself. Yet this was precisely what he intended to do, and in Vienna during the ensuing years he developed what he believed were the qualities that would enable him to rise in the world. They were, as Alan Bullock has reminded us, unattractive qualities:

> The ability to lie, twist, cheat and flatter; the elimination of sentimentality or loyalty in favour of ruthlessness ... above all, strength of will ... His lack of

scruple later took by surprise even those who prided themselves on their unscrupulousness. He learned to lie with conviction and dissemble with candour. To the end he refused to admit defeat and still held the belief that by the power of will alone he could transform events.

Characteristic of Hitler was his complete lack of sympathy – indeed, his contempt – for the working classes of Vienna and the miserable conditions which they were obliged to endure. How different was Churchill's reaction on walking through the slums of Manchester with Eddie Marsh in 1906. All his benevolence is aroused. 'Fancy,' he said to Marsh, 'living in one of these streets – never seeing anything beautiful – never eating anything savoury – never saying anything clever.' In that year Churchill was, at thirty-two, and as his son records, 'a fully equipped statesman. He knew how to get to the core of the matter, he knew how to express himself in lucid and compelling language, and he knew how to get things done. His over-mastering ambition and his prodigious powers of work and concentration seemed, although he was in a junior situation, to dominate everything he touched'. In 1921 at the same age of thirty-two Hitler was leader of the National Socialist German Workers' Party. He too could use compelling language. He too possessed an overriding ambition. He too was going to get things done. He too would dominate. But there the resemblance ended. And between 1906 and 1921 the world would have changed out of recognition.

Since Adolf Hitler was to have no influence whatever on the politics of Germany or anywhere else until the 1920s, we will continue to follow the astonishing career of Churchill up to the end of the Great War, when we must also glance at Hitler's own experiences as a soldier, which were to have a marked effect on his subsequent creation and use of a mighty military machine. In 1906 Churchill was to see something of the mighty military machine which had preceded that of Hitler's creation, for he succeeded in having himself invited to witness the Imperial German Army's manoeuvres in September of that year. The Under-Secretary for the Colonies had continued to take a great interest in military affairs and was in close touch with Haldane at the War Office, being particularly interested in the condition and future of the British Army. After attending the manoeuvres at Breslau, during which he had even had a talk with Kaiser Wilhelm II, Churchill wrote to his chief at the Colonial Office, Lord Elgin, recording how impressive they had been: 'There is a massive simplicity & force about German military arrangements which grows upon the observer; and although I do not think they have appreciated the terrible power of the weapons they hold & modern fire conditions, and have in that & in minor respects much to learn from our army, yet numbers, quality, discipline & organization are four good roads to victory.' This was not to be the last time that Churchill would attend Germany Army manoeuvres or have exchanges with the Kaiser. He was, moreover, already conscious of the German military menace, observing on his return that he was thankful there was a sea between the German Army and England.[1]

While in general the partnership between Lord Elgin and Churchill was both good-natured and fruitful, there were occasions when Elgin took exception to his subordinate's independence of mind and action. In one such instance, when Churchill caused the reply to a dispatch from Nairobi to be completed without reference to his chief, he received a mild reprimand, only to return a letter remarkable for the courtesy of its language, the inexorability of its logic and the dignity of its tone. It is worth quoting some of it as an example of Churchill's majestic style of writing:

> So much a matter of form did I regard the drafting of the despatch – so clearly marked were the lines upon which it should proceed – & marked by your decisions – that I gave no instructions of any kind verbal or written as to its tenor; nor did I alter a single word. The only decision I took upon myself was to direct that a despatch should be drafted for your approval in accordance with what I understand are in fact your views. This practice is adopted every day in the office by Assistant Secretaries & even by junior clerks . . . But if you do not wish me to exercise such a discretion, I am most ready to defer to your instructions . . .

Elgin returned a conciliatory note and the matter was closed. Churchill never had been and never would be so in awe of his superior officers or ministers that he would not stand up to them.

One of the most important items of business confronting Churchill at the end of 1906 and in the early part of the new year was arranging the Colonial Conference. This only took place in April 1907, and on 1 May Churchill was made a Privy Councillor for his part in it all, even though his views on what should be done at the conference were admirably summed up by Leo Amery as being 'that the Colonial Prime Ministers should be given a good time and sent away all banqueted, but empty-handed'. That summer, before setting off on a tour of East Africa, Churchill, who was always deeply interested in the handling of military forces, attended French Army manoeuvres. This time he was accompanied by the man who was to become one of his closest and most valued friends, F.E. Smith, whom he was later to describe as a great patriot, statesman, jurist, scholar; loyal, lovable and brilliant, possessing 'courage,

---

[1] Cf. Douglas Jerrold's comment, 'The best thing I know between France and England is – the sea.'

fidelity, vigilance, love of the chase', and whose versatility, command of the English language, wit and love of good living were not incomparable to Churchill's own. They served together in the Queen's Own Oxfordshire Hussars, for despite all his other preoccupations, Churchill found the time to command a squadron in this yeomanry regiment (the yeomanry were the Territorial Force's cavalry).

It was no surprise that Churchill found his tour of East Africa a source both of enormous interest in terms of his ministerial duties, but also one of great pleasure in viewing and hunting wild animals – to say nothing of the profit which came from writing magazine articles and a book, *My African Journey*. As was also his custom, Churchill sent home memoranda to the Colonial Office and other ministries, recommending that action should be taken on various matters arising from his tours of inspection. In this, however, he aroused the hostility of the Permanent Under-Secretary to the Colonial Office, Sir Francis Hopwood, who parted from the impartial loyalty expected in such senior civil servants by trying to make trouble between Churchill and Lord Elgin. While still in East Africa, Churchill received two particular pieces of news, one joyous – the engagement of his brother Jack to Lady Gwendeline Bertie – one disturbing – the illness of the Prime Minister, Campbell-Bannerman. This latter development, however, led to the appointment of Asquith as Prime Minister in April 1908 after Campbell-Bannerman's resignation, and in the same month Asquith offered Churchill the post of President of the Board of Trade, and thus at last – although he was still only thirty-three – a place in the Cabinet. He joined a distinguished body, containing such men as Sir Edward Grey, Haldane, the Marquess of Crewe, John Morley and Lloyd George.[1] Not that Churchill would have felt in any way overawed in such glittering company; on the contrary, he regarded himself as equally, if not more, talented.

April 1908 was a good month for Winston Churchill. It was then that he met Miss Clementine Hozier, and so speedy and successful was his courtship of her that five months later they married and, as he himself put it, 'lived happily ever after'. In between their meeting and marrying, however, there was another election, for in those days appointment to Cabinet rank required the newly promoted minister to be re-elected by his constituents. In this case, however, because many of the Irish Catholics chose not to support him, Churchill was defeated at Manchester. It proved to be but a temporary setback, for a safe seat was found at Dundee, and in May 1908 Churchill was returned with a substantial majority. One of the speeches he made during the campaign displayed sentiments and political beliefs that (if we substitute 'Labour' for 'Socialism'

---

[1] Respectively Foreign Secretary, Secretary for War, Secretary for the Colonies, Secretary for India, Chancellor of the Exchequer.

and 'Conservativism' for 'Liberalism') might be held to be as true today as they were nearly a century earlier:

> Socialism wants to pull down wealth, Liberalism seeks to raise up poverty. Socialism would destroy private interests – Liberalism would preserve them in the only way they could justly be preserved, by reconciling them with public rights. Socialism seeks to kill enterprise. Liberalism seeks to rescue enterprise from the trammels of privilege and preference. Socialism assails the maximum pre-eminence of the individual – Liberalism seeks to build up the minimum standard of the masses. Socialism attacks capital, Liberalism attacks monopoly.

Between 1908 and the outbreak of war in 1914, Churchill was a prominent member of the Cabinet – first as President of the Board of Trade, next as Home Secretary from 1910–11, and then as First Lord of the Admiralty. In all of them he played his familiar starring role, and in doing so made a profound impact on the principal political issues of the day. We may perhaps select some of these issues and the influence that Churchill exerted upon them before getting to grips with the business of war; a war, moreover, in which Churchill was to play so crucial and varied a part. He had already seen much of war at its tactical level during his time as a soldier, and he was to see much more of it in this role on the battlefield. Yet before long he would also be concerned with all the strategic complexities of a major conflict. His attitude to war was ambivalent. After again attending German Army manoeuvres at the Kaiser's invitation in the autumn of 1909, he wrote to his wife:

> This army is a terrible engine. It marches sometimes 35 miles in a day. It is in number as the sands of the sea – & with all the modern conveniences. There is a complete divorce between the two sides of German life – the Imperialists and the Socialists. Nothing unites them. They are two different nations . . . Much as war attracts me & fascinates my mind with its tremendous situations – I feel more deeply every year – & can measure the feeling here in the midst of arms – what a vile & wicked folly & barbarism it all is . . .

His son, Randolph, shrewdly observes in this connection that 'the public were intuitively to sense his first mood, and thus the myth of the warmonger was fostered; he was seldom given credit for the second.' The philosopher George Santayana once observed that for a soldier to delight in war was a merit, for a captain to do so was dangerous, and such delight in a statesman was a crime. In considering the latter point, we see at once how totally at odds were the sentiments of Hitler and Churchill. As Führer of the Third Reich and Supreme Commander of the Wehrmacht, Hitler did delight in war. He sought war, he waged war, he regarded it as an everyday business, a natural state of affairs, the summit of human achievement, the ultimate stage in man's historical development. Churchill's attitude was very different. Given that the condition of war existed, he was willing, indeed determined, to play a great part in it, to take the lead, to allow his gigantic historical and technological imagination full rein in combating the forces of evil and tyranny. What is more, he was himself as ready to fight on the field of battle as he was in the counsels of strategic policy. It is true that he regarded war as a great romantic adventure, and the doing of great things in war, the achievement of personal fame and glory, as things to be admired and sought after. Furthermore, he saw himself as a leading player on history's stage. But *au fond* Churchill was a man of peace, and one who believed passionately in order.

He was now well advanced in his pursuit of political power, and although the Board of Trade did not provide the challenge which subsequent posts did, he nevertheless was most active in promoting legislation for social reform. Of much greater significance was the constitutional crisis which, towards the end of 1909, arose from the refusal of the House of Lords to pass the Budget – the main opposition coming from Tory peers still hankering after tariff reform and from landowners concerned about their wealth being taxed. This refusal led to a general election in January 1910, at which Churchill was again returned for Dundee, although he defeated the Labour candidate by only 382 votes. As a result of the election in the House of Commons the Liberals had a majority over the Tories of only two, so that the Irish vote, with all that this meant for the prospects of Home Rule, again became critical. In a speech made in December 1910 Churchill set forth his views both on the possibility of coalition government – which was to come about six years later – and on what he believed the people of this country actually wanted:

After all, deep and wide as our party differences are, strong as are the contrasts of feeling and conviction, of temperament and interest, which mark and diversify our political life, the overwhelming majority of the British people stand true and clear for peace abroad, for law and order at home, for a reconciliation of races within the United Kingdom, for the unity and consolidation of the Empire, for a supreme and unchallengeable Navy, for a better, a fairer, juster and more scientific organization of the social life of the people, a due correction of the abuses of wealth and monopoly, religious equality and industrial progress.

Here was an impressive programme, and it would not be long before Churchill's own ministerial responsibilities would have much to do with most of its features, for he became Home Secretary in February 1910 and First Lord of the Admiralty twenty months later.

IV

It was while Churchill was still Home Secretary that the dangers of Imperial Germany's bellicosity became apparent. France and Germany came close to war in July 1911 when Germany sent a gunboat, *Panther*, to the small port of Agadir in Morocco as a riposte to French suppression of a rebellion at Fez. At the time Morocco, torn by revolt, was the subject of a secret agreement between France and Spain to partition the country between them; by championing Moroccan independence, Germany hoped to destabilize the Anglo-French Entente, although the ostensible reason for *Panther*'s presence was the protection of German interests in the face of French aggression. So alarmed were both Britain and France, not least at the prospect of Germany seizing a port so close to Gibraltar, that the Director of Military Operations, Brigadier-General Henry Wilson, hurried to Paris to discuss with General Augustin Dubail plans for military co-operation. Although there had already been discussions of this nature in London, the Wilson/Dubail meeting produced a memorandum, signed by Wilson, to the effect that should Britain intervene in a war between France and Germany, an expeditionary force of six infantry divisions and one cavalry division would move to France within two weeks of mobilization – a total of 150,000 men and 67,000 horses would then concentrate at Maubeuge and be ready for action immediately this concentration was complete. Here was a very clear answer to Haldane's question about what the army was for, but while General Wilson was in no doubt that his commitment to Dubail to provide two army corps to fight on the French Army's left flank was the correct policy, it was still necessary for this policy to be endorsed by the Government. In the following month, August 1911, there was a meeting of the Imperial Defence Committee, attended by Asquith, Lloyd-George, Reginald McKenna (then First Lord of the Admiralty), Haldane and Churchill, at which both General Wilson and the First Sea Lord, Admiral of the Fleet Sir Arthur Wilson, VC, were able to give their views. Churchill, never one to hang back in giving his colleagues the benefit of his opinion, had already circulated a memorandum to them in advance of the meeting. It was a remarkable document, so accurate in its forecast of what did actually happen three years later that it is worth recalling something of it. His assumptions that Britain, France and Russia would be at war with Germany and Austria-Hungary, and that the decisive element of the conflict would be the struggle between Germany and France, were precisely correct:

> The German army is at least equal in quality to the French, and mobilizes 2,200,000 against 1,700,000. The French must therefore seek for a situation of more equality. This can be found either before the full strength of the Germans has been brought to bear or after the German army has become

extended. The first might be reached between the ninth and thirteenth days; the latter about the fortieth.

The memorandum went on to prophesy that the Germans would breach the line of the River Meuse on the twentieth day, and that then the French Army would retire to the south, falling back on Paris. But, as the German advance continued, it would weaken for a number of reasons: the inevitable losses in battle; the need for flank guards and to protect lines of communication; the requirement of half a million men in order to invest Paris; the fact that the British Army would be taking a hand; pressure from Russian forces on the Eastern Front; in short, by the fortieth day the German Army would be in a bad strategic position. This in turn meant that there would then be opportunities for decisive counter-action. At the same time France's plight must be recognized – invasion by enemy troops, retirement to defensive positions – and therefore much would depend on Britain's ability to provide military support. Quite apart from sending an expeditionary force from this country, the British Army in India should send 100,000 men to France. Churchill's memorandum also dealt with the question of home defence, and sounded a note of optimism in asserting that after a year of war, British military strength should be such as to secure the country's interests outside Europe and enable her if necessary to continue the war alone. He had, of course, long made it plain that everything depended on naval supremacy – 'with a supreme Navy all unpreparedness can be redeemed; without it, no preparations, however careful, can avail'. Within three months of the Imperial Defence Committee's meeting, he would himself be responsible for this supremacy. Yet one disturbing failure of planning revealed during this meeting was the total lack of co-ordination between the British Army and the Royal Navy.

One reason for this lack was the fact that General Wilson and his naval namesake held totally different views. General Wilson, who was convinced that he was the only man present qualified to have an opinion (even though the future Chief of the Imperial General Staff, General Sir John French, who later commanded the British Expeditionary Force in France, was also there), took this opportunity to lecture the Cabinet members on what Germany would do if war should break out. He correctly predicted that the Germans would seek a quick decision in France by concentrating superior forces against the French Army, while conducting a holding operation on the Eastern Front where Russian mobilization would be slower. But being unfamiliar with the German Schlieffen Plan,[1] of which the essence was a very powerful right wing, Wilson

[1] The German operational war plan, prepared in 1905 by General Count Alfred von Schlieffen (1833–1913), and revised and updated each year subsequently. Schlieffen's last words are said to have been 'Keep the right strong.'

was quite wrong about *how* the German Army would attack France, suggesting that only four divisions would be launched west of the Meuse – in fact the Germans sent two armies there. Yet ironically, Wilson's proposal that the British Expeditionary Force should be positioned on the extreme French left – where it would be strong enough to resist the mythical four German divisions which he anticipated – turned out to be politically sound, though based on a faulty military appreciation, for in the event it ensured that the British Army would be heavily engaged from the outset.

Admiral Wilson's ideas, on the other hand, were so far removed from the army's that they inspired amazement and alarm among his audience. They were also so absurdly unrealistic that it was a simple matter for the Prime Minister to reject them. Wilson's predecessor as First Sea Lord had been Admiral of the Fleet Lord Fisher, who had always thought of the army as 'a shell to be fired by the Navy', and schooled in this doctrine, Admiral Wilson proposed that the BEF should be landed on the northern shores of Prussia, thereby causing such a distraction from the Western Front that the French would successfully resist the German attack there. This notion was swiftly discounted (although the broad strategic concept of such a landing on Germany's coastline was to recur during the war itself), and it was agreed that the army's role in the event of war between France and Germany would be as General Wilson had outlined. This was a crucial strategic decision, and enabled Churchill, when he became First Lord of the Admiralty in October 1911, to ensure that naval and military planning went hand in hand; it also allowed General Wilson to get on with the business of perfecting Anglo-French co-operation.

That Churchill was able to find the time to write strategic memoranda when his duties at the Home Office and in the House of Commons would have been more than sufficient for most men must excite special wonder. But as his son has observed, he 'had superabundant energy and could always find time for anything; he was never work-shy'. His relatively short term at the Home Office was marked by a number of issues and incidents which have figured prominently in the various accounts of his life – industrial unrest and the necessary measures to restore order (including the myth of Churchill's calling out the army to deal with striking miners who were rioting in Tonypandy, South Wales, November 1910); the so-called 'Siege of Sidney Street', in January 1911, when the police cornered a gang of 'anarchists' and troops really were called out, Churchill characteristically insisting on going to the scene of action; police operations against the suffragettes; as well as the less sensational matters of opening labour exchanges and embarking on prison reform – all these affairs commanded Churchill's customary dedication to duty. Another major political question which was to puzzle and frustrate not only Asquith's administration, but many subsequent ones, was that of Home Rule for Ireland and the enduring problem of Ulster. As Home Secretary Churchill was to deploy all his energy and skill in tackling the numerous tasks which came his way. But once he became First Lord of the Admiralty in October 1911, he was able to enter into his new duties heart and soul. Not only did these duties bring out all that was best in his strategic vision and determination to get things done, but they did so at a time when his country was about to face a more deadly peril than it had done for a hundred years.

It was in September 1911 that Asquith asked Churchill whether he would like to go to the Admiralty. 'Indeed I would,' was the reply, and so 'It was in a stern mood but with a buoyant heart,' writes his son, 'that Churchill embarked upon his new duties.' As we have seen from his memorandum for the Committee of Imperial Defence, he was well aware of the German threat to peace in Europe, and the longer he was in the post of First Lord of the Admiralty, the more certain he became that war with Germany was coming. Being well aware of the great need, in this eventuality, for a proper Naval War Staff, and being, like his predecessor, McKenna, unable to convince Admiral Wilson, the First Sea Lord, of this need, Churchill effected some important changes in the naval hierarchy – Admiral Sir Francis Bridgeman became First Sea Lord and Vice-Admiral Prince Louis of Battenberg Second Sea Lord. Churchill also appointed the dashing Rear-Admiral David Beatty – whose recipe for living properly was to work hard, play hard, love hard, fight hard, and who certaintly followed his own advice – as his Naval Secretary. It was now possible to set about creating a Naval War Staff, albeit belatedly. Churchill was soon to make his views about German naval strength known, and in a speech at Glasgow on 9 February 1912, drew a very clear distinction between the strategic requirements of the British and German Empires:

> The purposes of British naval power are essentially defensive. We have no thoughts, and we have never had any thoughts of aggression . . . There is, however, this difference between the British naval power and the naval power . . . of Germany. The British Navy is to us a necessity and, from some points of view, the German Navy is to them more in the nature of a luxury. Our naval power involves British existence. It is existence to us; it is expansion to them.

He went on to make it plain that whereas it was Britain's naval supremacy on which the fortunes of Britain and the Empire depended, Germany was a great power before having a navy of any sort. Moreover, Britain would not allow this naval supremacy to be challenged, and although she would welcome any reduction in naval building by European powers, if there were to be competition, she would respond in such a way as to augment her superiority, not reduce it. That

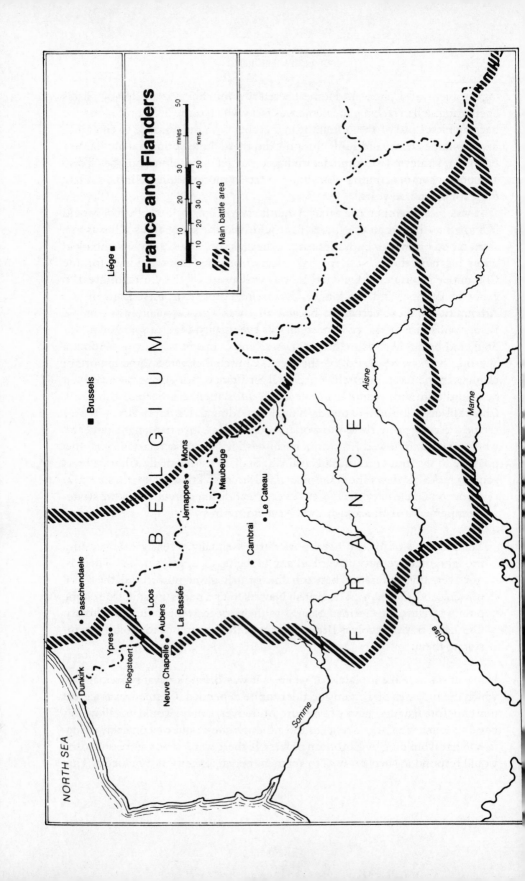

France and Flanders

Main battle area

NORTH SEA

BELGIUM

FRANCE

Liège

Brussels

Mons
Jemappes
Maubeuge
Le Cateau
Cambrai

Passchendaele
Ypres
Ploegsteert
Neuve Chapelle
Aubers
La Bassée
Loos

Dunkirk

Somme
Oise
Aisne
Marne

miles
kms

Churchill meant what he said was evident from his introduction of the Naval Estimates in the House of Commons a month later, when he declared that British naval policy would involve a 60 per cent advantage over Germany in dreadnoughts (battleships equipped solely with large-calibre guns) and that Britain would lay down two keels for every one ship built by the Germans. There was a predictably hostile reaction from Germany, the Kaiser both condemning Churchill for being arrogant, and at the same time making it clear that he had no intention of coming to an understanding with Great Britain by recalling the German Ambassador in London, Count Metternich, whose work had been directed towards reconciling differences between the two powers. Churchill's offer of a 'naval holiday' – that is, for both countries to call a temporary halt to naval construction – was dismissed by the Kaiser, with the result that, in July 1912, Churchill further emphasized the danger while addressing the Committee of Imperial Defence. The German fleet, he said, was such that it was clearly intended for the purposes of offensive action, particularly in the North Sea and North Atlantic, and therefore constituted a special threat to British naval power. Moreover, whereas the dangers of war on land were usually signalled by the preliminaries of mobilization, no such period of warning was to be expected in the event of naval aggression, for a ship which was manned and armed was ready for immediate action. So concerned were Churchill's colleagues in the Cabinet that he was able, that same month, to introduce Supplementary Estimates in the House of Commons, involving the addition of three battleships and one battle cruiser to the programme already under way. His speech outlining these plans brought him further golden opinions from the press, *The Times* praising the mastery over naval affairs which he had acquired in so short a time, and commenting also on the firmness with which he made it plain to Germany that he was well aware of the threat from that country. The *Daily Sketch*, meanwhile, compared him with the younger Pitt, to Churchill's advantage.

Only three months later, in October 1912, war in the Balkans between the 'Balkan League' of Bulgaria, Serbia, Greece and Montenegro, on the one hand, and Turkey on the other, brought to a head once more the conflict of interests between Russia (which encouraged the League), with her never-ending quest for access to warm-water ports through the Bosphorus and Dardanelles, and Austria-Hungary (backed by Germany), determined to maintain Turkey as a counter-force against Russia and the Slavs, and to keep Serbia landlocked and weak. Germany's position was of supreme importance, for her ambitions to establish a firm position from the Baltic to the Persian Gulf (this, the desire for eastward expansion, was the real meaning of that much misused phrase *Drang nach Osten*) depended essentially on keeping Russia out of the Golden Horn. 'The conflicts between these two thrusts,' wrote Sir Robert Ensor, 'the Russian north to south and the German west to east – was absolute. And it needs to be clearly grasped, because it was what motivated the war of 1914.'

The threat to British interests of the Balkan war was clear enough. If Russia went to war with the Germanic powers, France, as Russia's ally, would be drawn in and thus Great Britain would become involved. In any event, as British ministers had repeatedly declared, the prospect of a Germany, both powerful at sea and – by defeating France – having upset the European balance, was not to be tolerated. The Foreign Secretary, Sir Edward Grey, in convening a peace conference in London, sought not only immediate solutions to the Balkan dispute, but also longer-term agreements which would help remove the deeper dangers of major conflict. He succeeded in neither. Further conflict in the Balkans in June 1913 – when Bulgaria suddenly attacked Serbia and Greece, only to find herself invaded by Romanian and Turkish forces (the latter, to add to the confusion, being technically still at war with Greece and Serbia) – led at length to the Treaty of Bucharest in August. This agreement enlarged Greece and Serbia at the expense of Bulgaria, and also gave Adrianople back to the Turks. These arrangements did not augur well for a permanent settlement. Austria resented Serbia's expansion to such an extent that she actually proposed to her two partners in the Triple Alliance, Germany and Italy, that they should mount 'a defensive attack' on Serbia. Had this happened, it would presumably have brought forward the Great War by nearly a year. Italy, however, declined, and there for the time being the matter rested.

The greater danger lay in Germany's attitude. To those calling the tune in Berlin (and those with the loudest voices were soldiers of the General Staff, backed by the Kaiser, rather than politicians), the Bucharest settlement appeared to put another check on *Drang nach Osten* by imposing a Slav barrier between the Central Powers (defined, at that date, as Germany, Austria-Hungary and Italy) and Turkey. Yet German influence in Constantinople remained powerful, and not least because later that year a senior German officer, General Liman von Sanders, was appointed Inspector-General of the Ottoman Army with the Turkish rank of field marshal. It was an appointment that was to have profound consequences for the Gallipoli campaign in 1915, as also for the political fortunes of Winston Churchill. Germany also took action far more provocative than lending the Turks a general officer. Convinced that war between the Central Powers and the Dual Alliance of France and Russia had become inevitable, Germany took the unprecedented step of enlarging her standing army by 63,000 men. This decision caused Russia to add more than double this number to her army, while the French increased their two years' military service by one year. What the German Foreign Minister, Gottlieb von Jagow, had called 'this damned system of alliances' was becoming ever more menacing. It even appeared that the German General Staff might have their eyes on the summer of 1914 as the best time, from their point of view, at which to provoke war. By August of that year the German Army would be at its peak strength, would have been re-equipped and, with the likelihood of excellent campaigning weather, would be best placed to crush France in a lightning campaign – the Schlieffen Plan was designed to do this in six weeks – and then to turn back east to deal with Russia.

Although Germany, Russia and France had been concerned with increasing the size of their armies, in Britain Churchill, having in the previous year unsuccessfully proposed a 'naval holiday', was now again seeking such an agreement. In March 1913, and again seven months later, he suggested that the four capital ships to be laid down for the Royal Navy, and the two equivalent ships for the Imperial German Navy, should not be built. Germany turned down this proposal, no doubt bearing in mind the fact that by August 1914 the Kiel Canal, which would allow her dreadnought-class battleships to pass from the Baltic to the North Sea, would be completed. Although Churchill had been at odds with some of his Cabinet colleagues with regard to the naval programme, he did not allow political differences to prejudice his personal loyalties. To reinforce an understanding of his generous-hearted character, we may briefly recall that when suspicion fell on Lloyd George, Sir Rufus Isaacs and Herbert Samuel (respectively Chancellor of the Exchequer, Attorney-General and Postmaster-General at the time) concerning some questionable dealings in Marconi shares, Churchill was both energetic and vehemently eloquent in their defence, and successful in vindicating them. In August 1913, in a letter to Lloyd George, the Liberal Chief Whip (the Master of Elibank) declared that such action on Churchill's part was just like him: 'I have always regarded him as a really true friend who will always stand by one in foul or in fair weather – and that speech for its warmth of feeling for his injured friends and its scathing attack on their traducers will show to many what we already knew that in time of trouble Winston is the first to spring to the side of his friends . . .'

Perhaps the last man who might qualify for such admiration for loyalty, trueness, friendship and trust would be Adolf Hitler, who was far more likely to take petty pleasure in the discomfort of colleagues, and for whom, indeed, the word *Schadenfreude* (joy in others' misfortune), with all its undertones of malice, might have been invented. In the spring of 1913, at about the time when Churchill was making his proposal about capital ships, Hitler was leaving Vienna, where he had spent the last few years in obscurity, yet not without retaining his confidence in his own ability, nor losing his burning obsession with political matters. As Alan Bullock has emphasized, the future leader of the Nazi Party had much to learn from examining the methods and ideas of the three principal political parties which were active in Vienna during his years there – the Social Democrats, the Pan-German Nationalists and the Christian

Socialists. From the first of these Hitler came to see the need to appeal to and control the 'masses'; from the second sprang confirmation that German Nationalism was a programme in itself, one that also incorporated his anti-Jew, anti-Habsburg and anti-democracy views; from the third he realized the importance of winning over the lower-middle classes. Alan Bullock observes that although at the time of his leaving Vienna, Hitler had not formulated the ideas which he was later to set down in *Mein Kampf,* yet the seeds of National Socialism were already planted in him.

It was to Munich that Hitler went, finding lodgings in a poor part of the city and, rather as in Vienna, eking out an existence with his drawings, while still avoiding both regular employment and the making of friends. He later recorded his joy at being in a German city, but it seems that most of his time was spent idling, brooding, reading, frequenting taverns, studying the newspapers, arguing about politics. Although he never admitted to it, one reason for his going to Germany may have been to avoid military service with the Austrian Army. Ironically enough, when the authorities caught up with him and he was required to report to Salzburg for examination in February 1914, he was not considered medically fit for service. Yet he would soon be in uniform anyway, for by then war was not far off. Faced with that prospect, both Hitler and Churchill were, in their wholly different ways, exhilarated.

What was to make a lasting impression on Hitler was being a soldier at such a time and in such circumstances; he later wrote that the war had come as a deliverance from the distress of his youth. Carried away by nationalistic enthusiasm and by the idea of participating with the masses in a moment of 'historical greatness', of leaving resentful frustration behind him, of joining a community which would offer comradeship, discipline and, above all, purpose, he unashamedly went down on his knees to thank Heaven that he was living at such a time. Sentiments of this sort he no doubt shared with a million others. For Hitler, however, there was more to his feeling than mere patriotism, or the excitement of taking part in stirring events, of being identified with and protected by a great and growing organization. He identified himself with war itself and took upon himself – unasked, indeed, but still not insignificantly – responsibility for the military issues of the day, for advance and withdrawal, success and failure, victory and defeat. It was not only as a statesman, twenty-five years later, that Hitler delighted in war. He did so also as an ordinary soldier – a merit in a soldier, as George Santayana has it. His exaltation is to be seen by a curious chance at the very moment of the war's declaration, amongst the crowd photographed in the Odeons Platz in Munich on 1 August 1914.[1] When

---

[1] Germany declared war against Russia on that date, and against France two days later; on 4 August, Britain declared war against Germany and Austria-Hungary.

Hitler, the Austrian down-and-out, became Hitler, the German soldier, and donned the cherished uniform of his adopted country (uniform he was not to doff again for nearly six years), he had found his home. His years as a soldier were, therefore, immensely important in moulding his character and his creed.

Churchill knew all about soldiering already, and had distinguished himself in a number of actions. Now, as a Minister of the Crown in charge of the most powerful naval force the world had ever seen, he had been stretching every nerve to ensure that the Royal Navy would prove equal to the daunting task which lay before it. On 28 July 1914 we find him writing to his wife from the Admiralty:

> Everything tends towards catastrophe & collapse. I am interested, geared up & happy. Is it not horrible to be built like that? The preparations have a hideous fascination for me. I pray to God to forgive me for such fearful moods of levity. Yet I wd do my best for peace, & nothing wd induce me wrongfully to strike the blow. I cannot feel that we in this island are in any serious degree responsible for the wave of madness wh has swept the mind of Christendom. No one can measure the consequences ... We are putting the whole Navy into fighting trim ... Everything is ready as it has never been before. And we are awake to the tips of our fingers. But war is the Unknown & the Unexpected! God guard us and our long accumulated inheritance ... I feel sure however that if war comes we shall give them a good drubbing.[1]

War was coming all right. A month before Churchill wrote this letter the Archduke Franz Ferdinand nephew of the Emperor Franz Josef and heir to the throne of Austria-Hungary, and his wife had been assassinated by extremists in Sarajevo, the principal city of Bosnia, and the whole dreadful train of events began. Here, for Austria, which believed the plot to have been instigated by the Serbian Government, was the excuse to attack Serbia. German support was sought and obtained. On 23 July Austria's ultimatum to Serbia was presented, a document described by Grey, the British Foreign Secretary, as the most formidable ever addressed by one state to another. Two days later Serbia caved in, but, bent on war, Austria rejected Belgrade's request that some points should be submitted to the European Powers for their arbitration, and began to mobilize. Thereafter, despite flurries of diplomatic activity, Austria's actual attack on Serbia (28 July) led inexorably to general war. Great Britain's position was still equivocal, for she warned Germany not to rely on her neutrality and

---

[1] This brings to mind Captain Hallowell's remark to Admiral Sir John Jervis, who was quite unmoved by the odds against him at the impending battle off Cape St Vincent in 1797: 'By God, we shall give them a damn good licking'.

France not to rely on her support. On 29 July Russia began to mobilize along her borders with Austria and Germany – a move which Germany at once demanded should cease. Instead, Russia began full mobilization on the 31st, and her refusal to comply with Germany's demand resulted in the latter's declaration of war on 1 August. Two days later Germany declared war on France. Britain's support of France arose from Germany's demand (2 August) that Belgium should allow passage of her armies. On August 3 Belgium rejected this demand and their King appealed to King George V to intervene by diplomatic means. That same day mobilization of the British Army was authorized, and at a War Council also held that day it was decided to send four divisions of the Expeditionary Force to France. Next day, 4 August, the Germans invaded Belgium. The British Government demanded withdrawal, and when the time limit on the ultimatum expired at 11 pm without German compliance, Germany and the British Empire were at war. In only one respect was Britain anything like ready. In July there had been a trial mobilization of the Grand Fleet, and although the ships were supposed to have dispersed on July 24, when Prince Louis of Battenberg, by now First Sea Lord, heard that Austria had rejected Serbia's reply to her ultimatum, he boldly used his initiative and cancelled the Fleet's demobilization. Churchill at once endorsed this very timely decision.

The last page of the second volume of Randolph Churchill's life of his father reminds readers of the signal sent by the Admiralty to all HM ships and naval establishments at 11 pm on 4 August 1914: 'Commence Hostilities Against Germany'. Randolph Churchill also reminds us of all that his father had done to prepare the Royal Navy and the country for war, a war in which Winston Churchill himself would play so prominent a part not only as a statesman, but also as a strategist and a fighting soldier. The book ends by making the supremely important observation that Churchill was a romantic.

> Tears easily came to his eyes when he talked of the long story of Britain's achievement in the world and the many deeds of heroism which had adorned it . . . fortitude in distress warmed and comforted his heart in all that he was doing to keep Britain and her Empire safe and glorious. If his life had ended in 1914 in his fortieth year we can be sure that he would not have been denied a page in history and that his epitaph would have been
>
> When War Came
> The Fleet was Ready.

It can be seen, therefore, that Churchill had made his mark on world history before Hitler had been heard of, and was to do a good deal more during the Great War. The part he would play would, in the end, plunge him from being at the head of a ministry, concerned with the planning and execution of decisive strategic operations, to the relatively humble, if heroic, duty of commanding an infantry battalion on the Western Front. Before the war's end he would return to ministerial work, and in all these roles his courage, his commitment, his energy and his eloquence would remain unflagging. Moreover, what he did and suffered during the First World War would prove to be of infinite value and significance in fitting him for what he yet had to do and suffer when it came to the Second World War. This second conflict would, to a considerable extent, be a duel between himself and a man who, at the time of the Great War, was simply an unknown German soldier. Yet the second of these wars was in large measure brought about by the personal and political ambitions, the quest for power, of this same German soldier. Churchill's life from 1914 to 1918 was packed with labour, adventure, incident, controversy, and relationships, both stormy and heart-warming, with hundreds of people. Hitler's life during that same period was that of a conscientious and disciplined soldier. The latter, unlike the former, does not take long in the telling.

Hitler served as a battalion runner (*Meldegänger*) in the List Regiment. As such his job was to carry messages from Company to Regimental Headquarters and back again – dangerous enough employment, even if it was not that of the fighting infantryman in the actual trenches. He was, according to one of his comrades 'a peculiar fellow'. Not sharing a soldier's normal interests, not caring about leave or pleasure haunts, not even receiving letters or parcels from home, he was an odd man out. But he did his duty as a soldier bravely and well. Twice he was decorated for bravery, first in December 1914 with the Iron Cross, Second Class, and then again in August 1918 – for exactly what action is not clear – with the Iron Cross, First Class. Whatever the occasion, however, it was a most uncommon distinction for a mere lance-corporal, and Hitler was proud of it; indeed, later, as Chancellor, he invariably wore the medal when in uniform. In speculating about what sort of soldier Hitler was and why it was that he never rose above the rank of corporal, or even seemed to be interested in the idea of promotion (particularly when it is remembered that in former days he had been convinced of his own superiority over others and his right to take a lead), Alan Bullock concludes that it was probably because he was quite content with the position and job he had. His curious, eccentric behaviour did not endear him to his comrades, however much they may have acknowledged his conscientious performance of duty. 'He sat in the corner of our mess,' noted one of Hitler's fellow members of the List Regiment, 'holding his head between his hands, in deep contemplation. Suddenly he would leap up, and, running about excitedly, say that in spite of our big guns victory would be denied us, for the invisible foes of the German people were a greater danger than the biggest cannon of the enemy.' This uncharacteristic behaviour –

uncharacteristic, that is, when contrasted with the ordinary soldier's traditional concern with home leave, drink, women, grousing about food, living conditions, the army, the war itself, and so on – set him apart. He seemed to take too much upon himself, as if he had some personal involvement with his country's fortunes or misfortunes on the battlefield. To his fellow soldiers he took everything too seriously, would not join in with their condemnation of what was going on, and tended to sit silently brooding in the corner of the mess. Yet on Hitler himself, according to his later pronouncements, the war made a stupendous impression. It was 'the greatest of all experiences. For, that individual interest – the interest of one's own ego – could be subordinated to the common interest – that the great, heroic struggle of our people demonstrated in overwhelming fashion.' Alan Bullock also points out that the 'comradeship, discipline and excitement of life at the Front were vastly more attractive than the obscurity, aimlessness, and dull placidity of peace'. What was true for Hitler was true for many millions of Germans, so that 'the war, and the impact of war' upon these millions 'were among the essential conditions for the rise of Hitler and the Nazi Party'.

It was the aftermath of war which brought Hitler to prominence, and eventually to power. Churchill was at the centre of things from the very beginning, a position he relished. He was, as usual, bursting with ideas, nor did he confine his thoughts, suggestions or advice to the clearly defined areas of his own special responsibilities. As his great friend F.E. Smith subsequently commented: 'No one Department, hardly one war, was enough for him.' Indeed, Churchill's life during the Great War was so rich, so varied, so continuous and so influential on his future career that Martin Gilbert, in his incomparably majestic account of it, required almost a thousand pages in which to do it justice. This book cannot be so prodigal; instead, it will aim to illustrate this extraordinary activity by reference to five distinct periods: at the Admiralty, August 1914 to May 1915; as Chancellor of the Duchy of Lancaster, May to November 1915; as a soldier, November 1915 to May 1916; during the period when he was out of office, May 1916 to July 1917; and as Minister of Munitions, July 1917 until the war's end. Although this illustration cannot be comprehensive, it may perhaps be representative.

In the first months of the war there were both naval successes and setbacks. In the escorting of the British Expeditionary Force to France without loss lay ample proof of excellent planning and prudent execution. But the Royal Navy's failure to find and destroy the German battle cruiser *Goeben* and light cruiser *Breslau*, both of which evaded search and sailed to Constantinople, was a serious blow. The Turks, ostensibly neutral, knew that by harbouring the two warships, they were committing an act which Britain would regard as hostile (under international agreements, the ships of belligerents were meant to remain in neutral harbours no longer than forty-eight hours). That had been the German intention all along – to hasten Turkey's entry into the war on the side of the Central Powers. British disappointment at the escape of *Goeben* and *Breslau* was somewhat mitigated some two weeks later by a naval action in the Heligoland Bight on 28 August, during which three German cruisers were sunk and three others damaged without British loss. On land, however, things were going badly wrong. Five days earlier the British Expeditionary Force, deployed at Mons on the left of the French Fifth Army, was subjected to an attack by General von Kluck's First Army, containing four German corps and three cavalry divisions, in all some 160,000 men and 600 guns, most of it directed at General Sir Horace Smith-Dorrien's II Corps. The highly trained British riflemen, who were properly dug in, engaged the advancing enemy with fire of such accuracy and rapidity that the Germans believed they were facing machine-guns. So stubborn was the resistance of Smith-Dorrien's corps that although it was necessary to retire to a second line of defence a few miles further back – sheer weight of German numbers made this inevitable – it seemed to Field Marshal Sir John French, Commander-in-Chief of the BEF, that he could remain on the defensive. But when he heard that the French Fifth Army was withdrawing, he was obliged to conform with his ally's movements, and the classic retreat from Mons began. It was now clear that the BEF could have no independent role, and this point was further reinforced when the imperturbable General 'Papa' Joffre, the French Commander-in-Chief, began his counter-move against the advancing Germans on 5 September. The French Army, with the BEF in support, now halted the German advance on the line of the River Marne, east of Paris. Suddenly the German Army, which had come within thirty miles of the capital, began to retreat, dogged by the Allies who had at last put a stop to the seemingly endless series of retirements of the last weeks. As the French attack on the Marne had developed, a thirty-mile gap had been opened between the German First and Second Armies, and into this gap the BEF slowly and cautiously made its way. Apart from a few cavalry skirmishes, the British forces had little contact with the enemy, until on 9 September the German armies conducted a general withdrawal to the River Aisne. It was then that all manoeuvre and mobility came to an end. The Germans, as A.J.P. Taylor put it, had unwittingly 'stumbled on the discovery which shaped the First World War: men in trenches, with machine-guns, could beat off all but the most formidable attacks. The Allied advance ground to a halt. On September 16 French issued his first instructions for trench warfare.'

It was not to be supposed that Churchill would be content to deal only with naval affairs, although he was greatly cheered by his reception at a Guildhall dinner on 4 September, when the City audience demanded 'We want Churchill' despite the fact that he was not due to speak. It was the Heligoland Bight victory which prompted this demand and, speaking in response to it, Churchill was able to assure his audience that they could rely upon the Royal Navy. His concluding words would find an echo twenty-six years later when, as Prime Minister, he spoke to the nation at a time of far more deadly peril. At the Guildhall, that night in 1914, he said: 'Sure I am of this, that you have only to endure to conquer. You have only to persevere to save yourselves, and to save all those who rely on you. You have only to go right on, and at the end of the road, be it short or long, victory and honour will be found.' The road was indeed going to be long, although many efforts were to be made to shorten it. Two days before the Guildhall dinner, while things were still going badly in France, Churchill had recirculated the remarkable memorandum which he had prepared for the Imperial Defence Committee three years earlier while still at the Home Office. The war seemed to be going more or less exactly as he had predicted, and his colleagues were able to draw comfort from his conclusion that by the fortieth day – ten days distant from the date on which the memorandum was recirculated – the German strategic position would have deteriorated and the worst danger would have passed. So that when just this situation came about, Churchill's colleagues and friends were lavish in their praise. The Prime Minister, Asquith, confided in Haldane that Churchill was 'the equivalent of a large force in the field';[1] Haldane himself spoke of Churchill's courage and resolution which inspired them all; his old friend, General Sir Ian Hamilton, who was shortly to be involved in the Gallipoli campaign, was equally enthusiastic, while Admiral Lord Fisher (whom Churchill was soon to recall to duty as First Sea Lord) was both astonished and exhilarated; even Balfour, often a severe critic of Churchill, told Eddie Marsh that it was 'a triumph of prophecy'.

No one, however, had foreseen the ghastliness of trench warfare, the first horrors of which were tasted by the British in October and November at the First Battle of Ypres. It was there, in Flanders, to which the BEF had moved after the Aisne, that the German and British Armies collided as each strove to outflank the other. At Ypres, concentrated attacks by British troops on narrow fronts, with repeated reinforcement of failure, led first to the BEF's almost running out of supplies and ammunition, then to a breakthrough by the Germans which, however, they did not exploit, thus permitting French reserves to block the gap. After the battle had lasted for a month – from 12 October to 10 November – there was deadlock, leaving the British with a vulnerable salient jutting out into the German line. British attempts to 'level

---

[1] This would have particularly pleased Churchill, who greatly admired Napoleon, and sometimes likened his own power to raise morale to that of the French emperor, for Wellington had observed that Napoleon's presence on a battlefield made a difference of forty thousand men.

out' the salient, and to break out at Ypres and roll up the German line north-wards and southwards, led to two further battles there (April to May 1915 and July to November 1917), even more costly and indecisive than the first; the Third Battle of Ypres, better known as 'Passchendaele', was one of the costli-est battles of all those fought on the Western Front. Yet the cost of this first battle was heavy indeed, for as A.J.P. Taylor summed it up, 'the first battle of Ypres marked the end of the old British army. The BEF fought the Germans to a standstill, and itself out of existence.' As General Ludendorff is said to have declared, the British soldiers had fought like lions; fortunately for the Germans, the British generals had confirmed Colonel Hoffman's alleged rejoinder to Ludendorff, that they were lions led by donkeys. Having destroyed one British army, the generals would now need more soldiers in order to have another to destroy. Kitchener, now a field marshal and, since 5 August, Secretary of State for War in place of Asquith, would ensure by the voluntary recruiting campaign he instigated that there would be plenty more. Even he, however, did not know the answer to trench warfare: 'I don't know what is to be done; this isn't war.' Yet, by some brilliant flash of insight, he predicted that Britain would be required to deploy millions of men to fight for years in Continental battles.

This was hardly an attractive proposition, so that it was not surprising that before long the War Council was investigating alternative plans for prosecuting the war against the Central Powers, which now included – since 5 November – Turkey. Before we turn our eyes eastward, however, it is proper to recall a speech made by Churchill in London on 11 September, during which, as the *Manchester Guardian* reported, he compared the Royal Navy to a bulldog, whose nose is so shaped that it can breath without having to let go of whatever it has clamped its powerful jaws around. There were to be many occasions when Churchill was himself likened to a bulldog, and few who read the *Manchester Guardian* or who were present at the speech would have forgotten that 'At the moment of delivery, with extraordinary appositeness, it was particularly vivid, as the speaker was able by some histrionic gift to suggest quite the bulldog as he spoke.' Churchill was indefatigable both in his work at the Admiralty and in seeing for himself what went on in the field. His restless energy, his concern with every detail of his department's activities, his prodigious capacity for work, all meant that he bore a heavy load, but the very weight of his responsibilities was something he relished. He was still only thirty-nine, and when the opportunity for an active role in military operations presented itself, he at once was seized with enthusiasm to take command. It was the plight of the Belgian port of Antwerp which brought this about.

This longing for action was aggravated by the circumstances that the Royal Navy was not doing what Churchill and the country had expected of it; in short, the war at sea was providing the First Lord of the Admiralty with neither the excitement nor the glory he craved. The German High Seas Fleet seemed reluctant to leave port and engage Britain's Grand Fleet, and Churchill's frustration had been expressed in a speech made at Liverpool on 21 September, when he told his audience that 'if they do not come out and fight in time of war they will be dug out like rats in a hole'. This belligerence was not well received by the admirals, who deprecated anything that smacked of bombast or boasting; indeed, when, on the following day, three British cruisers were sunk on the Dogger Bank patrol by an enemy submarine, with the loss of nearly 1,500 lives, Churchill came in for much criticism. He took some comfort, however, in visiting the Royal Naval Air Service[1] squadrons which he had established at Dunkirk to bomb German targets and to assist with aerial reconnaissance for the BEF. He was also able to satisfy both his taste for battlefields and his gift for strategic reasoning by visiting Sir John French at his headquarters, where he represented Kitchener's views to the Commander-in-Chief, before going on to tour the front:

> Next day between daylight and dark I was able to traverse the entire British artillery front . . . I met everyone I wanted to meet and saw everything that could be seen without unnecessary danger . . . I saw for the first time what seemed to be the prodigy of a British aeroplane threading its way among the smoke-puffs of searching shells. I saw the big black German shells . . . bursting in Paissy village or among our patient, impassive batteries on the ridge . . . When darkness fell I saw the horizon lighted with the quick flashing of the cannonade. Such scenes were afterwards to become commonplace: but their first aspect was thrilling.

Churchill's thirst for visiting troops in the field did not always endear him to his colleagues, not least because often, when they wished to consult him about some urgent Admiralty matter, he was away. Nor was his advice about military matters that lay outside his responsibility always appreciated, since he appeared all too frequently to be making difficulties, or simply being meddlesome. Moreover, having got the bit between his teeth with regard to some particular problem, he was apt to give it precedence over wider and graver issues. A notable instance of this capricious behaviour was his action over the defence of Antwerp. Antwerp, Belgium's principal port, heavily fortified and defended by a ring of outlying forts, was dependent for its trade on passage of the River Scheldt, that is, the territorial waters of neutral Holland; its capture would deal

---

[1] For most of the war, Britain had two military air arms, the Royal Flying Corps and the Royal Naval Air Service. They were formally amalgamated into the Royal Air Force on 1 April 1918.

a severe blow to the Belgian economy. Furthermore, if it was lost to the Germans then there would be a further threat to Britain, so that when by the end of September it became clear that German forces were preparing for this very action, the British Government began to consider what might be done to assist in its defence. An additional danger arose from the German advance towards the Channel ports, an advance which would be made easier by the fall of Antwerp.

Churchill's involvement in the defence of Antwerp had begun in September when he responded to Grey's request for assistance to the Belgium forces by arranging for the dispatch of guns, ammunition and aircraft, but he was to become personally committed at the beginning of October. On 2 October he left by train to visit France, both to gauge the situation of the Royal Naval aircraft and armoured cars and the Royal Marine Brigade at Dunkirk, and to discuss their deployment with French. While he was on his way, however, Grey and Kitchener became so concerned about Antwerp that they gave instructions for the train to be stopped and for Churchill to return to London for consultation, the Prime Minister being away. After their discussion it was agreed that Churchill should himself go to Antwerp to report on the state of the city and the prospects for its successful defence, and that the Royal Marine Brigade should be sent there. We may perhaps note with wry tolerance Asquith's reaction to events on his return to London by recalling his note to his soulmate and confidante, Venetia Stanley (with whom he conducted a politically indiscreet correspondence throughout the war), to the effect that he had talked to Kitchener and that they were eagerly awaiting Churchill's report: 'I don't know how fluent he [Churchill] is in French [he was fluent enough, although his syntax and accent left something to be desired], but if he was able to do himself justice in a foreign tongue, the Belges will have listened to a discourse the like of which they have never heard before. I cannot but think that he will stiffen them up to the sticking point. Don't say anything of Winston's mission, at any rate at present; it is one of the many unconventional incidents of the war.' It was shortly to become even more unconventional.

In the event, Churchill *was* able to stiffen de Broqueville, the Belgian Prime Minister, sufficiently for him to undertake further resistance by Belgian forces provided their withdrawal routes were protected by Allied troops. Churchill further promised additional British reinforcements, and telegraphed to Kitchener that the two naval brigades (which were intended for home defence) should be sent with the appropriate supplies and ammunition. It is important to note here that he specified that the two brigades should come *without recruits*. Next day, 4 October, Churchill characteristically toured Antwerp's defences; the report, written by a naval rating, of this inspection shows the First Lord of the Admiralty savouring every aspect of being at the front:

Mr Churchill was energetic and imperative. He discussed the situation with his own staff and some of the Belgian officers, emphasizing his points with his walking stick . . . He appeared on occasions to criticize the siting and construction of the trenches . . .

To me it appeared that Mr Churchill dominated the proceedings and the impression formed that he was by no means satisfied with the position generally. He put forward his ideas forcefully, waving his stick and thumping the ground with it. After obviously pungent remarks, he would walk away a few steps and stare towards the enemy's direction . . .

The Royal Marine Brigade arrived in Antwerp on 4 October and did much to bolster the morale of its citizens, but its dispatch there had been strongly criticized by naval officers[1] who knew little of the political circumstances that had led to this decision. Not for the first time, or the last, political considerations overrode military prudence. Yet no one could have foreseen the next twist in the story which led Churchill, convinced that his own presence in Antwerp would provide the necessary stimulus to the city's continued resistance, quite apart from the responsibility which he felt for the two naval brigades shortly to arrive, to take upon himself command of the entire operation. 'The atmosphere of crisis and action excited him,' writes Martin Gilbert. 'The presence of troops, the immediacy of battle, and the importance of the outcome to the whole progress of the German advance, aroused his desire to participate and command.' It was with these things in mind that, on the morning of 5 October, Churchill sent a telegram to Asquith in which he offered to resign from the Cabinet in order to take charge of military affairs at Antwerp:

If it is thought by HM Government that I can be of service here, I am willing to resign my office and undertake command of relieving and defensive forces assigned to Antwerp in conjunction with Belgian Army, provided that I am given necessary military rank and authority, and full powers of a commander of a detached force in the field. I feel it my duty to offer my services, because I am sure this arrangement will afford the best prospects of a victorious result to an enterprise in which I am deeply involved . . .

Answering this fantastic proposal, Asquith told Churchill that much as his patriotic gesture was appreciated, he could not be spared from his duties at the Admiralty. The Prime Minister, however, was not above extracting as much fun as he could from this extraordinary state of affairs, writing to Venetia Stanley that when he informed his Cabinet colleagues of Churchill's offer, it was 'received with a Homeric laugh', adding that the would-be defender of

[1] Then, as now, the Corps of Royal Marines came under Royal Naval command.

Antwerp was but 'an ex-Lieutenant of Hussars'. Yet, as Martin Gilbert emphasizes, Asquith forbore to acknowledge that Churchill's experience of military affairs, his regular attendance at manoeuvres as a Territorial officer, his witnessing of the German Army on two occasions, his organization of naval air matters and Royal Marine brigades, his contribution to the Imperial Defence Committee's deliberations and his general grasp of strategic problems, all these entitled him to have made the offer in the first place, while Kitchener, for his part, was more than ready to grant Churchill the rank of lieutenant-general so that he should have the necessity authority. It should also be borne in mind that no other member of the Cabinet was likely to have risked life and limb – and reputation – in such a venture; furthermore, Churchill's conduct during his brief intervention in Antwerp's defence was admirably cool, as was recorded by an Italian war correspondent:

> I was in the battle line near Lierre, and in the midst of a group of officers stood a man. He was still young, and was enveloped in a cloak, and on his head wore a yachtsman's cap. He was tranquilly smoking a large cigar and looking at the progress of the battle under a rain of shrapnel, which I can only call fearful. It was Mr Churchill, who had come to view the situation himself. It must be confessed that it is not easy to find in the whole of Europe a Minister who would be capable of smoking peacefully under that shellfire. He smiled and looked quite satisfied.

As far as Antwerp itself was concerned, all was in vain, for the city surrendered to the Germans on 10 October. Losses to the Royal Naval Division were severe: apart from those killed and wounded, respectively 57 and 158, nearly 1,000 were made prisoners of war in Germany, while 1,500 were interned in Holland, to which they had withdrawn rather than surrender to the Germans. Much of the blame for these losses was levelled at Churchill himself, although the part he had played in delaying the enemy's advance received powerful support – both Kitchener and Albert, King of the Belgians, firmly believed that but for the defence, albeit for a short time, of Antwerp, the entire Belgian Army and the French Channel ports would have been captured by the Germans; Sir John French also wrote encouragingly about Churchill's 'splendid work at Antwerp'. But the seeds of doubt about his judgement had been sown, and a feeling that he would act with rashness and irresponsibility gained ground in both political and military circles, to say nothing of the opinions of the public and the press.

It was the *Morning Post*, under its editor, H.A. Gwynne, which published some of the most severe criticism, calling the Antwerp affair a costly blunder for which Churchill should be held responsible, and urging his colleagues in the

Government to restrain him so as to avoid further mischief of this sort. When other newspapers expressed support for the First Lord, the *Morning Post* returned to the charge by declaring that Churchill should understand that he was not 'a Napoleon', and that he should devote himself to his ministerial duties, rather than organizing or leading armies in the field, or seeking to impress the world with his gallantry. One of Churchill's supporters, writing about the Antwerp escapade, had made reference to Napoleon, and it is perhaps apposite to remind ourselves of a passage written by A.G. Gardiner which, although it appeared in a book published in 1913, is particularly apt to its subject, not only in terms of the Great War, but even more strikingly of the Second World War:

> He is always unconsciously playing a part – an heroic part. And he is himself his most astonished spectator. He sees himself moving through the smoke of battle – triumphant, terrible, his brow clothed with thunder, his legions looking to him for victory, and not looking in vain. He thinks of Napoleon; he thinks of his great ancestor [Marlborough]. Thus did they bear themselves; thus, in this most rugged and most awful crisis, will he bear himself. It is not make-believe, it is not insincerity: it is that in that fervid and picturesque imagination there are always great deeds afoot with himself cast by destiny in the Agamemnon role.

It would be difficult to coin a more compelling or comprehensive a portrait of Churchill in 1940 – when he was at last to fulfil his destiny – in so few words.

If there was considerable controversy as to Churchill's part in the Antwerp affair in 1914, it was to be as nothing to the controversy which would arise over the question of the Dardanelles in the following year. Before examining the circumstances leading to the Gallipoli campaign, however, three events of great moment to the Admiralty and its First Lord occurred. When anti-German prejudice made the position of Prince Louis of Battenberg as First Sea Lord intolerable (he resigned in October 1914; in 1917 he relinquished his German titles, changed the family name to Mountbatten, and was created first Marquess of Milford Haven), Churchill insisted – much against the wishes of King George V – on the recall of Lord Fisher, who had been First Sea Lord from 1904 to 1910, had devised the Dreadnought-class battleships and battle cruisers, and was probably as colourful, dynamic and loquacious a sailor as existed. Churchill was subsequently to rue the appointment, but initially it seemed a sound enough choice, for when, on 1 November, Vice-Admiral Count Maximilian von Spee's squadron destroyed a less powerful British force under Rear-Admiral Sir Christopher Cradock (who was lost with his flagship) off Coronel in Chilean waters, it was Fisher who persuaded Churchill that two battle cruisers, *Invincible* and *Inflexible* should be sent to South America. The decision resulted in the victory at the Falkland Islands on 8 December 1914, when Vice-Admiral Frederick Sturdee avenged Coronel by sinking all Spee's ships but one, *Dresden*, which was destroyed later; Spee, too, with two of his sons, died with his ship. Churchill, as always generous-hearted in victory as he was resolute in defeat, congratulated Fisher on his judgement, adding, 'Let us have some more victories together and confound all our foes abroad – and (don't forget) – at home.' Unhappily, the Dardanelles affair was to result in defeat for British forces abroad and victory for Churchill's foes at home.

In November 1914, when deadlock on the Western Front had laid its puzzling restraints on British strategists, who wished to avoid wasting millions of lives recapturing French territory (but nevertheless went on to do so in accordance with their ally's principal aim), and when the Ottoman Empire had entered the war on Germany's side, the appeal of the 'indirect approach' to these same strategists was extremely strong. There was nothing new about it. Over the centuries the British, when fighting huge Continental armies, had put their faith in sea power. Rather than resort to massed attack on land, and in any case lacking the means to indulge in it, they sought the open flank. Victory over German sea power on distant oceans and the apparent reluctance of the High Seas Fleet to venture from port as long as the Grand Fleet under Admiral Sir John Jellicoe barred its freedom of action, gave Britain the opportunity to seek a new theatre of action outside Europe. In short, the idea was to pursue a decision on the Continent, but in theatres of war away from the Continent, by exploiting the advantages which supremacy at sea offered in the way of concentration of effort, and of choosing time and place. During a meeting of the War Council on 25 November 1914, Maurice Hankey, the Secretary to the Imperial Defence Committee, noted what was proposed by the First Lord of the Admiralty with regard to countering the dangers posed by a Turkish army which was moving southwards through Palestine to threaten the Suez Canal: 'MR CHURCHILL suggested that the ideal method of defending Egypt was by an attack on the Gallipoli Peninsula. This, if successful, would give us control of the Dardanelles, and we could dictate terms at Constantinople. This, however, was a very difficult operation requiring a large force.'

There was an additional reason for Allied intervention against Turkey. Although in August the Russian armies had invaded East Prussia, the combined efforts of General Paul von Hindenburg and Ludendorff had brought about their crushing defeat at Tannenberg (26–30 August), followed in September by their rout at the Masurian Lakes, and the Grand Duke Nicholas, Chief of the Russian General Staff, had appealed to the Allies for assistance in his country's struggle with Turkey, which had invaded the Caucasus. It was not until January 1915, however, that the War Council made up its mind to mount an attack on the

Dardanelles, the Turkish-controlled channel between the Aegean and the Sea of Marmara. On the first day of that month the British Ambassador in Petrograd (as St Petersburg was called from 1914–24), Sir George Buchanan, telegraphed to the Foreign Secretary, Grey, passing on the Grand Duke's request that either a naval or a military demonstration against the Turks should be made in order to distract some of the Turkish forces operating in the Caucasus, thereby relieving the pressure on the Russians. Grey consulted Kitchener, who in turn consulted Churchill, asking if a *naval* demonstration could be made at the Dardanelles. Initially Churchill's reaction was that only a combined naval and military attack would have any chance of success, and he therefore urged Kitchener to find the soldiers necessary for a joint operation. After consulting his War Office staff, Kitchener confirmed to Churchill that 'we have no troops to land anywhere', and went on to say that he believed the only way to prevent Turkish troops reinforcing their front against the Russians would be by mounting a demonstration at the strategically vital Dardanelles, for if the straits were successfully stormed then Constantinople would be threatened. On the morning of 3 January, therefore, Churchill talked the matter over with his own experts, who shared his doubts about the practicability of an attack by naval vessels alone, since the straits were defended by minefields and by numerous well-sited shore batteries. Nevertheless, later that day he sent a signal to Vice-Admiral Sackville Carden, commanding the Royal Navy squadron blockading the Dardanelles, and asked whether it would be feasible to force the straits 'by ships alone', if necessary using old battleships and being prepared, in view of the high strategic stakes, to accept serious losses. Carden's reply, received on 5 January, stated that whereas he did not believe the Dardanelles could be rushed, he did consider that by using large numbers of ships and accepting an extended action, the straits might be forced. After further consideration Churchill telegraphed to Carden again on the next day, asking for details of what force would be needed and how it would carry out the operation.

Before moving on to Carden's reply, it is worth pausing for a moment to record the remarkable entry that Asquith's wife, Margot, had made in her diary on Churchill's fortieth birthday, just over a month earlier. She asked herself what it was that gave Winston his eminence, and answered herself by saying that it was not his mind, which was 'noisy', nor his judgement, which was frequently faulty, but his

> courage and colour . . . He never shirks, hedges, or *protects* himself – though he thinks of himself perpetually. *He takes huge risks.*[1] He is at his very best just now; when others are shrivelled with grief – apprehensive, silent, irascible

---

[1] Something Churchill was to share with Hitler in the Second World War.

and self-conscious morally; Winston is intrepid, valorous, passionately keen and sympathetic, longing to be in the trenches – dreaming of war, big, buoyant, happy even.[1] It is very extraordinary, he is a born soldier ...

These judicious comments do much to explain why his character and his actions sometimes upset Churchill's colleagues. His overall concern with the war's conduct, his sheer longing for action, his effusive spirits, his apparent lack of sensitivity to the grave and grievous nature of events – such things jarred on some of his fellow ministers, arousing their resentment. He appeared unaware of this, and continued to press for offensive action, supported in this respect by Fisher, who regarded the defensive strategy of the Royal Navy as bad for its morale.

The dilemma facing the War Council was aggravated by the belief of the BEF's Commander-in-Chief, French, that although the German defences in France seemed to be impenetrable, yet no dispersion of effort to other theatres should be made until the impossibility of a breakthrough on the Western Front had been incontrovertibly demonstrated. Kitchener, on the other hand, still had his eye on the Dardanelles, with its promise of establishing communications with Russia, and perhaps of persuading some of the Balkan powers to join the fight against Germany. Hankey supported this idea, and went so far as to suggest that breaching the Dardanelles might enable Allied sea power to exert pressure in Central Europe by making possible the advance of an army along the Danube. Kitchener was sufficiently enthusiastic, having previously declared that there were no troops to land anywhere, to volunteer the intuitive opinion that 150,000 troops would be capable of capturing the Gallipoli peninsula; he did not say, however, where those troops were to be found. At this time Churchill was still thinking of offensive action in Northern Europe, particularly in the Baltic and at Borkum (one of the East Frisian Islands, lying off the entrance to the Ems estuary), but Admiral Carden's reply to his signal, which reached the Admiralty on 12 January 1915, had a profound effect. The reply was nothing less than a detailed plan for forcing the straits 'by ships alone', thus threatening the Turkish capital, relieving the pressure on Russia, turning the Central Powers' flank, ensuring that the southern Balkan nations would rally to the Allies, and all without removing any troops from the Western Front. It is little wonder that the plan was so appealing, nor that it was immediately adopted. At the War Council next day, 13 January, one of the conclusions endorsed was that 'the Admiralty should also prepare for a naval expedition in February to bombard and take the Gallipoli peninsula, with Constantinople as its objective.'

---

[1] In a conversation with Margot Asquith on 10 January 1915, Churchill referred to 'this glorious delicious war'.

It was not long, however, before the First Sea Lord, Fisher, began to have misgivings about the whole operation. His principal concern was that Britain's naval strength should be concentrated in the North Sea and the Baltic, and should not be dissipated in sideshows in the Mediterranean. 'I just abominate the Dardanelles operation,' he wrote to Jellicoe, 'unless a great change is made and it is settled to be made a military operation, with 200,000 men in conjunction with the Fleet.' Wisdom after the event is common enough, but here was wisdom before it. The trouble was not merely that Kitchener continued to argue that there were no troops available, but that Carden's confidence in storming the Dardanelles with ships alone had so strong an appeal. Most of those concerned with the plan would have *liked* it to have been a combined operation, but were prepared to settle for a purely naval one. Before the War Council met again to discuss the Dardanelles on 28 January, there was encouraging news of a naval success off the Dogger Bank, where four days earlier British and German battle cruisers and their escorts had fought an engagement during which the *Blücher* was sunk and the rest of the enemy fleet forced to beat a retreat, some of its other ships having been heavily damaged. This was not, however, the decisive engagement for which Churchill had hoped, while for Fisher it was fuel for his concern that to jeopardize naval superiority over Britain's main enemy at sea, by detaching and risking ships and men in the Dardanelles, was to take an unwarrantable risk. He expressed his doubts to Churchill in a memorandum, accompanying it with the threat of resignation. The essential point of Fisher's argument was that British naval superiority in the North Sea was paramount and any action which threatened this superiority, which was designed to force a decision at sea, could not be justified. Churchill countered these points by asserting that the Grand Fleet could maintain the necessary superiority without resort to those warships which were required elsewhere in the world to pursue 'objectives of great strategic and political importance'. The truth was, of course, that whereas Fisher was wedded to a passive policy to aim at containing the enemy fleet – or destroying it – Churchill was set on mounting an offensive which would, above all, break the deadlock on the Western Front. Fisher pressed for his paper, and Churchill's counter to it, to be circulated to the War Council, but Asquith decided against doing so.

On 28 January Fisher wrote to both Asquith and Churchill. To the Prime Minister he expressed his disagreement with Churchill, his overriding concern with what might happen in the North Sea, his insistence that any naval bombardment operation, whether at the Dardanelles or Zeebrugge,[1] should be in co-operation with military forces, and that in view of the impossibility of his

---

[1] Situated on the coast at the head of the canal heading to the Belgian inland port of Bruges, from which the Germans were operating destroyers and submarines.

and Churchill's achieving a union of ideas, he, Fisher, would resign. To the First Lord he sent a comparable letter of resignation, concluding that he would not attend the War Council, scheduled for later that day. Churchill, however, persuaded Fisher that they should see Asquith together before the meeting started, and at this pre-Council discussion it was decided that the Dardanelles plan should be carried out. During the War Council, however, Fisher still made one more effort to dissent from this decision, even leaving the council table at one point. Kitchener reasoned with him, pointing out that the First Sea Lord was the only one in disagreement, and induced him to return to the discussion. Kitchener, Balfour (a member of the Committee for Imperial Defence, though without a Cabinet post at the time) and Grey all spoke in support of the Dardanelles operation, and Churchill outlined the plan, not overlooking the difficulties presented by mines and, even when the outer forts at the lower end of the Dardanelles had been dealt with, by the problems of attacking the Narrows (at the upper, eastern end of the channel, and heavily defended by shore batteries). After further deliberations – and doubts – the War Council agreed on the policy, which Churchill summed up by saying that the Admiralty would 'undertake the task with which the War Council has charged us so urgently . . . to make a naval attack at the Dardanelles'. It is important, therefore, to acknowledge here that this policy was one arrived at by the War Council as a whole, whatever doubts and fears might have been expressed. In this respect responsibility for failure cannot be laid at Churchill's door alone. It was later, at the time for decisions as to *how* the attack should be carried out, that charges against him could properly be made.

It is now worth stating briefly what did happen at the Dardanelles and Gallipoli and then – in view of the profound and lasting impact that the failure there was to have on Churchill's subsequent career – examining those special events which led to his bearing so much of the responsibility for what went wrong. After the War Council of 28 January, preparations were put in hand, but it was not long before Kitchener began to have doubts about the soundness of a purely naval expedition. Having been alerted to the dangers by a member of his intelligence staff, Captain Wyndham Deedes, who knew Turkey and its armed forces, Kitchener agreed on 16 February to make available the 29th Division, and it was further accepted by the War Council that the troops of the Australian and New Zealand Army Corps (Anzac) in Egypt could be moved to the Greek island of Lemnos to support the attack if needed. All this meant that, instead of the operation being a purely naval one, it was beginning to take on the character of a joint naval and military affair, a development greatly welcomed by Churchill. It meant, too, that henceforward rapid and fruitful co-operation between Churchill and Kitchener would be indispensable to success. This, however, proved to be asking too much. Moreover, Fisher was still intensely concerned that any dissipation of the Royal Navy's strength in the North Sea would seriously endanger the country. To Churchill's fury and consternation, Kitchener dithered, at one moment agreeing to dispatch the 29th Division, at the next withdrawing this agreement. Finally he decided not only to send this division as part of the military force, but also to appoint, as commander of that force, General Sir Ian Hamilton, who had been his Chief of Staff in South Africa, and who was also an old friend and associate of Churchill's. On 12 March 1915 Kitchener told Hamilton: 'We are sending a military force to support the Fleet now at the Dardanelles, and you are to have command.' It would include the Royal Naval Division, units from the Indian Army, French divisions and the Anzacs. First, however, the Royal Navy was, after all, to attempt to storm the Dardanelles with ships alone.

On 18 March the combined fleet – four French battleships took part, in addition to some dozen Royal Navy battleships, a battle cruiser, destroyer flotillas and minesweepers – under command of Rear-Admiral John de Robeck attempted to force the straits. The battle lasted all day and ended in absolute triumph for the Turkish defenders. Despite an intense pounding of the Turkish forts, only four guns were destroyed out of nearly one hundred and eighty deployed to defend the Dardanelles (the Turks had also sited mobile howitzers along the length of the straits). Not a single one of the four hundred or so mines was cleared. Three battleships were sunk and three more disabled. That incomparable chronicler of British Imperial fortunes and misfortunes, James (Jan) Morris vividly depicts the scene. Once it had become clear 'that the mystique of the Royal Navy could not force a passage through the Dardanelles, the great ships, turning heavily in the narrow waters of the straits, abandoned the assault and disappeared to sea, where presently the Turkish lookouts on the heights could see their dark silhouettes and billowing smoke-trails scattered among the islands of the archipelago.' Hamilton had watched the assault from one of the ships standing off and signalled to Kitchener his reluctant conclusion that the straits could not be forced by battleships, and that if his troops were to take part it would not be in a subsidiary role. The army would need to mount a deliberate attack in force on the Gallipoli peninsula to secure the northern shore of the Dardanelles and so clear a passage for the navy. This was a very different matter from what had at first been envisaged.

Kitchener agreed with Hamilton, who assumed this agreement to constitute a directive that he was to capture the Gallipoli peninsula. To prepare to do so, he took his army off to Alexandria to reorganize with a view to returning and effecting landings three weeks later. Obviously, by this time all hope of surprise had disappeared and the Turks reinforced their Gallipoli garrison threefold, bringing it up to a strength of six divisions. Moreover, the Turks had the additional advantages of General Liman von Sanders's genius for training and organization, and the bold and brilliant tactical command on the peninsula of Mustafa Kemal. Thus the British Army, already committed to a war of attrition on the Western Front, was about to indulge in an amphibious assault against unreconnoitred country defended by rather more soldiers than Hamilton had under his command at the outset. It was not precisely a recipe for success.

Hamilton himself has been described by Robert Rhodes James as an attractive, intelligent and sensitive man, but one who nevertheless lacked 'that element in a commander which is so difficult to define with exactitude, that inner confidence, that basic common sense, that understanding of reality . . . that mental and moral toughness . . .' These deficiencies were to have a damaging effect on the campaign. Right at the beginning there was dissension among the senior officers as to what should be done. Whereas Hamilton wanted the main effort to be directed against the Gallipoli peninsula itself, that is, the northern, European, shore of the Dardanelles, with the Anzacs landing south of Suvla Bay on the western side, and 29th Division either side of Cape Helles on the southern tip, Lieutenant-General William Birdwood, commanding the Anzacs, favoured the southern Asian, shore, where there would be so much more room for manoeuvre, while Major-General Aylmer Hunter-Weston, the 29th Division commander, was much concerned at the severe restriction of suitable landing beaches at Cape Helles. Hamilton had his way and, apart from diversionary landings by the Royal Naval Division at Bulair and by the French at Kum Kale on the Asiatic shore, the two main landings went in, on 25 April, south of Suvla (at what came to be called Anzac Cove) and at Helles.

The whole plan had major defects. Secrecy did not exist – everyone knew the expedition's destination. Moreover, there was a totally unwarranted assumption that all that was needed for success was to get ashore, and then, since the Turks were held to be negligible opponents, the rest of the invasion would look after itself. Administrative support was wholly inadequate. Above all, there was (to anticipate a phrase to which Montgomery became addicted) no master plan, no overall idea as to objectives or purpose which would have allowed commanders on the ground, comprehending what was being aimed at, to have taken the initiative without further guidance if clear orders from above were not forthcoming. There was also a fatal lack of air reconnaissance. Despite all these drawbacks, however, both the Anzacs and the 29th Division got ashore. But the reaction of the Turks under von Sanders and, more particularly, Mustafa Kemal, commanding the division facing the Anzacs, was swift and resolute. Hamilton's troops were simply pushed back and pinned to the shore; indeed, so bad was the Anzac situation that Birdwood recommended evacuation. Hamilton, while taking no grip at all of the battle during the first day, nevertheless refused to consider it and simply ordered the two beachheads, however precarious, to be held.

It soon became apparent that the British and Dominion forces, far from initiating a great strategic coup, turning the flank of the Central Powers and finding an alternative to the dreadful and pointless carnage of trench warfare in France and Flanders, had merely found another theatre of war in which to indulge in this same futile slaughter. Hamilton seemed incapable of anything but ordering fresh attacks, to which the Turks responded with further counter-attacks. In the south, attempts to reach Krithia resulted in the loss of nearly 7,000 men for a gain of 600 yards, reminiscent of the appallingly costly gains of useless, shattered ground which were being made in northern France. At Anzac Cove the conditions were so frightful that Aubrey Herbert (whom John Buchan portrayed as the romantic hero of his novel *Greenmantle*), who spoke Turkish fluently, arranged a truce so that each side could bury their dead. This temporary ceasefire took place on 24 May 1915, and Herbert later recorded that after passing through a cornfield filled with poppies 'the fearful smell of death began as we came across the scattered corpses . . . there lay about 4,000 Turkish dead. One was grateful for the rain and grey sky. The smell was appalling . . . One saw the result of machine-gun fire very clearly; entire companies annihilated . . . killed, their heads doubled under them with the impetus of their rush and both hands clasping their bayonets . . .'

Soldiers were not the only casualties. Failure at Gallipoli caused Fisher to resign as First Sea Lord and caused the Prime Minister, Asquith, to accept the need for a coalition. Those Unionists who had joined Asquith's government insisted that Churchill – regarded by many as the architect of the Gallipoli adventure, and thus the natural scapegoat – should go. He thus lost the Admiralty (to Balfour), becoming instead Chancellor of the Duchy of Lancaster. Before moving on to the dramatic days which led to Churchill's fall however, we must follow the Dardanelles campaign itself to its bitter end.

Hamilton was reinforced, as he had requested – the British were becoming very adept at reinforcing failure; they were, in all conscience, having enough practice at it on the Western Front – and in August another great effort was made when fresh troops landed at Suvla Bay with the elderly and incompetent Lieutenant-General the Hon. Sir Frederick Stopford nominally in command. The troops got ashore, the Turks occupied the hills dominating the landing places, more trenches were dug, the supporting Anzac attack almost, but not quite, broke through the Turkish lines – then furious counter-attacks under the personal leadership of Mustafa Kemal threw back the British and Anzac troops. Once more the stalemate resumed. The fault lay not with the troops, however, but with the generals, and notably with Hamilton, who, as the Official History justly put it: 'lacked the iron will and dominating personality of a truly great commander . . . He left too much to his subordinates and hesitated to override their plans, even when in his opinion they were missing opportunities.'

He paid the price, for in October 1915 he was replaced by General Sir Charles Monro (who immediately recommended evacuation of the entire expedition) and recalled; he was never to hold another command. In mid-December the Suvla and Anzac Cove beaches were evacuated, followed three weeks later by the Helles beaches. This was the most successful part of the entire enterprise, for the evacuation was carried out under the noses of the Turks without the loss of a single man. Yet of the half-million Allied soldiers who took part in the campaign, losses overall, including those from sickness, had amounted to almost half. Some 25,000 had been killed, 75,000 wounded, more than 10,000 were missing. And all for what? The campaign had simply demonstrated that the German Army on the Western Front could not be outflanked by Mediterranean adventures (although Churchill still clung to the idea during the Second World War), and the failure in the Dardanelles therefore lent great power to those British commanders like General Sir Douglas Haig and General Sir William Robertson who insisted that only in France and Flanders could the war be decided. But, as James Morris wrote: 'Long after the Empire had ended altogether, Britons would remember the names of Gallipoli and the Dardanelles.' So, for many years to come, would Winston Churchill.

Such is the bare outline of the campaign which led to Churchill's fall from power – not from office initially, but from any position central to controlling the war – a campaign ill-fated from the start, hampered by poor intelligence, confused purpose, dilatory planning, dithering delays, disgraceful security, uncertain objectives, weak command and flawed execution, and redeemed only by its imaginative strategic concept and the unquenchable valour of its participants. Now we may turn to the political and military in-fighting which brought about the fall of one of the campaign's most ardent advocates.

No one had supposed that an operation like the Dardanelles would be without attendant risk, Churchill least of all. He did, however, fervently believe in bold measures, and long after the Dardanelles fighting was over, in giving evidence to the Commission of Inquiry which looked into it, he emphasized the need in war for taking risks. 'It is not right,' he maintained, 'to condemn operations of war simply because they involve risk and uncertainty . . . For instance, the naval attack on the Dardanelles in its final and decisive phase was, of course, a sharp hazard of war. But so were a great many other things we had done successfully since the outbreak.' Churchill went on to recount that almost every naval action undertaken so far – concentrating the Fleet at its war station, escorting the BEF to France, the Falklands battle, deploying the Grand Fleet into German waters – 'All these operations, on which the successful prosecution of the naval war has been founded, were pervaded by grave elements of risk in matters of superior importance to the naval attack on the Dardanelles.'

It was, however, one thing to take risks, having calculated and accepted the

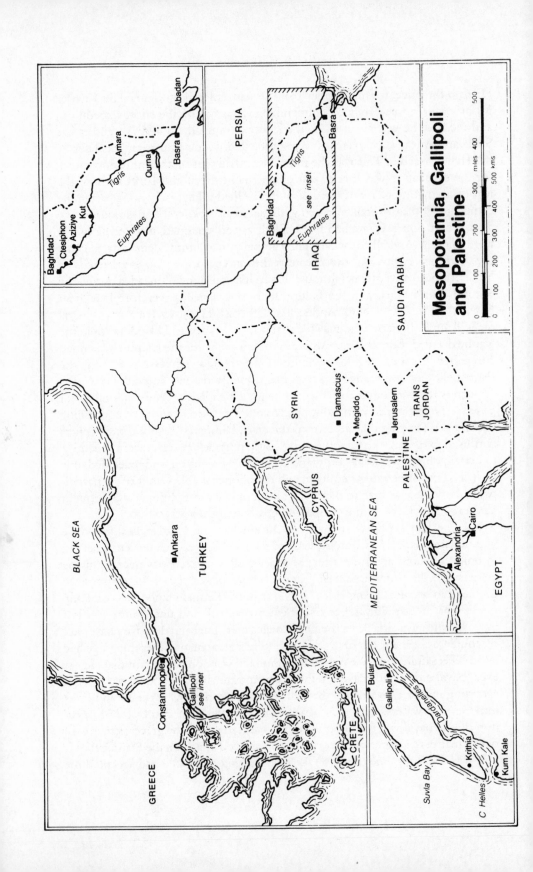

Mesopotamia, Gallipoli and Palestine

odds. It was another altogether to go on pressing for the execution of a plan, knowing that some of the resources believed to be necessary for its success would be lacking. Churchill had welcomed Kitchener's conversion to the idea of a joint naval-military operation; indeed, he had always thought that this was the proper way to undertake so hazardous an enterprise. It was hardly surprising, therefore, that when Kitchener, at the War Council of 26 February, again changed his mind and declared that the 29th Division could not be spared as it might be needed to reinforce the BEF, and further stated that he believed troops were unnecessary for the Dardanelles operation, Churchill protested vehemently. He therefore dissented absolutely from keeping the 29th Division at home, for its presence in the east might make all the difference, whereas this would not be so in the west. Kitchener was adamant, however, and the War Council supported him, 'to Winston's immense and unconcealed dudgeon,' as Asquith recorded. The root of the dilemma from Churchill's point of view was that he was so intensely committed to an attack on the Dardanelles that he was prepared, albeit against his better judgement, to endorse an attempt by ships alone, even though he was convinced that the proper way to do it was with a military force as well. Martin Gilbert sums it up with perfect perception:

Churchill had helped to add to the War Council's self-deception by his earlier willingness to make the operation purely naval; he now believed that ships alone would be inadequate, and that the more troops that could be found, the greater chance there would be of victory. But he so believed in the need for victory that he was prepared to go ahead with the plans for an entirely naval attack. However much he continued to argue that these plans might fail, by agreeing to go ahead with them, he made himself responsible for the very disaster that he forecast.

In another passage, Gilbert points out that the result of this attack would be crucial to Churchill's future career. No matter how often and how strongly he had argued for a powerful army to mount a joint operation with naval forces, he had in the end been prepared to pin hopes on a victory by ships without this military support. 'If the battleships assembled at the mouth of the Dardanelles could blast their way past the forts and mines of the Narrows into the Sea of Marmara, and thence to Constantinople, Churchill's impetuosity, his pushing, his petulance, his ambition, his youth, would find their vindication.' But, as we have seen, they did not. Moreover, the military operation which followed itself failed, Fisher's resignation produced a political crisis, and Churchill himself was obliged to step down. There is little point in giving the full details of the political intrigue which led to Churchill's quitting the Admiralty. It is enough to say that Fisher's repeated threats to resign, coupled with his megalomaniac demand to be allowed to run the naval war without Churchill, indeed, without any ministerial interference at all, ensured that he, Fisher, would go. The First Sea Lord's departure, underlining the Dardanelles débâcle, together with a report in *The Times* about the shortage of shells in France, gave Bonar Law, leader of the Conservatives, his chance to signal his party's unwillingness to continue to support Asquith's Liberal Government unless certain changes were made. On 17 May he made it clear to the Chancellor, Lloyd George, that whereas 'it was essential to avoid any division in the nation in face of the enemy' it was impossible to allow 'Mr Churchill to remain at the Admiralty if Lord Fisher persisted in his resignation'. On this particular point the Opposition, no matter what the danger, would 'force a Parliamentary challenge'. Lloyd George[1] at once put the case to Asquith that a coalition government was greatly to be preferred to conflict between the opposing parties. The Prime Minister agreed. The principal reason for his almost instant acquiescence, however, was that his own spirit had been broken by the news from Venetia Stanley (whose affection he so cherished, in whom he had so frequently confided – 'soul of my life', as he called her – who gave him 'the life blood of all that I do, or can ever hope to do'), was to marry Edwin Montagu, the Financial Secretary to the Treasury. Later that day Churchill heard in the House of Commons, first from Lloyd George, that a coalition was absolutely necessary and could not be delayed, and second from Asquith himself, who told Churchill that he had 'decided to form a National Government by a coalition with the Unionists, and a very much larger reconstruction will be required . . . What are we to do with you?' This meant, of course, that Churchill's remaining days at the Admiralty were numbered to very few.

Although Churchill fought hard to remain as First Lord of the Admiralty, and continued with his duties there cheerfully and conscientiously, he could not at times conceal his disappointment and bitterness, accusing Lloyd George at one point of not caring what became of him or his reputation, or whether he were trampled on by his enemies – only to receive the rejoinder that neither did Lloyd George care for his own reputation at that time, but only for winning the war. It was the prospect of being away from the centre of things which so grieved Churchill, and he told the newspaper proprietor Sir George Riddell on 20 May that he was the victim of political intrigue and was finished. Riddell, a close friend of Lloyd George's, remonstrated with him, arguing that someone with his remarkable powers was certainly not finished at forty. 'Yes,' Churchill replied. 'Finished in respect of all I care for – the waging of war; the defeat of the Germans . . . This is what I live for . . .' As it happened, he need not have

---

[1] In the Coalition Government, Lloyd George became Minister of Munitions, and McKenna Chancellor of the Exchequer.

worried. There was still plenty of 'the waging of war' in front of him – between 1915 and 1918 as a soldier in the front line, as a member of the War Council and as Minister of Munitions, while twenty-five years later, as Prime Minister, he would tell the House of Commons, in answer to his own rhetorical question as to what his government's policy was: 'It is to wage war.'

On 21 May, five days before Churchill finally left the Admiralty, he wrote one last appeal to Asquith in which, among other points, he desperately pleaded to be allowed to see the Dardanelles business through, not from self-interest, but because he wished to continue with his 'task' and his 'duty'. Since, he said, it was Asquith who knew the whole background and knew too that he, Churchill, could carry the burden successfully, 'I can only look to you. Let me stand or fall by the Dardanelles – but do not take it from my hands.' Asquith's reply, however, made it quite plain that Churchill would not remain at the Admiralty, but that his services as a member of the Cabinet – the post not yet specified – would be retained. An actual offer of a post quickly followed, that of the Chancellorship of the Duchy of Lancaster, with a seat in the Cabinet and on the War Council – an offer which Churchill accepted. Nor, however great his disappointment, could he have failed to have been consoled by James Garvin's appreciation of all that he had done. Among other instances of praise, Garvin wrote in the *Observer*, of which he was the editor:

Our sea-power has obtained in ten months a more unchallengeable mastery of the sea than it ever obtained in centuries past after years of successful warfare ... to Mr Churchill, and to Mr Churchill alone, belongs the praise for having used it at the very outbreak of hostility so promptly and so resolutely that the decisive victory was won before a shot had been fired ...

We have suffered losses; there have been, no doubt, mistakes. Mr Churchill may have made his share. But that he should have been malignantly and ungenerously attacked and made the scapegoat for all of them is an injustice which must rouse the blood of any man with a spark of the sense of justice ...

If the nation is yet able to appreciate great qualities it will testify in no uncertain way its appreciation of the zeal, courage and tireless devotion which Mr Churchill has displayed during the war. He has earned its undying gratitude; he has set an example of faith and resolution which none of the arm-chair critics who have assailed him can ever hope to approach ...

He is young. He has lion-hearted courage. No number of enemies can fight down his ability and force. His hour of triumph will come.

Churchill might have been consoled, but no newspaper article could compensate for his grievous loss of position, of executive responsibility, and of the power to influence the policy by which the war would be conducted. Above all, perhaps, there was the knowledge that the Dardanelles campaign was still under way, still held out at this time the glittering prospect of success, but that he could have no influence upon it. Martin Gilbert has recorded that Clementine Churchill told him that the Dardanelles campaign haunted her husband 'for the rest of his life. He always believed in it. When he left the Admiralty he thought he was finished . . . I thought he would never get over the Dardanelles. I thought he would die of grief.'

V

We now come to the second of the five phases of Churchill's war, his time as Chancellor of the Duchy of Lancaster. It can be passed over fairly quickly, for it was only a short interlude, nor did Churchill much enjoy it. In particular, he did not relish having collective responsibility as a member of the War Council without personal authority over the execution of policy – policy which, if he had had his way, would have been conceived and recommended by himself. Nevertheless, he remained ceaselessly active, and made some profoundly significant contributions to the war effort during this period. Nor, even in adversity, did his sense of humour desert him. As one of the duties of his new office was the appointment of county magistrates, he wrote to his old friend, John Seely, that the Duchy of Lancaster had been mobilized and that 'a strong flotilla of magistrates for the 1915 programme will shortly be laid down'.

Although Churchill realized that, in spite of being a member of the War Council (since the formation of the Coalition known as the Dardanelles Committee), his influence on its decision-making was much reduced, he continued to offer his opinions and advice – not only with reference to what was happening in the eastern Mediterranean, but also to events on the Western Front. In particular, he pressed for more submarines to be sent to reinforce Admiral de Robeck, and for certain protective measures against enemy submarines to be revived. His views on the utter uselessness and tragic waste of lives which invariably resulted from frontal assaults against the German trenches were particularly relevant, especially when it is remembered that at Neuve Chapelle in March 1915 the British Army captured a shattered salient, 2 miles wide and about 900 yards deep, and of no tactical value whatever, at the cost of 600 officers and more than 12,000 men. The British High Command failed utterly to see that the narrower the front of the attack, the easier it was for the Germans to concentrate against it; and that it was not the volume and duration of the attackers' supporting artillery bombardment which mattered so much as the speed with which an attack was followed up by the reserve infantry, so that a gap made in the German defences could be properly exploited. Yet the mistakes made at Neuve Chapelle were to be repeated time after time. At Aubers Ridge in May 1915 the same tactics were employed. On this occasion the wretched infantry were subjected not only to the customary dangers of shells, barbed wire and machine-guns, but also to the added misery of poison gas (which the Germans had first used during the Second Battle of Ypres, April to May 1915). The attack at Aubers might have failed with heavy losses – that much was acknowledged by the British High Command. No matter – they would plan another attack. Attrition was the key to success, or so the received wisdom ran. On 1 June Churchill circulated to his colleagues a note decrying the absolute futility of this strategy:

> Although attacks prepared by immense concentrations of artillery have been locally successful in causing alterations of the line, the effort required is so great and the advance so small that the attack and advance, however organized and nourished, are exhausted before penetration deep enough and wide enough to produce a strategic effect has been made. The enemy must always have some knowledge of the concentration before the attack. They will always have time to rectify their line afterwards. At an utterly disproportionate cost the line will be merely bent . . .
>
> We should be ill-advised to squander our new armies [the divisions of Kitchener's 'New Army', at this time mostly undergoing training in Britain, which had been raised in enthusiastic response to his call for volunteers in 1914] in frantic and sterile efforts to pierce the German lines. To do so is to play the German game.

This view was endorsed by the Chief of the German General Staff, Falkenhayn, who, while acknowledging the bravery and endurance of British troops, was confident that they could achieve nothing decisive against the German Army because they 'have proved so clumsy in action'. Would that the Chief of the Imperial General Staff (CIGS), Robertson, or the BEF's Commander-in-Chief, French, had heeded either Churchill or Falkenhayn. But they did not, persisting instead with the same old recipe, so that at Loos in September 1915 the familiar pattern was repeated. As soon as the first momentum of the attack faltered, as falter it always did once the Germans realized what was happening and took the appropriate counter-measures, any renewal of the assault – that is, a reinforcement of failure – simply resulted in greater and greater losses with nothing to show for them. So it was at Loos, and when two of Kitchener's unblooded new divisions, the 21st and 24th, went into action on the second day, advancing over open country towards the intact defences of the German line, the enemy machine-guns simply mowed them down in their hundreds. The affair lasted three and a half hours until at length, despite incredible courage and perseverance, and having endured terrible losses (of about 10,000 soldiers in this attack, 385 officers and 7,861 men were killed or wounded), the pitiful survivors made their way back to their own trenches – and while they did so no further shots were fired by the Germans, who called the battleground *das Leichenfeld von Loos* – the corpse-field of Loos. If, after nearly a year of trench warfare, this was the best the British Army's generals could do, there would be little likelihood of the policy of attrition bringing forth the fruits of victory.

Two months after Loos Churchill was to find himself – at his own special wish – back in military uniform and in action at the front. Until then, however, he still had some other axes to grind. One of these showed once again how his eloquence could appeal to the nation. Another was a practical solution to a military problem which had puzzled the tacticians for a year, a solution which was to revolutionize war and to provide Hitler with one of the ingredients of the Wehrmacht's astonishing blitzkrieg triumphs in the war still to come.

At a speech in Dundee on 5 June Churchill displayed his particular penchant for posing a rhetorical question and then, to the huge satisfaction of his audience, answering it. 'What does the nation expect of the new National Government?' he demanded.

I can answer my question. I am going to answer it in one word – action . . . Action – action, not hesitation; action, not words; action, not agitation. The nation waits its orders. The duty lies upon the Government to declare what should be done, to propose to Parliament, and to stand or fall by the result. That is the message which you wish me to take back to London – Act; act now; act with faith and courage. Trust the people. They have never failed you yet . . . Above all, let us be of good cheer . . . The valour of our soldiers has won general respect in all the Armies of Europe . . . I would advise you from time to time, when you are anxious or depressed, to dwell a little on the colour and light of the terrible war pictures now presented to the eye . . . Look further, and, across the smoke and carnage of the immense battlefield, look forward to the vision of a united British Empire on the calm background of a liberated Europe . . . The times are harsh, the need is dire, the agony of Europe is infinite, but the might of Britain hurled united into the conflict will be irresistible . . .

These splendid sentences, which were received with equal enthusiasm by both the press and the public (and which might almost have been a rehearsal of the words with which he was to reassure and inspire the nation twenty-five years later), brought Churchill much praise. Moreover, his call for action was one that he was determined to answer himself. Though he was still much concerned with the conduct of the Dardanelles campaign, and never hesitated to shower advice and recommendations on his fellow ministers, he was by now seriously considering taking up arms again himself. Before he did so, however, he had turned his hand to something that was to bring him great solace and pleasure – painting. Some years later he recorded in his own inimitable way how, in July 1915, he came to dominate the canvas in front of him when bringing himself to try painting in oils. The sheer exuberance of his language, the absolute joy with which he fell to attacking the canvas before him – to find that it could not retaliate – does much to explain why painting became such an agreeable pastime for him, while such phrases as those describing how the canvas before him grinned helplessly – 'I seized the largest brush and fell upon my victim with Berserk fury. I have never felt in awe of a canvas since' – are characteristic of the man's relish in living life to the full and finding in every experience deep satisfaction born of total commitment. It would be impossible to imagine a greater contrast in attitude towards painting, towards people, towards the purpose of endeavour, towards the goal of struggle, indeed, towards life itself, than that between Churchill and Hitler.

In September 1915 he returned again to the question of military activity, and actually asked the Prime Minister for command of a brigade in France. Asquith was inclined to agree. Kitchener was not, and in this field Kitchener was not to be gainsaid. But as it became clearer to Churchill that he was without political allies, he increasingly felt that he should quit the Government and serve in the trenches. Almost exactly a year later – after he had commanded a battalion on active service in France – something else made its appearance in the trenches, largely because of an initiative he had promoted two years earlier while he had been at the Admiralty. As early as September 1914 Churchill, conscious of the need for something to restore movement to the battlefield in the face of trenches, machine-guns and artillery fire, had ordered work to be started on what was initially conceived of as a trench-spanning vehicle. Some months later, as a result of reading a paper written by Colonel Swinton (a War Office representative at the BEF's headquarters) in which a similar proposal was outlined, Churchill went further and urged the Prime Minister to authorize the necessary expenditure to construct a prototype of what later became known as the 'tank'. His note to Asquith is remarkable for its vision. When it is remembered that this proposal was written in January 1915, and yet the first tanks did not go into action until September 1916 – and were then misused, being deployed in small numbers without decisive results (not least because many of them broke down), thus forfeiting the element of surprise which, if it had been properly exploited, might have brought about real decision on the Western Front – it has to be conceded that Churchill's tactical flair was of no mean order. This is what he wrote to Asquith:

It would be quite easy in a short time to fit up a number of steam tractors with small armoured shelters, in which men and machine guns could be placed, which would be bullet-proof. Used at night, they would not be affected by artillery fire to any extent. The caterpillar [tracked] system would enable trenches to be crossed quite easily, and the weight of the machine would destroy all wire entanglements.

Forty or fifty of these engines, prepared secretly and brought into position at nightfall, could advance quite certainly into the enemy's trenches, smashing away all the obstructions, and sweeping the trenches with their machine-gun fire, and with grenades thrown out of the top. They would then make so many *points d'appuis* for the British supporting infantry to rush forward and rally on them. They can then move forward to attack the second line of trenches.

Those who disparage Churchill's grasp of military affairs at this time might well ask themselves who else among the political and military chiefs in January 1915 was able to see the future role of the tank in battle so clearly. Indeed, just over a year later, in February 1916, Kitchener dismissed a demonstration tank as 'a pretty mechanical toy' (although there were those who said that he made this remark for reasons of security). By then Haig had replaced French as Commander-in-Chief of the BEF, while Robertson was CIGS. It cannot be said that either of them saw the tank's potential. Haig himself had long argued that the 'shock action' of cavalry was superior to the firepower of rifle and machine-gun, and at first had been wholly unable to appreciate the immense military value of the aeroplane. For his part, Robertson – who had made it a condition of his accepting the appointment of CIGS that *he* would determine strategy and decide how to conduct the war – was wedded to the belief that the main theatre of war would be France, and therefore it would be in France that the bulk of the British Army would fight. This view, although largely accurate, nevertheless blinkered him in his consideration of new strategies and new weapons.

If there was ever a time when Churchill's initiative for creating the 'tank' had needed to be energetically taken up again and pursued, it was in September 1915. Then, as we have seen, the ghastly failure at Loos – a frontal attack against strong German defences, whose machine-guns simply mowed down thousands of British soldiers with utterly negligible gains in territory; in other words, the very sort of attack against which Churchill had warned three months earlier – reinforced his view that something needed to be done to break the deadlock of trench warfare. Indeed, two days before the battle of Loos he had written to the Under-Secretary of State for the Colonies, Arthur Steel-Maitland, to express his impatience that not more was being done to speed up the project. He pointed out that while still at the Admiralty he had ordered a dozen experimental machines to be produced, as he believed they would enable trenches to be taken with minimal losses to the infantry. While himself no longer in a position to foster the idea, he advised Steel-Maitland how to proceed, and compared the new machines with 'elephants of Roman times. These are mechanical elephants.' Churchill concluded by suggesting that the machine's merits would be appreciated after the war was over. Here he erred, however, for at Cambrai in November 1917 their value was dramatically demonstrated. Unhappily, as their success surprised the British almost as much as it did the Germans, their gains were not exploited.

At the beginning of October 1915 Churchill was still undecided as to whether to continue in politics or to take an active part in the fighting. He continued to bombard Asquith and others with memoranda about the conduct of the war, and about who should be in command of various expeditions and in various theatres. His themes varied from the need to remove Kitchener from the War Office; what to do at Gallipoli – one decision, taken on 16 October, was to recall Hamilton and replace him by General Monro, who recommended evacuation ('he came, he saw, he capitulated' was Churchill's comment); there was even a four-point plan for an attack against Bulgaria, which had joined the war on the side of the Central Powers. There was so much criticism of government policy – and not only from Churchill – that towards the end of October Asquith put an end to the Dardanelles Committee, formerly the War Council, which had been responsible for the general conduct of the war, and replaced it with a group numbering only three – himself, Kitchener and Balfour. This move left Churchill completely out in the cold as far as war policy went, and since he was offered no alternative post which would enable him to play a significant part in determining such policy, he decided to go. He wrote two letters of resignation to Asquith.

The first dated 30 October, expressed agreement with the three-man War Council, but added that as this arrangement excluded Churchill himself, he felt that he could no longer serve usefully and therefore should not remain in office. He deplored the delays in decision-making, and the faulty execution of policy. His own views on what should be done were on record. He could not accept responsibility without power, and must take leave of the Prime Minister. He still urged, however, that the truth about the initiation of the Dardanelles campaign should be made public. As Asquith was shortly to report to Parliament about the war situation, he asked Churchill to delay his resignation, and the latter, hoping that the report would vindicate his own conduct, agreed. Meanwhile Monro, after only a few days at the Dardanelles, had, as we have seen, recommended an end to the campaign. Apart from his conviction that little could be achieved there, he was a supporter of Haig and Robertson in regarding France and Flanders as the proper place for British soldiers to be – killing Germans. His recommendation to evacuate the Gallipoli peninsula was not, however, instantly accepted by the War Council. Instead, Kitchener was dispatched to the Dardanelles to report – a move designed more to get the Secretary for War out of the way than anything else – and then, on 11 November, Asquith set up another War Committee, adding Bonar Law (who had been appointed Secretary for the Colonies) and Reginald McKenna (the new Chancellor, Lloyd George having become Minister of Munitions in May) to himself, Lloyd George and Balfour. Churchill, thus finally and completely excluded, on that same day sent to Asquith his second resignation letter. He reiterated both his agreement with the new Cabinet War Committee, and the point that his own counsel was well known and on record. He confirmed yet again his unwillingness to accept general responsibility for war policy without a voice in its formulation, asked that his resignation should be submitted to the King, and as an officer on the Reserve placed himself 'unreservedly at the disposal of the military authorities', his regiment, the Oxfordshire Hussars, being in France. Asquith accepted his resignation.

It was not to be expected that Churchill's resignation speech in the House of Commons on 15 November would be without either vindicatory or stirring comment, and so it proved. He pointed out with absolute justice that as far as criticism of naval operations was concerned, had the First Sea Lord refused his consent to any of them, they would not have taken place. With the Dardanelles clearly in mind, Churchill perhaps underplayed his own ability to persuade Fisher to a course of action he instinctively disliked, but in essence he was right.[1] He was completely open in stating that his advice to the Government regarding general strategy had consistently urged that no western offensives should be undertaken which would prove more costly to the Allies than to the enemy – counsel that was as consistently ignored – and he admitted that he had just as consistently counselled that in the east, Constantinople should be taken – by ships, by soldiers, by any means militarily sound – and that it should still be taken was, to his mind, worth every effort towards that end that could be made. He also had words of encouragement for the House. No doubt the country was passing through a bad time, and things might become worse before they were better, 'but that it will be better, if we only endure and persevere, I have no doubt whatever'. The war could be won without sensational successes; it could be won even though there might be vexations and disappointments. 'It is not necessary for us to win the War to push the German lines back over all the territory they have absorbed, or to pierce them . . . Germany may be defeated

---

[1] As Prime Minister from 1940–45 Churchill often prodded the Chiefs of Staff towards a particular course of action, but if opposed did not overrule them.

more fatally in the second or third year of the War than if the Allied Armies had entered Berlin in the first.' Churchill was not quite right about the year of Germany's defeat, but he was right about the nature of that defeat. Now the moment had come for him to assist in bringing about Germany's surrender in the front line. On the morning of 18 November 1915 he crossed over to France to join his regiment, the Oxfordshire Hussars, and thereby to enter the third phase of his war service.

Churchill's six months on the Western Front were remarkable in many ways: for his dedication to the task in hand; his courage in action; his capacity for command; his care for his men and determination to share their dangers; for the absorbing letters he wrote and received; for his concern as to what was happening on the wider military and political stage; and for his eventual conviction that after having done his duty as a soldier, his proper place in order best to serve the country was at home in the House of Commons – if possible as a minister. Right from the start he is resolved to put his heart into the business of soldiering, and no sooner is he in France than he writes to his wife saying he is sure he will be happy and at peace; he must try and win his way as 'a good and sincere soldier', but will not run foolish risks. First he must learn, and in order to do so, he asked and was allowed to do his training with the 2nd Battalion, Grenadier Guards. On 21 November he tells Clementine that he is in the line; tells her, too, what life is like, how excellent the commanding officer is, and that 'the system of the Guards – discipline & hard work – must be seen at close quarters to be admired as it deserves.' He also asks her to send out some footwear and clothing to make things more agreeable. He insists on being in the trenches as far forward as possible, and describes to his wife the filth and desolation, with graves revealing their contents, bats gliding about, shelling, bullets whirring overhead, and concludes that 'amid these surroundings, aided by wet & cold, & every minor discomfort, I have found happiness & content such as I have not known for many months.'

His wife's letters to him were a source of great comfort, not only for the love and concern they expressed, but also because they kept him informed about events and people at home. Her concern for his safety was not misplaced. On 26 November, while sitting in the dugout of No 1 Company HQ, Churchill was sent for by the corps commander. Arriving after a hazardous, uncomfortable walk across muddy fields, he found that the proposed meeting had been changed; on his return to the trenches, however, he discovered that, just fifteen minutes after he had left it, the dugout had received a direct hit from a shell which had burst only a few feet from where he had been sitting. His annoyance at his seemingly purposeless hike across sodden fields was somewhat diminished by this discovery. But he was wholly philosophical about the dangers of war, in which, as he later wrote, 'chance casts aside all veils and disguises and presents herself nakedly from moment to moment as the direct arbiter over all persons and events . . .' Churchill remained with the 2nd Grenadiers until the end of November, and learned a good deal. He then spent a few days at St Omer, GHQ of the British Expeditionary Force, where he had the opportunity to discuss with General Sir Henry Wilson his ideas for breaking the deadlock of trench warfare; in particular, he advocated his former notion of a kind of caterpillar-tracked mobile shield which would protect soldiers from machine-gun fire.

There was at this time much talk of Churchill's being given a brigade to command, and on 3 December Sir John French, just returned from London, persuaded him to accept one, although Churchill insisted that before taking command he wished to visit other sectors of the front and to go back into the line with the Grenadiers. He was also aware that French's own position was uncertain, for the Cabinet had lost confidence in him, and his subordinate, Haig, had long been intriguing against him in order to secure the overall command for himself. In the event both French and Churchill were the losers. On 17 December it was made clear that French was to hand over command to Sir Douglas Haig, and that Churchill – because Asquith had vetoed the idea – would not get a brigade. In his note to French, Asquith had written: 'Perhaps you might give him a battalion.' Churchill's initial reaction, apart from his bitterness at Asquith's treatment of him, was not enthusiastic, but when Haig, explaining that there was no immediate prospect of a brigade, reiterated the offer of a battalion, Churchill accepted.

Before examining Churchill's service as a battalion commander, it is necessary to acknowledge that the political intriguing which had gone on to deprive him of command of a brigade had sharply reawakened his longing to be back at the centre of political affairs. It was by no means clear when or whether he would again have a voice in war-making policy, but about his obsession with politics there was no doubt. Martin Gilbert stresses that however keen Churchill may have been to play his part in the military world – and, indeed, to try to effect a change that would greatly reduce the cost, in human terms of trench warfare and futile frontal offensives – he could not escape the lure of political life and the claims it made upon him. Many of his friends – F.E. Smith and Sir Max Aitken[1] among them – kept his political hopes alive, while his wife was ever active at home. In the meantime, on the first day of 1916, while he was still at St Omer, he learned that he was to command the 6th Battalion, The Royal Scots Fusiliers.

At this same time a great change took place in the method of recruiting for the army. In January 1916 Asquith gave way to political pressure for the intro-

---

[1] Later Lord Beaverbrook.

duction of conscription, with the result that the Miliary Service Act was passed, effective from February. As A.J.P. Taylor has so forcibly pointed out this measure, although it made military service compulsory for men between the ages of eighteen and forty, did not at once increase the number of men available for that service. Rather, it reduced this number, for whereas those working in essential jobs such as manufacturing munitions or mining coal could not be prevented from volunteering, they could not be conscripted. It had been thought that between 600,000 and 700,000 so-called 'slackers' would be rounded up for compulsory service. The authorities found instead that about three-quarters of a million men claimed exemption on one ground or another. It was not until the battles of 1917 that huge numbers of conscripted men would make their presence felt, although by the summer of 1916 volunteers had built up the BEF to some sixty divisions, enough for its new C-in-C, Haig, who believed that if sufficient artillery were used, a hole really could be punched in the German defences, allowing infantry to exploit the gap and make way for the cavalry – Haig's cherished illusion – to break through and 'crack about' in open country. This would be the first really 'big push' by the British Army. In this fashion Haig had convinced himself that a major offensive could win the war. The place eventually chosen for this great battle was the Somme.

But this is to anticipate, for by then Churchill had served his time in the trenches and was back in England. He proved a brave and successful commanding officer of the 6th Royal Scots Fusiliers. Soon after taking command he had won the confidence of his officers and men, as Second Lieutenant McDavid made clear:

> After a very brief period he had accelerated the morale of officers and men to an almost unbelievable degree. It was sheer personality . . . He had a unique approach which did wonders to us. He let everyone under his command see that he was responsible, from the very moment he arrived, that they understood not only *what* they were supposed to do, but *why* they had to do it . . .
>
> No detail of our daily life was too small for him to ignore. He overlooked nothing . . . I have never known an officer take such pains to inspire confidence or to gain confidence; indeed he inspired confidence in gaining it.

This was high praise indeed, and no officer serving in the army today could do better than follow in Churchill's footsteps, for 90 per cent of the business of command is knowing those you command, training them well, looking to their welfare, their equipment, their employment, and leading them boldly and successfully on operations. During his months of front-line service, Churchill was constantly in the thick of things. McDavid also recalled that the first time the Colonel visited the battalion's front-line posts, he showed a fine contempt for danger, and nearly brought about a major action. Churchill was moving in front of McDavid, wearing trenchcoat, boots and steel helmet and carrying a revolver and a flashlamp, when just as they had almost reached an outpost, enemy machine-gun fire forced them to dive into a shell crater. Then a sudden glare in the crater produced an order from the Colonel to 'Put out that bloody light!', only for him to discover that it was his own lamp which was the guilty party – luckily without reaction from the enemy. Another of Churchill's officers, Lieutenant Edmund Hakewill-Smith, remembered the nerve-racking experiences of going into no man's land with him: 'He was like a baby-elephant . . . He would call out in his loud, gruff voice – far too loud it seemed to us – "You go that way, I will go this . . . Come here, I have found a gap in the German wire. Come over here at once!" . . . He never fell when a shell went off; he never ducked when a bullet went past with its loud crack. He used to say, after watching me duck: "It's no damn use ducking; the bullet has gone a long way past you now."'

Churchill did not hesitate to criticize the military machine when it failed to live up to his expectations, which was often, since in his view the army's administration totally lacked the necessary drive. The sacrifice of brave and conscientious infantry soldiers would never, he argued, be an effective means of fighting a war which depended on brainpower and mechanical devices. He felt deeply for his men, forced to live in the trenches under such harsh conditions, exposed to needless death, in danger of being worn down by despair. He did all he could to lighten their burden, and reserved his anger for those in authority. In a phrase reminiscent of King Lear[1] he wrote to his wife: 'By God, I wd make them skip if I had the power – even for a month.' During the four months that Churchill commanded the 6th Royal Scots Fusiliers in and out of the line at Ploegsteert, just south of the Ypres Salient, he wrote innumerable letters to his wife and treasured her equally numerous replies. Some of his contained requests for material comforts, asking her, among other things, for Stilton cheese, hams, sardines, beefsteak pie; at the end he would sign himself 'Your loving and devoted – greedy though I fear you will say, W'.

All soldiers admire an apparent indifference to danger coupled with a dash of eccentricity in their commanding officers. Churchill, who had both qualities in abundance, certainly lived up to this admiration. 'He wanted his men to feel that he was one of them,' writes Martin Gilbert, 'that where the danger was there he would be, that when they needed guidance or good cheer or courage he would be at hand, and that he would not fail them in their hour of need . . . He was determined that they should trust him.' His imperturbability, sitting in

[1] 'I have seen the day, with my good biting falchion,/I would have made them skip.'

the open at his headquarters, Laurence Farm, with shells bursting every now and then, even setting up a canvas and painting, attracted both amazement and admiration – and particularly because he was so well-known a figure, and a politician at that (for he was, of course, still an MP). The dangers he seemed to disdain were real enough, however. Writing to his wife Churchill tells her of a lucky escape:

> We had just finished an excellent lunch and were all seated round the table at coffee & port wine, when a shell burst at no gt distance making the window jump. Archie [Major Sir Archibald Sinclair, a great friend and Churchill's second-in-command] said that at the next one we wd go into our dugout in the barn just opposite & we were discussing this when there was a tremendous crash, dust & splinters came flying through the room, plates were smashed, chairs broken . . . A shell had struck the roof and burst in the next room – mine & Archie's. We did not take long in reaching our shelter – wh is a good one. My bedroom presented a woe-begone appearance . . . The wonderful good luck is that the shell (a 4.2) did not – & cd not have – burst properly. Otherwise we shd have had the wall thrown in on us – and some of us wd surely have been hurt.

Clementine, on getting this news – at a time when Churchill is temporarily commanding the brigade in the absence of the actual brigadier-general – hastens to urge him to arrange a safer headquarters for himself, which he does at another farm about half a mile further back. Some ten days later, while Churchill was investigating with a young Engineer officer how to strengthen his battalion's trenches and dugouts, the two of them standing together in front of one of the most forward trenches and thus exposed to enemy fire, a German machine-gun opened up. Churchill's companion immediately urged him to keep still, 'But he didn't take the slightest notice. He was a man who had no physical fear of dying.'

Many of the soldiers who served under Churchill spoke of his determination to do whatever he could to make life better. He would ensure, for example, that a man whose boots were in bad condition was instantly supplied with a new pair, although at the same time he would punish any ill discipline with an iron hand. What also impressed all who saw him was the way in which he threw himself into the business of soldiering with such ardour and commitment. At one stage Clementine reports that soldiers on leave from the front talk about the vast improvements he has effected in the battalion, and hopes that, as a result, he will soon be given a brigade.

By now, his letters home had become a lifeline. Although his wife was consistently active in keeping abreast of political affairs, and Churchill himself took every opportunity of communicating with Lloyd George, F.E. Smith and others, neither he nor Clementine was sanguine as to his prospects of finding a place in the Government. None the less, she should, as he wrote to her, 'Keep in touch with those smug swine at home.' As it turned out, he was soon to be able to do so in person, for on 2 March, after his battalion had been relieved in the line, he went home on leave, and while there, having decided to speak in the forthcoming naval debate, made contact again with Fisher – much to Clementine's dismay, who felt that Fisher had ruined her husband once and must not be allowed to do so again. But Churchill confided in Fisher that in his speech in the House of Commons he would not only criticize Balfour's handling, as First Lord of the Admiralty, of naval affairs, but would also appeal for Fisher's return as First Sea Lord. The prospect so delighted Fisher that on 6 March, in a highly emotional, almost hysterical, letter, he urged Churchill to lead an opposition to Asquith's government, even writing '*you can be Prime Minister if you like!*' What Fisher had to say was no doubt what Churchill wanted to hear. But as Martin Gilbert so judiciously observes, the former First Sea Lord's advice bore 'the mark of lunacy'. Churchill was out of touch with the political ins and outs of the day, and had in any case been subject to the strains of active service in the trenches. 'Now he was told that he was on the verge of a great personal triumph which might lead him forward to power. All the vociferous forces of faction and discontent were pressing him to go forward. He failed to see that he was about to prove to every critic and to most friends that he lacked the mature judgement of statesmanship.'

Thus when he rose to speak in the naval debate on 7 March 1916, he not only lamented the failure of the Admiralty to pursue with vigour the programme of shipbuilding that had been laid down when he had been First Lord, and suggested that there was a serious danger that Germany was outbuilding this country in capital ships, but he also drew attention to the menace both of the submarine and of the Zeppelin raids against England, all in the face of a thoroughly negative policy on the Admiralty's part. Thus far, Churchill commanded the respect and attention of the House, whose members began to understand that unless corrective action were taken, Britain might face naval defeat. Had Churchill stopped there the effect of his speech might have been at once salutary and enduring. But when he concluded by calling for the return of Lord Fisher as First Sea Lord, not only did he destroy the impact of his just criticism of Admiralty policy, but he left himself open to ridicule, scorn and humiliation. Some very unkind things were said in the House of Commons that same evening, notably by Admiral of the Fleet Sir Hedworth Meux,[1] who, having

---

[1] As Commander-in-Chief, Portsmouth, in 1914, Meux had been responsible for securing the safe passage of the BEF to France.

poured scorn on the idea of Fisher's return, wished Churchill every success in France, and expressed the hope that he would stay there. Then, on the following day, Balfour, employing all his mastery 'of Parliamentary sword-play and of every dialectial art', both rejected Churchill's criticism and made every possible use of the Fisher point to deliver a tirade remarkable for its savage sarcasm, and thereby rendered the challenge to the Government's handling of the war that Churchill had sought to foster utterly without force or conviction.

For some days Churchill was uncertain whether or not to pursue his opposition or to return to Flanders. His close friend Violet Bonham Carter (whose *Winston Churchill As I Knew Him* is one of the most just, well-written and revealing books about him) talked to him on 8 March, and saw that 'he had hopelessly failed to accomplish what he had set out to do . . . What he had conceived as a great gesture of magnanimity – the forgiveness of the wrongs Fisher had done to him, for the sake of a greater aim, our naval supremacy – had not been interpreted as such. It was regarded instead as a clumsy gambler's throw for his own ends . . .' In the end, Churchill's decision to return to the trenches was strongly influenced by his receiving from Asquith agreement that should he wish to return to political life, no military obstacle would be placed in his way, and indeed, as he made his way back to Flanders, he was already convinced that his future lay with politics. It was really a question of when to make that return. Back in the line with his battalion on 20 March, he shortly afterwards received in a letter from his wife the excellent advice to be patient and wait for the right moment.

It is impossible to exaggerate the importance of the letters that passed between Winston and Clementine Churchill while he was at the front. In replying to one of hers, in which she speaks of time 'stealing love away and leaving only friendship', all the passion and longing that he feels for her are revealed:

> . . . Oh my darling do not write of 'friendship' to me – I love you more each month that passes and feel the need of you & all your beauty. My precious charming Clemmie – I too feel sometimes the longing for rest & peace. So much effort, so many years of ceaseless fighting & worry, so much excitement & now this rough fierce life here under the hammer of Thor, makes my older mind turn – for the first time I think to other things than action . . .
>
> But I am not going to give in or tire at all. I am going on fighting to the vy end in any station open to me from wh I can most effectively drive on this war to victory. If I were somehow persuaded that I was not fit for a wider scope I shd be quite content here – whatever happened. If I am equally persuaded that my worth lies elsewhere I will not be turned from it by any blast of malice or criticism.

Churchill's intense desire to be once more at the centre of war policy-making was further stimulated by what was going on on the Western Front, particularly at Verdun, where the long-drawn-out battle between the French and German armies seemed to achieve nothing but the spilling of blood and the draining of morale. To Churchill it vindicated 'all I have ever said or written about the offensive by either side in the West'. His mind was never far from his great longing to return to politics. He urged Clementine to keep in touch with Lloyd George, whom he saw as the key to his own future position, and she in turn urged him not to leave the front prematurely:

> ... If I were sure that you would come thro' unscathed I would say 'wait wait have patience, don't pluck the fruit before it is ripe. Everything will come to you if you don't snatch at it'. To be great one's actions must be able to be understood by simple people. Your motive for going to the Front was easy to understand. Your motive for coming back requires explanation.

In the event the amalgamation of the 6th and 7th Battalions of the Royal Scots Fusiliers seemed, to Churchill, a sensible time at which to leave the trenches, since his own command disappeared in the reorganization. Even though offered a brigade by Haig, he had come to feel strongly that he could do most for the war effort by returning to Parliament. His proper war station was there. When he left the battalion on 7 May 1916, the Adjutant, speaking for all the officers, made plain what it had meant to them to have served under his command, and how they regarded his going as a personal loss. Yet Churchill's return to England did not herald an instant revival of his political fortunes, although, in regarding Lloyd George as like to be influential in his own future, he was not wide of the mark.

The great political issue of the day was, of course, the conduct of the war. Churchill, back in the House of Commons, made his strong and, it must be stressed, strategically sound views known both on 17 May, when he spoke about the establishment of an Air Department, and again on 23 May, when he made a passionate appeal that lives should not be thrown away in useless frontal offensives in France. On the first occasion he pointed out that the air service (at that time still two separate arms, naval and military) would become 'the dominating arm of war' and that air supremacy would yield untold advantages both to armies in the field and to fleets at sea. Whereas mines and submarines had robbed the navy of its freedom of action, and the power of defences on land had made offensives immensely difficult and costly, the air was open to all, and there was nothing to stand in the way of Britain acquiring air supremacy, which was perhaps 'the most obvious and the most practical step towards a victorious issue from the increasing dangers of the War'. Even more telling and urgently relevant to matters in 1916 was his condemnation six days later, of premature offensives on the Western Front:

> Many of our difficulties in the West at the present time spring from the unfortunate offensive to which we committed ourselves last autumn ... Only think if we had kept that tremendous effort ever accumulating for the true tactical moment . . . if we had held in reserve the energies which were expended at Loos, Arras, and in Champagne – kept them to discharge at some moment during the protracted and ill-starred German attack on Verdun! Might we not then have recovered at a stroke the strategic initiative without which victory lags long on the road?
>
> Let us not repeat that error. Do not let us be drawn into any course of action not justified by purely military considerations ...

Churchill was not being wise after the event, but was reiterating views he had held from the very outset. In September 1914 he had grasped the futility of frontal attacks by infantry against strong, well-sited and well-supported defences protected by wire and machine-guns, and had advocated the development of what became the tank. Yet in spite of his passionate plea, Haig did repeat the error. At the beginning of July the Somme offensive began, an operation aimed at relieving the pressure on the French at Verdun by drawing German reserves away from that sector to meet the threat in the north. It was an unmitigated disaster. The British planners' tactics were based on a totally false conception – and one that had already been shown to be false by previous offensives – namely, that a prolonged and powerful artillery bombardment would fall with such force upon the German defences that it would 'leave nothing alive', so allowing the attacking infantry to follow up and capture their objectives without a fight. In fact, even after a week of pounding, the artillery shells did not as much as cut the German wire (one of the main purposes of the barrage), had no effect whatever on the deep dugouts occupied by the enemy machine-gunners, and simply provided them with additional craters to which they deployed when the bombardment lifted, where they found themselves admirably placed to deal with the slowly advancing British infantry, mowing down line after line. On the first day of the battle, 1 July 1916, the British Army suffered more casualties in a single day than it ever had before or has since – nearly 60,000 in all, of whom not quite 20,000 were killed.

For this ghastly sacrifice about a mile of strategically useless ground had been gained. Yet Haig persisted. Another major assault was mounted on 14 July. The same futile tactics were employed. 'Brave helpless soldiers, blundering obstinate generals,' as A.J.P. Taylor described it, 'Nothing achieved.' But Haig would not give up. In September he even tried using the new tanks, but on far too small a scale to have more than a local effect, other than to throw away the benefit of surprise which their employment in mass might have had in contributing to a real breakthrough and a decisive victory. When the battle finally ended in mid-November, the overall gain amounted to a strip of land some 6 miles deep by 20 miles wide, while the Allied losses totalled more than 600,000 (420,000 British and Dominion, 200,000 French); estimates of German casualties range between 437,000 and 680,000, but are generally held to have been around 450,000. By then, the whole offensive had bogged down in mud; for, ironically enough, it was the weather and the conditions, not the enemy, and certainly not the British generals, which finally halted the 'big push'. Meanwhile, of course, Kitchener's New Army had been virtually destroyed. It was clear that Haig and GHQ could think of nothing but repeated attacks against the German lines in order to exhaust the enemy's reserves and crack his morale, whereas what was really needed was a radical change in tactics. Churchill was sharply critical of Haig's premature and abortive use of tanks. 'The ruthless desire for a decision at all costs,' he wrote, 'led in September to a most improvident disclosure of the caterpillar vehicles.' Lloyd George, who had taken over as Secretary for War after Kitchener's death in June,[1] thought he had the answer to the problems of war policy-making – a War Council of three, with himself in charge. All this led to such controversy between Bonar Law (leader of the Unionist, in other words the Conservative, Party), Cecil, Chamberlain and Curzon on the one hand, and Asquith on the other that both Lloyd George and Asquith resigned, and as Asquith subsequently refused to serve under Bonar Law, it was Lloyd George who, in December 1916, became Prime Minister in his place, heading a coalition government and forming his own War Cabinet – himself, Bonar Law, Arthur Henderson (the Labour leader), Curzon and Lord Milner (as the former High Commissioner for South Africa had become). There was no place for Churchill; indeed, one of the conditions under which the Unionists agreed to join the Government was that Churchill should be excluded. Another was that Haig should remain as Commander-in-Chief in France.

'The implacable hostility and suspicion of the Conservatives,' wrote Martin Gilbert, 'Asquith's refusal to allow the facts about the Dardanelles to be published, and the isolation imposed by a year without office, combined to keep Churchill from power.' Thus all his hopes of becoming a war leader, all the confidence that he had in his own abilities, his grasp of strategic affairs, his drive and determination, his sheer zeal for waging war – all these, instead of resulting in his being called to direct, or at least help to direct, war policy, had

---

[1] Kitchener was drowned on 5 June 1916 when the *Hampshire* hit a mine. Lord Northcliffe's comment was that Providence was after all on the British Empire's side.

for the time being at least been ignored. The fact was that Churchill's longing to be at the centre of things, his overbearing manner, his impatience at lack of decision in others, his enthusiasm for action, his relish for war itself, created mistrust. His judgement was suspect, and among the Unionists there were many whose hostility was not lightly to be overcome, a hostility which he himself could not fully comprehend. Conscious of his own energy and ability, confident of his grasp of military affairs and his flair for command, convinced of his own indispensability to the pursuit of victory, burning to be active, he could not understand why he should be excluded. 'Is it not damnable,' he had asked in a letter to his brother, 'that I should be denied all real scope to serve this country, in this tremendous hour?'

There were still nearly two years of the war to run, and although in December 1916 Churchill's return to power seemed unlikely, he was still to have a major role to play in the war's prosecution, and one which would, moreover, give free rein to his multitudinous talents. That, however, still lay in the future. Meanwhile he thought little of those who were in charge, condemning the Government as weak and the War Council as being composed of those – with the exception of Lloyd George – who had no aptitude for war; furthermore, to have excluded the Admiralty and the War Office from that council he regarded as incomprehensible. The difficulties, he knew, were enormous and for many months to come only disasters lay ahead (a phrase he was to reiterate in 1940). As to Churchill's own ambitions, the Dardanelles Commission continued its work, and on its report much would depend in terms of his future employment. In the event his political prospects were improved by the report, which made it clear that Asquith had been in favour of the attack on the Dardanelles and that Kitchener had been at fault in not keeping his colleagues fully informed of military plans. Churchill himself was not an especial target for blame in the report, a point which undoubtedly enhanced his chances of making a comeback. In the House of Commons, apart from speaking during the Dardanelles debate, he had again given his views about campaigning on the Western Front, advocating once more the use of 'machine-power' and new 'manoeuvre devices' as opposed to a repetition of the tactics of attrition so dear to the heart of Haig and his generals. Yet in April 1917 Haig's offensive east of Arras, which did little more than gain a few miles of useless ground, was just such a repetition and was to lead to the tragic and futile Third Battle of Ypres, better known as Passchendaele which began some three months later. By then, however, Churchill would be back in office, this time as Minister of Munitions.

There were many who opposed his rejoining the Government, including the influential Lord Esher who, in a letter to Haig, described Churchill's power for both good and evil as very great, suggested that his views on naval matters were valuable, but on army affairs valueless, and judged that he lacked 'those puissant qualities that are essential in a man who is to conduct the business of our country through the coming year'. Equally opposed to Churchill's return to ministerial office were Lords Derby, Curzon and Milner (the former being the Secretary for War, the two latter, among other appointments, being members of the War Council). Derby complained to Lloyd George that Churchill's presence in the Cabinet would weaken it, and was only prepared to accept it if Churchill's position was a minor one, adding that the new minister (if such he became) was unlikely to agree to 'do his own work without interfering with other peoples'. Curzon reminded his own party leader, Bonar Law, that he had only agreed to join the Government if Churchill were excluded; he also told Lloyd George that while Churchill might be dangerous in opposition, he would be more so as a member of the Government. Milner talked of resigning over the issue. But, as Frances Stevenson (Lloyd George's mistress, later his second wife) so clearly saw, the Prime Minister needed someone cheerful, optimistic and energetic to support him, someone who was full of drive, who would take part of the great burden off his shoulders – even though, as Lloyd George put it, referring to Churchill's conceit, 'He has spoilt himself by reading about Napoleon.'

Despite opposition and his own consciousness of Churchill's high opinion of himself, Lloyd George *did* invite him to join the Government, and on 16 July 1917 Churchill became Minister of Munitions. There was continued hostility – Lord Cowdray, a leading businessman and an influential Liberal, had described him as 'a dangerously ambitious man', and the *Morning Post*, complaining about the appointment, referred to Churchill's 'overwhelming conceit' which 'led him to imagine he was a Nelson at sea and a Napoleon on land'. (This was indeed how Churchill saw himself, and does much to explain why it was that years later, at his home in Kent, Chartwell, there were in his study busts of Nelson and Napoleon.) Despite such antagonism, as a minister once more Churchill now had something to get his teeth into, and with his great relish for work, his organizing ability and the clarity with which he was able to see how things should be done, he completely reorganized his department, setting up a Munitions Council which was ready for action early in September. 'What is your war plan?' he asked his main advisers, explaining that once the plan was clear, allocation of resources would follow. He emphasized the need to expand the aircraft programme, and with a characteristic oversimplification, stated that the two ways of winning the war both began with A – aeroplanes and America. Twenty-four years later a similar formula, albeit with the addition of the Soviet Union, would recommend itself to him.

Before tracing Churchill's part in the winning of the Great War, we may perhaps briefly pick out some of the main features of its course. The tragedy of

Passchendaele dragged on from July 1917 until the autumn. The village itself was insignificant, but as it overlooked the Ypres Salient and was held in strength by the Germans it became an objective. The plan called for it to be taken within a day or two at the start of the offensive, the aim of which was to drive a hole in the German line and advance to clear the Belgian coast, meanwhile relieving pressure on the French Army which, after a series of disastous operations, had suffered from a massive fall in its morale, which in some areas had led to mutiny. In the event it took the British, Australian and Canadian troops 100 days to capture Passchendaele, and by the time it had been taken, the butcher's bill totalled 250,000 casualties among those troops (and about the same number among the Germans), while the whole purpose of the operation had long been forfeited. It had been shown that the German defences were well nigh impregnable, with row after row of concrete pillboxes housing maching-gun emplacements. The preparatory bombardment had simply churned the ground over which the troops advanced into bogland. This part of Flanders was in fact reclaimed bog, sodden even before the rains started – and it rained continuously from August onwards, so that the soldiers were required to advance through liquid mud. Moreover, they were being asked to attack a citadel. The countless deaths were not caused by bullets and shells alone. Many drowned in the mud. 'To the tank crews bogged down in the swamp,' wrote Lyn Macdonald, 'to the infantry slogging inch by inch up the grisly ridges, to the gunners labouring to drag the guns forward through the slough, to the signallers struggling to lay the wires that were cut to pieces as quickly as they spooled them out, even Passchendaele a mile or so away seemed as unattainable as the mountains of the moon. For the rest of their lives the men who came out of the battle remembered it with horror.' Churchill's view at the time, when visiting Haig in the field, was one of doubt that the war could be won on the Western Front. Haig in turn thought it could, and hoped that Churchill would concentrate on providing the army with what it needed and stop meddling with tactical and strategic matters.

Yet despite the totally unexpected breakthrough by the Tank Corps at Cambrai, east of the old Somme sector, in November, this time using tanks *en masse* (as Churchill had always advocated) – indeed so unexpected that no arrangements to exploit success had been made (most of the ground taken was soon recaptured by the Germans) – Haig's war-ending offensive of 1917 had resulted in utter failure. Moreover, in March of that year the Russian Revolution, followed in November by the Bolshevik Revolution which, under Lenin, seized power from the Provisional Government established in March, had more or less removed the threat to Germany from the east, although another threat – America's declaration of war against the Central Powers in April – albeit a distant one, had appeared. Also in April, Lloyd George's insistence on introducing the convoy system for merchant vessels, against the advice of Sir Edward Carson, the First Lord of the Admiralty, and of Jellicoe, the First Sea Lord, had made a dramatic difference in the U-boat war, shipping losses dropping from 25 per cent to a mere 1 per cent. Additionally, in October 1917 the Commandant of the Royal Flying Corps, Lieutenant-General Hugh Trenchard, created the Independent Air Force specifically for the purpose of strategic bombing; with it was born the myth that air power alone could win wars, a myth which was to be exploded, while causing death and grievous destruction to all participants, during the war still to come. The Great War still had a year to run. At the beginning of 1918 Haig demanded a further 600,000 men, but initially received only 60,000 as higher priority was given to the other armed services, the merchant fleet, the coal mines and other vital war production industries. He longed to milk the large British armies in the Middle East, where General Sir Edmund Allenby had already – by Christmas 1917 – won great victories, and was to win more by bringing to utter defeat the Turkish armies in Palestine. In this he was aided by Lawrence of Arabia, who fought as a liaison officer with the forces of the Arab Revolt, those Arabs who had seen the upheaval caused by the war as the means by which they might throw off Ottoman rule, in which they were supported by the Allies, and especially Britain. It says much for Allenby that he was able to recognize the guerrilla-organizing ability of Lawrence, despite suspecting that he was something of a charlatan. Churchill, always seeing war as a huge romantic adventure, wrote of Lawrence in *Great Contemporaries*: 'His audacious, desperate, romantic assaults . . . Grim camel-rides through sun-scorched, blasted lands, where the extreme desolation of nature appals the traveller . . . carried dynamite to destroy railway bridges and win the war . . . Lawrence rousing the fierce peoples of the desert, penetrating the mysteries of their thought, leading them to the selected points of action and as often as not firing the mine [to destroy Turkish railway tracks and other communications] himself.' Elsewhere, in Mesopotamia (*now* Iraq), after a disastrous start British and Indian Army forces had driven the Turks northwards beyond Baghdad, and were beginning to threaten Turkey itself. By January 1918, whatever the situation on the Western Front, it was clear that the days of the Ottoman Empire were numbered.

In February 1918 Lloyd George at last got rid of Robertson, with whom he did not see eye to eye, and appointed Henry Wilson CIGS in his place. Haig remained as C-in-C in France, and was soon faced with crisis when, on 21 March, Ludendorff launched Operation Michael, the first of his great offensives to divide the French and British armies and seize the Channel ports. Three weeks later the British Army had been driven back forty miles and faced defeat. Haig issued his famous 'backs to the wall' Special Order of the Day, General Ferdinand Foch was appointed overall Commander-in-Chief of the

Allied forces; the British Army was reinforced to the tune of half a million men; the French, their morale stiffened since the mutinies of 1917, held firm; the Americans were beginning to make their weight felt – eventually Allied strength and pressure began to tell, and by July the German offensives ran out of steam. From then on the initiative passed to the Allies, never again to be lost. In August and September they were everywhere attacking and advancing. On 23 October, after Ludendorff had insisted that an armistice be sought, Germany accepted President Wilson's 'Fourteen Points'. On 11 November, in a railway carriage in the Forest of Compiègne, the armistice was signed. The comment made by a trooper of Churchill's old regiment, the 4th Hussars, was laconic, to say the least: 'Thank God that's over.'

Churchill's own contribution to victory was of profound importance. After only three months as Minister of Munitions he had made a great impression, and Leo Amery (at that time Under-Secretary for the Colonies, later First Lord of the Admiralty) praised his energy and foresight, and his skill in getting things done to produce more and better trench mortars and tanks, noting what a difference it made to see at work 'a man of real brains and imagination' compared with 'second-rate men like Haig and Robertson, who still live in the intellectual trench in which they have been fighting'. Churchill, who was never content unless he saw matters for himself, repeatedly visited the Western Front, and was greatly impressed by the French Prime Minister, Georges Clemenceau, describing him later – in what might almost be thought of as a self-portrait – as growling and going into action like a 'ferocious, aged, dauntless beast of prey'. Always bursting with ideas, Churchill recommends in November 1917 that shortages of steel for war production should be made up by park and garden railings (as happened in 1940), girders from construction sites, even shell remnants lying about on the battlefields. Being in France during the Cambrai battle that same November, when the tanks were at last properly used, he had some penetrating recommendations to make thereafter. He pointed out that armour was 'an indispensable adjunct to infantry', that it could be decisively used not only in the offensive, but in counter-attack, and that – all the more remarkable coming from a cavalryman – the 'cavalry myth is exploded . . . I am pressing that the cavalry shd be put by regiments into the Tanks, both heavy and chasers [light tanks] . . . It wd be a thousand pities if the cavalry were simply dispersed as drafts [i.e. reinforcements] among the infantry. The future life of this arm after the war depends upon their discarding the obsolete horse, & becoming associated with some form of military machinery having a scientific & real war value.' In this last point he was wholly right, although it would take twenty years and more before this change was effected completely in the British Army.

Churchill even anticipated the 'Ludendorff Offensive' of March to July 1918, realizing that in the wake of the collapse and surrender of Russia[1] the Germans would be able to transfer huge numbers of men and vast amounts of weaponry and equipment from the Eastern Front, and that unless the Allies both increased their strength and their defensive capability with mechanical weapons, their whole position in the west might crumble. In February 1918 he is constantly in France, discussing matters with army commanders, seeing about the supply of tanks, ammunition and gas, visiting the front line, and writing to his wife to describe what the Ypres Salient looked like:

> I had not been in Ypres for 3 years. It has largely ceased to exist. As for the country round & towards the enemy – there is absolutely nothing except for a few tree stumps in acres of brown soil pockmarked with shell holes touching one another. This continues in every direction for 7 or 8 miles. Across this scene of desolation wind duckboard tracks many of them in full view of the enemy; & all about it as we walked now here now there occasional shells were pitching or bursting in the air, & our guns hidden in mud holes flashing bright yellow flames in reply.

Churchill's technological foresight was remarkable. On hearing of the CIGS's concern that land mines would seriously disrupt the advance of tanks, he instantly turned his mind to finding an answer to the problem – namely 'an ordinary tank might push a heavy roller or series of rollers, in front of it', or 'A large steel hammer . . . could strike the ground heavy blows' to detonate the mines. Such was the idea which led, in the Second World War, to the development of the 'flail' tank, which was used to clear paths through minefields. It required a fertile mind indeed to put forward the notion as early as 1918, but such ideas were characteristic of Churchill.

It was equally characteristic of the man, and wholly fitting to his position, that he should be in France and well forward at the headquarters of the 9th Division (in which he had served when commanding a battalion a year before) when Ludendorff's offensive actually began on the morning of 21 March 1918. He had crossed over to France three days earlier to discuss with Haig and others his plans for tank production and to attend a meeting about chemical warfare. From Divisional HQ Churchill, after the 'most tremendous cannonade I shall ever hear' watched the German infantry in their attack, which was

---

[1] Severe losses in action, appalling conditions at the front, internal strife at home, and the revolutions of 1917 brought the Russian armies to the point of collapse, and in November of that year the Bolshevik Government ordered a ceasefire on all fronts. On 3 December, at Brest-Litovsk, German and Bolshevik delegates met to discuss the terms of the Russian surrender, and the treaty, named after the town in which they met, was finally signed on 3 March 1918.

successfully breaking through the British Fifth Army's positions. Although Churchill proposed to stay with the 9th Division, he was persuaded otherwise and after further meetings at St Omer, returned to London on 23 March, where, at a meeting of the War Cabinet and in subsequent talks with Lloyd George and the CIGS, Wilson, his resolve, confidence and immediate action did much to steady the nerve of his colleagues. During the days of crisis – we have already seen that the Allied line held in the end and that the German offensive exhausted itself – Churchill was repeatedly in France, and later recalled his impressions of both Foch and Clemenceau. He wrote of Foch's 'extraordinary methods of exposition; his animation, his gestures, his habit of using his whole body to emphasize and illustrate as far as possible the action which he was describing or the argument which he was evolving, his vivid descriptiveness, his violence and vehemence of utterance'. At the end of this particular conference on 30 March, Foch expressed his certainty that the position would be stabilized; as to what happened afterwards, 'That is my affair'. Later that day Clemenceau, having promised to support Haig with French reinforcements, insisted on seeing the battle, and in company with Churchill and others went forward in the British sector, where, just behind the front line itself, they surveyed the scene from a small mound overlooking the Bois de Moreuil. From here, in a phrase reminiscent of Stendhal,[1] Churchill recalled: 'From here we could see as much as you can ever see of a modern engagement without being actually in the firing line, that is to say, very little indeed.' But the 'Tiger' seemed pleased by the sight of the shells bursting near by and by a bleeding, riderless horse which trotted by, and whose bridle he instantly seized, before somewhat reluctantly agreeing to move on, while muttering to Churchill, 'Quel moment délicieux!'

Throughout April 1918 Churchill continued to assist Haig by ensuring that British losses in guns, machine-guns and tanks were more than replaced and also, realizing as he did that manpower had become the greatest problem of all, by making more men available for the army. Haig acknowledged his efforts, recording in his diary on 30 April that Churchill was doing all he could to help the army, in that he had greatly increased the output of munitions, while displaying great energy in his efforts to get men released from industry for service in France. He was customarily eloquent in one speech to the House of Commons in which he dealt with the military and munitions problems; he was also full of confidence resulting 'from everything I learn' of 'the strength, the massive solidity, and the inexhaustible resources of this great nation, this wonderful Island, battling for its life and for the life of the world'. Yet Churchill

---

[1] 'From noon until three o'clock, we had an excellent view of all that can be seen of a battle – i.e. nothing at all.'

still pined for a greater say in policy, and advised the Prime Minister to widen his War Cabinet, as he believed the present one was too narrow and unrepresentative to determine 'the high policy of the State'. Lloyd George, however, was content with his own way of running things, and as a result Churchill decided to spend more time in France, where he could keep in touch with the armies' needs and co-ordinate production matters with the Allies (there were by now considerable numbers of US Army troops in France). He even set up, with Haig's agreement, his own headquarters in France, and was there when the last of the German offensives in the British sector was launched in June. He was constantly hurrying back to England and then to France again, advising Lloyd George on policy, visiting the front, making speeches, welcoming American participation, and making it clear that although there could be no peace before victory, once Germany was beaten – knew and felt that she was beaten – then, when the war was over, Germany must be treated 'with wisdom and justice'.

It was nearly over now. The Allies recovered, the French and British began to push back the Germans, and increasingly the Americans took their part, winning some notable victories. In August the British Army began its series of attacks on the German lines. One of them, at Amiens on 8 August, employed between four and five hundred tanks, the very weapon that Churchill had helped to develop, and had for so long and so passionately championed. There was, however, no attempt to exploit a single break in the line. Rather, Haig had by now realized that repeated attacks on a wide front would more quickly use up the German reserves. So it proved, and, learning from their own experiences, the French adopted similar tactics. By September Haig was noting in his diary, after capturing nearly 80,000 German prisoners and 800 heavy guns, that there had never been such a victory before, that the enemy's discipline was going, that it seemed to him 'to be the beginning of the end'. Yet in spite of successes by the French and British, their offensives, expensive in casualties, were simply pushing the enemy lines back, neither outflanking the German Army nor achieving a decisive breakthrough. Instead, it was what was happening elsewhere – in the Middle East, on the Italian front and in the Balkans (a vindication of what Churchill had always steadfastly maintained) – that finally convinced Ludendorff that there was no longer any possibility of avoiding defeat. Allenby had destroyed the Turks at Megiddo in September and entered Damascus a few weeks afterwards. On 26 October Turkey began armistice negotiations with the British; on the 30th the Ottoman Empire capitulated. Bulgaria sued for an armistice on 28 September as the Allied armies moved northwards from Salonika, and surrendered two days later. On the Italian front, the Austro-Hungarian forces, driven back by repeated attacks, began to collapse; on 29 October Austria-Hungary asked the Allies for an armistice, which came into effect on 4 November. Thus the road to Central Europe was open to the Allies, and the Germans could find no troops to counter them. Accordingly, as has already been seen, Ludendorff told the German Government that an armistice must be sought. On 7 November a German delegation crossed the lines in France to begin negotiations with the Allied delegates, the discussions taking place in the carriage of a special train halted near Rethondes, in the Forest of Compiègne. On 9 November, with the greatest reluctance, the Kaiser abdicated, fleeing to sanctuary in Holland on the following day. On 11 November 1918, the signing of the Armistice finally brought an end to the fighting, with effect from 11 o'clock that morning.

Throughout these last months of the war Churchill is as active as ever. In September, having failed to get home to see his wife on their tenth wedding anniversary, he writes to her explaining why, adding that his work in France, of which he has so much to do, is 'just the sort of life I like . . . I do not chafe at adverse political combinations, or at not being able to direct general policy. I am content to be associated with the splendid machines of the British Army & to feel how many ways there are open to me to serve them.' His contentment with his lot seemed to be confirmed a few days later when, in a conversation with Siegfried Sassoon, the soldier-poet is deeply impressed by Churchill's character and eloquence; pays him the greatest of compliments by reflecting that he is the sort of man whom 'I should like to have as my company commander in the front line'; wonders if Churchill is serious when he says that war is the normal occupation of man (just the sentiments of Hitler and of General Hans von Seeckt, the architect for the rebuilding of the Germany Army between the wars); and concludes that even though Churchill qualifies this 'normality' by adding 'and gardening', war is for him 'the finest activity on earth'.

Back at home, while the armistice was being negotiated, Churchill had become obsessed with his need to be reassured by Lloyd George that there would be a place for him in the post-war Cabinet, and a number of letters were exchanged. The Prime Minister was determined to keep the Coalition in being, but was not prepared initially to give Churchill the reassurance he sought. The latter's reflections as the war actually ended on 11 November were recorded in his book *The World Crisis*. 'I was conscious of reaction rather than elation . . . My mind mechanically persisted in exploring the problems of demobilization . . . How long would it take to bring the Armies home? What would they do when they got home? . . .' These questions were soon to be of special significance to him, for in January 1919 he was made Secretary of State for War and Air, an appointment of which the *Morning Post* strongly disapproved, suggesting that it 'makes us tremble for the future'. Also in 1919, a German soldier, by then demobilized from the army, was so shocked by Germany's defeat and humiliation that he decided 'to take up political work'. Here indeed was something which would make anyone tremble for the future. The soldier's name was Adolf Hitler.

CHAPTER 3

Seesaw of Power

No doubt Hitler regarded himself as Nietzsche's super-
man, 'beyond good and evil'. He certainly incarnated
the monstrous assertion of the will and the will to dominate.

A.L. ROWSE

We have seen that Hitler's identification with the German Army, the German
Reich, the German people, with the justice of their cause, the invincibility of
their armed forces, with the certainty that they would prevail, was absolute.
What, then, must have been the effect on him when all these hopes and certainties suddenly collapsed, without warning, without expectation, and with catastrophic results for Germany? We may ignore the motives behind the
exaggeration which manipulated the wording of *Mein Kampf*, without doubting
that Germany's surrender did profoundly shock Hitler, and was, for him, a
deeply felt experience which influenced the path he would shortly take and the
goal he would set himself:

> Everything went black before my eyes as I staggered back to my ward[1] and
> buried my aching head between the blankets and pillow . . . The following
> days were terrible to bear and the nights still worse . . . During these nights
> my hatred increased, hatred for the originators of this dastardly crime.

It was not only the collapse of all he believed in which dealt Hitler so devastating a blow. It was the emergence of the despised Social Democrats at the
head of a democratic German Federal Republic[2] that lent a spur to his decision

---

[1] He was in hospital in Germany at the time, having been temporarily blinded in a gas
attack launched by the British south of Ypres on the night of 13–14 October.
[2] Generally called the Weimar Republic, after the town in which the newly created National
Assembly was first convened in February 1919.

to 'take up political work'. During his years in Vienna and Munich Hitler had, as we have seen, developed his own wholly unoriginal political philosophy. It was a philosophy of hatred. He hated the Jews, the Habsburgs, the leaders of religion, and even the working men who belonged to those despicable organs of equality and organization, the trade unions and the Social Democratic Party. In spite of his subsequent proud reiteration that he himself had sprung from the masses, in spite also of his quick understanding that a man who was able to manipulate the masses inherited power, in spite even of his own uncanny gift for such manipulating, and thus his reliance, as it were, on them, it was the masses themselves for whom Hitler felt a special contempt. According to the Austrian critic and writer Karl Kraus, a demagogue's secret lay in making himself as stupid as his audience, thereby inducing the belief that they were as clever as he. Whether or not Hitler was familiar with this belief, it was almost echoed by his own contention that 'everybody who properly estimates the political intelligence of the masses can easily see that this is not sufficiently developed to enable them to form general political judgements on their own account.' So that when Hitler found the masses disparaging all that he believed in – the nation, the concept of the Fatherland, above all authority – and asked himself whether such men 'were worthy to belong to a great people', he was able to put the blame for such systematic poisoning of the masses on others: on the leaders of the Social Democratic Party, who exploited the workers for their own cynical purposes, and on the Jews with their 'Marxist' doctrine which 'repudiates the aristocratic principle of nature and substitutes for it and the eternal privilege of force and energy, numerical mass and its dead weight'. The worth of personality, the significance of nationhood and race – these, to Hitler, were the foundations of existence and civilization. Nietzsche had not propounded the theory of the *Übermenschen* (supermen) for nothing, and Hitler was in no doubt that he belonged to the *Herrenvolk*, the master race. The other side of that coin, of course, was that he also believed in the existence of the *Untermenschen* (subhumans), a class of people for whom he had nothing but the profoundest contempt.

It is now necessary briefly to trace Hitler's rise to power, and in particular his relationship with the German Army during that rise, for once he was in power it was by the use of military force that he intended to extend Germany's power – indeed, to embark on a *Griff nach der Weltmacht* – seizure of world power. It was this aggressive foreign policy of Hitler's which at length brought Winston Churchill out of the political wilderness in which, after ten post-war years in office, from 1919 to 1929, he found himself. It would be soon after Churchill's return to power that he and Hitler would find themselves at the centre of world affairs – even of world history.

The position of the German Army was always a crucial factor in the nation's politics. Hitler was much addicted to condemning the so-called 'November criminals', that is the Social Democrats who, in a country facing defeat and riven by unrest, formed a government on 9 November 1918, two days before the Armistice. In charging these men with betraying the nation, Hitler was, of course, founding his propaganda on what Alan Bullock has called 'a fraudulent lie'. They were in fact doing what they thought was for the good of the nation, and the irony of it was that in doing so they were aided and abetted by the very instrument of state which they were later accused of stabbing in the back – the army. When Ludendorff's successor as First Quartermaster-General, General Wilhelm Gröner, and the first Chancellor of the German Republic, Friedrich Ebert, allied themselves to save the country from the extremes of revolution, a bargain was struck. The army would prevent anarchy and see to it that order was maintained. The Government would provision the army and help the officer corps both to suppress Bolshevism and preserve discipline. In this way two parties, each faced with the collapse of all they stood for and believed in, made a pact. Gröner wished to have the best of all worlds. Of course, he respected the constitutional authority which Ebert's government represented, but he was determined that responsibility as the ultimate guarantor of the State should, in accordance with (largely Prussian) tradition, continue to rest with the officer corps. At the same time, responsibility for the Armistice would be firmly in the lap of the civilian government. The General succeeded in every respect. The German Army, within six months of having been on the point of capitulation, had achieved what Gröner had promised; indeed, had even done more. It had prevented civil war, preserved the country's unity, and, most important of all for its own leaders, had re-established its reputation and influence to such a degree that it was once again a force which could not be ignored politically.

Furthermore, there was no doubting that it was with the Government, not the army, that the responsibility for making peace lay, and the Allied terms were harsher than the most pessimistic German had ever contemplated. The Government itself described them as unbearable, yet it had to endure both the terms themselves and the odium which accompanied their imposition, odium slow to be dissipated. In a characteristic denuniciation of the Government and the peace terms, Hitler harped time and again on the same old theme:

We want to call to account the November Criminals of 1918. It cannot be that two million Germans should have fallen in vain and that afterwards one should sit down as friends at the same table with traitors. No, we do not pardon, we demand – vengeance! The dishonouring of the nation must cease. For betrayers of the Fatherland and informers, the gallows is the proper place.

However harsh the terms, it is hard to imagine what Hitler would have done without the Treaty of Versailles,[1] so often did he make use of it to further his own passage to power. One of the messages of *Mein Kampf* was 'the destruction of Versailles', and this message commanded support from most shades of German opinion. There had been many shades of Allied opinion about what terms should be imposed on Germany, and Churchill, as was customary with him in dealing with a defeated enemy, was strongly in favour of moderation; he would, in fact, have preferred a negotiated settlement, rather than one which was both imposed and harsh. 'We must proceed with great care and vigilance,' he had argued in a speech to his constituents at Dundee shortly after the war's end, 'seeking so to influence matters that a government might be created in Germany strong enough to shoulder the burden of reparation and yet not capable of renewing the war.' He was convinced that it would be wrong to impose on Germany the sort of terms which Germany had imposed on France in 1871 by the Treaty of Frankfurt, which ended the Franco-Prussian War. Then, Germany's annexation of Alsace-Lorraine, against the will of those who lived there and who wanted the two provinces to remain part of France, had done much to bring about the Great War. It would therefore be quite wrong now to put Germans who wished to remain citizens of Germany under some foreign government, and so run exactly the same risk of bringing about yet another conflict. Yet this is just what the Allies did do (several areas of the pre-Great War Germany were ceded, under the Versailles Treaty, to other states), and so provided Hitler with a motive for his murder of Europe. 'The first war,' declared A.J.P. Taylor, 'explains the second and, in fact, caused it, in so far as one event causes another.' Hitler himself constantly repeated his belief that the Second World War grew naturally out of what happened in the First.

It was in November 1941, during the second war, that Hitler explained how, on returning to Germany from the front in 1918, he brought back with him his war experiences, and out of these experiences he built his National Socialist community among the people at home; so now, in 1941, with the nation at war again, this same National Socialist community had taken *its* place at the front. Whatever the determinist view of history may be, there is little doubt that the second war was one of Hitler's making. Although motives, like metaphors, may be both subtle and mixed, Hitler's underlying motive for everything was both

[1] The Treaty of Versailles resulting, from the Paris Peace Conference of 18 January 1919 to 20 January 1920, formally ended the war with Germany and set out the terms imposed by the Allies. It was signed on 28 June 1919. The treaties ending the war against Germany's co-belligerents were respectively: of St Germain (Austria), 10 September 1919; of Neuilly (Bulgaria), 27 November 1919; of Lirianon (Hungary), 4 June 1920; of Sèvres (Turkey), 10 August 1920. The latter was revised by the Treaty of Lausanne, 24 July 1923, the Turkish republican movement under Mustafa Kemal having rejected the original treaty.

simple and unmixed – power, power primarily for himself to wield, but at the same time on behalf of his adopted nation. The opportunities both for achieving this power and then for wielding it were inextricably woven with the means by which power most nakedly expresses itself – force of arms. It is, therefore, the way in which Hitler dealt with the armed forces during his rise to power – for had he not handled this aspect of affairs skilfully, he would not have achieved power – which commands our special attention. We must also trace his political beginnings, since without that early start he would never have been in a position to build the National Socialist Party into the irresistible force it became.

Hitler's opportunity to 'take up political work' presented itself in Munich, where he had been sent in March 1919 while still serving in the army. It was in Munich that an example of the army's methods of maintaining order and preventing anarchy occurred. A Communist uprising in the spring of 1919 had been bloodily suppressed by the army and the so-called Freikorps (armed bands of volunteers originally recruited to assist the Reichswehr[1] in maintaining order, and for the protection of Germany's eastern frontier), and Hitler, now a Bildungsoffizier or education officer, was sent to Munich to investigate the goings-on of political groups there. In September he was told to attend a meeting of the German Workers' Party, and while there was so infuriated by the words of a Bavarian separatist that he leapt to his feet to answer the speaker. He spoke so well that the party's leader, Drexler, asked Hitler to join, and a few days later invited him to attend a committee meeting. Hitler did so, and while recognizing the insignificance of the German Workers' Party at this time, he regarded that as an advantage, in that he would be able to secure its leadership without much opposition. By February 1920 he had begun to organize mass meetings, at which he was the most compelling speaker, had introduced a new name – National Socialist German Workers' Party (also known by its initials, NSDAP) – and, after leaving the army in April 1920, began to devote all his energies to building up the party. In the summer of 1921 he became its leader.

It is important to understand how much the success of the National Socialist Party owed to Hitler's own energy and political genius, which, as Alan Bullock has pointed out, 'lay in his unequalled grasp of what could be done by propaganda, and his flair for seeing how to do it'. It was a hard task and involved countless meetings under every kind of circumstance, but Hitler had the uncanny gift of reading the minds of his audience and then concentrating on the grievances, ideas and aspirations which he sensed to be at the forefront of those minds. Moreover, he travelled so widely in Germany that he came to

[1] Literally, 'Reich defence', the name given to the German armed forces in 1919, and used until 1933, when the name Wehrmacht ('defence forces') was adopted.

know the country and the German people better than any politician had ever done before. 'By the time he came to power in 1933 there were few towns of any size in the Reich where he had not spoken'. What is more, 'his experience of politics, not in the Chancellery or the Reichstag, but in the street, the level at which elections are won,' was unmatched.

If, while he was mounting the first rungs of his political ladder in Munich, Hitler had not been tolerated and, to some extent, at least, supported by the army, it may be doubted whether he would have made any progress at all. For the protection which was thus afforded to his career of violent agitation, he was principally indebted to one man, a man who later figured even more dramatically in Hitler's deal with the army. This was Major Ernst Röhm, like Hitler a member of the German Workers' Party but, unlike him, a member of the officer corps. Any organization which seemed likely to further Röhm's dream of re-establishing a powerful united Fatherland commanded his allegiance, and Röhm, differing here from most other members of the officer corps, saw that this dream was unattainable without capturing support from the masses. He was also realistic enough to have abandoned the idea that the army should remain aloof from politics; indeed, as he viewed it, the very reverse was needed. If the sort of state in which the army could thrive and enjoy all its former privileges were to come about, then the army must play an active political role in order to secure just this circumstance. In short Röhm, like Hitler, wanted to do away with Versailles. The two men had much in common as far as methods went, and even as far as the dream of creating a revolutionary nationalistic state was concerned. It was in the use to which the state would thereafter be put that their paths diverged. In the early stages of their partnership Röhm did more than act as a powerful liaison officer between the army in Bavaria and the man who was building the National Socialist German Workers' Party. He helped build up the Party himself, and took steps which led to the creation, under his leadership, of the Party's own army – the SA (Sturmabteilung, literally, 'storm unit', hence the common usage 'storm troopers') or strong-arm squads, and thereby enabled Hitler to proceed with his methods of intimidation.

Yet these advantages, solid though they were, did little to aid Hitler at the time of his first real confrontation with the army in 1923. The year had seemed to be one full of opportunity. Given that National Socialism could only prosper under conditions of economic distress and internal instability, 1923 appeared to be peculiarly propitious. The catastrophic collapse of the mark, which brought ruin and misery to millions, touched off, or at least accelerated, as it was by the French and Belgian occupation of the Ruhr in January in retaliation for Germany's failure to fulfil reparations payments, lent weight to Hitler's reiterated denunciation of the German Weimar Republic. He was able to condemn once more the 'November criminals' in terms which everyone understood. Acceptance of the Versailles Treaty had brought personal affliction into the context of national humiliation. Hitler's dilemma was how to turn the opportunities presented by general discontent and unrest to his own advantage. At this stage in his career, as he confirmed in 1936, he was thinking of 'nothing else than a *coup d'état*', that is, the overthrow of the Republic, and aimed, first, to unite those Bavarian groups hostile to it, and second (provided always that he then had sufficient power at his disposal), to march on Berlin. It was at about this same time, too, that General von Seeckt observed that, as Commander-in-Chief of the Reichswehr, *he* was the only man in Germany who could instigate a putsch (by which he meant a successful one), and that he assuredly would never do so. In November 1922 Hitler had excitedly shouted to Schweyer, the Bavarian Minister of the Interior, who had warned him against incitement, that he too would never, so long as he lived, organize a putsch. Shortly afterwards he set about doing just that.

In January 1923 Hitler addressed his storm troopers at Munich. He made it plain in his speech that his attitude to French occupation of the Ruhr was not that the Reich should present a united front in order successfully to resist the French, but that this further instance of 'betrayal' and 'crime' should provide a lever for unseating the guilty men. In extolling a passionate enthusiasm for the glory of the Fatherland, he proclaimed:

> Whoever wants this fire [i.e. ardent patriotism] to consume every single German must realize that first of all the arch-enemies of German freedom, namely the betrayers of the German Fatherland, must be done away with ... Down with the perpetrators of the November crime. And here the great mission of our movement begins.

What exactly was this mission? A month earlier, in a conversation with two of his party's financial backers, Hitler had outlined his thoughts and aims. He expressed his absolute hostility to Bolshevism and his confidence that his own movement would prevail. Prohibition of the Nazi[1] Party by provincial authorities had simply enhanced its support. Moreover, its military strength was growing; every week saw the formation of two more brigades of storm troopers as volunteers flocked to the Party. Now the SA had seventeen brigades. Not that he would resort to force unless it seemed that no further expansion of support was likely. In that case, however, the 'dynamic and coherent force' at his disposal would be able to suppress any opposition. Turning to Europe, Hitler expressed the belief that Britain would not be hostile to a stable German

---

[1] The contraction was formed from the German phonetic spelling of the first two syllables of *Nationalsozialist*, the first word (in English, two words) of the NSDAP's full title.

government, although she would oppose Germany's becoming a great power again. France, on the other hand, would wish Germany's destabilization to continue in order to keep the upper hand in the Ruhr and the Rhineland (the latter, under the terms of the Versailles Treaty, was to be occupied by Allied troops for fifteen years and permanently demilitarized). Once Germany was strong and stable again there would be a choice between a global or a Continental strategy, and as the former would mean collision with Britain, the latter was to be preferred. In particular, Bolshevik Russia was a danger and therefore it was 'vital to splinter the Russian empire and to divide up her territories and soil, to be settled by German settlers and tilled by the German plough'. (In seeking to fulfil this part of his mission, Hitler was to show absolute consistency.) By maintaining good relations with Britain, the French problem could be solved; besides, Germany would certainly be on the march against France again within twenty or thirty years. There was also the question of what was to become one of Hitler's principal rallying cries – living space (*Lebensraum*): 'that is our top priority . . . Only then can our government again begin working in the national interest toward a nationalist war.' To achieve all this, and to solve Germany's financial problems, government had to be brutal. What Germany needed, what her people urgently required, was another Bismarck, 'a full-blooded and ruthless ruler . . . a monarch-like idol'.

Hitler's mission thus becomes clear – expansionist nationalism, but (and this was the most important point of all) essentially as a means of revolution, and in this sense revolution was just another word for power, his own and the Party's. This in turn explains why the SA was so vital, and underlines the contrast between how Röhm and Hitler intended to use the SA. To Röhm, every inch a soldier, its purpose was clear. It was one more clandestine army, like the Freikorps and the Defence Leagues, just one more disciplined and trained body of military men, one more reserve, which, if a point of open or guerrilla war with France were ever to be reached, would swell the ranks of that small, 100,000-strong Reichswehr which was all the army Germany was permitted by the terms of Versailles. Thus, for Röhm, the SA's military efficiency was paramount. To Hitler, however, the situation appeared in a very different light. There might one day be wars of revenge against France, but it was not for the SA to fight them. Its role was far more important, far more historic, far more likely to lead in the end to a reversal of the harsh humiliation of Versailles, far more liable to make world history – its role was nothing less than to hoist Adolf Hitler into power. The SA troopers were political soldiers, and they were to be employed to gain political ends. Once these ends had been achieved, once the political power of the state was in his hands, then he could turn to other objectives – building up the state's military strength, avenging Versailles and making Germany once more great, once more feared in Europe.

Priorities, then, were clearly defined. Party came first. The army, indispens-able though it no doubt was, had to be harnessed to party. But in order to put party first he had to have his own soldiers, for too great a dependence on the Reichswehr would be counter-productive. The nature of these personal, polit-ical troops is lucidly explained in *Mein Kampf*: 'The SA must not be either a mili-tary defence organization or a secret society . . . Its training must not be organized from the military standpoint, but from the standpoint of what is most practical for Party purposes'. There was, however, still a great difficulty to be overcome. The dilemma facing Hitler in 1923 was how to carry out a coup d'état which could only hope to succeed with the army's tacit, if not explicit, support, yet which must not be so dependent on the army that its fruits might be denied him.

It was in this same year, 1923, that the two men who had both abjured any idea of instigating a putsch, Seeckt and Hitler, met. It was not a meeting of true minds, and it soon became apparent that there were obstacles to any such understanding. After listening with distaste to Hitler's ferocious vilification of the French and his familiar condemnation of the German Republic, as well as his demand for action against them, General von Seeckt, a man who possessed both the precision of the soldier and the *savoir-faire* of the enlightened man, asked a most pertinent question, namely, what were his visitor's views as to the soldier's oath of allegiance? Seeckt found Hitler's answer was so unsatisfactory that he brought the discussion to an end by coldly observing: 'You and I, Herr Hitler, have nothing more to say to each other.'

It was not long before the relevance and power of the soldier's position, and the matter of his duty of loyalty, were again forcibly brought to Hitler's atten-tion. On 1 May 1923, having succeeded in arming the SA for the purpose of breaking up the socialists' and trade-unionists' May Day parade in Munich, he was obliged under humiliating circumstances to hand back the arms and abandon the whole plan, in spite of there being 20,000 of the SA on parade. In the face of the army's hostility, his bluff called, Hitler gave way. Reliance on the army's neutrality had failed him and he had been forced to capitulate. Yet six months later he was to capture the limelight as never before, and although he was to suffer another defeat as far as force of arms went, it was a military defeat which turned itself into a political victory. The events leading to this next attempt began with the Stresemann government's decision to abandon the policy of passive resistance in the Ruhr. (Gustav Stresemann was leader of the liberal German People's Party; in the event, however, he was only Chancellor from August to November 1923, although he was then a highly effective Foreign Minister until his death in 1929.) However wise a move this may have been, it rapidly provoked vituperation from nationalists, who in any case opposed Stresemann because of his belief in 'fulfilment' of the terms of the

Versailles Treaty, which, he held, was the only way by which Germany might regain the confidence of the other western powers. Hitler spoke of subservience, sacrifice of national dignity, cowardice, ready acceptance of every human humiliation.

First he alerted 15,000 of the SA and announced that fourteen mass meetings would forthwith be held in Munich. The Bavarian Government were naturally alarmed and appointed the right-wing Gustav von Kahr State Commissioner with appropriately sweeping powers. Kahr thereupon banned the meetings, unmoved by Hitler's threats and ravings of revolution. These ravings were not hollow, however, for they led to the putsch of 8–9 November. It was not that the putsch failed that was remarkable; it was that it occurred at all. The situation can be summarized thus: on the one hand, Hitler was calling for a new German regime; on the other, the central government in Berlin, while thoroughly alive to the dangers of civil war, was fortunate enough to enjoy the unequivocal support of Seeckt. Since an attempted coup by Hitler would be opposed by all the strength of Seeckt's Reichswehr, the result could not be in doubt; indeed, it was only because Hitler found unexpected support in Bavaria itself that things went as far as they did. Two events command special interest – Hitler's 'formation' of a new German government, and his march on the headquarters of General von Lossow, the army commander in Bavaria. The first of these, arising as it did from a combination of bluff and oratory, had enabled Hitler to announce, amongst other things: 'I propose that, until accounts have been finally settled with the November criminals, the direction of policy in the National Government be taken over by me.' There is perhaps nothing to be wondered at in Hitler's brazen effrontery. What is astonishing, however, is that such senior figures as Kahr, Ludendorff and Lossow all acquiesced in his outrageous proposal, and joined him in his actions. To have commanded the support of such men was no mean achievement for a former lance-corporal.

The second event hardly displayed Hitler in a heroic light. On 8 November, having marched on Munich with the idea of usurping the power of the Bavarian State Government, before marching on Berlin and establishing a right-wing government, the plans of Hitler and his supporters were brought to an abrupt end as the march reached Munich's Feldeherrnhalle. A few shots from a police detachment halted and dispersed the overwhelmingly stronger SA column at whose head Hitler marched. Sixteen of his supporters were killed; he himself ignominiously made his escape, although Ludendorff – who had not commanded the German Imperial Army for nothing – marched on and brushed his way through the line of police carbines. Hitler, however, in his explanation of the business – namely, that there had never been any intention to use force, nor any question of fighting it out with the army ('we never thought to carry through a revolt against the Army; it was *with it* that we

[131]

believed we should succeed') – turned the whole affair to his advantage. Arrested and charged with treason, at his trial he appealed again to the army. 'Never was Hitler's political ability more clearly shown,' writes Alan Bullock, 'than in the way he recovered from this set-back. For the man who, on November 9 1923, appeared to be broken and finished as a political leader – and had himself believed this to be so – succeeded by April 1924 in making himself one of the most talked-of figures in Germany, and turned his trial into a political triumph.' Of major importance was his revived idea for allying himself and his party with the army. In recording his satisfaction that it had been the police, not the army, which had fired on the marchers and that the Reichswehr was thus untarnished, he predicted an hour when this same Reichswehr would stand at his side. Having defended himself at the trial, in his closing address to the court he made it clear that another court, the eternal one of history, would judge him and his fellows

> as Germans who wanted only the good of their own people and Fatherland; who wanted to fight and die. You may pronounce us guilty a thousand times over, but the goddess of the eternal court of history will smile and tear to tatters the brief of the State Prosecutor and the sentences of this court. For she acquits us.

He was not, however, acquitted by 'this court'. Sentenced to five years in gaol, he was imprisoned in the fortress of Landsberg, some thirty miles west of Munich, until 24 December 1924 (a review had reduced his sentence to six months, plus four years' probation), thus giving him the opportunity to compose *Mein Kampf*, which he largely dictated to a fellow prisoner, or disciple whose name was to become almost as well known as Hitler's – Rudolf Hess. If no other example were sought of the utter contrast in character, taste, talent, humanity and proper sense of history between Hitler and Churchill, it would be enough to put their writings side by side. Churchill's conception of events and of life itself was essentially adventurous, romantic, overflowing with the joys of nature, art, family, friendship, of hard work, of political rivalry, of action, of meeting great difficulties and challenges with vigour, hope and courage. The language he used, both in writing and speaking, reflected his vivid imagination, his sense of history, his love of literature, his formal presentation of ideas with a combination of stylistic solemnity and sheer grandeur. To read his speeches, his memoranda, his letters, his books is to live with the history of Britain, the Empire and the world. It is to be constantly amazed and delighted with the depth of his experience, the fertility of his imagination, the power of his intellect, the sweep of his style and the puckish nature of his wit. As a result, to turn then to the turgid philosophical nonsense churned out by Hitler is to experience a profound sense of deterioration. Norman Stone describes *Mein Kampf*[1] as 'long-winded, self-important, and written in an extraordinarily opaque jargon'. The book is, of course, violently anti-Semitic, full of hatred, of vindictive racialism. It makes plain that Germany's foreign policy should be aimed essentially at conquering an empire in the east at the expense of Russia. It reveals that Hitler's political strategy was one of opportunism, which recognized that Germany's problems could in the end only be resolved by force, and that the use of force always carried with it – risk. As a warning of what might happen if Hitler and his party ever came to power, it was no doubt important. It was, however, so difficult to read and so dull that few had the patience to do so. The first volume of *Mein Kampf*, published in 1925 (the second volume appeared the following year) sold a mere nine thousand or so copies. After Hitler came to power reading (or at least possessing) the book was more or less compulsory, and by 1940 6 million copies had been sold.

Nine years were to pass between Hitler's imprisonment and his becoming Chancellor. The army's compliance was always a condition of his success, and during those nine years the game between them went on. One of the game's most important rules was Hitler's insistence that he intended to achieve power legally, and herein lay the key to relations between the Nazi Party and the army. A speech at Munich in March 1929 underlined the need, as he saw it, for the army not to stand aside from politics in the Seeckt tradition; not to continue to 'go along with the Social Democrats', a course which could end only in the army's dissolution; above all not to oppose the very party which would, as Hitler so often pledged, expand the army and so give back both to it and the nation their former greatness. In September 1929 Hitler had another opportunity to appeal to the generals, and by this time the generals were willing to listen, for that month's elections had left Hitler as the leader of the second most powerful party in Germany. The Nazis had polled nearly 6.5 million votes and had 107 members in the Reichstag. So that when Hitler gave evidence during the trial of three officers accused of spreading Nazi propaganda in the army, the generals sat up and took note. He did much to reassure them, first by brushing aside any idea that the SA was there to fight against or replace the army, second by dismissing the notion that he contemplated any disintegration of the army itself. On the contrary, 'when we come to power, out of the present Reichswehr a great German People's Army shall arise.' As for legality, Hitler insisted on maintaining his basic principle that any Party regulation which was in conflict with the law would not be enforced. The 'German National Revolution' was to be considered a revolution only in the political

---

[1] His first proposed title for the book was *My Four-and-a-Half-Years' Struggle Against Lies, Stupidity and Cowardice*, which he later reduced to *My Struggle – Mein Kampf*.

sense. It was an uprising of oppressed peoples, but the uprising would tolerate no illegal means, no use of force. 'But when we do possess constitutional rights, then we will form the State in the manner which we consider to be the right one.' The menace that this simple statement contained, plain though it was, had yet to be comprehended.

Yet there were contradictions in all this talk of legality. If the movement were to shed its revolutionary appeal, how many would wish to belong to it? The balance was a nice one, and since it was the SA which most strikingly personified the Nazi Party's revolutionary character, control of the SA was all important. In October 1930 Hitler succeeded in getting Röhm, who had resigned in 1925, to return to the SA and reorganize it. Numbers alone spoke loudly of his success. By 1931 it had trebled its strength to a total of 300,000 – exactly three times the permitted size of the Reichswehr. Heinrich Himmler's SS (Schutzstaffel, 'protection detachments'), the elite, black-shirted troops who swore personal allegiance to the Führer, also came under Röhm.[1] Hitler's difficulty with regard to the SA was well pointed in a statement by Adolf Wagner, a Party Deputy, to the effect that the Nazis would never leave the German people alone or in peace until power was theirs. And the way in which the people would be harassed would be by means of ceaseless propaganda, backed by the threat of force – that is, the force of the SA. They were, as Alan Bullock puts it, to be 'the shock troops of a revolution that was never to be made'. How far to use the SA to trick and bully his way into power, yet at the same time avoid a clash with the Reichswehr – this was the Führer's problem.

Hitler was greatly assisted in the resolution of this problem, albeit unwittingly, by General Kurt von Schleicher, who was head of the Ministeramt (ministerial office) in General Gröner's Defence Ministry. Schleicher, like Gröner and the President, Hindenburg, was opposed to suppressing the Nazi movement by force. Rather, he sought to harness them to the machinery of government. Whereas Schleicher's intention was to 'tame' the Nazis by granting them participation in government, to Hitler such participation might offer the very means of achieving power which other paths – force, which he had rejected, or an elected majority, which still eluded him – did not. Hitler was quick to see the possibilities which Germany's present method of government – decrees by President Hindenburg, which were necessary because of the inability of the Chancellor, Heinrich Brüning, to command a parliamentary majority – might be turned to his own advantage. If Hindenburg could rule by decree, why should not Hitler?

[1] The SS originated in 1923 as Hitler's bodyguard. Himmler, a poultry farmer who was an early adherent of the Nazi Party, was appointed head of the SS in 1929 and turned it into a powerful Party weapon.

Thus, if he could gain the co-operation of those men closest to the President – Schleicher, Oskar Hindenburg (the President's son), Brüning, the present Chancellor or, after 1 June 1932, his successor, Franz von Papen – might not he become Chancellor himself, and like those before him make use of the President's emergency powers to govern by decree? However unlikely such an arrangement might have seemed, negotiations between this group of men on the one side, and Hitler with his principal advisers on the other, began in the autumn of 1931. Hitler's first meetings with Brüning and Hindenburg were not auspicious. Yet it was the President's reluctance to continue, unless his term of office could be extended without resort to re-election, which induced Brüning to seek Hitler's support in securing this extension. Hitler's rejection of this offer resulted in his taking the remarkable step of challenging Hindenburg for the Presidency itself. In the elections of March and April 1932, Hindenburg won and Brüning remained Chancellor, although not for long. The intrigues of Schleicher led first to Papen becoming Chancellor and then, on 2 December, Schleicher himself. Each of these Chancellorships was short-lived, and during them Hitler survived one of his most serious reverses. His demand, at the time of negotiating with Schleicher and Papen in August 1932, that he should himself become Chancellor on the grounds that he led the largest party in the Reichstag[1] was refused. In offering him the Vice-Chancellorship, Hindenburg coldly made it clear that Hitler and his party were acceptable only as part of a coalition. He was, in short, not 'good enough' to be Chancellor.

Hitler refused the Vice-Chancellor's post, and in doing so, as well as in restraining Party pressure to abandon the apparently descredited policy of legality and attempt to seize power by force, he faced and overcame great difficulties. (This legality was relative, however. There had been clashes between Nazis and the police, and between the Nazis and Communists, as well as 'acts of violence committed by Hitler's followers against those who were of a different opinion, excesses against Jews and other illegal acts'. The violence had been escalating for some time, and would continue to do so.) He stuck to his guns and waited. In December 1932 Schleicher replaced Papen as Chancellor, drawing heavily in the process on his great authority as Minister of Defence (he had engineered Gröner's resignation) and as spokesman for the army. He made it clear that the army could no longer support Papen, since the continuing and growing unrest put the country at risk of civil war. Once more the army had shown its hand as kingmaker. But Schleicher, the arch-intriguer, for once intrigued too much, for he both overestimated the popularity of his

---

[1] Elections on 31 July 1932, called by Papen, resulted in a resounding victory for the Nazi Party, which won 230 of the 608 seats – although it still had no majority, any more than any other party did.

own programme and underestimated the strength of opposition to it. He even went so far as to boast that Hitler's movement was of no danger to him; the Nazi problem was 'a thing of the past'. While it is true that Hitler's fortunes – including the little matter of Party finances – were at a low ebb, a change of tide and of luck was at hand.

This time the principal intriguer, apart from Hitler himself, was Papen. The issue was unchanged – how to achieve government by parliamentary majority and put an end to rule by emergency decrees. Early in 1933 Hindenburg agreed to allow Papen to negotiate with Hitler with a view to the latter forming a new government. On the understanding that he had the Chancellorship himself, Hitler was willing on this occasion to compromise in allowing certain ministries – Foreign, Defence, Finance – to be headed by Hindenburg's men, and to seek a coalition with other parties which would enjoy a parliamentary majority. Once again the army held the key to success, but it was a key wielded by Hindenburg himself, and Hindenburg had by now accepted Hitler as Chancellor. What is more, the President chose General Werner von Blomberg as Minister of Defence, and on Blomberg's support, and thus that of the army as a whole, too, Hitler could count. Later that year, in September, he recorded his debt, declaring how important it was to remember 'the part played by our Army, for we all know well that if, in the days of our revolution, the Army had not stood on our side, then we should not be standing here today'. But he was standing there as Chancellor of the German Reich. The unlikely had come about. The former drop-out of Vienna, the lance-corporal *Meldegänger* of the Imperial German Army, the political agitator whose *Weltanschauung* could be contained in two words – 'Force Rules' – was now at the head of a nation, which a former Chancellor, Prince Otto von Bismarck, had shown to be more than ready to embark on, and certainly capable of doing so, a *Griff nach der Weltmacht* by ruthlessly exploiting the potentialities of, in Bismarck's phrase, '*Blut und Eisen*' – Blood and Iron. Hitler, as A.L. Rowse declared, thought of himself, like Nietzsche's *Obermensch*, as 'beyond good and evil'. His will to dominate had always been there. Now he had the power, too, and it would not be long before the domination began.

When Hitler became Chancellor in January 1933, Churchill had been out of office for a little more than three and a half years. He had not been inactive, however; indeed, he was incapable of inactivity. Moreover, his warnings as to the dire consequences of Hitler's rise to power had been both persistent and compelling. Before we see what they were, however, we must return to his appointment as Secretary of State for War and Air in January 1919 – the year in which Adolf Hitler had turned his mind to taking up political work. There was a certain mischievous irony about Churchill's becoming War Minister just after the war against Germany had ended. In fact, he himself had had doubts about accepting the post, asking what was the use of being War Minister without a war, and receiving the cutting rejoinder from Bonar Law that he would never have been offered the position had there been a war. What many of Churchill's colleagues at that time failed to discern was his resilience and realism. Even at that time his insistence on magnanimity in victory was as plain as his former defiance in defeat, and he threw his weight behind those who sought some measure of reconciliation in dealing with the Central Powers. Furthermore, despite his eagerness to support the Tsarist forces, which were still engaged in a bloody civil war against the Bolsheviks, with further British commitment, he was quick to recognize that no such wish existed among the British soldiers longing for demobilization, and thereupon took steps to speed up their return to civilian life. But these sensible measures in no way affected his suspicion of and hatred for Bolshevism. In this last respect he had something in common with Hitler, although for different reasons. Churchill, wrote Piers Brendon, 'saw all acts hostile to Britain, whether in Ireland, the Middle East or India, as part of an international revolutionary conspiracy directed against the victorious empire'. Russia, India, Ireland, the Middle East – all were to figure largely in Churchill's ministerial responsibilities and initiatives both at the War Office and, later, at the Colonial Office.

By the end of January 1919 a million soldiers, officers and other ranks, had been demobilized, but in presenting his Army Estimates to the House of Commons on 3 March, Churchill sounded several notes of warning. In declaring that 'We are half way between peace and war', he pointed out that most of Europe and Asia were still racked by 'disorder and anarchy'. 'Hunger, bankruptcy and revolution' were widespread. Even the victors were exhaused, not least financially, and it was finance that would now determine the shape and size of Britain's armed forces in the future. It would therefore be necessary, he said, to seek reductions in these forces in order to secure sound finance. Yet these reductions must never be carried too far. In making his case for the right balance, Churchill expounded two maxims of victory – not to be 'carried away by success into demanding or taking more than is right or prudent', and not to 'disband your army until you have got your terms'. Substantial military power, albeit employed with moderation, was a necessary condition for preserving the country's position in the world. Thus along with the demobilization of those who had won the war would go continued compulsory service in order to man an Army of Occupation in Germany, accompanied by a volunteer army of Regulars, and recruiting for a post-war army made up of young, well-trained, well-found recruits 'who have to reach the age of twenty before they can be sent to the East'. The success of Churchill's policy and its execution may perhaps best be gauged by recording that military costs in September 1919 were little more than a quarter of what they had been at the beginning of the year, and at the same time the country was able satisfactorily to discharge its military responsibilities.

As Churchill was also the Secretary of State for Air, he had the additional task of ensuring that both the autonomy and the efficiency of the air force were properly seen to. In asking Sir Hugh Trenchard to become Chief of the Air Staff,[1] he could hardly have made a more important or effective choice, and Trenchard's views on what the future Royal Air Force, at that time not yet eighteen months old, should be like, what it would do and how it should be managed, were very like Churchill's own. Churchill relished his joint responsibilities in relation to both the army and the air force. In particular, he was far-sighted enough to appreciate the way in which aeroplanes would in the future be able to take over certain internal security duties in the Empire and other dependent territories from the soldiers who hitherto had performed them, and moreover do so much more economically and effectively. At the same time he was determined to foster the RAF's independence, and indeed 'to enhance its distinctive character by every reasonable means'. This not only involved such things as uniforms and rank titles, but Churchill – conscious as he was of the huge advantages of the army's regimental system which so firmly built up comradeship, pride and fighting spirit – wanted to preserve 'the identities of the more famous squadrons' and establish 'definite units of a permanent character possessing their own *esprit de corps*'. In planning how RAF officers should be trained, he laid down that, apart, obviously, from being taught to fly, they should have the proper bearing and discipline, be schooled in war studies, and have special mechanical instruction.

It was characteristic of Churchill that he should at this time himself resume flying lessons, which he had taken while at the Admiralty before the war, but had given up in 1914, shortly before he would have qualified for a pilot's licence. The whole thing nearly ended in disaster when in July 1919 Churchill was having a flying lesson at Croydon with a Colonel Scott, a Royal Flying Corps veteran with whom Churchill had often flown. He had taken off successfully and was attempting to gain height by a series of turns, only to find that with the aeroplane only about ninety feet from the ground, and at an angle of some forty-five degrees, it failed to respond to the controls. Colonel Scott took over, but it was too late. Churchill later recorded what happened:

> The aeroplane was just turning from its side-slip into the nose dive when it struck the ground at perhaps fifty miles an hour with terrific force. Its left

---

[1] General Trenchard, who had commanded the Royal Flying Corps in France, 1915–18, had actually been Chief of the Air Staff from January to April 1918, at the time when the RAF was being formed, but had resigned after disagreements with Lord Rothermere, then the Air Minister.

wing crumpled, and its propeller and nose plunged into the earth. Again I felt myself driven forward as if in some new dimension by a frightful and over-whelming force, through a space I could not measure. There was a sense of unendurable oppression across my chest as the belt took the strain. Streams of petrol vapour rushed past in the opposite direction . . . Suddenly the pressure ceased, the belt parted and I fell forward quite gently on to the dial board in front of me. Safe! was the instantaneous realization. I leapt out of the shattered fuselage and ran to my companion. He was senseless and bleeding. I stood by ready to try to pull him out should the machine catch fire. Otherwise it was better to leave him till skilled help arrived.

It was fortunate that Colonel Scott had prevented an explosion by switching off the engine just before it hit the ground. It was fortunate, too, that Scott recovered, and indeed seemed to have overcome a former injury caused by a wartime flying accident. But as a result of the pleading of his friends Churchill gave up trying to gain a pilot's licence.

Some months previously he had again demonstrated his extraordinary instinct for anticipating future requirements by advocating the formation of a Ministry of Defence, from which a single minister would run the three services. Churchill acknowledged, however, that such a step could not be taken until 'you have created a staff of extra-officers who have grown up year after year having studied the question of war and the defence of the Empire . . . and unless that staff have gradually gained the confidence of their respective branches . . . It is a matter for a good many years' work.' Indeed it was. Twenty-one years later he himself would become Minister of Defence as well as Prime Minister; later still a Joint Services Staff College would be established; and in 1964, not quite a year before his death, the all-powerful Ministry of Defence was at last established.

Churchill's vision of how imperial defence could be run more cheaply and efficiently by using air power, instead of troops, for internal security purposes was first put into practice in what was then – in 1920 – still known as Mesopotamia.[1] In this field the imaginative ideas of Churchill stimulated the practical schemes of Trenchard, and between them they produced a policy, which was endorsed by the Cabinet, whereby the Royal Air Force would exercise control over Mesopotamia. Churchill foresaw a system of air bases, suitably protected by both static defences and mobile fire power provided by tanks or armoured cars, and where possible sited so that they were also accessible by river. In their peacekeeping role, the RAF squadrons would not only be

[1] The former possession of the Ottoman Empire was a British mandate from 1920–33, and in 1921 it became a kingdom under Feisal I, the leader of the Arab Revolt during the Great War. In 1932, as Iraq, it became an independent kingdom, and a republic in 1958.

required to subdue hostile bases by bombs and machine-gun fire, but also to transport infantry soldiers to threatened areas and then maintain them there by air supply. Churchill even suggested the employment of chemical weapons which 'are not destructive of human life but which inflict various degrees of minor annoyance'. In responding to this strategic concept, Trenchard pointed out that it would be necessary to develop aeroplanes which were suitable for transporting stores to remote posts, as well as troop-carrying machines. Between them, these two enthusiasts for the development of air power were anticipating what became a major feature of both German and Allied strategy in the Second World War. There was, however, one drawback to this emphasis on both economy and the priority of *military* aviation, for the needs of civil aviation and the development of air routes to the Middle East, Africa, India and Australia, although pursued, were nevertheless very much subsidiary to the requirements of the RAF.

Of much greater moment during Churchill's service as War Minister was the problem of Russia. Even before taking over this office he had been passionately concerned to support the anti-Bolshevik forces in the civil war that was still raging there, and did everything in his power to convince his political colleagues that Bolshevism must be overthrown. Within the War Cabinet, however, in spite of initial concord, there was little sign of lasting agreement as to a consistent British policy towards Russia. Two days after the armistice with Germany, a meeting between Balfour, Milner and Cecil had produced a number of decisions which were, as Martin Gilbert writes, 'in favour of continued British intervention in Russia'. Murmansk and Archangel were still to be occupied; the anti-Bolshevik Russians established at Omsk were to be recognized; British troops would stay in Siberia; the anti-Bolshevik armies under General Anton Denikin in southern Russia were to be supported; the Baku-Batum railway line would be occupied; Latvia, Lithuania and Estonia would receive munitions. These broad lines of policy were accepted by the War Cabinet, who were at least in agreement about two principles: first, that Britain should support anti-Bolshevik movements in so far as it was in the interests of the British Empire to do so; second, that the broader dangers of Bolshevism, which might influence Britain's own easily roused industrial workers, must be understood and kept at bay. Churchill, in customarily extravagant language, made known his own concern about the Bolshevik menace in a speech to his constituents, explaining to them the chaos and havoc of civil war in Russia. 'Civilization,' he declared, 'is being completely extinguished over gigantic areas, while Bolsheviks hop and caper like troops of ferocious baboons amid the ruins of cities and the corpses of their victims.'

The difficulties facing the British Government and the other nations involved in shoring up the White Russian forces sprang from both the degree of their existing commitment of troops – nearly 200,000 soldiers from eight Allied countries were positioned in what had been Imperial Russia – and the variety and dispersion of the various White Russian armies, totalling more than 300,000 men, which had to be supplied with weapons and other sinews of war if they were to maintain their anti-Bolshevik campaigns. Everywhere that British soldiers had been sent to back up Russian troops in their fight against Germany, they now found themselves involved in civil war. Churchill made plain in a memorandum written shortly before he became War Minister that while Britain did not wish to have another war on her hands so soon after having fought and won a war with Germany, and while the whole country wished to bring soldiers home and to economize, yet events in Russia were such that they could not be pushed aside – 'We may abandon Russia; but Russia will not abandon us.' Churchill, therefore, was a firm supporter of the Allies acting together to bring about a proper settlement. Yet he did not believe that such a settlement – by which he meant a democratic government, as opposed to a Bolshevik dictatorship – would be achieved unless the Allies were prepared to use force. Against this position the Prime Minister, Lloyd George, firmly set his face. He argued that such an undertaking, that is military intervention, was simply to invite soldiers of the interventionist forces to become irretrievably stuck in a morass. If Russia could by her own efforts free herself from Bolshevism, well and good. But for Allied armies to attempt it would be dis-astrous, and more likely to spread Bolshevism than to suppress it. 'To send our soldiers to shoot down the Bolsheviks would be to create Bolsheviks here. The best thing was to let Bolshevism fail of itself and act as a deterrent to the world . . .' While the Imperial War Cabinet, like Lloyd George, was willing to assist Russia's border states in maintaining their independence, it was agreed by its members on the last day of 1918 that there was no question of trying to over-throw the Bolshevik regime by force. Yet the problem presented by the mere presence of British troops in North Russia and elsewhere remained.

As Secretary of State for War, Churchill was particularly concerned with this problem, and at a War Cabinet meeting on 10 January 1919 – the very day he assumed office – Churchill not only spoke up for the idea put foward by Marshal Foch that Britain and France should aid Poland against Bolshevik incursion, but went so far as to suggest that the German Army should be used for this purpose. He also opposed the withdrawal of two British battalions from Omsk in Western Siberia on the grounds that if the British went, so would the Czechs and the French, and the anti-Bolshevik forces commanded by Vice-Admiral Alexander Kolchak (who from November 1918 to December 1919 styled himself 'Supreme Ruler' of Russia) would disintegrate. Churchill's principal military adviser was, of course, the CIGS, General Sir Henry Wilson (he was promoted Field Marshal that year), who had a very high opinion of his own abilities, both in the military and political fields, and this high opinion was matched only by his low opinion of most politicians. Such an attitude was unlikely to have much effect on Churchill, whose confidence in his own political *and* military powers was unbounded. The two men were bound to disagree about certain aspects of policy, and one of them was whether or not British troops should be in Russia. Two days after the War Cabinet meeting, Wilson noted in his diary his conviction that the British should keep out of Russia and on the following day recorded that the Imperial War Cabinet, meeting this time in Paris, was not in favour of sending troops to fight Bolshevism, but did support the policy of helping independent states against Russia by supplying arms.

Churchill, who had inherited from his predecessor the somewhat uncomfortable circumstance that British troops, some 14,000 of them, were already deployed in Russia, was nevertheless of the opinion that they should stay there, even though it was far from clear what they were supposed to be doing. He still believed in the valuable moral effect of keeping British troops in Russia, although he and Wilson were at one in deprecating the lack of clear policy, and Churchill, further exasperated when he heard that Lloyd George was willing to receive the Bolsheviks for peace talks, pressed the Prime Minister for both a decision and a declaration about British policy. In choosing between evacuation and reinforcement, Churchill recommended that whereas British forces in North Russia should be sustained until it was possible to withdraw them when the ice allowed, those in South Russia, Transcaspia and Western Siberia should continue to support the anti-Bolshevik armies with weapons, supplies and volunteer soldiers. The arguments continued to fluctuate between evacuation and reinforcement until the War Cabinet made up its mind that the policy would be withdrawal while continuing to supply General Denikin in the south with munitions and other war material. In a letter to Lloyd George on 9 March 1919, Churchill summed up the decisions that had been taken by the War Cabinet and which he and the Prime Minister had further discussed on the previous day. Murmansk and Archangel were to be evacuated as soon as the White Sea ice melted. British troops in the Caucasus were also to be withdrawn, as were the battalions at Omsk. Denikin was to be helped both by the supply of arms and a British military mission composed of volunteers for service in Russia. In concluding his letter, Churchill undertook to 'be responsible for carrying out the policy on which you and the War Cabinet have decided'. That, however, was not to say that he approved of the policy. On the contrary, he had wanted the Allies jointly to intervene in Russia in order to destroy Bolshevism. But as Martin Gilbert observes: 'After March 8, despite his personal distaste for the policy, he had no alternative, except resignation, than to supervise the withdrawal of British troops from every Russian war zone, and the limitation of

British involvement to the despatch of arms, and a small military mission, to Denikin. Here at last was a clear policy, such as he had been demanding for over eight weeks. Much as he disliked this policy, he had accepted it; he had now to carry it out.'

The business dragged on for the best part of a year. It was not until the autumn of 1919 that the bulk of British troops had been withdrawn, and supplies of arms to the anti-Bolshevik forces dwindled as the Red Army gradually overcame all resistance. It is interesting to note some of the observations made by and about Churchill during this melancholy process. As early as February 1919, while still awaiting the determination of a policy towards Russia, Churchill had warned: 'When we have abandoned Russia, she will be restored by Germany and Japan, and these three powers together will constitute a menace for Britain, France and the United States very similar to that which existed before the present war.' Not every politician had had such vision. Although Churchill had accepted the policy of withdrawal, he did not like it, and in April 1919 told the historian H.A.L. Fisher, at that time the Education Minister, that he would consider resignation rather than submit to 'ignominious withdrawal from Russia', adding that 'After conquering all the huns – tigers of the world – I will not submit to be beaten by the baboons!' He did not resign, but when a month later there came news that General Denikin was enjoying some success, he spoke in the House of Commons, praising the continuing British assistance to the anti-Bolshevik forces and earning a note of congratulation from Sir Samuel Hoare: 'For the last six months I have been convinced that the whole future of Europe, and indeed of the world, depends upon a Russian settlement and the destruction of Bolshevism. If I may say so, you alone of the Allied Ministers have consistently held and expressed the same view.'

The making of economies was, of course, still a political priority, and in August 1919 the Cabinet Committee on Finance made an important decision, and one which was to affect Churchill's activities not only at the time, but again some years later, when he would have special responsibilities for the country's finances. This was the establishment of the 'Ten-Year Rule', under which the estimates for all military expenditure were to be based on the assumption that there would be 'no great war for ten years, no increase to the naval shipbuilding ... the army to be organized only for the maintenance of order in India, Egypt, Palestine & Mesopotamia & for support of the civil power in Great Britain & Ireland ...' Churchill did not like these limits on expenditure, and in voicing his disagreement provoked from Maurice Hankey the comment that 'Churchill obviously does not care to be a War Minister without a war in prospect.' It was his continued advocacy of 'making war upon the Bolshevists by every means in our power' and his pressure for further assistance to Denikin that prompted the press to talk of 'Mr Churchill's Private War,' and goaded Lloyd George into likening Churchill to counsel engaged by a solicitor not so much because he was the best available, but because 'he would be dangerous on the other side'.

By October 1919 it was clear that the Red Army was driving back the anti-Bolshevik forces on all fronts, despite the earlier successes of Denikin and of General Nikolai Yudenich. In a House of Commons debate the following month Churchill defended his policy against an attack not only on Denikin's anti-semitism but also on the reactionary nature of all the anti-Bolshevik leaders. He pointed out that Bolshevism aimed at worldwide revolution, and that its poison had already, like a terrible disease, torn 'to pieces every institution on which the Russian State and nation depended'. Afterwards Balfour told Churchill how much he admired 'the exaggerated way you tell the truth'. But truth, however exaggerated, or not, in the end all Churchill's efforts to promote an active British or Allied policy against the Bolsheviks came to nothing, largely because of Lloyd George's opposition. In acknowledging this, Churchill told the Prime Minister that he could not help admiring the strategy the latter had employed in defeating him: 'You have downed me and my policy . . . You have gone on consistently, never varying, but always with the same fixed idea. I fought you, & you have beaten me.'

In January 1920, however, another proposal to intervene more actively was made by the British High Commissioner for South Russia, Sir Halford Mackinder. This amounted to a plan which would co-ordinate all the anti-Bolshevik forces then in Russia and on Russia's borders, and in which British troops would participate. On 29 January the Cabinet rejected any such idea, making it plain that Britain would not make war on the Bolsheviks, but that neither would peace negotiations with them be undertaken until they could conduct their own affairs properly and ceased to interfere with their neighbours. Moreover, the border states (Latvia, Lithuania, Estonia, Finland – until 1917 a Russian Grand Duchy – and Poland) would have to decide for themselves between peace and war, and although they might be helped to defend themselves, they could not be encouraged or aided in any aggression against Russia. Specifically, the Cabinet endorsed Lloyd George's declaration that Poland (which had been reconstituted as an independent republic in 1918, absorbing so much former Russian territory that it became the largest state in Eastern Europe) would not be given military assistance for an attack on Russia. Churchill was never one to give up, but when, at a Cabinet meeting on 9 February, he again complained that there was no Russian policy, Lloyd George sharply put him down by saying that their policy 'was to try to escape the results of the evil policy which [Churchill] had persuaded the Cabinet to adopt'. In March 1920 there came an extraordinary proposal from General Ludendorff that he and Churchill should meet to discuss the Bolshevik threat, and although

Churchill privately endorsed the idea of 'a strong but peaceful Germany wh will not attack our French allies, but will at the same time act as a moral bulwark against the Bolshevism of Russia,' nothing came of it. It is an ironical reflection that before long the Soviet Union would be helping to build up, train and equip the German armed forces so that they could attack France and Britain. Meanwhile the British forces continued to withdraw from Russia, while the remnants of Denikin's army reached the Crimea. On 29 March the CIGS, Wilson, noted that 'another of Winston's military attempts' had ended 'in practical disaster. First Antwerp, then the Dardanelles, now Denikin. His judgment is always at fault, & he is hopeless when in power.' It was not a view shared by one of Wilson's successors, General Sir Alan Brooke, twenty years later when Churchill at last enjoyed the power necessary for the waging of war according to his own strategic ideas.

In April and May 1920 crises were sufficiently frequent to satisfy even Churchill's craving for action and excitement. Early in April the German Government sent troops to the Ruhr to deal with a revolutionary insurrection there, an action which had so infuriated France that she in turn occupied four German towns. Churchill, in discussing the matter with his French opposite number, M. Lefèvre, made it clear that whereas the British would always be ready to come to the aid of France if she were attacked, they could not support, nor would they tolerate, arrogant triumphing over a defeated enemy which was trying to keep order in its own house. Churchill's warning and arguments for moderation prevailed. The French not only agreed to consult their allies in future over such matters, but agreed to withdraw their troops when the Germans withdrew theirs from the Ruhr. With the Ruhr uprising suppressed, these withdrawals duly took place in mid-May. This incident showed once more Churchill's concern for fairness and magnanimity in dealing with the Germans; moreover, he had no patience with France's chauvinistic antics.

His tolerance was much less evident, however, when it came to the matter of receiving a Soviet representative to discuss the question of resuming trade with Russia. He allowed full rein to his eloquence when finding fault with Curzon's objection to Maximilian Litvinov, the man who controlled Soviet foreign policy, as one of the Russian delegation which would negotiate with the Allies. Churchill spoke of the Foreign Secretary's objection as a very small consideration in relation to other Bolshevik misdemeanors:

> The Bolsheviks deserted the Allied cause and let loose a million Germans on our front. They have repudiated their obligations in every direction and torn up every treaty. They murdered Commander Cromie, the British Naval Attaché in Petrograd, at the door of the British Embassy, which they sacked. The essence of their policy is to produce world-wide revolution, and that is

their only chance of permanent life. They are engaged in wholesale extermination in their own country of the upper and middle classes and to a very large extent of the educated class. They have committed and are committing unspeakable atrocities and are maintaining themselves in power by terrorism on an unprecedented scale and by a denial of the most elementary rights of citizenship and freedom.

If, Churchill's memorandum to the Cabinet went on, Britain could put up with all this, and then start talking to the Bolsheviks, ask them to come to London, make friends with them and do business with them, surely to deny the presence of a lightweight like Litvinov was going too far? 'No doubt one must draw the line somewhere, but I should have thought it hardly worthwhile drawing it here . . .' On this occasion his eloquence was ineffectual. Litvinov was excluded (in 1917 he had become the first Bolshevik representative in London, where he had lived since 1908, but had been deported in September the following year).

Fears of Russian expansionism were not confined to Europe. There was the question of whether the Bolsheviks would threaten Persia (now Iran), India and Mesopotamia. This in turn affected whether or not the British garrisons at Batum on the Black Sea and at Enzeli on the Caspian Sea should remain or be withdrawn. Wilson pressed for the withdrawal of both in May 1920; at a Cabinet meeting on the 5th, Churchill tried hard to get agreement to evacuate Enzeli, but on Curzon's insistence both garrisons stayed where they were. These matters were, however, thrown in the shade by Poland's attack on the Bolsheviks in the Ukraine, the Polish aim being, according to their provisional head of state, Marshal Józef Pilsudski, not the enlargement of Poland, but the preservation of an independent Ukraine. This was not as altruistic as it sounded; the Ukraine was (and is) the 'granary of Russia', and the Bolsheviks had halted or reduced exports of grain from there to other countries, including Poland. With the collapse of Tsarist Russia in 1917 the Ukraine had declared itself an independent republic allied to the Central Powers, and the Germans had established a regime there which fell with the war's end. Poland, anxious to have a buffer state between her eastern border and Russia, invaded and annexed the western Ukraine; the remainder was conquered by the Red Army in 1920. There was no question of British aid to Poland, although at the same time – 11 May – as Churchill was saying just that in the House of Commons, a ship at the London docks was being loaded with munitions for Poland as a result of an agreement made in the previous October. Protests from both dockers and the Labour Party caused the munitions to be unloaded from the ship, however. Churchill was himself in favour of allowing the establishment of an independent Ukraine, while warning that the Bolsheviks would certainly attempt to overrun the province, so that the export of grain to the rest of Europe would again become unlikely. Meanwhile, events further south had again raised the matter of the Batum and Enzeli garrisons, for the latter had been surrounded by the Bolsheviks and its defenders imprisoned. Both Wilson, who had for months been recommending withdrawal from the Causasus and Persia, and Churchill, who felt that withdrawal was preferable to 'disaster and shameful incidents' brought about by staying there, pressed the Cabinet for a decision, and on 21 May got one – British troops were to be withdrawn from northern Persia, and the Batum garrison would withdraw when General Sir George Milne, who had overall command of all British forces in the region, judged it to be in danger. Despite all these disturbances, negotiations between Britain and Russia got under way when, on the last day of May 1920, Leonid Krasin and Lloyd George met for the first time. Curzon had expressed the wish that when discussions began in earnest – with trade foremost on the agenda – the opportunity should be taken 'to come to an understanding concerning the many points on which the British Government were at issue with the Soviet Government in different parts of Europe and the East'. This aim was endorsed by ministers, although Churchill's plea that the anti-Bolshevik forces of Denikin's successor, General Baron Peter von Wrangel, in the Crimea should enjoy immunity from attack for at least one year – this to be a condition of any Soviet-British agreement – was not accepted.

Churchill could always be relied upon to lend decisive support to the Government when himself in office (or for that matter to deliver decisive blows against it when in opposition), and in July 1920 he again displayed his powers in the debate about the massacre at Amritsar which had occurred more than a year earlier, in April 1919. At that time, with nationalist feelings riding high in India, there had been rioting and deaths in the Punjab, and in the state's capital, Amritsar, public meetings had been forbidden, a curfew had been established, and martial law had been declared. When, in defiance of the first order, hundreds of people assembled in the confined space of the Jallianwala Bagh, a sort of public garden in the centre of Amritsar, with only a few narrow exits, the local commander, Brigadier-General Reginald Dyer, had felt it necessary to reassert the Raj's authority over the political demonstrators, among whom tension was so charged and emotion so inflamed that they would be unlikely to listen to reason. Indeed, they were far too occupied listening to the oratory pouring from the mouth of the speaker addressing them, so that the arrival of British armoured cars and some 100 infantrymen (Gurkhas and soldiers from two other Indian Army regiments), under British officers, and with Dyer himself in command, and their deployment at one end of the square, went almost unnoticed. But when the command to fire was given and the Gurkhas and sepoys began impassively to shoot at point-blank range into the crowd, the panic was terrible and the slaughter worse. In six minutes' shooting some 400 people were killed and 1,500 wounded. Dyer was obliged to resign as a result of his condemnation by the Hunter Commission, which conducted the official inquiry in the autumn of 1919, and was given no further military employment. This last decision was strongly backed by Churchill himself.

During the debate itself the Secretary of State for India, Edwin Montagu, spoke in support of Dyer's dismissal, labelling his actions as smacking of terrorism, and even going so far as to question the whole nature of British rule in India. So 'provocative and violent' was Montagu's address that he aroused passionate hostility among the Conservative members, whose feelings were further stimulated by Carson's defence of Dyer, which was both reasonable and clever. At this point it was clear that the Coalition Government was in serious trouble, and although it had been intended that Churchill would speak later, Bonar Law now asked him to speak next. He did so with such effect that the motions against the Government were easily defeated. Having expounded the legal position of an officer in circumstances similar to those in which Dyer had found himself, and established that in this particular case the customary procedure had been properly adhered to, and furthermore that Dyer had been informed that there could be 'no prospect of further employment for him under the Government of India', Churchill was at pains to emphasize the extraordinary nature of the massacre itself:

> That is an episode which appears to me to be without precedent or parallel in the modern history of the British Empire. It is an event of an entirely different order from any of those tragical occurrences which take place when troops are brought into collision with the civil population. It is an extraordinary event, a monstrous event, an event which stands in singular and sinister isolation.

He then went on to argue that justification for such severity of action could only be upheld if an officer faced with a hostile mob could establish, first, that the mob was armed, and second, that it was attacking or about to attack those in authority. General Dyer's contention that he was confronted by a revolutionary army hardly tallied with the facts (quite apart from anything else, large numbers of those in the Jallianwala Bagh were people from the surrounding countryside who had come to attend a local fair). There was also the point – and it was a major point of principle – that in such internal-security situations as this, it was essential that the rule of minimum force should be stringently applied. In describing once more the details of the Amritsar shooting and the fact that the shooting went on while the crowd was desperately trying to escape through only one narrow exit (one other being locked, and the last, the main gate, being blocked by the soldiers), Churchill reiterated the need to condemn

Dyer's action and to make 'it absolutely clear, some way or another, that this is not the British way of doing business'. He went on to dismiss the claim that Dyer's use of force had prevented another Indian Mutiny, and pointed out that Britain's reign in India could not be based on the employment of force alone, but 'has always meant and implied close and effectual cooperation with the people of the country'.[1] Admiration and praise for Churchill's speech, which 'seemed to all who listened to have saved the Government from the danger of a serious set-back', was widespread. Indeed it was described by the Archbishop of Canterbury as 'unanswerable'.

Churchill did not have the same success in his support for a campaign against the Bolsheviks, who defeated the Polish forces in July 1920, and advanced to threaten Warsaw itself. Moves to intervene on the Polish side by French and British forces caused such a stir from the Labour Party – which made plans for a general strike and was even prepared to challenge the British constitution itself – that Lloyd George was able to resist the pressure from Churchill and others to support the Poles. In the event the Poles turned the tables on the Red Army, allowing Churchill to take a leaf from Pitt's book and record that 'Poland has saved herself by her exertions & will as I trust save Europe by her example.' But the whole crisis had made it clear that public opinion would not support war with the Soviet Union. As A.J.P. Taylor put it, the war weariness of the British people had drawn a limit to 'the sanctity of parliamentary government'; the cry of '"No More War" was irresistible'. All Churchill's advocacy of intervention in Russia had done him no good polit-ically, for its failure simply increased his own bitterness, as well as others' dis-trust of him. His persistent and vocal resolve to do away with Bolshevism put him at odds with his ministerial colleagues, particularly the Prime Minister, who sought some reconciliation with the Soviet Union. 'In the public mind,' says Martin Gilbert, 'it was yet further proof that he [Churchill] was a man who delighted in war.' Yet his hostility to Bolshevism continued.

We have seen that in 1920 and thereafter Hitler was to make much of the Treaty of Versailles and the need for its 'destruction'. Churchill too, in his search for a barrier against Bolshevism, foresaw the need for some modification of Versailles, involving nothing less than 'a working agreement between Britain, France and Germany in regard to the arrangements for the pacification and reconstruction of Europe'. While recognizing extreme reluc-

[1] The contribution India had made to victory in the Great War had been recognized by a British agreement to institute reforms that would lead to a measure of Indian self-deter-mination. When these reforms were not forthcoming, there was considerable unrest in the country, which resulted in the Rowlatt Acts, draconian measures introduced in 1919 to suppress 'sedition'. It was against these that the protestors in the Punjab had, in the main, been rebelling.

tance of the French to allow a resurgence of Germany's influence, Churchill put this down to France's concern at her possible isolation against forces threatening her from the east. Reassurance, however, could be provided by offering France an alliance with Britain and Germany. What was needed, therefore, was 'a tripartite arrangement between Great Britain, France and Germany for the re-construction of Europe and the pacification of its Eastern regions. This implies a profound revision of the Treaty of Versailles and the acceptance of Germany as an equal partner in the future guidance of Europe . . .' If anything like this had come about, many of the grievances which so filled Hitler's political propaganda would have been removed. But Churchill was making these proposals at a time when there was still a danger of Russia's destroying Poland, and with the removal of this threat his arguments lost much of their force.

Churchill was, however, still highly suspicious of the activities of Lev Kamenev and Krasin, leaders of the Soviet Mission, whom Churchill believed were fostering Bolshevik agitation in Britain. Indeed, he was so violently opposed to the whole idea of Anglo-Soviet trade, a policy which had, in general, the support of the Government ministers, that during a Cabinet meeting on 17 November 1920, he sent a note to Lord Birkenhead (as F.E. Smith had become in 1919) indicating that if trade with Russia went ahead, he would resign. It required all his old friend's persuasive powers – pointing out that public opinion was not opposed to trade with Russia, that it was not an issue which would justify Churchill's parting with colleagues with whom he agreed on most great matters, and that there would be little support for him among these colleagues – to convince Churchill that he should remain in office. None the less, he continued to speak in public against the Bolshevik regime – he had sought the Cabinet's agreement to do so – calling, in a speech at the Oxford Union, for example, for 'the overthrow and destruction of that criminal regime'.

Much nearer home, the Irish Nationalists were once more taking up arms to overthrow what they regarded as a criminal regime, that is, the rule of the British. During the Easter Rising of 1916, a small group of armed Irishmen had taken possession of the Dublin General Post Office and other buildings and declared an Irish Republic. Fighting between the Irish Nationalists and the British Army caused heavy casualties – 100 British soldiers and 450 Irishmen were killed. After five days the remaining rebels, besieged in the Post Office, surrendered after the building had been all but destroyed. The men who had signed the declaration of independence, together with most of the Irish Volunteer commanders (except Eamon de Valéra) were shot. All attempts while the Great War was still in progress – attempts by Asquith, Lloyd George, Carson (leader of the Ulster Unionists) and John Redmond (a moderate Irish

Nationalist political leader) – to set up Home Rule for Ireland, less six of the nine counties of Ulster,[1] failed. An Irish Republic would have to wait, but the Irish Nationalists grew stronger, and in 1919 resumed their campaign of violence. It was not until December 1922 that the Irish Free State was established, and by then Churchill had served as Colonial Secretary for almost two years and had then, also in 1922, lost his seat in the House of Commons after Lloyd George's Coalition Government ended. Throughout the three years from 1919 to 1922 he had had much to do with Ireland, and we will now briefly survey events there and then look more closely at Churchill's part in them.

One of the measures taken, late in 1919, to combat terrorism, a measure which had Churchill's support, was a form of counter-terrorism in the shape of the notorious 'Black and Tans', originally demobilized British soldiers recruited in England for the Royal Irish Constabulary (RIC).[2] The Irish 'troubles' were characterized by brutality on both sides. The Irish Republic Army – the armed force of the Nationalist party Sinn Féin – which at any one time could call on perhaps 5,000 men for 'active service' (an expression that has become all too familiar in Britain since 1969) was fighting against what the Nationalists regarded as British occupation. They would collect together in small groups to attack army convoys and seize arms, or would stage assaults on isolated police barracks, not wearing uniform, but usually identifiable by their trench coats; then, after a raid was over, they would disperse again to their homes or hiding places. The British Army deployed some 50,000 men against the IRA and the Royal Irish Constabulary about 10,000. The Government forces slowly learned and put into practice anti-guerrilla tactics, and some units, notably the Black and Tans, with far more vicious zeal than was either justified or sensible. There was no question of pacification or restoration of law and order. The affair simply dragged on – about 700 Irishmen were killed and a similar number of soldiers and policemen – hardly helped by the Black and Tans or by the Auxiliary Division of the RIC (raised from among demobilized British Army officers), whose activities merely increased hatred, resentment and bitterness. Throughout it all, the problem of Loyalist Ulster persisted.

In 1921 the CIGS, Field Marshal Sir Henry Wilson (who was to be assassinated by the IRA in London a year later) gave it as his view that to subdue Ireland would demand the deployment of 100,000 specially recruited soldiers

---

[1] Cavan, Donegal and Monaghan became part of the Republic of Ireland when the country was partitioned in 1921, and today form the province of Ulster within the Republic. The remaining six counties form Northern Ireland.

[2] They took their name because a shortage of the dark-green RIC uniforms led to their wearing a mixture of that and khaki service dress (and later khaki with black hats and belts). 'Black and Tans' is the name of a famous Irish pack of foxhounds.

to wage full-scale war. Lloyd George, urged by Field Marshal Smuts and strongly supported by King George V, sought reconciliation, and after prolonged negotiations and endless disagreements – plus fighting between the various representatives of Sinn Féin and the IRA – the country was partitioned after elections in 1921, while the Treaty establishing an Irish Free State of twenty-six Counties (that is, excluding six counties of Ulster) was accepted by both the Irish and the British in December 1922. British troops left Ireland in the same month, and to the regret of many some of the most renowned fighting regiments of the British Army – those that were based in and recruited from southern Ireland – were disbanded, and so disappeared from the order of battle.

Churchill did much to defend the army's position in Ireland against criticism in the House of Commons. He pointed out during the February 1920 debate on the Army Estimates that the War Office was not answerable for the way in which Ireland was governed – this was for the Irish Secretary – but simply for providing troops as needed. He also spoke up for the soldiers themselves, declaring that it was not only wrong, but dangerous, 'to shoot soldiers who fought in the War, who have come home from the War expecting to have a period of rest and peace, and who do not expect to be murdered from behind hedgerows in a civilized country by a population for whose defence they risked their lives during the War'. In 1919, as the situation worsened, the Prime Minister had appealed to Churchill for his help, in particular to provide more men, as had been recommended by Major-General Sir Nevil Macready, commanding the British forces in Ireland. Churchill responded by proposing to raise a special force of 8,000 men that would be quite separate from the Regular Army which was, as usual, overstretched. Thus was born the organization known as the Black and Tans. Few bodies of troops – for 'the Tans' were effectively irregular troops, despite coming nominally under the RIC – have created such controversy. Henry Wilson condemned their reprisals against the IRA and appealed to Churchill to put a stop to their activities, but Churchill did not agree, and in this he had the support of Lloyd George.

There were many who sought reconciliation between the various Irish factions, among them Churchill's cousin, Shane Leslie, a notable literary figure and passionate advocate of a peaceful solution to Ireland's problems, who had asked Churchill what advice could be offered to Sinn Féin. In answering him, Churchill produced something reminiscent of his much later 'Jaw jaw is better than War war', for he replied 'Quit murdering and start arguing' (a sentiment which has infinite relevance to the situation in Northern Ireland in 1997). But although Sinn Féin at this time was determined to continue with its programme of insurrection, intimidation and murder, despite the inevitable response of repression and counter-murder, Lloyd George pressed on with his

Government of Ireland Bill, which intended to give a comparable degree of Home Rule to both the south and the north of the country.

That Churchill's concerns with military affairs were not confined to Ireland was made plain by his speech in the House of Commons in December 1920 when he expressed his surprise 'that the expenditure we have been put to in Ireland, compared with the expenditure we have been put to in the more distant regions of the Middle East should be so remarkably small . . . There is far larger skill involved; a far greater loss of life, I am sorry to say, and a far greater expenditure of money takes place in the more distant but much more loosely connected parts of the British Empire which do not seem to us to raise problems nearly so formidable.' Yet the problems in the most distant parts of the British Empire were formidable enough, and were to become more so. Even though Churchill left the War Office at the beginning of 1921, he became even more committed to Britain's responsibilities both in the Empire and elsewhere overseas, particularly the intractable ones of the Middle East and the former Turkish dependencies, for in February 1921 he became Colonial Secretary. It was an office that was to give him far more scope and satisfaction than that of Secretary for War. Martin Gilbert sums up Churchill's disappointment with his time at the War Office by saying that he 'found himself in charge of a War Office without a war, committed to economies, withdrawals and, in Ireland, reprisals'. On this last point his wife had pleaded with him to exert his influence to try to persuade the Government to follow a policy of justice and moderation towards Ireland. 'It always makes me unhappy & disappointed,' she wrote to him, 'when I see you *inclined* to take for granted that the rough, iron-fisted "Hunnish" way will prevail.'

Before accepting the office of Secretary of State for the Colonies, which Lloyd George offered him on 1 January 1921, Churchill asked that certain conditions should first be met or agreed. He was particularly concerned that expenditure in the Middle East should be reduced, that a Middle East Department should be set up under the Colonial Secretary, and that his responsibilities should include the administration, both civil and military, of Mesopotamia and Palestine. In setting out these conditions as part of some notes made for the Prime Minister, Churchill was as characterically effusive as he could be in his covering letter:

While I feel some misgivings about the political consequences to myself of taking on my shoulders the burden & the odium of the Mesopotamia entanglement, I am deeply sensible of the greatness of the sphere you are confiding to my charge, of the honour which you have done me in choosing me for such critical employment, and also of the many acts of personal kindness by which you have marked our long friendship & political association.

Once in office, of course, Churchill revelled in the 'burden & odium' of his responsibilities. Recognizing, too, how important it was to have the active co-operation of the Foreign Secretary, Curzon, if he were to solve Britain's problems in the Middle East, he wrote to ask for the advice and help of Curzon himself, as well as that of the Foreign Office as a whole. He also enlisted the aid of T.E. Lawrence to advise him on Arabian matters. Lawrence, at that time a research Fellow at All Souls, Oxford, thus became a political adviser to the newly created Middle East Department of the Colonial Office.

Following on his decision to set up that department, Churchill was determined to go to the Middle East himself. At first he was inclined to travel directly to Mesopotamia, but on 6 February decided instead to go to Cairo and summon there what he himself described as 'practically all the experts and authorities on the Middle East'. In *Farewell the Trumpets* James Morris drily comments that 'of the thirty-eight participants, thirty-six were British and two Arab', thus illustrating how the British regarded Arab expertise at that time. Churchill explained to his advisers that he wished to confer with Field Marshal Lord Allenby (as he had become), the High Commissioner for Egypt, and would visit Jerusalem to confer with Sir Herbert Samuel, the High Commissioner for Palestine; Sir Percy Cox, the High Commissioner for Mesopotamia, was to attend the conference. The purpose of the Cairo Conference was to settle, at least in theory, Arab affairs in accordance with the decisions set out in the clauses of the Treaty of Versailles which established the League of Nations, and also in the terms of the abortive Treaty of Sèvres (intended to settle the war with Turkey) and later retained in its successor, the Treaty of Lausanne. In practice, what resulted was increased British control in the Arab world. The conference began on 12 March and lasted for ten days. Two new Arab kingdoms were to be created – Iraq and Transjordan (now Jordan), and each would have a Hashemite monarch – Feisal in Baghdad, and his brother Abdullah (who had also been one of the leaders of the Arab Revolt) in Amman. Palestine would be a Mandated Territory, but would continue to be governed under the aegis of the Colonial Office. During his visit to Jerusalem Churchill had seen for himself the impressive work done in the Jewish settlements, where desert had been transformed into beautiful and fertile vineyards and orange groves. He was also thoroughly conscious of the absolute Arab hostility to the Jewish settlers.

While Churchill was in Cairo, Bonar Law resigned on the grounds of ill health. His successor as Leader of the House was Austen Chamberlain, who thus left vacant the post of Chancellor of the Exchequer, which he had held since 1919. Churchill was still in the Middle East when Sir Robert Horne was promoted from the Board of Trade to be Chancellor of the Exchequer, Stanley Baldwin going to replace Horne. Churchill, never one to hide his feelings and profoundly disappointed that *he* had not been chosen to succeed Chamberlain as Chancellor, was, according to Frances Stevenson, 'still very vexed with the P.M. . . . It was the joke of the moment his being away when all the changes were made.' She noted, too, that whereas Churchill had previously begun his letters to the Prime Minister by writing 'Dear David' or 'Dear LlG', it now became 'Dear Prime Minister'. Not concealing his disappointment, Churchill spoke of resigning, but in the end confined himself to adopting an attitude of hostility towards Lloyd George. The result was that each of them became dissatisfied with the other. Frances Stevenson recorded that 'D. is so sick with C. I don't think he cares if he does go,' while the editor of the *Daily Mail* noted 'Winston is fed up with Lloyd George. He wanted to be Chancellor but Ll.G. refused to give him the job.' Churchill particularly resented having to go to Horne, who had only recently risen to ministerial office, for money, when he himself was relatively so much more senior.

While it is true that Churchill could behave like a spoilt child when the mood took him, nothing could or would prevent his doing his duty properly, not even personal tragedy, and 1921 had its share of this for him, for his mother, Lady Randolph, died in June, and his youngest child, Marigold, in November. But, also in June, he had another triumph in the House of Commons when he made a statement about the Middle East. In tracing the circumstances that had led to Britain's position there, he reminded the House that during the conquest of Palestine and Mesopotamia by their armies, the British had succeeded in enlisting the Arabs and other local inhabitants to help them against the Turks, and having overrun these former provinces of the Ottoman Empire, had pledged that Arab 'influence and authority' would be restored. In addition, Great Britain had made promises to the Zionists, under the Balfour Declaration of November 1917,[1] to the effect that a Jewish national home would be established in Palestine on the condition that the rights of non-Jewish communities there would be safeguarded. As was customary with him, Churchill clothed his justification of government policy in the most extravagantly rich garments:

> We cannot repudiate light-heartedly these undertakings. We cannot turn round and march our armies hastily to the coast and leave the inhabitants, for whose safety and well-being we have made ourselves responsible in the most public and solemn manner, a prey to anarchy and confusion of the worst description. We cannot, after what we have said and done, leave the Jews in Palestine to be maltreated by the Arabs who have been inflamed

[1] The Declaration, signed by Arthur Balfour, the Foreign Secretary of the time, was a communication sent to Lord Rothschild, a leader of Zionism. The Zionist movement's principal aim was 'to secure for the Jewish people a home in Palestine guaranteed by public law'.

against them, nor can we leave the great and historic city of Baghdad and other cities and towns in Mesopotamia to be pillaged by the wild Bedouins of the desert.

After declaring that there was no useful purpose in arguing whether or not Britain should have acquired such responsibilities, Churchill went on to say that they 'were bound to make a sincere, honest, patient, resolute effort to redeem our obligations' whether it were popular or not. Having explained how it came about that Middle Eastern matters had been placed under one minister – himself – he went on to outline the course of the Cairo Conference and the economies that had been and were to be realized, and to present the details of the settlement. Iraq (the former Mesopotamia) would have an Arab ruler and an Arab army, as would the new kingdom of Transjordan. Ibn Saud, Emir of the Nejd, would – in return for an annual subsidy amounting to no more than the cost of maintaining one Indian Army infantry battalion – guarantee peace in that region (a part of what is now Saudi Arabia). Air power would play its part in exercising British control of Iraq. Palestine was a more difficult problem, largely because of British support for the Zionist movement and Arab hostility to Jewish immigration. The British garrison there had been reduced, but because of unrest in the country could not be reduced further. Churchill then suggested – wrongly, as subsequent events were to show – that although the Palestinian Arabs feared that they would be 'swamped by scores of thousands of immigrants from Central Europe, who will push them off the land, eat up the scanty substance of the country and eventually gain absolute control of its institutions and destinies . . . these fears are illusory.'

The Colonial Secretary was careful to emphasize that the Middle East settlement would, in the end, depend on 'a peaceful and lasting' agreement with Turkey, who could easily stir up trouble on her borders and throughout the area. Peace with Turkey (where the Sultanate had accepted the terms of the Treaty of Sèvres, only to have them rejected by the Nationalists), therefore, was of supreme importance. He concluded his speech by saying that what was being done was designed both to bring peace and save money, and in believing that they would do so, he invited the House to give its support. Praise and admiration for the excellence of his speech were lavish, notably from both Curzon and Lloyd George. Churchill's anxiety to negotiate with the Turks was aggravated by the hostility of the Greeks and Lloyd George's support for them. But the Prime Minister was to find that the new leader of Turkey, Mustafa Kemal – the general who had commanded Turkish troops so skilfully and successfully against the British during the Gallipoli campaign and who had led a Nationalist revolt since 1919, setting up a provisional government of Ankara in May 1920 – was not a man to be trifled with. His leadership inspired the

Turks to a new and virile national spirit, to such an extent that France and Italy, which under the peace agreements had been allotted areas of Asia Minor, made peace with Kemal and withdrew their claims. Russia too had come to an agreement with Kemal, but Greece not only remained in Smyrna (now Izmir), which she had been granted in the post-war dismemberment of the Ottoman Empire, but threatened to seize Constantinople. The British occupied various posts on the Asian side of the Dardanelles, principally at Chanak. While Churchill was still seeking to come to an agreement with Kemal, in which he was supported by both Birkenhead (by now Lord Chancellor) and Curzon, Lloyd George still sat on the fence. But when, in August 1922, Kemal attacked the Greeks, overwhelmed them, with Smyrna suffering the most appalling scenes of massacre and conflagration, and then advanced towards the Dardanelles themselves, threatening the British positions at Chanak, something had to be done.

When the British Cabinet met on 15 September 1922 they decided that the Neutral Zone – of which Chanak was part – should be defended by force. The garrison there was reinforced and it was also decided that a telegram should be sent to the Dominions both to inform them of this decision and to ask for their assistance in the form of military forces. Unhappily, this last matter was badly mishandled. The telegram to Dominion Prime Ministers, drafted by Churchill, outlined the position created by the advancing Turks, explained the numbers of Turkish soldiers involved – 60,000 to 70,000 – and stated that proper countermeasures were essential. It went on: 'Grave consequences in India and among other Mohammedan populations for which we are responsible might result from a defeat or from a humiliating exodus of the Allies from Constantinople [an Allied Army of Occupation was stationed in the capital, and also guarded the approaches through the Dardanelles and the Bosphorus] . . . The announcement of an offer from all or any of the Dominions to send a contingent even of moderate size would undoubtedly exercise in itself a most favourable influence on the situation.' This was a reasonable request, and was in any case intended to be in the nature of an 'inquiry'. But, believing that the public should be made aware of the crisis, the Cabinet also agreed that a communiqué should be released to the press. The text of this statement, while stressing the British intention of securing peace with Turkey, made it plain that Mustafa Kemal had been told that the Neutral Zone must be respected, and that adequate Allied forces must be maintained there to protect the freedom of the straits from Turkish aggression. Britain's allies had therefore been appealed to for support, and the Government had asked the Dominions to send forces 'in the defence of interests for which they have already made enormous sacrifices and of soil which is hallowed by immortal memories of the Anzacs'. This high-flown language was all very well – the trouble was, however, that the communique was published in Dominion newspapers before Lloyd George's secret telegram to the Prime Ministers had been decoded, and the latter were understandably incensed by the apparent British presumption, as it appeared from reports in the press, since there had been no previous consultation. 'The Dominions,' wrote James Morris, 'were tired of European squabble, intrigue and bloodshed, and they were notably disinclined to send their young men once again to the Dardanelles, where so many of their brothers lay uselessly buried.' Although New Zealand and Newfoundland[1] agreed to send troops should they be needed, Australia's response was grudging, South Africa ignored the whole business, and Canada made it clear that her involvement in such matters could be decided only by the Canadian Parliament. Indeed, the incident prompted from the Canadian Prime Minister, William Mackenzie King, the revealing reflection that, 'If membership in the British Empire means participation by the Dominions in any and every war in which Great Britain becomes involved, without consultation, conference or agreement of any kind in advance, I can see no hope for an enduring relationship.'

It was fortunate for the British, and indeed for all those involved, that the officer commanding the Allied Forces of Occupation in Turkey, Lieutenant-General Sir Charles ('Tim') Harington, was both stalwart and wise. By 27 September the Turks had violated the Neutral Zone. British and Turkish troops were actually confronting each other, and at Chanak 23,000 Turks faced some 3,500 British, though the latter had in addition powerful naval support. The British demand for Turkish withdrawal from the Neutral Zone was rejected by Kemal on the 27th, and two days later the Cabinet instructed Harington to send the Turks an ultimatum to the effect that unless they withdrew from the Neutral Zone by a time to be chosen by Harington himself, 'all the forces at our disposal – naval, military and aerial – will open fire'. It was then that Harington showed the stuff he was made of. He declined to obey orders, and his reasons for doing so were contained in a telegram which the Cabinet received on the morning of 1 October. It was a model of sound military judgement and of reassuring, reasoned confidence:

I share Cabinet's desire to end procrastinations of Kemal and I note decision of Cabinet but I would earnestly beg that matter be left to my judgment for moment . . . To me it seems very inadvisable just at moment when within reach of distance of meeting between Allied Generals and Kemal . . . that I should launch Avalanche of fire which will put a match to mine here and everywhere else . . . Confidence has re-appeared in last few days since rein-

---

[1] From 1855 to 1949, when it was federated as a province of Canada, Newfoundland was a self-governing British colony.

forcements marched in and I was every day feeling more hopeful that I might see the end with principle of the neutral zones preserved without firing a shot...

These hopes were not misplaced, and later that day the Cabinet heard that Mustafa Kemal and General Harington had agreed to meet at Mudania to discuss the whole question of the Neutral Zone. The Cabinet then agreed that the ultimatum need not be sent and Harington was informed accordingly. It is worth noting that during the Second World War, Churchill frequently chided his generals for their caution and reluctance to mount offensives. In the resolution of the Chanak affair, however, he and his colleagues had every reason to be grateful for the prudence, negotiating skills and firm military stance of General Harington. Mustafa Kemal also showed wisdom and restraint, confident that the peace arrangements which would follow the pact of Mudania – which was agreed on 11 October and which guaranteed that the Neutral Zone would be respected – would return to Turkey what was no more than her own territory.

Thus the Chanak Crisis ended without war – for which, indeed, no one except Lloyd George, Birkenhead and Churchill had shown any enthusiasm. Such was the misreading of the public mood by the Prime Minister and his Cabinet, however, that they decided to call a general election, planning to keep the Coalition in being. Bonar Law thought otherwise, deplored Lloyd George's adventurous policies – 'We cannot act alone as the policemen of the world' – emerged from retirement to persuade the Conservatives to end the Coalition and, at the general election, to appeal to the country as a party in its own right, and wholly independent. Lloyd George thereupon resigned, Bonar Law was elected leader of the Conservative Party and then, after the Conservatives won the election, became Prime Minister, while Churchill, together with Lloyd George's other ministers, lost office. As it happened on 18 October he had been operated on for appendicitis, and so was unable, one week later, to be present at Buckingham Palace to hand over with his colleagues the Seals of Office. The King's Private Secretary, Lord Stamfordham, sent a sympathetic message both on the monarch's behalf and his own. Colonal Richard Meinertzhagen, Churchill's military adviser on Middle Eastern affairs at the Colonial Office, paid his chief a great tribute when he recorded in his diary how sorry he was that Winston had gone: 'He has a brilliant brain and is as quick as lightning,' acting largely by instinct, usually right, a hard master, tremendously hard-working himself, and expecting the same from his staff. Twenty years later, there were to be many others who would have endorsed absolutely Meinertzhagen's admirable résumé of Churchill's qualities in high office.

In his brilliant essay on *Mr Churchill in 1940*, Isaiah Berlin emphasized with great clarity and force his subject's remarkable consistency. Churchill may have changed party – and was shortly to do so again – but 'Far from changing his opinions too often, Mr Churchill has scarcely, during a long and stormy career, altered them at all.' One of his enduring beliefs was in the importance of national unity and the integrity of the Empire. In March 1922 he gave voice to this belief while supporting his old friend, Major-General Edward Spears, as a National Liberal candidate at Loughborough: 'I am for unity and Coalition . . . I look forward to the day when out of the Coalition there shall arise a strong, united, permanent National Party, liberal, progressive and pacific in its outlook at home and abroad, but resolute also to uphold the traditions of the State and the power and unity of the Empire.' It was true that there would in the next decade be several national *governments* – although Churchill would not be a member of one until world war came again – but no National *Party*.

Apart from the Middle East and Turkey, the other great issue confronting the Coalition was, of course, Ireland. By May 1921 it had become plain that some form of reconciliation with Sinn Féin was to be preferred to the continuance of coercion and violence. One of the questions of the day was whether or not to proceed with elections in both the south and the north, and while it was recognized that in the south, elections would almost certainly return Sinn Féin, rather than the Government, Churchill pointed out in Cabinet that if this happened 'a wave of feeling will sweep over the nationalist world that the movement is passing from murderous to non-murderous, from non-constitutional to constitutional. The election would be a new situation which might lead to negotiations.' In a sense this was true, for despite the virtual separation of the north from the south as a result of elections, King George V's appeal, on opening the newly created Parliament of Northern Ireland in Belfast in June 1921, that all Irishmen should 'pause, to stretch out the hand of forbearance and conciliation, to forgive and to forget, and to join in making for the land which they love a new era of peace, contentment, and goodwill,' had its effect. On 11 July a truce came into being, and five days later de Valera (who had been elected President of Sinn Féin in 1917) and Lloyd George met at 10 Downing Street. The British offer of Limited Home Rule for Ireland as a British Dominion was rejected by de Valera; for Sinn Féin (the phrase means 'Ourselves Alone') nothing short of total independence was acceptable. After months of negotiation, renewed threats of war, devious proposals by Lloyd George to lead the south into believing that, by redrawing boundaries, the six Loyalist counties of Ulster would be anxious to join the Irish Free State, the 'Articles of Agreement for a Treaty between Great Britain and Ireland' – which conferred Dominion status on Ireland except for six of Ulster's nine counties, which were granted limited self-government as 'Northern Ireland' –were signed on 6 December 1921. 'The settlement with Ireland,' wrote A.J.P. Taylor, 'was a great achievement, despite its faults.' Yet, he added, 'Ireland ruined Lloyd

George, as it had ruined Peel and Gladstone before him. But at least he was ruined by success, they by failure.' When the Irish Free State was at last formally declared in December 1922, Churchill had been out of office for some six weeks, and indeed had lost his Dundee seat in the House of Commons in the previous month's general election. Yet his part in bringing about the creation of the Irish Republic had been a major one. 'He had,' says Martin Gilbert,

> worked for nearly a year to reconcile the conflicting passions of North and South. He had believed in, and sought to further, a United Ireland under the British Crown. He had guided complex legislation through a divided Parliament. He had stood firm against the extremists in both South and North. He had refused to be deflected from supporting the Treaty by error or by the threat of war. At Lloyd George's personal request, he had conducted delicate and prolonged negotiations with the Free State leaders. He had piloted the Treaty through the House of Commons, and had acted in Cabinet as the advocate and spokesman of political compromises, based upon a permanent constitutional link between Britain and Southern Ireland.

If Churchill had done nothing else during his time – all but two years – as Colonial Secretary, he would have earned his place in British history as a consummately skilful politician, a great patriot, and a leader of formidable power and endurance. But he had, as we have seen, achieved other great things in the more distant parts of the world where Britain had Imperial or other responsibilities. Moreover, if losing both high office and his seat in Parliament were severe disappointments, there was some solace to be found elsewhere. In September 1922 he acquired Chartwell, the country house at Westerham in Kent which was to give him and his family so much peace and pleasure. He had, too, made great strides with the completion of and arrangements for the publication of *The World Crisis*, his memoirs of the Great War, which he himself thought of as 'a gt chance to put my whole case', and others referred to as 'Winston's autobiography about the Great War'. Whatever else might be said about *The World Crisis*, it convinced many that Churchill's part in the Dardanelles affair had not been as blameworthy as had become widely accepted. The book also brought him some money when it was published in 1923, money doubly welcome at a time when he was out of office. There was also one other source of great comfort to Churchill, for his youngest child, Mary, was born in September 1922,[1] just as he was negotiating to buy Chartwell.

By 1922 Churchill had already made a substantial contribution to world, as

---

[1] Diana had been born in 1909, Randolph in 1911, and Sarah in 1914. Churchill's fourth child, Marigold, as has been said, died in November 1921, aged three and a half.

well as to British, history, and was to make an even greater one. Shortly before he lost his Dundee seat in November 1922, T.E. Lawrence (by now Aircraftman John Hume Ross, Royal Air Force) had written of him that he was 'as brave as six, as good-humoured, shrewd, self-confident & considerate as a statesman can be', and had added that Churchill was also apt to 'chuck the statesmanlike course & do the honest thing instead'. There were not many politicians of whom that could be said. During his time as a minister in Lloyd George's administration, whether as minister of Munitions, or at the War Office or Colonial Office, it was Churchill's outstanding courage which gave such significant support to the Prime Minister – during the crisis on the Western Front in March 1918, over Ireland, the Middle East or Turkey. Churchill, like Nelson, believed that the boldest measures were the safest. 'I am sure the path of courage,' he told Lloyd George in June 1921 referring to the Irish question, 'is the path of safety,' and again in February 1922 he insisted that action must be determined by what was best for the nation and the Empire: 'Decisions must be taken, & those who take them must not shirk from facing the consequences.' Apart from his courage and the sheer range of his responsibilities, he excelled as an administrator and won golden opinions from subordinates and colleagues alike for the skilful way in which he ran his various departments. As an orator, too he was in a class of his own, most particularly in the House of Commons. He showed himself to be a superb parliamentarian, prompting Austen Chamberlain to commend to the King Churchill's contribution to a debate on Ireland as being 'a speech faultless in manner and wording, profoundly impressive in its delivery and of the first consequence as a statement of policy. It gripped the attention of the House from the opening sentences and held it, breathlessly intent, to the end.'

In the same year of Churchill's fall from office, Adolf Hitler was just beginning to make felt the force of his oratory, and the strength of his will. Hitler's demagogy was somewhat cruder than Churchill's. In November 1922 he told an audience in Munich:

The Marxists taught – If you will not be my brother, I will bash your skull in. Our motto shall be – If you will not be a German, I will bash your skull in. For we are convinced that we cannot succeed without a struggle. We have to fight with ideas, but, if necessary, also with our fists.

Such inflammatory stuff earned him a rebuke from the Bavarian Minister of the Interior, Franz Schweyer, and although Hitler assured the Minister that he would not 'make a putsch', Schweyer warned him that if he went on making such speeches, 'the stream will one day burst loose of its own accord . . . and you will swim with it.' Hitler, however, continued to spout his propaganda, and although there were still many years of waiting, when the stream did burst loose, it was not against Hitler, but for him.

Churchill's defeat in the general election of November 1922 had one significant benefit – it gave him time, time to rest, time to ponder, time to paint and to write, and time to oversee the rebuilding of Chartwell into the home he wanted. For about a year after losing his seat he lay fairly low on the political scene, but by November 1923 he was eager to re-enter the House of Commons, still in the Liberal interest. During this year the two volumes of his *The World Crisis* had been published. Sales were good, reviews numerous and generally favourable. T.E. Lawrence called it 'the best war-book' he had read in any language. The Prime Minister, Stanley Baldwin (who had succeeded the ailing Bonar Law in May), to whom Churchill had sent a copy of the second volume, wrote to express his thanks and observed that if he himself could write as Churchill did, he would not bother to make speeches. On one of the principal political issues of the day, however, Baldwin and Churchill were at odds. On 25 October 1923 – anniversary of the Battle of Angincourt and of the Charge of the Light Brigade at Balaclava, in which Churchill's regiment, then the 4th Light Dragoons had played a leading part – Baldwin had declared that there must be a return to protectionism in order to reduce unemployment, and a little more than two weeks later made it known that he was going to hold a general election. Churchill, who had always been a firm advocate of free trade, had reiterated his view that its continuance was 'vital to the British people and indispensable to the recovery of their prosperity'. He accepted the invitation of the West Leicester Liberal Association to stand as their candidate in the election, but on 6 December, when the poll was held, he was defeated by the Labour candidate, Frederick Pethwick-Lawrence, to whom Churchill then observed that 'it is a victory for Free Trade'. Although he had at this time adhered to the Liberal Party, six months earlier, when asked by Sir Robert Horne (whose appointment as Chancellor of the Exchequer under Lloyd George had so irritated Churchill), about his political position, Churchill had replied that he was what he had always been, 'a Tory Democrat', and that although circumstances had obliged him to serve with others, 'my views have never changed, and I should be glad to give effect to them by rejoining the conservatives'. The opportunity to do so was not to be long in coming.

Although Baldwin's Conservative government remained in power after the election despite the loss of nearly a hundred seats, in January 1924 it was defeated in the House of Commons, and Ramsay MacDonald formed the country's first Labour government. Two months later Churchill stood in the by-election for the Abbey Division of Westminster, but despite his declarations of wishing 'to work effectually with the Conservative Party in resistance to the rapid advance of Socialism', and the support of many leading Tories, the local Conservative Association had selected Otho Nicholson as its candidate. It was therefore difficult for the Conservative supporters to vote against their party's chosen candidate in favour of Churchill, who was standing 'on his own', and Nicholson won by the narrow margin of forty-three votes.

In August and September 1924, while Churchill was working away at Chartwell – creating a new lake, observing that the moorhens were migrating there and writing to his wife that the Chartwell pigs were earning their keep in the sales, taking his son, Randolph, to lunch with Lord Rosebery, where they discussed the prospect of Churchill's writing a biography of his great ancestor, the first Duke of Marlborough – the offer of a seat in the Conservative interest at Epping was made to him. He accepted it. Later in September, he spoke at a meeting of Scottish Conservatives in Edinburgh. In that speech, he declared that Liberals and Conservatives – between whom there was no difference of principle – should join to defeat the Labour Party, which by making a treaty with the Soviet Government had aided terror and tyranny in Russia. The policy of the Labour Government was such that, 'We are to render these tyrannies possible by lending to their authors money to pay for the ammunition to murder the Georgians, to enable the Soviet sect to keep its stranglehold on the dumb Russian nation, and to poison the world, and as far as they can the British Empire, with their filthy propaganda. That is what we are asked to take upon ourselves. It is an outrage on the British name.' Churchill further contrasted Labour's warm attitude to Britain's enemies with its coldness towards the Dominions, and firmly called for opposition to such a policy. This speech, says Martin Gilbert, 'marked his public emergence as a supporter of the Conservative Party, and heralded his return to full-time politics'. Churchill did not confine his warnings to spoken condemnation of the Labour Party, but in a magazine article – for whose technical data he had received the help of Professor Frederick Lindemann, who was to play such a prominent part in Churchill's wartime premiership – wrote not only of the dangers of further European conflict but also of the potential and frightening power of new weapons. Quite apart from Russian ambitions of regaining territory,

From one end of Germany to the other an intense hatred of France unites the whole population. This passion is fanned continuously by the action of the French Government. The enormous contingents of German youth growing to military manhood year by year are inspired by the fiercest sentiments, and the soul of Germany smoulders with dreams of a War of Liberation or Revenge.

It was precisely these sentiments which, at this same time, Hitler sought further to arouse by the very propaganda he was making about the Treaty of

Versailles and the November criminals. In his article, Churchill went on to say that although France was well armed and Germany largely disarmed, yet 'physical force alone, unsustained by world opinion, affords no durable foundation for security. Germany is a far stronger entity than France, and cannot be kept in permanent subjugation.' In 1924, not many men in public life were predicting the future with such uncanny accuracy. Moreover, Churchill actually foresaw both the power of the atomic bomb and the devastating menace of what the world would come to know as Hitler's V weapons (from *Vergeltungswaffe*, revenge weapon), the V-1 pilotless aircraft and V-2 guided rocket:

> May there not be methods of using explosive energy incomparably more intense than anything heretofore discovered? Might not a bomb no bigger than an orange be found to possess a secret power to destroy a whole block of buildings – nay to concentrate the force of a thousand tons of cordite and blast a township at a stroke? Could not explosives even of the existing type be guided automatically in flying machines by wireless or other rays, without a human pilot, in ceaseless procession upon a hostile city, arsenal, camp, or dockyard?

His article even warned of the dangers of chemical warfare, and, in stressing how crucial it was to avoid future war, particularly in the light of such terrible advances in military technology, spoke out with great force on the vital need to support the League of Nations,[1] despite America's indifference, Russia's contumely, Italy's rejection, the uncertainty of France and Germany – and, indeed, his own hitherto apparent neglect. Although it was not yet in a position to safeguard the world: 'To sustain and aid the League of Nations is the duty of all. To reinforce it and bring it into vital and practical relation with actual world-politics by sincere agreements and understanding between the Great Powers, between the leading races, should be the first aim of all who wish to spare their children torments and disasters compared to which those we have suffered will be but a pale preliminary.' Alas, like so many of the warnings Churchill was to give in the coming years, this one, although widely distributed and enthusiastically read, had little practical effect.

When Churchill was next in a position actively to influence affairs, he found himself more concerned with financial matters and making economies than with military strategy on the world stage, although he maintained, as always, a

---

[1] An international organization, established at the Paris Peace Conference in April 1919 to maintain peace and settle disputes between nations without recourse to war. Having no armed force, it relied on sanctions to bring agressor states under control – a system which proved singularly ineffective. Although both weak and largely discredited, the League did enjoy some successes.

deep interest in foreign and defence policy. When the Labour Government was defeated in the House of Commons on 8 October 1924 – the issue was the Government's reluctance to prosecute the editor of a Communist newspaper who had urged soldiers to disobey orders – Ramsay MacDonald called for a general election. During the lead-up to the election itself on 29 October, Churchill made it clear that he supported the Conservative Party whole-heartedly, and the election resulted not only in his being handsomely returned for Epping (his majority was almost 10,000), but also in a triumphant victory for the Conservatives. On 4 November King George V asked Baldwin to form a government, and on the following day the latter talked with Churchill.

After an exchange of pleasantries, Baldwin asked Churchill if he were willing to help, and received the reply, 'Yes, if you really want me.' He was, however, determined that he would only join the Government if a position of real standing were offered to him, but even he was surprised when the Prime Minister asked if he would serve as Chancellor of the Exchequer. After some further exchanges Baldwin repeated his question, and Churchill said: 'This fulfils my ambition. I still have my father's robe as Chancellor. I shall be proud to serve you in this splendid Office.' There was some criticism of Baldwin's choice, but Churchill's friends rejoiced, and the Liberal politician George Lambert (a former Civil Lord of the Admiralty), in congratulating both Churchill and the country, declared that he was the 'fittest man in England' to be Chancellor. 'Winston, my boy,' Lambert wrote in his letter, 'I have got a fair instinct for politics. I think I shall live to see you Prime Minister.' As Lambert lived until 1958, he was able to see his friend fill that office not once, but twice.

In the fifth volume of his incomparable biography, Martin Gilbert tells us that during his almost five years as Chancellor – October 1924 to June 1929 – Churchill

> introduced five budgets, launched important measures of social reform, brought Britain back on to the Gold Standard, organized the Government's newspaper at the time of the General Strike, led the Government's negotiations for a settlement in the coal industry, and embarked upon a vast scheme of the de-rating of industry in order to stimulate and revive the economy. He also took a leading part in the Cabinet's discussions on defence and foreign affairs. These five years at the Exchequer marked a high point of Churchill's political influence, of his parliamentary skills, and of his personal contentment.

Gilbert devotes 265 pages to his account of Churchill's years as Chancellor. Here we must be content with selecting some of his actions, his speeches and his writings to illustrate his superhuman capacity for work, and for life.

Churchill's first Budget, which he introduced on 28 April 1925, had been eagerly awaited, and during its preparation the new Chancellor had been determined both to introduce social reform and to resist what he regarded as unnecessary naval expenditure. There was also the question of a return to the gold standard, and on this point Churchill was at first undecided, weighing most carefully the arguments for and against, but in the end – gloomy forecasts by the great economist, John Maynard Keynes, notwithstanding – acceded to the advice of his Treasury experts and, making it plain that a return to the gold standard was not 'entirely an economic matter; it is a political decision', agreed that the country should go back to it. In resisting the Admiralty's demand for a new construction programme to reinforce the Far East Fleet, Churchill dismissed the possibility of war with Japan: 'Why should there be a war with Japan? I do not believe there is the slightest chance of it in our lifetime.' As might be expected, he was just as imaginative in his ideas for not spending money on warships while Chancellor as he had been for doing just the reverse and expanding the navy when at the Admiralty. One of his more compelling arguments with regard to the defence of Singapore, important both for its naval base and as a centre of trade, was that the best way to protect the island 'was by the expansion of aerial defence rather than by the more expensive method proposed by the Admiralty of an enlarged submarine defence'. Nor did he like the idea of huge, static gun batteries for Singapore's security. He advocated heavy bombers in preference, suggesting that it would be much better to have money invested 'in mobile air squadrons rather than tied up forever to one spot on two heavy batteries'. (It may be wondered whether Singapore would have fallen to the Japanese in February 1942 quite so easily – or indeed at all – had Churchill's idea of deploying substantial air resources there been taken up and vigorously pursued.) In preparing his 1925 Budget, Churchill was anxious to save money on defence in order to drive through his proposals for health insurance and pensions, together with a reduction in income tax. In his Budget speech he stressed his endeavour to 'balance it fairly in the scale of social justice as between one class and another', so that its benefits would be 'national'. He hoped that income tax relief would produce more wealth for the expansion of industry, and that the security for the 'mass of wage-earners, their wives and children', enhanced by the insurance and pension schemes, would 'promote contentment and stability, and make our Island more truly a home for all these people'.

His speech was acclaimed by many, not least by the Prime Minister in his letter to the King. Baldwin wrote of Churchill's endurance – he spoke for more than two and a half hours – his lucidity in explaining financial details, and when it came to tariff reform, a subject on which Churchill had always held strong views, 'he indulged in witty levity and humour which come as a refreshing relief in the dry atmosphere of a Budget speech'. It can have been no surprise to those who were familiar with the Chancellor's style of speaking that, when it came to expounding his pension scheme for widows and mothers, he should have 'soared into emotional flights of rhetoric in which he has few equals'. It was an illustration not only of what a great parliamentarian Churchill was, but that he also possessed 'the versatility of an actor'. Lord Mildmay found it the only Budget speech of the forty he had heard which had held his interest throughout. Two weeks after his presentation of the Budget, when speaking at the British Bankers' Association dinner, Churchill emphasized the need for a policy which would not simply be one of party, but should be national. He made it clear that the Government's aim was to 'help every class and section' of the country and, what is more to build 'financial and social plans upon a three or four years' basis instead of a few months' basis'. He was at least in office long enough to pursue this aim, although his interests and activities inevitably stretched to far wider horizons.

Any objective commentator must constantly be filled both with wonder and admiration at Churchill's capacity for work, and the range of his vision. While his duties in 1925 varied from organizing a settlement of the mining industry, negotiating with France and the United States about the repayment of war debts, and preparing the ground for his next Budget, he was also pondering the problems of Britain's international obligations and how to minimize the risk of further European conflict. In giving his opinion at meetings of the Committee of Imperial Defence, Churchill warned his colleagues that whereas Germany might be willing to tolerate the Versailles terms governing her western frontier, this would certainly not be so where her eastern border was concerned. He recommended the establishment of demilitarized zones between Germany and France, and Germany and Poland. Moreover, he said, the historical rivalry of France and Germany had not disappeared; what guarantee was there that they would not again find themselves at war? 'It may not be for twenty years, certainly not until Germany has been able to acquire some methods of waging war.' Churchill's view was that the Versailles Treaty would have to be amended, particularly with regard to Germany's eastern frontiers – which, of course, could affect both Poland and Czechoslovakia (the latter, like the former, a new republic established in 1918). He was opposed to a unilateral undertaking to come to France's assistance in the event of attack, for a war between France and Germany, an 'Armageddon No 2', would be such that 'victory . . . would compass our ruin scarcely less surely than defeat'.

Eric Hoffer observed that 'the only way to predict the future is to have power to shape the future'. He went on to say that those who possessed absolute power could prophesy, and make their prophecies come true; they could even tell lies and make these become truths. In 1925 Churchill certainly did not have anything like absolute power, yet he had a most uncanny knack of making prophecies which came true. We find him saying that sooner or later Germany would rearm, and then, because of German military adventure, possibly 'aggression against Poland', Britain would be drawn into war against Germany by her obligation to support France. This in turn could lead to German control of the Channel ports. What would then happen would depend on who possessed the most effective weapons. In another remarkable prophecy, Churchill continued: 'If in addition to sea superiority we had air supremacy, we might maintain ourselves as we did in the days of Napoleon for indefinite periods, even when all the Channel ports and all the Low Countries were in the hands of a vast hostile military power . . . It should never be admitted in this argument that England cannot, if the worst comes to the worst, stand alone.' Fifteen years later he was to show that with himself at the head of the country's affairs he could make this claim come true. Another observation he made at this time was perhaps more prosaic, but none the less equally important, and in view of his office of more immediate significance then. 'The main object of all Governments,' he maintained in a speech at the Mansion House on 15 July, 'was to effect a continuous rise in the comfort level of the mass of the nation'.

It would, it must be said, be difficult to imagine two men more unlike in appearance, inclination, habit, distraction, friendships, beliefs and character than Winston Churchill and Neville Chamberlain, the Minister of Health in 1925. Yet the latter – having himself been Chancellor from 1923 to 1924, a post he was to hold again under Baldwin from 1931 to 1937 – astutely summed up several of the former's great qualities in writing to the Prime Minister about Churchill's performance during his first nine months as Chancellor. Chamberlain commented on Churchill's ability to exert influence in Cabinet, without either attempting to dominate or intrigue for the leadership, and acknowledged his strength in debate in the House of Commons and his general contribution to the Government's prestige. 'What a brilliant creature he is! But there is somehow a great gulf fixed between him and me which I don't think I shall ever cross. I like him. I like his humour and his vitality. I like his courage . . . But not for all the joys of Paradise would I be a member of his staff! Mercurial! a much abused word, but it is the literal description of his temperament.' It must be said, too, that Churchill himself would not have been displeased to read these comments. Nor would he have been dissatisfied to learn that Beaverbrook, by now nearing the height of his influence as a newspaper owner, had told Mackenzie King, the Canadian Prime Minister, that Churchill was gaining more and more influence over Baldwin, going so far as to say that the Chancellor 'practically is the Government'.

Shortly after Churchill had introduced his second Budget in April 1926, a dispute between mine owners and the miners – caused by the miners' fear that their wages would be reduced – a fear that had been exacerbated by the report of a Royal Commission, the Samuel Report, in March, which recommended changes and reforms, but also called for a cut in wages – came to a head. While the owners insisted on a wage reduction in order to minimize their losses, the miners' requirement was for a minimum wage nationwide, and they rejected a proposal for longer hours for the same wage. On 1 May not only did the miners reject the owners' wage-reduction plans, but the Executive of the Trades Union Congress declared that a general strike, in which transport workers, printers, builders, heavy industrial workers and engineers would be called out in support, would begin at 11.59 pm on 3 May. For the Cabinet the issue became one of an unconstitutional threat to parliamentary democracy, and when it became clear that the threatened strike would affect either the content or even the printing of national newspapers, it was determined that an emergency news-sheet should be published with the assistance of newspaper editors. It was hardly surprising that into the production of what was to be called the *British Gazette* Churchill threw himself with all the energy, zeal and administrative skills of which he was capable – taking command of every difficulty, dictating articles, organizing newsprint, almost forcibly enlisting expert printing technicians, and generally behaving, as the editor of the *Morning Post*, H.A. Gwynne, put it, like Napoleon. But throughout it all Churchill drew an important distinction between the question of defeating a general strike – which was essential for the survival of parliamentary government – and the settlement of the coal dispute, which could be done by negotiation. Moreover, to ensure, where necessary, the security of communications and installations, he proposed that units of the Territorial Army (as the Territorial Force had been renamed in 1922) should be incorporated into the volunteer police forces. The men would wear not uniform but armbands, and be equipped with truncheons, not firearms. This thoroughly practical, common-sense proposal to employ what was effectively a non-military force was accepted by the Prime Minister. The *British Gazette* was duly published and distributed, and by 11 May more than a million copies were being read daily by the public. That day's issue made it plain that things were going well for the Government – supplies reaching their destinations, railways running (albeit only partially), ships unloading at the docks, special constables plentiful, lorry convoys moving with armoured-car escorts, newspapers printing again. On the following day the TUC decided to call off the General Strike.

In anticipating this result, Churchill characteristically advised the Prime Minister that once the strike was abandoned, a resumption of negotiations with the miners could be contemplated; the two must not be concurrent, however. (Always ready with the telling phrase, 'Tonight surrender. Tomorrow magnanimity' was how he put it.) The last issue of the *British Gazette*, which appeared on 13 May and sold over 2 million copies, inevitably contained an article by Churchill, which announced that the newspaper had fulfilled its purpose: 'It becomes a memory; but it remains a monument.' His own contribution to its success was recorded by John Davidson, the Parliamentary and Financial Secretary to the Admiralty (and a former Chancellor of the Duchy of Lancaster), who wrote of Winston's boundless energy and his desire to produce a newspaper which would rival the great organs of normal times: 'The result was, I think, quite good, and the energy and vitality of Winston were very largely responsible for it. He is the sort of man, whom, if I wanted a mountain to be removed, I should send for at once . . .' Churchill's teasing sense of fun was never far from the surface, and when he spoke in the House of Commons about the production of the *British Gazette* during the General Strike, and referred to the possibility of another such strike and another trial of strength, working himself into an attitude of solemn defiance of the Labour benches and with a manner pregnant with drama, he threatened them with 'another *British Gazette*', whereupon the House collapsed with laughter. In describing the scene to the King, Baldwin's letter summed the moment up thus: 'Mr Churchill's whole attitude had led the Labour Party to believe that they might expect one of his fulminatory and warlike declarations with reference to tanks, machine-guns and all the armed forces of the State, and the complete bathos contained in his final words was a consummate jest which no one appreciated more than the victims at whose expense it was effected. It was a happy ending to a good-humoured debate.'

The General Strike did not help the miners in their struggle for shorter hours, better wages and other concessions; indeed, starvation obliged them to return to work without gaining any of their objectives. The overall effect was that strikes throughout industry became rarer. Wages remained stable and unemployment fell. The cost of living was reduced, and 'as a result,' writes A.J.P. Taylor, 'the British working man, except for the miner, was better off in 1929 than he had ever been before'. Taylor goes on to point out that between 1924 and 1929 Baldwin's government was firmly established by its 'safety first' policy, a euphemism for a style of government of which Lord Melbourne would have approved – do as little as possible. Yet this period of economic stability, even relative prosperity, was accompanied by an increase in production and high interest rates. Taylor is not kind, however, about Churchill's handling of affairs, and says that his 'budgets were balanced only by sleight of hand. He raided the Road fund which had accumulated a surplus; juggled with the sinking fund;[1] advanced the date for the payment of income tax; and

---

[1] Government revenues invested as a reserve with which to meet long-term debts or charges.

allowed the unemployment insurance fund to run steadily into debt. His budget speeches provided much entertainment and some futile expedients, such as the attempt to tax betting. Churchill's years at the Treasury were indeed the weakest in his varied career.'

It is doubtful whether Churchill himself would have endorsed this view for, as was customary with him when he was in office, he thoroughly enjoyed his five years as Chancellor. As usual he was bouncing with energy, enthusiasm and activity. In January 1927 he leaves for a cruise of the Mediterranean, taking his son, Randolph, with him (not long before he had told Randolph, on receiving a birthday present from him, how much he would prefer to 'hear something creditable about you' from his masters at Eton). During this trip he works on the third volume of *The World Crisis*, plays polo (for the last time) in Malta, and meets Mussolini. His first impressions of the Italian dictator and of Fascism itself are surprisingly favourable, and his saying so publicly causes the inevitable criticism from the left-wing press at home. On his return, Churchill introduces his third Budget in April with such obvious enjoyment – his speech being notable for its dramatic eloquence, mischievous buoyancy and financial dexterity – that the press begins to carry cartoons of 'the smiling Chancellor', while Baldwin writes to the King that 'his enemies will say that this year's budget is a mischievous piece of manipulation and juggling with the country's finance, but his friends will say that it is a masterpiece of ingenuity'.

During the rest of 1927 Churchill wrestled with schemes for improving the country's economic position; spent time at Chartwell painting, building, enjoying his friends' visits, starting work on the book which became *My Early Life*; and spoke often in the House of Commons, thereby giving much entertainment to all its members – Neville Chamberlain recalled an occasion when, because of the Opposition's repeated interruptions, Churchill once more turned events to his advantage:

> 'Of course it is perfectly possible,' he said, 'for Hon'ble members to prevent my speaking, and indeed I do not want to cast my pearls before . . .' he paused and then concluded 'those who do not want them,' in a roar of delight that lasted several minutes.

Chamberlain conceded that Churchill was unequalled as a speaker in the House of Commons. Certainly his speeches were looked forward to by members as superb entertainment, if nothing else, a point confirmed by Baldwin, who wrote 'Winston's position is curious. Our people like him. They loved listening to him in the House, look on him as a star turn and settle down in the stalls with anticipatory grins. But for the leadership, they would turn him down every time . . .'

One of Churchill's pet schemes for reviving the economy was to reduce the burden of local rate charges, and especially those affecting certain industries. In order to compensate for the loss of revenue, however, it would be necessary to cut government expenditure elsewhere, and his eye turned once more to defence costs, particularly those of the Royal Navy. Although he did not succeed in getting agreement to all the economies he sought, the naval programme was sufficiently modified for him to press ahead with his de-rating proposals. Another of his concerns at this time was the cost of the mechanization of cavalry regiments, as tanks and armoured cars replaced horses, and he summed up the whole question of the Defence Estimates in a note to his wife: 'No more airships, half the cavalry, and only one-third of the cruisers.' There was considerable disagreement between Churchill and Chamberlain (who, as Minister of Health, was also concerned with reforms in local government, one of which was the de-rating proposal) as to exactly how the de-rating scheme should be applied. Churchill wanted agriculture to be totally free of rates, while industry and the railways would enjoy relief of three-quarters of the rate levied. As the revenue thus forfeited would be made up by the Government and by ratepayers who did not qualify as contributing to the nation's 'production', the whole scheme was, as A.J.P. Taylor pointed out, a devious method 'of subsidizing industry at the expense of the taxpayer'. Broadly, Churchill's views prevailed, and in his Budget speech of April 1928, his fourth, he was able to propound his ideas to the House and the nation:

Under our present arrangement, unemployment, distress, and pauperism increase, and to meet that the rates are raised. Industry flies from these districts or else withers and dies. Who would start a new industry in such a district? . . . We have to face the fact that unemployment remains obstinately chronic round the dismal figure of 1,000,000, and all those basic industries which used to be the glory of these islands are under a serious eclipse . . . We cannot possibly give the reliefs which are needed to industry, unless in reimbursing the local authorities, we put ourselves, the central Exchequer, in a firm and secure financial position . . . You cannot have the new reliefs without the new taxes and the new reforms. No one can take out of this scheme the parts he likes and reject the parts that do not suit him. Everyone who approves of the general plan must take the rough with the smooth . . .

Once again Churchill received widespread praise for his performance, which had lasted for a formidable three and a half hours. Both Lord Tyrrell (a senior diplomat) and Lord Derby (who had been Secretary for War for the second time from 1922 to 1924) described it as statesmanlike. Illness with influenza prevented Churchill from being in the House of Commons until 5 June, when the Budget debate opened. His introduction of the Finance Bill on that day and his closing speech three days later won further praise from the Prime Minister, whose letter to the King referred to the restraint, competence and clarity with which the Chancellor explained the benefits of his plan and demolished the Opposition's criticism. But already Churchill was preparing for his fifth Budget, and once again the vexed question of defence expenditure was foremost in his mind. At a meeting of the Imperial Defence Committee on 5 July 1928, he brought up the Ten-Year Rule, proposing that its principle should be confirmed, that it should advance from day to day (in other words, that the ten years should run from each succeeding year), and be reviewed every year by the Committee. In response to a request from Baldwin, the Foreign Secretary, Austen Chamberlain, reviewed the world situation, and gave it as his opinion that war with France or Italy or Germany was not to be imagined, that Japan was not at that time a menace, and that the one area of uncertainty was Russia. The Committee concluded, therefore, that 'it should be assumed for the purpose of framing the Estimates of the Fighting Services, that at any given date there will be no major war for ten years'. As it turned out, this was a valid assumption for the year 1928, and certainly from Churchill's point of view ensured that there would be no unnecessary extravagance in defence spending. Whether the assumption could properly or sensibly be renewed annually was another question, as was also the notion that sticking to the Ten-Year Rule would guarantee the country's security. Nor would it be long before Churchill was both out of office and beginning to sound a series of warnings to those in power that the country's security was being culpably jeopardized.

Even before this, he had become conscious of the hostility that some of his attitudes and pronouncements were arousing amongst his colleagues, one of the main issues involved being the old chestnut of protection versus free trade. There was also the matter of Churchill's personality and character, for which he was by no means universally admired. Although he might tell his wife in a letter: 'Really I feel vy independent of them all,' this hostility was to have a profound effect on the question of who would succeed Baldwin as leader of the Conservative Party, and thus, sooner or later, become Prime Minister. Neville Chamberlain was particularly concerned when Sir Douglas Hogg, at that time the Attorney-General, went to the House of Lords (as the first Baron, later first Viscount, Hailsham), as he had regarded Hogg as the best successor to Baldwin, and with this new development, there emerged a 'dangerous possibility – *viz* the acceptance of Winston as leader'. Chamberlain's attitude to Churchill was ambivalent. On the one hand he recognized him as 'a real man of genius' whose speeches were in a class by themselves because of their 'sparkling humour and the torrent of picturesque adjectives'. There was, Chamberlain sagely observed in his letter to Irwin 'no subject on which he is not prepared to propound some novel theory and to sustain and illustrate his theory with cogent and convincing arguments. So quickly does his mind work in building up a case that it frequently carries him off his own feet.' Chamberlain also shrewdly commented that in considering matters Churchill tended to rely on his instinct for novelty and to prefer the broad brush rather than precise knowledge and careful reasoning. 'He is a brilliant wayward child who compels admiration but who wears out his guardians with the constant strain he puts upon them.' In comparing himself with Churchill, Chamberlain pointed to the deep difference between their natures. This was in 1928. Twelve years later this difference would become apparent to the entire world.

There can be few who do not admire Churchill's astonishing zest for life and versatility. During the summer recess of 1928 we find him working away at yet another volume of *The World Crisis* – this one dealing with the Versailles Treaty and the years immediately following it – while at Chartwell, where he also plays bezique, builds walls, is a generous and voluble host, and *talks*. One of his guests, James Scrymgeour-Wedderburn, puts the unique quality of Churchill's overflowing gift for enthusiastic reminiscence, and his encouragement of the young, in a nutshell when he recalls an evening at Chartwell, during which he enjoyed two hours' conversation with the great man. Having answered Churchill's question about his age by admitting to twenty-six, his host instantly seized on it as the age at which Napoleon commanded the Army of Italy, 'and he then discoursed for some time on the changes in military tactics and strategy since 1795 [in fact Napoleon took command in 1796] and stressed the importance of the revolution brought about by the invention of tanks and armoured cars, which were incomparably superior to cavalry for all purposes'. Scrymgeour-Wedderburn went on to note that when Churchill 'becomes engrossed in his subject, he strides up and down the room with his head thrust forward and this thumbs in the armholes of his waistcoat, as if he were trying to keep pace with his own eloquence. If he shows signs of slowing down, all you have to do is to make some moderately intelligent observation, and off he goes again.' It is arguable that not many men of such stature and with such responsibilities would have taken the trouble to engage a young man with his fascinating talk, or to have shown such kindliness. With Churchill it was not unusual; indeed, it was customary. He is, of course, just as much at home in royal company, writing to his wife from Balmoral in September 1928 that the Princess Elizabeth, aged two, is 'a character. She has an air of authority & reflectiveness astonishing in an infant'. In the same letter he displays not only his affectionate concern for Clementine's problems with household staff, but a practical common sense in giving advice about tackling small irritants. He points out that servants are there not to give trouble, but to save it. 'Nothing is worse than worrying about trifles. The big things do not chafe as much: & if they are rightly settled the rest will fall in its place.' Yet he would have been the first to endorse Hamlet's contention:

> Rightly to be great
> Is not to stir without great argument,
> But greatly to find quarrel in a straw,
> When honour's at the stake.

In October 1928 it was decided in Cabinet that the general election should be held on 4 June 1929. Meanwhile, there were few times when Churchill was not in some way or another concerned with defence matters and the balance of power in Europe. At this time he was opposed to the idea, sponsored by the United States, that there should be a general disarming by the Great Powers. In particular he objected to the weakening of France, which had abandoned the Rhine frontier in return for guarantees by both Britain and the United States of assistance in the event of German attack. Since it was the strength of the French Army which protected Britain from the danger of having to intervene in a European conflict, it was necessary to maintain that strength. Churchill was equally concerned with what had been revealed about the growing power of German naval forces, and especially a new type of German battle cruiser, which both for range and fire power would outclass the planned British warships of comparable size. He therefore pressed for a delay in the British cruiser plans in order to take full advantage of developing technology.

As the time of the general election approached there was much speculation as to Churchill's future; indeed, there was great uncertainty as to the likely outcome of the election itself, with both the Liberals and Labour launching sharp attacks on Government policy. It was clear that within the Conservative Party itself there was still much opposition to Churchill's succeeding to the leadership. Yet when Baldwin and Neville Chamberlain were discussing what would be done were the election to result in a stalemate, which would mean that, to survive, the Conservatives would have to serve with Lloyd George and the Liberals. Both men made it clear that they themselves would not do this, and Baldwin therefore supposed that in such an event 'the leadership would go to Winston'.

Churchill himself had published *The World Crisis: The Aftermath* in March 1929. It sold well, and received much praise from former colleagues and friends to whom the author had sent personal copies, including Rosebery, Balfour and T.E. Lawrence (the latter urging him once more to write a biography of the first Duke of Marlborough, an idea which rapidly developed into a contractual agreement. Reviews of *The Aftermath* were generally favourable, as indeed were those of most volumes of *The World Crisis*. Isaiah Berlin has, however, reminded us that there was one critic of Churchill's great work who, writing in the previous year, had 'condemned it root and branch,' because in his view 'Such eloquence is false because it is artificial . . . the images are stale, the metaphors violent, the whole passage exhales a false dramatic atmosphere . . . a volley of rhetorical imperatives.' 'He went on to describe Mr Churchill's prose,' Berlin tells us, 'as being high-sounding, redundant, falsely eloquent, declamatory, derived from undue "aggrandization of the self" instead of "aggrandization of the theme".' Yet Berlin is quick to show how wrong this critic was: 'What he . . . denounced as so much tinsel and hollow pasteboard was in reality solid: it was this author's natural means for the expression of his heroic, highly coloured, sometimes over-simple and even naïve, but always genuine, vision of life.' Few men have been better qualified to pronounce this judgement than Sir Isaiah Berlin; there are fewer still who have succeeded so triumphantly in both making and writing world history than the subject of this particular controversy.

There was still one more Budget for Churchill to work on and present to the House of Commons, which he did on 15 April. Like some of his previous budgets, it was more noteworthy for the brilliance of its delivery than the appeal of its content. There was a tax concession on tea and an end to the betting tax, but duties were to be imposed on alcohol and tobacco manufacture. As usual, his speech was praised by his colleagues. It was no easy thing to keep 'the House fascinated and enthralled by its wit, audacity, adroitness and power' – Neville Chamberlain's words – in a speech lasting almost three hours. Churchill's great gift of oratory was further illustrated by an election broadcast, which the *Daily Express* called 'superb'. The report went on: 'His voice was edged alternatively with sarcasm and warning. There was a note in it of extraordinary intimacy with his audience. He began with statistics, merged with derision of his political opponents and ended high on the pinnacle of perfervid patriotism.' Within ten years Churchill's broadcasting skills, combined with his resolution and confidence, would do more than win the approval of newspaper reporters – they would inspire the nation. Not all his eloquence, however, could win the 1929 election for the Conservatives. As a result of the polling on 30 May, Labour won 288 seats, as opposed to 260 for the Conservatives, with the Liberals trailing at 59. After a Cabinet discussion on 3 June, Baldwin determined to resign. Churchill held his own seat, but having, together with his colleagues, handed back the Seals of Office on 7 June, he once more found himself a Member of Parliament, but not a minister. In a letter predicting that Churchill would make a strong comeback, T.E. Lawrence reiterated his wish that he should become Prime Minister.

There now followed ten years during which Churchill held no political office. During the first four of these years – from 1929 to 1933 – Adolf Hitler, who had endured many years of waiting for circumstances to develop in his favour, and had not only never lost faith in his own destiny, but had also succeeded in retaining his followers' loyalty and belief in him, at last began to savour the spoils of opportunity. It is the way in which he exploited this opportunity, together with its effect on Churchill's activities and political fortunes, which now commands attention.

There was, as has already been noted a profound difference in the views held by General von Seeckt and Hitler as regards the position of the German Army and political parties. For Seeckt, the Reichswehr was above party – 'The Army serves the State'. In his eyes the army's self-indentification with the state was absolute. He must, therefore, have felt an infinite satisfaction when, during the period of passive resistance to Allied occupation of the Ruhr in 1923, Friedrich Ebert[1] appealed to him, asking if the army would stick to the republic. 'Die Reichswehr,' he replied, 'steht hinter mir' ('The Army will stick to me'). It was in this sense, as the ultimate protector of the Reich, ready to do whatever was necessary for the Reich, that the army was non-political. This did not alter the reality of its independence, however, for it had become, in a phrase immortalized by Seeckt himself, 'a state within the State'. Hitler, on the other hand, always conscious of his need for the army's support, or at least its non-interference, in his bid for power, challenged Seeckt's doctrine that the army must distance itself from politics. In a speech he made at Munich in March 1929, he argued that it was no use for officers of the Germany Army to tolerate the ideology of social-democracy, for to do so would simply lead to the army's own dissolution. What was needed was an attitude on the part of officers which would tie them to the future of the German people. In other words, the army must support the political party which embodied the strength of the people, who in turn 'are prepared and who wish to bind themselves to this Army, in order to aid the Army some day in defending the interests of the people'. Hitler developed this argument further in his new monthly publication, *Deutscher Wehrgeist* (*German Military Spirit*), seeking to appeal to the young officers of the Reichswehr with promises of expanding the army and giving it back its prominent, honoured position when he came to power. By not supporting his nationalist movement – so went his reasoning – the army was failing to be loyal to its own traditions and was damaging itself.

These arguments clearly had some effect, for in September 1930 three officers of the Reichswehr were tried at Leipzig before the Supreme Tribunal on the charge of trying to enlist support for the Nazi Party within the army. As the Nazi Party was, by the time of the trial, the second most powerful such organization in Germany, the proceedings were bound to be of great interest

[1] Ebert remained President until his death in 1925.

to the army's generals, and this interest was further stimulated by Hitler's being called to give evidence. Hitler himself seized the opportunity to give reassurances to the army's leaders, in particular with reference to the SA. He insisted that the SA's purpose was to use its propaganda to protect the Party, not to set itself against the state; indeed, he had done all he could to stop the SA from being military in character. There was no question of trying to replace the army. What he did want, however, was that the German people and the country should 'be imbued with a new spirit', something which would come about when his party was in power, at which time a 'great German People's Army' would arise from the present Reichswehr. In answering questions put by the Court's President, Hitler stressed that power would be achieved by legal, constitutional means. Again, in explaining what he meant by the 'German National Revolution', he dismissed the need for force, since the revolution would spring from propaganda, which by itself would bring about an uprising of the German people. 'The time will come when the German nation will get to know of our ideas; then thirty-five million Germans will stand behind me.' Hitler even went so far as to say that once in power, the formation of the state in 'the manner which we consider to be the right one' would be effected by constitutional means.

In his unrivalled study of Hitler, Alan Bullock makes it clear that by the end of the year 1930, with Party members totalling some 400,000 and more than 6 million Germans voting for the Nazis in that year's elections, producing a strength of 107 in the Reichstag, 'success no longer seemed impossible. This was the measure of his achievement in 1930. He had reached the threshold of power.' There were still two years to go before he stepped over that threshold. Then, as we have seen, after Röhm had reorganized the SA, Hitler was able to make use of the threat of force, rather than force itself, together with the mass support he enjoyed and the effectiveness of his party's propaganda, to persuade President Hindenburg and his colleagues in government to enter into partnership with him, and so allow the Nazis to achieve power, so to speak, by the back door.

While Hitler was moving steadily towards the position of power which he so coveted, Churchill was beginning to isolate himself from the leaders of the Conservative Party, although his doings remained as varied and vigorous as ever. Visits to Canada and the United States occupied the three months from August to October 1929; in addition, he gave lectures, wrote articles, worked on his biography of Marlborough, and, in Parliament, expressed his concern both at the Government's policy in Egypt and at his own party's attitude to Labour's proposals for self-government and Dominion status for India. It was not only India which was a cause of Churchill's growing isolation from his former colleagues, but once more the old question of protection versus free trade. Yet his literary endeavours were not only formidable in range and volume – in the summer of 1930 he was engaged with three books: his life of Marlborough; yet another, and final, volume of *The World Crisis*; and *My Early Life* (perhaps his most universally popular book), to say nothing of newspaper and magazine articles – but formidable, too, in bringing in a substantial income.

Amidst all this political and literary activity, there occurred a great sadness in Churchill's life – the death of his old friend, Lord Birkenhead, on 30 September. A month later, at a meeting of the Other Club, which the two of them had founded almost twenty years earlier, Churchill spoke of the loss of 'our dear friend F.E.,' emphasizing that this loss was one to be felt both by Birkenhead's close associates and the country at large:

> We miss his wisdom, his gaiety, the broad human companionship and comradeship which he always displayed and excited from his friends. We admired his grand intellect and massive good sense. He was a rock . . . He loved this Club. He was always happy here . . . The country is the poorer. Just at a time when we feel that our public men are lacking in the power to dominate events, he has been taken. This was the occasion and these were the very years for the full fruition of his service to our country.[1] He had the calmness of age while still retaining the force and power of his prime, and the questions which are now most grave and urgent are the very ones in which his influence and advice, his experience, his sagacity, his long trained judgment, would have been precious.

One of the great political questions of the day was, of course, India, and Churchill had been hoping to enlist Birkenhead's support for his own opposition to the Labour Government's move towards granting Indian independence. It was over this issue, and in opposition to this policy, that in January 1931, Churchill decided to speak in the House of Commons, and thus found himself speaking against the policy of the Conservative Party. When, therefore, Baldwin spoke in favour of implementing the Indian Constitution which the London Round Table Conference[2] (which that month had been attended by the Congress Party leaders) had recommended, Churchill felt that the differences between him and his party leader, now made public, obliged him formally to resign from the so-called 'Business Committee' of Conservative leaders, which met for discussion and the formation of policy, and over which

[1] Birkenhead's last post in government had been as Secretary of State for India from 1924 to 1928.

[2] A series of conferences, beginning in November 1930, to discuss the future constitutional status of India. A number of prominent members of the Indian Congress Party, including its leader, Gandhi, attended the conference held in January 1931. The last of these round-table discussions was in 1932.

Baldwin presided. A few weeks earlier Churchill had written of the chilling of his relations with Baldwin, of his own hostility to being part of a future Baldwin administration which would pursue protectionist policies at home and what he regarded as fatal policies for India. 'I shall be much more able to help the country from outside,' he said. Baldwin accepted his decision, which meant, as Martin Gilbert puts it, that 'For the first time since November 1924 Churchill was cut off from the central workings of the Conservative Party, and from the formulation of its policies.' This breach, however, in no way prevented Churchill from making known his views about the Indian problem, nor from voicing his increasing disquiet about the activities and growing strength of the National Socialist Party in Germany.

As early as October 1930 Churchill had told the German Ambassador in London, Prince Otto von Bismarck (a descendant of the Iron Chancellor and father of modern Germany), of his concern about the way in which Hitler and the Nazi Party had brought about a dangerous worsening of Germany's external relations, and in particular with France and Poland. Although France had a large army, the mere fact that work on the construction of the Maginot Line along her eastern frontier had started in 1929 was an expression of her inherent fear of Germany. As to Poland, when that country was established as an independent republic in 1918, the city of Danzig (now Gdansk), then in East Prussia, was declared a Free City under the Treaty of Versailles, and came under the administration of a League of Nations Commissioner. The purpose was to give Poland a sea port, and access was provided by a 'corridor' to the city from Poland, also guaranteed under the terms of Versailles. German objections to the Polish Corridor were not justified, however, for Poland required 'an outlet to the sea'; moreover, railway traffic between East Prussia and the rest of Germany passed freely across the Corridor. Bismarck recorded that although 'Hitler had admittedly declared that he had no intention of waging a war of aggression; he, Churchill, was convinced that Hitler or his followers would seize the first available opportunity to resort to armed force.' Churchill's foresight, we might say, was as powerful and accurate as the Führer's *Vorhersehung.* Both of them had an eye on the *Anschluss* – literally, union, but in this case meaning Germany's planned annexation of Austria – but they looked at it from very different points of view. Even before Hitler became Chancellor, Austria and Germany had, in March 1931, established a Customs Union. Churchill instantly saw the dangers which might arise, for (as he wrote in a newspaper article) the Customs Union could herald 'union between the German mass and the remains of Austria,' and once these two countries were one, two other European states would feel themselves threatened – France and Czechoslovakia. In the case of France, the prospect of a 'solid German block of seventy millions producing far more than twice her number of military males each year, towering up grim and grisly, luckily as yet largely unarmed,' was not something to be treated lightly. After having been repeatedly invaded by Germany and having 'only escaped destruction the last time because nearly all the other nations of the world came to [France's] aid, which they certainly do not mean to do again, [the French] cannot help feeling anxious about this ponderous mass of Teutonic humanity piling up beyond the frontier.' As for Czechoslovakia, she had three and a half million subjects who were Austrian or German – if the Anschluss were to take place she would effectively be threatened by Germans from three sides.

In his article, Churchill was as good as predicting exactly what Hitler would do when, first, he had come to power, and, second, had built up his armed forces so that he could make that power felt outside Germany. The accuracy of Churchill's vision may be judged by a discourse Hitler made to his War Minister, the Commanders-in-Chief of the three armed services, and his Foreign Minister at the Reich Chancellery in November 1937 (which will be examined more closely later), during which he expressed his determination to solve Germany's problem of *Lebensraum* (living space). The precise date at which he would launch this operation would depend on circumstances, he said, but might be as early as 1938; the principal and most urgent objectives would be the overthrow of Austria and Czechoslovakia. These two countries were not just milestones on the road to a Greater German Reich, but furnished critical strategic advantages in denying the West opportunities to threaten Germany from her southern flank, to say nothing of Austria's twelve divisions or Czechoslovakia's economic and armament resources. Of course there might be risk, but the Great Powers would, Hitler persuaded himself, do nothing, certainly not in concert. The will was lacking. In any case, Austria and Czechoslovakia must be acquired *blitzartig schnell*, at lightning speed.

All this lay in the future, however. In June 1931 Ramsay MacDonald, the Prime Minister, told the House of Commons that he would be seeking European armament reductions at a forthcoming conference, only to be warned by Churchill that Britain's armed forces were already dangerously weak – the army little more than a 'glorified police force' and the air force a fraction of what it should be. Britain, he insisted, must be properly armed, otherwise her 'hour of weakness' would be 'Europe's hour of danger'. Two months later he was repeating in a newspaper article a point that he had often made before – 'German youth mounting in its broad swelling flood will never accept the conditions and implications of the Treaty of Versailles.' He was echoing Hitler.

The growing economic crisis in Europe during the summer of 1931 – although it strengthened Hitler's growing appeal to many Germans – produced in Britain proposals for an all-party National Government. This was duly formed under MacDonald in August, with many Conservatives agreeing to serve in a coalition with Labour. Churchill was not asked to join the administration, but so serious did he regard the economic distress that, recognizing the need to restrict the importation of foreign goods, he even relinquished his lifelong belief in free trade and recommended that tariffs should be imposed. He also tried to persuade the Liberals to support the National Government. When Lloyd George declined to commit his party to such a course, MacDonald called a general election, which was held on 27 October. As a result the Conservatives gained hugely, Labour lost more than 200 seats, the Liberal Party was split, and the National Government was confirmed in office. Although MacDonald remained Prime Minister, it was Baldwin and the Conservatives who were the real power in the administration. Churchill, who had strongly supported the National Government during his election campaign, doubled his majority, but was not included in the Government. In December he left England for the United States where, soon after his arrival, he had a serious accident, being struck by a car while crossing New York's Fifth Avenue. This meant a spell in hospital and an enforced rest for some weeks, but he was soon writing articles and lecturing again. He returned to England in March 1932, then resting at Chartwell, although still working on his biography of Marlborough and writing more articles for the newspapers. His illness in September – it was paratyphoid brought about by the accident in America – found him at Chartwell again, continuing to dictate chapters of *Marlborough* and already planning to write *A History of the English-Speaking Peoples*. One of his old friends, Professor Lindemann – who was to give Churchill such invaluable advice during the Second World War – visited him and, as Churchill's daughter, Sarah, recorded, gave him much comfort. 'He was part of our Chartwell life,' she wrote of 'the Prof'. 'It is hard to remember an occasion on which he was not present'. But as 1932 advanced more sombre matters arose, in particular what was happening in Germany.

We have already followed the process by which Hitler became Chancellor. In the summer of 1932, when the Nazis won more seats in the Reichstag than any other party, Churchill's son, Randolph, reporting on the German elections for the *Sunday Graphic*, wrote that the Nazis' success would 'sooner or later mean war', as they were determined to avenge Germany's humiliation in 1918. Once they had an army again – that is, an army restored to its former size and power, and which was one of their aims, 'they will not hesitate to use it'. While he was still in Germany Randolph Churchill tried to arrange a meeting between his father, who was touring some of Marlborough's battlefields, and Hitler. In this he was helped by Ernst ('Putzi') Hanfstaengel, a confidant of Hitler who had also helped with the publication of the *Völkischer Beobachter*,[1] the Nazi news-

---

[1] *National Observer* – in Nazi parlance, however, the adjective *völkisch* carried deliberate anti-Semitic overtones.

paper, and who was at this time very much under the Führer's spell. Nothing came of this plan in the end, for although Churchill was willing, Hitler was reluctant to meet someone 'whom he knew to be his equal in political ability'. Moreover, Churchill was no longer in office, but in opposition; 'What part does he play?' Hitler asked Hanfstaengel. 'No one pays any attention to him'. It is interesting to reflect on what might have resulted from such a meeting. Hitler, no doubt, would have realized that the British politician was not, as he subsequently described him, 'a superannuated drunkard supported by Jewish gold'. Whether he would have grasped that Churchill was, like himself, one of the most unyielding, even ruthless, men in centuries is rather less certain, but he could hardly have failed to appreciate the other's grip, range, largeness of personality and resolution. In his turn, Churchill would almost certainly have been repelled by Hitler's fanaticism, arrogance and coarseness, always supposing that the interview would not have been abruptly concluded by the Führer flying into a rage at one of Churchill's wise remarks or shafts of wit.

In November 1932, shortly after Hitler had made it clear to President Hindenburg that he and his party would support a government only if he were appointed Chancellor, Churchill warned the House of Commons to have no illusions about Germany's intentions. It was not equality of armaments or status with the other Great Powers that Germany sought:

> All these bands of sturdy Teutonic youths, marching through the streets and roads of Germany, with the light of desire in their eyes to suffer for their Fatherland, are not looking for status. They are looking for weapons, and, when they have the weapons, believe me they will then ask for the return of lost territories and lost colonies, and when that demand is made it cannot fail to shake and possibly shatter to their foundations every one of the countries I have mentioned [France, Belgium, Poland, Romania, Czechoslovakia and Yugoslavia], and some other countries I have not mentioned.

Hitler himself could hardly have summarized his own programme more succinctly. 'Wir wollen wieder Waffen!' ('We will have arms again!') had long been his cry. With weapons he would abolish the Treaty of Versailles, and extend the Reich's frontiers to include *all* Germans in territories which were now outside those borders. What Churchill was urging was to 'Tell the truth to the British people.' Yet he was, as he always had been, conscious of the need to remove the 'just grievances of the vanquished', which the *Daily Mail* argued was a far more practical way of seeking peace than pursuing the chimera of disarmament. At the same time Churchill was strongly opposed to Britain's weakening her own military position, and in a speech during the Air Estimates debate in March 1933 (that is, some six weeks *after* Hitler had become Chancellor of Germany) he spoke of the need to strengthen the country's own naval and air forces, if the British were to continue to be the 'judges' of their own future. He also urged the ending of the Ten-Year Rule. In attacking the Prime Minister, however (although it is true to say that MacDonald was largely a figurehead in the predominantly Conservative National Government), Churchill antagonized many MPs, which inevitably weakened the impact of his warnings. Undeterred, in a further speech the following month he referred to the dangers of Hitler's clear intention to rearm: 'The rise of Germany to anything like military equality with France,' he said, 'or the rise of Germany or some ally or other to anything like military equality with France, Poland or the small states, means a renewal of a general European war.' He commented, too, on the 'odious conditions now ruling in Germany' – Hitler's Enabling Bill, passed by the Reichstag in March, had given him absolute dictatorial powers, and the persecution of Jews in Germany was now plain for all to see – conditions which one day might extend to Poland. There was, of course, no question of Hitler's embarking on such an extension without having the military means to do so. But no sooner had he achieved absolute power than he embarked upon what Alan Bullock called 'Revolution after Power', a process that was to include the creation of a revolutionary Wehrmacht.

CHAPTER 4

Hitler's Path to War

I want war. To me all means will be right. My motto is
not: 'Don't whatever you do annoy the enemy!' My
motto is: 'Destroy him by all and any means!' I am the
one who will wage the war.

ADOLF HITLER

'The next war,' declared Hitler in 1932, 'will be quite different from the last
world war. Infantry attacks and mass formations are obsolete. Interlocked
frontal struggles lasting for years on petrified fronts will not return. I guarantee
that . . . We shall regain the superiority of free operations.' In the event, Hitler
more than lived up to that promise. That he did so was due to the efforts of two
men in particular – Seeckt and Guderian. General von Seeckt was Commander-
in-Chief of the 100,000-strong Reichswehr from 1920 to 1926, and during
these years he imbued it with two priceless qualities concerned essentially with
the winning of battles. The first was leadership, the second tactical doctrine. In
forming and training the Reichswehr he set out to create an army, not of
mercenaries, but of leaders – 'Nicht ein Söldnerheer, sondern ein Führerheer'.
In other words, he trained his majors and colonels so that later they could
command divisions, his lieutenants and captains so that they could command
battalions and regiments. Each sergeant and corporal was ready to become an
officer, each private and trooper an NCO. At one time, out of the total 100,000
men, nearly half were NCOs. Seeckt's great achievement was to preserve the
kernel of a greatly expanded army within the nutshell of a tiny restricted one.
Moreover, he virtually outflanked and evaded the Allied purpose of doing away
with the great German General Staff, which had been specifically outlawed by
the Treaty of Versailles.

He did even more than this, however. He had all the military training pam-
phlets rewritten, not merely so that they could serve a rearmed and powerful

German Reich, but in accordance with a principle which had in the past shown itself to be fundamental to successful military operations, and was to do so again with even greater effect. Whatever might be said to the contrary, the essence of combat does not change. Its elements have always been, are now, and will remain – fire power, movement and signalling. The need to move about, control and apply agents of violence in order to dismay or disable your opponent persists. The method and agents may change, but not the precept. And the principle which Seeckt laid down and practised was that all the major fighting arms must be closely integrated and must operate as a team. Here was the seed which later gave birth to the mixed panzer groups which perfected mobile warfare and proved so formidable in action. There was nothing new about the co-operation of horse, foot and guns – it had been the practice for centuries. But much of it had been forgotten or submerged in the mud of Flanders. Although there had even then been piecemeal tank, infantry and artillery co-operation, the need for this process to be continuous had been neglected. What Seeckt had done was to restore this battle procedure to its position of precedence. He had also brought it up to date by insisting that mechanized cavalry, infantry and artillery should not merely work as one, but should enjoy also the intimate support of anti-tank guns and aircraft. This system of battle groups – *Kampfgruppen* – combining as it did the essential elements of combat – fire power, movement and signalling – was to be a consistent feature of the new Wehrmacht from its creation, and was to prove to be as effective in defence as in attack. Not only was it the basis for Hitler's great blitzkrieg campaigns of conquest, but its application also explains how, with the initiative lost, he was able vastly to augment the Wehrmacht's capacity for resistance.

As the key to success in battle, Seeckt had always believed in mobility – in rapid movement, in the need to restore to attacking forces their rightful predominance by grand, sweeping operations which would penetrate, engulf, paralyse and annihilate the defences opposing them. Writing about warfare in the future soon after he became Commander-in-Chief, he argued that what would be paramount would be the use of relatively small but highly trained and extremely mobile armies working in co-operation with aircraft. These ideas were not sown on infertile ground, for they were taken up, studied and further developed by the man who became an outstanding panzer leader and eventually Hitler's Chief of General Staff – Heinz Guderian. Unlike many a great general before and since, Guderian was generous in attributing the sources of his tactical ideas to others, notably to the British soldier-writers and theoreticians of warfare, Fuller, Martel and Liddell Hart. These men all advocated use of the tank as an essentially offensive weapon to be supported by other arms, as opposed to its being deployed in a secondary role *in support of* these other arms. It was the tank, they insisted, properly designed, supported and employed that would restore mobility to the battlefield. In particular, Liddell Hart emphasized how effectively armoured forces could be used in long-range operations to attack the enemy's communications and support areas. He even went so far as to propose the very type of division that Guderian had in mind and would create, containing what the latter called 'panzer and panzer-infantry units'.

In developing his tactical theories Guderian hit upon the formula, both for effecting a breakthrough and exploiting it, that was to surprise, shock and cripple every European army subjected to it. To get the most out of tanks, he argued, you had to use them in mass and move them so fast that they reached the enemy's main defence zone before the guns there could intervene effectively; at the same time, enemy tanks attempting to counter this penetration must be stopped, either by overwhelming them with superior numbers or by using tactical air forces, which at all times would closely support the armoured forces, acting as a kind of mobile, instantly available artillery. This was only the prelude, however. Once the breakthrough had been made, tank and infantry teams would be deployed to mop up the artillery areas and reserve defence positions. The unique part of the whole theory lay in the concept of expanding initial depth on a relatively narrow front to a *combination of depth and width*, thus disrupting the entire enemy defensive zone. Guderian summed it all up by saying that the essentials of a decisive panzer attack were 'suitable terrain, surprise and mass deployment in the necessary width and depth'. When theory was turned into practice, as it was with the astonishing blitzkrieg successes of the Wehrmacht between 1939 and 1942, all that Guderian had foreseen came about. What is more, once Hitler had lost the initiative and was fighting defensive battles during the last two years of the war, while the British, Americans and Russians were attacking and advancing, what Guderian had said about the way to counter penetration was also shown to be true.

Guderian's revolutionary ideas about the application of speed and violence were exactly in accordance with Hitler's own concepts of waging war. Even before he saw Guderian's tank prototypes and heard him explain his tactical theories, Hitler had been expounding his own intentions: 'I shall never start a war without the certainty that a demoralized enemy will succumb to the first stroke of a single gigantic attack.' Force and fraud, as Thomas Hobbes so succinctly put it, were what mattered in war. Not only would Hitler indulge in deception and surprise, not only would he hurl himself upon the enemy 'like a flash of lightning' – hence the noun *Blitzkrieg*, lightning war – but the force and the fraud would be on unprecedented scales. In the air, he vowed, they would be supreme. A single blow would do the business, the launching of overwhelming attacks on every weak point, stupendous in their effect, a 'gigantic all-destroying blow'. What enemy, already demoralized, his will broken before the battle even started, would be able to resist? Besides, Hitler himself would be the one who would make war, not the generals. He would decide the time and place of attack. He would shrink from nothing. It might be that the war would be the most inhuman that the world had yet seen because it would be total, yet its very brevity would make it the most humane.

It was hardly surprising, therefore, harbouring ideas like these, that in 1933, when Hitler, as Chancellor, saw a demonstration of the then Colonel Guderian's blitzkrieg methods, illustrated by armoured vehicles, his enthusiasm knew no bounds. 'That's what I need,' he cried, as he watched the prototype tanks being put through their paces, 'that's what I want to have.' Here were the very weapons[1] that would carry through his designs on Europe. In *Mein Kampf* he had made frequent reference to weapons, equipment, rearmament, for without them he would never be able to carry out his aim of annulling the shameful Treaty of Versailles. Not that the reversal of Versailles would by itself bring to fruition the programme that Hitler had set himself, for he was after bigger game. Not only was he determined to get back for Germany territory that was 'rightfully' hers, but he planned more, much more – in other words, a deliberate programme of expansion. This was Hitler's foreign policy for Germany, and the goal, in the end, was Russia. *Mein Kampf* had explicitly called for a stop to the endless German drive to the south or west and for the nation to turn its gaze instead to the east, where Russia's vast empire was 'ripe for dissolution'. Despite this supposed end to westward-looking policies, however, *Mein Kampf* also called for a final reckoning, a last decisive struggle with France, but to achieve any of these objectives, east or west, Germany had to be rearmed. What is more, a new expanded Wehrmacht would have to be wholly subordinate to Hitler's will – a will which proved to be so powerful and implacable that it overrode, time after time, all the objections the German General Staff was to make.

Hitler was – or pretended to be – a great believer in pursuing the way that Providence dictated, and he followed this way 'with the assurance of a sleepwalker'. But there was much more to it than this. His leadership was bolstered by an uncanny ability to calculate the odds, a cynical disregard for both 'expert' advice and Western 'solidarity', a remarkable intuition as to what his adversaries would think and do – all coupled with the *absolute* power he attained. Believing, as he did, that force, or the threat of it, could solve any problem, he was not likely to hold back in the further creation of the very force which was

---

[1] These were the first armoured vehicles produced in Germany since the Treaty of Versailles had banned the German Army from having tanks. In 1931, Guderian had been given his first command – of a motorized battalion armed with dummy tanks and anti-tank guns.

indispensable to the realization of his aims. Within a year of coming to power, therefore, Hitler gave orders that by October 1934 the army's strength would be trebled to 300,000. Yet there was still the problem of what to do about the SA. A choice had to be made between the old army and the new, between the military force and the political one. In making this choice Hitler was profoundly influenced by the question of who would succeed the old and ailing President von Hindenburg, who was Commander-in-Chief of the Armed Forces and as such enjoyed the soldiers' loyalty owed to that office through the oath of allegiance. It was this, the sworn allegiance of every serviceman, that Hitler coveted and was determined to have for himself. Herein lay the basis of a deal between the Führer and his top military men. During naval manoeuvres in April 1934, Hitler was attended by General Werner von Blomberg, Minister of Defence, General Baron Werner von Fritsch, C-in-C Army, and Admiral Erich Raeder, C-in-C Navy. Between them a bargain was struck. On the one hand all the nonsense that Ernst Röhm had talked about the new army being based on the SA was to be scrapped so that the position of the army and navy as the Armed Forces of the State would be unchallengeable; on the other hand, Adolf Hitler would succeed Hindenburg as C-in-C Armed Forces. It did not take long to turn the idea into fact. On the night of 29/30 June, and for two days afterwards, the SA was subjected to a sudden and savagely violent 'blood purge', which came to be known, in a phrase Hitler himself first used, as 'the Night of the Long Knives'. Röhm and some scores of others from the SA were summarily shot by Himmler's SS; also killed were other rivals within the Party who were not SA, such as Gregor Strasser, non-Nazi figures like Generals Schleicher (Hitler's predecessor as Chancellor) and Kurt von Bredow, and others with whom the Führer felt he had a score to settle, such as Gustav von Kahr, who had suppressed the Munich putsch. The reason given for this welter of blood-letting was that the senior SA men, and others, had been plotting against the state – and for his action Hitler received Hindenburg's thanks for 'nipping treason in the bud and rescuing the German people from great danger'. The truth was, of course, that Hitler had crushed any potential opposition within the Party, and thereby confirmed himself as its indisputable leader; in addition, in crushing the older, more radical elements of Nazism, he had made the Party more acceptable to Germany's officer corps.

The other half of the bargain followed close upon the purge. On 2 August Hindeburg died. Within hours it was announced that Hitler would become Head of State, in which post the offices of Chancellor and President would be merged. He would also become Supreme Commander-in-Chief of the Armed Forces of the Reich; furthermore, on that very day the entire German Army swore a new oath of allegiance to Hitler *personally*: 'I swear by God this holy oath: I will render unconditional obedience to the Führer of the German Reich and People, Adolf Hitler, the Supreme Commander of the Armed Forces, and will be ready, as a brave soldier, to stake my life at any time for this oath.' 'Thou hast it now:' soliloquized Banquo of Macbeth, 'King, Cawdor, Glamis, all, . . . and, I fear, Thou playd'st most foully for't.' Hitler, too, had it all now – Führer, Chancellor, President, Commander-in-Chief – and there had never been any doubt about the foul play. Nor was there any doubt about the German people's compliance, which confirmed acceptance of the Führer by plebiscite on 19 August. And, by this time, the armed forces had grown into services of which it was worth being Commander-in-Chief.

By October the expansion of the army was well under way. Twenty-one infantry divisions had been formed, as had one panzer brigade – a year later this brigade had itself been expanded to form three panzer divisions, one of them commanded by Guderian. These divisions were all that Seeckt had foreseen – strong in tanks, and each supported by a panzer grenadier brigade (that is, motorized infantry), as well as reconnaissance, artillery, engineer, signal and anti-tank units, all themselves motorized. The principal striking power of the division was its panzer brigade of 561 tanks, but the whole formation was designed and trained for fast, bold, thrusting operations. In March 1935 Hitler announced that the German Army would in future derive its recruits from compulsory military service, and that it would total thirty-six divisions in peacetime. At the same time he also made it known to the world that the Luftwaffe – the air force which, like the tanks, Versailles had forbidden – was already at a strength of 1,000 operational aircraft, manufactured under the same clandestine rearmament programme as the tanks. He was fulfilling his promise that 'in the air we shall of course be supreme'. Hermann Göring, a distinguished fighter pilot in the Great War, had been charged with the business of creating the Luftwaffe, which was essentially a part of the blitzkrieg concept; that is to say, it was designed to support the army in the field in order to win fast-moving, short-lived offensive campaigns. It was not a strategic force consisting of long-range bombers to strike at distant targets, combined with fighter aircraft to win air superiority. What Göring had done was to concentrate on a few types of aircraft and then have them built in large numbers. There were twin-engined bombers, the Heinkel He-111 and Junkers Ju-88; single- and twin-engined fighters, the Messerschmitt Me-109 and Me-110, respectively; transport aircraft, including the famous three-engined workhorse, the Junkers Ju-52; and the notorious Junkers Ju-87 Stuka (from *Sturzkampfflugzeug*, literally, 'dive-attack aeroplane'), which combined accurate attack with machine-guns or bombs together with a terrifying, screeching howl, emitted when it dived, for phychological effect. This new German Air Force, its pilots trained under the auspices of apparently innocent sport-flying programmes, was capable of delivering accurate fire power over great distances and thus filled a gap, at least until the widespread introduction of self-propelled artillery some years later, in Guderian's concept of an all-arms team. That team now had, in the panzer and the Stuka, weapons formidable enough in their own right; together, however, they were all but invincible.

Thus the Wehrmacht[1] had acquired two revolutionary instruments of warfare, together with a revolutionary tactical doctrine to extract from them the most rewarding dividend. By now, too, it was imbued with a spirit to match its leader's intentions. In September 1935, when Hitler addressed the Party rally at Nuremberg, he seized the opportunity to make much both of Germany's great military tradition and of the army's new units parading before him. The army, he declared, was in war the nation's defiance; in peace it was 'the splendid school of our people'. 'It is the Army,' he went on, 'which has made men of us all, and when we looked upon the Army, our faith in the future of our people was always reinforced. This old glorious Army is not dead; it only slept, and now it has arisen again in you.' Yet it was in fact a very different army. The mere nature of the Nuremberg rallies themselves was sufficient to illustrate the change that had taken place. These rallies were such that they inspired all those who attended them with an indescribably powerful ardour, which was at once nationalistic and revolutionary. And, of course, the appeal of these master-pieces of mass psychology was at its greatest among the very youth of the nation which was now filling the ranks of the Wehrmacht. 'To see the films of the Nuremberg rallies even today,' wrote Alan Bullock,

> is to be recaptured by the hypnotic effect of thousands of men marching in perfect order, the music of the massed bands, the forest of standards and flags, the vast perspectives of the stadium, the smoking torches, the dome of searchlights. The sense of power, of force and unity was irresistible, and all converged with a mounting crescendo of excitement on the supreme moment – when the Führer made his entry. Paradoxically, the man who was most affected by such spectacles was the originator, Hitler himself . . .

Apart from these manifestations of power and unity, it is important to remember that in the Nazi state the entire male population from the age of six onwards was to be trained to acquire those qualities needed to become members of a revolutionary Wehrmacht – discipline, hardness, marksmanship (and other skills, such as parachuting), teamwork, leadership, and absolute devotion to the person of Adolf Hitler. The whole of their schooling from the

---

[1] On 21 May 1935, under a secret law, the Reichswehr became officially the Wehrmacht, thus symbolically severing the armed forces' links with the Weimar Republic – which itself came to an end in 1933 when Hitler assumed the Chancellorship.

Churchill as an Officer in the 4th Hussars
1895

Churchill with his mother, Lady
Randolph

Churchill family portrait
Winston, Diana, Clementine, Sarah (on lap), Randolph, Lady Randolph,
Peregrine (on lap), Lady Gwendeline, John-George, Jack

Churchill in April 1916 when a Lieutenant-Colonel

Churchill in the Cabinet Room at 10 Downing Street, 20 November 1940

On board the *Prince of Wales* at Argentia, August 1941
Front row: Sir Wilfred Freeman, Sir Dudley Pound, Churchill,
Sir John Dill, Sir Alexander Cadogen

Algiers, 3 June 1943
Left to right: Anthony Eden, Gen. Brooke, ACM Tedder,
Admiral Cunningham (behind Churchill), Gen. Alexander,
Gen. Marshall, Gen. Eisenhower, Gen. Montgomery

Churchill with General Alexander, 26 August 1944

Yalta, February 1945

Churchill at 10 Downing Street, 8 May 1945

time these young boys joined the Deutsches Jungvolk (German Young Folk) and went on to be members of the Hitlerjugend (Hitler Youth) – itself closely co-ordinated with the Wehrmacht – until, at eighteen, they actually became soldiers, was one of continuous indoctrination. It was all part of Hitler's own contention that education should be designed to produce potential soldiers. Nietzsche had spoken of the German people's readiness to be intoxicated by a leader who held before them the prospects of splendid victories and conquests. It was no surprise, therefore, that when Hitler embarked upon a series of bloodless triumphs, annexing large tracts of contiguous territory during the period 1935 to 1939, the young officers of the army were, in General Erwin von Witzleben's words 'drunk' with Hitler.[1]

In suppressing the SA (which, largely leaderless, had rapidly dwindled) Hitler had satisfied the generals on the point that the army should be the sole bearer of arms within the state, but in the event Himmler's SS, detached from the SA as a reward for its part in the purge, remained in being; and under the Reichsführer-SS (as he was now styled) also came all Germany's police forces. Despite the bargains Hitler had made, therefore, possession of the SS gave him his political army after all – and the SS contained the sort of men who would kill with a smile. The army itself was growing still, the result of Hitler's decree of March 1935 establishing universal military service and a peacetime army of twelve corps. By 1937 the number of divisions was in fact thirty-nine, three more than had originally been planned, but potentially the total was far greater, as was shown by the expansion to over a hundred divisions on mobilization in August 1939. Yet in 1935 all Hitler's talk was of peace. Hitler was adept at combining acts of menace with words of reassurance. On the very day, 21 May 1935, on which he announced the reorganization of the command structure of the armed forces – and on which the Reichswehr was formally renamed the Wehrmacht (there was menace even in the name) – with himself as Supreme Commander and each of the three services, Heer, Marine and Luftwaffe, having its own C-in-C, Hitler's speech to the Reichstag drew attention to the fact that all the blood-letting in European wars had not changed the characters of nations nor their actual existence. Thus Germany did not seek to conquer other nations. Germany both wanted and needed peace, and in its pursuit of that aim was willing to make bilateral non-aggression pacts with her neighbours. In spite of her rearmament, Germany 'respected' the non-military clauses of the Versailles Treaty. In this display of being 'reasonable', Hitler declared:

[1] In 1938, Witzleben (later a field marshal) commanded the Third Military District, which included Berlin. He was one of the conspirators who, before the Munich Agreement, planned to seize Hitler and put him on trial if he attacked Czechoslovakia. After the July 1944 attempt to assassinate the Führer, Witzleben, who was involved in the plot, was executed.

Germany has solemnly recognized and guaranteed France her frontiers as determined after the Saar plebiscite . . . We thereby finally renounce all claims to Alsace-Lorraine . . . Germany has concluded a non-aggression pact with Poland . . . We shall adhere to it unconditionally . . . Germany neither intends nor wishes to interfere in the internal affairs of Austria, to annex Austria, or to conclude an Anschluss.

This was the sort of language the Western democracies wanted to hear, and *The Times* expressed the hope that the speech would everywhere be taken as 'a sincere and well-considered utterance meaning precisely what it says'. That, in turn, was exactly the sort of reaction Hitler was hoping for. Whereas Vegetius advised that those who desire peace should prepare for war, Hitler's line was that those who desire war should persuade others to prepare for peace. This talk of peace was simply a part of his tactics in the diplomatic game, a game at which he excelled; it was just a ruse to disguise when and where he would first indulge in warlike acts. François-Poncet, the French Ambassador in Berlin, observed of what he saw as Hitler's intention to reoccupy the Rhineland that the Führer hesitated only because he was deciding when would be the right time to take action. Meanwhile, what had Churchill to say about all this? A great deal, as it happened, and most of it very much to the point.

Churchill's alarm at Nazi intentions surfaced as early as April 1933, when he warned the House of Commons of the dangers inherent in the sweeping away of Germany parliamentary democracy and its replacement by dictatorship, with all its accompanying militarism which so appealed to 'every form of fighting spirit'. In that same month he spoke elsewhere of a different sort of danger caused by Britain's own tendency to drift into an attitude of defeatism, to abandon faith in herself and be ruled by the impractical, self-wounded theories embraced by intellectuals. He asserted that nothing could save England if she did not save herself, for to lose faith in her own capacity and her own will would be to write finis to her greatness. (This might almost have been taken from that grand declaration by Philip Faulconbridge, quoted in the first chapter, that naught would make us rue, if England to itself did rest but true.) 'If, while on all sides foreign nations are everyday asserting a more aggressive and militant nationalism by arms and trade, we remain paralysed by our own theoretical doctrines or plunged into the stupor of after-war exhaustion, then indeed all that the croakers predict will come true, and our ruin will be swift and final . . .' There was not much doubt about the aggressive militancy of Nazi Germany. Quite apart from the reports received from the British Embassy in Berlin, which showed, amongst other things, that Germany was in breach of the Versailles Treaty by manufacturing military aircraft, Churchill's apprehensions were reinforced by a letter from his old friend, Alfred Duff Cooper, who had recently driven through Germany and had everywhere seen uniformed troops marching and training. 'They are preparing for war,' he wrote to Churchill, 'with more general enthusiasm than a whole nation has ever before put into such preparation.' In England, however, the political talk was all of disarmament, and the Foreign Secretary, Sir John Simon, was pressing for international agreement not only for a general reduction in armies, but also for the absolute abolition of certain categories of weapon. In the House of Commons debate of 7 November Churchill pointed out the absurdity of expecting France and other countries which felt threatened to disarm at the same time as Germany was being permitted to rearm (or, at least, was not being prevented from rearming).

During the last months of 1933 and the early ones of 1934, Churchill went on with his writing. The first volume of his *Marlborough* received the same kind of warm praise as his previous books, one admirer, Lord Riddell, making the shrewd observation that if things went on as they were Churchill would one day be writing the history of the 'Second Great War'. He continued to warn of the dangers posed by German rearmament and Nazi doctrine, pointing to the grave responsibilities of British defence ministers in providing for the country's security, and recommending, despite Hitler's having withdrawn Germany from the League of Nations, that it was to the League that they should look for some sort of international peacekeeping, not by pursuing the fruitless aim of disarmament. There was, he said, no time to lose.

In the articles he wrote and the speeches he made, Churchill consistently warned the Government against disarmament and again urged them to abandon the Ten-Year Rule, which, he said, might have been all very well in mellower days, but was quite inappropriate to the changed situation of a covertly rearming Nazi Germany. He even predicted that unless Britain put her defence arrangements in order, a situation could arise in which 'the crash of bombs exploding in London and cataracts of masonry and fire and smoke' would make plain the deficiences in the country's air defence. It was inconceivable that Britain could allow herself to reach a position where her air force was not at least the equal of 'that of any Power that can get at us'. The Government's response, however, was to propose expenditure on the Royal Air Force at a figure *lower* than that of three years earlier. Besides deprecating the state of the country's defences, Churchill again recommended the creation of a Ministry of Defence so that planning for the future of all three services could be put under a single minister. In this way it would be possible to effect the proper co-ordination necessary to counter any threat from Germany. But the Government was in no mood to adopt Churchill's ideas, however courteously they might listen to what he had to say. Lord Beaverbrook even suggested that Churchill, in speaking 'better than for years past', had come to terms with 'the part of a farewell tour of politics'. He could not have been more mistaken. Churchill's finest hour was still to come – and was not now far distant.

Churchill's sixtieth birthday fell in 1934, and even though in that same year Lady Lambton, in deprecating his own reference to himself as old, wrote that to her he was 'still a promising lad', he was deeply saddened by the death of another close friend, his cousin, the Duke of Marlborough. Whatever his personal worries or sadnesses, however, he pressed on with his warnings about Germany's growing strength and Britain's relative weakness, particularly with regard to air forces. Indeed, so concerned was Churchill about Britain's air strength, so consistent in his reasoning, so authoritative in the presentation of facts and figures (in this he was greatly helped by Government officials), so conscientious in marshalling statistics of Germany's actual and potential striking power, and so persistent in ensuring that both Parliament and the general public were aware of the dangers, that in the end even the most sceptical, reluctant and pacific-minded of his audiences were convinced that he was in the right. But it took a long time. In a debate in the House of Commons on 30 July 1934, he put before the Government four statements, all of which were unpalatable. In the first place Germany's military air force was already two-thirds the size of the RAF in Britain; second, as Germany was continuing to augment her air forces, they would by the end of 1935 be almost equal to the RAF's home strength; third, if Germany went on at the same pace – and Britain did nothing to counter the threat – by 1936 Germany would be stronger; and finally, once Germany had gained this lead, they would maintain it. In emphasizing the overriding importance to Britain of having a strong air force, Churchill said that he regarded it as the only way in which Germany could be deterred from the path of aggression. Government ministers paid little attention, however, and even Maurice Hankey, who, as Secretary both to the Cabinet and to the Committee of Imperial Defence, was well versed in such matters, gave it as his view that the imminence of the German threat was overrated: 'The peril is there all right, but will take much more than 5 years to develop in the military and air sense.' Less than two years later Hitler began his programme of expansion by marching troops into the Rhineland.

There never seemed to be a time when Churchill did not continue with his astonishing literary and journalistic output. In August he is making progress with the third volume of *Marlborough*, writing newspaper articles, embarking on his *History of the English-Speaking Peoples*, agreeing to write a film script about George V's reign, and even writing to his wife that he must find time to write a biography of Napoleon before he dies. On this last point, it may perhaps be observed that his books about himself portrayed a soldier-statesman of

Napoleonic stature. Which was just as well, for, as we have seen, in that same month Hitler had assumed supreme political and military power, and he, unlike Churchill, had Napoleonic designs. Later that year, in November, Churchill repeated his warnings to the nation, this time in a broadcast about the causes of war. Once more he pointed out that disarmament was no way to deter aggression; on the contrary, it encouraged it. The nation's choice, therefore, was the old one between submission and preparation. There could, of course, be no doubt as to the correct choice, but it had to be understood that preparation would involve 'statesmanship, expense and exertion'. Moreover, peace would depend on the collective strength of armed forces, and if an appropriate structure 'could be built up by the League of Nations at the present time – and there may still be time – it would, I believe, enable us to get through the next ten years without a horrible and fatal catastrophe, and in that interval, in that blessed breathing space, we might be able to reconstruct the life of Europe and reunite in justice and goodwill our sundered and quaking civilization.' His broadcast touched a chord in many listeners, and its effect was soon to be reinforced by his speech in the House of Commons on 28 November, when he once again stressed the need for Britain to put its air defences in order. In drawing attention to what German air superiority could mean to this country in terms of death, destruction and damage, he painted a strikingly horrifying picture (one which was to come all too vividly to life at a time when he was at last in charge of the nation's affairs): 'However calmly surveyed, the danger of an attack from the air must appear most formidable.' Such an attack, he continued, might encompass the prolonged and intensive bombing of London, with tens of thousands of people being killed, while incendiary bombs would set fire to buildings. Nor would London be the only target – industrial towns, dockyards, storage depots would all be vulnerable. It was essential, therefore, not only to adopt new technological developments, but also to build up a powerful air force which would wreak as much damage on an enemy as he was capable of inflicting, and thereby deter attack. What was necessary, therefore, was a decision 'to maintain at all costs in the next ten years an air force substantially stronger than that of Germany, and that it should be considered a high crime against the State, whatever Government is in power, if that force is allowed to fall substantially below, even for a month, the potential force which may be possessed by that country abroad'. Baldwin, at that time Lord President of the Council, made a characteristically cautious reply for the Government, questioning Churchill's figures and reiterating the progress that would be made in increasing the number of aircraft, aerodromes and pilots. Then, having – to his own satisfaction, if to few others' – declared Churchill's claims to be exaggerated, he gave the House a pledge that His Majesty's Government would not accept 'any position of inferiority with regard to what air force may be raised by

Germany in the future'. But, as one of Churchill's advisers, Major Desmond Morton (who headed the Imperial Defence Committee's Industrial Intelligence Centre, and was an expert in such matters) explained in a memorandum to Churchill, Baldwin's figures were wrong.

While working on the next volume of *Marlborough* during the Christmas holidays, Churchill writes to his wife, who is cruising in Far Eastern waters, and observes 'What a downy bird' his great ancestor was. His adaptability, lack of pride and adroitness in 'stooping to conquer' were of great value in helping 'his world schemes and in raising England to the heights she has never since lost', although there was something pitiful in his behaviour when he was out of favour and out of power. Yet 'it is only on the field and in his love for Sarah that he rises to the sublime. Still Mars and Venus are two of the most important deities in the classical heaven.'

In his continued opposition to the India Home Rule Bill, Churchill 'linked the Government's India proposals with the threat of German rearmament' and in a broadcast about the Bill in January 1935, condemned the proposed legislation for what it was: 'It is a gigantic quilt of jumbled crochet work. There is no theme; there is no pattern; there is no agreement; there is no conviction; there is no simplicity; there is no courage. It is a monstrous monument of shame built by the pygmies.' Beyond that, however, he also pointed out that other European countries, friendly to Britain, were flabbergasted at what appeared to them to be absolute folly. 'The storm clouds are gathering over the European scene,' he declared.

> Our defences have been neglected. Danger is in the air . . . The mighty discontented nations are reaching out with the strong hands to regain what they have lost; nay, to gain a predominance which they have never had . . . Is this, then, the time to plunge our vast dependency of India into the melting pot? Is this the time fatally to dishearten by such a policy all those strong clean forces at home upon which the strength and future of Britain depends?

It was Curzon who had long before declared that as long as Britain ruled India, she would remain the greatest power in the world, but that if India were lost, this country would at once decline to the status of a third-rate power. All the ports and coaling stations, the dockyards and fortresses, the Crown colonies and protectorates would go – 'For either they will be unnecessary, or the tollgates and barbicans of an Empire that has vanished.' In supporting his son Randolph's attempt to win, in a by-election set for January 1935, the constituency of Wavertree as an Independent Conservative, Churchill spoke in a comparable vein for, like Curzon, he too regarded the potential loss of India as something only to be contemplated with the very deepest anxiety and distress about our country and its future. There are times when I, and many of you, must feel it may be impossible to stem the adverse tide; but then there always comes back across our minds a surge of strong and unquenchable faith that we can do it if we try, the confidence that our destiny is still in our own hands, and the consolation that if we do our best while life and strength remain, we shall be guiltless before history of a catastrophe which will shake the world.

His support for Randolph, however, was unavailing; indeed, by splitting the Conservative vote, his son had succeeded only in letting the Labour candidate in and arousing the ire of his own party. Yet if this incident provoked only dissatisfaction with his son, Churchill was grateful to him in another respect, in that Randolph had persuaded his father to speak in the House of Commons in a more conversational manner, and to eschew the more grandiloquent and literary style which he had been at such pains to cultivate over the years.

By March 1935 it was clear that some of Churchill's warnings about Britain's defence deficiencies had found their mark, for the Government White Paper on the subject heralded the expenditure of a further £10 million, which so angered Hitler that he refused to receive the Foreign Secretary, Simon, whose proposed visit to Berlin was thereby delayed. Although Churchill described this modest addition to defence spending as a sign that the Government 'tardily, timidly and inadequately have at last woken up to the rapidly increasing German peril,' he supported the Government in the debate about it on 11 March. By the time he was once more urging the Government to do more about air defence, Hitler had, as we have already noted, declared his policy of military conscription and the consequent expansion of the German Army, which he claimed amounted even then to half a million men. All the more relevant, therefore, was Churchill's reminding the House of Commons, during the Air Estimates debate a few days later, that had the Government paid attention to his recommendations two years earlier, and again in 1934, to increase the size of the air force, the British would not now find themselves 'in our present extremely dangerous position'. It was ironic to learn that, shortly after this debate, Hitler himself confirmed all that Churchill had been saying. While talking to Sir John Simon and Anthony Eden, (at that time Minister without Portfolio for League of Nations Affairs) in Berlin, the Führer declared that Germany had achieved air parity with Britain. In a letter to his wife Churchill called this a 'political sensation' vindicating all that he had said. His suspicion that in fact Germany was already well ahead of Britain, and was building aircraft so rapidly that this superiority would continue to grow, was soon confirmed by further reports from Berlin, and in another letter to Clementine, dated 11 April, he repeated the point that his statements of the previous November had been as accurate as Baldwin's denials had been false. 'There is no doubt,' he wrote, 'that the Germans are already substantially superior to us in the air, and that they are manufacturing at such a rate that we cannot catch them up.' He went on to say how discreditable it was for the Government to have allowed itself to have been so misled, and to have misled the country in a matter so vital to its security. Germany was now the greatest armed power in Europe, and it could only be hoped that joint Allied action would prevent her from seeking 'a plunge into a terrible contest'.

Although the need for some sort of collective action was clear enough, *A Statement Relating to Defence*, the White Paper just referred to, was designed to make the country wake up to the dangers with which Japan, Italy and Germany were confronting the world by putting its faith and effort, not in collective security, but in armed force. In this design it was largely ineffectual, for neither the increase in defence spending, nor indeed the international reaction to what the European dictators were actually doing, did anything to deter Hitler and Mussolini from taking further risks and embarking on new adventures. Hitler's announcement that the new German Army of thirty-six divisions would be based on conscription and that the Luftwaffe, which already had a thousand operational aircraft, would be further expanded, should have sounded warning enough. The response from Britain and France was feeble. It is true that a conference at Stresa, attended by British, French and Italian Prime Ministers and their Foreign Secretaries in April 1935, which aimed to discuss forming a common front against Germany in the light of Hitler's refusal to be bound any longer by the Versailles-imposed limitations on rearmament, produced plenty in the way of words about preventing the breach of international treaties, but nothing in the way of action. The three powers may have reiterated their allegiance to the Locarno Treaty (which in 1925 had guaranteed both the Franco-German and Belgian-German borders), but the means to enforce such guarantees were simply not there. The only significant steps taken to check aggression were the pacts of mutual aid concluded between France and the Soviet Union, and between the Soviet Union and Czechoslovakia. Hitler, meanwhile, made one of his speeches to the Reichstag, deploring war, appealing to the longing of the Western democracies for peace, and offering to limit German naval strength to 35 per cent of that of the Royal Navy. Britain's readiness to be deceived was illustrated by the signing of just such a naval treaty in June 1935. In the same month Baldwin replaced MacDonald as Prime Minister when the former resigned. There were few Cabinet changes. Sir Samuel Hoare became Foreign Secretary and Philip Cunliffe-Lister (who became Lord Swinton that year) Secretary of State for Air, but, as he had himself foreseen, there was no place for Churchill. Indeed, he condemned the Anglo-German naval treaty, and continued, especially after becoming a member of the Air Defence Research Sub-Committee, to press for urgent action both in developing radiolocation[1] of hostile aircraft and in setting to rights Britain's air offensive capability. 'Every day counts,' he told Cunliffe-Lister. 'We are moving into dangers greater than any I have seen in my lifetime; and it may be that fearful experiences lie before us.'

Quite apart from the German menace, Churchill had made it clear that ever since the Stresa Conference, it had been apparent that Italy was preparing to embark on the conquest of Abyssinia. Furthermore, he added, even if Britain attempted to persuade Mussolini that such a course of action would result in her hostility, it would do little good because 'Mussolini, like Hitler, regarded Britannia as a frightened, flabby old woman . . . incapable of making war.' Equally undeterred by the condemnation of the League of Nations, and its imposition of limited sanctions, Mussolini duly invaded Abyssinia, without a declaration of war, on 4 October, which as it happened was the opening day of the Conservative Party Conference at Bournemouth, at which Churchill took the opportunity to press once more for rearmament while there was still time, urging that the necessary measures should include reaching air parity with Germany, strengthening the Royal Navy and organizing British industry so that it could rapidly adjust to war production. He also paid generous tribute to Baldwin, and in a subsequent exchange of letters advised the Prime Minister 'to go to the country at the earliest moment', meanwhile pledging his support.

As the general election, set for 14 November, approached, Churchill continued with his warnings about Germany – which he stressed was a far greater danger than Italy – both in his speeches and articles. One particular article in the *Strand* magazine was very blunt about Hitler himself, and brought complaints from German officials in London. In it, Churchill properly pointed out that the Führer's rise to power, and his exercise of it, had been boosted not just by love of Germany, but by hatred of other countries, and indeed of Germany's own people if they were also Jews or intellectuals or socialists or trade unionists. Churchill also drew attention to the manner in which these two hatreds manifested themselves – on the one hand, the establishment of great training areas for Hitler's revolutionary army, together with innumerable airfields for the ever expanding Luftwaffe; on the other, the use of concentration camps to subdue those Germans who fell victim to Hitler's totalitarianism. The great question, therefore, was what would Hitler do. Would he, in his triumph at the head of a great and powerful state, nurse these hatreds and

[1] A former name for what came to be universally known as 'radar' – RAdio Detection And Ranging.

grievances, or would he turn away from the ideas of aggression and struggle? For Churchill, though, whatever 'words of reassurance' Hitler might utter, there were still 'the rifles, the cannon, the tanks, the shot and shell, the air-bombs, the poison-gas cylinders, the aeroplanes, the submarines'. And soon Churchill would himself put paid to any remaining doubts about Nazi Germany's belligerent intentions by predicting Hitler's next aggressive move. Before that, however, the general election was held, resulting in a Conservative victory and, for Churchill himself, an increased majority. He continued, too, with his literary work, now helped by 'a young man of great historical distinction,' Bill Deakin (who was later to distinguish himself both as a gallant soldier in war and a brilliant academic in peace[1]). In January 1936 while on holiday in Morocco, Churchill calculated that Hitler would before long put his own strength and the Western democracies' weakness to the test by reoccupying the Rhineland, something – like German rearmament – specifically forbidden by the Treaty of Versailles. On 20 January, King George V died and was succeeded by his son, Edward VIII. Churchill was still in Morocco at the time, but returned to England a few days later. It would not be long before all his warnings about Hitler's intentions, and Nazi Germany's military capabilities, were to be direly realized.

Adolf Hitler had always believed in the policy of force and fraud described in the seventeenth century by Hobbes, and in his next political manoeuvre he pulled off one of the most colossal pieces of bluff in history. He had long adopted the technique of disguising his aggression as a programme designed essentially for the defence and security of the Reich. Thus it was that his withdrawal of Germany from the League of Nations and its Disarmament Conference in October 1933 had been presented as a reluctant response to Allied recalcitrance in limiting armaments: peaceloving Germany, saddened by the failure of her efforts to promote international disarmament, was obliged to quit Geneva, and the League (she had only been a member for seven years). It was the level of Allied military strength, combined with France's prolongation of compulsory military service, that had made German rearmament necessary in the first place – to restore her equality of rights, to underwrite her sovereignty, to put an end to intolerable humiliation. But if Hitler's pacific protestations were one thing, his actual strategy was another. One of his favourite expressions, used to define how he would achieve his aims, was 'so oder so,' in this way or in that. In other words, if one method failed to solve a problem, he would try another. One feature, however, would remain common to any method – force, or the threat of force, had to be a part of it. All those statesmen from other European states who took comfort from Hitler's soft words

[1] And with whom, many years later, I had a most enjoyable lunch at Brooks's.

and 'peace overtures' would have thought again if they had heard what he had confided to his friend Hermann Rauschning:[1]

> I am willing to sign anything. I will do anything to facilitate the success of my policy. I am prepared to guarantee all frontiers and to make non-aggression pacts and friendly alliances with anybody. It would be sheer stupidity to refuse to make use of such measures merely because one might possibly be driven into a position where a solemn promise would have to be broken. There has never been a sworn treaty which has not sooner or later been broken or become untenable. There is no such thing as an everlasting treaty. Anyone whose conscience is so tender that he will not sign a treaty unless he can feel sure he can keep it in all and any circumstances is a fool. Why should one not please others and facilitate matters for oneself by signing pacts if the others believe that something is thereby accomplished or regulated? Why should I not make an agreement in good faith today and unhesitatingly break it tomorrow if the future of the German people demands it?[2]

It was in this spirit that Hitler set about realizing his aim of reoccupying the Rhineland. In his conciliatory speech of 21 May 1935 he not only pledged that Germany would 'uphold and fulfil all obligations arising out of the Locarno Treaty', but specifically promised that the Rhineland would not be remilitarized. Three weeks *before* his speech, the Defence Minister, General von Blomberg, had on Hitler's orders issued a directive to the armed services for the preparation of plans to reoccupy the demilitarized zone of the Rhineland. All that remained was for the Führer to choose the timing for an operation which would, by now, have been planned in the greatest detail. That timing would in turn depend upon either inventing or seizing some pretext to justify an act of aggression long since determined on.

Hitler's excuse for defying the Locarno Pact[3] soon presented itself. He had already condemned the Franco-Soviet mutual aid pact of the year before as being incompatible with Locarno's undertakings, and when the French

---

[1] Before the war, Rauschning was for a time leader of the Nazis in Danzig. Once a close friend of Hitler, he repudiated him and Nazism, and fled Germany.

[2] Rauschning's evidence might be borne in mind by John Charmley and Alan Clark, and other revisionists who maintain that Churchill should have made peace with Germany in 1941. Can anyone really suppose that with Russia subdued, Hitler, with all his new weapons, would not have turned his attention back to Britain? See later.

[3] The series of treaties resulting from the Locarno Conference were all signed on 1 December 1925. The most important of these guaranteed the French-German and Belgian-German borders and the demilitarized Rhineland; it was signed by Belgium, France and Germany, with Britain and Italy as guarantors.

Chamber of Deputies ratified this treaty on 27 February 1936, Hitler had his pretext and was able to determine his timing. On 7 March one division of German troops occupied the Rhineland; a much smaller force, three battalions only, moved west of the Rhine to Trier, Saarbrücken and Aachen (Aix-la-Chapelle). This move had not been welcomed initially by the German General Staff. The generals and the Führer regarded the army in very different, even opposing, lights. For Hitler, the army's purpose was to prepare for and wage war, not just to guarantee peace, and for this purpose it had to be imbued with the proper sort of spirit and dedication. Generals, however, like most soldiers in history, were all for avoiding war. A large, honoured, privileged and powerful army supporting a strong and respected Reich, to that they would agree; even to rapid, limited, military success; but by and large they counselled caution. When, in this instance, the Chief of General Staff, General Ludwig Beck, advised Hitler to declare that no defences would be constructed west of the Rhine, and the Defence Minister, Blomberg, wished to come to some under-standing with the French under which both countries would agree not to garri-son the border areas, Hitler contemptuously dismissed such weak-kneedness. Moreover, the outcome of the reoccupation (and remilitarization) of the Rhineland seemed wholly to justify his aggressive boldness.

When, at midday on 7 March, Hitler announced to the Reichstag that Locarno was invalidated and that German troops were re-entering the Rhineland – all part, mind you, of Germany's quest for a peaceful solution to Europe's problems – the effect on the assembled members, as recalled by William Shirer, was all that the Führer could have wished for:

> All the militarism in their German blood surges to their heads. They spring, yelling and crying, to their feet . . . Their hands are raised in slavish salute, their faces now contorted with hysteria, their mouths wide open, shouting, shouting, their eyes, burning with fanaticism, glued on the new god, the Messiah.

Although Hitler is vowing, first, never to allow the German people's honour to be compromised by force; second, to work tirelessly for an understanding with Germany's western neighbours, meanwhile giving assurances that he would make no more territorial demands in Europe and that Germany would never break the peace – even while he is saying all this, the French Ambassador (who, together with his British and Italian colleagues, had been briefed by Baron Konstantin von Neurath, the German Foreign Minister, about the invalidation of Locarno and the need to remilitarize the Rhineland) is sourly commenting that even as Hitler struck his adversary in the face, he made fresh overtures for peace. The cheering of the Reichstag members was not echoed by the generals, who simply could not believe that France, with her overwhelmingly more powerful army, would not take military action to oppose and reverse Hitler's move. Yet she did not.[1] The fact that they did not do so represented a triumph for Hitler – not simply over the Western political and military leaders, whose lack of resolution and timidity for action he had so sagely diagnosed. It was, too, a triumph over his own generals, and immeasurably added to his predominance over them when it came to contemplating further aggressive adventures. Sir John Wheeler-Bennett makes the point that although, after the Rhineland gamble, which in Hitler's eyes paid off so handsomely, the generals might continue to express their professional doubts as to the Führer's intuition and *Vorhersehung*, 'they made their protest with an increased lack of assurance and with the growing and sickening fear that he was right and they were wrong'.

Yet even Hitler was to concede that had the French made a move in strength, he would have had no choice but to withdraw again. While making this admission, however, he was not slow to emphasize that it was only his own 'unshakable obstinacy and amazing aplomb,' together with his iron nerve, which had enabled him to make threats that unless the situation eased, he would send a further six divisions into the Rhineland, when in fact he had only four brigades (that is, one division plus three battalions) in place. Hitler was one of the few men who would bluff by exaggerating his military strength, where most others tend to bluff by concealing their actual hand. In the event France, like Britain and her co-guarantor of Locarno, Italy, preoccupied with the Abyssinian crisis, did nothing except reinforce the Maginot Line – a wholly defensive and ineffectual gesture. By reoccupying the Rhineland Hitler had gained a major strategic advantage. When war finally came his principal strategic problem was how to enjoy security on one front while waging war on another – and it was possession of the Rhineland – that is, a measure of security on his western front – which started off the whole grim sequence of events.

Churchill, always possessed of a sure grasp of strategy, was quick to see it. Two days after Hitler's move, he spoke in a debate on the Defence White Paper (which had heralded increases in all three services and recognized the need for joint security with other states), welcoming this as a step in the proper direction. Although shortly afterwards – to his own disappointment and his friends' disgust – Sir Thomas Inskip was appointed to the post of Minister for Co-ordination of Defence, when Churchill spoke again in the House of Commons on 6 April, he put his finger on the peril now facing Europe as a result of the Rhineland's reoccupation. He foretold the building of the Siegfried Line, along

---

[1] In his *English History 1914–1945*, A.J.P. Taylor maintains that the French never intended to oppose the German move, as they were militarily incapable of doing so. Certainly the French Army's performance in 1940 does much to support this contention.

Germany's western frontier, and with it not just the fact that the Germans would be able to economize on forces in the Rhineland in the event of war, or strike strongly through Belgium and Holland from there, but also – more imminently dangerous, if less directly so to the west – German security in the west augured ill for the Baltic states, Poland, Czechoslovakia, Yugoslavia, Romania and Austria. In short, he said, the whole strategic balance in Central Europe would now be changed.

Before examining how Hitler set about changing the strategic balance in Germany's favour to such an extent that it seemed as though *Weltmacht* (world power) might actually be within his grasp, and how it came about that it evaded his grasp, in large measure because of the courage, defiance and resolution of Churchill, it is perhaps helpful to recall the nature of these two men, so wholly different in character, in taste and in purpose. Alan Bullock, in his great study of the Nazi dictator, tells us of Hitler's view of himself as a man who knew all about painting, architecture and music. He would always attend the Bayreuth Festival (he all but worshipped Wagner), liked operettas and films, eating cream cakes and chocolates, flowers, pretty women, but above all he liked talking, preferably at the Berghof (the vast villa he had built at Berchtesgaden in southeastern Bavaria, on the border with Austria) or in the Chancellery in Berlin. 'There he sat and talked about every subject under the sun until two or three o'clock in the morning, often later. For long periods the conversation would lapse into a monologue, but to yawn or whisper was to incur immediate disfavour.' Hitler cared little for, indeed, was indifferent to, what might be called the pleasures of life – clothes, food, tobacco, wine, tender emotions, good company, social gatherings. What interested him was power, and he had no scruples about either getting it or using it. His creed hinged upon the leadership principle, the *Führerprinzip*, which Seeckt had so nurtured in the Reichswehr, and which in the end meant, as Hans Frank expressed it, that the German Constitution was 'the will of the Führer'. About Hitler's extraordinary willpower and its effect on others there was never any doubt. Soldiers like Guderian and Colonel-General Franz Halder[1], who opposed his strategic recklessness and were prepared to say so to his face, were united in acknowledging it. Admiral Dönitz made a point of avoiding Hitler's headquarters in order to stay away from his uncanny powers of persuasion, and Göring freely admitted that when face to face with the Führer and determined to oppose some project of his, he dared not do so for 'my heart sinks into my boots' – this, moreover,

---

[1] Halder, Chief of the General Staff at the time, was sacked for disagreeing with Hitler over the attack on Stalingrad in July 1942. Implicated in the plot against Hitler almost exactly two years later, he was first kept in solitary confinement for several months before being sent to Dachau concentration camp, from which he was liberated by US forces in 1945.

from a man decorated with the coveted Pour le Mérite (Germany's highest gallantry award) for exceptional bravery in action. Alan Bullock calls Hitler 'a consummate actor' who possessed the 'ability to express the most rapidly changing moods, at one moment smiling and charming, at another cold and imperious, cynical and sarcastic, or swollen and livid with rage'. However cynical he may have been about the manipulation of others, about the use of psychology, surprise and force, about the inferiority of the masses, about morality or human suffering, he was never in any doubt about his own historical greatness, about his mission. It is Bullock again who points out that while this sense of mission was combined with the ability ruthlessly to calculate the odds, Hitler was successful. It was when success went so much to his head, when his previously intuitive foresight was so overshadowed and expelled by belief in his own infallibility, that, like Napoleon, he began to live in a world created by his own imagination, to ignore facts and to embark upon military adventures absurd in concept and doomed in execution. Once his longing for *Weltmacht* had been proved to be clearly unattainable, its alternative, *Niedergang* – ruin – took its place as an aim in itself. Never was Hitler's evil character more starkly illustrated than by the blood lust which accompanied his last days, and indeed had been a feature of his entire conduct of war. Whether revelling in the destruction of Warsaw in 1939, at a time when its fall was already certain, or whether indulging in bloody revenge after the July Plot of 1944, his lust for blood seemed insatiable. Heavy casualties in his own personal bodyguard division in Russia brought from him the exultant cry: 'Losses can never be too high! They sow the seeds of future greatness'. It is little wonder that Churchill called Hitler 'this monstrous abortion of hatred and defeat'.

To turn the gaze on Churchill himself – or perhaps for a moment to see him through the eyes of Bill Deakin – is to bring an utterly different human being into view. During a conversation with Martin Gilbert in 1976, Deakin recalled what it had been like to work for the great man at Chartwell forty years earlier:

> He would start the day at eight o'clock in bed, reading things, reading proofs. Then he started with his mail, which he would clear fairly rapidly before going back to what interested him . . . If there was something he wanted to hear about I would sit at the desk in his library and read to him. At luncheon he did not come downstairs until the guests were there . . .
>
> His lunchtime conversation was quite magnificent. It was absolutely free for all. He did not restrain himself. After lunch if people were there he would shut off completely from politics, from writing. If he had guests he would take them around the garden. If there were no guests he would potter off into his room . . . Between five and 7 he would clear the mail he had dictated

in the morning and sign letters but still there would be no work. He might play cards with his wife or Randolph. At seven he would bath and change for dinner.

Dinner at 8.30 was the event of the day. In very good form he could hold forth on any subject – memories of Harrow, or the western front – depending on the guests. After the ladies had left he might sit up with his male guests until midnight . . .

At midnight when the guests left, *then* he would start work . . . to three or four in the morning. One felt so exhilarated. Part of the secret was his phenomenal power to concentrate – the fantastic power of concentrating on what he was doing – which he communicated. You were absolutely a part of it – swept into it.

Even this relatively miniature portrait of Churchill at his home, wholly organized and adhering to a disciplined timetable, provides evidence of his sheer humanity and versatility. When we add to it Sir Isaiah Berlin's contention that 'no man has ever loved life more vehemently and infused so much of it into everyone and everything that he has touched,' we see at once how utterly different was Churchill's love of life – of pleasure, of people, of work, of creating his own vivid, exuberant, rich and solid world, full of achievement, enjoyment and historical significance – how different this was from Hitler's *Weltanschauung*[1] of hatred, revenge and destruction. Hitler sought to create world history by turning everything upside-down, by building a sort of life for the few out of the deaths of the many. Churchill stood essentially for peace and order.

Although reoccupation of the Rhineland in 1936 did not in actual fact turn the world upside-down, it was the first step along the road to doing so. Hitler was always concerned to show that his power was based on support from the masses, and as with all his subsequent aggressive foreign-policy coups, he invited the German people to pass judgement on this one by plebiscite. Nearly 99 per cent approved. It was, of course, an easy matter for the Germans to adjust themselves to the changing balance of power in Europe. The process was less agreeable for Germany's neighbours. Meanwhile, there was a distraction, which not only divided opinion in the Western democracies, but gave Hitler and Mussolini the opportunity to try out some of their latest weapons of war. In July 1936 there began the Spanish Civil War.

German intervention in Spain on the Nationalist side provided the Wehrmacht with an opportunity to try out in practice some of the basic blitzkrieg tactics that Guderian had so eloquently propounded in theory. The

---

[1] World-view, hence a comprehensive philosophy of life and the universe.

nature of the country and the type of fighting did not allow panzers to be used to their maximum effect, however – that is, in large numbers – yet this very restriction had its own benefit for the Germans. Allied tactical thinking was profoundly influenced, in that the French Chief of Staff, General Maurice Gamelin, drew comfort from his conviction that there could be no armoured breakthroughs, for the tanks were not sufficiently independent of other arms and anti-tank guns would always stop them – or so he deduced from the panzers' performance in Spain. The British CIGS, Field Marshal Sir Cyril Deverell, thought likewise, and dismissed German tanks as fit only for the scrap heap. With the Stuka, however, it was a very different story. Not only was its effect in the hands of the Condor Legion shattering, but the Luftwaffe was able to practise the business of keeping up with the leading troops by exploiting the mobility provided by transport aircraft. The lessons thereby learned by the Germans – and later practised only by them – were to pay large dividends later.

Despite Gamelin's inability to see the potential of armoured forces boldly used *en masse*, Churchill, who accompanied Gamelin during French manoeuvres in September 1936, was impressed by what he saw and recorded his feeling that the 'strength of the nation resides in its army'. Hitler's view was a very different one, and as he was later to say: 'I place a low value on the French Army's will to fight. Every army is a mirror of its people . . . After the first setbacks it will swiftly crack up.' It was a prediction which, when it came to the test, was to prove all too accurate, while Churchill's faith in the French Army was to be utterly shaken. (Whatever his admiration for France's army, it cannot have been much comfort to him to hear that, in that same month, his old friend and colleague, Lloyd George, during a visit to Hitler at Berchtesgaden, had called the Führer 'the greatest German of the age', although it is certain that the recipient of this fulsome tribute, whose vanity was limitless, wholly agreed with it.) He continued, however, with his campaign of urging the Western democracies to prepare themselves to oppose aggression, no matter from what quarter. He did so in a speech in Paris, and again in the House of Commons in November, when he stressed the need for Anglo-French co-operation and for a joint front to be established against possible aggression, for without such combined action there could be no settlement. 'All the nations of Europe will just be driven helter-skelter across the diplomatic chessboard until the limits of retreat are exhausted, and then out of desperation, perhaps in some most unlikely quarter, the explosion of war will take place, probably under conditions not very favourable to those who have been engaged in this long retreat.' He could hardly have painted more vividly or more accurately a picture of what was to occur in less than three years' time.

Churchill reiterated the urgent need to make good serious deficiencies in

Britain's forces during the defence debate of 11 and 12 November. He pointed to the army's deplorable lack of modern weapons, particularly tanks, anti-tank and anti-aircraft guns and wireless sets. Both in quantity and quality British equipment was far inferior to that of other European armies, as well as the US Army. Moreover, the Government's continued refusal to create a Ministry of Supply could only further aggravate the problem of ensuring a proper flow of munitions. He again drew the House's attention to Britain's dangerous inferiority to Germany in the air. In sum, Churchill's speech was a comprehensive assault on the Government's defence policy – or lack of proper policy – as it had persisted for years. He asserted that the Government's primary duty – to ensure national security – had been neglected, and added that, given the substantial Parliamentary majorities which the Government enjoyed, there could be no justification for the prolonged delay in putting Britain's defences in order. He could hardly believe that the House of Commons could have failed for so long to react to the continued errors made by the Government, and unless it did so soon, 'it will have committed an act of abdication of duty without parallel in its long history'.

It was during another act of abdication and all the controversy accompanying it – when King Edward VIII decided to give up the throne in order to marry the twice-divorced American socialite Wallis Simpson, – that Churchill showed once more how loyal a friend he could be, even at the expense of antagonizing many of his political colleagues and personal friends. In standing by the King, however, Churchill wholly misjudged the mood of the House of Commons, and when he pleaded for 'time and patience' at Question Time on 7 December, the hostility was such that Lord Winterton called it 'one of the angriest manifestations I have every heard directed against any man in the House of Commons'. Churchill himself was badly shaken, although his subsequent speech on 10 December, by which time the abdication had been decided on (it was formally announced on the following day), did much to mitigate the ill effects of his earlier intervention. After paying tribute to the King's personal qualities, he referred to the overriding need to look forward and 'to give to His Majesty's successor that strength which can only come from the love of a united nation and Empire,' for 'Danger gathers upon our path.'

Churchill was not exaggerating, for the danger was growing. In January 1937, having completed his first four years as Chancellor, Hitler was able to indulge in a self-adulatory address to the Reichstag during which he thanked Providence for assisting him, once an unknown soldier in the war, successfully to restore to Germany her honour and her rights. There was, of course, more to the restoration of Germany than this enhanced standing amongst the world's nations; there was also the economic miracle, which was unequalled by any other country. It may be commented here that this economic recovery was not brought about simply for the health of the nation. Its purpose was to enable the strongest and most effective Wehrmacht to be created in the shortest possible time. The armament programme was the key issue of German politics – arms, munitions, matériel of every kind were to be manufactured rapidly and in quantity. Everything else was to be subordinated to this purpose, provided this purpose was not itself compromised by the neglect of other matters. It is from this point – Hitler's clear priority to build the Wehrmacht into an instrument indispensable to a policy of expansionism – that it may be judged whether or not he was bent on war.

While Hitler is congratulating himself in the Reichstag, Churchill is working on Marlborough, painting, and urging the Government to hasten its armament programme. He is also mourning the loss of another great friend, Ralph Wigram, who, as an assistant Under-Secretary at the Foreign Office, had been very diligent in supplying his friend with information that would assist him in his fight for the nation's security; according to his widow, Wigram had regarded Churchill as 'the greatest Englishman alive'. That same month Churchill also hears from Lord Rothermere, who has seen Hitler at Berchtesgaden, that the Führer claims the German Army to be better than it was in 1914, and the Luftwaffe to be the strongest air force anywhere. In February, although there is a general welcome for the Defence White Paper which announces expenditure of £1,500 million over the next five years, Churchill warns the House of Commons that plans to spend money will not change the actual dangers of 1937 and the following two years. He could not have picked with greater accuracy the years of Hitler's bloodless victories, which were to be followed by naked aggression and blood-spilling war. In March another great friend and former colleague, Austen Chamberlain, dies and in writing to his widow Churchill speaks of their long association of nearly forty years: 'I feel that almost the one remaining link with the old days indeed the great days has snapped.' Another change is imminent. Baldwin announces in April that he will give up the premiership after King George VI's coronation,[1] and on 26 May he is succeeded by the Chancellor of the Exchequer, Neville Chamberlain; there is, however, still no post for Churchill. Now approaching his sixty-third birthday, he is beginning to find that he has reached an age at which friends and colleagues begin to die. But if further proof of his magnanimity were required, it is shown by what he wrote about the Labour politician Lord Snowden on his death. In thanking him for his obituary notice, Lady Snowden refers to Churchill's 'generosity to a political opponent [which] marks you for ever in my eyes the "great gentleman" I have always thought you'; she adds that there is no

[1] On Edward VIII's abdication his brother, Prince Albert, Duke of York, was proclaimed King. He was crowned as George VI on 12 May 1937.

one to whom she can turn with more confidence were she to be in trouble. Herein, once again, is the utter contrast between Churchill's innate generosity of spirit and the vindictiveness of Hitler's nature.

As it happened, that vindictiveness was about to be put into practice, for in July 1937 Blomberg issued, on Hitler's orders, a directive to the three Commanders-in-Chief which specified deploying a panzer army to 'eliminate' Austria or Czechoslovakia. The cynical opportunism of this directive is well illustrated by such wording as: 'The politically fluid world situation... demands constant preparedness for war on the part of the German armed forces... to make possible the military exploitation of politically favourable opportunities should they occur.' The directive went so far as to make plans for several circumstances of general war. A French attack on Germany – *Fall Rot*, Case (Operation) Red – would mean that the main German effort would be in the west; *Fall Grün*, Case Green, was designed for 'a surprise German operation against Czechoslovakia in order to parry the imminent attack of a superior enemy coalition. The necessary conditions to justify such an action politically and in the eyes of international law must be created *beforehand*'; a third option, *Fall Otto*, catered for armed intervention in Austria. All this pre-planning was not to be wasted. Since one of the principal aims of Hitler's foreign policy was the incorporation into the Reich of *all* Germans, Austria and Czechoslovakia (the latter with its large population of German-speaking former Austrian subjects in the Sudetenland) were clearly primary targets. The neighbours of both countries, notably Italy and Poland, would have to be mollified, but this should not be too difficult. Cementing the Berlin-Rome Axis should assist with a takeover of Austria, and reassuring negotiations with Poland should ease the passage of any operations against Czechoslovakia. 'Danzig,' Hitler told Colonel Józef Beck, Poland's Foreign Minister, 'ist mit Poland verbunden' – 'Danzig is tied up with Poland.'

While Hitler's military plans were thus in course of preparation, Churchill was still arguing that the British Government was not only guilty of underestimating the dangers, but by its general attitude of non-intervention, as well as the country's weakness in armaments, was actually encouraging 'those savages to acts of aggression and violence of every kind'. He is nonetheless determined 'to go my own way and to act independently in order to further the safety of our country and of the civilization without which we cannot survive as a nation'. Meanwhile his truly astonishing literary output continued – *Marlborough*, *A History of the English-Speaking Peoples* and *Great Contemporaries* were all in the process of being written or revised, while at the same time he wrote numerous articles for newspapers and magazines, many of which were concerned with defence matters and the likely behaviour of Germany. His private correspondence was equally prolific, and often equally concerned with those subjects. In replying to Lord Londonderry[1] who had written saying how he wished Chamberlain had made Churchill Minister of Defence, as he would have seen that the country developed the strength necessary to deal with Hitler and Mussolini, Churchill once more put his finger on the German dictator's intentions:

> We certainly do not wish to pursue a policy inimical to the legitimate interests of Germany, but you must surely be aware that when the German Government speaks of friendship with England, what they mean is that we shall give them back their former Colonies,[2] and also agree to their having a free hand so far as we are concerned in Central and Southern Europe. This means that they would devour Austria and Czecho-Slovakia as a preliminary to making a gigantic middle Europe-block. It would certainly not be in our interests to connive at such policies of aggression.

It was somewhat ironical that at this time Maurice Hankey, the Cabinet Secretary, and a man just as concerned as Churchill about the deficiencies in Britain's defence programme, should have taken exception to what he regarded as Churchill's use of confidential information supplied to him by Government officials in attacking the policies of the very Government which these same officials served. Hankey sent what Churchill described as 'a lengthy lecture' on the subject; as Martin Gilbert points out, however, the whole issue depended upon an interpretation of where duty lay. The officials concerned felt it was their duty to keep informed the one man with whom so-called 'official secrets' were safe and who would make such valuable use of them in the national interest; while Churchill was in no doubt that it was *his* duty to spur the Government into action. 'Churchill had long warned,' writes Gilbert, 'that 1938 would be the year when Hitler could do what he wanted, unless there were a radical change of attitude and planning in Whitehall. These changes had not taken place . . . On every major issue of defence, Churchill's facts had proved accurate, and his persistent warnings vindicated.' Those warnings continued. At the beginning of November 1937 he was predicting that because of the failure to take proper measures in 1934 and 1935, the consequences of this failure would shortly be felt. As was always the case with him, however, Churchill did not despair, for he judged that 'the spirit of Britain is reviving. The working people are ready to defend the cause of Liberty with their lives.' He added that what he wanted was

---

[1] The Marquess of Londonderry had been Secretary of State for Air from 1931 to 1935.

[2] These were (as they were then known): Cameroons, New Guinea, Samoa, South-West-Africa, Tanganyika and Togoland. In 1919 they were ceded to the Allied Powers under the Treaty of Versailles, to be ruled as League of Nations mandates.

'to see the British Empire preserved for a few more generations in its strength and splendour,' although this would only be achieved by 'the most prodigious exertions of British genius'.

Without doubt, all these exertions were going to be needed, for at about the same time as Churchill was reflecting as to how history could guide one's day-to-day judgement and courses of action, Hitler was holding forth on his intended future policy, the policy which was so profoundly to affect world history. A relatively small audience – except for Colonel Friedrich Hossbach, his adjutant, only five men, the War Minister and C-in-C of the Wehrmacht, Blomberg, the three service Cs-in-C, Fritsch, Raeder and Göring, and the Foreign Minister, Neurath – heard Hitler's proposals on 5 November. These amounted to nothing less than a blueprint for acquiring the *Lebensraum* of which Hitler had so often spoken. The aim was to secure, preserve and enlarge the racial community. Space must be carved out of the heart of Europe from territory contiguous with the Reich, and the problem would be where to carve out the greatest gain at the smallest cost. There would be antagonists to cope with, notably France and Britain, and since dealing with them would mean the use of force, there would be risk. The actual date for the commencement of operations would depend on circumstances, but might be as early as 1938. The first objectives would be to overthrow Austria and Czechoslovakia, which were not only milestones on the road to a Greater German Reich, but which offered significant strategic advantages by gaining Austria's twelve divisions and Czechoslovakia's military and industrial resources, as well as securing Germany's southern flank. In gauging the risks involved, Hitler posed the question: what would the Great Powers – Russia, France, Britain, Italy – do in the face of such German aggression? In answering his own question at some length (as might be expected, only one of those present did much talking), Hitler was able to convince himself that they would do nothing. Italy would be too much taken up with Britain and France. Russia was in thrall to Japan. Concerted action by the Powers was improbable; the will to act decisively did not exist. In any event, Austria and Czechoslovakia must be seized, and seized, moreover, with lightning speed – *blitzartig schnell*.

It has never been easy to judge precisely Hitler's real intentions in calling this meeting, and in announcing in such detail the programme he had in mind. There are several possible interpretations, ranging from the theory that he was conducting an exercise in domestic politics to that he was promulgating an irreversible decision to make war. The great rearmament programme which he had brought about had to be maintained, not only to guarantee full employment, but to keep the whole momentum of the National Socialist movement in being. Hitler's review of policy would justify the continuation of rearmament and even call for the pace to be accelerated. This is not to say, however, that at the meeting he was setting out an exact timetable for the realization of his aims. That was not his style. His political strategy was based essentially on exploiting opportunity, of waiting for the right moment, of profiting by other's mistakes, of letting others do his work for him (at the time of Munich, less than a year later, Chamberlain showed himself to be especially biddable in this respect), of getting all he wanted without resorting to war. In one sense, therefore, there was nothing very new in what Hitler was proposing. It was all written down in *Mein Kampf.* What was perhaps new was that in repeating his intention to use force to resolve Germany's problems – something that he had always maintained would be necessary – he was raising the stakes, confident in the power now at his disposal and which had increased by virtue of the success he had enjoyed; he was, too, willing to threaten more violently, gamble more openly, rely more fully on resorting to force simply because he had more of it. Thus it may be said that at this meeting it became clear that Hitler's mind was made up as to *what* was to be done; exactly *how* and *when* still had to be determined.

In an attempt to improve relations between Britain and Nazi Germany, Lord Halifax, then Lord President of the Council, with Chamberlain's active encouragement, visited Hitler at the Berghof some two weeks after this meeting. His conversation with the Führer would have done nothing to deter the latter from his aggressive intentions, however, just as his later report to the Cabinet did nothing to spur Chamberlain to spend more money on armaments. Halifax, while admitting that he might have misjudged the situation, expressed the belief that Germany was not going to embark on an adventurous policy and that Czechoslovakia had nothing to fear provided the Germans living there were well treated. Moreover, although Germany might pursue her aims in Central Europe, she would not do so in such a way as to warrant interference. As if this were not enough, Halifax even spoke of Hitler's disarmament proposals and his rejection of the idea that 'the world was in a dangerous state'. Before the debate on foreign policy in the House of Commons on 21 December, Churchill had had the opportunity to have a talk both with the Foreign Secretary, Eden,[1] during which they agreed that European matters must take precedence over Far Eastern ones – Japan's operations in China[2] – and to General Sir Edmund Ironside, C-in-C Eastern Command, who deprecated the lack of clear War Office policy and found himself in agreement with Churchill that although the French Army was powerful, by 1940 the Germans would have a great superiority, and that that year would be 'a very bad time for

---

[1] Eden resigned on 18 February because Chamberlain failed to support him in taking a firm line with Italy, which, having completed its conquest of Abyssinia in 1936, was seeking expansion elsewhere. He was succeeded as Foreign Secretary by Lord Halifax.

[2] Japan had occupied Manchuria in 1931, and in July 1937 launched a full-scale invasion of China.

us'. During the foreign policy debate itself, Churchill stressed the awful dangers which would arise if Britain bargained for her own security at the expense of the freedom or safety of other nations (the very course of action which Chamberlain would soon adopt), again put his faith in Anglo-French co-opera-tion, and pointed out that in spite of all his urgings for 'guns, aeroplanes, muni-tions . . . I am quite sure that British armaments alone will never protect us in the times through which we may have to pass'. There were also, he said, 'the moral forces involved', for by now the brutal and totalitarian nature of the Nazi regime was only too apparent to observers who chose to see it. Shortly after this Churchill left for a holiday in France, and by the time he returned to England in early February 1938, Hitler had shown his hand, and had begun to put the policy outlined at his meeting three months earlier into drastic effect.

He had started by tightening his grip on the reins of both economic and strategic power. At the end of 1937 he had removed Dr Hjalmar Schacht from the post of Minister of Economics and War Economy, and replaced him with Göring, whom he also promoted Field Marshal (Schacht remained a minister 'without portfolio' and President of the Reichsbank, however.) Blomberg, Fritsch and Neurath, all of whom were regarded by Hitler as 'dead wood', were sacked on one pretext or another. The vain and pliant champagne salesman, Joachim von Ribbentrop, became Foreign Minister and General Walther von Brauchitsch who, although in awe of Hitler, was acceptable to the General Staff, was appointed Army C-in-C, in Fritsch's place. The most significant appointment, however, was that of Hitler himself as Minister of Defence and Commander-in-Chief of the Armed Forces. The announcement of this change had an ominous ring:

> From henceforth I exercise personally the immediate command over the whole armed forces. The former Wehrmacht Office in the War Ministry becomes the High Command of the Armed Forces [Oberkommando der Wehrmacht or OKW] and comes immediately under my command as my military staff. At the head of the Staff of the High Command stands the former chief of the Wehrmacht Office [General Wilhelm Keitel]. He is accorded the rank equivalent to that of Reich Minister. The High Command of the Armed Forces also takes over the functions of the War Ministry, and the Chief of the High Command exercises, as my deputy, the powers hith-erto held by the Reich War Minister.

Hitler had in this way established a new command structure, so that his own orders, whether concerned with military or other matters, would be trans-mitted, as Hugh Trevor-Roper put it, 'through the whole war-machine of the Reich without the possibility of legal opposition; and it was through this machinery that he applied and controlled his strategy throughout the war'. On the very same day, 4 February 1938, on which he began to exercise supreme command of the Wehrmacht, the Führer set in train the events which led to the Anschluss with Austria. For some years Austrian Nazis had been agitating for union with Germany; unrest had grown, and there were increasing numbers of violent incidents, especially killings and bomb outrages, as well as factional fighting. Now Franz von Papen (who, having narrowly escaped being purged during the Night of the Long Knives, had been appointed the Führer's minister in Austria) was recalled from Vienna, saw Hitler next day at Berchtesgaden and proposed a meeting between the latter and Dr Kurt von Schuschnigg, the Austrian Chancellor.[1] This audience – for that was what it was – took place a week later at the Berghof. Hitler's combination of shouting, bullying, sending for General Keitel, threatening to order his troops to march into Austria – 'You don't seriously believe that you can stop me,' he told Schuschnigg, 'or even delay me for half an hour, do you?' – had its effect. The Austrian Chancellor, though a brave and decent man, was caught effectively between two hard choices; he therefore signed a protocol which agreed to far-reaching demands. His subsequent resolution to hold a plebiscite so that the Austrian people might declare whether or not they were in favour of a free, independent and united Austria, simply provoked Hitler into issuing orders for military action.

But the Führer also sent Prince Philip of Hesse (who was married to the daughter of Victor Emmanuel III, the all but puppet King of Italy) to Mussolini with a letter designed to secure Italy's neutrality. In it, referring to the Anschluss, he spoke of restoring law and order in his homeland, said that he was acting in national self-defence, reminded the Duce of his, Hitler's, steadfastness in Italy's critical hour during the Abyssinian crisis, and drew a definite boundary between Italy and Germany, the Brenner Pass, thus reassuring Mussolini about fears for the southern Tyrol (which, under Versailles, had been ceded from Austria to Italy). While this appeal was being made in Rome, the movement of German troops to occupy Austria continued. Before they crossed the frontier, Hitler had his answer from Mussolini. Prince Philip of Hesse telephoned to say that the Duce had 'accepted the whole thing in a very friendly manner' and sent his regards. The Führer's response was one of effusive gratitude: 'Tell Mussolini I will never forget him for this . . . never, never, never, whatever happens . . . I shall be ready to go with him through thick and thin . . . You may tell him that I thank him ever so much . . . If he

---

[1] In July 1934 Schuschnigg's predecessor, Engelbert Dollfuss, who sought to impose fascism on Austria while keeping the country independent of Germany, was assassinated by Austrian Nazis during an unsuccessful coup d'état. A part of Papen's task in Austria had been to smooth over the resulting diplomatic mess.

should ever need any help or be in any danger, he can be convinced that I shall stick to him, whatever may happen, even if the whole world were against him.' In this last respect, at least, Hitler was to be as good as his word.

On 11 March 1938 Schuschnigg, after yet more pressure and further threats, resigned, having done everything in his power to halt the Anschluss. A pro-Nazi traitor in his Cabinet, Dr Artur von Seyss-Inquart, a leader of the Austrian Nazis, became Chancellor, and German panzer units crossed the frontier into Austria. The following day Hitler himself crossed the border at his former home, Linz, to an enthusiastic reception, and told the assembled people about the 'mission given to me by destiny that I should bring my home country back to the great German Reich. I have believed in this mission and I have fulfilled it.' Hitler's own enthusiasm for the performance of his panzer units was not enhanced by the fact that so many of them broke down on the road from Salzburg and Passau to Vienna. The same unreliability caused a monumental traffic jam between Linz and the capital, which further enraged Hitler. His fury at this poor showing resulted in some valuable lessons being learned for the future, however. Guderian had much to say about the need for proper maintenance, fuel supply and march discipline, which was to pay great dividends when next the Wehrmacht set forth upon the path of invasion and occupation. But in any event, for two panzer divisions to have motored between 400 and 600 miles in two days was a remarkable achievement for unpractised troops and staff to have pulled off. Nevertheless, the military prizes were dwarfed by the political ones. Hitler did hold a plebiscite after all, but far from asking the people to decide for or against an independent Austria, it was an appeal, in which the entire new Grossdeutschland (Greater Germany) was to participate by voting, for him to be accorded four more years in power. The people of Germany and Austria gave their overwhelming approval for Hitler's policies and the Anschluss – 99 per cent said Yes.

It was clear that among the 1 per cent who did not approve were some of the generals. After the war, Blomberg explained that before 1938, the senior German generals had not opposed Hitler's policies because he was getting the results they wanted. By 1939, however, it was another matter, and it was then that they – or some of them, at least – began to question his judgement, as well as deploring his methods. The problem for these dissenters, however, was that he went on being so successful, even after the outbreak of war, with the result that, having so often overruled them and been proved right, he came to ignore or dismiss their advice. He condemned their thinking as sterile, their brains ossified by their own experience. They were imprisoned by their own professional training and knowledge, incapable of grasping the new, the unusual, the unorthodox. A creative genius like himself, on the other hand, dwelt outside the enclosure of expertise, unhindered by preconceived ideas or formulas based upon not necessarily typical experiences. He had 'the gift of reducing all problems to their simplest foundation'. It was not simply Hitler's unorthodoxy, however, which so influenced his strategic thinking. It was also his insistence on the value of surprise. Surprise was all part of the technique of blitzkrieg, a major factor in winning the psychological battle which, in turn, made winning the military battle so much easier. The Anschluss had been won without resort to actual fighting; moreover, it had been conducted in a way which marked a departure from his former tactics. The 'union' with Austria – in fact, annexation – was no reversal of the humiliation of Versailles. It had nothing to do with Germany's rights, and everything to do with naked aggression. The myth of righteousness was exploded, the mask of injured morality down, all pretence of legality put aside, all three replaced by the reality of the jackboot. The Anschluss marked the beginning of the murder of Europe. The three ingredients of murder – motive, means, opportunity – all were now to hand.

It was force that had worked the trick, a use of force so serious that it could no longer be ignored. On 14 March, during the House of Commons debate on the Anschluss, Chamberlain condemned the Nazi move and promised that there would be a further review of Britain's defences with a view to increasing or strengthening them. Churchill was far more robust:

> The gravity of the event of March 12 cannot be exaggerated. Europe is confronted with a programme of aggression, nicely calculated and timed, unfolding stage by stage, and there is only one choice open, not only to us but to other countries, either to submit like Austria, or else take effective measures while time remains to ward off the danger, and if it cannot be warded off to cope with it . . . A long stretch of the Danube is now in German hands. This mastery of Vienna gives to Nazi Germany military and economic control of the whole of the communications of South eastern Europe, by road, by river, and by rail. What is the effect of this on the structure of Europe? What is the effect of it upon what is called the balance of power . . .?
>
> Czechoslovakia is at this moment isolated, both in the economic and in the military sense . . . How many potential allies shall we see go one by one down the grisly gulf? How many times will bluff succeed until behind bluff ever-gathering forces have accumulated reality? Where are we going to be two years hence, for instance, when the German Army will certainly be much larger than the French Army?

Although Germany's army was not yet as large as France's, it was more than powerful enough. It was also growing fast, not only in numbers, also in quality. With Guderian in charge of the training and organization of mobile troops, and with the new PzKw[1] III and IV tanks (which would become famous, once the shooting started, as Mark IIIs and IVs) coming into service, it had become incomparably superior. The purpose behind the German Army's power was clear enough. Being wholly subordinate to Hitler's will, it would supply the force, whether threatened or actual, that would further policy. There would be plenty for the military planners to think about. One week after Churchill's speech, Hitler gave instructions to General Keitel to polish up the plans for *Fall Grün*, the codename for an assault on Czechoslavakia.

During the crisis over Czechoslovakia which led to the Munich Agreement of September 1938, whereas Churchill was constantly pressing for a 'Grand Alliance' between France and Britain, for bringing Russia into the game too, and for making it plain that if Germany marched against Czechoslovakia, she would have Britain and France to reckon with, the two Prime Ministers of these countries, Chamberlain and Edouard Daladier, seemed to be convinced that all Hitler was after was the return of the Sudeten Germans to the Fatherland. Both leaders failed initially to appreciate that what Hitler really intended was to 'smash the Czechs', to destroy the whole state and simply absorb it into the Reich. It was this failure to comprehend Hitler's true intentions that greatly influenced the various manoeuvrings that followed, for once the Führer saw the leaders of Britain and France at work, he pronounced them to be 'little worms'. The first draft of *Fall Grün*, produced on 20 May 1938, was such that it permitted Hitler to keep his options open. Whereas the plan did not envisage immediate military action to 'smash Czechoslovakia' unless events dictated or conditions favoured it, nonetheless the directive outlined how the army and Luftwaffe would destroy the Czech Army and occupy Bohemia and Moravia. Moreover, war was to be total, with every propaganda and economic card being played to undermine resistance and hasten Czechoslovakia's collapse.

On the same day, 20 May, and following Lord Swinton's[2] resignation as Secretary of State for Air – which prompted many to believe that Churchill would now be brought into the Cabinet (Chamberlain declined to invite him) – Churchill was telling the editor of the *Sunday Referee*, R.J. Minney, that he did not believe he had shown any particular wish to be a member of the Government. To others he confided that Parliament would take no effective action over the Czechoslovak crisis, adding that 'We are in an awful mess', and that if the situation worsened 'something in the nature of a National Government may be forced upon us, but events, and great events alone will decide.' Great events

---

[1] PzKv: abbrevation for Panzerkampfwagen, armoured fighting vehicle.
[2] Sir Philip Cunliffe-Lister had been created Viscount Swinton in 1935. The title was later raised to an earldom.

were not long in coming. Although reports of German troop concentrations had alarmed the Czechs, who ordered partial mobilization, and although the French and British Governments warned of the dangers – the French, with Russian support, even going so far as to promise aid to the Czechs – Hitler retained his patience, if not his temper. Reassurances were given at the same time as German military preparations were hastened. Fall Grün was amended to encompass the smashing of Czechoslovakia 'in the near future' – this latter phrase specifying a date not later than 1 October. Such readiness for military action was not welcome to the generals; in particular, the Chief of the Army General Staff, General Ludwig Beck, was convinced that Hitler's expansionist policies would lead to war with France, Britain and Russia, with the United States becoming an arsenal for the democracies, a war that Germany, by virtue of limited economic and military resources, would be bound to lose. But his stand against Hitler simply resulted in his resignation and replacement by Halder. Furthermore, when, in August 1938, Hitler indulged in the rare luxury of lecturing the generals about his politico-military theories, and one of them pointed out that if the bulk of German forces were fighting in Czechoslovakia, the West Wall (the fortifications along Germany's western frontier, known to the Allies as the Siegfried Line) could be held for only three weeks, the Führer lost his temper and bellowed that it would be held 'for three months and three years'. He had no time for faint-hearted generals, with no morale, no vision and, worst of all, no faith in his genius.

After revising the General Staff plans for invading Czechoslovakia – substituting a bold, concentrated breakthrough for the cautious, conservative ideas of the military men – Hitler once again demonstrated that his 'intuition' and bullying tactics paid off, for after a venomous attack on Czechoslovakia in his speech at the Nuremberg Rally on 12 September, during which he demanded justice for the Sudeten Germans, the French Government's nerve failed, and Daladier, appealed to Chamberlain to prevent German troops entering Czechoslovakia, at the same time giving the British Prime Minister a free hand to negotiate with Hitler. On 14 September, despite Churchill's urging that Germany should be told that any incursion into Czechoslovakia would mean war with Britain, Chamberlain informed the Cabinet of his intention to go to Germany to see Hitler, and that he would support the idea of a plebiscite in the Sudetenland.

At this first meeting with the Führer at Berchtesgaden on 15 September Chamberlain conceded a point of principle from which the rest of the surrender sprang – 'he [Chamberlain] could state personally that he recognized the principle of the detachment of the Sudeten areas . . . He wished to return to England to report to the Government and secure their approval of his personal attitude.' From then on the game went inexorably Hitler's way. On 22

September Chamberlain returned to Germany and at Bad Godesberg presented Hitler with the joint British, French and Czech agreement to transfer the Sudetenland to Germany, whereupon Hitler upped the stakes, rejecting the offer and insisting that the Sudetenland be *occupied* by German troops at once. After an argument as to which country, Germany or Czechoslovakia, had mobilized first, Hitler 'conceded' that he would delay the German occupation and the evacuation of the Sudetenland's Czech population until 1 October, this being his original plan and thus no concession at all. Moreover, the Czechs must accept these terms by '2pm on September 28'. Further bullying followed. Hitler's speech of 26 September in Berlin's Sportpalast was filled with raving invective, and on the following day he shouted at one of Chamberlain's advisers, Sir Horace Wilson, that he would 'destroy' Czechoslovakia. Sliding from extremes of fury to moderation, Hitler then wrote to Chamberlain – the letter arrived on the evening of 27 September – expressing his willingness to guarantee the security and sovereignty of the rest of Czechoslovakia and to negotiate details with the Czechs. This was just the sort of language Chamberlain wanted to hear, and in his vain search for 'peace with honour', he suggested to the Führer that he could get what he wanted 'without war and without delay', and recommended a meeting at which Italy, France and Czechoslovakia would also be represented. He then sent a telegram to Mussolini asking him to urge Hitler to accept this proposal. On 28 September invitations were sent from Germany to the heads of the Italian, French and British Governments to meet the Führer in Munich at noon on the following day.

While Chamberlain flew to Munich on the morning of 29 September, Churchill was in London. He attended a luncheon at the Savoy given by the Freedom and Peace Movement, and remained there for a further meeting at which there prevailed a sense of despair at the evident inability of the movement, and of other like-minded people, to stop Chamberlain making further concessions to the Nazis. At dinner that evening Churchill was so overcome by anger and gloom that he demanded to know from the two Government ministers present, Duff Cooper and Walter Elliot (respectively First Lord of the Admiralty and Minister of Health) – this as reported by the journalist Colin Coote[1] – 'How could honourable men with wide experience and fine records in the Great War condone a policy so cowardly? It was sordid, squalid, sub-human and suicidal . . . The sequel to the sacrifice of honour would be the sacrifice of lives, our people's lives.' But Chamberlain was already signing away Britain's honour.

---

[1] At the time, Coote (later Sir Colin, Editor of the *Daily Telegraph* 1950–64) was a leader writer on *The Times*. Disagreeing with that paper's support for appeasement, he confined his leaders to home topics.

At Munich, Hitler gained even more than he had demanded at Bad Godesberg. Under the agreement signed that day by the leaders of the four Powers represented at the conference – Hitler, Chamberlain, Daladier and Mussolini – the Sudetenland, with its formidable fortifications, economic resources, and control of communications, was transferred to Germany. Polish and Hungarian claims to slices of territory were also settled, so that the Czech nation was dislocated. No representative of its government had been present at the conference, but what remained of the country was guaranteed by the four signatory Powers. Strategically and industrially Czechoslovakia had been broken, however, and now lay at the mercy – and mercy was not a quality he was renowned for – of the Führer. For Hitler, there were other causes for satisfaction. The military operation had gone smoothly – the planning, the execution, the mastery of detail, all had gone to show what Teutonic thoroughness coupled to Hitler's intuition and foresight could achieve. Moreover, any ideas the generals might have had about bringing off a coup d'état[1] to oust Hitler were now simply laughable. Colonel Alfred Jodl, Chief of Operations at OKW Headquarters, summed it all up by announcing that, 'The genius of the Führer and his determination not to shun even a world war have again won victory without the use of force.' 'Legality' – in the form of an internationally guaranteed 'agreement' – allied to the ever-present threat of force had once more paid off. Adolf Hitler's policies had been dramatically vindicated.

Not surprisingly, rather less enthusiasm was displayed for the Munich Agreement in the House of Commons. Duff Cooper resigned from the Admiralty; Clement Attlee the Labour leader, spoke of humiliation and the triumph of brute force, and the leader of the Liberals, Churchill's friend and former adjutant, Sir Archibald Sinclair, of surrender and injustice that could never lead to lasting peace; Richard Law (Bonar Law's son, and a vociferous opponent of appeasement) pointed out that Europe was now dominated by a single power, the very circumstance which 'we have fought four wars to prevent happening'. Churchill himself did not speak in the debate until its third day, 5 October (although, in a newspaper article published on the 4th, he made a rather curious reference to Hitler in a passage in which he called for proper leadership which must not lack 'something of the spirit of that Austrian corporal who when all had fallen into ruins about him, and when Germany seemed to have sunk for ever into chaos, did not hesitate to march forth against the vast array of victorious nations, and has already turned the tables so decisively upon them'). When he came to make his own speech, apart from deploring the

---

[1] There was such a conspiracy among the army's senior commanders at the time, among them Beck and Halder, who were perfectly well aware that if Hitler's bluff were called, and Germany went to war, in 1938, with Czechoslovakia, France, Britain and (probably) Russia, she would be heavily defeated.

Munich Agreement in the strongest terms, he pointed to the Government's consistent failure to prevent such dangerous conditions coming about. They had failed to prevent Germany's rearmament, failed to rearm their own country, 'quarrelled with Italy without saving Ethiopia . . . exploited and discredited the vast institution of the League of Nations,' and completely failed either to build collective alliances or to strengthen national defence. He went on:

> We are in the presence of a disaster of the first magnitude which has befallen Britain and France. Do not let us blind ourselves to that. It must now be accepted that all the countries of Central and Eastern Europe will make the best terms they can with the triumphant Nazi Power . . .

Moreover, he continued, the time would come when Hitler would 'look westward', and then Britain would find that she had not just compromised Czechoslovakia, but had also endangered 'the safety and even the independence of Great Britain and France'. However much it might be the wish of the Government to be on good terms with Germany, the nature of the Nazi regime, which, he warned, 'cheers its onward course by a barbarous paganism, which vaunts the spirit of aggression and conquest, which derives strength and perverted pleasure from persecution, and uses, as we have seen, with pitiless brutality the threat of murderous force,' made it impossible. He could not, he said, endure the prospect that Britain might somehow come to be in thrall to Nazi Germany, and it was to prevent this that he had for so long been urging the strengthening of the country's defences, not only by creating an air force stronger than any other which might threaten Britain, but by building alliances which would be powerful enough to keep Nazi Germany in check. But his efforts had not succeeded. The country had 'sustained a defeat without a war' – and it should not be supposed that this was the end of the story. 'This is only the first sip, the first foretaste of a bitter cup which will be preferred to us year by year unless by a supreme recovery of moral health and martial vigour, we arise again and take our stand for freedom as in the olden time.'

All too soon, Hitler was to prove Churchill right by his determination to 'smash' what remained of Czechoslovakia and ride in triumph through Bohemia. In doing so, however, he aroused even the supine Chamberlain administration to recover some of its moral health and martial vigour. On 21 October 1938 Hitler issued a further directive to his military commanders, which spoke of setting out future tasks for the armed forces, and of the *conduct of war*. Meanwhile, everything must be ready to secure Germany's frontiers, to liquidate the rest of Czechoslovakia, and to occupy Memel (a port on the Baltic, ceded to Lithuania from Germany under the Versailles Treaty). More directives followed – one, in November, envisaged the occupation of Danzig;

another in the following month ordered that the plans for the occupation of Czechoslovakia were to be based on the assumption that there would be virtually no resistance. Three months later, in March 1939, this last directive was executed, and that there was no resistance was due in large measure to the literal, physical collapse of Czechoslovakia's President, Emil Hácha. With Czechoslovakia, what remained of it, by then in a state of largely Nazi-orchestrated disintegration, Hácha asked for a meeting with Hitler in Berlin. Arriving on 14 March with his Foreign Minister, František Chvalkovsky, the poor old man was subjected to such a bullying by Hitler and Göring that he fainted, and had to be revived by the sinister Dr Theodor Morell (who was later to administer such dangerous drugs to Hitler himself). The Führer made it clear that whether or not the German Army would invade was not the issue. The only question was whether or not there would be a fight – if there were, the Czech Army would cease to exist – or whether German troops would enter peaceably. If the latter, the Führer would be generous; otherwise, not only would Prague be destroyed by Göring's bombers, but for every Czech *battalion* that might be deployed a German *division* would oppose it. Hácha, wholly unable to withstand such an onslaught, signed a paper which effectively placed his country and his people in the hands of the Führer of the German Reich. On 15 March 1939 the German Army poured through Bohemia and Moravia. Hitler had triumphed again, while the guarantors of Czech sovereignty – Britain, France and Italy – did nothing.

In spite of this latest Nazi success, however, in Britain some things were changing. Programmes which Churchill had been advocating for more than five years were beginning to emerge – a more resolute foreign policy and a more positive defence policy, in particular. It was not lost even on Chamberlain that Hitler's rape of Czechoslovakia was hardly in the spirit of the Munich Agreement, and what was more, for the first time Hitler had now incorporated non-Germanic peoples in his Greater Reich. Was it, Chamberlain asked in a speech at Birmingham two days after Hitler's triumph, 'a step in the direction of an attempt to dominate the world by force?' Indeed it was, nor would the next step be long in coming. Although Chamberlain resisted pressure to form a National Government – which would, of course, have included those who most sternly criticized his policy, like Churchill, Eden and Duff Cooper – he did at least take the step of 'guaranteeing' Poland; in other words, Britain would give Poland all the support she could 'in the event of any action which clearly threatened Polish independence, and which the Polish Government accordingly considered it vital to resist'. It would not be many months before the British Government was required to honour this undertaking, even though the support actually given to Poland would prove to be negligible. Chamberlain's resolve was not weakened by Germany's annexation of Memel on 23 March, nor by Italy's invasion of Albania on 7 April. Shortly before this invasion Churchill had deplored the fact that the British Mediterranean Fleet, instead of being on station in the Adriatic Sea to prevent such an occurrence, had been 'lolling in the Bay of Naples,' with its commander being 'entertained no doubt on the orders of Mussolini himself at the Naples Yacht Club'.

Slowly but surely the British Government was beginning to come to its senses, and to adopt measures which Churchill had for so long been advocating. In April it was at last agreed that a Ministry of Supply was to be established, prompting a comment from his friend and protégé Brendan Bracken[1] that 'Winston has won his long fight . . . No public man in our time has shown more foresight, and I believe that his long, lonely struggle to expose the dangers of the dictatorships will prove to be the best chapter in his crowded life.' While Churchill was still working on his *History of the English-Speaking Peoples* with the aid of Bill Deakin and others, pressure for his inclusion in the Government continued to be exerted on his behalf. Although Chamberlain still did not take this step, he did introduce, on 27 April, the Military Training Bill, which heralded compulsory military service. While he supported this measure, Churchill still deplored, nevertheless, the slowness of rearmament. Early in May in a *Daily Telegraph* article, he predicted, once again with unerring accuracy, Hitler would perpetrate a 'new outrage or invasion', suggesting 'that the glare of Nazi Germany is to be turned on Poland'. Such an outrage would indeed be a grave matter in view of the British Government's change of policy.

Hitler himself was in no doubt about the seriousness of his intentions. In the same month, May 1939, he again addressed a meeting of his generals and admirals at which he expressed the view that war was inevitable. The problem was still *Lebensraum*. The solution was still expansion eastwards:

We are left with the decision: To attack Poland at the first suitable opportunity. We cannot expect a repetition of the Czech affair. There will be war. Our task is to isolate Poland. The success of this isolation will be decisive . . . There must be no simultaneous conflict with the Western Powers. If it is not certain that German-Polish conflict will not lead to war in the west, the fight must be primarily against England and France.

He went on to outline how Britain, Germany's most dangerous enemy, might best be attacked. It was no longer necessary to invade her in order to

---

[1] Bracken, the founder, owner or co-owner of a number of journals, including the *Financial News* and *The Economist*, was a Conservative MP at the time; he became Churchill's Parliamentary Private Secretary when the latter became First Lord of the Admiralty for a second time at the outbreak of war.

conquer: cut off her supplies and capitulation must follow. The army must therefore take those strategic points that bordered or were close to the English Channel or the North Sea, from which the Kriegsmarine and Luftwaffe would be able to strangle the United Kingdom's lifeline. This in turn meant occupying Belgium and Holland, as well as defeating France, thereby establishing the conditions necessary for a successful war against Britain. If the generals and admirals who were listening had looked back on this meeting a year later, they would have been obliged to acknowledge that Hitler's strategic survey was astonishingly prescient. So too was his argument that, had the German Army conducted a wheeling movement towards the Channel ports in 1914 and not aimed to encircle Paris, the result would have been a decisive defeat of the Allies. Precisely this strategic decision was to be his in 1940. To predict with such uncanny accuracy the course that a future war will take speaks of no common strategic gift. Hitler warned also that a conflict with the British might be a long one, something which was also to be confirmed by events. The error into which he fell, however, was that he did not design and prepare his armed forces for a long war with Britain and her Empire. He relied instead on what he regarded as the overwhelmingly decisive effects of blitzkrieg.

While Hitler was stressing the need to isolate Poland, Churchill was doing his best to ensure that this isolation did not come about by urging the Government to enter into a Triple Alliance with France and Russia. In July 1939 the press was again demanding that Churchill be given ministerial office, but Chamberlain was still opposed to it, arguing that the former's inclusion in the Cabinet would not make his own task as Prime Minister any easier. Yet even in the German hierarchy itself, as Martin Gilbert has reminded us, there was one man, Count Lutz Schwerin von Krosigk, the Reichsfinanzminister – and, like some of the generals, anxious to avoid war – who advised senior British officers that Churchill's inclusion in the Cabinet would contribute immeasurably to the avoidance of trouble, adding that he was the only Englishman of whom Hitler was afraid. Chamberlain and Halifax were not regarded seriously, but Churchill was seen as being in the same class as the President of the United States, Franklin D. Roosevelt; simply by the fact of his being given a senior ministerial post, Hitler would understand that the British were going to stand up to him. Churchill himself continued to work on his *History* (observing at one point what a comfort it was in such difficult times to 'retire into past centuries'), and to urge in newspaper articles the formation of 'a solid, binding, all-in alliance between Britain, France and Russia'. Delay in doing so, he argued, would 'aggravate the danger of a wrong decision by Herr Hitler'.

Hitler had, of course, already made the 'wrong' decision. When he had heard of the French and British guarantee to Poland, he had lost his temper, promised to 'cook them a stew that they'll choke on,' and issued a new directive for *Fall Weiss* (Operation White), war with Poland. This directive was uncompromising in its language and precise in its reference to timing:

> The aim will be to destroy Polish military strength and create in the East a situation which satisfies the requirements of national defence ... The political leaders consider it their task ... to limit the war to Poland only ... The isolation of Poland will be all the more easily maintained even after the outbreak of hostilities, if we succeed in starting the war with sudden, heavy blows and in gaining rapid successes ... The task of the Wehrmacht is to destroy the Polish armed forces. To this end a surprise attack is to be aimed at and prepared.

There were three additional points: everything must be prepared so that the operation could be carried out from 1 September onwards: OKW would produce an exact timetable which would be used to co-ordinate the operations of all three services; and detailed plans must be submitted by 1 May. Once more Hitler had set himself a precise date for military action. Once more he was to stick to it. There was still, however, something to be done about Poland's isolation, if the condition Hitler had laid down of limiting the war to Poland only were to be realized, and in doing so, Hitler took another leaf from General von Seeckt's book.[1] In a memorandum written in 1922 Seeckt had laid down that the obliteration of Poland – a fundamental principle of German foreign policy – was to be obtained with Russia's help. Hitler had already cemented his military alliance with Italy by the Pact of Steel, signed in Berlin on 22 May, of which one of the articles made it clear that if one party were involved in war, the other would lend military assistance at once. Only two days later, as has already been touched on, Hitler delivered his lecture to the generals and admirals about attacking Poland, and at which he had stated that he judged an alliance between Britain and France, on the one hand, and Russia, on the other, to be unlikely; indeed, Russia was more likely to show an interest in the destruction of Poland. Here was the old principle of *so oder so*: since Poland was not to be a willing tool to assist Germany in the dissolution of Russia, the reverse side of the coin – Russian participation in the swallowing-up of Poland – began to look more attractive. However, if Hitler were to stick to his timetable of attacking Poland on 1 September, there was not much time left in which to complete that country's isolation.

[1] Seeckt had retired in October 1926, largely as the result of President von Hindenburg's jealousy. In 1934 and 1935 he was military adviser to General Chiang Kai-shek in China; he died in Germany in 1936, and so was never to see in action the army which, more than any other single person, he had been responsible for creating.

Just as Hitler had told his senior military officers that war was now inevitable, so Churchill was convinced of it, telling General Ironside[1] at Chartwell on 24 July that it was 'now too late for any appeasement. The deed was signed, and Hitler is going to make war.' He even outlined what would happen when war came – Poland would be annihilated; Italy would create diversions and attempt to capture Egypt; the Germans would make for the Black Sea through Romania; that there would be a Russo-German alliance. Three days later Ironside recalled his discussions at Chartwell, seeing his host as 'a man who knows that you must act to win. You cannot remain supine and allow yourself to be hit indefinitely.' To the General, Churchill was 'full of patriotism and ideas for saving the Empire' – it would not be long before he would be able to put some of his ideas to the test.

Churchill was again to display his remarkable strategic grasp when, on 14 August, in company with his old friend General Spears, he lunched with the French General Joseph Georges (who, in 1940, would command the French armies opposite the Ardennes). They agreed that Hitler had made excellent use of the year since Munich by strengthening the West Wall, which boasted defences in depth, as opposed to France's linear Maginot Line. In discussing this point, Churchill made the discerning comment 'that it would be very unwise to think the Ardennes were impassable to strong forces.[2] "Remember," he said, "that we are faced with a new weapon, armour in great strength, on which the Germans are no doubt concentrating, and that forests will be particularly tempting to such forces since they will offer concealment from the air".' He might have been putting words in the mouth of General Fritz Erich von Manstein, who was later to propose just such a plan to Hitler – who eagerly seized upon it – a plan which led to the overwhelming of the French Army, the evacuation of the BEF from Dunkirk, and the capitulation of France.

Nine days later, on 23 August 1939, a treaty of non-aggression between Germany and the Soviet Union, the Nazi-Soviet Pact, was signed secretly in Moscow by Ribbentrop and the Russian Foreign Minister, Vyacheslav Molotov. Stalin, who wished to avoid war with Germany, or at least to postpone it, had not been averse to buying those priceless strategic commodities, time and space, at Poland's expense. However cynical the arrangement, no one should have been surprised by it, for the West's ideas of an alliance with Russia had never been, from his viewpoint, sufficiently tempting, and when Litvinov – who had advocated collective security with the West – was replaced as Foreign

---

[1] By now, Ironside was Inspector-General, Overseas Forces.
[2] It was widely held among the French High Command that the Ardennes, the forested plateau, bisected by the River Meuse, that lies in south-east Belgium, north-east France and northern Luxembourg, was impenetrable to armour.

Minister by Molotov in May, the path to an understanding with Germany was made smoother. The last ten days of August were eventful. On the 22nd Ribbentrop had flown to Moscow to complete negotiations of the Nazi-Soviet Pact of Non-Aggression, which was signed the following evening; Count Ciano, the Italian Foreign Minister, noted in his diary that with this pact Germany had struck 'a master blow – the European situation is upset'.[1] Meanwhile at the Berghof, also on 22 August, Hitler again harangued the generals: 'There will probably never again be a man with such authority or who has the confidence of the whole German people as I have. My existence is therefore a factor of great value. But I can be eliminated at any moment by a criminal or a lunatic. There is no time to lose. War must come in my lifetime.' Yet he admitted that Germany's economic situation was such that she could only hold out for a few years. In making this admission, although doing so to support the need for action there and then, Hitler also pointed to the fundamental weakness of the blitzkrieg strategy, which could only succeed if *all* Germany's enemies were quickly overcome. But in any event, iron resolution was required. 'Close your eyes to pity. Act brutally. 80 million people must obtain what is their right. Their existence must be made secure. The strongest man is right.' A definite date was then set for the invasion of Poland – 26 August, four days away – and Hitler then told his assembled commanders that the chances of intervention by Britain and France were negligible. If by this he meant interference with the actual military overrunning of Poland, he was right. If he doubted the resolution of Britain and France to stick to their undertaking to support Poland in the longer term, he miscalculated. For on 25 August the British Government confirmed its intention of coming to the Poles' aid with a formal Treaty of Alliance. Hitler was sufficiently taken aback to postpone the invasion. But not for long, for the Führer simply set a new zero hour for *Fall Weiss*, and on 31 August, when everything was ready, and German-engineered 'frontier incidents' having provided an appropriate propaganda reason, Hitler signed Directive No 1 for the Conduct of the War:

> 1. Since the situation on Germany's Eastern frontier has become intolerable and all political possibilities of peaceful settlement have been exhausted, I have decided upon a *solution by force*.

[1] Apart from being a treaty of non-aggression, the pact also contained pledges that either country would remain neutral if the other were at war, as well as secret terms allowing Germany a free hand in Lithuania and western Poland, and Russia the same latitude in Finland, Estonia, Latvia, Bessarabia (a disputed province straddling the border between the Ukraine and Romania) and eastern Poland. A secret amendment a month later increased the German 'area' of Poland in return for Lithuania passing into the Russian sphere of influence.

2. *The attack on Poland* will be undertaken in accordance with the preparations made for Case White, with such variations as may be necessitated by the build-up of the Army which is now virtually complete . . .

> Date of attack 1 September 1939.
> Time of attack 4.45 am.
> This time also applies to operations at Gdynia, in the Bay of Danzig, and at the Dirschau bridge.[1]

3. In the *West* it is important to leave the responsibility for opening hostilities unmistakably to England and France . . .

4. *Should England and France open hostilities* against Germany, it will be the duty of the Armed Forces operating in the West . . . to maintain conditions for the successful conclusion of operations against Poland . . .

This last point once more put Hitler's strategy for the whole war in a nutshell – hold in the west, blitzkrieg in the east; next, secure the east, and let loose the blitzkrieg in the west; once more defend the west and then, finally, a decisive blitzkrieg in the east. Although the Führer had declared that he would never fight a war on two fronts, this is precisely what, in the end, he did – and it was to prove too much even for the astonishing skill, power and endurance of the Wehrmacht.

At the very time when Hitler's panzers were cutting their way into Poland, Churchill was at Chartwell, where he had been working on his book. On hearing the news he drove to London and was asked by the Prime Minister to call at No 10 Downing Street, where Chamberlain, who now saw no possibility of avoiding war, asked him to become a member of the small War Cabinet he proposed to form, it being agreed that Churchill would become Minister without Portfolio. Over the next two days there was much excitement in the House of Commons, particularly when Chamberlain vainly spoke of the possibility of further negotiations with Germany. There was, too, much impatience on the part of Churchill, who according to his secretary, Mrs Hill, spent much of 2 September 'pacing up and down like a lion in a cage. He was expecting a call, but the call never came.' And there was much fury on Hitler's part when, having declared to the Reichstag that henceforth he was 'just the first soldier of the German Reich' and would devote his life to his people, he com-

---

[1] Gdynia, a port lying a few miles north-west of Danzig, was established in 1920 to give Poland an outlet to the sea, Danzig having become a Free City under Versailles. The bridge over the Vistula (now Wisla) lay to the south of Danzig; in the event, the Poles demolished it before the Germans could seize it.

pletely lost his temper with Birger Dahlerus,[1] the mediator from neutral Sweden, shouting that if Britain wanted to fight for one year or two, so would he. 'He paused and then yelled, his voice rising to a shrill scream and his arms milling wildly: "If England wants to fight for three years, I shall fight for three years . . ." The movement of his body now began to follow those of his arms, and when he finally bellowed: "Und wenn es erforderlich ist, will *ich zehn Jahre kämpfen*" ['And, if necessary, I will fight for ten years'], he brandished his fist and bent down so that it nearly touched the floor.' It was hardly demonstrative of that quality so indispensable to the successful execution of high command – calm – yet for the first two years of the war practically everything was to go Hitler's way.

After the British ultimatum to Germany, which required the Germans to halt their attack on Poland, had been sent to Berlin at nine o'clock on the morning of 3 September, and after it had failed, within the two-hour deadline, to produce any such cessation of hostilities, Chamberlain declared to the nation in a broadcast at a quarter-past eleven that a state of war existed between Britain and Germany. Almost at once the air-raid warning sounded, and in a characteristic gesture Churchill went up to the roof of his London house to see what was happening, and then he and his wife descended to the basement 'armed with a bottle of brandy and other appropriate medical comforts'. Later, in the House of Commons, he was conscious of the very condition so notably lacking in Hitler during his talk with Dahlerus. 'A very strong sense of calm came over me,' he remembered, 'after the intense passions and excitements of the last few days . . .' In his own speech to the House, while recalling all the efforts the British had made for peace, emphasizing the dangers and setbacks that might lie ahead and expressing confidence in their own strength, he pointed out that, even leaving the guarantees to Poland aside, 'We are fighting to save the whole world from the pestilence of Nazi tyranny and in defence of all that is most sacred to man.' When the speeches were over Churchill saw Chamberlain and was offered the post of First Lord of the Admiralty, which, not unnaturally, he accepted. Great was the rejoicing among Churchill's supporters, and indeed among the nation at large. It was, perhaps, the Board of Admiralty which, in a signal to the Fleet, succinctly and suitably summed up such a satisfactory and necessary turn of events: 'Winston is back.'

---

[1] Dahlerus, a Swedish businessman, was a friend of Göring who, over the weeks, had become involved as a kind of unofficial arbitrator between the British Foreign Office and the Nazis. If his naïvety about German intentions bordered on the idiotic, he was nevertheless good-hearted, genuinely desirous of preserving peace, and utterly tireless in his efforts.

CHAPTER 5

1939–1940 – Hitler's Blitzkrieg, Churchill's Finest Hour

When I warned them [the French Government] that Britain would fight on alone whatever they did, their Generals told their Prime Minister [Paul Reynaud] and his divided Cabinet, 'In three weeks England will have her neck wrung like a chicken.'

Some chicken! Some neck!

WINSTON CHURCHILL

A few weeks before Hitler launched the Wehrmacht against Poland, he had explained to Count Ciano how it would all be done. The Italian Foreign Minister noted in his diary that although the Führer was very cordial, he would not listen to the former's attempts to dissuade him from taking the final steps to war. He was both impassive and implacable, and with the aid of maps displayed profound military knowledge in explaining how Germany's superior strategic position and methods would quickly conquer Poland. Germany would then rapidly deploy a hundred divisions in the west, preparatory to engaging in general conflict there. (By November 1939, only two months after the Polish campaign, it was estimated by Allied intelligence that Germany had concentrated from ninety-seven to ninety-nine divisions on the western front, facing Holland, Belgium, Luxembourg and France.) Hitler's confidence, in any case great, soon received an additional boost from the Wehrmacht's actual performance on the battlefield. Even though it had expanded far more quickly than the General Staff had advised and taken on tasks which some had judged too risky, it showed itself to be one of the most efficient and adaptable war machines that the world had yet seen. Explanations for this were not hard to find – a combination of excellent new weapons, revolutionary tactics, proper leadership at all levels, together with the bold strategy and driving willpower of the Führer himself, proved irresistible. What is more, the sheer spirit of this revolutionary Wehrmacht – which had sprung from Seeckt's *Führerheer* ideas, so that it really was an army of leaders and, moreover, one which believed all the propaganda about *Herrenvolk* – was such that the whole war machine was confident that the master race would demonstrate to the *Untermenschen* of Poland how swiftly a campaign could be fought and won. Hitler estimated that it would take a fortnight. He was only a few days out.

As has been demonstrated, the principles of blitzkrieg were surprise, speed and concentration. Each was aided by the other: surprise made for speed; speed abetted surprise; concentration bolstered both. In the Polish campaign each had its own particular manifestation. Surprise was further reinforced by diplomatic negotiations with the Poles until the last moment, and then attacking without even a declaration of war. Quite apart from crushingly powerful *Schwerpunkte*, which provided the necessary concentration, the Luftwaffe both destroyed the Polish Air Force (which in any case was equipped with slow, ill-armed and outdated aircraft, many of them biplanes) and pulverized the enemy's centres of command and communications, thus enabling such defences as there were to be torn open by the German armoured columns. These thrust deep into the artillery and supply areas and brought about that very paralysis which makes for a battle of annihilation, a type of battle classified by Clausewitz[1] as one in which the enemy's moral and material resources are exhausted to the point where he is no longer able to wage war.

In any case, the Polish strategic position was hopeless from the start, for Germany was able to attack from three sides and thus outflank any forces which the Poles might deploy to the west of the Vistula – the only natural defensive line. Thus the great Polish salient which jutted out westwards could be threatened from the north by German troops in Pomerania and East Prussia, and from the south by those in Silesia and Slovakia. At the same time, to abandon this salient would be for the Poles to give up the very warmaking commodities – oil, coal, armaments, industry – indispensable to her armed forces. The Polish Commander-in-Chief, Marshal Eduard Smigly-Rydz, adopted the defensive posture which best suited his enemies by stringing out his armies along the frontier, while keeping something in reserve near Warsaw. Such a deployment was wholly incapable of resisting the two massive pincer movements executed by the German armies (which comprised forty-five divisions), one to envelop and destroy Polish forces west of the Vistula, the second

---

[1] Karl Marie von Clausewitz (1780–1831), Prussian soldier, military theorist and writer. His most famous work, *Vom Kriege* (*On War*, 1833) has had, and continues to have, a major influence on strategy.

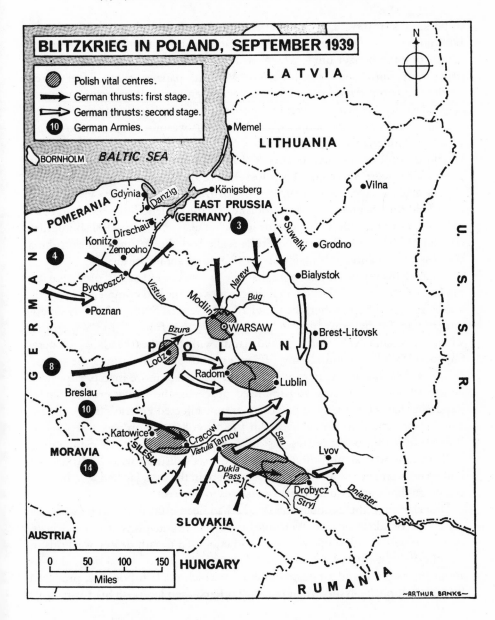

driving east of Warsaw and cutting off all Poland west of the line from Bialystok, through Brest-Litovsk to the River Bug.

The campaign progressed as Liddell Hart had imagined and as Guderian had so thoroughly trained for. Up to this time blitzkrieg had been but an idea. Now it became a reality. The Luftwaffe commanded the skies, reconnoitring, bombing, terrorizing, paralysing, the screaming Stukas bombing and strafing, supporting the panzer units, which easily broke through the Polish lines and drove deep into enemy territory. Nor were the panzers alone. Mechanized artillery and motorized infantry kept up with them; even the marching infantry seemed to advance with frightening speed. Such an onslaught was all too much for the Poles, who were simply overwhelmed. It was not for lack of courage, however. Guderian reported that on 3 September, during the battle for the Corridor, some of his tank regiments were charged by a Polish cavalry brigade armed with sword and lance. Their losses were appalling. So too were those of Polish artillery regiments overrun by panzers. Even Hitler, visiting the battlefield on 5 September, was astonished by the destruction which had been wreaked, not only among the enemy guns, but also among the Polish infantry and supply columns. Panzer and Stuka really had shown themselves to be a peerless combination in bringing about a battle of annihilation.

It was all over in not much more than the two weeks Hitler had predicted. By the end of the first week the initial pincer movement had completed its work, and as early as 7 September, the Chief of the General Staff, Halder, was planning to transfer divisions from Poland to the western front. On 17 September, when Guderian's XIX Corps joined hands with the spearheads of General Sigmund List's Fourteenth Army, fifty miles south of Brest-Litovsk the second pincer was closed. It was here at Brest-Litovsk, where more than twenty years before Imperial Germany had imposed peace on the newly created Soviet Republic, that the Soviet and Nazi armies now effected Poland's last partition. The bill presented to Hitler by Stalin for his collaboration was steep – half Poland and the Baltic states Estonia, Latvia and (from 28 September) Lithuania, as well as non-interference in Russia's dispute with Finland.[1] But Hitler could afford to wait for a final settlement in the east. He had won his first campaign there, and could now turn his eyes to the west.

Hitler's part in the conquest of Poland had been crucial. It was he who had set about building up the Wehrmacht on the foundations laid by Seeckt, imbued it with revolutionary ardour, and equipped it with deadly weapons; it was the Führer, too, who had fostered the whole idea of blitzkrieg, brought about the political and strategic conditions which made it possible, procured Russia's complicity, issued the necessary orders, then let loose his formations

---

[1] A Russian Grand Duchy until the Revolution of 1917, Finland had become a republic in 1919. Disputes with Russia over Finland's eastern frontier, which in the south was only eighteen miles from Leningrad (as Petrograd had been renamed in 1924), culminated in Soviet demands for military bases and a revision of the border in Russia's favour. The Finns rejected these demands, and war broke out on 30 November 1939.

and conquered. His grip on the armed forces, in or out of action, was absolute. By his various directives he determined what, militarily, was to be done, when it was to be done, and, to the consternation of the General Staff, even *how* it was to be done. The manner in which military operations were to be conducted was a province which the generals thought of as peculiarly their own, in which belief, however, they were sadly mistaken – having called for detailed plans for the execution of *Fall Weiss*, Hitler was not content to confine himself to political and strategic matters; he went through all the operation orders, down to regimental level, for the first phase of the attack, and then not only found fault with, but altered, them. Here was the Supreme Commander positively dictating to the General Staff on the subject of tactics. *Unerhört!*[1] Had his decisions and orders been wrong, the subsequent battles in Norway, the Low Countries, France, Greece, Africa, Russia, Italy, and the campaigns in North-West and Eastern Europe and in Germany itself, might have been conducted very differently, if they had taken place at all. But he was not wrong, at least not so far as the Polish campaign was concerned. He foresaw a far more rapid and complete breakthrough than had his generals, a circumstance unlikely to be of much comfort to these officers, or to enhance their Supreme Commander's confidence in them. So that when the campaign was over, Hitler was not inclined to be 'lectured' by the generals. Quite the contrary, indeed – and a further shock awaited them when he announced his intention, since it had become clear that the Western Allies were not prepared to make peace, of attacking them as soon as possible. Indeed on the very day on which Warsaw capitulated, 27 September, after being ruthlessly – and from the military point of view needlessly – bombed (an action which was in every way characteristic of Hitler's lust for blood and destruction), he actually told the three Wehrmacht Commanders-in-Chief that the date for assaulting the Franco-British armies would be 12 November. Throughout the campaign Hitler had been very much at the forefront. His special train had a so-called 'command coach' in which conferences would take place and from which orders would be issued. By 9 September this train was in Silesia, and from there Hitler would tour the battle areas, taking great enjoyment from the scenes he saw and, according to his secretary, careless of his personal safety. 'The Chief', she wrote, 'has taken to driving around as though he were in Germany, standing up in his open car even in the most hazardous areas . . . Obviously it gives the soldiers' morale a colossal boost to see the F. in the thick of the danger with them, but I still think it's too risky.' One of those who often accompanied Hitler, and who came to be greatly admired by British soldiers and by Churchill himself, was the commander of the Führer's bodyguard, Colonel Erwin Rommel, who

[1] Unheard of, unprecedented; thus, shocking.

reported that 'The Führer is in the best of moods . . . He says that in eight or ten days it'll all be over in the east and then our entire battle-hardened Wehrmacht will move west'. One week after a triumphant visit to Danzig on 19 September, Hitler's train returned to Berlin. By now he was contemplating the next move.

While Hitler and his armies swept through Poland, Churchill threw himself into the tasks confronting him. His prime responsibility was, of course, the war at sea, but as might have been expected this did not deter him from giving his opinion about other matters. At a meeting of the War Cabinet on 4 September he suggested that the Siegfried Line should be attacked by the Royal Air Force and the French Army in order to lessen German pressure on the Polish front. To this the Cabinet agreed, but in the event nothing was done. Churchill's method of obtaining information and initiating either action or discussion was unique, and consisted, as Martin Gilbert reminds us, of sending out minutes to his numerous advisers or colleagues in government. These notes would often propose some strategic plan or ask questions in order to encourage an exchange of ideas. 'Some contain words of rebuke,' writes Gilbert, 'some words of encouragement; some are stern, some witty; some are weighty, some light. But from each of his minutes, Churchill expected to learn what was happening over the full range of his responsibilities, and to probe every area of potential war policy and action.' When he became Prime Minister, he kept up this flow of minutes, many of them marked with his bright red label, 'ACTION THIS DAY', which spurred those to whom they were addressed into taking the appropriate action. Churchill's drive, imagination and range of experience, as well as his sheer confidence in, and determination to achieve, victory, had a profound effect on many of those accustomed to a more leisurely way of prosecuting government business, who now found themselves prodded into action by these minutes. 'They galvanized with a sense of personal responsibility, and a sense of the urgency of the perils through which the country was steering the Ministers and civil servants to whom they were addressed. "It was as though the machine had overnight acquired one or two new gears, capable of far higher speeds than had ever before been thought possible."'

One of the principal dangers at sea which Churchill had to face was, of course, that presented by the German U-boats, and he therefore made haste to put into effect the convoy system of protecting merchant shipping with escorting warships, which had served the country so well in the last two years of the Great War. While concerning himself with every aspect of naval equipment, policy and morale – whether it were building dummy ships to deceive air reconnaissance; looking into the question of guns for British cruisers, or that of Scapa Flow's air defences; providing leisure amenities for sailors in shore establishments; setting up a proper map room at the Admiralty to chart all shipping near British shores; having all naval vessels fitted with radar; or visiting and sailing in such craft – Churchill was also a member of the Land Forces Committee, whose first and principal task was to decide on the future size of the army and the date by which it should reach that size. The committee's decision, based on the assumption that the war would last for at least three years, was to equip fifty-five divisions by the end of 1941, twenty of which would be ready a year earlier. This plan was very much in line with Churchill's firmly expressed views.

What was to be done with this army once it had actually come into existence was another matter altogether, however. It was clear to all that Hitler held the initiative, nor was there a grand Anglo-French strategy for the conduct of war. The first eight months from September 1939 to May 1940 have been called 'Sitzkrieg', justly so, for the Allied armies in France simply sat down and waited to see what would happen. The French manned the Maginot Line and made a few half-hearted reconnaissance patrols into German territory, while the British Expeditionary Force slowly built up its strength and dug some inadequate defensive positions on the Franco-Belgian frontier.[1] If there were little offensive thinking being done by the BEF's Commander-in-Chief, General Lord Gort, VC, or by the sixty-eight-year-old French C-in-C, General Gamelin – who insisted that the blitzkrieg which had overwhelmed Poland could not happen in France (he was shortly to be shown to be wholly mistaken) – there was, as we have noted, plenty of such thinking being done by the Supreme Commander of the Wehrmacht and his staff at OKW, the results of which pushed France out of the war, and Churchill into the position to which he was, in every respect, best suited.

In the Admiralty there was never any lack of activity. The mere passage of the BEF to France without any interference by the enemy spoke loudly for the Royal Navy's strength and skill. For Churchill it was a repetition of what had happened in 1914, when in the same post he had been responsible for the safe passage of British troops to take their place beside the French Army. Although he took steps to investigate the feasibility of mass-producing small, cheap anti-submarine ships in order to relieve destroyers for other duties, he was urging the First Sea Lord, Admiral Sir Dudley Pound, and his colleagues to plan a British naval attack in the Baltic which, if carried out effectively, would deny Germany sea communications with Scandinavia (especially vital, since much of her iron ore came from Sweden). He regarded such an operation as the most important 'naval offensive open to the Royal Navy', for its successful

---

[1] The BEF that began to land in France in September was at first pitifully small; by 11 October it amounted only to four divisions.

execution would deny Norwegian and Swedish war material to Germany and perhaps even bring these countries in on the Allied side, besides having a profound effect on Russia. In the event, however, Britain's adventures in these northern waters were to have very mixed results. Another strategic area of great interest to Churchill was the Middle East, and he was disturbed to note in a Foreign Office telegram a suggestion that Egypt might not become involved in the war as an ally of Great Britain.[1] In seeking to maintain Egyptian support, he was to have the significant backing of the recently appointed Commander-in-Chief, Middle East, General Sir Archibald Wavell. The strategic importance of the Middle East and the Mediterranean to the British conduct of war cannot be overstated, and was to find expression in Churchill's bold reinforcement of that theatre at a time when Britain's own security was still in doubt. In August 1939 Wavell had appreciated that in the event of war, Germany would seek to dominate Eastern and South-Eastern Europe, while Italy, which already controlled Libya, Abyssinia and Eritrea, would attempt to do the same in North Africa and the Mediterranean. Control of the Mediterranean would therefore be a cardinal feature of British strategy, not only in order to secure British interests there – communications and oil among them – but to permit offensives to be mounted from air, sea and land bases against both Italy and Germany. To Wavell all this meant that his task was to secure Egypt and the Canal, control the Eastern Mediterranean, clear the Red Sea littoral and eventually develop operations on land against the Axis powers. It was not, however, until Italy declared war – on 10 June 1940, while France was on the point of collapsing – that Wavell began to put all these ideas into practice. When he did he met with some startling successes, and – goaded by Churchill to undertake too much with too little – some equally dramatic reverses.

The second half of September 1939 brought mostly bad news. The CIGS, General Ironside, reported to the War Cabinet that the French expected an attack on the Western Front within a month or so – it will be recalled that Hitler had told his generals that just such an attack was to be launched on 12 November – but Churchill was doubtful about its likelihood, although he recognized the need for establishing anti-tank obstacles and minefields at France's frontier with Belgium. While visiting the Fleet on 17 September he was subject to uncharacteristically gloomy meditation, recalling the losses and oppressions

[1] Egypt had been governed by British civil agents since the 1880s, but had been granted nominal independence in 1922. In 1936 Britain promised the country full independence and the phased withdrawal of all British troops (with the exception of the Canal Zone); this was delayed by the outbreak of war and, in 1940, by Italy's invasion of Egypt from Libya. Egypt was ostensibly neutral during the war, but was an important British base, and thus its government conformed to be British-directed.

of the previous war and noting that he was now subject to such uncertainties once more. And the international scene was bleak indeed – with Poland conquered, France unwarlike, Russia of no comfort to the Allied cause, Japan hostile, America uncertain. 'The British Empire remained intact and gloriously united, but ill-prepared, unready. We still had command of the sea. We were woefully outmatched in numbers in this new mortal weapon of the air.' Curiously enough, it was to be through victory in the air a year later that Britain was to get her second wind, and thereby be able to turn away from the problem of avoiding defeat to that of inflicting it. Back in London, having recovered from these harsh recollections, Churchill was once more urging upon his admirals the need for a naval offensive.

He did not, however, confine himself solely to naval matters, and during the last days of September the strategic ideas he expressed in the War Cabinet, the sheer activity of his mind, and the force and eloquence of his speeches in the House of Commons began to bring increasing acknowledgement of his leadership and of the likelihood of his becoming Prime Minister. His first wartime broadcast, made on 1 October, was received with enthusiasm and greatly praised. In it, he reviewed the position in Poland ('she will rise again like a rock') and in Russia ('It is a riddle wrapped in a mystery inside an enigma'); praised the Royal Navy's vigilance and zeal; explained how the country was preparing for the war to last at least three years, and that great ordeals, particularly from the air, must be faced and would be faced; and stated that Britain would fight on to the end. John Colville, who was to become Churchill's Private Secretary, spoke of him as 'the only man in the country who commands anything like universal respect,' while calling his broadcast 'inspiring' and predicting that he would become Prime Minister. An old friend, Lady Desborough, wrote to Churchill that his broadcast had been 'a touchstone, lifting up our hearts . . . You made one feel that all that matters most is unconquerable . . .' It was the first of many broadcasts which would inspire and uplift the nation.

During the first week of October two events of profound significance occurred: the first of what was to become a long-lasting series of exchanges between Churchill and President Roosevelt took place; and Hitler made the first of his peace overtures to Britain. On 6 October the Führer announced to the Reichstag that he had offered peace to the West provided those nations recognized the legitimacy of his conquest of Poland. Even before the predictably unenthusiastic replies from France and Britain, he seemed to have abandoned this peace offensive, for on 10 October he again summoned his senior commanders and read them a memorandum which he had drawn up the previous day. Its language was uncompromising. The German war aim was military settlement with the West, and by settlement he meant the removal of the democracies' ability to interfere with German domination of Europe. Hitler's War Directive No 6 gave the necessary guidance:

1. Should it become evident in the near future that England, and, under her influence, France also, are not disposed to bring the war to an end, I have decided, without further loss of time, to go over to the offensive . . .

3. I therefore issue the following orders for the further conduct of military operations:

(a)   An offensive will be planned on the northern flank of the Western front, through Luxembourg, Belgium, and Holland. This offensive must be launched at the earliest possible moment and in greatest possible strength.

(b)   The purpose of this offensive will be to defeat as much as possible of the French Army and of the forces of the allies fighting on her side, and at the same time to win as much territory as possible in Holland, Belgium, and Northern France, to serve as a base for the successful prosecution of the air and sea war against England and as a wide protective area for the economically vital Ruhr.

(c)   The time of the attack will depend upon the readiness for action of the armoured and motorized units involved. These units are to be made ready with all speed. It will depend also upon the weather conditions obtaining and foreseeable at the time . . .

8. I request Commanders-in-Chief to submit to me their detailed plans based on this directive at the earliest moment . . .

The Commanders-in-Chief did not object to the strategic idea. It was the proposed timing to which they took exception, and they were loath to commit the army to an operation which they believed would fail. The Army C-in-C, Brauchitsch, was therefore chosen for the unenviable task of reasoning with the Führer on two counts: first, that a major offensive in November, given the likelihood, if not the certainty, of poor prevailing weather conditions then, was quite out of the question; second – and still more explosive an issue – that the army commanders should be left alone to conduct military operations in the way they thought fit, without interference from Hitler's headquarters. Neither proposition was well received by the Führer, but when Brauchitsch was unwise enough to question the performance and spirit of the German soldier in Poland, he was subjected to such a tirade of invective from Hitler, who accused the army of disloyalty, defeatism, sabotage, lack of belief in his genius, even cowardice, that the unfortunate C-in-C bent before the storm and retired, vanquished, to OKH headquarters at Zossen, incoherent and in a state of severe shock. In the event Hitler did postpone the attack, because of bad weather, but it was not long before he returned to the charge.[1]

Meanwhile, Churchill himself was considering what reply he should make to a letter he had received from Roosevelt. The American President had written to express his pleasure that Churchill was again at the Admiralty and to say that he would welcome the First Lord's keeping in personal touch with him by diplomatic bag, and passing on any information that he or Chamberlain felt Roosevelt should have. In his reply, Churchill endorsed the idea of the establishment of a zone extending for 300 miles from American shores, in which submarines of any belligerent country should not be allowed to take action, while pointing out that Britain could only accept the arrangement if it were the United States Navy that enforced the guarantee of safety for passenger and merchant ships within the zone. Churchill also pledged Britain's help in trying to keep the war away from American waters. So began the flow of telegrams between these two men, which were to have such a profound influence on Anglo-American co-operation, Allied joint strategy, and, in the end, both the conduct and the outcome of the war.

It was just as well that Churchill *was* at the Admiralty, for at this stage of the war about the only real military activity was at sea. On the same day on which Chamberlain formally rejected Hitler's peace offer in a House of Commons statement, Churchill warned that the weeks ahead would be full of danger, particularly at sea. He was right. German U-boats were hard at work, and two days later one penetrated the Scapa Flow defences and sank the battleship *Royal Oak* – more than eight hundred officers and men were drowned. In stark contrast to Hitler's 'Close your eyes to pity' was Churchill's reception of the news; 'Poor fellows,' he murmured, tears in his eyes. He had, however, little time for mourning, so continuous, so comprehensive and so compelling was his work. His tasks ranged from studying all the War Cabinet papers, urging a greater flow of aircraft from factory to squadron, grappling with the problem of Italy and the Mediterranean, pondering the Nazis' next move – it appeared that there might be a German plan to invade England – wrestling with the matter of Eire's neutrality, visiting France to talk to Generals Gamelin and Georges, sending telegrams to Roosevelt, giving accounts of naval operations to the House of Commons, and again broadcasting to the nation. In this second talk he praised the calm, businesslike way in which the people were carrying on, spoke of the

---

[1] It may be noted here that although Churchill, once he became Prime Minister, could goad and prod his generals when their (as he saw it) lack of drive and boldness exasperated him, he was never either as unreasonable or as unkind to his senior commanders as was Hitler to his.

country's improved military situation, pointed to Germany's lack of allies, and reiterated his confidence that if Britain were to have to face 'violent and dire events', she would do so 'with resolution'.

One of Churchill's main concerns at the Admiralty was the loss of merchant shipping, not only from enemy submarines, but from a new menace – the magnetic mine, Hitler's so-called 'secret weapon' which had first been used in September 1939, and the mystery of which was not solved for three months. Nor was this problem of shipping losses confined to mine and submarine or to home waters. In the South Atlantic the German pocket battleship *Graf Spee*, had been enjoying spectacular successes against merchant shipping until she was found and engaged by three British cruisers on 13 December, and obliged to take refuge in Montevideo in neutral Uruguayan waters. Under international laws governing neutrality, she was only permitted seventy-two hours in a neutral port before she had to put to sea again. Grievously damaged, and it being impossible to complete repairs within the time limit, she was blown up by her own crew. Churchill was much cheered by this successful offensive action and remembered later how exciting it had been to 'follow the drama of this brilliant action from the Admiralty War Room'.

Winston Churchill was now sixty-five, Adolf Hitler fifty. Both were full of vigour and eloquence. Hitler even went to the extent of telling his generals on 23 November – in yet another lecture at the Reich Chancellery – how convinced he was of his own powers of intellect and decision, that he himself was irreplaceable and that his decision was unchangeable: 'I shall attack France and England at the most favourable and quickest moment . . . Every hope of compromise is childish . . . I have to choose between victory and destruction. I choose victory . . .' The trouble with German leaders in the past, men like Bismarck and Moltke,[1] was that they had not been hard enough, unlike himself – 'the hardest man in centuries'. What Hitler did not understand, however, and could not have prophesied, was that his attack in the west would prove to be the very act which would bring about Churchill's leading and inspiring the British nation in the conduct of war. To the Führer, though, his offensive in the west would be 'the end of the World War, not just a single action'. Here he was on uncertain ground, for by attacking there he would be embarking on the first of the real battles for Europe. Far from ending the world war, it would lead to precisely that. Hitler's War Directive No 8, issued on 20 November, laid down that a high state of readiness must be preserved so that the offensive could rapidly

---

[1] Prince Otto von Bismarck (1815–1898), Prussian and German Chancellor, who brought about creation of the German Empire in 1871 by means of Prussia's wars with Denmark (1863–4), Austria (1866) and France (1870–71) – wars whose strategy was framed by Field Marshal Count Helmuth von Moltke (1800–91), Chief of Prussian General Staff from 1857.

be mounted once the weather was favourable. The directive also contained a significant modification to the former plan in that it ordered that provision must be made for the main weight of the attack to be switched from the north to the centre should enemy dispositions indicate that greater success would thereby be achieved. When *Fall Gelb* (Operation Yellow) was at last executed, it was to be this very switch which was decisive in bringing about Hitler's most startling victory, and since by then he had convinced himself, not wholly without reason, that it was his own plan, one more step was taken on the road to absolute belief in his own infallibility, and thus to megalomania and ruin.

Whereas Hitler was able to decide what was to be done and had the power to put his decisions into effect, Churchill was able only to recommend action, and usually found that either his War Cabinet colleagues or the Chiefs of Staff opposed his plans. A.J.P. Taylor admirably sums up the position when he writes: 'The government were still moving into war backwards, with their eyes tightly closed. Churchill was the one exception, a cuckoo in the nest, as restless against inaction and as fertile with proposals as Lloyd George had been in Asquith's war government.' The First Lord's proposals included both the launching of floating mines down the Rhine, and also the mining of Norwegian territorial waters, which German ships would have to use to move Swedish iron ore in winter, when ice closed the Baltic. Churchill had long been obsessed with the idea of action in Norway, and this was further reinforced after the Soviet Union's invasion of Finland in November, when for a time British ministers toyed with the intention of coming to Finland's aid with a joint Anglo-French expeditionary force, which on its way would seize the Norwegian port of Narvik[1] and from there wreck Swedish iron ore mines – exactly what had been in Churchill's mind for some time. In March 1940, before anything could be done, however, Finland, hugely outnumbered and outgunned, and having put up a very gallant defence, gave up the fight and made peace with Russia. One result of this was that the cautious Daladier was replaced as French Premier by Paul Reynaud, who revived the Anglo-French resolution to act together. When action was at last taken it was too late, although there had been one successful incident in Norwegian waters in which Churchill had played a direct part, and whose outcome greatly cheered him. This had come about when, on 16 February, he had received intelligence that the German supply ship *Altmark* was inside Norwegian territorial waters, bearing in her hold some three hundred British merchant seamen who had been captured as a result of the *Graf Spee*'s former raiding activities. Churchill

---

[1] In winter, when ice closed the seaways from Swedish ports across the Baltic to Germany, iron ore was sent by rail to Narvik, where it was loaded on to ships for transport to open German ports.

thereupon gave orders to Royal Naval cruisers and destroyers which were nearby to go to the rescue.

HMS *Cossack*, commanded by Captain (later Admiral of the Fleet Sir) Philip Vian – a man after Churchill's heart, and who possessed some of Nelson's 'touch and take' attributes – was the first to sight the *Altmark*. The British warships followed the German vessel to Jösing Fiord, only to find when Vian attempted to send boarding parties that Norwegian gunboats, whose commander claimed that there were no British prisoners in the Germany ship, had orders to resist. Vian signalled the Admiralty and Churchill himself, after consulting the Foreign Secretary, Halifax, sent instructions. Unless the Norwegians (at that date still neutral) would conduct the German ship to Bergen with Anglo-Norwegian guards and escort, 'you should board *Altmark*, liberate the prisoners and take possession of the ship pending further instructions'. If the Norwegians interfered to the extent of attacking the British ships, appropriate defensive action was to be taken. In the event *Altmark* ran aground, *Cossack*'s boarding party killed 4 Germans and wounded 5, the rest surrendering or escaping, and 299 British prisoners were released and taken aboard the destroyer, which then sailed for England. It may have been a minor triumph, but it was a triumph just the same. Britain rejoiced, and Lord Lloyd gave credit where it was due – to Churchill, commenting that any other minister's courage would have failed him. To cap it all, there was another, albeit less spectacular, success when two transatlantic convoys completed their passage from Canada without loss.

Churchill's qualities of leadership were not, of course, confined to boldness in proposing action and taking decisions. It was the way he worked which won admiration, even devotion, from people of all sorts. His sheer presence inspired, his capacity for work was astonishing, yet he was intensely human, making his staff feel that they were all part of a great team; when he was at the Admiralty, his secretary recalled, everything buzzed, when he was touring, the place was dead. It was clear to all who worked with him that he wanted to take over the direction of the whole war. Because of the action that Hitler was about to initiate, it would not be long before he did so.

At the same time as Churchill was receiving congratulations for the outcome of the *Altmark* incident, Hitler was listening enthralled to the tactical ideas of General von Manstein, Chief of Staff of General Gerd von Rundstedt's Army Group A. Hitler had already confounded Brauchitsch and Halder when, in October 1939, he had suggested that a main attack from south of Namur to Amiens might 'cut off and annihilate the enemy'. However, in January 1940 secret German documents giving the operational plans for invading Holland and Belgium had been captured when a German aircraft made a forced landing at Mechelen, which gave the Führer cause to think again. Being already dissatisfied with OKH's ideas for limited, frontal attacks, he again took up the notion that the principal *Schwerpunkt* should strike through the Ardennes to Sedan, and drive on into the heart of France from there. Nothing could have been better designed to bring about a rapid and decisive victory, for Gamelin's plan for France's defence, the soundness of which had in his view been confirmed by the captured German plans, was based on a strong right flank, the Maginot Line, a strong left flank for the Dyle-Breda position, and a weak centre opposite the Belgian Ardennes, with little or nothing behind it. 'What a standing temptation,' wrote Alistair Horne, 'the spectacle of this French Line, then, so weak in the centre, might present to an opposing captain of audacity and genius.' There was little doubt about Hitler's audacity, nor, in his own estimation, his genius. The whole concept coincided with his ideas about the value of surprise, of boldness, of risk, of sudden, unexpected, hammer-like blows, paralysing in their strength and velocity. When he heard Manstein's detailed proposals for just such an offensive, therefore, an offensive which would utterly smash all resistance and which would prove decisive because it would penetrate behind the Allied defences and then cut them off at the roots, as a sickle cuts corn (*Sichelschnitt*, 'Cut of the Sickle', was the plan's codename), he received them with rapt enthusiasm, and shortly afterwards a new directive for *Fall Gelb* emerged:

> The objective of offensive Yellow is to deny Holland and Belgium to the English by swiftly occupying them; to defeat, by an attack through Belgian and Luxembourg territory, the largest possible forces of the Anglo-French army; and thereby to pave the way for the destruction of the military strength of the enemy. The main weight of the attack across Belgium and Luxembourg will be south of the line Liège-Charleroi.

The broad plan that was to result from all this was that General Fedor von Bock's Army Group B, with some twenty-nine divisions, was to be the bait to draw Anglo-French forces into Holland and Belgium, thereby allowing Rundstedt's Army Group A of forty-five divisions, including seven panzer divisions, to smash through the Ardennes and swarm over the River Meuse between Dinant and Sedan. In the van, properly enough, would be Guderian's XIX Panzer Corps. At the same time General Ritter Wilhelm von Leeb's Army Group C would threaten the Maginot Line. When Guderian was explaining his detailed plans to Hitler and the generals of Army Group A in March 1940, it was the Führer who asked the panzer commander what he would do after crossing the Meuse, a vitally important question, as Guderian observed. His reply was that unless ordered otherwise he would drive on westwards, and gave it as his opinion that his objective should be Amiens, not Paris. Hitler indicated his agreement.

Before discussing the comprehensive success of the whole German invasion of France and the Low Countries, it is necessary to turn back to Scandinavia, for, as if Hitler had not already demonstrated how bold a strategist he could be, he was to do so further by launching an attack on Denmark and Norway. On 1 March he had signed his directive for this attack, the purpose of which was to forestall British action there, secure Swedish iron ore for Germany and provide both the Luftwaffe and the Kriegsmarine with additional bases from which to operate against the United Kingdom. As small a force as possible was to be employed; surprise, speed and skill were to make up for numbers. They did. In two ways the operation's success was remarkable. First, it seemed to show that Germany could do what she liked, when she liked, and that the Allies, indecisive, feeble in conflict, were helpless to stop her; second, it seemed, despite severe German naval losses, that even Britain's traditional naval omnipotence counted for nothing in the face of the Wehrmacht.

On 8 April Hitler launched his invasion, which began on the following day. Surprise, speed and sheer military skill paid great dividends. Denmark was overrun with only a minor skirmish or two, capitulating on the 9th, and all the important Norwegian ports were captured by the Germans, while Allied intervention was a catalogue of confusion, contradictory orders and failure. Although Narvik was captured at the end of May by British, French and Polish troops after six weeks of fighting, it was taken only to be evacuated again, while the two principal landings at Namsos and Åndalsnes, aimed at recapturing the important harbour at Trondheim, fared even worse. The British Army was having its first lesson in the impossibility of conducting amphibious operations without enjoying two of such a venture's indispensable conditions – absolute clarity of purpose in the co-ordination of the various services, and complete air and naval superiority. Of course there were gains too, in that the German Navy suffered heavy losses – three cruisers and ten destroyers, together with two battle cruisers and a battleship severely disabled. But the fact was that in this first encounter with Germany's armed forces, and in circumstances where it might have been supposed that the Royal Navy's strength and traditions would be decisive, the British Army had been put ashore, only to be beaten and chased out again. Not only had the Germans demonstrated how effective air power could be when properly used in conjunction with land forces, but the German Army itself had shown that it had been excellently trained and was supremely well led. Churchill summed up the German qualities, and the Allied failures, thus:

At Narvik a mixed and improvised German force, barely six thousand strong, held at bay for six weeks some twenty thousand Allied troops, and though driven out of the town lived to see them depart. The Narvik attack, so brilliantly opened by the Navy, was paralysed by the refusal of the military commander[1] to run what was admittedly a desperate risk. The division of our resources between Narvik and Trondheim was injurious to both our plans . . . At Namsos there was a muddy waddle forward and back. Only at Aandalsnes did we bite. The Germans traversed in seven days the road from Namsos to Mosjoen, which the French and British had declared impassable . . . We, who had command of the sea and could pounce anywhere on an undefended coast, were outpaced by the enemy moving by land across very large distances in the face of every obstacle. In this Norwegian encounter, our finest troops, the Scots and Irish Guards, were baffled by the vigour, enterprise, and training of Hitler's young men.

In *The Gathering Storm* Churchill emphasizes that in her struggle with Britain's navy, Germany all but destroyed her own, for in June 1940, after Narvik had been evacuated, all that the Kriegsmarine could effectively put to sea in the way of surface vessels of any size were seven warships – three cruisers, two of them light, and four destroyers. This was to have a profound influence on the aftermath of the British Army's next confrontation with the Wehrmacht. There was, of course, another supremely important consequence of the Norwegian campaign, one which wholly altered the course the war was to take. Severely criticized for the failures in Norway, Chamberlain resigned and was succeeded as Prime Minister by Churchill on 10 May, the very day on which the Germans began to destroy both the French Army and the French people's will to fight. It is these events which must now be examined more closely.

The measure of Neville Chamberlain's grip on strategic matters may perhaps be gauged by his assertion on 4 April 1940, speaking of Allied military strength in France and Belgium, that 'Hitler has missed the bus'. Four days later the German invasions of Denmark and Norway began, and were rapidly successful. Allied intervention, primarily British, and under British command, was, as we have seen, dogged by contradictory orders, lack of joint-service action, and inability to operate effectively in the face of German air power, so that by 2 May (except for Narvik, which was not abandoned until 8 June, by which time the dangers to Britain herself had become incalculably greater, and much closer) British troops had been evacuated from Norway. But although the campaign had ended in almost ignominious defeat, it was not without something on the credit side – severe damage to the German Navy, of which

---

[1] Major-General P.J. Mackesy. He was replaced at the end of April by Lieutenant-General Claude Anchinleck; by then, however, it was too late for the military situation in Norway to be retrieved.

the benefits were to be felt when, about a month later, there came the 'miracle' of Dunkirk, and when later still the combined integrity of the Royal Navy and Royal Air Force put paid to any German invasion of Britain. There was, too, the not insignificant matter of a million or so tons of Norwegian merchant shipping, and some naval vessels, which sailed for Britain when the situation in Norway was seen to be hopeless; with those ships there also sailed a good number of Norwegian seamen and servicemen, most of whom would fight in the Allied cause.

As A.J.P. Taylor has pointed out, however, as far as the British people were concerned, such small gains were of little consolation, and although it could be argued that Churchill had had far more to do with the Norwegian campaign in the first place, and far more influence over strategic matters generally, than had Chamberlain, 'their wrath turned against Chamberlain; their enthusiasm towards Churchill . . . Public opinion . . . judged men by their spirit.' It was much the same in the House of Commons, where a debate on the Government's handling of the Norwegian campaign began on 7 May. It was a crucial affair, and Harold Nicolson[1] noted in his diary that Chamberlain's reference, in a feeble speech, to complacency was greeted with ironic cheers; that the speech by the Labour leader, Attlee, was also weak; and that the speech by the Liberal leader, Churchill's old friend, Sir Archibald Sinclair, was powerfully damaging (he used a phrase, which Churchill was subsequently to echo, to the effect that wars are not won by evacuations). Even more devastating for Chamberlain, however, was the Conservative Member for North Portsmouth, Admiral of the Fleet Sir Roger Keyes – in full naval uniform, covered in medal ribbons – who told the House how dreadfully bad had been the conduct of naval operations during the Narvik affair, only to be followed by Leo Amery who, with powerful effect, quoted Oliver Cromwell's terrible indictment of the Long Parliament's unfitness to manage the nation's affairs: 'Depart, I say, and let us have done with you. In the name of God, go!'

There was a good deal of coming and going during the next three days. On the second day of the debate Labour divided the House. Churchill spoke with his customary fire, eloquence and loyalty, but the Government's majority fell sharply and Chamberlain's attempts next day to reinforce his position by appealing to Conservative rebels resulted in their making it clear that members of the opposition parties, Labour and the Liberals, must be brought into the Government. Since such men were unlikely to be willing to serve under Chamberlain himself, a successor must be sought. But who should that successor be? The choice lay between Churchill and Halifax. Although it might seem strange to us now, many leading men of the day were willing to accept Halifax

[1] Nicolson was the National Labour MP for West Leicester from 1935–45.

as Prime Minister. Things came to a head on the afternoon of 9 May at a meeting between Chamberlain, Halifax, Churchill and the Conservative Chief Whip, David Margesson. Although Churchill had repeatedly expressed his willingness to serve under any leader at a time of such national peril, he had heard from his friend Brendan Bracken that Labour would not be unwilling to join a government led by himself. When, therefore, Chamberlain asked the crucial question as to whether Churchill would serve under Halifax, the First Lord remained silent, and Halifax then broke the deadlock by conceding that it would hardly be fitting under the prevailing war conditions for the Prime Minister to sit in the House of Lords (he had succeeded to the viscountcy in 1934). When, later that day, the Labour leaders confirmed that they would not wish to join Chamberlain's government, but would probably do so under a new leader, the Prime Minister's position was further weakened, and even the news during the early hours of 10 May that the German invasion of Belgium and Holland was under way could not save him. Sir Kingsley Wood, Secretary of State for Air, told Chamberlain he must go. With Labour's confirmation that they would serve under a new leader, the latter resigned, and having told King George VI that Halifax (whom the King would have preferred) 'was not enthusiastic', it was agreed that Churchill must become Prime Minister. In a telephone conversation the previous evening Churchill had told his son, Randolph, that he thought he would be Prime Minister on the next day. By six o'clock on the evening of 10 May, he was. 'As soon as Churchill had returned to his room at the Admiralty,' writes Martin Gilbert, 'he began the work of forming a Government. He was sixty-five years old. For more than forty years he had believed that the destiny of Britain would be well guarded in his hands . . . Now all his qualities, all his energies, all his experience, and his faith in himself, were to be put to the test.'

On that same day, Adolf Hitler, the man who for some twenty years had believed that the destiny of Germany would be well guarded in *his* hands was at his field headquarters at Münstereifel, overseeing the launch of *Fall Gelb* – that one last decisive battle with France, for which he had called in *Mein Kampf*. 'Germany's decisive struggle has begun' and 'The Führer at the Western Front' proclaimed the headlines in that day's edition of the *Völkischer Beobachter*, and from the reports that began to come in to Hitler's headquarters as 10 May wore on, it seemed that this particular battle was going to be decisive, for he heard that the French and British armies *were* advancing into Belgium, were in fact falling into the very trap prepared for them, the Allies believing that the German offensive was to be a repeat of the old Schlieffen Plan that they had faced in 1914. Before the part Hitler played in it, and Churchill's reaction to it, it might be helpful quickly to summarize *Sichelschnitt*. The essential point was that the plan worked, and it worked far better and far faster than the Germans could ever have believed likely. Holland was swiftly overrun and formally capitulated on 15 May. Hitler's ideas about special operations to seize fortifications and river and canal crossings were completely vindicated. The supposedly impregnable Belgian fortress of Eben-Emael, commanding the junction of the Meuse with the Albert Canal, fell to airborne attack by a tiny force in little more than a day's fighting. The main thrust of Army Group A to the Meuse and beyond was brilliantly successful. Guderian's corps poured through a hole made in the French line, with panzer and Stuka once more demonstrating their performance in action. In ten days German spearheads reached Abbeville, three days later Boulogne. On 28 May Belgium surrendered. British forces, sandwiched between Army Groups A and B, fell back on Dunkirk, from which, together with many French units, they were evacuated by 4 June. The Germans then set about finishing off the French who, true to Hitler's prediction that they would not have the will to withstand setbacks, surrendered on 16 June. Meanwhile Italy, eager to be in at the kill, had declared war against the Allies on 10 June.

The most startling of all these tactical successes was Guderian's crossing of the Meuse on 13 May, and his expanding of the hole thus made into a huge fifty-mile gap through which the panzers flooded, reaching the English Channel a week later and splitting the Allied armies. With Rommel, now a major-general commanding 7th Panzer Division on the right (that is, the north) of General Ewald von Kleist's Panzer Group,[1] it might have been expected that, leading from the front as he did, and taking personal command of his forward battalion, any temporary delay in the tempo of getting his division over the Meuse would soon be overcome. So it proved, and once the Germans had gained sufficient space on the west bank to develop the leverage of manoeuvre they quickly prised open the French defences. The speed and magnitude of the victory was ample proof of what could be achieved when blitzkrieg tactics were coupled with bold leadership. Guderian's theories had triumphed in practice and he now expected – as he had suggested to Hitler in March – to continue advancing until his XIX Panzer Corps reached the Channel. But greatly to his chagrin and surprise Kleist, acting upon orders from Führer headquarters, ordered him to halt, so as to allow some of the infantry formations to come up. This was the very negation of the whole blitzkrieg idea, and after Guderian had made the understandable protests and threats to resign, he was permitted to carry out further 'reconnaissance in

---

[1] Rommel's division was part of General Hermann Hoth's XV Panzer Corps, in turn part of General Günther von Kluge's Fourth Army. Kleist's Panzer Group comprised two panzer corps, including Guderian's, and a motorized corps, drawn from two different armies.

force'. That permission was all he needed, for a reconnaissance in force is open to all sorts of interpretation. By 18 May his panzers had reached St Quentin; next day they were forcing the Somme; on the 20th Guderian himself was on the outskirts of Amiens watching 1st Panzer Division's attack; the day after that a unit of 2nd Panzer Division was at the mouth of the River Somme, on the Channel coast. All that Guderian had promised had come about. Why and how had it happened? The BEF, separated from the bulk of the French armies by the panzers' breakthrough, did its best with a spirited counter-attack south-wards towards Arras on 21 May, which assisted in a more general withdrawal towards Dunkirk, fifty or so miles to the north, but the French Army, as was noted in Chapter 1, was 'smashed to pieces, cut to shreds by the tanks, nailed to the ground by the enemy's Stukas'. The truth was that in almost every aspect of strategy and tactics; of combining fire power and manoeuvre; of initiative, boldness, improvisation and exploiting opportunity; of co-ordinating air and ground forces; of leadership, morale and spirit; the Germans were vastly super-ior to the Allies. Their concentration, speed, risk-taking, momentum and sheer confidence overwhelmed the Allied forces, which were strung out without proper mutually supporting defensive positions, without defence in depth, and without the necessary counter-penetration and counter-attack reserves to hand and ready for immediate action. Hitler was thoroughly justified in congratulat-ing his soldiers and airmen on their great victory. Although there was still some fighting to do after his 5 June order of the day about Dunkirk's fall (see p. 5), French capitulation soon followed; as Rommel put it, 'the war has gradually turned into a lightning tour of France.'

As to Hitler's own part in it all, the question is whether he had also justified his own position as Supreme Commander of the Wehrmacht. There are perhaps two answers here. In his conception and adoption of the overall plan for *Sichelschnitt*, he had been emphatically vindicated. In its execution, however, there are two areas of doubt: firstly, his orders on 16 May to halt the panzer divisions, which so angered and frustrated Guderian; secondly, the question of why the British Army, together with many French units, was allowed to get away at Dunkirk, when with even more speed and boldness on the part of the Germans, the entire force might have been put in the bag. As it turned out, the former hesitancy did not matter much; the halting of the panzers on 24 May, however, was a blunder of incalculable proportions.

When, on 16 May, Hitler became worried about Guderian's flanks and the danger of a counter-attack against them from the south, his behaviour in the Führer headquarters was not that of a commander possessed of that indis-pensable quality of calm – a commander who, having issued his orders with confidence in them, himself retires to rest. Quite the contrary – excitable, talk-ative, ever ready to blame others, it was clear that Hitler, who prided himself on his iron nerve, completely lost it, as Halder recalled on 17 May: 'Führer is terribly nervous. Frightened by his own success, he is afraid to take any chance and so would rather pull the reins on us'; and again on the following day: 'Führer keeps worrying about south flank. He rages and screams that we are on the way to ruin the whole campaign. He won't have any part in continuing the operation in a westward direction.' As we have seen, his interference was evaded by Guderian's 'reconnaissance in force', but it is interesting to note that here Hitler was missing the whole point of all that Guderian had for so long been stressing – that once a panzer thrust had got going, it must maintain momentum night and day. It must never halt, for to do so would allow it to be located, checked, counter-attacked. The enemy must be subjected continuously to unexpected, ever-deepening, ever-broadening thrusts, disrupting reserves, communications, headquarters, supply areas, by a never-ending yet ever more paralysing flow of integrated panzer, motorized infantry and artillery groups with the Stukas and transport aircraft to keep them supported and supplied. All this was fundamental. Yet the very proof of the blitzkrieg's triumphant success had reduced almost to panic the military genius who had promised to restore the superiority of free operations.

The question of halting the panzers later on is a different one, and here Hitler's fault lay not so much in interfering, as in *not* having done so. On 23 May Kluge, commanding Fourth Army with most of the panzer divisions, proposed to Rundstedt, Commanding Army Group A, that his formations should 'halt and close up'. The latter, convinced that the Allied armies were trapped between his own army group and Bock's Army Group B to the north, therefore agreed, Fourth Army's War Diary noting that 'the Army will, in the main, halt tomorrow [24 May] in accordance with Colonel-General von Rundstedt's order.' Thus far, it is clear that the order was given, on the suggestion of Fourth Army's commander, by the Army Group commander. But Hitler, visiting Rundstedt on 24 May, endorsed it. There was at the time considerable disagreement between various general officers. The Army C-in-C, Brauchitsch, wanted the advance to continue by putting Fourth Army under Bock, who would then continue to attack the Allies from east, south and west. Halder disagreed, however, and Rundstedt supported him, believing that there was still plenty of time in which to trap the Allied force, while Bock had his own fish to fry. It follows, therefore, that Hitler's error was not in initiating the order to halt, but in allowing it to stand, in failing to see – after Guderian's triumphant demonstration of the rightness of his own theories of armoured warfare – that the one thing, as Supreme Commander, he must not allow to happen was for the panzers to halt. He should have made sure, given that he had the supreme tactical authority, that the relentless drive went on until the enemy annihilation was absolute. It was in this respect that he failed, but it was a failure of *in*action.

Moreover, this inaction persisted for two days. Not until 26 May did he give the order for the attacks to continue. By then it was too late. In the end, of course, the allocation of blame is irrelevant. The Wehrmacht did its best to prevent the BEF and other forces from escaping via Dunkirk, but the British Army's doggedness, the gallantry of the Royal Navy and of the crews of the small ships that sailed to Dunkirk to lend their assistance, and the Royal Air Force were too much for them. For the Third Reich it was a most serious blunder, but it did not stop Hitler, flushed with victory, from creating twelve field marshals[1] on 19 July, nor from being looked upon by his generals 'as a military genius and also as a fount of honour. There were no doubts in 1940.'

If there were no doubt in anyone's mind that Hitler was in charge of the German war machine, there was soon to be little doubt that it was Churchill who intended to run British military affairs. The War Cabinet itself was small – Chamberlain, Attlee, Halifax and Arthur Greenwood[2] with Churchill, as both Prime Minister *and* Minister of Defence in the chair. Relatively few changes were made among ministers of Cabinet rank, outside the War Cabinet, although most importantly Ernest Bevin became Minister of Labour and Beaverbrook Minister of Aircraft Production. But, as A.J.P. Taylor so forcefully points out, Churchill's appointment of himself to the additional post of Defence Minister was of profound significance. 'He did not seek parliamentary approval for this. He acquired no statutory powers. He had no staff other than the military wing of the war cabinet secretariat, the head of which, General [Sir Hastings – 'Pug' –] Ismay, became a member of the chief of staff's committee as Churchill's watchdog. The name itself was enough. It made Churchill supreme director of the war on the military side.' What is more, the Minister of Defence regarded himself as peculiarly suited to such a role. He was in this own view expertly qualified to direct the operations of all three services. He had taken part in several military campaigns as a young army officer, and had commanded a battalion in the Great War; he had twice been in charge at the Admiralty and had concerned himself closely with both naval weapons and naval strategy; he had from the very outset interested himself in military aviation, very nearly earned his wings as a pilot, and had been Secretary of State for Air – indeed, he frequently dressed up as an air commodore (equivalent in rank to a commodore in the Royal Navy or a brigadier in the army), actually sporting 'honorary wings' on his tunic; his knowledge of military history was extensive and his writing of it prolific. 'His mind teemed with original, often with dangerous, ideas, and he could sustain them with technical arguments. The chiefs of

[1] Among them Brauchitsch, Keitel, Rundstedt, Bock, Leeb and Kluge; Göring was promoted to the specially created rank of Reich Marshal, of which he was the only one.
[2] Respectively Lord President of the Council, Lord Privy Seal, Foreign Secretary and Minister without Portfolio.

staff had difficulty in resisting him . . . [they] had to answer Churchill's proposals with objections equally technical and even more carefully thought out. This was a wearing business, especially when Churchill, in his romantic way, suggested that the conduct of the war would be much improved if some generals, or even some chiefs of staff, were shot.' Yet in the day-to-day business of running the war, Churchill, amateur strategist though he may have been, succeeded in winning both the admiration and affection of his various Chiefs or Staff, and he in his turn was disinclined to overturn professional opinion when it was cogently presented.

As he presided over his first War Cabinet on 11 May 1940, there was little military news to cheer him. Things were going badly in Norway, and next day not only were the reports from that theatre 'far from satisfactory', but the Chief of the Air Staff, Air Chief Marshal Sir Cyril Newall, suggested that the German invasion of Belgium and Holland might be a preliminary to the establishment of bases from which the Luftwaffe would mount air attacks against Britain – precisely the idea contained in Hitler's War Directive No 6. At a meeting of the Chiefs of Staff Committee on the 13th, at which Churchill presided, there arose the question of whether more air support should be provided from Britain for the Allied armies in France and Belgium, but no decision was taken. It was a full day for Churchill, for he was completing his ministerial appointments for the new government, and that afternoon, having already confided to his ministers that he had 'nothing to offer but blood, toil, tears and sweat', repeated this offer to the House of Commons, together with those splendid sentences, quoted at the beginning of this narrative (see p. 4) as to the government's policy and aim. The purpose of victory was clear enough and it certainly would not be achieved without the policy of waging war, but for the time being it was also clear that any war waging would be defensive, and more concerned with the avoidance of defeat than with the imposition of it upon the enemy. Although the news from Norway continued to worsen, Churchill was – on 13 May, at any rate – more sanguine about the Western Front, as he was not convinced that a great battle was yet emerging. He was soon to be disillusioned, for the French Premier, Reynaud, telephoned on the next day to report that the Germans had effected a breakthrough at Sedan, and requested ten additional British fighter squadrons to help stiffen French resistance (the French Air Force, wholly outclassed in equipment and performance, had been all but destroyed by the Luftwaffe). Neither Newall nor Churchill was inclined further to weaken Britain's air defences,' however, and Reynaud was accordingly informed. Who can now doubt that this decision was correct? On 15 May tidings were still worse, with

---

' The RAF had already suffered heavy losses in the battle for France, especially among the obsolescent light and medium bombers, which were completely outclassed.

Reynaud excitedly telephoning Churchill to report that the battle was lost, the road to Paris open and begging for help. It was at this point that Churchill told Reynaud of his resolution 'that whatever the French might do, we should continue the fight – if necessary alone'.

When, later that morning, Churchill met the Chiefs of Staff, he told them of a further telephone conversation he had had, this time with General Georges, who commanded in the sector opposite the German breakthrough, and that Georges had seemed calm. In spite of this Churchill told them that he might feel it necessary to go to Paris himself in order 'to sustain the French Government'. The question of British fighter squadrons to aid French troops again came up, and Air Chief Marshal Sir Hugh Dowding, C-in-C Fighter Command, reiterated the point that as Britain might well have to face German attacks from France and Holland, he did not wish to part with a single fighter to help France. Such assistance would do little to affect the decision there, and might seriously damage Britain's ability to resist a German attack. Churchill still had much to do before he could go to France, however. A message was sent to Mussolini expressing the hope that Italy (still nominally neutral) and Britain would not find themselves in conflict, but it prompted a dusty, indeed a harsh, answer; Churchill was also still completing appointments to his administration, and sent too a message to all Royal Navy personnel expressing his regret at leaving the Admiralty, although he added, 'I shall not be far away'; furthermore, he sent a telegram to Roosevelt, this time not just to inform the President of the situation, but also to ask for help both in the way of weaponry and of American diplomatic pressure upon the Germans. In this, his first telegram to Roosevelt as Prime Minister, Churchill did not hesitate to show how badly things were going: 'the small countries . . . smashed up', France uneasy against German air power and new tactics, Italy likely to cash in, Britain herself, although liable to air and airborne attack, ready to fight on alone. As a result of Britain's likely isolation, he appealed for support, other than with armed forces. Specifically, he asked for forty or fifty old US destroyers to be lent to Britain, some hundreds of new aircraft, iron ore, anti-aircraft weapons, and for US warships to visit Ireland to deter German action there; he also asked that America use her best efforts to keep Japan from taking action against British interests in the Far East.

Next morning the news from the Western Front was so serious – the Germans having breached the Maginot Line – that the decision not to send fighter squadrons from Britain was reversed, even though it was recognized what risks were involved. The War Cabinet agreed that four squadrons should go, and, perhaps even more significantly, that Churchill himself should leave for France that very afternoon in order to discover what the precise military position was, and in particular to discuss with the French their proposal to withdraw from the present line, a withdrawal which would expose British troops to further risk. Churchill was accompanied on his visit to Paris by two senior army officers, General Sir John Dill, Vice-Chief of the General Staff, and Ismay, to whom it was at once clear, when he saw the faces of Reynaud, Daladier[1] and Gamelin at the French Foreign Office on the Quai d'Orsay, that the French were already beaten. Dejection was written all over them. It was at this time that Churchill asked Gamelin about the French Army's strategic reserve – 'la masse de manoeuvre', as he put it – only to receive the depressing response that there wasn't one. Indeed it seemed to the British officers present at the meeting that the French did not themselves know what the real state of the game was. Apart from talking of withdrawal and of moving troops from the southern flank to fill the breach, the main French argument was for more British air support, especially fighters, a plea, Ismay recalled later, that was to be constantly reiterated until France fell. That evening Churchill telegraphed the War Cabinet from the British Embassy, explaining the grave military position – a thirty-mile-wide penetration of the French line – and recommending that further fighter support should be given to their allies. A sensible solution was arrived at. Three squadrons of Hawker Hurricanes would operate in France from dawn until noon of each day, and on returning to their airfields in Kent, be relieved by another three squadrons. The French ministers were emotionally grateful, Daladier silently wringing Churchill's hand on receiving the news. Churchill flew back to London on the morning of 17 May and reported to his War Cabinet colleagues about the French Ninth Army's defeat,[2] stating that the resulting situation was uncertain, and that if the French would really fight hard and were allowed some relief from constant air attack, they might rally, but unless they did, Britain could not jeopardize its own security by dispatching more fighter squadrons to France. If there was little comfort for Churchill from France, nor was there any from the United States with regard to the loan of destroyers, although the American President was able to be more helpful about the export of steel, aircraft and anti-aircraft weapons to Britain. If ever there were a man who knew how to make sweet use of adversity, however, it was Winston Churchill, and even though on that same day he called for a study of how to withdraw the BEF from Channel ports, by the next morning he was telling his son that not only could he see his way to avoiding defeat, but to beating Germany. When Randolph expressed his inability to see how this could come about, his father, so certain was he that sooner or later the United States would eventually join in the struggle against Germany, declared: 'I shall drag the United States in.'

[1] Having resigned in March 1940 because of the public outcry over France's failure to go to Finland's aid, Daladier was successively War Minister and Foreign Minister. He was arrested when France fell, and was interned until 1945.
[2] It was on this army's front near Sedan that the main panzer blow had fallen.

No one would have levelled against Neville Chamberlain the charge that he was the sort of man who would champion harsh, even ruthless, methods of making war, yet he showed great clear-sightedness and courage in recommending to the War Cabinet that in the event of France's defeat, it would be necessary for Britain to adopt almost totalitarian measures, for prosecuting the fight and for controlling the country; moreover, Chamberlain added, Churchill should tell the nation so. The former Prime Minister therefore advocated that his successor should broadcast to the people on 19 May, to say, amongst other things, 'that we were in a tight fix and that no personal considerations must be allowed to stand in the way of measures necessary for victory'. Before Churchill made this, his first broadcast as Prime Minister, the War Cabinet had agreed that in view of the worsening situation in France, Lord Gort, commanding the BEF, should attempt to link up with the French Army by moving his forces in a south-westerly direction, even though Gort himself had recommended that should the French fall back further – as in the event they did – he would base his army on Dunkirk and fight it out there, clearly with a view to evacuation if necessary. In his broadcast that evening, Churchill did not conceal the extreme 'gravity of the hour', and warned the nation that it would not be long before German military force was turned upon Britain. He then continued:

I am sure I speak for all when I say we are ready to face it; to endure it; and to retaliate against it – to any extent that the unwritten laws of war permit. There will be many men and many women in this Island who when the ordeal comes upon them, as come it will, will feel comfort, and even a pride, that they are sharing the perils of our lads at the Front – soldiers, sailors and airmen, God bless them – and are drawing away from them a part at least of the onslaught they have to bear. Is not this the appointed time for all to make the utmost exertions in their power?

From that exhortation, he went on to warn that in the coming struggle it would be necessary to take the most drastic steps 'to call forth from our people the last ounce and the last inch of effort of which they are capable. The interests of property, the hours of labour, are nothing compared with the struggle for life and honour, for right and freedom, to which we have vowed ourselves.' He ended this resolute speech by referring to the joint action being taken by the French and British people to rescue not only those states that had been broken by Nazi tyranny, but the whole of mankind. In order to save them all from barbarism, their task was to conquer this tyranny 'as conquer we must, as conquer we shall'. The British people, their imagination fired by this call for endurance during times of suffering, deprivation, sorrow and setback, were to respond in a way that astonished the world, and indeed themselves. These bad and dangerous times were not quite upon them yet, but they soon would be. Then they would display their extraordinary gift for screwing their courage to the sticking-place and simply carrying on. It was seen that every man and every woman was willing, even eager, to do his or her bit. Apart from the armed services themselves, the firemen, air-raid wardens, ambulance men and women, police, Home Guard, land girls, merchant seamen, drivers, railway staff, nurses and doctors, Royal Observer Corps, factory workers – all these, and many more, made it possible for Churchill to speak years later of 'the buoyant and imperturbable temper of Britain which I had the honour to express', adding that 'It was the nation that had the lion's heart. I had the luck to be called upon to give the roar.' That was still in the future, however, for the Battle of France was not yet over. It would not be long, though, before it was.

It may perhaps be helpful to summarize the events which led to the evacuation of the BEF from Dunkirk before looking at Churchill's part in the operation. General Maxime Weygand had replaced Gamelin as Allied Commander-in-Chief[1] on 19 May, but took no action. Ironside, CIGS still (although not for much longer), had gone to France to confirm to Gort the War Cabinet's direction that the BEF should advance southwards to Amiens and attempt to link up with the French. But when the latter made it clear that nearly all his force, seven out of nine divisions, was engaged in fighting the Germans on the Scheldt, Ironside realized that no such southward attack was possible, and reported accordingly to London. It may be said that Gort, although he has never figured in the history books as one of the great generals of the Second World War, by sticking to his guns here and plainly seeing what, at the time, many others did not – that French plans for restoring the situation either did not exist or were chimerical – saved the BEF, gave the British Army the opportunity to fight another day, and probably saved Britain from a far more dangerous and prolonged assault than in the event occurred (an assault which in all likelihood would have seriously prejudiced Britain's ability to resume the struggle so quickly and effectively). By the same token, it must also be conceded that he thereby rendered his country and the cause of freedom an immeasurably great service.

Weygand did eventually make a plan: under it, British and French forces north of the gap driven into the Allied line by the panzers would advance towards Bapaume and Cambrai with a view to taking Amiens and so link up

---

[1] As in the Great War, the BEF and its C-in-C nominally came under the overall command of the French; Gort, however, had instructions that he might appeal to the British Government if he felt his orders from the French endangered or might endanger his army. As it proved, the value of this instruction was incalculable.

with other French forces moving up from the south. But even though Churchill approved this scheme during another visit to France on 22 May, nothing happened. Weygand's plans might have been all right in theory. No one knew what might have been their worth in action, for there was no action and in any case it had become clear that Gort was now intent on keeping the BEF intact, and was not going to conform to any of Weygand's paper plans. It will be remembered that it was at about this time, 23 May, that it was agreed by Rundstedt, backed by Hitler, that the German panzer drive should halt, and the advance did not resume until three days later. On 25 May Dill replaced Ironside as CIGS and next morning, after a meeting between Reynaud and Churchill in London – in the course of which Churchill obtained the agreement of the French – orders were telegraphed to Gort to withdraw his forces towards the ports. At six o'clock that evening, 26 May, after a further War Cabinet (at which Churchill, speculating on the probability that France would make peace with Germany, told his colleagues that in that case Britain must part company with France and show Hitler that 'he could not conquer this country') a signal was sent from the Admiralty to Vice-Admiral Bertram Ramsay, commanding at Dover: 'Operation Dynamo is to commence.' 'Dynamo' was the codeword for the evacuation of the BEF from Dunkirk. The operation began next morning.

The 'miracle' of Dunkirk was an astonishing affair. It cannot be compared with any other withdrawal of British forces by sea in the past, no matter how many of these there have been (and there have been several, not least Corunna in 1809 and Gallipoli in 1915–16), for it was not only the warships of the Royal Navy that took the men home, but countless small fishing boats, ferries, pleasure cruisers, yachts, even sailing dinghies – in all, 860 vessels took part. The evacuation, shielded by a defensive perimeter of British and French troops (the former and about two-thirds of the latter were progressively withdrawn to the beaches and harbour as the operation proceeded), lasted until 3 June, and in the end nearly 340,000 men (of whom about 139,000 were French) were shipped from the beaches near Dunkirk or from the town's harbour back to England. This side of it was indeed a miracle, a triumph only made possible by the dogged defence of the perimeter by British and French troops under the overall command of Major-General Harold Alexander (to whom Gort had handed over on 31 May; until then, Alexander had commanded the 1st Division), by the gallantry of the Royal Navy and the crews of the 'little ships', and by the unflagging skill and courage of the RAF's bomber and fighter pilots, who committed themselves wholeheartedly to bombing the German units encircling the Dunkirk perimeter and to driving off enemy aircraft trying to destroy the BEF. Yet the losses were grievous, too – more than 250 vessels of all kinds, including 6 British and 2 French destroyers sunk, and 19 damaged, and there were inevitably casualties from bombing, shelling and strafing among the soldiers of the BEF and the French troops that had reached Dunkirk. In the Battle of France as a whole, the Royal Air Force lost more than 900 aircraft, 477 of them precious fighters; while, besides thousands of soldiers killed, wounded, missing or made prisoner, the BEF lost all its tanks, guns and heavy equipment, most of these left behind at Dunkirk.

Well before the extent of the operation's success was known, Churchill was already giving tongue both to his defiance and his confidence. On 28 May, after the Belgian surrender and when only some 14,000 men had been evacuated from Dunkirk, he reported the gravity of the situation to the House of Commons, and then declared:

> I have only to add that nothing which may happen in this battle can in any way relieve us of our duty to defend the world cause to which we have vowed ourselves; nor should it destroy our confidence in our power to make our way, as on former occasions in our history, through disaster and through grief to the ultimate defeat of our enemies.

After this speech, Churchill held two meetings in his room in the House of Commons, both gatherings remarkable for the effect that he had on his colleagues. At the first, attended by just the other four members of the War Cabinet, they discussed the question of whether negotiations with Germany should even be contemplated. Chamberlain and Halifax suggested that they might, while Churchill himself emphatically disagreed, as indeed did Attlee and Greenwood. That Britain, under Churchill's leadership, would fight on no matter what happened was powerfully endorsed by the meeting which immediately followed, and which was attended by all other ministers, twenty-five of them. Martin Gilbert calls it 'one of the most extraordinary scenes of the war', and quotes Hugh Dalton's version of events, which is so striking that it deserves to be included here. Having explained that Germany would probably take Paris and then offer some terms for peace, and that Italy would be likely to join in the war on the German side, also offering terms, Churchill stated that there was no doubt 'that we must decline anything like this and fight on'. 'He was quite magnificent,' noted Dalton. 'The man, and the only man we have for this hour.' Churchill then gave an account of all that was happening, explaining that the BEF would fight its way to the coast and evacuate as many of its men as possible. Fifty thousand should certainly get away, twice that number would be better than anyone dared hope. Dunkirk was the only port left. He would now have to prepare the British people for bad news. The war would come to these islands – the enemy would attempt an invasion, although that would be difficult, and made more so by British defensive measures:

And then he said: 'I have thought carefully in these last days whether it was part of my duty to consider entering into negotiations with That Man.' But it was idle to think that, if we tried to make peace now, we should get better terms than if we fought it out. The Germans would demand our fleet – that would be called 'disarmament' – our naval bases, and much else. We should become a slave state, though a British Government which would be Hitler's puppet would be set up – 'under Mosley[1] or some such person'. And where should we be at the end of all that? On the other hand, we had immense reserves and advantages.

'And I am convinced,' he concluded, 'that every man of you would rise up and tear me down from my place if I were for one moment to contemplate parley or surrender. If this long island story of ours is to end at last, let it end only when each one of us lies choking in his own blood upon the ground.'

His words were greeted with the most enthusiastic acclaim, and Dalton, according to his own account, actually patted Churchill on the back when they all got up from the table, saying to him: 'Well done, Prime Minister! You ought to get behind that cartoon of Low,[2] showing us all rolling up our sleeves and falling in behind you, and frame it and stick it up there.' He answered with a broad grin, 'Yes, that was a good one, wasn't it?' In the light of such support, and indeed of subsequent events, no one can seriously doubt[3] that Churchill was right to dismiss utterly the idea of negotiation with the Nazis.

In recalling later the days of Dunkirk, Churchill wrote: 'Had I at this juncture faltered at all in the leading of the nation, I should have been hurled out of office. I was sure that every Minister was ready to be killed quite soon, and have all his family and possessions destroyed, rather than give in. In this they represented the House of Commons and almost all the people.' He went on to record how in the days and months that followed it was left to him to express the feelings of the British people, which he was able to do because he shared

---

[1] Sir Oswald Mosley (1896–1980) entered Parliament as a Conservative in 1918, became an Independent in 1922, and then sat as a Labour MP, 1926–31. In 1932 he founded the British Union of Fascists, having been impressed by Mussolini during a visit to Rome that same year. The BUF became progressively more anti-Semitic and Hitlerite, although its membership declined after 1936, when the Government introduced legislation outlawing political uniforms and private armies. From 1940–3 Mosely was interned as a potential threat to Britain's war aims.

[2] David (later Sir David) Low (1891–1963) was the political cartoonist of the *Evening Standard* from 1927–50. Among much else, he created the character of Colonel Blimp, the fatuously complacent and reactionary officer whose name has now gone into the language.

[3] Except, it seems, revisionists like John Charmley.

them so completely. What he failed to add to these recollections, but which many others have since said, was that by his leadership, by his indomitable spirit, and by the sheer simple grandeur and historic appeal of his words, he played an indispensable part in creating in the British people that very glow of defiance, confidence and pride which he remembered with such gratification. There is, therefore, something in Piers Brendon's claim that Churchill's oratory was his greatest single contribution to the war effort, that he galvanized his people by the power of rhetoric alone. Yet it was, of course, far more than this. Churchill himself conceded that rhetoric could not guarantee survival. Constant activity, eternal vigilance, the undimmed offensive spirit, defiance in spite of all the odds, fertility of imagination, the spurring of all manner of people into action, boldness – above all, inspiring leadership – these were the ingredients of survival. And as a war leader Churchill was unique. Despite some will-o'-the-wisp notions from time to time, he was a master of strategy. He really believed he understood the business of war, and with reason – after all, what other Prime Minister (and Minister of Defence) had fought on the North-West Frontier, charged at Omdurman, stood on the bloodied heights of Spion Kop, commanded a battalion in the trenches, been First Lord of the Admiralty (twice), Secretary for Munitions and for War and Air, voraciously studied the technicalities of ships, aircraft and guns, thought, written and debated about war for nearly half a century?

While the Dunkirk operation proceeded, the French will to resist continued to wither, as Churchill found when he again visited France on 31 May, only to find that newcomers to Reynaud's government, the ancient Marshal Henri Philippe Pétain and Weygand, were already thinking in terms of an armistice. But in his outpourings to the Supreme War Council in Paris, Churchill not only made it clear that if Italy entered the contest, the Allies must strike at her at once and as hard as possible; he also reiterated his determination to continue the struggle no matter what the cost. He did his best to raise the spirits of the French leaders, urging that both Britain and France must present 'an unflinching front against all their enemies,' that they must act together, must carry on the fight, and that 'even if one of them were struck down, the other must not abandon the struggle'. In any event, 'the British people will fight on until the New World reconquers the Old. Better far that the last of the English should fall fighting and finis to be written to our history than to linger on as vassals and slaves.' At the same time, since Britain would resist invasion if it came, she must have enough troops with which to fight; only then could further help be rendered to the French. In spite of all that Churchill had to say in his attempts to stiffen French morale, his old friend, General Spears, recorded that the Prime Minister 'realized in his heart that the French were beaten, that they knew it, and were resigned to defeat'.

As far as helping the French went, Churchill was as good as his word, for despite the ever deteriorating situation of the French Army, two British divisions were sent to France under Lieutenant-General Sir Alan Brooke[1] (who had commanded II Corps of the BEF in the campaign that ended at Dunkirk), although Brooke himself quickly saw that the gesture was a futile one, and on 14 June he was given the authority to act as he thought fit, which meant further evacuation. Although the 51st Highland Division was trapped at St Valery-en-Caux, on the Channel coast west of Dieppe, unable to get away because of fog, most of its men and its commander being captured, nearly 200,000 soldiers, of whom more than 140,000 were British, were successfully brought back to England. Some of these British soldiers belonged to Brooke's force, others were the administrative remnants of the original BEF which had been positioned further back when the battle for France started. Among the non-British soldiers were both Frenchmen and Poles, and this second great exodus brought the total number of men to be successfully evacuated from France to nearly 560,000, of which about 369,000 were British.

Churchill was indefatigable in responding to the French leaders' calls for him to go to France for discussions, but from the French point of view the issue was no longer how to continue resistance, but how to slide out of it. Churchill met Reynaud and his colleagues on 11 June at General Weygand's headquarters, the Château du Muguet, near Briare. It was the day after Italy's declaration of war, and it soon became clear as the Supreme War Council began its meeting that all fight had gone out of the principal French leaders, who were dismayed to learn that the planned bombing by the RAF of objectives in northern Italy could not – as the French wanted, fearing German reprisals – be called off.[2] Churchill's plea for French forces to continue to hold out, while Britain steadily built up her own forces so as to be able to come to her ally's aid, did nothing to stiffen French resolve. Indeed, Weygand gave it as his opinion that the military situation was hopeless. He had no reserves. Nothing could now stop the Germans from taking Paris and driving beyond it – 'C'est la dislocation.' Yet even in the face of this bleak pronouncement, Churchill did not abandon his attempts to put some backbone in the French leaders. All his efforts, and those of Dill, the CIGS – even offering Weygand freedom to make what use he thought best of the British divisions arriving under Brooke's command; recalling how the tide had turned in the Great War both at the Marne in 1914 and after Ludendorff's offensive in March 1918; suggesting, as Churchill did, that Paris, by now imminently threatened, should conduct its own defence, rather

---

[1] Of all British generals of that war the soundest, not excluding Montgomery and Slim.
[2] In the event British bombers were prevented from taking off when the French obstructed the runways.

than meekly allowing itself to be occupied (a point received with notable lack of enthusiasm by the French) – none of these had any effect on Weygand's attitude of defeatism. The Germans were almost at the gates of Paris; they had crossed the Seine and Marne; they were covering fifty miles a day; there were no reserves to stop them; all talk of delaying them by weeks or months was futile, for it was now a question of hours. Only substantial fighter reinforcement from Britain could turn the scales, and, as General Ismay recalled, Weygand suggested that every single fighter aircraft in Britain should be sent to France, thereby conforming with the fundamental strategic rule of concentrating force at the decisive point and the decisive time. Ismay remembered, too, his concern that Churchill's generosity of spirit and courage born of optimism would get the better of his military judgement, and of the unequivocal advice given by Dowding that no more fighters could be spared from Britain if her own defence were not to be fatally prejudiced. But Churchill took up Weygand's strategic argument and reversed it, as Ismay noted:

> After a pause, and speaking very slowly, he [Churchill] said, 'This is not the decisive point. This is not the decisive moment. The decisive moment will come when Hitler hurls his Luftwaffe against Britain. If we can keep command of the air over our own island – that is all I ask – we will win it all back for you.'
>
> After another long pause, he continued magnificently, 'Of course if it is best for France in her agony that her Army should capitulate, let there be no hesitation on our account. Whatever happens here, we are resolved to fight on and on for ever and ever and ever.' Reynaud, obviously moved, said: 'If we capitulate, all the great might of Germany will be concentrated upon invading England. And then what will you do?' Whereupon Churchill with his jaw thrust well forward, rejoined that he had not thought that out very carefully, but that broadly speaking he would propose to drown as many as possible of them on the way over, and then to '*frapper sur la tête*' anyone who managed to crawl ashore.

Churchill had still not done, for he soon repeated to Reynaud that no matter what happened Britain 'would fight on and on and on, *toujours*, all the time, everywhere, *partout, pas de grâce*, no mercy. *Puis la victoire!*'

It was also at this meeting that Churchill was able to respond to a proposal made by General Charles de Gaulle, formerly the commander of the French 4th Armoured Division, and now in Reynaud's Cabinet as Under-Secretary for Defence, to the effect that there should be an amalgamation of British and French armoured formations, whose different types of tank would complement each other. Churchill was greatly impressed by de

Gaulle,[1] but even though he responded enthusiastically, nothing could prevail against the mood of hopelessness which had gripped Weygand and Pétain, and the British Prime Minister's further schemes for holding bridgeheads on the Atlantic coast, or for 'guerrilla warfare on a gigantic scale throughout France', merely annoyed the French leaders. Yet even though it was clear that all Churchill's efforts to rally them had failed, he himself reiterated that Britain would willingly stand up to whatever malicious fury the Nazis might turn against her. Therefore 'Great Britain would carry on, if necessary for years . . . if she could survive the next three or four months then she would be in a position to wage war for as long as was necessary to smash the German domination. She would fight in the air, she would fight with her unbeaten navy, and she would fight with the blockade weapon.' The question of fighting at sea highlighted a matter of great concern to Churchill – if France were to capitulate, what would happen to the French Navy? This vital question was to recur, and its resolution would bring both tragedy and vilification.

Next morning, before the Supreme War Council resumed its deliberations, there occurred at the Château du Muguet one of those bizarre incidents which will always endear Churchill to people as a man who, even under the greatest stress of responsibility, could display an eccentric simplicity in his day-to-day activities. General Spears reported the astonishment, alarm even, of two French officers, who had been drinking coffee in the dining room when the double doors were flung open and they were suddenly confronted by 'an apparition which they said resembled an angry Japanese genie, in long, flowing red silk kimono over other similar but white garments, girdled with a white belt of like material, stood there, sparse hair on end, and said with every sign of anger: "*Uh ay ma bain?*"' Before retiring for the night on 11 June, Churchill had been told by Reynaud that Pétain had confided in him that an armistice would have to be sought. Nor did the Supreme War Council of 12 June bring any comfort to anyone, even though Churchill once more tried to bolster the French by putting forward a number of ideas phrased as questions: could not Paris provide an obstacle to delay the enemy, and could not a counter-stroke then be mounted; if, by an end to conventional conflict, the enemy became dispersed, could not an attack on their communications be organized; was it not possible to hold on and resist until the United States joined in? But Weygand rejected all these suggestions. (It was during these meetings at Briare that Weygand had confided to Reynaud that Britain would have her neck wrung like a chicken.) Churchill, meanwhile, had undertaken to convey a message to

---

[1] During the campaign in Belgium and Northern France, de Gaulle had commanded his division with considerable *élan*, counter-attacking the panzers at Crécy-sur-Serre and again near Abbeville. He had only been appointed to the command on 11 May.

Roosevelt, and flew back to England later in the morning, reporting to the War Cabinet that afternoon. 'It was clear,' he said, 'that France was near the end of organized resistance.' Therefore, even though support for the French might have to continue for a time, it would now be necessary to concentrate on the defence of Britain itself; there was, however, still the matter of the French colonies and the French fleet. Finally, he added that although France might still be able to put up some resistance, it would not as 'a great land power'. After the War Cabinet meeting, Churchill sent messages first to Roosevelt, then to Reynaud and Weygand. In his telegram to the American President, he gave warning of the probability of France's concluding an armistice, while suggesting that the moment had come for Roosevelt to speak up in favour of continued French resistance. He also assured the President that the French well understood Britain's resolution to fight on whatever happened: 'Hitler could not win the war or the mastery of the world until he had disposed of us, which has not been found easy in the past, and which perhaps will not be found easy now.' To the French, Churchill promised further support by the RAF, both from fighters and bombers operating from airfields in Britain and from aircraft stationed in France; to the War Cabinet he expressed his favourable impressions of General de Gaulle.

At Admiralty House shortly after midnight, while Churchill was preparing to go to bed, he was called to the telephone to speak to Reynaud, who had moved to Tours and wanted Churchill to fly over to see him on that same afternoon, 13 June. This was to be the Prime Minister's fifth – and as it turned out, last – visit to France (until four years later, that is) since the German assault, and it was to achieve nothing. While Reynaud spoke of a separate peace, Churchill reiterated Britain's determination to fight on – 'She had not and would not alter her resolve: no terms: no surrender' – for her it was to be death or victory. It was clear that there was no meeting of minds. While Churchill was emphasizing that the war would go on, and that as a result there would be great hardships to be endured – France occupied by the Germans; the British naval blockade wreaking its terrible effects; the prospect of 'bitter antagonism between the French and English peoples' – Reynaud, who had previously displayed some degree of robustness, seemed totally to have changed his position, dwelling on what would happen if the French collapsed, and if Britain exacerbated their suffering by blockade. He expressed the hope 'that Great Britain would, in recognition of the untold sacrifices of French men and women, make some gesture that would obviate the risk of an antagonism, the later consequences of which he considered fatal'. This idea, that even in the event of a separate peace there would be some degree of solidarity between the two countries, alarmed General Spears (one of several advisers in Churchill's party), who had begun to suspect that the French might even side with the Germans were not Britain to

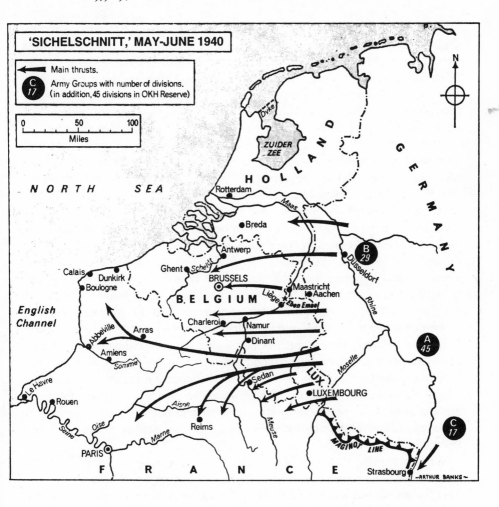

make some pledge not to harm France – a pledge that clearly could not possibly be given. The one thing that had been agreed during this last meeting of the Supreme War Council was that Reynaud should explain France's position to Roosevelt, and see what comfort might be obtained from America. For the rest of it, so concerned were Churchill and his British colleagues that they conferred alone before returning to the Council. It was the voice of Beaverbrook which sounded an admirable realism, advising Churchill to say no more until Roosevelt had been consulted. 'Don't commit yourself to anything. We shall gain a little time and see how those Frenchmen sort themselves out. We are doing no good here. In fact, listening to these declarations of Reynaud's only does harm. Let's get along home.' The Supreme War Council broke up in the hope that Roosevelt's response would be positive. Before Churchill's aircraft actually took off from the airfield at Tours, he learned from Spears that Paul Baudouin, the French War Cabinet Secretary, had been circulating a story to the effect that Churchill had signified his agreement to France's concluding a separate peace, if that were to become necessary. This muddle turned on the French interpretation of the Prime Minister's answer to Reynaud, 'Je comprends', by which he had meant, of course, that he understood the words being used; it did *not*, however, imply that he agreed with such a step. Since de Gaulle[1] had expressed his concern about this, Spears was anxious to obtain from Churchill his confirmation – which, emphatically, he gave – that at no time had he indicated his consent to a separate peace between France and Germany.

At that evening's meeting of the War Cabinet, Churchill expressed his confidence that since Roosevelt had informed Reynaud that the American Government would do all it could to assist the French with the material they needed, and had (in an earlier message) welcomed Reynaud's declaration that France would continue the fight, this meant that the President intended to bring the United States into the war on the Allies' side. Churchill then tried (unsuccessfully, as it turned out) to secure agreement for Roosevelt's statement to be published, and sent a further telegram to Reynaud once more urging France to continue the struggle, as she would soon be joined by the United States. He then sent a message to the French people themselves, praising their heroism, pledging Britain's aid – indeed, proclaiming union of their two nations and empires – and reiterating Britain's resolve 'never to turn from the conflict until France stands safe and erect in all her grandeur, until the wronged enslaved States and peoples have been liberated and until civilization is freed from the nightmare of Nazidom'.

Whatever might have been the optimism of 13 June, however, it was soon shattered by the events of the following day. Roosevelt refused permission for his message to Reynaud to be published – not that it would have made any difference, for the French were about to give in anyway; the German Army entered Paris as triumphant conquerors; General Brooke, whom Churchill had tried to persuade by telephone to continue supporting the French, reversed the position and convinced the Prime Minister that his 150,000 or so troops must be evacuated – the appropriate orders were then given; and Churchill now had to accept the unpleasant fact that French military action in France itself was about to cease altogether. Never one to despair, in a telegram to Roosevelt sent on 15 June he bluntly described the situation that would prevail were Britain to become subject to the power of the Nazi regime, not leaving out the conse-

---

[1] As Churchill was leaving for the airfield at Tours, he spoke to de Gaulle, calling him '*l'homme du destin*' which the General, though he made no reply, was certainly to become.

quences for America were the British Fleet to fall into the wrong hands, and then renewed his previous plea for the loan of American destroyers – thirty-five, this time – until British construction could fill the gap. Churchill also sent a message to the Dominion Prime Ministers, explaining that in the event of France's fall, Britain would fight on. He assured them that the country would overcome air attacks or any other assaults, and that although the outcome was unpredictable, Britain would enter upon 'a life-and-death struggle . . . in good heart'. He reiterated his determination to 'go on to the end' and even if 'we should be beaten down through the superior numbers of the enemy's Air Force it will always be possible . . . to send our fleets across the oceans, where they will protect the Empire and enable it to continue the war and the blockade, I trust in conjunction with the United States, until the Hitler régime breaks under the strain'.

After the War Cabinet had approved these two messages on June 15, the question of 'real unity between Great Britain and France' was again raised, this time by Chamberlain. Churchill's reaction was that while it might be valuable to have some statement prepared in appropriately dramatic form, such as would appeal to the French people, the most important issue at stake was 'to secure the French Fleet'. The matter was further discussed with two members of the French Economic Mission and it was agreed that General de Gaulle, who was also in London, dealing with an arms shipment from America, should be consulted as to the wording of a possible proclamation about union between France and Britain. In addition, Churchill was also contending with the urgent need to secure American destroyers, an issue very much bound up, of course, with the future of the French fleet. Back in 10 Downing Street (where the Churchills had now moved from Admiralty House) Churchill sent another telegram to Roosevelt, stressing that with the imminence of a French collapse, all would turn on the defence of Britain; it was essential, therefore, that she be reinforced by the destroyers he had asked for. The whole problem was further aggravated by Reynaud's making it clear that if the United States did not declare its intention of coming into the war, France would not even be able to continue fighting from overseas, thus making it even more probable that the French fleet would pass into German hands. Yet another telegram from Churchill to Roosevelt made this dire possibility plain, but realistically added that the Prime Minister himself did not anticipate that the United States would respond by sending an expeditionary force. It was rather that an American decision to participate would have a profound moral effect on both sides in the conflict – indeed, on the whole world. With a touch wholly characteristic of his ability to lighten even the sternest moment, Churchill, whose earlier telegram to the Dominion Prime Ministers had given him 'a glow of sober confidence', read it out to Colville, his Private Secretary, and commented that 'if words counted, we should win this war'. That night at Chequers, as Churchill retired for the night, the imminent fall of France weighed heavily upon him, and he later confessed to Eden that at this time, despite the usual buoyancy with which he met every danger or difficulty, he would wake 'with dread in my heart'.

The sixteenth of June was a day when the air was cleared. After the War Cabinet had met at Downing Street in the morning, Reynaud, whose government was now at Bordeaux, was informed that Britain would release France from her undertaking not to negotiate with Germany only if 'the French Fleet is sailed forthwith for British harbours pending negotiations'. Later that morning Churchill and de Gaulle conferred further on the question of the two countries' union, and while a draft declaration was being discussed and revised, it became clear when the two men were together in Downing Street that afternoon that de Gaulle was being thought of as the next French Commander-in-Chief. It was then agreed that de Gaulle would take the completed Declaration of Union to France, and that Churchill, accompanied by Attlee, Sinclair, Ismay and the Chiefs of Staff, would themselves sail to France that evening to discuss the whole matter with Reynaud. The Declaration, apart from proposing indissoluble union under a single government, common citizenship and associated parliaments, was designed to enable Reynaud to hold on to his position and to continue resistance; indeed it even contained a statement about concentrating everything against the enemy no matter where the fighting might be, and thus conquering. These were bold words, but they were only words. French actions were somewhat different: Reynaud resigned, and Pétain formed a new government and asked the Germans for an armistice. Next day, 17 June, while the War Cabinet was meeting, the news came though that the French ceasefire had taken place at 12.40 pm. Churchill, however concerned he may still have been about what would happen to France's navy and air force, and to her colonies, was undaunted, and broadcast that afternoon to the nation, telling the people how bad the news from France was and the grief he felt for her gallant people, who would surely rise again. Moreover, he added, what had happened would not change Britain's position. 'We have become the sole champions now in arms to defend the world cause. We shall do our best to be worthy of this high honour. We shall defend our Island home, and with the British Empire we shall fight on unconquerable until the curse of Hitler is lifted from the brows of mankind. We are sure that in the end all will come right.'

In order to make sure that all would come right, he now set about tackling some of the innumerable strategic problems which faced Britain. The large-scale supply of guns and ammunition was to be seen to by Morrison, the Minister of Supply; the naval forces must be so deployed that an Italian threat to Egypt (soon to develop) could be countered and any hostile moves by Spain be checked; France's leaders must be left in no doubt about the urgency of sailing the French fleet to friendly ports; de Gaulle was to return to Britain from Bordeaux. At Bordeaux itself on 18 June, the First Lord of the Admiralty, Alexander, and the First Sea Lord, Pound, made a further attempt to ensure that the French fleet did not fall into German hands by appealing to Admiral Darlan himself, and they seemed to receive proper reassurances. Although it was necessary for Churchill to put all defensive measures into practice, as the prospect of invasion now had to be faced, he was already thinking of how to turn to the offensive, and on that same day[1] he was demanding to know what General Paget, C-in-C Home Forces, was proposing to do about forming storm troops, suggesting that 'there ought to be at least twenty thousand Storm Troops or "Leopards" [later they were called Commandos] drawn from existing units, ready to spring at the throat of any small landings or descents. These officers and men should be armed with the latest equipment, tommy guns, grenades, etc., and should be given great facilities in motor-cycles and armoured cars.' Nor did Churchill stop at organizing these aggressive counter-checks. Seeing that the British Army had been turned out of France, he was soon wanting to mount 'a vigorous, enterprising and ceaseless offensive against the whole German-occupied coastline', raiding deep inland, destroying vital installations, 'butchering' Germans, and then 'bolting'. He therefore required the Chiefs of Staff to let him have their proposals for raising Commandos from the army and the Royal Marines; for raising a minimum of 5,000 parachute troops; for espionage and intelligence arrangements; and for transporting tanks to the beaches. He told Mountbatten to turn the south of England into a springboard for attack. As we have seen, all these ideas, streaming from his ever-active mind in the form of memos, often marked 'Action This Day', followed by discussions with his military chiefs (during which he mercilessly harangued them), were to give new and urgent life to the whole machinery of directing the war.

It was also on 18 June that Churchill made one of his most memorable speeches in the House of Commons – a speech which was later broadcast to the nation and in which he spoke of what Britain had done during the Battle of France, of the need to put aside any question of recrimination as to the past or present, of the present government's unity and authority to conduct the country's affairs. He was confident that the Royal Air Force would successfully counter air attacks, just as the Royal Navy and the army would prevail against any invading forces, although the ordeal which lay before the nation would be extreme. He was confident, too, that his countrymen would stand up to it all. It would be a time when 'every man and every woman will have the chance to

---

[1] As it happened, 18 June 1940 was the one-hundred-and-twenty-fifth anniversary of the Battle of Waterloo.

show the fine qualities of their race and render the highest service to their cause'. Of course Britain's situation had worsened, but although the Germans controlled Western Europe, its resources and much of its coastline, with all the air and naval threats which this promised, Britain would draw supplies from the arsenals of America and from the Dominions. Therefore, although he saw 'great reason for intense vigilance and exertion', he saw none for 'panic or despair'. Britain would survive the fall of France, but was now faced with the threat of attack from the air, and invasion. The Battle of France was over, and the Battle of Britain about to begin:

> Upon this battle depends the survival of Christian civilization. Upon it depends our own British life and the long continuity of our institutions and our Empire. The whole fury and might of the enemy must very soon be turned on us. Hitler knows that he will have to break us in this island or lose the war. If we can stand up to him, all Europe may be free, and the life of the world may move forward into broad, sunlit uplands; but if we fail, then the whole world, including the United States, and all that we have known and cared for, will sink into the abyss of a new dark age made more sinister, and perhaps more protracted, by the lights of a perverted science.
>
> Let us therefore brace ourselves to our duty and so bear ourselves that if the British Empire and its Commonwealth lasts for a thousand years men still will say, 'This was their finest hour.'

It is perhaps worth remarking here that it looks very much as if the Commonwealth, even if not the Empire, *will* last for a long time yet, and that judging by the general acclaim witnessed in 1995 at the fiftieth anniversary of VE-Day, men still are saying that Britain's defiance and endurance in those dark days did represent the nation's finest hour.

While Churchill was being defiant, Hitler was being exultant. When he heard at his military headquarters that Pétain had asked for armistice terms, he gave, according to a member of OKW, a hop of delight. Certainly he had cause. It was he who had insisted that a campaign in the west would pay great dividends; it was he who had caused the plan to be changed and who had bullied the generals into executing it; and it was, as Jodl put it, his will that had triumphed. In discussing armistice terms for the French with Mussolini and Ciano at Munich on 18 and 19 June, it was Hitler who was inclined to be moderate, Mussolini who wished to acquire huge gains at the expense of France and Britain. As was customary in their dealings, the Führer decided what was to happen, and the Duce meekly complied. In this particular instance, while Mussolini wanted mastery of the Mediterranean and a good deal of French North Africa, to say nothing of Malta, Egypt and the Sudan, Hitler persuaded him that territorial claims should await the war's conclusion. And whereas the Duce wanted all France to be occupied and the French fleet surrendered, the Führer proclaimed that only northern and western France should be occupied, the rest remaining under Pétain's control, while the French fleet (which must, of course, not join the British) would be partly left to the French, provided that they made no warlike use of it, and partly decommissioned. The French colonies would remain as they were. Thus far it might almost be said that Hitler had shown a degree of magnanimity, though this was, of course, calculated – in the hope that it might have some effect on Great Britain's attitude towards coming to some negotiated settlement.

Not all the Führer's actions were magnanimous, however, for, as was noted in Chapter 1, Hitler chose for the actual signing of the armistice the humiliating condition that the railway carriage in which the German representatives had signed the Armistice of 1918 should move from its Paris museum to the same spot in the Forest of Compiègne; he himself sat in Foch's chair inside the carriage, relishing the absolute turning of the tables, and even danced a victory jig. After receiving the French delegation without a word, and having listened to the reading of the preamble to the armistice terms and arrangements, Hitler gave his own particular version of a salute, left the carriage accompanied by his staff, and made his way back to where cars were waiting, while a military band added to the triumph with 'Deutschland über Alles' and the Nazi Horst Wessel Song. Hitler had fulfilled his undertaking to avenge the Treaty of Versailles; now he would fulfil another ambition – he would feast his eyes on the architectural wonders of Paris, visiting that city for the first time and, moreover, as a conqueror. Perhaps not surprisingly, it was Napoleon's tomb in Les Invalides which impressed him most. Appropriately enough, in his strategic handling of the great obstacle to his quest for world power – Great Britain – he was about to make the same mistakes as the French Emperor.

For now, however, the initiative clearly lay with Hitler. The question that confronted him was what he was to do with it, and in the end it resolved itself into the strategic choice that was to recur time after time – *entweder, oder; so oder so* – the choice between east or west. At first Hitler toyed with both. Although by the end of June he had formed the opinion that the British were determined to fight on, an opinion powerfully reinforced when on 3 July, and on Churchill's orders – he called it 'a hateful decision' – the main part of the French fleet was attacked in its base at Mers-el-Kébir in Algeria by the Royal Navy (two battleships and a battle cruiser were destroyed, and some 1,300 French sailors killed), nevertheless plans were being prepared by the OKW for the invasion of Britain, *and* at the same time 'some operational thinking' was under way at the OKH (the Army High Command) for a campaign against Russia. This was the offensive which was most dear to Hitler's heart, and although he continued to play with the idea of subduing Britain first, much of the planning for 'Sea Lion' (as the operation to invade England came to be called) was designed to bring the British to their senses, and thus to negotiate some settlement.

There was, of course, another factor to be taken into account – one that in the end was gravely to prejudice Hitler's freedom of action – the entry of Italy into the war. On 26 June 1940 we find Mussolini writing from Rome: 'Führer! Now that the time has come to thrash England, I remind you of what I said to you at Munich about the direct participation of Italy in the assault of the Isle. I am ready to take part in this with land and air forces, and you know how much I desire it. I pray you to reply in order that I can pass into the phase of action. Awaiting this day, I send you my salute of comradeship.' Hitler treated this bombastic nonsense with understandable contempt, but he was no nearer to solving the strategic dilemma of what to do next. Of one thing he could be sure. However active Great Britain might be at sea and however formidable she might become in the air, there was no danger of a British offensive against Hitler's Europe. Yet, as Michael Howard has so forcibly pointed out, 'there was a subsidiary theatre where British forces could be employed to harass the enemy and perhaps inflict serious damage. Italy's entry into the war had turned the Middle East into an active theatre of operations. As a centre of gravity of British forces it was second only to the United Kingdom itself.' No sooner had Italy declared war than British forces under Lieutenant-General Richard O'Connor were harassing Italian units in Libya and dominating that country's frontier with Egypt in preparation for what was later to be a triumphant conquest of Cyrenaica[1] and the Italian Tenth Army.

In Britain itself the measures being taken were essentially defensive. The Home Guard[2] – the name was Churchill's own choice – was established, with many of its soldiers equipped with rifles supplied by Roosevelt as 'surplus to American requirements'; the army – initially under Ironside's command, then from 20 July under the far more competent Brooke – prepared itself to meet and repulse a German invasion, though it was very weak in tanks and anti-tank guns. Sea defences were another matter, however, and were largely provided by light cruisers and destroyers (at length in September Churchill did get the loan of fifty American destroyers, although only a few were operational in 1940).

---

[1] The Italian colony of Libya was divided into two provinces: Tripolitania in the west, and Cyrenaica in the east.

[2] This had originally been formed as the Local Defence Volunteers, and consisted of men aged between seventeen and sixty-five who had not been called up; unpaid, they worked at their normal occupations, and underwent training in their spare time. The Home Guard formed part of the armed forces of the Crown, and was subject to military law; although it never saw action, it did relieve the rest of the army of many duties. By 1944 it was over 2 million strong.

Moreover, what was to prove decisive in the forthcoming Battle of Britain was, of course, Fighter Command under the clear-sighted and strong-minded Dowding, who knew exactly how the battle should be fought – he stuck to the age-old military maxim that one should engage the enemy under conditions which favour oneself, not him – and had the strength of character to insist that he knew best. Over all reigned Winston Churchill, delving into every matter, his strategic horizon unlimited, his courage never flagging – though at times under sufficient strain as to make him unkind to his colleagues and to provoke a mild rebuke from his wife, Clementine, who reported the concern of a friend about his rudeness and sarcasm, urging him to temper his power with urbanity and calm – at one moment resisting dissipation of British troops and aircraft to remote areas; then encouraging the bombing of German targets whenever and wherever possible; at another, pursuing his notion of 'Leopard' groups, ready to spring rapidly on any lodgements made by enemy forces which might have slipped through the sea defences; next, sending a telegram to Lord Lothian, the British Ambassador in Washington, assuring him of his confidence that Britain would repel invasion, and telling him: 'Your mood should be bland and phlegmatic. No one is downhearted here.'

That confidence would soon be put to the test, for on 16 July Hitler signed his War Directive No 16 for the invasion of England, Operation Sea Lion, which he himself pronounced 'an exceptionally bold and daring undertaking'. The directive laid down that air mastery would be a prerequisite of the operation, that the enemy's air force must be so reduced both in numbers and in spirit that it could not significantly interfere with the sea crossing of the invading troops. It was a condition never to be fulfilled. Indeed, Hitler only signed the directive reluctantly. Apart from not really having much faith in the invasion plan, apart also from the fact that his eyes were still being drawn to the east, he was even now hoping that some sort of accommodation with Great Britain might be reached. As a result, in his address to the Reichstag on 19 July he was able to combine his supposed regret that war with Britain must continue with a personal appeal that it might be ended:

It almost causes me pain to think that I should have been selected by Fate to deal the final blow to the structure which these men [Churchill and the other British 'warmongers'] have already set tottering . . . Mr Churchill ought perhaps, for once, to believe me when I prophesy that a great Empire will be destroyed – an Empire which it was never my intention to destroy or even to harm . . .

In this hour, I feel it to be my duty before my own conscience to appeal once more to reason and common sense in Great Britain as much as elsewhere. I consider myself in a position to make this appeal since I am not the

vanquished begging favours, but the victor speaking in the name of reason. I
can see no reason why this war must go on.

Hitler may have had his doubts about the likelihood of such an appeal succeeding, and if he did, they were soon confirmed. It had become clear to
Churchill by the end of June that attacks on Great Britain were being planned
in detail, for the deciphering staff at Bletchley Park in Oxfordshire had already
decoded Enigma messages, indicating that Luftwaffe units had put in requests
for large numbers of maps of France, England and Ireland. Later, of course,
the Enigma decrypts – intelligence collectively known as 'Ultra' – were comprehensive and the knowledge thereby gained of German plans and intentions
was of vital importance to British and Allied policy and action.[1] Being aware, as
he was, that an attempted invasion could shortly be expected, Churchill and the
War Cabinet had decided on 3 July that what he called an 'admonition' should
be sent out to all those, both military and civil, who held senior positions in the
country, making it plain to them that defeatism or fears in the face of imminent
attack must be suppressed and overcome. The message was signed by the
Prime Minister himself, and informed all those in responsible positions that it
was 'their duty to maintain a spirit of alert and confident energy'. It expressed
confidence in the ability of the three services to prevent a landing, and
exhorted 'all His Majesty's servants in high places to set an example of steadiness and resolution'. What was more, all ill-advised talk must be checked; those
guilty of spreading 'alarm and despondency' were if necessary to be removed;
all must be worthy of the men doing the fighting. Next day, 4 July, Churchill
made a statement about the naval action at Oran[2] to the House of Commons,
repeated there his admonition to senior officials, and then – this was well
before Hitler's peace appeal – concluded:

> The action we have already taken should be, in itself, sufficient to dispose
> once and for all of the lies and rumours which have been so industriously
> spread by German propaganda and Fifth Column activities that we have the
> slightest intention of entering into negotiations in any form and through any
> channel with the German and Italian Governments. We shall, on the con-
> trary, prosecute the war with the utmost vigour by all the means that are
> open to us until the righteous purposes for which we entered upon it have
> been fulfilled.

The whole House cheered him. And when, later, he was asked whether he
wanted to respond to Hitler's 19 July offer to negotiate with Britain for an end

---

[1] Churchill referred to the Ultra messages as his 'golden eggs'.
[2] Mers-el-Kébir is in the Gulf of Oran.

to the war, his answer was: 'I do not propose to say anything in reply to Herr Hitler's speech, not being on speaking terms with him.'

As far as the invasion of England was concerned, Hitler tended to say different things to different people. He told Rundstedt on 19 July that he had no intention of invading, and at the same time ordered Brauchitsch to get on with planning an attack on Russia. Two days later, before leaving Berlin for a tour of Weimar and Bayreuth, he declared that unless preparations for the cross-Channel assault were complete by the beginning of September, other plans would have to be looked at. Meanwhile the C-in-C Navy, Raeder, was required to report on the naval aspects of such an invasion, which he did both on 25 July and on the 31st, advising strongly against it that autumn, both on grounds of likely bad weather during suitable moon and tide periods and because more German battleships would be in service by the spring. No doubt these arguments were the more acceptable to Hitler simply because one of the other plans – the defeat of Russia – was uppermost in his mind, not only for ideological reasons, but for strategic ones, since the supply of grain and oil from Russia and Romania might dry up unless they came under Germany's control. Yet Hitler's arguments, touched on in the first chapter, for choosing to subdue Russia before dealing with Britain fall down when set against the strategic circumstances of the time. In late 1940, even in early 1941, Germany was not at war with Russia (although relations between the two countries cooled in the late summer of 1940, as the Soviet Union increased its demands in south-eastern Europe), and Hitler failed to see, or perhaps would not allow himself to see, that England's subjection was not a corollary of an attack on Russia. It was in fact an indispensable condition of German victory, as Churchill told the world when he said that Hitler knew he must conquer Britain or lose the war. There was, of course, an alternative to attacking either Russia or Britain by direct assault, and this – as Raeder so frequently, yet so unsuccessfully, urged upon the Führer – was to concentrate on war against the British in the Middle East and Mediterranean. It is a sobering reflection that had Germany turned the great power of the Wehrmacht against the British position in Egypt and its neighbours by seizing North Africa – possibly with the aid of Vichy France and Spain – before Churchill so boldly reinforced the Middle East; had in fact the entire Middle East, the pivot of the British Empire, and the Eastern Mediterranean fallen into Axis hands, it is difficult to see how offensive action against Italy or Germany, other than by sea and air attacks, could have been mounted. It was the huge distraction created by British and later Allied action in the Mediterranean, the Balkans, North Africa and southern Europe which robbed Germany first of her ability to finish off Russia, second of her strength to resist successfully the violation of *Festung Europa* ('Fortress Europe'). Hitler's mind, however, did not work in such a way as to permit him to see this. Intuition, willpower, world-history-making strategic ideas – these were his gifts. In August 1940 he decided to attack Britain with the Luftwaffe, *and* to prepare to invade the Soviet Union.

While Hitler is contemplating which country to invade and when, Churchill is both preparing for an attack on Britain and seeking ways in which to take the offensive. He consults the Air Secretary, Sinclair, about bombing Germany, including, if required, Berlin; he explains to those concerned about the defence of the West Country that the combination of Home Guard units, backed by mobile reserves of Regular troops, coastal defence guns, constant naval patrols supported by more powerful warships, to say nothing of the Royal Air Force, would be available to counter enemy landings; he appoints Brooke as C-in-C Home Forces; makes plans for seizing the Azores and for protecting Britain's position in Palestine if Germany attacks Turkey; he is, as Brooke notes, 'full of offensive thoughts' and 'of the most marvellous courage considering the burden he is bearing'. His thoughts and proposals range as far afield as the Dutch East Indies, causing him to warn Japan that an attack on them would mean war with Britain; he is, too, in favour of bringing about an arrangement whereby French North Africa's government will be committed to 'continuing the war' against Germany. Martin Gilbert sums matters up by saying that Churchill was sure that from his innumerable ideas would come something that would hasten victory. 'His ability to produce schemes covering every aspect of war policy was well matched by the ability of his advisers to sift, mould, and if necessary to reject those schemes. But it was the spirit behind them that gave them their strength, and animated all who received them.' Nor was it just general war policy that the Prime Minister took such a deep interest in – the exact state of equipment for infantry divisions; aircraft losses; civilian casualties caused by German air raids; the establishment of an underground Cabinet War Room at Storey's Gate; further pleas to Roosevelt for destroyers (finally to meet with agreement in September, as has been said); the protection of vulnerable points in the event of invasion, including Whitehall and Chequers; inspection of coastal defences; talks to shipyard workers – no detail was too insignificant. Amidst all these warlike preparations at a time when invasion seemed imminent, Churchill examined the proposed Foreign Office reply to a suggestion made by Sweden's King Gustaf V to George VI that the possibilities of making peace should be examined. The Prime Minister's reaction to the Foreign Office draft was that it erred 'in trying to be too clever, and to enter into refinements of policy unsuited to the tragic simplicity and grandeur of the times and the issues at stake'.

It was, of course, Churchill's own superb coalition of simplicity and grandeur in his speeches that prompted such high praise, notably after his 30

July statement to the House of Commons about the perils facing the country, which prompted Henry 'Chips' Channon's comment, 'magnificent oratory and artistry,' and Harold Nicolson's 'Winston surpassed even himself'; while the Archbishop of Canterbury, Cosmo Lang, observed: 'His qualities of drive and courage, and his powers of glowing speech are a great public asset.' On the last day of July intelligence sources reported that invasion was imminent, and as if in confirmation of this, on 1 August Hitler's War Directive No 17 was issued. It called for the establishment of conditions necessary for the conquest of Britain. To this end the Luftwaffe was required to 'overpower the English Air Force' as quickly as possible, using all its strength. This intensification of air activity was to start 'on or after August 5'. More specifically, the attacks were 'to be directed primarily against flying units, their ground installations, and their supply organizations, but also against the aircraft industry . . .' Had the Luftwaffe stuck to this part of their directive, the story might have been a very different one, and the Germans might have reached that further part of their instructions as to what to do after achieving air superiority. But they did not, as will be seen from the following brief account of the course of the Battle of Britain.

Although there had been many previous encounters between the Luftwaffe and the Royal Air Force – on 8 August, for example, the RAF intercepted 300 German aircraft over the Isle of Wight – it was not until 12 August that Göring, who had told Hitler that he required three days of favourable weather in order to launch the opening phase of an attack on British fighter defences, actually gave orders for Operation Eagle to begin. Next day 1,500 German aircraft opened the attempt to destroy the RAF, and these attacks continued in varying degrees of intensity until the middle of September. Fortunately for Britain, Göring's strategy had two fundamental flaws. In the first place he did not concentrate on Fighter Command's radar stations; secondly, at a time when persisting with the bombing of the RAF's fighter airfields might have turned the scales, he switched his attacks to London. These two mistakes, together with the skilful husbanding and direction of Britain's fighter aircraft, and the spirit and courage of the pilots themselves, led to a decisive victory for the RAF on 15 September. Fighter Command, which had been close to exhaustion, was able to benefit from the respite accorded to its airfields and defences by the switching of the German target to London (a change of policy brought about partially in response to the British bombing of Berlin in late August, and also as a deliberate campaign of terror), and so mustered sufficient strength to break up the concentrated force of German bombers on 15 September, driving them off with severe losses. At the time it was claimed that 185 German aircraft had been shot down. This was a gross exaggeration, however. The figure was more like 60, as opposed to RAF losses of some 26 aircraft. But taken with other

German losses – some 225 between 30 August and 6 September – it was enough to convince Hitler that the Luftwaffe had not won, and would not win, air superiority. On 17 September he postponed Operation Sea Lion, and on 12 October cancelled it for the winter months.

Well before this decisive day in the Battle of Britain, Churchill had made his immortal tribute to the Royal Air Force pilots. In his review of the war given to the House of Commons on 20 August, he drew a distinction between the two world wars, emphasizing that unlike the 'prodigious slaughter' of the Great War, the present conflict was more concerned with 'strategy, organization, technical apparatus, science, mechanics and morale'. Britain's position and her ability to employ sea power to muster resources from around the world would allow her to undertake amphibious operations for the forthcoming campaigns of the next two years. However hard the struggle or long the road to victory might be, 'we mean to reach our journey's end'. The nation's defences against invasion bristled. Air power, in particular, was growing fast, and Britain 'would continue the air struggle indefinitely and as long as the enemy pleases'. It was then that Churchill produced the sentence which has lived on ever since, and will continue to do so:

> The gratitude of every home in our Island, in our Empire, and indeed throughout the world, except in the abodes of the guilty, goes out to the British airmen who, undaunted by odds, unwearied in their constant challenge and mortal danger, are turning the tide of war by their prowess and by their devotion. Never in the field of human conflict was so much owed by so many to so few.[1]

It was not only in the defence of Britain that the RAF was so active, but also in the continual bombing of German targets, which demanded from the bomber squadrons the greatest skill and endurance. This bombing campaign, Churchill continued, designed to disrupt the German war-making economy and the military bases from which attacks on this country were mounted, was 'the most certain . . . of all the roads to victory'. He even spoke of the post-war world, but stressed that the first task was to gain the victory. He touched also on the agreement that had been reached with the United States in leasing British Caribbean bases to the Americans in return for the loan of destroyers; he spoke, too – a matter dear to his heart – of the inevitable coming-together of these two great English-speaking democracies. He had no misgivings about

---

[1] No doubt Churchill recalled the then Lieutenant-Colonel John Moore's tribute to the men who captured Calvi, in Corsica, from the French in 1793: 'Never was so much work done by so few men.'

this process: 'Let it roll on full flood, inexorable, irresistible, benignant, to broader lands and better days.' Those who nowadays aim critical darts at Churchill's policy of bringing the United States ever closer to Britain, even at the cost of mortgaging substantial British assets, would do well to ask themselves what sensible alternative there was, if indeed any such alternative existed.

It was not just the defeat of the Luftwaffe which was of such moment to Churchill during the second half of August, for he was also enthusiastic about a plan to mount a landing by Free French forces at Dakar, the chief port and seat of government of French West Africa. Greatly concerned, too, about the Italian threat to Egypt (the Italians, much to the Prime Minister's displeasure, had turned the British out of Somaliland and his vexation was not alleviated by General Wavell's rejoinder to one of his pugnacious cables, that heavy casualties were not evidence of tactical sense), and therefore took the bold measure of reinforcing the Middle East command with an armoured brigade and many other armaments at a time when Britain itself was dangerously threatened – to say nothing of the risk to the convoy at sea. Although Wavell admired Churchill's boldness and foresight, he did not relish the Prime Minister's interference in tactical matters, a department which, reasonably, he regarded as peculiarly his own. The two men never really saw eye to eye. Churchill was not satisfied that Wavell was making the best use of his resources, and found he could not *like* the general, who was too cool, too unemotional, too independent. Besides, he did not wish to leave things to his Commander-in-Chief Middle East. He wanted to run them himself, particularly as here was a theatre of war where it would be possible to take some aggressive action, even though that might at first be part of a defensive campaign. He therefore gave Wavell a directive which contained detailed tactical instructions showing, as the General said, that 'Winston did not trust me to run my own show and was set on his ideas.' The document, dated 16 August, was important in that it laid down strategic priorities, but it also set in train a series of telegrams between C-in-C – no matter which one – and Prime Minister which was to be a persistent feature of the North African campaign. Having stated that the invasion of Egypt from Libya was to be expected at any time, Wavell was directed to assemble the largest possible force on Egypt's western frontier, told broadly how to deploy it, and guided as to priorities concerning the Sudan and Kenya; the directive also referred, in characteristically romantic terms, to 'the Army of the Delta'. Everything was to be ready by 1 October. 'The campaign for the defence of the Delta therefore resolves itself into strong defence with the left arm from Alexandria inland, and a reaching out with the right hand using sea power upon his [the enemy's] communications. At the same time it is hoped that our reinforcements acting from Malta will hamper the sending of further reinforcements – Italian or German – from Europe into Africa.' In this last sentence Churchill put his finger on the nub of the whole struggle for North Africa, which became in the end a battle of supplies, a battle in which Malta was to pay an absolutely crucial part, thereby enabling Britain to win the campaign. In the event, the Italians attacked in North Africa before 1 October, and as the British response to this was to have a profound effect on Hitler's next moves, and indeed upon the entire course of the war, it is as well to look at what happened. North Africa was, after all, the only theatre in which the British could engage Axis forces on land, and Wavell, as he was shortly to demonstrate, was thinking just as offensively as Churchill could have desired. The C-in-C Middle East was soon to inflict such a reverse on the Italians that, when it was taken in conjunction with Mussolini's pitiful blunderings in the Balkans, Hitler was obliged to *react* to what others, including his ally, were doing rather than retain absolutely the initiative for himself.

On 13 September 1940 the Italian Tenth Army under Marshal Rodolfo Graziani, Governor of Libya, made its ponderous advance into Egypt – Ciano having commented that no military commander had ever undertaken a military operation with so much reluctance – and having reached Sidi Barrani six days later, sat down and began to construct a series of defensive positions. There had been little opposition, since Graziani's four divisions had been opposed by little more than a battalion group, although the Italian columns received some attention from the RAF. The principal drawback for the British squadrons was that they could not now use the airfields at Sidi Barrani, thus robbing them of refuelling facilities and shortening the range at which they could operate. As this latter meant that Hurricane fighters from North Africa could no longer reach Malta, the strengthening or enhancing of that island's defensive and offensive capabilities – the last being especially important to the harassing of Italian lines of communication – became even more urgent. The Chiefs of Staff in London therefore reinforced Malta with fighters, reconnaissance aircraft and anti-aircraft guns, while continuing to strengthen the Middle East theatre generally. As the threat of invasion at home lessened, so the regularity of these reinforcements grew. This was just as well, for quite apart from Wavell's eagerness to mount an offensive in the Western Desert as soon as his forces were strong enough, Mussolini was about to take a step which would land him in serious trouble, and which, as a result of Germany's subsequent moves to retrieve the situation, would also turn Wavell's priorities upside-down.

On 28 October the Italian Government presented an ultimatum to Greece. It was immediately rejected, and from this time forth, nothing went right for Italy. Invading from Albania, which they had occupied in the spring of 1939, the Italians were disastrously defeated and thrown back out of Greece. Less than two weeks later Swordfish[1] aircraft from HMS *Illustrious*, a part of the Mediterranean Fleet commanded by Admiral Sir Andrew Cunningham, crippled half the Italian battle fleet in Taranto harbour at a single blow. This change in the balance of sea power reduced the threat to British shipping in the Eastern Mediterranean and enabled the Royal Navy to run convoys through to Malta, although the island's striking forces were still insufficient to prevent Italy reinforcing Libya by sea. Meanwhile the War Cabinet in London had decided to afford some help to the Greeks by sending RAF bombers and fighters, plus anti-aircraft batteries, to Greece from Egypt. These forces came under the overall command of Wavell, who also became responsible for the security of Crete. His strategic foresight was again well illustrated when he predicted that Germany could not afford to see Italy defeated in Greece, and would probably assist her ally with air forces shortly. Whereas Germany might not wish to push Bulgaria into the war or to invade Yugoslavia, she might be forced to do so, and, given her interior lines of communication, could attack Greece or Turkey more quickly than Britain could support them. Most of these predictions came about, yet in spite of so disagreeable a prospect, Wavell was determined to attack the Italian Tenth Army in the Western Desert before Greece became too great a drain upon his resources. On his orders, therefore, Operation Compass began on 7 December, lasted until 8 February 1941, and resulted in the absolute annihilation of Graziani's army. Under the command of the brilliant General O'Connor, after a series of swift, bold manoeuvres, and hard fighting by 7th Armoured Division (the 'Deserts Rats'), 4th Indian Division and Australian troops, with a classic outflanking armoured pursuit, Wavell's forces succeeded in winning what O'Connor termed 'a complete victory as none of the enemy escaped'. The fruits of this victory passed all expectations. In two months two British divisions had advanced 500 miles and routed an army of 10 divisions. In doing so they had suffered about 2,000 casualties, but had captured 130,000 enemy soldiers, nearly 400 tanks and over 800 guns. The Royal Air Force had established mastery of the skies, destroying about 150 enemy aircraft, and so had allowed the tanks and armoured cars of O'Connor's tiny force to outflank the enemy and to emerge unsuspected behind them.

O'Connor wanted to follow up his victory by executing the plan he had already made for an advance to Sirte and Tripoli, and Wavell backed him in his signal to London of 10 February, albeit with certain understandable reservations:

[1] A feat made all the more remarkable by the fact that the Fairey Swordfish was a three-seat *biplane* torpedo bomber of pre-war design and manufacture. Extremely slow, it was also extremely robust, and despite its obsolescence would achieve other notable successes before the war's end.

Extent of Italian defeat at Benghazi makes it seem possible that Tripoli might yield to small force if dispatched without undue delay. Am working out commitment involved but hesitate to advance further in view of Balkan situation [German forces destined for Greece had begun to move through Hungary into Romania early in January for an attack on Greece planned for the beginning of April] unless you think capture of Tripoli might have favourable effect on attitude of French North Africa.

Further advance will also involve naval and air commitments and we are already far stretched. Navy would hate having to feed us at Tripoli and Air Force to protect us. On other hand possession of this coast might be useful to both. [Those making strategic plans in London were soon directing their military and political efforts to the conquest of North Africa with its profound benefits of controlling the Mediterranean and releasing untold quantities of shipping.]

Will make plans for capture of Sirte which must be first step; meanwhile cable me most immediate your views as to effect on Weygand and war situation generally.

It was all in vain. The die was already cast. Greece's acceptance of Britain's offer to aid her had made priorities clear to Churchill. There was to be no further advance to Tripoli; Greece was to be 'succoured' and that was the end of it. Dill, the CIGS, recalled that when he tried to convince the Prime Minister that all the troops in the Middle East were fully committed and that none could be spared for Greece, Churchill turned on him, blood rushing to suffuse his great neck, eyes darting fury, and began to talk of courts martial and firing squads in Cairo. Dill regretted not having thought until later of asking Churchill whom he wanted to shoot.

It is now necessary to look back a little to see how the Prime Minister was wrestling with the problems of conducting – and thus of winning – the war, and how Hitler – 'That Man' – was coming to terms with the realization that the problems created by his Axis partner in the Balkans were beginning to prejudice his freedom of action. First Hitler, for there was no doubt that in terms of sheer military power (as well as of military successes), he still held the initiative. Having abandoned, at least for the time being, any idea of mounting Operation Sea Lion against Great Britain, where was the Wehrmacht to go? Could it turn east and leave an unsubdued foe behind it? Could indirect attack on Britain succeed where direct attack had failed? Italy was a partner in the war, fighting notably half-heartedly and inconclusively in Greece and North Africa. Would decision in the Mediterranean and Middle East, as Raeder so urgently and eloquently advocated, be a substitute for no decision in the skies over southern England? Or would Hitler's moves in the Mediterranean be designed

[286]

simply to prop up Mussolini and to guard his own southern flank while seeking in the east that decision which had eluded him in the west? In short, where was the war's real centre of gravity? Where did the real line of operations which would lead to decisive, total victory lie – through London or through Moscow? In his discourse to the Commanders-in-Chief in July, Hitler had persuaded himself that Russia's destruction must lead to the isolation of Britain, since America would become obsessed with Japan's consequently enhanced power, yet during this harangue the Führer left out what was perhaps the most powerful strategic argument for doing what he proposed.

Blitzkrieg in the west, for all the victories and gains it had brought, had been inconclusive. German naval and air forces were inadequate to crush Britain. Most of the Third Reich's military strength, in both men and material, was tied up in the army. The machine could not suddenly be switched to conduct a wholly different type of war. Moreover, it seemed that the war was not to be a short one after all. If that were the case, the economic resources needed both for prosecuting a long war and sustaining a largely occupied Europe could only be guaranteed by securing control of the Balkans – in September Romania, with its vital oilfields, was occupied by German troops – and by ensuring the continued supply of oil and grain from the Soviet Union. Yet the great enterprise of conquering Russia was to be seriously prejudiced by the sheer necessity of holding down great tracts of Europe, which was shortly to be added to by the need for precautionary and protective moves in the Mediterranean area. It was almost as if Hitler, like Macbeth, was to feel 'his secret murders sticking on his hands,' and 'his title Hang loose about him, like a giant's robe Upon a dwarfish thief'. He may have hoped that by continuing to harass Britain, and in attempting to close the Mediterranean to her shipping, he might persuade her to give in. But he can hardly have had much confidence in such an outcome when direct assault had served only to strengthen British resolution and defiance. What is more he was already beginning to be concerned about the future integrity of his *Festung Europa*. 'For all her glittering victories,' observed Arthur Bryant in the *Illustrated London News*, 'the Third Reich is encircled by steel. And the instrument of that encirclement is the sea-power of the British Empire and its still passive but very real and potent supporter, the United States of America. Germany must break that ring or go down as surely in the end as she did in 1918.' In the Battle of the Atlantic Hitler tried to break it by offensive means. In his plans for the Mediterranean – as we saw from his War Directive No 18 (touched on in Chapter 1) – his ideas were pre-emptive: block the Western Mediterranean, seize Gibraltar and secure French North Africa. If Germany could do this the use of these areas would be denied to the British as stepping-stones back into Europe, and the spectre of war on two fronts would be laid. That things did not quite go this way owed much to Hitler's 'allies'. But whereas the prudence of Spain and Vichy France robbed him of an opportunity which, had Raeder's great plan proved fully exploitable, might have been decisive, the rashness of Italy provoked a rescue operation which was as untimely as it was expensive. The price Franco demanded for Spain's participation was too high, while Pétain turned out to be better at collaborating with words rather than deeds, so that in the Western Mediterranean, Hitler's plans stalled, even though he was greatly cheered by Vichy's defeat in September of de Gaulle's attempt, with British naval assistance, to seize Dakar. At the other end of the Mediterranean Mussolini, by attacking Greece, had precipitated the very crisis Hitler wished to avoid. This unwelcome upsetting of equilibrium – which enraged the Führer, since he had been confident of absorbing the Balkans 'peacefully' – was, of course, looked upon as a gift by another leader whose strategic dilemma was no less profound – Churchill.

Churchill had already stated publicly that wars are not won by evacuations, although he was to arrange a few more of them, and was always searching for a way 'not of avoiding defeat, but inflicting it'. Where could British forces best inflict damage on the Axis? The answer was not hard to find. As Raeder predicted, no sooner had Italy declared war on Great Britain than the British sought ways of harassing Italy's military forces in the Mediterranean and North Africa. Moreover, since this was the only theatre in which Great Britain could engage the enemy on land, Churchill began to build up Wavell's forces. The Royal Navy soon established ascendancy in the Mediterranean, while the Desert Rats teased Graziani's Tenth Army. This activity did not greatly harm Britain's principal foe, and at first Wavell was able to do little more than block the Italians on land while naval and air forces attacked their communications with Africa, Malta playing a key role in this harassment. But Wavell was contemplating 'such measures of offence as will enable us and our Allies to dominate the Mediterranean at the earliest possible moment; and thereafter take the offensive against Germany in Eastern or S.E. Europe'. His great offensives against the Italians in Cyrenaica and East Africa,[1] together with his containing operations against pro-German elements in Iraq and the Vichy French in Syria, plus, of course, Admiral Cunningham's triumphs against the Italian Navy at Taranto and off Cape Matapan,[2] did much if not to dominate, at least to contest, the Mediterranean and Middle East. When it came to arguing the toss with the Germans, however, it was not so much a matter of taking the

---

[1] In 1941, a British and Colonial force under Lieutenant-General Alan Cunningham (brother of the admiral) reconquered Abyssinia and British Somaliland, taking 50,000 Italian prisoners for the loss of 500 casualties.

[2] On 28 March 1941 Cunningham's ships engaged the Italian fleet off the southern tip of Greece, destroying an enemy squadron.

offensive, but rather of coming to the assistance of allies, like Greece, who were being overwhelmed. Furthermore, because Wavell's Middle East Command was desperately overstretched, that assistance was given with insufficient strength. In the end, he was obliged to intervene, as we shall see, in both Greece and Crete, only to incur grievous losses and be forced to order further withdrawals.

Yet the instinct of both Churchill and Wavell to fight for the Middle East as far forward as possible was sound. The mere fact of British successes in Libya and intervention on the mainland of Europe (that is, in Greece) was so disturbing to Hitler that it produced the precise effects which British Mediterranean strategy was intended to have. It was not in this theatre that decision in the struggle for Europe was to be found. But by inducing Hitler to begin dissipating the Wehrmacht, by managing to create the opportunity for attrition, to provide a colossal distraction, to enforce a division of effort, to pose and go on posing a threat which Germany could neither eliminate nor ignore – this was to wield sea power both traditionally and advantageously. It was a policy which, in the end, was not only to account for as many Axis soldiers as were lost to Hitler at Stalingrad; it would also provide a springboard from which to arrange and carry out the overthrow of a fortress.

During the autumn of 1940 Churchill had cause to take comfort from some successes – the defeat of the Luftwaffe, the growing activities of Bomber Command, naval action in the Mediterranean, the intelligence derived from Ultra – and he was confident that his troops would see off the Italians in North Africa. He was greatly encouraged when he heard from the Chief of Air Staff at a War Cabinet on 22 September that 100 heavy bombers were to attack Berlin, while others would be giving their attention to the Channel ports, where German invasion barges were still positioned. Churchill longed for offensive action against the Axis, telling Colville that the enemy must never be maltreated by halves: 'Once the battle is joined, let 'em have it.' But the threat of invasion had not dissolved, the operation to seize Dakar had to be abandoned, German U-boats were still sinking merchant ships in the Atlantic, and the Blitz on London by German bombers was destroying houses and businesses and killing people. It was characteristic of Churchill that he visited the worst-hit areas (Hitler never did so when German cities were getting their own taste of destruction from the air). The Prime Minister's coming to see them and his evident concern were greatly appreciated – 'You see, he really cares', one woman was heard to say during his visit to the London Docks on 8 September, 'he's crying.' Others welcomed him with shouts of approval, saying that they could take it and urging 'Winnie' to administer the same medicine to the Germans. Commenting on the Blitz in a speech in the House of Commons on 8 October – it was the occasion of the introduction of his son, Randolph, as

Member for Preston – Churchill spoke of the great length of time it would take for London's houses to be demolished, of the intention to rebuild better ones, of what would be happening to Hitler and his regime meanwhile, and referred to his visits to those areas badly hit:

> In all my life, I have never been treated with so much kindness as by the people who have suffered most. One would think one had brought some great benefit to them, instead of the blood and tears, the toil and sweat which is all I have ever promised. On every side, there is the cry, 'We can take it,' but, with it there is also the cry, 'Give it 'em back'.

He would do so, but made it clear that for the present British air attacks would concentrate on military targets. At the same time, he said, it must be understood that the danger of invasion was not over, and that even though the autumn weather was uncertain, there would be periods of calm when barges, perhaps aided by fog, could make the crossing. All the armed forces must build up their strength, aided by resources from the United States. Vigilance must be the order of the day. The setback at Dakar in no way altered the Government's support of General de Gaulle, support which would continue until his cause was merged 'as merged it will be, in the larger cause of France'. While the world now recognized Britain's resilience and purpose, no one must be in doubt about the great perils which still faced the country, nor about the need for unflagging and undaunted efforts:

> No one can predict, no one can even imagine, how this terrible war against German and Nazi aggression will run its course or how far it will spread or how long it will last. Long, dark months of trials and tribulations lie before us. Not only great dangers, but many more misfortunes, many shortcomings, many mistakes, many disappointments will surely be our lot. Death and sorrow will be the companions of our journey; hardship our garment; constancy and valour our only shield. We must be united, we must be undaunted, we must be inflexible. Our qualities and deeds must burn and glow through the gloom of Europe until they become the veritable beacon of its salvation.

Amidst all his own trials and tribulations Churchill's irrepressible lightness of heart enables him to reprove his cat, Nelson, for being unworthy of his great name by showing, even in the basement of 10 Downing Street – now a dining room – his dislike of anti-aircraft guns. Nelson is firmly told by his master to remember what the boys in the RAF are doing.

During the second week of October 1940, we find the Prime Minister accepting leadership of the Conservative Party, spending a weekend at

Chequers, where his grandson, Winston is born, and discussing the war situation with Dill and Brooke. The latter notes in his diary what 'a wonderful vitality' Churchill has and how 'he bears his heavy burden remarkably well. It would be impossible to find a man to fill his place at present.' The bombing of London continued, and although some Londoners voluntarily evacuated themselves and others slept every night in the Underground stations, civilian morale on the whole held up, bolstered from time to time by either Churchill or the King appearing on the scene after a severe raid. Indeed, Churchill commented that this was the sort of war that he thought suited the British people, sharing the dangers in the front line rather than, as in the Great War, helplessly hearing about the appalling slaughters on the Western Front. In his *English History 1914–1945*, A.J.P. Taylor makes the point that the British people's spirit was unshaken. He describes how, when a motion was brought forward in the House of Commons in December for the negotiation of peace, it was defeated by 341 votes to 4, and further declares that in spite of all the suffering and hardship caused by the Blitz, the raids 'cemented national unity' and did away with any possible resentment felt by the fighting men against civilians. The mere fact that the British people could 'take it', as they repeatedly told Churchill, made them feel that the war could be won. How it was to be won was another matter, and one that was constantly in the Prime Minister's mind. He was deeply concerned that the bomber force should be expanded and that as great a tonnage of bombs as possible should be dropped on Germany. But he still insists that German military targets should be attacked, not civilians, and rebukes Robert Cary in the Smoking Room of the House of Commons when he demands reprisals for raids on London. 'This is a military and not a civilian war,' he says, adding that others might wish to kill women and children, but he and his colleagues preferred to destroy enemy military objectives. His motto, he said, was 'Business before Pleasure'. Harold Nicolson, who is present during this exchange, reports that those present drift away, thinking 'That was a man'.

The problem of Vichy France still weighed heavily with Churchill, and he made every effort to influence its leaders, firstly by conveying through Britain's Ambassador to Spain, Sir Samuel Hoare, to the latter's Vichy contacts, his conviction that Hitler, no matter how much he might ravage Western Europe, was in the end doomed to defeat; secondly by broadcasting to France *in French*. In fact, the speech was broadcast on the evening of 21 October (whether those concerned recalled that this was the anniversary of the Battle of Trafalgar has not been recorded) in both French and English. It contained some marvellous Churchillian cries: 'We are waiting for the long-promised invasion. So are the fishes;' 'Frenchmen – rearm your spirits before it is too late.' He reminded the people of France of what Napoleon had said about the Prussians; told them that the British and their friends across the Atlantic Ocean would destroy

Hitler and his gang; and exhorted them: 'Therefore have hope and faith, for all will come right . . . *Vive la France!*' This broadcast, Churchill's French painter friend, Paul Maze, told him, was like a blood transfusion.

Whenever he could Churchill visited the troops and sailors, inspecting the Polish forces under General Wladyslaw Sikorski, head of the Polish Government-in-Exile, and the battleship, *King George V*, often accompanied by Dill and Brooke. He found time to intervene in the appointment of senior officers, and in particular that of Major-General Hobart, whose original ideas made such a contribution to the development of specialized armour. In defending Hobart's unconventional ideas, he pointed out that conventional soldiers rarely possessed the genius of such men as Cromwell, Wolfe, Clive and Gordon, and that the very qualities which were sometimes condemned as defects were in fact those of greatness. He had his way.

In wrestling with the Vichy difficulties, Churchill found himself able to recognize qualities of greatness in General de Gaulle, commanding the Free French forces at Libreville in French Equatorial Africa. On 27 October the General made what became known as the 'Brazzaville declaration'. In utterly condemning the Vichy regime as 'unconstitutional and in subjection to the invader . . . an instrument used by the enemies of France against the honour and interests of the country,' de Gaulle was talking the language that Churchill understood, and the latter was further impressed by de Gaulle's calling to war 'all the men and all the women of the French territories which have rallied to me,' who together with the Allies would work 'towards restoring the independence and greatness of France . . .' While conscious of the need to keep the Vichy option open, Churchill responded by signalling to the Free French leader that Britain was trying to reach 'some *modus vivendi* with Vichy which will minimize the risk of incidents and will enable favourable forces in France to develop'. At the same time, he added, hostile action by Vichy would provoke an instant and persistent response.

Although the threat of invasion appeared to have diminished, Churchill informed President Roosevelt that, both at home and in the Middle East, Britain was still under great strain, and therefore all assistance possible from the United States would be most welcome. An agreement reached between Sir Walter Layton and General George C. Marshall, United States Army Chief of Staff, arranged for the equipping of ten British divisions, and further agreements for aircraft and aero engines were made. In appealing to Roosevelt to speed up delivery of this vital equipment, Churchill stressed the varied and growing dangers which Britain faced – a hostile Vichy; the extension of war in the Middle East and Eastern Mediterranean; the ever-present requirements of home defence; and the menace of German U-boat and air attacks on sea communications, 'our only remaining life-line'. He was, however, confident that, given all the weapons and ammunition required, Britain would be able to 'carry the war on to a successful conclusion'.

It was *how* to do so which so exercised Churchill at the Defence Committee meeting of 31 October 1940, which, again, we touched on in Chapter 1. There was, of course, no simple answer to the problem of how to win the war. Britain, except for the bombing of Germany and Italy, and leaving aside Wavell's intention to attack Graziani's Tenth Army in the Western Desert, was still reacting to German moves. The threat of imminent invasion might be lessening, but the requirement to counter an increased submarine danger to shipping in the North-Western Approaches was such that naval forces would have to be diverted from anti-invasion duties for this purpose. Moreover, the situation in South-East Europe, aggravated by Italy's invasion of Greece, made it even more necessary to reinforce the Middle East. In reviewing how the war might now develop, Churchill acknowledged the freedom of action enjoyed by Germany, which could, if she wished, attack Spain or Turkey, or even Russia, whereas Britain would not be in a position to undertake any major offensive until 1942. Nevertheless, the aim was to have fifty-five divisions fully equipped by the end of 1941, and a further ten, as has been said, to be furnished with weapons and equipment by the United States. In addition, the bomber force would enable Britain to attack the Axis powers, particularly Germany, 'to the greatest extent possible'. In this last respect Churchill left no doubt in the mind of Portal, Chief of the Air Staff, that he was dissatisfied with progress being made in the expansion of Bomber Command and its bomb-dropping capacity, which he regarded as 'lamentably small'. At the beginning of November Churchill was urging both Dill and Eden, who was in Cairo, that the maximum aid should be given to Greece with land, sea and air forces. Eden objected that to do so would imperil the whole Middle East position, and a good deal of signalling to and fro resulted, but by 3 November the policy of aid to Greece had been accepted by the Chiefs of Staff, who instructed the Cs-in-C, Middle East,[1] to send maximum possible military support to Greece, even though it would greatly weaken Egypt until further forces and supplies could be sent there. British intervention in Greece was to increase during the coming months, to the extent that it prejudiced Wavell's ability to mount further offensives in the Western Desert; it also caused severe losses in all three services, as well as further weakening Britain's prestige. Both morally and strategically, however, this intervention must be counted as sound, in so far as it hampered Hitler's principal plans for 1941, as well as exerting a profound influence on Greek popular opinion.

In a statement to the House of Commons on 5 November, Churchill's

[1] That is, Wavell, the overall Commander-in-Chief, and the commanders of the naval, army and air forces in the theatre.

review of the war situation was hardly sanguine. On the contrary, with its tale of losses at sea, of problems developing in the Eastern Mediterranean, of casualties in the Blitz at home, it painted a grim picture. Yet in putting over to the House both the unattractive facts and a statement of Britain's continued resolution, in the unique manner in which he was able to confront the worst, Churchill cheered those who heard him. 'I have never admired him more,' noted Harold Nicolson, while Chips Channon admired his 'pluck, his courageous energy and magnificent English'.

Not all the news in these early days of November 1940 was bad. Roosevelt had been re-elected President of the United States, with all that that meant in terms of further support for Britain, and when Eden came back from his visit to the Middle East, he brought with him the information that Wavell and O'Connor were intending to embark on Operation Compass which, as has already been outlined, led to the destruction of Graziani's Tenth Army. The mere prospect of an offensive was a source of great delight to Churchill ('I purred like six cats'); what he referred to as 'the intolerable shackles of the defensive' were at last to be thrown off. The subsequent success of Compass was to increase his delight, even though the further reinforcing of Greece robbed Wavell and O'Connor of the opportunity to exploit Italy's defeat in the desert, and indeed were to lead to such frustration over Wavell's apparent inability to restore the British position there that Churchill eventually decided to replace him. By that time, of course, there were new players in the game – General Rommel and the Afrika Korps. For the time being, however, Churchill's elation was augmented by the Royal Navy's raid on the Italian base at Taranto.

The Prime Minister's capacity to switch his concentration, and his eloquence, from one matter to another, together with his generosity of spirit, were further illustrated by his tribute to Neville Chamberlain, who long ill, had died on 9 November. Even though Chamberlain's hopes had been disappointed and his expectations contradicted by events, the aims he had set himself, the hopes he had cherished, the faith he had had were, Churchill said,

> surely among the most noble and benevolent instincts of the human heart – the love of peace, the toil for peace, the strife for peace, the pursuit of peace, even at great peril and certainly to the utter disdain of popularity or clamour . . . We can be sure that Neville Chamberlain acted with perfect sincerity according to his lights and strove to the utmost of his capacity and authority . . . to save the world from the awful, devastating struggle in which we are now engaged.

He was equally capable of administering a Reproof Valiant when circumstances demanded. War, as is well known, is an option of difficulties, and in trying to balance the conflicting needs of Greece and Egypt, Churchill had difficulties enough. He was thus understandably incensed on reading a telegram from the British Ambassador to Egypt, Sir Miles Lampson (who enjoyed immense power and who had formed a very high opinion of his own abilities) to the effect that sending military supplies to Greece was 'completely crazy'. The reproof took the form of telling Lampson that he should not use such expressions 'when applied by you to grave decisions of policy taken by the Defence Committee and the War Cabinet after considering an altogether wider range of requirements and assets than you can possibly be aware of.'

The intelligence resulting from the reading of Enigma signals – Ultra – was able to give Churchill and others warnings of impending German air raids on British cities. It was wholly in keeping with the Prime Minister's wish to share the dangers undergone by the people that when, just as he was on the point of leaving London for the country on the afternoon on 14 November, he was handed information that a heavy German air raid was expected that night, and assuming that London was the target, he instantly changed his plans on the grounds that 'he was not going to spend the night peacefully in the country while the metropolis was under heavy attack'. There were to be many occasions in the future when Churchill, just as he had during the Great War, insisted on getting as close to the front line as possible, whether in Africa, Italy, Normandy or Germany – indeed, sometimes he had to be restrained. Hitler, on the other hand, kept well away from the bombs and the fighting, until his final decision to remain in Berlin and 'die fighting at the head of his troops'. As it turned out the German raid on the night of 14 November was against Coventry, not London, and was a most savage attack, soon to be followed by further raids on London and Birmingham. Churchill's extraordinary concern and compassion were once more illustrated by his urging of the Home Secretary, Herbert Morrison, to look into the question of improving the people's air-raid shelters, especially in view of the coming winter, and providing them with 'gramophones and wireless'. Similarly, he wanted to raise the status of mayors of badly bombed cities, by awarding these cities the honour of having Lord Mayors. His attention to the details of ordinary Britons' lives, when burdened with the great strategic issues of the day, was remarkable. Harold Nicolson noted at about this time that Churchill seemed in good health, but that his eyes were 'glaucous, vigilant, angry, combative, visionary and tragic. In a way they are the eyes of a man who is much preoccupied and is unable to rivet his attention on minor things . . . [In fact, as we have seen, Churchill *did* attend to what might have been thought of as minor things. They were not minor to him.] But in another sense they are the eyes of a man faced by an ordeal or tragedy, and combining vision, truculence, resolution and great unhappiness.'

There was no doubt about the vision or the resolution. His vision encompassed the dangers which would arise if Spain, suffering from food shortages as a result of the war, should come in on the German side (and he urged Roosevelt to provide supplies in exchange for Spain's undertaking to remain neutral), with the threat that this would present to Britain's naval position at the Straits of Gibraltar. He saw, too, danger in the Balkans, where German concentrations in Romania and Bulgaria pointed to a possible attack on Turkey with all the consequent danger to Britain's hold on the Middle East. Yet the prospects of Wavell's forthcoming offensive in Libya held out hopes of encouraging Turkey; timing was all important, for the Germans were in a position to strike at Greece as well, and Churchill therefore signalled Wavell advocating that Operation Compass should be launched during the first two weeks of December. It was, and we have seen with what glittering success. In anticipating this success, Churchill brimmed with ideas as to how it was to be exploited. He was already conscious that there might not be time enough to finish the business in Libya before having to move to Greece, while among his more bizarre ideas are those of sending four British divisions to land on the African shore of the Straits of Gibraltar, and another for making a landing on the island of Pantelleria, between Tunisia and Sicily!

On 30 November Winston Churchill was sixty-six. He had been Prime Minister for rather more than six months and had told Anthony Eden earlier in the week that he had never felt more equal to his work. He would need to be, for the next two years would bring with them some terrible trials and tribulations, fortunately not unmixed with the acquisition of allies in the struggle with Germany that in the end brought about the utter ruin of Hitler's Third Reich.

While, in December 1940, Churchill was viewing with confidence the situation in the Eastern Mediterranean, where Britain's capability had been enhanced by the establishment of sea and air bases in Crete, he was by no means encouraged by what he regarded as the failure of the United States to assist in control of the seas in such a way as would ensure that Britain could both import essential supplies and munitions *and* move its military forces about to engage the Axis powers. He therefore requested Roosevelt to help protect convoys engaged in 'lawful trading on the high seas' with United States warships, by giving or lending further warships to Britain, and by providing more merchant shipping. There was also the continued need to equip British divisions. As for payment, Churchill made a powerful plea for some alternative to the paying of cash – which was fast running out – for such shipping and supplies:

> I believe you will agree that it would be wrong in principle and mutually disadvantageous in effect if at the height of this struggle Great Britain were to be divested of all saleable assets, so that after the victory was won with our

blood, civilization saved and the time gained for the United States to be fully armed against all eventualities, we should stand stripped to the bone. Such a course would not be in the moral or economic interests of either of our countries.

Churchill's appeal led, by an Act of Congress in March 1941, to the 'Lend-Lease' arrangement, under which supplies and equipment from America would be lent or leased to countries 'whose defense the President deems to be vital to the defense of the United States,' without payment in cash. It sounded admirable in theory. It was of less immediate financial advantage in practice, for the bulk of military equipment received in 1941 was paid for in dollars. But the real virtue of lend-lease was that Britain's survival would not be put at risk because of shortages of war-making material. At the same time the United States would not be a disinterested benefactor. Lend-lease was essentially 'to promote the defense of the United States,' and indeed it enabled America's industry to be set upon a war footing eight months before she joined the war. As A.J.P. Taylor writes: 'The Americans insisted that they were aiding Britain so that she should fight Germany and not to maintain her as an industrial power . . . Thanks to lend-lease Great Britain virtually ceased to be an exporting country. She sacrificed her postwar future for the sake of the war.'[1]

It was a question of survival. It seemed that Britain could just about keep the supplies coming across the Atlantic, could damage the Italian army and navy, could supply some help to new allies, like Greece, could support de Gaulle's Free French movement, and take what was coming in the continued Blitz – while mounting bombing campaigns against both Axis powers and building up her military strength in the Middle East for further offensive action in southern Europe later – but she could not match the power of the Wehrmacht. As it turned out mere survival – until Hitler's obsession with making world history caused him to take on both the Soviet Union and the United States – proved to be Britain's indispensable contribution to the ultimate defeat of the Third Reich. She was to make many other contributions, too, but this survival against all the odds was the one without which the others would not have been possible. And without Churchill it may be doubted whether all this would have come about.

As 1940 drew to a close Churchill witnessed the damage done to the House of Commons in the air raid of 7 December; rejoiced in the success of Compass, although, as was customary with him, he became impatient that

---

[1] When academics like John Charmley criticize Churchill for bankrupting the country, they fail to show how Great Britain could have carried on the war without some such arrangement as lend-lease.

Wavell was not pursuing the enemy with sufficient speed and vigour; appointed Halifax to be British Ambassador in Washington on the death of Lothian, making Eden Foreign Secretary; enjoyed himself by visiting his old school, Harrow; and continued to wrestle with the problems presented by powerful German troop concentrations in the Balkans, by the uncertainties as to whether it would be possible to collaborate with Vichy France, and by the urgent need to improve Whitehall security, whether telephonic or documentary. 'As 1940 ended,' observes Martin Gilbert, 'many of Churchill's hopes for 1941 were based on the United States: its material and its moral support, and its possible direct participation in the war . . .' Yet also in December 1940, Hitler at last came to a decision which was to result in the world's strategic balance being turned upside-down.

It was said of Napoleon that his frequent, decisive victories became more comprehensible when the consideration that he was rarely encumbered with allies was taken into account. Hitler might have been excused for harbouring some such sentiment in the autumn of 1940 as a result of his conferences with Franco, Pétain and Mussolini. It is curious that the Führer's undoubted strategic gifts did not extend to grasping – or perhaps he was unwilling to acknowledge – the truly enormous potential of gaining complete control of the Middle East, the Mediterranean and North Africa. Quite apart from striking a near-mortal blow at Britain, Hitler's sole enemy at the end of 1940 (although admittedly backed by the not inconsiderable resources of the Dominions and Empire), by robbing her of freedom to employ sea power in the theatre, there was the almost unlimited supply of oil to exploit. Moreover, Germany's allies (either actual or latent), Italy, Spain and Vichy France, were all capable of deploying military forces in this area, to say nothing of what the Wehrmacht itself could do. We have only to think of what Rommel's relatively tiny Afrika Korps, together with the deployment of Luftwaffe squadrons in Sicily and North Africa, did achieve. Yet Hitler's objectives in the Mediterranean and North Africa were preventative rather than decision-seeking. He wanted both to inhibit the British maritime freedom of action there and at the same time establish some sort of defence against the use of North-West Africa as a stepping-stone for the British – and any allies they might acquire – to mount an attack against southern Europe. And to do these things, he needed the help of others. None of the meetings he had with his fellow dictators and with Pétain was, however, satisfactory.

The first of these meetings, with Mussolini on 4 October, revealed the dilemma Hitler faced with regard to French North Africa, if he were not to antagonize one or other of the possible beneficiaries of its disposal. He knew that Franco's terms for joining in the war included the ceding of French Morocco to Spain, but not only did Hitler want to retain control of the

Moroccan coast as a means of access to his planned German empire in Central Africa, but he feared that giving French Morocco to Spain would so aggravate opinion there and elsewhere that the whole of French North-West Africa would rally to de Gaulle. Moreover, Hitler was equally unwilling to risk any development of that sort by acceding to Mussolini's ambitions with regard to the French colonial empire. Hitler determined therefore to tackle Franco and Pétain in person. His nine hours' talk with Franco at the Spanish border on 23 October got him nowhere. Franco's demands were excessive, his commitment vague, and to his intense irritation Hitler found himself quite incapable of impressing the Caudillo with either his own dominant personality or with Germany's capability of defeating England. Things went more smoothly and agreeably with Pétain, but although the old warrior may have agreed to the idea of collaboration in principle, nothing concrete was agreed, details being left for subsequent discussion which, as Pétain so significantly observed later, would take six months – and another six months to forget.

Hitler's second meeting with Mussolini, in Florence on 28 October, unlike the earlier one, did lead to decisive action, but not of the sort Hitler had planned, for when the Führer's train arrived at Florence station, to his intense annoyance the Duce greeted him with the news that Italy's attack on Greece had begun: 'Führer, wir marschieren!' This was in direct opposition to Hitler's wishes, and it had a profound effect on the conduct of the war thereafter. It was the beginning of a gigantic distraction for Axis and Western Allies alike from the two main theatres of operation which were to develop and where the fate of the Wehrmacht and the Third Reich were to be decided – the Eastern Front and North-West Europe. The magnitude of Italy's strategic blunder was such that Hitler never trusted the Italians again. Meanwhile, however, something had to be done, and the Führer's War Directive No 18 dated 12 November (touched on in Chapter 1) illustrated that the dissipation of the Wehrmacht over wide areas and subsidiary objectives was about to take place. The directive called for action by France to secure their African possessions; preparations to seize Gibraltar; employment of German forces, including a panzer division, to assist the Italians in Egypt; plans for occupying Greece from Bulgaria; a campaign against Russia – there was even reference to Operation Sea Lion. All this variety reflected Hitler's uncertain strategic intentions; and revealed, too, the first signs of relinquishing the initiative. The directive spelled out *re*action to what the British and Greeks were doing to the Italians. David Irving calls Mussolini's invasion of Greece – for, as has been said, his divisions were quickly thrown back – the sowing of the first seeds of later defeat.

One more meeting took place before Hitler came to a decision as to what to do about Russia. This was with the Soviet Foreign Minister, Molotov, and so outrageous were his demands in Hitler's view – 'military bases on Danish soil on the outlets to the North Sea . . . Constantinople, Romania, Bulgaria and Finland – and *we* were supposed to be the victors!' was the way he later recalled it – that the Führer was in little further doubt. A month later he signed War Directive No 21, Operation Barbarossa, whose opening sentence must have sent a shiver down the spine of those who read it at OKW and at the three service headquarters and who remembered a former war on two fronts: 'The German Armed Forces must be prepared, even before the conclusion of the war against England, to crush Soviet Russia in a rapid campaign.' Everything was to be ready by mid-May 1941. Hitler had therefore declared: 'The Mediterranean question must be liquidated this winter . . . I must have my German troops back in the spring, not later than May 1st'. The Mediterranean question was not liquidated in the winter of 1940–1. From the German point of view it was never liquidated, and in both 1941 and 1942, Churchill's insistence on reinforcing the Middle East and conducting a Mediterranean strategy, despite some disappointing delays and heavy setbacks, began to pay substantial dividends.

CHAPTER 6

1941 – The War's Outcome is Decided

─────────────

When *Barbarossa* begins, the world will hold its breath and make no comment.

ADOLF HITLER, February 1941

Any man or state who fights on against Nazidom will have our aid . . . It follows therefore that we shall give whatever help we can to Russia and the Russian people.

WINSTON CHURCHILL, June 1941

On 8 and 9 January 1941 Hitler held another of his war councils at the Berghof. As was customary with him his review of the situation ranged wide. Italy was to be supported in Africa and in Albania; Operation Marita – an attack on Greece by twenty-four divisions which would assemble in Romania in order to advance through Bulgaria as soon as the weather was suitable – would now be mounted at the end of March; Russia would have to be crushed as soon as possible, for Stalin was a 'cold-blooded blackmailer' and would not give up his claims in Eastern Europe. Yet, Hitler reflected, if both Russia and the United States made war on Germany – the very situation which during this year he was himself (albeit with Japanese connivance) to bring about – things 'would become very complicated'. Yet in spite of this gloomy prognostication, his survey of grand strategy was wreathed in confidence: 'The situation in Europe can no longer develop unfavourably for Germany even if we should lose the whole of North Africa.' The British could only hope to win by defeating Germany on the Continent, and this the Führer considered to be out of the question. All these considerations were translated into another War Directive, No 22. This showed to what an extent Hitler was at this time concerned with the Mediterranean, for it dealt largely with German support for battles in this theatre. Libya's western province Tripolitania was to be held (Cyrenaica by now being in British hands), and an Italian collapse on the Albanian front averted. German Army units would therefore be made ready to move to Libya in February, and the Luftwaffe's X Fliegerkorps would remain in Sicily and take on a new offensive role – to attack British naval forces, communications and supply installations in the Mediterranean area. An entire army corps would be made available to stiffen the Albanian front, enable the Italians to break through the Greek defences, and support the German army, commanded by Field Marshal Sigmund List, which was moving south into Bulgaria. All this went to show the lengths to which Hitler was prepared to go to help Mussolini, whose compliance at the time of the Anschluss had earned him the Führer's undying gratitude. In the end, of course, Hitler's support did Mussolini no good at all, even though it prolonged Italy's participation in the war for the best part of two and a half years.

While Hitler is making his grand strategic plans, Churchill is conferring with President Roosevelt's personal emissary, Harry Hopkins. Their first meeting on 10 January at Downing Street was auspicious in that each was greatly impressed by the other. Churchill was very frank in their exchanges, telling the American that Greece would probably be lost, even though the British were reinforcing there at the expense of the Western Desert Force,[1] but that they would continue to harass Italy, would control the Mediterranean, and would hang on to Africa. The instant understanding and liking that grew up between the two men, and which were reinforced during the coming weeks, were profoundly important to the co-operation between their two countries. It was made clear by Hopkins that Roosevelt was determined to supply Britain with 'the means of survival and of victory'. It was equally clear that the United States's leaders were as resolved as Churchill himself that Hitler must be defeated. Hopkins, in writing to Roosevelt, praised both the Prime Minister and the British people themselves:

People here are amazing from Churchill down, and if courage alone can win, the result will be inevitable. But they need help desperately, and I am sure you will permit nothing to stand in the way ... *Churchill* is the gov't in every sense of the word – he controls the grand strategy and often the details – labour trusts him – the army, navy, air force are behind him to a man. The politicians and upper crust pretend to like him. I cannot emphasize too strongly that he is the one and only person over here with whom you need to have a full meeting of minds.'

Hopkins stressed that Britain needed American aid at once, and that it should be all that could be given.

---

[1] Later renamed Eighth Army.

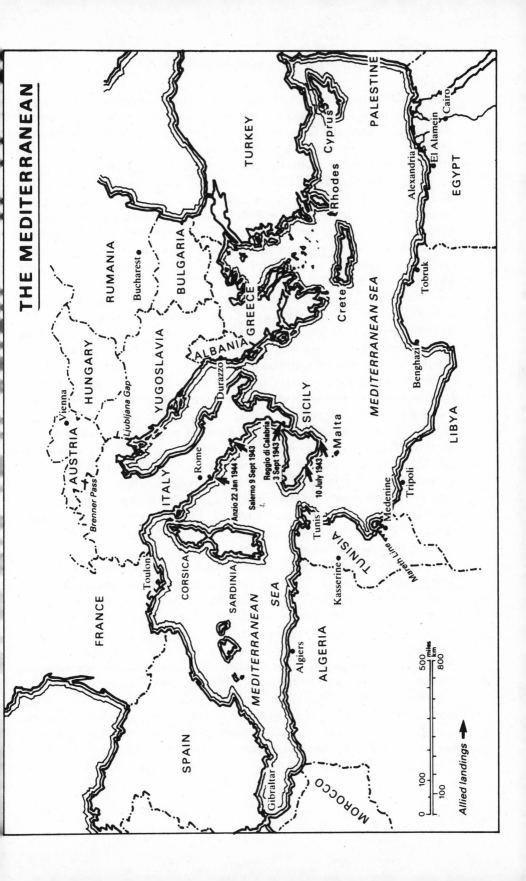

The relationship between Hopkins and Churchill continued to flourish. They visited Scapa Flow, spent a night on board the battleship *King George V*, went to Edinburgh and Glasgow, where Churchill, in one of those extempore speeches he was so good at, told his audience about the purpose behind Hopkins's visit, and that what Britain needed was not large armies to help, but weapons, ships, aircraft; he added that he had no doubt about final victory, however long and hard the road might be. Later, at a dinner, Hopkins responded by saying that he would report to the President the absolute harmony between their two countries. (On another occasion Hopkins told Churchill, much to his pleasure, that at Dover he had heard one working man say to his companion as the Prime Minister passed them: 'There goes the bloody British Empire.') All in all, the Hopkins visit was immensely reassuring for Churchill as it convinced him that Roosevelt's support, particularly in the dangerous months that lay ahead, would be solid and bountiful, and that although he might see America's immediate role as being that of an arsenal for the provision of weapons with which to fight Hitler, Roosevelt would not shrink from war itself, should it become necessary.

On 19 and 20 January 1941 Hitler and Mussolini again conferred at the Berghof, the former, as usual, doing most of the talking. He greatly impressed his audience with his 'mastery' of all strategic contingencies, as if he were in firm control of any situations which might develop. Ciano recorded that Hitler spent two hours explaining his coming intervention in Greece, dealing primarily with the military side of the operation, yet fitting it all in with political considerations. The Italian Foreign Minister conceded that it was brilliantly done and greatly impressed Italy's military experts. At the same time – and this was illustrative of the limited trust Hitler had for his partners – while taking an extremely anti-Russian attitude, he said nothing to Mussolini or Ciano about his intention to attack Russia.

During the spring of 1941 the war's centre of gravity was clearly in the Mediterranean, although Churchill was so concerned about the Battle of the Atlantic and the 'terrifying' losses in ships and cargoes – 'this mortal danger to our life-line gnawed my bowels' – that he saw little hope of victory or even of the country's survival through 1942 without millions more tons of shipping from the United States. It is as well, however, to look first at what happened in the Mediterranean theatre, before Hitler turned away from it for his great mission in the east, both by tracing broadly what happened and by following the actions of the two principals. Churchill had hopes of forming a Balkan front to include Greece, Yugoslavia and Turkey, all adding up, with the inclusion of the armed forces of those countries, to a force of some fifty divisions – a nut, as he called it, for the Germans to crack. Alas, the nut proved to be neither large nor solid. Intervention in Greece simply robbed Wavell of sufficient strength in the Western Desert for decisive results there, while proving inadequate to stem the Germans in Greece. Hitler, on the other hand, showed how quickly and decisively the Wehrmacht could act under his direction. In order to turn the British out of Greece, he required either the co-operation or the compliance of Romania, Hungary, Bulgaria and Yugoslavia. The first three did not hesitate to comply, Romania and Hungary joining the Axis alliance in November 1940, Bulgaria in March 1941. Yugoslavia, however, not only hesitated, but a successful military coup in Belgrade disassociated the new government there from the Axis. Such opposition was the very thing to arouse all Hitler's fury and ruthlessness. Yugoslavia would be 'smashed with merciless brutality' – and was. Orders given on 27 March led to the invasion of that country early in April, at the same time as the Germans attacked Greece, and within a fortnight Yugoslavia capitulated. A week after this Field Marshal List had completed the conquest of Greece, forcing yet one more evacuation by a British army. The Germans' subsequent invasion and capture of Crete completed Axis mastery of the northern shores of the Mediterranean, and led to a further British evacuation. But even worse things were happening on the desert flank, described by Churchill as 'the peg on which all else hung'.

In late March a new player on the Middle East stage, Lieutenant-General Erwin Rommel, who had arrived in Tripoli a month earlier with 15th Panzer Division and 5th Light Motorized Division, brought a fresh set of rules to desert fighting. With a combination of speed, daring, surprise and great tactical skill, together with a penchant, not shared by his British counterparts, for leading from the front, Rommel succeeded in bundling the British right out of Cyrenaica and back to Egypt, leaving only the garrison of the port of Tobruk, isolated and besieged, as the remaining prize of all O'Connor's conquests earlier that year. As Rommel himself put it:

> We've been attacking with dazzling success. There'll be consternation amongst our masters in Tripoli and Rome, perhaps in Berlin too. I took the risk against all orders and instructions because the opportunity seemed favourable. No doubt it will be pronounced good later and they'll all say they'd have done exactly the same in my place. We've already [3 April 1941] reached our first objective [Benghazi] which we weren't supposed to get to until the end of May . . . The British are falling over themselves to get away.

How Churchill would have relished having as one of his generals a soldier like Rommel, with all his dash, boldness, daring and charismatic leadership! Instead, he had to make do over the next year and more with the overworked Wavell, the conventional Auchinleck, the glamorous Alexander and, under the latter, the cautious Montgomery. But although Rommel was so brilliantly successful at winning battles in his encounters with the British until finally starved of supplies and air support in the summer and autumn of 1942, he was highly critical of Hitler's strategy, claiming later that had Germany kept her hands off Greece and concentrated on North Africa, she might have secured the entire Mediterranean and Middle East. It was Malta, not Crete, that should have been seized, for Malta was the key to lines of supply between Italy and North Africa. The prize would have been all the Middle Eastern oil and bases from which to threaten Russia. When we consider what Rommel did achieve with relatively puny forces, it may hardly be imagined what he might have done with even a tenth of the weight which Hitler was shortly to put into Barbarossa to crush the Soviet Union.

Churchill too was in no doubt about the absolutely crucial importance of Egypt and the Middle East, whose loss, he wrote in a War Cabinet directive dated 28 April, 'would be a disaster of the first magnitude to Great Britain, second only to successful invasion and final conquest!' He went on:

> Every effort is to be made to reinforce General Wavell with military and Air forces, and if Admiral Cunningham requires more ships, the Admiralty will make proposals for supplying them. It is to be impressed upon all ranks, especially the highest, that the life and honour of Great Britain depends upon the successful defence of Egypt.
>
> It is not to be expected that the British forces of the land, sea and air in the Mediterranean would wish to survive so vast and shameful a defeat as would be entailed by our expulsion from Egypt, having regard to the difficulties of the enemy and his comparatively small numbers. Not only must Egypt be defended, but the Germans have to be beaten and thrown out of Cyrenaica.

It was to be another eighteen months before this was to come about, and had Admiral Raeder been able to convince Hitler in May 1941 – when the former renewed his proposal for 'a decisive Egypt-Suez offensive for the autumn of 1941 which would be more deadly to the British Empire than the capture of London' – it might never have done so. If the Wehrmacht had been ordered to concentrate against the British position in the Middle East there and then, they would have found Wavell and his fellow Cs-in-C more stretched in their resources than at any other time. Although the East African campaign was soon to reach its successful conclusion in the total conquest of the Italian Empire there, it was not yet over; Greece and Crete had caused grievous losses; in Iraq the pro-German revolt led by Rashid Ali had to be dealt with; Syria had to be wrested from the Vichy French; and the 'Desert Fox' was at the gates of Egypt. What might not have been achieved, had Hitler only listened to Raeder.

Happily the Führer refused to see it, and his Directive No 30 made it plain that the whole question of mounting an offensive finally to break the British position in the Middle East could not be decided until after Barbarossa. The British Official History of the campaigns in the Mediterranean and Middle East observes that 'had the Eastern Mediterranean arena not been successfully held during the lean years, in which case, for want of bases, no British fleet or air forces could have even disputed the control of the Mediterranean sea communications, the task of the Allies in gaining a foothold in Europe would have been rendered immensely more difficult; indeed it might well have proved to be beyond their powers.' Fortunately, however, in June 1941 Germany turned away from the Mediterranean. Hitler had achieved his immediate aims. Italy was still fighting. The Balkans were secure. The British were more or less at bay. He could turn to his great mission of eradicating the Soviet Union. He had not consulted Mussolini, who heard about it only on the eve of the attack, wakened in the middle of the night by an urgent message from the Führer, which explained and justified his great decision. There was little in the message to reassure Mussolini. 'Whatever may now come, Duce, our situation cannot become worse as a result of this step; it can only improve.' The situation was to improve – *for Great Britain* – albeit only very slowly, and not before it had first become rather worse. Germany might turn away from the Mediterranean, but Italy could not. Nor could the British. Not only was it the only theatre where they could engage Axis forces on land, but as the CIGS, General Sir Alan Brooke, was to put it later that year: 'I am positive that our policy for the conduct of the war should be to direct both military and political efforts towards the early conquest of North Africa. From there we shall be able to reopen the Mediterranean and stage offensive operations against Italy.' In other words, the blueprint for British strategy was becoming clear, and it was a strategy which had Churchill's wholehearted support. He was never short of ideas, and having somewhat reluctantly accepted the view of the Chiefs of Staff that the capture of the Italian island of Pantelleria, in the Sicilian Channel midway between Tunisia and Sicily, could not at present be mounted without undue risk, invited them to study instead a plan for taking Sardinia. When speaking in the House of Commons towards the end of January, he spoke of the victories then being won by O'Connor in Cyrenaica, but warned against taking too optimistic a view of these events. At the same time he wished it to be known that 'this great nation is getting into its war stride. It is accomplishing the transition from the days of peace and comfort to those of supreme, organized, indomitable exertion.' His continuing worries about the Balkan situation prompted him to try to persuade Turkey to allow the stationing of British fighter and bomber squadrons on Turkish airfields, but it was clear from their response that the Turkish Government, conscious of their country's inadequate defences, were not prepared to take action which might provoke the

Germans into attacking them. On 9 February Churchill once again broadcast to the nation. He gave praise to the people for standing up under the Blitz, and to the armed forces – the RAF's great efforts, the desert army's triumphs in securing the Middle East base – and also to the United States of America for her sympathy and assistance. He reiterated his belief that Hitler would have to overcome Britain to win the war, and no matter what conquests he might make elsewhere – in Russia, the Balkans, around the Caspian Sea – this he could not do, for, 'masters of the sea and air, the British Empire ... will be on his track, bearing with them the sword of justice'. In sending an answer to President Roosevelt, in the name of the British people, he would ask for America's continued confidence in Britain: 'We shall not fail or falter; we shall not weaken or tire. Neither the sudden shock of battle, nor the long-drawn trials of vigilance and exertion will wear us down.' And Churchill, with his unerring talent for the pithy phrase likely to appeal to every sort of listener, summed up his message to the American people (in a broadcast that February) thus: 'Give us the tools, and we will finish the job.'

In Cyrenaica, however, the job was by no means finished, and would not be for a good while. Although the Italian Army there had been defeated, and although General Cunningham was also successfully clearing up the Italians in East Africa, the need to succour Greece – a policy endorsed by both the War Cabinet and by Churchill's envoys on the spot, Eden and Dill, who were supported by Wavell – took precedence over any idea of advancing to Tripoli. It was therefore agreed that Wavell's forces would not proceed westwards further than El Agheila, with the intention of holding Cyrenaica, while mustering what could be spared in the way of army and air force units for Greece. This was a time when Churchill was severely exercised by having too many strategic commitments – the Middle East, the Balkans, the air attacks on Britain, the appalling losses of shipping, the nagging worry of what Germany might do next – with resources wholly inadequate to meeting them properly. Yet his spirit remained undaunted, and as one of his visitors at this time, the Australian Prime Minister Robert Menzies, noted on 1 March, however much Churchill might paint a gloomy picture of the war situation, he would always 'fight his way out' again. Menzies recalled Churchill's reference to times like this not as being 'years lost out of our lives,' but rather as being those of the greatest interest. It seemed that no matter how great the extent to which he might use sheer eloquence to mask unpleasant fact, underlying it all was a firm conviction that 'you are going to win a war and that you're damned if anything will stand in your way'. There was no defeat in Churchill's heart, Menzies concluded; his course was set.

But although there was no defeat in Churchill's heart, there was plenty of it on the field of battle. Rommel's attack on 30 March overwhelmed the dispersed and ill-equipped British troops – their tanks were hopelessly inferior to the

Germans' – and by 11 April he had cleared Cyrenaica, except for Tobruk. There was also the point that fighting the Germans in the desert was a very different matter from fighting the Italians. The Africa Korps's tactical mastery and bold thrusts – they were particularly skilled at operating in all-arms teams of tanks, motorized infantry, self-propelled guns and anti-tank guns (including the dreaded 88mm) – were too much for the slower-moving and thinking British formations, while the decision to aid Greece had gravely weakened Wavell's ability to stem Rommel's advance. There might have been some consolation in this if the campaign in Greece had been successful. Far from being so, however, it was catastrophic. Having overrun Yugoslavia, the German Army reached Greece before the British had had time to deploy properly. They hardly engaged the Germans at all. Rather more than 60,000 British soldiers were landed in Greece, and between 24 April and 1 May some 50,000 were evacuated by the ever-ready and ever-gallant Royal Navy, although, as at Dunkirk, most of the heavier weapons and equipment were left behind. Among the units which suffered was Churchill's (and the author's) old regiment, the 4th Hussars, when, surrounded by panzers and airborne units, it lost over 400 men and most of the senior officers, all taken prisoner. The regiment re-formed in Egypt and fought on throughout the desert and Italian campaigns.[1]

It was hardly surprising that all these reverses of fortune led to further disparagement of Churchill's leadership, and in a House of Commons debate on 7 May he countered this criticism with his customary vigour, confidence and eloquence. He accepted total responsibility for policy decisions, while assuring the House that in making such decisions the opinions both of the Chiefs of Staff and of commanders in the field were properly respected. He had never underestimated the dangers facing the country, but reminded the House that the Germans had their problems too. When he looked back on all 'the perils which have been overcome' he felt sure that the tempest need not be feared: 'Let it roar, and let it rage. We shall come through.' Churchill was greatly cheered when the Government won a vote of confidence by 477 votes to 3, he himself earning 'an ovation such as he had never yet received'.

The early days of May 1941 were filled with dramatic incidents both at home and in the Middle East. On 10 May the Germans made one of the worst raids against London – the debating chamber of the House of Commons was destroyed,[2] together with many factories and docks, and fires raged for three nights. On the next evening came the extraordinary flight of Hitler's deputy,

---

[1] To the great joy and pride of all ranks, Churchill became Colonel of the Regiment shortly after the Greek disaster, visiting it four times during the next three years, and remaining Colonel until his death.

[2] From then on, the House of Commons met in Church House.

Rudolph Hess, from Germany to Scotland, undertaken without Hitler's approval and with the fantastic, and fruitless, idea of arranging peace with Great Britain provided Germany had a free hand in Eastern Europe. Hess achieved little more than arousing Hitler's fury and Churchill's incredulity. On 12 May the 'Tiger' convoy of ships carrying tanks and Hurricanes, which Churchill, despite the Admiralty's apprehensions, had insisted should sail through the Mediterranean – so urgent did he regard the reinforcement of Wavell in order to guarantee the Middle East's security – arrived at Alexandria. During the naval operations designed to ensure the safe passage of this vital convoy, Admiral Cunningham was able to resupply Malta with oil, food and aircraft, as well as mounting a raid on Benghazi where his warships sunk a number of Rommel's ammunition carriers. Yet in another encounter with the Germans – for Hitler had not been satisfied with capturing Greece, he wanted Crete, too, and on 20 May launched a great airborne operation to take the island – the Royal Navy suffered grievous losses. Between 20 and 31 May the battle for Crete demonstrated once more that no matter how resolute or skilful troops or seamen might be, and none could have been more so than the Australian, New Zealand and British soldiers commanded by Major-General Bernard Freyberg, VC, or the sailors in Admiral Glennie's and Admiral King's destroyers and cruisers, their operations simply could not prevail against an enemy who enjoyed absolute air superiority. The Germans used some 700 fighter, bomber and reconnaissance aircraft and 500 transports plus 72 gliders, and once General Kurt Student's XI Fliegerkorps had seized and held Maleme airfield, their build-up ensured superiority of numbers over Freyberg's forces. (This in itself was a controversial matter, for Ultra had given information about the likely German objectives, but to endanger this source of intelligence by anticipating – that is, by deploying defensively in the indicated landing areas – was, it seems, regarded as too risky.) Yet although casualties in Crete were considerable – the British lost about 14,000 men, mostly prisoners, out of 32,000 engaged, and 9 warships were sunk, with 17 damaged – they were not one-sided. Student's Fliegerkorps had ceased to exist as a fighting formation, having suffered 6,000 casualties. It had been a near-run thing, and as a result the Germans never tried airborne invasion again, which augured well for Malta, whose role in severing sea communications between Italy and Africa became more prominent than ever. Churchill, despite his having signalled to Wavell on 26 May that 'Victory in Crete is essential at this turning point in the war,' accepted – in view of the overwhelming enemy strength in the air – that the latter's insistence that the troops must be withdrawn should prevail, and Wavell was ordered to act accordingly. But no sooner was the Battle of Crete over than Churchill was urging the C-in-C to resume the offensive in Cyrenaica. There were compelling strategic reasons for doing so. German possession of Crete enabled the Axis to open sea communications with Cyrenaica via western Greece. Shipping using this route must therefore be harried and, where possible, destroyed. In order to do this, to help Malta and to go on attacking the Tripoli route, airfields in eastern Cyrenaica must be recaptured, which in turn meant that the enemy in the Western Desert must be brought to battle and destroyed. Despite his shortage of resources and commitments elsewhere – East Africa, Syria, Iraq – Wavell's preparations for this offensive against Rommel, codenamed Operation Battleaxe, went ahead, the initial assault being set to start on 15 June. This, however, was not the only matter to receive Churchill's attention at a Defence Committee meeting on 27 May for there were also the questions of raising an airborne division and of increasing tank production. The CIGS, Brooke, commented at this time how surprisingly light-hearted the Prime Minister remained through all these heavily burdened days – though the burden had been somewhat lightened by Churchill's announcement in the House of Commons that the German battleship, *Bismarck*, had been sunk that day – and remarked on what a wonderful man he was. 'Occasionally such human beings make their appearance on this earth,' Brooke wrote in his diary, 'human beings who stand out head and shoulders above all others.'[1]

Before Battleaxe was launched Churchill made several speeches: one in the House of Commons defending the need for and conduct of the Crete campaign; another to representatives of 'Allied Governments'; and a third which was broadcast to the United States. They all rang with splendid and defiant phrases. In Crete the Germans had encountered severe and fierce fighting hitherto unexperienced by them; Hitler might ravish Europe, advance in Africa and Asia, but 'it is here, in this island fortress, that he will have to reckon in the end ... We shall be on his track wherever he goes. Our air power will continue to teach the German homeland that war is not all loot and triumph'; and to the United States:

> For more than a year we British have stood alone, uplifted by your sympathy and respect and sustained by our own unconquerable will-power and by the increasing growth and hopes of your massive aid. In these British Islands that look so small upon the map we stand, the faithful guardians of the rights and dearest hopes of a dozen States and nations now gripped and tormented in a base and cruel servitude. Whatever happens we shall endure to the end.

To do so Britain would continue to rely on America's aid with merchant shipping and air transport of equipment via Brazil and West Africa to the Middle

---

[1] A sentiment which Hitler would have endorsed totally – indeed, did endorse – with regard to himself.

East base. In Hopkins, Wendell Willkie and Averell Harriman[1] Churchill had invaluable friendly contacts who would tirelessly press for more and more shipping and war material to assist Britain.

Battleaxe was duly launched on 15 June, and failed. The Afrika Korps was ready for an attack – indeed, Rommel had been expecting one, and disposed his armour in conjunction with anti-tank guns, fighting a highly successful defensive battle, so that even after two days, Wavell was obliged to withdraw with the loss of more than a hundred tanks. This failure was a severe blow to Churchill, who had placed such high hopes on what he called his 'Tiger Cubs'; when he heard about it, he retired to Chartwell and wandered disconsolately about the valley there. The reverse determined him to make a change in Commanders-in-Chief, something he had been contemplating for the last month. His ensuing cable to Wavell of 21 June began: 'I have come to the conclusion that public interest will best be served by appointment of General Auchinleck to relieve you in command of Armies of Middle East.' Wavell's reply was characteristic of his generous nature: 'I think you are wise to make change and get new ideas and action on the many problems in the Middle East and am sure Auchinleck will be successful choice.' So Wavell went to India as C-in-C there in Auchinleck's place, and 'the Auk' took over in Cairo at the end of June.

Meanwhile, Hitler was about to take the step which would prove to be an irretrievable blunder and which, together with what he was to do six months later, was to ensure that the outcome of the war would end the so-called 'New Order' and bring the Thousand-Year Reich crashing down after a mere dozen years. On the same day that Battleaxe started Churchill had signalled to Roosevelt the information that intelligence sources indicated a German attack on Russia was imminent, and that should it occur Britain would give what help it could spare to the Russians. No matter what anti-communist views Churchill may have held, his purpose was Hitler's destruction, and 'If Hitler invaded Hell he [Churchill] would at least make a favourable reference to the Devil!'

On 21 June, the day before Barbarossa began, an article by Arthur Bryant appeared in the *Illustrated London News*. This analysed the strategic disadvantages under which Germany laboured in spite of all her conquests, all her strength and all her freedom of choice. Hitler had to maintain the offensive; he could not sit back and wait to be attacked; he must himself attack and since he had already overrun so much of Europe – all of which must be either held down or sustained – wherever he now advanced would take him further and further from his homeland bases. To break out of Europe meant either wresting mastery of the seas from the British – and this particular battle was already

---

[1] Willkie, a lawyer and politician, was a semi-official envoy for Roosevelt; Harriman, a financier and, later, diplomat, was the administrator of lend-lease from 1941–3.

raging in the Atlantic – or thrusting through Russia into Asia and Africa. The article did not mention the Raeder option of assaulting the Middle East through Libya and Egypt. It seemed to Bryant that Russia was the 'easier' road, 'but such desperate steps cannot be taken without evoking human and racial imponderables which may well benefit us far more than the enemy. Hitler knows this, and his hour of decision is at hand. It is his fate to strike, and ours to resist and strike back.'

With the initiative still in Hitler's grasp – and this was the last time that it would be, for from now on he would be obliged to respond more and more to Allied moves – it was supremely important that he used it decisively. In other words, having chosen which campaign to conduct, it was essential next to select the crucial objective of that campaign and then concentrate on gaining it. No sideshows, however desirable in terms of political propaganda or personal prestige, must be permitted to distract from that purpose. Hitler's War Directive No 21 seemed to have taken in this fundamental requirement, for it was designed to prevent the possibility of any Russian army remaining in being: 'The Bulk of the Russian Army stationed in Western Russia will be destroyed by daring operations led by deeply penetrating spearheads. Russian forces still capable of giving battle will be prevented from withdrawing into the depths of Russia.' In spite of laying down a final objective – to erect a barrier against Asiatic Russia on the general line Caspian Sea-Archangel – the directive did not say exactly where and how the Russian armies were to be destroyed. It was not meant to: that was left for detailed military planning. But the directive did outline generally how operations were to be conducted. North of the Pripet Marshes two army groups would deliver the main weight of the attack to destroy all enemy forces in White Russia and the Baltic area; south of the marshes a third army group would account for all Russian forces west of the Dnieper in the Ukraine. When these battles were ended – and the northern one was to include capturing Leningrad and Kronstadt – then, and only then, would the pursuit be ordered, a pursuit whose aims were Moscow ('an important centre of communications and of the armaments industry') and the Donets basin. The directive invited commanders-in-chief to submit their detailed plans. When Hitler first saw these plans in February 1941, he reiterated the overriding need to 'wipe out large sections of the enemy and not put them to flight,' yet added the curiously incompatible footnote that the main aim was to 'gain possession of the Baltic States and Leningrad'. It is clear, therefore, that while still in the planning stages and four months before Barbarossa began, there is already some doubt about precise objectives. That absolutely indispensable factor, singleness of aim – a necessary end, and beginning, for proper concentration of forces – was absent. And because of this absence, the struggle became a gigantic encounter battle, which for the Germans, for all the vast distances covered, for all the unthinkable destruction or capture of Russian men and material, was marred by fatal compromises.

The assault upon the Soviet Union was to be the blitzkrieg to end all blitzkriegs, was to shackle accidents and bolt up change. With Russia struck down, Britain impotent and the United States unwilling actually to enter the war, the Thousand-Year Reich would be assured. Excluding Finnish and Romanian forces, 120 divisions, 17 of which were panzer and 12 motorized, were organized into three army groups, commanded by Leeb in the north, Bock in the centre (it was here that the main panzer groups were – one of them commanded by Guderian) and Rundstedt in the south, three great *Schwerpunkte* directed roughly at Leningrad, Smolensk and Kiev. At dawn on 22 June 1941 panzer and Stuka swept forward. 'What an appalling moment in time this is,' wrote Alan Clark in his study of the Russian-German conflict, 'the head-on crash of the two greatest armies, the two most absolute systems, in the world. No battle in history compares with it . . . In terms of numbers of men, weight of ammunition, length of front, the desperate *crescendo* of fighting, there will never be another day like the 22nd June 1941.'

Eleven days previously Hitler had issued one of the most remarkable of his many directives, No 32; remarkable not for its execution, but for its conception. It laid down how the war was to be conducted after Russia had been conquered. It showed that Hitler was planning to fulfil his former promise to Raeder that he would finish off Great Britain. The British position in the Middle East would be strangled by converging attacks from Libya through Egypt, from Bulgaria through Turkey, and from Transcaucasia through Iran. In addition, the Western Mediterranean would be closed by seizing Gibraltar. Planning was to begin 'so that I may issue final directives before the campaign in the east is over'.

As soon as Churchill heard that Germany had attacked Russia – it was about eight o'clock on the morning of 22 June when his Private Secretary broke the news to him at Chequers and was instructed to tell the BBC that the Prime Minister would broadcast to the nation that evening – he made up his mind that Britain would give Russia all the aid in its power. In coming to this decision Churchill did not consult the Cabinet, although he did talk to both Beaverbrook, the Minister of Supply, and Sir Stafford Cripps, the Ambassador to Moscow. The truth was that he had determined what he would do in advance of the event. His broadcast of 22 June contained some stirring stuff. After conceding that he had consistently opposed Communism in the past and that he had no wish to contradict his former views, he stated that a totally new situation had now arisen. Then, in declaring HMG's decision and policy, he reiterated the country's aim of destroying Hitler and the Nazi regime, that nothing would turn the nation from this resolve, that the British would never negotiate with the Nazis, but would fight on land, on sea and in the air 'until, with God's help, we have rid the earth of his [Hitler's] shadow and liberated its people from his yoke. Any man or state who fights on against Nazidom will have our aid. Any man or state who marches with Hitler is our foe. That is our policy and our declaration. It follows therefore that we shall give whatever help we can to Russia and the Russian people.' He went on to warn that the German attack on Russia was but a prelude to further attempts against Britain. Thus Russia, Britain – and indeed the United States – all shared a common danger, and therefore must be united both in their exertions and in their counter-strokes. Harold Nicolson noted after hearing the broadcast that in spite of admitting the possibility of Russia's early defeat, with all that might mean for the rest of the world, Churchill had produced another masterpiece, which 'somehow leaves us with the impression that we are quite certain to win this war'. (Those of us who took part in the war and look back now on what we thought in 1941 and in the subsequent war years, can confirm that this was our impression, too. Such was the magic of Churchill's leadership; such also was our own confidence in him, and that of our military comrades, our allies, actual or potential, and the British people as a whole.)

As Barbarossa proceeded it soon became clear that Hitler's prediction about the whole rotten structure of the Soviet Union coming crashing down when the door was kicked in was wholly misguided. In spite of huge advances and sensational victories, this was to be no blitzkrieg on the lines of those that had gone before. The Red Army, which proved to be also a mirror of the Russian people, did not crack up after the first setbacks, though there was no shortage of these. It fought back wherever and whenever it could. Bock, in the centre, executed a gigantic pincer movement which converged on Minsk, and on 10 July the Germans claimed over 300,000 prisoners. A week later the battle for Smolensk was joined and lasted three weeks; a further 300,000 Russian prisoners were taken, but Bock's armies had suffered such losses that they had to refit and regroup. There was no further advance from Smolensk before 2 October. In the north, Leeb pushed through Estonia, reaching Nava and Pskov by 20 August, but he was repulsed at Leningrad in mid-September, and had to be content with investing the city. In the south, during the first two weeks of September the great encirclement of Kiev took place. Two army groups were involved – from Bock's command north of Kiev were Weich's army and Guderian's panzer group, and from Rundstedt's to the south were Field Marshal Walter von Reichenau's army and Kleist's panzer group. The pincers closed at Lokvitsa on 14 September, when Guderian and Kleist joined hands 120 miles east of Kiev. The bag was nearly 700,000 prisoners. Hitler called it 'the greatest battle in the history of the world'. Halder, the Army Chief of Staff, condemned it as the principal strategic blunder of the campaign.

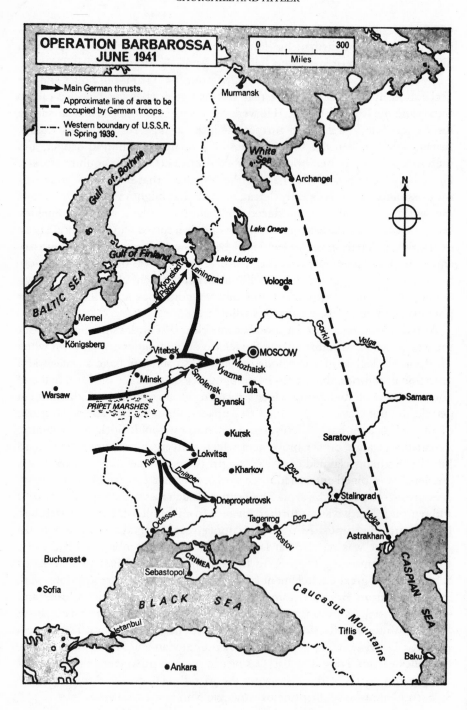

**OPERATION BARBAROSSA
JUNE 1941**

0   300
Miles

Main German thrusts.

Approximate line of area to be
occupied by German troops.

Western boundary of U.S.S.R.
in Spring 1939.

Murmansk

White
Sea

Archangel

Gulf of Bothnia

Lake Onega

Gulf of Finland

Lake Ladoga

Kronstadt

Pskov

Leningrad

Vologda

BALTIC SEA

Memel

Königsberg

Vitebsk

MOSCOW

Gorki

Volga

Mozhaisk

Vyazma

Smolensk

Tula

Minsk

Bryanski

Warsaw

PRIPET MARSHES

Samara

Kursk

Saratov

Lokvitsa

Kiev

Kharkov

Dnieper

Don

Stalingrad

Dnepropetrovsk

Odessa

Tagenrog

Don

Volga

Rostov

Astrakhan

Bucharest

CRIMEA

Sebastopol

CASPIAN SEA

Sofia

BLACK   SEA

Caucasus Mountains

Istanbul

Tiflis

Baku

Ankara

There followed further advances and further spectacular successes – Manstein got as far as Sebastopol; Kleist reached Rostov; Rundstedt's army group occupied the general line Tagenrog-Kharkov-Kursk; Bock set off from Smolensk on 2 October, trapped another 600,000 Russians between Vyazma and Bryanski, and actually got to Klin, only 35 miles west of Moscow, by 5 December. But despite all this – despite a total of some 2 million Russian soldiers killed or captured, and despite the sensational announcement by Dr Otto Dietrich, the Nazis' principal press officer, on 8 October that Soviet Russia as a military power was done for, and that the war in the east was over – none of the basic aims which Hitler had laid down was achieved. Moscow had not been captured, nor Leningrad, nor the Caucasian oilfields, nor the Archangel railway; above all, the Russian armies as a whole had not been destroyed or prevented from withdrawing. The very diversity of these aims was the cause of the failure to achieve them, diversity well-nigh inevitable because of the sheer width of front. Yet as early as 3 February 1941, when plans were first being discussed, Hitler had answered the General Staff's objection that a successful advance to a general line from the Black Sea to the Gulf of Finland would double the frontage by claiming that, since the entire Russian armies would by that time have ceased to exist, it did not matter how wide the front or how great the distance beyond, for there would be nothing to stop the German forces.

In actual fact, the Russians' performance was in stark contrast to Hitler's prophecies. Not only was the individual Soviet soldier as fanatically tough and brave as the most ardent Nazi; not only were the partisans already fighting in the areas from which the Red Army itself had withdrawn; not only was the organization from which the partisans came, the Osoaviakhim, 36 million strong and spread over the whole nation; not only was the raising of new armies done at prodigious speed, and their equipment as efficient as it was seemingly inexhaustible, but the proof of Russian resilience was such that, on 6 December Marshal Georgi Zhukov counter-attacked in the central sector of the front with *17 armies*[1] – and winter had set in! At this the Wehrmacht wavered, and something like despair swept over the ordinary German soldier.

Hitler, however, did not despair. But what had been his part in all this? In the first place, his interference in the conduct of the campaign, whether from his East Prussia headquarters, the Wolfsschanze ('wolf's lair'), near Rastenburg, or when visiting commanders at their headquarters, was more radical and more continuous than in any that had gone before. Moreover, it was soon to become absolute. During the first weeks of spectacular success there was no cause for major disagreement between Hitler and his generals. But when it came to deciding what to do after the great Smolensk battle, the scene changed. Leaving

---

[1] About a hundred divisions.

aside for a moment the ever-present requirement of destroying Russia's armies, Hitler's original directive had laid down that in the north Moscow would be occupied only after the capture of Leningrad, while in the south the Ukraine, with its large industrial and agricultural resources, would be seized. The question in August, faced with these three possible objectives, was which of them, singly or together, to go for.

The professional soldiers, Brauchitsch, Halder, Bock, Guderian among them, were convinced that by concentrating their effort and pushing on to Moscow, they would not only be aiming at a great communications, armaments and political centre, but would also stand the best chance of achieving the primary object – destruction of the main Russian armies, including the newly formed ones, which would dispute their passage. Hitler disagreed. He had his eye on different political and economic objectives – Leningrad and the Ukraine. 'Only completely ossified brains, absorbed in the ideas of past centuries,' he angrily declared, 'could see any worthwhile objective in taking the capital.' Brauchitsch's objection that the main Russian armies contesting the road to Moscow could not be destroyed by any other means than engaging them – a reasonable argument – was brushed impatiently aside. The fact was that, by mid-July, Hitler was so confident as a result of the Wehrmacht's initial successes, that Russia's defeat was assured that he supplemented Directive No 32 with another, which actually proposed to reduce the army, limit naval activity to what was necessary for prosecuting the war against England (and possibly America), and greatly strengthen the Luftwaffe. Yet the first of a series of crises was about to break over the Führer's head, crises which only an infinitely more powerful army could have resolved.

The controversy as to which objectives were to be pursued was, of course, decided by Hitler. The Ukraine and Leningrad gave way to the former alone. The Ukraine was to receive the main attention, and the results were dazzling. Halder's comment that this was the greatest strategic error of the campaign demands explanation, not least since possession of the Ukraine and 665,000 prisoners cannot be dismissed as insignificant. But it is when this stroke is looked at in conjunction with Hitler's second refusal to concentrate on one objective that we see how fatal his repudiation of strategy's master rules could be. On 2 October Bock's Army Group Centre resumed the advance. Within a week another huge pincer movement between Vyazma and Bryansk had accounted for a further 600,000 Russian soldiers, and by 15 October the panzer spearheads were at Mozhaisk, a mere 65 miles from Moscow. It was then that the supreme tactical error was made. At this point, in spite of the time the Russians had been given, in spite of deteriorating weather, victory, if by victory we mean what the German General Staff meant – destruction of the Russian armies disputing the road to Moscow and capture of the capital itself – was probably still in Hitler's grasp.

But failing once more to observe those prime principles of war – singleness of aim, concentration of forces – failing to select the decisive objective and go for it with all the terrifying weight of fire power that was available, Hitler chose to go for three, absurd in their dispersion and sheer unattainability.

Leeb was to capture Leningrad and, having linked up with the Finnish Army under Field Marshal Carl Gustaf Mannerheim,[1] push on to the Murmansk railway; Bock was to press forward to Moscow; Rundstedt (who records that he laughed aloud when he received the orders, so unrealistic were they) was to clear the Black Sea coast and advance beyond Rostov to the Caucasus. None of these objectives was achieved, yet it may be imagined that had Leeb's and Rundstedt's forces been relegated to holding operations on their fronts, and the entire weight of the panzer groups, air effort and logistic support been welded into one colossal *Schwerpunkt* under Bock for the drive on Moscow, the city would have fallen. Even with the crazy dispersion Hitler insisted on, the city's suburbs were reached. Had the effort been trebled, Moscow might well have been taken, and even though this might not have produced absolute decision, it would have been such a blow – moral, economic, political and strategic – that the future shape of Soviet resistance must have been altered. As it was, Hitler told his people that 'the enemy in the east has been struck down and will never rise again'.

It was perhaps just as well for Hitler that he thought so, for his enemy in the west was showing further signs of revival. Churchill was longing to mount some British military action to aid the Russians, and his proposals to the Chiefs of Staff, apart from increased bombing of German positions in Occupied France, envisaged an actual raid by up to 30,000 commandos and others, an idea which had also been put forward by Ivan Maisky, the Soviet Ambassador in London. At the same time Churchill was concerned that the possibility of a German defeat of Russia would release formidable forces to attack the British either at home or in the Middle East, and in order to counter such threats he urged Roosevelt to assist in the provision of more tanks, adding that the quality of these tanks should be superior to that of the German armour – something which the Allies never achieved throughout the course of the entire war. He did succeed, however, in persuading the President to garrison Iceland, thus releasing British troops and shipping.

Above all, the Prime Minister was greatly frustrated by Britain's inability to help her new ally, the Soviet Union, at this time. Not only was the equipment which the Russians had asked for (aircraft, bombs, anti-aircraft guns) not avail-

---

[1] In June 1941, when the Germans invaded the Soviet Union, Mannerheim allied Finland with Germany and led the Finnish Army against the Russians. He negotiated an armistice with Russia when faced with defeat in September 1944, and in March 1945, by which time he was President, took Finland into the war against Germany.

able, but any idea of a substantial commando raid on northern France was soon shown to be impracticable. As the news from the Russian front revealed continued German successes and advances, Churchill took steps to tighten up anti-invasion measures, and again urged Roosevelt both to increase the ship-building programme and to provide a greater number of American escorts for the convoys, for, as he pointed out, the rate of sinkings had to be reduced. There was, however, a welcome change of policy by the United States in respect of her naval operations to protect shipping delivering material to 'nations whose security is essential to the defense of the United States'. This meant that Axis naval or air forces which threatened such shipping in the western hemisphere would be attacked, although the American authorities regarded such action 'as a measure short of war' which would not necessarily lead to war with the Axis powers. In July Churchill received the good news that a further large number of light and medium tanks – 1,600 to 2,000 – would be supplied by the United States, and that British tank crews could be trained over there. Also in that month the Anglo-Soviet Agreement, which pledged both mutual aid and that neither ally would make peace separately with Germany, was signed in Moscow, and in an attempt to draw some Luftwaffe strength away from the Russian front Churchill requested the Chief of the Air Staff, Portal, to have Bomber Command devastate German cities; as a result, Hanover, Hamburg, Frankfurt, Mannheim, Wilhelmshaven and Berlin were all heavily attacked.

Churchill's mind was never far away from what was happening in the Middle East, and his frustration at not being able to give significant aid to Russia was aggravated by the attitude of the new C-in-C there, Auchinleck, who refused to contemplate a renewed offensive in the Western Desert before he was ready – which meant November. Churchill had been hoping for a much earlier date; indeed, he was concerned that even mid-September, by which time further tank reinforcements would have reached Auchinleck, was too late, in view of the dangers of Russia's front collapsing. Britain's impotence to aid Russia was further illustrated by Churchill's reply to Stalin's plea for two 'second fronts' – in northern France and the Arctic. He explained that any major landing in France would simply invite 'a bloody repulse', and reminded Stalin that Britain had been 'fighting alone for more than a year' and that although growing in strength, 'we are at the utmost strain both at home and in the Middle East by land and air, and also that the Battle of the Atlantic, on which our life depends, and the movement of all our convoys in the teeth of the U-boat and Focke-Wulf[1] blockade, strains our naval resources, great though they be, to the utmost

---

[1] The Focke-Wulf FW200 Kondor was Germany's only four-engined bomber. Possessed of a good range, it was deployed to 'shadow' Allied convoys and report their positions and headings, so that U-boats or surface vessels could be sent to attack them; it was also used to bomb convoys.

limit'. But he did promise the Soviet leader help in the Arctic with both naval and air forces.

In August 1941 Churchill had the first of his many wartime meetings with President Roosevelt held at Placentia Bay in Newfoundland. Before sailing on the battleship *Prince of Wales* to attend the meeting, he discussed the Middle East situation with General Auchinleck. Churchill tried his best to convince the latter that an early offensive should be mounted, but did not succeed. Auchinleck had already signalled from Cairo on 23 July that provided he had 150 more cruiser tanks and retained air superiority, and that there were no substantial enemy reinforcements or an Axis move against Syria (Vichy forces there had surrendered on 12 July), a limited offensive to relieve Tobruk should be possible in November; however, given an additional 150 American tanks, plus trained crews and extra transport, both lorried and air, he could mount an operation to recapture Cyrenaica in mid-November. Before Churchill and Auchinleck talked privately together on 2 August at Chequers, Ismay, the Military Secretary to the Cabinet, had thought it wise to explain to the C-in-C Middle East what sort of man Churchill was, and what he had to say is remarkably revealing in its insight into the Prime Minister's character, commitment and methods. Ismay really knew his man, and some of his comments are central to an understanding of Churchill's conduct of military affairs:

> Churchill could not be judged by ordinary standards; he was different from anyone we had ever met before, or were ever likely to meet again. As a war leader, he was head and shoulders above anyone that the British or any other nation could produce. He was indispensable and completely irreplaceable.
>
> The idea that he was rude, arrogant, and self-seeking was entirely wrong. He was none of these things. He was certainly frank in speech and writing, but he expected others to be equally frank with him . . .
>
> He was a child of nature. He venerated tradition, but ridiculed convention. When the occasion demanded, he could be the personification of dignity; when the spirit moved him, he could be a *gamin*. His courage, enthusiasm and industry were boundless, and his loyalty was absolute. No commander who engaged the enemy need ever fear that he would not be supported. His knowledge of military history was encyclopaedic, and his grasp of the broad sweep of strategy unrivalled . . .

But, Auchinleck was told, Churchill did not fully understand how mechanization had so complicated logistics and why so large a 'tail'[1] was now required.

---

[1] The rear-echelon units, providing transport, resupply, workshops, medical facilities, and so on, as distinct from the 'teeth', the fighting soldiers.

While respecting an experienced military view, the Prime Minister did not sub-
scribe to the idea that generals were always right. He was dedicated to battle,
longed for the offensive, and although he might send a stream of telegrams to
his commanders in the field, Auchinleck must understand, Ismay said, that they
sprang from Churchill's wish to know how to allot resources between theatres
and according to the overall strategy which was demanded, and he must not be
irritated by all these messages. Churchill as Prime Minister and Minister of
Defence had 'the primary responsibility' for conducting affairs 'in the best
interests of the war effort as a whole'.

But even Churchill could not move Auchinleck from his decision that there
could be no great offensive before November, and although the Prime Minister
was 'appalled by the proposal to remain passive all this time, when the golden
opportunity may be lost' while Germany was so heavily committed to the
Russian campaign, he had on this occasion to accept the former's opinion.

As might have been expected, Churchill revelled in his voyage aboard *Prince
of Wales* from Scotland to Placentia Bay – composing memoranda for the
Chiefs of Staff, dictating to shorthand writers, reading *Captain Hornblower RN*
by C.S. Forester (just the sort of book to suit his mood), signalling to Attlee
that the Free French were not to be allowed 'to mess up our Syrian position and
spoil our relations with Arabs', watching the film *Lady Hamilton* (a great
favourite of his, and one which he had already seen many times) – until at last
on 9 August he crossed by barge to the American battleship USS *Augusta*,
where President Roosevelt awaited him. Next day Roosevelt and his staff came
aboard *Prince of Wales* for Divine Service, for which Churchill chose the hymns;
it was a moving occasion. As for the conference itself (which had been given
the codename 'Argentia'), much was achieved in the way of strengthening
friendly relations between Churchill and Roosevelt, and of establishing them
between the Chiefs of Staff of both countries. The Americans were unconvinced that bombing alone would defeat Germany – a campaign on land would
be essential; nor did they at first regard the Middle East as anything but a liabil-
ity, although the British believed that they were able to persuade their counterparts that their strategy there was sound. If Churchill had been expecting some
agreement about future strategy, however, he was disappointed, for Roosevelt
was unwilling to discuss the war's future course, except with regard to helping
Russia. Nevertheless, Argentia's contribution here was important, for it
resulted in the setting up of the Anglo-American Mission to Russia, with
Beaverbrook and Harriman playing leading roles (the industrialist Arthur
Purvis, who had already done so much to organize British supply purchases in
America, and who was to have encouraged similar help for Russia, had been
killed in an air crash just after taking off from Scotland for Newfoundland, a
loss Churchill described as 'most grievous'). The so-called Atlantic Charter

which emerged from the Argentia Conference – a joint declaration by Roosevelt and Churchill – dealt essentially with principles, although, as the latter pointed out in *The Second World War*, its reference to 'the final destruction of the Nazi tyranny' was remarkable given that the United States was at this time still a neutral power. In a joint telegram to Stalin the two leaders stressed the importance of Russian resistance in the struggle to defeat Hitlerism, and pledged their commitment to providing aid.

On his return from this meeting, Churchill was able to give the War Cabinet some encouraging impressions of the US President's attitude to the war. He believed that Roosevelt was 'determined that they should come in'; indeed, the President had told him that 'he would wage war, but not declare it'. In practical terms this meant that American destroyers would escort British convoys and that these escorts would be authorized to attack U-boats even if they were several hundred miles from the convoy. Indeed, US Chief of Naval Operations, Admiral Harold Stark, went so far as to tell Churchill that he would approve the action of any of his escort commanders who sank a U-boat, and would even attempt to provoke an incident. This was clearly a great advance in waging that absolutely vital struggle, the Battle of the Atlantic. While he was still on his way back from the meeting with Roosevelt, the Prime Minister addressed the crew of one of the loaned American destroyers, renamed *Churchill*, responsible for escorting Atlantic convoys. He told the sailors 'that the war would last another three years at least and that hard times lay ahead. He told us that we were carrying out one of the most vital jobs of war ensuring that the food and supplies without which Britain could not survive reached us from North America. He would not deny that this was one of the bleakest times in Britain's history, but he was confident that we would survive, and with right on our side and help from allies . . . we should win through to a great and glorious victory.'

That Churchill had not exaggerated in his reference to bleak times was clear enough as he reviewed the war situation after his return. Bomber losses over Germany were heavy; Britain could do little to aid Russia, which might well collapse; the Germans were reinforcing Cyrenaica, and still there was no prospect of Auchinleck attacking Rommel's army before November; there was a further commitment in Persia, into which British and Soviet forces moved late in August in order to prevent any pro-German movement there. The two principal considerations which nagged him most, however, were when America would enter the war, and how to help Russia. At the end of August, when the American Ambassador, J.G. Winant, is dining with him at Chequers, Churchill refers to the Atlantic Charter and tells Winant that 'America could not honourably stay out'. It would, he said, be far better for the United States to enter the war now 'and give us no supplies for six months than stay out and double her supplies. If she came in, the conviction of an allied victory would be founded in a dozen countries.' Without American belligerency, although Britain would not be defeated, the war could go on for four or five years, 'and civilization and culture would be wiped out. If America came in, she could stop this. She alone could bring the war to an end.' Winant was unable to give Churchill the assurances he sought.

Nor was there much satisfaction for the Prime Minister during his meeting with the Soviet Ambassador, Maisky, who on 4 September delivered to Churchill a letter from Stalin, which demanded that a second front be established *that year* in France or the Balkans to draw German divisions from the Eastern Front. Stalin also required supplies – hundreds of aircraft and tanks every month. Without a second front, Maisky went on, Russia might fall, and then how could Britain hope to defeat Germany? In his reply, Churchill made it clear to the Ambassador – and later to Stalin himself – that there was little Britain could do in the next few months other than increase the flow of supplies. There was no possibility of a landing in France, nor could there be a Balkan front without Turkey's participation on the Allied side. But in surveying the strategic potential for 1942, he suggested that once the British forces in the Middle East had been strengthened enough to turn the Axis forces out of North Africa, these forces could be applied to Russia's southern flank. In making this prediction as early as September 1941, Churchill was outlining exactly what was to happen in 1942, 1943 and the first half of 1944. Adding to this prescience, in his message to Stalin he had added that he had formed the impression that 'the culminating violence of the German invasion is over and that winter will give your heroic armies a breathing space'. A few days later there was snow on the Russian front.

It would not be long before the Russian winter played its hand in the game. Guderian, the boldest and most resolute of panzer leaders, was deeply depressed during the drive on Moscow in November. The cold affected both men and machines. Tank tracks required special fittings, which were not available; gunsights became useless; fuels froze; machine-guns would not fire. The Russian T-34 tanks, of which there seemed to be limitless numbers, were invulnerable to many of the German tank and anti-tank guns. 'The icy cold,' Guderian wrote, 'the lack of shelter, the shortage of clothing, the heavy losses of men and equipment, the wretched state of our fuel supplies – all this makes the duties of a commander a misery, and the longer it goes on the more I am crushed by the enormous responsibility I have to bear.' Only those who served in the campaign, he said, could judge the feelings of those who 'saw the endless expanse of Russian snow during the winter of our misery and felt the icy wind that blew across it, burying in snow every object in its path; who drive for hour after hour through the no man's land only at last to find too thin shelter with insufficiently clothed, half-starved men; and who also saw by contrast the well-fed, warmly clad and fresh Siberians, fully equipped for winter fighting.' All this was bound to have its effect. When Kluge's Fourth Army, although it had reached the outskirts of Moscow, was forced to withdraw without reaching its objective in the first week of December, even the fanatically brave and highly skilled German soldiers faltered, and something like paralysis – the sort of helplessness that, in the past, blitzkrieg had induced in the Wehrmacht's enemies – gripped the High Command. Hitler had talked of finishing the job in five months. More than five months had passed, but the job was nowhere near finished.

The great offensive had not just bogged down; it looked perilously like turning into another retreat from Moscow, another panic, another rout. Hitler, however, did not despair; instead, he showed once more that willpower is all. 'He rose,' wrote Alan Bullock, 'to the occasion. By a remarkable display of determination he succeeded in holding the German lines firm. Whatever his responsibility for the desperate situation in which the German Army now found itself, and whatever the ultimate consequences of his intervention, in its immediate effects it was his greatest achievement as a war leader.' The Führer's order was uncompromising: there was to be no withdrawal. Nothing could have been simpler than that. And so in keeping with Hitler's character was the enforcement of this order that there was nothing he would not sacrifice to see that it was obeyed. Thousands of German soldiers, scores of German generals whose loyalty or obedience was deemed to be in question – these could be dispensed with, but not an inch of ground was to be given up.

Hitler also resorted to the age-old rule of sacking those in the High Command who clearly thought his handling of the campaign was faulty. Rundstedt was replaced by Reichenau, Bock by Kluge, Guderian and Höppner were dismissed, and many other senior commanders who had either acted without the Führer's agreement, or had argued with him, were sent packing in disgrace. Even the compliant Keitel received such a scolding when he recommended a general withdrawal that he tried to resign, but was persuaded to stay. The Army C-in-C, however, Brauchitsch, twice offered his resignation, and on the second occasion, 17 December, Hitler accepted it, and took over command of the army himself! Now he had supreme control of all military operations. As Army C-in-C with the OKH staff he ran the war in Russia, and as Armed Forces C-in-C with the OKW staff, he directed operations on all other fronts. What this meant in practice was that the Führer, and only the Führer, had in his grasp the overall strategic direction of the war. Yet by assuming command of the army, while still having responsibility for strategic decisions, Hitler involved himself in the day-to-day business of operations; in a conversation with Halder, still the Army Chief of Staff, he referred to operational command as 'this little affair . . . that anybody can do,' adding that the C-in-C's task was 'to educate the Army in the idea of National Socialism,' and who else could do it in the way that he wanted it done? This assumption of army command was perhaps one of the greatest mistakes Hitler made in relation to the war's direction, for whereas his gifts did in some ways fit him for the role of Supreme Commander concerned primarily with major strategic decisions – where startling successes often resulted from his unorthodoxy, his grip of psychological warfare, his boldness in exploiting the value of surprise, and in striking cripplingly swift and audacious strokes – all this intuition was not applicable to the hard-and-fast execution of military plans. He was also astonishingly knowledgeable about weapons and technology, but what he lacked was experience of command in the field, of the actual handling and supply of armies, the drills and battle deployment which do so much to win actions at the lower level. This detailed knowledge of weapon performance, and the preoccupation with technicalities, were out of place, and took his mind off the broader operational issues appropriate to one in so exalted a position.

Opinions differed as to the merits or otherwise of Hitler's taking over and exercising command of the army. Halder condemned it absolutely, pointing out that what army group and army commanders needed were broad, long-term directives which would enable them to act with some independence within the framework of a general unified plan. Moreover, since the very essence of tactics was *movement* combined with fire power, Hitler's refusal to contemplate planned withdrawal to stronger defensive positions was absurd. Simply to order the army to stand and fight where it was with no regard for tactically sensible positions was simply to invite heavy losses in men and material which could have been avoided – this was, in Halder's view, the sum of Hitler's leadership. Other generals disagreed. General Günther Blumentritt, Kluge's Chief of Staff in the battle, regarded Hitler's order to stand fast as correct, given that there were no proper positions to withdraw to, and that to have done so haphazardly would have led to the sort of dissolution of the army which Napoleon had suffered. Alan Clark's judgement is similar; indeed, he calls this Hitler's finest hour: 'He had done more than save the German Army; he had achieved a complete personal ascendancy over its ruling class.'

Yet this very ascendancy was greatly to contribute to his undoing. He had always been impatient of the General Staff's professionalism, its conservatism, its readiness to point out difficulties and disregard his own genius. He underrated the need to turn grand campaign plans into practical staff propositions. His own ability to reduce all problems to simple terms, his own iron willpower were no substitute for careful analyses of opposing military strengths, of enemy capability and intentions, of logistic matters, of the effect which time and space invariably had on the deployment of armies, of settling which objectives were both attainable and necessary so that a combined effort could be concentrated to attain them. Rarely was Hitler capable of seeing any point of view but his own, and so confident was he of his own infallibility that his success in holding firm the German Army's line in the winter of 1941–1942 led him to believe that the Wehrmacht's failure to achieve all its objectives had been the General Staff's fault, not his. It also encouraged him to believe that a new offensive in Russia in 1942 under his own direction would be the knock-out blow that would end the war in the east.

Churchill too was already thinking about 1942, and in particular the Middle East campaign, and his urging of Auchinleck to mount an offensive as soon as possible went on. He was to suffer a further disappointment, however, when the latter telegraphed seeking agreement to a postponement of his offensive, 'Crusader', from 1 November until 18 November. In his reply, Churchill's exasperation was clear enough:

> It is impossible to explain to Parliament and the nation how it is our Middle East armies had to stand for 4½ months without engaging the enemy while all the time Russia is being battered to pieces. I have hitherto managed to prevent public discussion, but at any time it may break out. Moreover, the few precious weeks that remain to us for the exploitation of any success are passing. No warning has been given to me of your further delay, and no reasons . . .

But Auchinleck would not be hurried, and on 21 October Churchill accepted the new date, albeit with great reluctance. When the battle did start, Auchinleck had much in his favour. Tobruk was tying down four Italian divisions and three German battalions. The savaging of Axis convoys by attacks from Malta and elsewhere was having serious consequences for Rommel: 35 per cent of his supplies and reinforcements dispatched to North Africa were lost in August; 63 per cent in October. Moreover, the newly named British Eighth Army consisted of two powerful corps – XXX, which was strong in armour, and XIII, in which were such famous formations as the 4th Indian Division and the New Zealand Division. Fresh from his triumphs in East Africa, General Cunningham was in command of Eighth Army. He planned a battle which would oblige Rommel to do what he, Cunningham, wanted him to do. It turned out otherwise.

There were four main phases of the battle. First, on 18 November three British armoured brigades advanced with the idea of concentrating at Sidi Rezegh and drawing Rommel's panzers to their destruction. Instead, they got the worst of the encounter. Next Rommel put himself at the head of the Afrika Korps and made a dash to the Egyptian frontier, which so dismayed

Cunningham that, in the light of events and given his tank losses, he recommended breaking off the battle. Auchinleck quite properly insisted on continuing with the offensive in order to force Rommel back to his supply bases. This worked, but because he believed Cunningham was now 'thinking defensively', Auchinleck relieved him and appointed the little-known Major-General Neil Ritchie[1] in his place. The third phase saw more heavy fighting at Sidi Rezegh, and then finally Rommel cut his losses and withdrew to El Agheila. Eighth Army was thus left in possession of the battlefield, but it was clear that its commanders had got two vital things wrong. Firstly, they seemed incapable of controlling large forces in fast-moving operations; secondly – and this was the cause of the first – command arrangements were themselves faulty, not only in the mechanics of such arrangements, but in the personalities involved. Auchinleck had sacked one Commander Eighth Army in the middle of the battle and appointed another; before long he was to do so again in circumstances far more dangerous and difficult. Yet he could draw some comfort from the results of Crusader – he had relieved Tobruk, inflicted a sort of reverse on Rommel, and reoccupied Cyrenaica.

Throughout the Crusader battles, of course, the Prime Minister had not been neglectful in offering his comments and advice. Churchill had all along been hoping that a British victory over Rommel would lead to a change in attitude in the Vichy authorities in French North Africa. Two days after Crusader started he had signalled to Roosevelt to seek his aid in influencing the Vichy Government to keep Weygand in his North Africa command, and not have him 'replaced by some pro-Hun officer just at the moment when we are likely to be in a position to influence events in North Africa'. Churchill followed the ups and downs of Auchinleck's operation, his mood varying, but becoming one of great confidence when he hears of Rommel's fuel shortages and Auchinleck's 25 November Order of the Day: 'Attack and pursue. All out everywhere.' Indeed, so great is his confidence by then that he invites the Chiefs of Staff to study exploitation options for advancing to Tunisia or taking the war into Sicily, and asks Roosevelt to consider sending 150,000 troops to Morocco to bolster the French. At the same time, however, he was thinking of what might have to be done if Crusader failed and the Germans gained control of French North Africa.

While never overruling Auchinleck when Ritchie replaced Cunningham, Churchill strongly advised the C-in-C to take a personal grip of the battle. In offering this advice, he anticipated exactly what had to be done some six months later, when Rommel once again gave the British a lesson in what bold, aggressive and fast-moving tactics could achieve. For the time being, however,

[1] At the time, Ritchie was Deputy Chief of Staff at GHQ in Cairo.

Auchinleck was able to report favourably, and on 30 November, Churchill's birthday (he was sixty-seven), sent a message to the Prime Minister hoping that the difficulties being experienced by 21st Panzer and the Italian Ariete Divisions would 'develop into a real Birthday present for you'. Other messages included one from Beaverbrook, who wrote that 'to be known as Churchill's man' would be glory enough for anyone who had served with him; another old friend, Leo Amery, described Churchill as 'the spirit of old England incarnate, with its unshakeable self-confidence, its unfailing sense of humour, its underlying moral earnestness, its unflinching tenacity'. All these great qualities would be required in the coming year, for Britain was to face greater dangers – in North Africa, in the Mediterranean, in the Atlantic and in the Far East – than she had ever faced before, and Churchill himself, struggling to cope with repeated military setbacks, was to find himself facing political trouble at home. On the other side of the balance sheet, however, late in 1941 Britain would acquire the ally that Churchill had for so long been seeking, waiting for, and encouraging – the United States of America.

On 7 December 1941 Japan attacked both the United States at Pearl Harbor and Great Britain in Malaya, Hong Kong and Singapore. What an unlooked-for bonus this might have been for Hitler! What an opportunity to wring the maximum benefit from a situation in which either Japan would be able to keep both Britain and the United States busy in the Far East, or he would be able to demand from Japan an offensive against Russia in exchange for Germany's active support. An attack by Japan on Russia – and the Japanese had met with crushing military success in their war against the Russians of 1904–1905 – might have turned the scales in the struggle between Germany and the Soviet Union. Yet Hitler neither sought such intervention by Japan, nor refrained from intervening himself in the Japanese-American conflict. For a number of reasons – the United States's undisguised support for Britain, his belief that this was one more decadent and unmilitary democracy whose defeat would be swift – and by further stimulation of his sense of his own historic destiny to decide the fate of the world, Hitler declared war on the United States four days after Pearl Harbor. Italy followed suit.

A.J.P. Taylor makes the telling point that when the British people, having defied Hitler, found they were not strong enough to unseat him, he himself came to their assistance. 'His success depended on the isolation of Europe from the rest of the world. He gratuitously destroyed the source of this success. In 1941 he attacked Soviet Russia and declared war on the United States, two World Powers who asked only to be left alone. In this way a real World War began.' If attacking Russia were an irretrievable blunder, declaring war on the United States must run it a close second. By taking on the world's three greatest powers – and without having succeeded in developing an atomic bomb before the Allies – Hitler as early as 1941 determined the war's outcome. He took the very steps that would ensure Germany would lose it.

Yet when we examine his conversation or his speeches of this period we are struck by the extraordinary contrast between megalomaniac claptrap and strategic vision of the first order. On one day, 11 December, in his speech declaring war on America he is buoyed up by his great role as Man of Destiny: 'I can only be grateful to Providence that it entrusted me with the leadership in this historic struggle which, for the next five hundred or a thousand years, will be described as decisive, not only for the history of Germany, but for the whole of Europe and indeed the whole world . . . A historical revision on a unique scale has been imposed on us by the Creator.' It is strange and somehow ridiculous to find Hitler putting forward the determinist view of history when no better example exists of events being subordinated to human will than his own. Yet on the next day, at the Führer Naval Conference of 12 December, we find him talking in a very different vein to Raeder. 'Is there any possibility,' he asks, 'that the United States and Britain will abandon East Asia for a time in order to crush Germany and Italy first?' The prescience of such a question is made plain when we observe that within a matter of weeks the US and British Combined Chiefs of Staff are framing just such a strategy – Japan will be denied the means to wage war while the Allies concentrate on Germany's defeat, tightening the ring round the latter country by sustaining Russia, strengthening the Middle East and winning and holding the whole North African coast. However, during this conference Raeder assures the Führer that the British cannot put India at risk nor the Americans abandon the Pacific to the Japanese Navy. The Admiral then tries to press on Hitler once more his favourite strategic plan. While the Allies are preoccupied elsewhere, now is the time to seize Malta and the Suez Canal with a view to linking up with the Japanese in the Indian Ocean: 'The favourable situation in the Mediterranean, so pronounced at the present time, will probably never occur again.' It was in fact to occur once more, but then as now Hitler was not interested. The struggle with Russia had him in thrall.

If Hitler was not interested in the Middle East at this time, Churchill could not have been more so. A few days before Japan's attack, he heard that Ethiopia had finally been liberated with the defeat of remaining Italian forces there. Crusader continued, and although it was developing into what Churchill called a 'prolonged, wearing-down battle' with little prospect of breaking through to Tripoli or advacing to Tunisia, the very nature of the struggle was drawing in Axis resources from elsewhere and thus bringing some measure of relief to the Russian front. At the same time Axis reinforcements for the Mediterranean, while they were thus prevented from being sent to Russia, made things more difficult for Auchinleck, the Eighth Army and British naval and air forces in the theatre. In particular, when Fliegerkorps II was transferred from Russia to Sicily and more U-boats were dispatched to the Mediterranean, the battle of supplies and of Axis communications to Libya was intensified. German and Italian naval successes against Royal Navy warships allowed reinforcements of tanks, armoured cars, anti-tank guns and the vital fuel for armour and transport to reach Rommel, enabling him to plan, and some months later to execute, a spoiling attack on Eighth Army, the spectacular results of which surpassed even Rommel's own ebullient expectations. Moreover the Japanese attacks on Malaya and elsewhere were to rob Auchinleck not only of powerful reinforcements he was expecting to receive, but also units from his existing order of battle, including tanks and aircraft. Thus in December 1941 the general situation in the Mediterranean and Middle East was nicely balanced. Churchill was sanguine, and although deeply saddened by the loss of the battleships *Prince of Wales* and *Repulse*, sunk by Japanese air attacks with bombs and torpedoes off the Malayan coast on 10 December, he had been immensely heartened by Roosevelt's declaration of war on Japan and his message to the Prime Minister of 8 December: 'Today all of us are in the same boat with you and the people of the Empire, and it is a ship which will not and cannot be sunk.' After Hitler's declaration of war on America on 11 December, Churchill signalled to Roosevelt: 'I am enormously relieved at turn world events have taken.' He was confident that with America in the war, 'time and patience will give certain victory'. In any event, he told his Private Secretary 'We must just KBO [keep buggering on].'

Having made arrangements to meet President Roosevelt in Washington, Churchill set sail in HMS *Duke of York* on 13 December, accompanied by Beaverbrook, the Chiefs of the Naval and Air Staffs, Field Marshal Dill[1] and others. Nothing could have suited more this 'Former Naval Person' – as he so frequently styled himself in his telegrams to Roosevelt – than to be on board a British battleship, within range of U-boats and Focke-Wulf Kondors, spending much of his time dictating memoranda on the future conduct of the war as a basis for the forthcoming meetings with the United States President and his military advisers. These memoranda illustrated the extraordinary range of Churchill's strategic vision, his absolute confidence in victory over the Axis powers, and his ability to list the practical military means by which this victory would be achieved. Indeed, many of the measures which he proposed were to come about more or less exactly as he was now advocating. In examining what he called the 'Atlantic Front', Churchill made it clear that a top priority for

---

[1] Dill had just relinquished his post as CIGS, and been replaced by Brooke. At this time he was Governor-designate of Bombay, but in the event he remained in the USA as senior British representative on the Combined Chiefs of Staff Committee in Washington.

Britain and America would be to ensure Russia was supplied with war material to keep her fighting and to maintain some leverage with Stalin. French North Africa must be won over, and in order to do so British and American troops must be landed there *in 1942* and be assisted in their campaign by Eighth Army's advance from the east. If the Vichy Government co-operated, France could be 're-established' – if not, de Gaulle's movement would have to be supported and employed. In order to deter any German attempts on Ireland, United States troops should be stationed in Ulster. United States bomber forces should be deployed in Britain from where they could 'come into action against Germany' as 'the most direct and effective reply' to the latter's declaration of war against America.

Churchill was less hopeful about developments in the Far East – which was probably just as well, for some terrible disasters were awaiting the British there. Much would depend on the United States's ability to regain command of the Pacific, but it had to be expected that Allied strongpoints in the Far East theatre would fall to the Japanese, and it was far from certain that Singapore and the Philippines (an American possession, and very vulnerable to a Japanese invasion) would hold out for long. Even at this stage Churchill foresaw the building-up of Allied air power against Japan. Although he could not have envisaged what was to happen in 1945, Churchill noted that 'the burning of Japanese cities by incendiary bombs will bring home in a most effective way to the people of Japan the dangers of the course to which they have committed themselves . . .' In speculating about the relative priorities of the European and Pacific theatres of war, Churchill was in favour of the United States concentrating on naval power in the Pacific, so that the main American military effort would be available for liberating Europe. This, broadly, was the way things were to fall out.

Perhaps the most interesting of Churchill's memoranda was the one dealing with the year 1943. By then, he argued, the whole of North Africa would be in Allied hands, and landings might have been made in Sicily and Italy 'with reactions inside Italy which might be highly favourable'. There was, however, still the question of defeating the German armies, for any notion of 'internal convulsions in Germany produced by the unfavourable course of the war, economic privations and the Allied bombing offensive' was not something to be counted on. Indeed, it was necessary to assume that the German Army and Air Force would continue the struggle and that the U-boat offensive would probably increase. Therefore the Allies would have to prepare for landing British and American armies in western and southern Europe to liberate the countries which had been overrun by Germany. Churchill went so far as to suggest that such landings might be effected as early as the summer of 1943, and that this might lead actually to winning the war by the end of that year, or by 1944.

The most important point to emerge from all these speculative memoranda was Churchill's insistence that the Allies should concentrate on Europe first, and then deal with the Far East, even though the re-establishment of the Allied naval position in the Pacific must remain a high priority. It was, of course, of great value to the British position that all these matters could be studied by the Chiefs of Staff while *Duke of York* was still making her way to America. The Chiefs were able to comment on Churchill's memoranda, and in doing so made clear their view that late 1943 or early 1944 was a more realistic date for landing strong Allied forces in Europe, and that proper emphasis should be given to the bombing programme against Germany in 1943. Moreover, it had to be expected that until the Axis powers in Europe had been dealt with, Japan would have a fairly free hand in the Western Pacific. Churchill's reaction to their comments reflected his persistent determination to think offensively, and he insisted that even though it might be necessary to postpone the actual landings on the Continent until 1944, plans and preparations for an invasion must be put in hand now. He was not prepared to agree that such landings must wait until Germany had been 'so weakened by night air-bombing as not to be able to offer any effective resistance to liberating armies'. It was important, he said, to consider Hitler's difficulties – an enormous coastline to defend, Allied freedom of choice as to where to strike, a huge commitment in Russia, the Mediterranean distraction, air forces weaker than those of the Allies, the morale of the German people faced with 'a bad winter . . . slaughter in Russia and the entry of the United States . . .' – all these things led Churchill to the view that landings on the Continent would be possible in the summer of 1943. (As far as Sicily and Italy went, Churchill was proved right, but the main invasion of Continental Europe, as the Chiefs of Staff had suspected, would not be until a year later.) What mattered in all this, however, was that Churchill and his military advisers had studied all the strategic problems, and when they met their American counterparts, they were ready with a prepared and broadly agreed position.

Churchill reached Washington on 22 December, and on that very evening in the White House he was able to discuss with Roosevelt – both men had their advisers present, Beaverbrook and Halifax in Churchill's case, Cordell Hull, Sumner Welles[1] and Hopkins in Roosevelt's – the very strategic matters he had explored in his memoranda. Churchill was greatly reassured by Roosevelt's ready agreement to the plan for a joint landing in North-West Africa and by the President's offer to station US divisions in Northern Ireland. While these discussions were in progress, a meeting between the American and British Chiefs of Staff confirmed the American view, which coincided so completely with Churchill's, that the decisive theatre of war – the Japanese attacks notwith-

[1] Hull was Secretary of State, Welles the Under-Secretary of State.

standing – was that of the Atlantic and Europe. Germany was regarded as 'the key to victory'; once she was defeated, the other Axis powers' defeat would follow. Such hopeful prospects were not exactly enlivened by events in the Far East, for on that same day the Philippines were invaded by Japanese troops, and on Christmas Day Hong Kong surrendered. Churchill was deeply concerned as to the fate of Singapore, and since the news from Libya continued to be encouraging – Auchinleck had signalled on Christmas Eve that armoured cars of the Royal Dragoons had occupied Benghazi, and he sent the Prime Minister Christmas greetings from 'the Army of the Nile' – he asked the C-in-C Middle East to release both fighter squadrons and an armoured brigade for the Far East, going so far as to warn that 'All our success in the West would be nullified by the fall of Singapore.'

On 26 December Churchill delivered his celebrated speech to the Senate and House of Representatives in which he made his claim that 'If my father had been American and my mother British, instead of the other way round, I might have got here on my own,' and thus his audience would have heard his voice before. He expressed his confidence that their two peoples would in the future, both for their own and everyone else's security and wellbeing, 'walk together side by side in majesty, in justice, and in peace'. He received the prolonged cheers of Senators and Congressmen. It was also at this time that he suffered an attack of angina. It did not prevent him from continuing with his heavy programme of work, and on 28 December he went by train to Ottawa for discussions with the Canadian War Cabinet and, on the 30th, to make a speech to the Canadian Parliament. Once more he reiterated that no matter how long or severe the struggle might be, the people of the British Empire would never weary or give up, and he referred to the time (mentioned previously) some eighteen months earlier when he had told the French Government that no matter what they did, Britain would fight on alone, and that the French generals had predicted to their government ministers that 'In three weeks England will have her neck wrung like a chicken.' After a pause, he uttered his never to be forgotten retort: 'Some chicken! Some neck!' While still in Ottawa, Churchill was asked at a press conference on December 31 whether he thought Singapore could hold on, and answered with a most emphatic affirmative. Alas, six weeks later he was to be proved tragically wrong; indeed, for Churchill and the British, the first half of 1942 was to prove a voyage bound in shallows and in miseries. Yet even formidable dangers, defeats, disasters could not in the end shake his indomitable spirit, so that when, in the latter half of 1942, there was a perceptible turning of the tide, by taking the current when it served, Churchill's ventures began to prosper.

CHAPTER 7

1942 – End of the Beginning

It does not seem likely that in 1942 any large-scale land
offensive against Germany except on the Russian front
will be possible . . .

ALLIED GRAND STRATEGY MEMORANDUM

Our aim is to wipe out the entire defence potential
remaining to the Soviets, and to cut them off, as far as
possible, from their most important centres of war
industry.

ADOLF HITLER, WAR DIRECTIVE NO 41, April 1942

Churchill returned to Washington from Canada on 1 January 1942. He still had
business to do with Roosevelt, agreeing to the President's declaration by the
'United Nations' (which was signed by twenty-six nations who undertook to do
all within their power to defeat the Axis powers and after complete victory to
'defend life, liberty, independence, and religious freedom, and to preserve
human rights and justice in their own lands as well as in other lands'), and co-
presiding with Roosevelt at a meeting to determine the scales of American war
production. From 5 to 10 January he both rested and worked in Florida, before
returning to Washington for final talks with the President and a meeting of the
Combined Chiefs of Staff. Although the deteriorating position in the Far East
meant that fewer American troops than had at first been planned would be
available for Iceland and Northern Ireland, Churchill derived great satisfaction
from Roosevelt's strong support for a joint Anglo-American landing in North
Africa, and his pledge to supply American troops for Australia's defence should
a Japanese threat develop there. Before Churchill left Washington to return
home, the news from Malaya was such that he formed the opinion that the
peninsula could not be successfully defended, while still placing great hopes on
Singapore, despite Wavell's warning that the battle there would be, like
Waterloo, a near-run thing. Although he had originally intended to sail back in

Duke of York, on his arrival in Bermuda by flying boat, Churchill decided in view of what was happening in Malaya to fly on. He reached Plymouth on 17 January and was able to report to the War Cabinet that evening the results of his conferences in Washington. Churchill had every reason to be pleased that he had obtained such whole-hearted co-operation from the United States, and in particular agreement for early joint action in French North Africa. Bad tidings on several fronts, however, were soon to dim his optimism and to rule out any such early action.

Hitler, too, might have felt some satisfaction in having stabilized the Russian front. Indeed, in mid-January he felt able to allow Kluge to effect some tactical withdrawals to prepared positions for those of his units which were too exposed. Moreover, warmer clothing was being provided, some reserves were coming forward, and heavy weapons had been recovered. But the losses of Barbarossa had already been grievous. Between 22 June – when the panzers had cut through the Soviet defenders and galloped across the Russian plains while the Stukas above destroyed aircraft, tanks, fuel dumps and soldiers on the march – and February 1942 – when the Russian counter-offensive had died down and Halder, worried about the sagging front, had complained that troops do not hold ground when the temperature is 30 degrees below zero – the Germans had lost over a million men killed, wounded and missing, almost a third of the total which they had started the campaign with. What had been planned, and indeed had started out, as a five-month battle of conquest was beginning to turn into a four-year struggle of attrition. Yet Hitler had great hopes for 1942. Although he had recognized that his gamble of crushing Russia by blitzkrieg had not come off, he set himself ambitious goals – the Caucasus in March or April, Vologda or Gorki (respectively 300 miles north-east and east of Moscow) in May. The question of building an 'East Wall' remained open.

In 1942, therefore, it seemed that Hitler's battles for Europe were still to be ones of conquest. What transpired was that despite the most spectacular advances, perhaps of the whole war, in both Russia and Africa, despite visions of the most gigantic pincer movement ever executed by panzer and Stuka, despite reaching the very zenith of conquest, the year was to witness both the peak and the turning point of his career, together with his final forfeiture of the initiative. Then the rot would set in, and the battles of resistance begin. It was by now clear to Hitler that all ideas of a short war were illusory. The fallacy of blitzkrieg was exposed. In spite of the triumphs of 1939 and 1940, his great mission in the east had bogged down, and moreover had robbed him of his former freedom to turn east or west at will. He therefore had to seek decision in the east before the United States and Britain could open another front in the west, to say nothing of what might happen in the south. Besides, Germany had

Hitler in Munich, August 1914

Hitler as a soldier in the First World War

Hindenburg and Hitler on his appointment as Chancellor; standing behind Hitler, Göring and Raeder

Munich 1938

Hitler and Rommel in Poland, 1939

Himmler and Hitler

Hitler's victory "jig" at
Compiègne

The Dictators

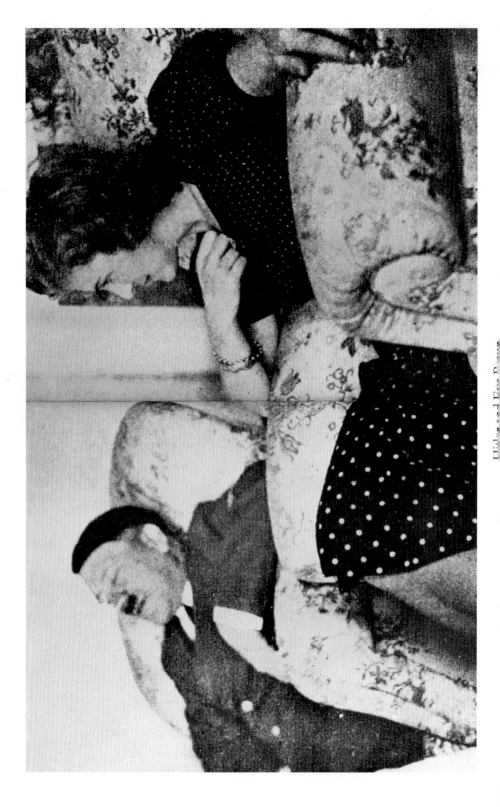

to have more oil. On the eve of the offensive by which he hoped to gain it, Hitler told General Friedrich von Paulus, commander of the Sixth Army (which was to perish in the attempt), that if he did not get the Caucasus oilfields, Germany must end the war.

By this time, however, Hitler was beginning to do what Marmont accused the great Napoleon of doing – he began to live in a world created by his own imagination, to close his eyes to hard military facts and rely instead upon his own intuition and willpower. He refused to accept that however much human will might complement and direct military strength, it was no substitute for that strength. This obstinate refusal to face facts was illustrated by his reception of intelligence about the Soviet Union's growing numbers of soldiers and weapons. When wholly reliable sources revealed that in 1942 Stalin would muster a further 1¼ million men in the region north of Stalingrad and west of the Volga, with at least ½ million more in the eastern Caucasus, and that Russian tank output was some 1,200 a month, Hitler, according to Halder, 'flew with clenched fists and foam at the corners of his mouth at the one who was reading this statement, and forbade such idiotic twaddle'. It was not only Russian military strength which was of such concern, however, but also the state of the Wehrmacht itself. In March 1942 only 8 out of 162 divisions on the Eastern Front were operationally fit, while the 16 so-called panzer divisions had between them only 150 tanks. But if Hitler could do little except harbour his own illusions about growing Russian numbers, where his own numbers and equipment were concerned he could and did act. In February 1942 he made an appointment which, perhaps more than any other, enabled him to go on waging war beyond the point in 1943 when many of his associates believed it to be lost: Albert Speer became Minister of Armaments and Munitions. Quite unlike the general run of Nazi ruffians, Speer, an architect by training, showed an astonishing flair for organization, for mustering labour, and for devising or improving methods of production. Faced with ever-increasing difficulties, he actually succeeded in expanding the output of arms in 1942 and 1943.

There was also the question of more troops. For these Hitler turned to his allies, and so successful was he that for the coming summer offensive no fewer than fifty divisions were raised, mainly from Romania, Hungary and Italy. To one of his principal allies, Mussolini, who was disturbed by Germany's setback in Russia, Hitler gave another of his interminable lectures when the two leaders met at Salzburg on 29–30 April. Ciano recalled Mussolini's misery: 'Hitler talks, talks, talks, talks. Mussolini suffers – he, who is in the habit of talking himself, and who, instead, has to remain silent.' None the less, the Duce agreed to provide nine divisions. What was the Führer's intention this time? His main objectives were as comprehensive as their capture was fanciful – the Caucasus oil, the Donbass industry[1] and Stalingrad. Directive No 41, which laid down that the entire Soviet defence capability was to be wiped out, explained that all available forces would be employed (although security in the west and north would be maintained), and went on:

> In pursuit of the original plan for the Eastern campaign, the Armies of the Central sector will stand fast, those in the North will capture Leningrad and link up with the Finns, while those on the southern flank will break through into the Caucasus . . . all available forces will be concentrated on the main operations in the southern sector, with the aim of destroying the enemy before the Don, in order to secure the Caucasian oilfields and the passes through the Caucasus mountains themselves.

These were formidable tasks, yet the trouble with this directive did not lie in what it ordered, but rather in its failure to reveal the master plan behind the operations it described. What Hitler had in mind was that if he succeeded in destroying the Russian armies in the south and in destroying or taking over the region's oil and war economy, he would have a choice – either to exploit further south to Baku (on the Caspian Sea, close to the Persian border), or, much more promising in terms of gaining a real decision, turn north to outflank and destroy Soviet forces in the centre protecting Moscow. In this way he might smash Russian resistance once and for all. Whilst it could not be claimed that had the subordinate army commanders known this, the offensive would necessarily have succeeded, it is far more likely that, had they been fully aware of the intentions behind the plan, they would have operated in a way designed to contribute to Hitler's ultimate aim. As it was, there was a fatal misunderstanding as to what the role of Stalingrad was to be, and this led, as we shall see, to the loss of Paulus's Sixth Army.

While Hitler was wrestling with the expansion and consolidation of his empire in the east, Churchill was equally perturbed by the imminent collapse of the British Empire in the Far East. It may perhaps be said that the greatest humiliation suffered by British arms during the Second World War was not being chased out of Europe by the Wehrmacht nor being chased round the Western Desert by Rommel. It was not even the premature capitulation of Tobruk (which in this story we have yet to witness). It was the surrender of Singapore to the Japanese. 'The fall of Singapore,' wrote James Morris, 'presaged unmistakably the end of Empire itself.' Churchill was well aware of Singapore's importance, both strategically and in terms of prestige, and had been deeply disturbed to receive from Wavell, who had been appointed

[1] Some 60 per cent of Soviet industry was concentrated in the Donets basin.

Supreme Commander, South-West Pacific in December 1941, information as to the ill-preparedness of Singapore's defences and the doubtful quality of some of the troops there. He was especially 'staggered' to learn that there were no proper defences against a Japanese attack from the north, that is, from the southern Malayan state of Johore, and he told the Chiefs of Staff that there could be no excuse for having only seaward-facing batteries on the island. He urged the immediate making of a proper plan so that 'the whole island must be fought for until every single Unit and every single strong point has been separately destroyed'. Singapore must become a citadel which would be defended to the death – 'the Commander, Staffs and principal Officers are expected to perish at their posts'. On 21 January, however, when he saw a signal from Wavell which held out little prospect of a lengthy defence of Singapore, he began to question the soundness of reinforcing the island if it were to be for a mere few weeks. Would it not be better to send reinforcements to Burma, to keep open the road to the Chinese so that they could continue their fight against the Japanese?[1]

It was not only from Malaya, where the rapid Japanese advance continued, that the news was bad, however, but from Libya too, for Rommel launched a spoiling attack on 21 January, and so successfully did he exploit its initial success that by early February he had succeeded in pushing Eighth Army back to the Gazala-Bir Hacheim line, so robbing Auchinleck of Crusader's fruits, particularly the airfields of western Cyrenaica. Because of criticism in the House of Commons, Churchill had decided to seek a vote of confidence, and in winding up a three-day debate on 29 January, he claimed that the policy pursued by the Government of aiding Russia, attacking in Libya, while accepting dangers in the Far East had been soundly based, and that subsequent setbacks did not change this. He was confident that although more misfortunes might occur, the conflict would be brought to a satisfactory conclusion. His confidence was echoed resoundingly by the House – 464 Members voted in support of the Government, with only one, the Chairman of the Independent Labour Party, James Maxton, against.

About the further misfortunes to come there was no doubt either, for arrangements to defend Singapore proved hopeless. Even while the Japanese Twenty-Fifth Army was making swift advances down the Malayan peninsula, so unseriously did the authorities in Singapore view the danger that when the

[1] In July 1937 Japan launched a full-scale invasion of China, and by October 1938 had gained control of the entire eastern seaboard. The Chinese Government under its President, General Chiang Kai-shek, withdrew to Chungking, from where the defence of China continued to be organized, with the help of supplies from the Allies brought in from Burma.

army proposed constructing defensive positions on the golf club, they were informed that this was a matter to be put to the Club Committee! There was universal muddle, clashes between military and civilians as to what was to be done, protocol and outdated orders taking precedence over demands of the moment, and a general lack of initiative. Under such circumstances defeat was no surprise, despite all Churchill's talk of defence to the death and the Empire's fighting reputation and honour. Preceded by shelling and bombing, the Japanese crossed the Johore Strait on 8 February, attacking the weakly held north-west of the island, the main defences being in the north-east. Threatened by General Tomoyuki Yamashita that he would mount annihilating bombardments, the C-in-C, Lieutenant-General Arthur Percival, signalled Wavell on 14 February that his troops 'were incapable of further counter-attack', and the latter, with Churchill's authority, instructed him to surrender, which he did on the following day. In commenting on this humiliation, James Morris recorded that 'Asians were never to look upon Englishmen in quite the same way again. The Royal Navy had failed; the British armies had been out-classed; white men had been seen in states of panic . . . the legend had collapsed . . . even the courage was less than universal.' This last point was made by Wavell in his report to Churchill on the whole débâcle of Malaya and Singapore, which included such phrases as 'lack of real fighting spirit' and 'neither British, Australians or Indians have shown any real toughness of mind or body', and went on to comment that although fighting conditions had been hard, they 'should not have been insuperable'. These words must have made uncomfort-able reading for Churchill, who a few days earlier had had to endure the further humiliating news that the German battle cruisers *Scharnhorst* and *Gneisenau*, with the heavy cruiser *Prinz Eugen*, had left Brest, sailed through the English Channel in broad daylight and reached German ports despite some damage inflicted by British aircraft, many of which were lost in the attacks against the ships. Yet in fact the withdrawal of these German warships could only aid the British strategic position at sea, for it was the Battle of the Atlantic which counted.

Churchill felt it necessary to broadcast to the nation on 15 February about the fall of Singapore (the surrender took place that day), although he had little of comfort for his listeners. He was, however, able to produce comprehensible reasons for weakness in the Far East – the demands of the Middle East, not just in the Western Desert, but also in East Africa, Iraq, Persia, Palestine and Syria; the requirement of aiding Russia; the problems of sea transport and supply; the need to sustain Britain herself – all these commitments had meant that Britain had been unable to withstand the Japanese onslaught. Yet with the United States as an ally, with Russia still fighting Hitler's armies, with the British Commonwealth itself, although there would still be losses, troubles, worries to face, the only real crime would be 'a weakening of our purpose and therefore in our unity'. Martin Gilbert makes the point that whereas at the time of Dunkirk, Churchill's words of defiance and hope had somehow inspired the nation, in the face of this further disaster 'he seemed unable to turn the tide of depression':

I speak to you all under the shadow of a heavy and far-reaching military defeat. It is a British and Imperial defeat. Singapore has fallen. All the Malay Peninsula has been overrun. Other dangers gather about us out there, and none of the dangers which we have hitherto successfully withstood at home and in the East are in any way diminished.

This, therefore, is one of those moments when the British race and nation can show their quality and their genius. This is one of those moments when it can draw from the heart of misfortune the vital impulses of victory. Here is the moment to display that calm and poise combined with grim determination which not so long ago brought us out of the very jaws of death. Here is another occasion to show – as so often in our long story – that we can meet reverses with dignity and with renewed accessions of strength.

We must remember that we are no longer alone. We are in the midst of a great company. Three-quarters of the human race are now moving with us. The whole future of mankind may depend upon our action and upon our conduct. So far we have not failed. We shall not fail now. Let us move forward steadfastly together into the storm and through the storm.

As they had before the British people did show their quality and their genius. They soldiered on. There were, however, even more reverses they would have to meet with dignity, both in Burma and in North Africa. In the days immediately following Singapore's fall, Churchill himself was not at his most dignified or most robust. Having told the House of Commons on 17 February that the escape of the German warships was something that would be properly looked into, he then deplored the idea of recriminations with regard to the fall of Singapore. But there was no escaping the fact that both Members of Parliament and those they represented were 'immensely disturbed'. All this added to Churchill's depression, and he even spoke to one of his staff about how irksome he found it to have to bear both the bad news itself and the criticism of others, so much so that he was becoming tired of it and 'very seriously thinking of handing over his responsibilities to other shoulders'. At this Captain Pim, who ran the Map Room at the 10 Downing Street Annexe, instantly gave a reply which the nation would have echoed: 'But, my God, sir, you cannot do that'. Happily he did not, but he did reconstruct the Government. Beaverbrook went, at his own request and much to Churchill's regret. In their exchange of letters Beaverbrook acknowledged his debt to the other's loyalty to and confidence in him, calling the Prime Minister 'leader of the nation, saviour of our people, symbol of resistance in the free world'; in his reply Churchill referred to the decisive work done by Beaverbrook as Minister of Aircraft Production, at the Ministry of Supply and in aiding the Russians – he was 'one of our few fighting men of genius'. Arthur Greenwood and Sir Kingsley Wood left the War Cabinet, Oliver Lyttelton and Sir Stafford Cripps joined it (as Minister of Production and Minister of Aircraft Production, respectively). *The Times* approved of the changes, which would 'be capable of re-invigorating the conduct of the war and public confidence'.

As for the war, Churchill could have been forgiven for recalling Claudius's 'When sorrows come, they come not single spies, But in battalions,' for in the Far East everything was going wrong. On 24 February the Prime Minister told the House of Commons that if a nation found itself struggling with two strongly armed countries, of which one possessed 'the most powerful military machine in the world', and then when fully engaged a third, militarily superior enemy attacks you too, 'your [the nation's] task is heavy and your immediate experiences will be disagreeable'. They were certainly disagreeable in Burma, where the Japanese invasion lasted from January 1942 until May, when the monsoon put paid to further advances, by which time they had reached the frontier with India. There had never been a chance that the British would be able to defend Burma successfully. In the first place, they had always assumed that, because of the mountainous country to the east and north, any attack would come from the south or west. The Japanese chose otherwise. Secondly, there were not enough troops, and those that there were had inadequate training and equipment. Thirdly, the British, Indian and Chinese troops seemed unable to combat Japanese tactics of frontal assault combined with wide outflanking movements which established strong positions *behind* the defenders. By 20 February the 17th Division had retreated to the Sittang River, and only one of its brigades crossed before the bridge was blown because it was thought to be in danger of being taken intact by the Japanese. Of eight battalions thus cut off, fewer than two thousand officers and men reached the west bank. Churchill had sent General Alexander to take command in Burma, but not only could he not save Rangoon, which was abandoned on 7 March, but he was fortunate to get his forces away towards Prome. 'The loss of Rangoon,' wrote Churchill, 'meant the loss of Burma, and the rest of the campaign was a grim race between the Japanese and the approaching rains.'

It was the robust, articulate and tactically brilliant Lieutenant-General William Slim who commanded the Burma Corps during the retreat, but he was unable to prevent the Japanese from cutting the Burma Road, that vital link between Lashio and Chiang Kai-shek's capital, Chunking. There seemed to be no stopping the Japanese advance. By late March they had pushed the Chinese out of Toungoo and were advancing against the British at Prome. A month later the Chinese had been turned out of Burma – some into China itself, some under the American General Joseph ('Vinegar Joe') Stilwell into India astride the Irrawaddy. The British and Indian forces under Alexander and Slim had withdrawn to Kelewa, and the final retreat from there to Imphal, where the routes into India could be blocked, was, under the full fury of the monsoon, an incalculably miserable affair. This was in mid-May 1942. Although some doubts had been cast on the fighting spirit of the British Army, both because of Singapore and some of the Burma fighting, doubts echoed by the Viceroy of India, Lord Linlithgow, and even by Churchill himself, the British soldier totally redeemed his reputation in the subsequent reconquest of Burma. But quite apart from their conquest of Burma, the Japanese had invaded Java on 28 February, with heavy naval losses for the British – 4 destroyers and a cruiser – and when the Dutch surrendered ten days later, a total of 13,000 British, American and Australian airmen and soldiers became prisoners of war. Yet Churchill's astonishing robustness – or so it seemed to those about him – would never allow disasters over and done with to deter him from facing and trying to avert further dangers. The defence of Ceylon is instantly his concern as Java falls; he is angered when he hears that Auchinleck is not proposing to return to the offensive before June; the U-boat menace is aggravated by their having adopted a new signal code which Bletchley Park cannot decipher, and also by their operating more powerfully in the Western Atlantic and Caribbean, with the result that shipping losses are again alarmingly high. Yet as his doctor, Charles Wilson, noted, Churchill would bear his dreadful burden without saying anything to discourage others. For his part, the CIGS, Brooke, tells a friend that 'Winston is a marvel. I can't imagine how he sticks it.'

In March 1942, very conscious of the need to reassure Russia as to the intentions of Britain and America, not only in continuing to supply aid, but also in creating strategic diversions, and to satisfy Stalin about Russia's post-war frontiers, Churchill began to make plans to meet the Soviet leader himself. One of the difficult aspects of the frontier problem was the question of the Baltic states and Russia's occupation of eastern Poland, but Churchill failed in his efforts to persuade President Roosevelt of the need to play along with Stalin's territorial demands. More encouraging was Roosevelt's enthusiasm for 'the establishment of a new front this summer on the European continent, certainly for air and raids'. The President, it seemed, was even prepared to accept that losses would be great on the grounds that such casualties would be 'compensated for by at least equal German losses and by compelling Germans to divert large forces of all kinds from Russian fronts.'

The trouble with any such idea was that the conflicting demands of the various fronts on which the Western Allies were engaged, to say nothing of the need to aid Russia, meant that the actual application of military force anywhere was a matter of priorities. Churchill was particularly worried that at the very time when a major German offensive on the Russian front was likely – that is, in the early part of the summer, Auchinleck was insisting that his forces would still be on the defensive. Such delays exasperated Churchill, who found it 'intolerable that the 635,000 men on your ration strength should remain unengaged preparing for another set-piece battle in July'. Such considerations strengthened his determination to descend on Auchinleck in person, before going on to see Stalin. He even threatened to remove fifteen air squadrons from Auchinleck's command, in order to help the Soviets in the Caucasus area, for if this part of the Russian front should collapse, the whole Middle East position could face a further threat by a German drive through Syria. Reviewing the general situation on 26 March, Churchill found little to draw comfort from, and in speaking to the Conservative Party Central Council he referred to 'an almost unbroken series of military misfortunes' – in the Mediterranean, in the Far East, in the Atlantic, even in Cyrenaica, there was uncertainty. Late in March a successful naval and commando raid on the dry dock and U-boat pens at St Nazaire, which had been planned by Vice-Admiral Lord Louis Mountbatten, Chief of Combined Operations and since early March a member of the Chiefs of Staff Committee, together with further attacks on U-boat bases did something to redress the balance, but at the beginning of April Churchill was obliged to admit to Roosevelt that even though his government's position was sound, 'with nothing but disaster to show for all one's work, people were restive in Parliament and the Press'.

On 2 April Roosevelt had informed Churchill that he was dispatching the US Army Chief of Staff, General Marshall, and Hopkins to England to explain a plan which he had formulated, and which he hoped would be greatly welcomed by Russia. When his special envoys arrived six days later and revealed this plan it turned out to be nothing less than a proposal to invade France on beaches between Le Havre and Boulogne, employing thirty American and eighteen British divisions, supported by nearly 6,000 aircraft, with Antwerp as the objective. Not only would this all take place in 1943, but if necessary – that is, to prevent a Russian collapse – a smaller invasion force would be prepared to assault in the autumn of that very year, 1942. It did not take the British military experts, Brooke, Mountbatten and Portal, very long to show that the small force which was all that could be made available in 1942 would not even be able to secure a bridgehead against the weight of numbers and armament with which the Germans would attack it. The proposal for 1943, on the other hand, deserved serious consideration. During the discussions, a fundamental difference of attitudes between the two Allied nations became plain. Whereas the British tended to deploy their military forces wherever they could, and indeed had no other option if they were to wage war at all – for example, armies in the Middle East, naval forces in the Atlantic and the Mediterranean, and both in the Far East – and then assumed that circumstances would dictate where and when decisive battles would occur, the Americans preferred to decide first where a decision was to be sought and then deploy the necessary forces there to gain that decision. Each of them thought the other wrong, the Americans instinctively distrusting the British preference for what they saw as indirect, indecisive strategies – often designed to prop up or expand the British Empire – while the British, wearied by former experience, were unconvinced that the direct approach could be successful without a good deal of wearing-down of the enemy's strength elsewhere beforehand. And one of the key questions which faced the two Allies during 1942 and 1943 as to how their various resources should be employed was admirably framed by Michael Howard: 'Above all, should Allied resources be used to extend the conflict in the Mediterranean, or concentrated in preparation for a cross-Channel attack?' It was the resolution of this question which so vexed Allied counsels at this time.

Meanwhile there were plenty of questions to vex Churchill. While agreeing in principle with Roosevelt's plan for a second front, he could not accept the American President's ideas about the setting-up of a nationalist government in India, and indeed felt that the allocation of resources for pursuing any offensive in Europe must be balanced against the demands of ensuring the security of India and the Middle East. Churchill was still deeply worried about the situation in Cyrenaica, for the intensity of air attacks on Malta had gravely reduced that island's ability to strike at the convoys supplying Rommel and the Afrika Korps. He had obtained Roosevelt's agreement to the employment of a United States aircraft carrier, *Wasp*, with the result that during the first week of May Malta received sixty Spitfires, flown in off the carrier, as well as General Lord Gort from Gibraltar, whom Churchill had appointed Governor, C-in-C and Supreme Commander of Malta, confident that Gort was 'the man to save the fortress'. Malta was, of course, crucial to the whole battle for North Africa. Just as the island's ability to provide the means for sinking Axis shipping was a necessary ingredient to the Eighth Army's success against Rommel, so was the Eighth Army's success indispensable to Malta's continued campaign to rob Rommel of the sinews of war. Auchinleck could not win without Malta's aid, and Malta could not survive without Auchinleck's. It was a vicious circle indeed. So seriously was this whole matter regarded – aggravated as it was by Auchinleck's intention to delay any offensive against Rommel until mid-June, when all the intelligence sources pointed to an attack *by* the Afrika Korps well before this date – that when the War Cabinet discussed it on May 8 it was agreed that the drawbacks of postponing an attack were greater than those of attacking early. In particular, the question of Malta's needs was paramount, and Churchill signalled Auchinleck that since the loss of Malta would be disastrous and could be 'fatal . . . to the defence of the Nile valley', the latter was to 'fight a major battle' against the enemy in May. We shall see shortly that despite all this urging, it was Rommel who held and then took the initiative, and in doing so very nearly triumphed.

That he did so at that particular time was a result of orders from the Führer himself. Although Hitler had repeatedly laid down that the war could only be won in the east, and although he regarded the Mediterranean theatre as a side-show whose value could be measured in terms of 'tying down enemy forces' (thus we have the singular circumstance that both sides in the world conflict are arguing that operations in the Mediterranean are being conducted in order to distract the other side from more important activities elsewhere), Hitler did nevertheless want Rommel to mount his offensive before the British could start theirs, and he therefore instructed OKW that the Axis attack should take place at the end of May. Operation Hercules, the conquest of Malta, for which the Italians had been pressing so hard, could wait, although Hitler did promise German parachute forces to assist. Before we see how Hitler got on with seeking decision in the east, we may briefly follow Rommel's fortunes, which in May and June 1942 reached the highest point of his reign in the desert.

Attacking the British Gazala position on 26 May, Rommel brought about the sort of pell-mell battle at which he and the Afrika Korps excelled. By 13 June they had defeated the Eighth Army and sent it scurrying back to the Alamein line, and on 21 June they had *taken* Tobruk. (Churchill was in Washington at the time, conferring with Roosevelt; his reaction will be recorded shortly.) Egypt now beckoned Rommel, for El Alamein was only some 65 miles from Alexandria and the Nile delta. Had he then remembered his own previous warning, that 'without Malta the Axis will end by losing control of North Africa,' Egypt might have been his, and with it the Suez Canal, the Levant, Iraq, the Gulf oil – everything. Mussolini, not always renowned as a strategist, saw what had to be done, however. He at once advised Hitler that this was the moment to launch Operation Hercules, the assault on Malta, and that Rommel should pause until after its capture. But the latter was riding high, and the sheer abundance of supplies which fell into his hands at Tobruk, among them some 2,000 tons of fuel and 2,000 vehicles, his two principal needs, closed his eyes to logistic realities. Besides, he thought the British were beaten; delay would simply allow them to recover. The arch-opportunist, he refused to acknowledge that there are times when an opportunity must be forgone in order to create an ever greater one. His sentiments were matched exactly by those of the Führer, a gambler if ever there was one. To Hitler the prospect of Rommel's further success persuaded him that Hercules, a venture he had never favoured, would now be unnecessary. He could not see that it was an indispensable preliminary to the Desert Fox's continued success.

He therefore telegraphed to Mussolini in Rome in suitably dramatic langauge, talking of Rommel's victory with German and Italian troops as a turning point, arguing that the Eighth Army had been shattered and that the supply problem could be eased by using the British railway from Tobruk to Egypt. He ended his telegram in extravagant style. There is no record as to whether Hitler was a student of Shakespeare; Nietzsche, Schopenhauer and Hegel were more to his taste. Yet in this ending he gave a fair paraphrase of the comment which Brutus makes to Cassius before Philippi:[1] 'The battle's Goddess of Fortune draws nigh upon the commanders only once; he who does not grasp her at that moment will seldom come to grips with her again.' In short, Rommel (whom Hitler promoted field marshal the day after he captured Tobruk) was told to get on and take Egypt. Hercules would have to wait. In allowing himself to be persuaded from his former prudence, Mussolini consoled himself with the alluring notion of riding in triumph through Alexandria mounted on a white charger. Two days after capturing Tobruk Rommel and his Panzerarmee crossed the frontier into Egypt.

The British, however, never more dangerous than when everyone else thinks they are beaten, were preparing to stand at the Alamein line, which could not be outflanked,[2] and where a battle, not of manoeuvre (at which the Afrika Korps excelled and Eighth Army did not), but of attrition, would have to be fought. For such a battle the British already enjoyed considerable advantages. In the first place Auchinleck, confident of himself and his army, had dismissed Ritchie and taken personal command; secondly, Malta had been reprieved, and its aircraft and naval units were already doing great harm to Axis supply convoys; thirdly, Churchill had extracted 300 Sherman tanks and a hundred 105mm self-propelled guns from Roosevelt; fourthly, the air situation was turning to favour the British; lastly, Eighth Army would be fighting near its sources of supply, and with secure lines of communication, while Rommel would be at the very end of extremely long and insecure supply lines. Never was the point that the battle for North Africa was a battle of supplies to be more strikingly demonstrated. In the event Auchinleck was successful not merely in stopping Rommel at what is sometimes known as the First Battle of Alamein, which lasted from 30 June to 27 July. He began to mount his own counter-attacks. Yet his command in the Middle East was shortly to end, and to

[1] *Julius Caesar*, III, iii, 216–22.
[2] To the north lay the Mediterranean; to the south the Qattara Depression, a 7,000-square-mile wilderness of soft sand, salt lakes and salt marches, impassable to vehicles.

see how and why this came about we must return to Churchill's activities – in London, in Washington and in Cairo.

On 21 May Molotov, the Soviet Foreign Minister, began discussing the Anglo-Russian treaty with Churchill in London. It was not a marriage of true minds. Not only would Churchill not give way to Molotov's demand that Russia's future frontiers must include eastern Poland, but he would not yield either to Stalin's pressure for a second front in time to distract the German Army from its eastern offensive, which was known to be imminent. If the Soviet line failed to hold firm, Churchill told Molotov, 'we should fight on, and, with the help of the United States . . . build up overwhelming air superiority which would enable us to put down a devastating weight of air attack on the German cities and industries . . . Ultimately the power of Great Britain and the United States would prevail.' Yet he also assured Molotov how earnestly the British nation hoped for a Russian victory and how eagerly they wished to engage the enemy and help the Russians. The treaty was successfully concluded (Eden's part in the negotiations having been extensive and invaluable), though without resolution of the frontier problem.

Despite Churchill's unwillingness to commit Great Britain to a European landing operation in order to create the second front that the Russians were asking for, his fertile mind was already grappling with the question of how to effect large-scale landings on the French coast; in essence, he was laying down the principle of using prefabricated floating pontoons to form an artificial harbour, telling Mountbatten not to argue the matter, but simply produce a solution.[1] At the same time General Sir Bernard Paget, C-in-C Home Forces, and Mountbatten were working on the practicalities of launching a seaborne attack on Western Europe – in 1942 and 1943. The main limitation was one of landing craft, and at the time of this planning, May 1942, only some 4,300 men and 160 tanks could be disembarked in the initial landings – a force quite inadequate to establishing a proper bridgehead. By May 1943 the position would be very different, however. More landing craft would allow an initial assault of 100,000 men and 1,800 vehicles. Churchill made it plain that he was not prepared to authorize a landing which would bring no significant help to the Russians, and might draw a terrible retribution down upon any French patriots who rose against the Germans in support of a landing which might fail.

Molotov went next to Washington, and as a result of his talks with the President and his advisers, Roosevelt's enthusiasm for mounting an offensive operation in Western Europe in 1942 was greatly stimulated; on 1 June he sig-

---

[1] What eventually resulted, of course, were the highly successful Mulberry harbours of the Normandy invasion in June 1944. Two were built in Britain, towed across the Channel and bolted in place.

nalled to Churchill that the plan to concentrate United States troops and equipment in the United Kingdom – the codename for this build-up was Bolero – with a view to a cross-Channel landing in 1942 should proceed as rapidly as possible. In these heady days there was an abundance of codewords for various operations. What the Americans really wanted – an invasion of Europe in 1942 – had the codename Sledgehammer, but even its most ardent advocate, General Marshall, had talked of it as an emergency attack, one which would only be justified if 'the situation on the Russian front became desperate' or if 'the German situation in Western Europe becomes critically weakened'. Yet the US Chiefs of Staff were under pressure from their own President to do something in view of the enormous burden being borne by the Russians. 'The necessities of the case,' declared Roosevelt, 'called for action in 1942, not 1943.' So strongly did the President hold this view that during Molotov's visit to Washington, he gave the Soviet Foreign Minister an assurance which, in the language of the communiqué issued later, stated that 'in the course of conversations full understanding was reached with regard to the urgent task of creating a Second Front in Europe in 1942'. In other words, the Americans pledged themselves to send their forces into battle against the Germans on land somewhere before the end of the year. This undertaking was to have a profound influence over Allied strategy.

It was gradually to become clear that if Roosevelt's undertaking were to be honoured, there would be only one sound course of action – to revert to an idea put forward by Churchill as early as December 1941 for a landing in French North Africa, Operation Gymnast. At first the Combined Chiefs of Staff were opposed to Gymnast which, they pointed out, would represent a dangerous dispersion of the whole Allied strategic activity. Therefore, they argued, the Allies would do better to concentrate on speeding up Bolero and continue to examine the possibilities of a Continental operation in 1942 in case conditions favourable for such an operation arose. In actual fact, what the Chiefs of Staff were really saying was that there should be no such operation in 1942 at all. Here, however, they fell foul of their political masters.

Churchill now felt it necessary to pay another visit to Roosevelt. He signalled to this effect on 13 June, and flew to America four days later, accompanied by Brooke and Ismay, among others. Perhaps the most important issue for decision was that of a second front, and in a paper he prepared for the President he maintained that Sledgehammer was impossible, and that because of this the Allies should be preparing 'within the general structure of *Bolero* some other operation by which we may gain position of advantage and also directly or indirectly take some weight off Russia'. It was in this light, Churchill concluded, that Gymnast should be looked at again.

It was while he and Roosevelt were talking together on the morning of 21

June that Churchill received the devastating news of Tobruk's surrender. He described it as one of the heaviest blows of the whole war; reflecting later, when contemplating the fall of both Singapore and Tobruk to inferior enemy numbers, he wrote of the bitterness of that moment, observing: 'Defeat is one thing; disgrace is another.' Yet some benefit was derived from even this military disaster, for Roosevelt's generous offer of help resulted in the dispatch of 300 Sherman tanks[1] to Egypt, together with 100 105mm self-propelled guns, which were to have a major effect on the forthcoming crucial battle for Egypt. Meanwhile the Combined Chiefs of Staff continued to examine the various strategic options, remaining for the time being in favour of a cross-Channel operation, while recognizing that if its success were improbable, some alternative plan for 1942 would be necessary.

Before this matter was finally resolved, Churchill had to face on his return home a vote of censure in the House of Commons. On the first day of this debate, 1 July, the news from the war fronts was not exactly encouraging, for Rommel had reached the El Alamein line, while on the Eastern Front the Germans had captured Sebastopol. In putting the case that 'this House ... has no confidence in the central direction of the war' Sir John Wardlaw-Milne, a leading Tory backbencher, made the ludicrous suggestion that the Duke of Gloucester should be the army's Commander-in-Chief, which so reduced members to 'disrespectful laughter' that his subsequent ideas about a more effective leader carried little weight. Yet Admiral Keyes was not only convinced that Churchill must stay – 'It would,' he said, 'be a deplorable disaster if he had to go' – he argued for more decisive leadership from the Prime Minister, who should if necessary override the cautious fears of his military advisers. On the other hand, Leslie Hore-Belisha (a Liberal, and formerly Secretary for War from 1937 to January 1940) criticized Churchill's military judgement, pointing to the various defeats in the Far East and the Middle East, while the Labour MP Aneurin Bevan suggested that although the Prime Minister might win debates, he kept on losing battles. Churchill, however, was not only resoundingly to win this debate too, but shortly would have some victories to his credit as well. In his spirited and responsible reply he explained the processes of decision-making – the activities of the Chiefs of Staff, at the service departments, his own position as Minister of Defence and Prime Minister, the War Cabinet itself, the actual record of decisions. He was, he said, content to be judged by

---

[1] The M-4 Sherman had a 75mm gun as main armament, and was to become the mainstay of the Allied armoured forces. Although a vast improvement over British tanks of the time, it was still inferior, in armour, performance and armament, to the later marks of German tanks; moreover, some Shermans were powered by petrol engines, making them more susceptible to 'brewing up'.

this record. Yet he was the House's servant and they had the right to dismiss him. What they could not ask of him was that he should 'bear responsibilities without the power of effective action'. The vote was, he added, of great importance in assuring Britain's friends that she had 'a strong solid Government'; if it were to be 'converted to a vote of censure upon its authors, make no mistake, a cheer will go up from every friend of Britain and every faithful servant of our cause, and the knell of disappointment will ring in the ears of the tyrants we are striving to overthrow'. The motion was defeated by 475 votes to 25, and both Roosevelt and Hopkins sent their delighted congratulations.

It was not long, however, before Churchill needed more from Roosevelt than friendly encouragement. Their joint concern that aid to Russia must be maintained as a top priority could only be exacerbated by the disastrous fate which overtook PQ17, a convoy of war material which had left Iceland on 27 June headed for Archangel. So heavy had been the air attacks on the escorts, and so likely seemed the threat of interference by the German battleship *Tirpitz*, that the First Sea Lord, Admiral Sir Dudley Pound, ordered the escorts to withdraw and the convoy to disperse. Scattered and unescorted, the merchant ships were at the mercy of the U-boats and Kondors; two-thirds of the vessels were sunk, so that only one-third of the 200,000 tons of supplies reached port. In communicating with Roosevelt, Churchill stressed the difficulties the Russian convoys faced, and the necessity of maintaining contact with the Soviet Union. He was, he added, shortly to have the opportunity to propose a visit by himself to Stalin. Before this it had been established by the British Chiefs of Staff that since Sledgehammer had no chance of success, and would moreover put paid to any idea of executing Round-Up in 1943, Gymnast would not merely be the *best* method of bringing some relief to the Russian front, it was virtually the *only* practicable operation for 1942. On 8 July, therefore, Churchill signalled to Roosevelt that Gymnast 'is the true Second Front of 1942'. Eight days later General Marshall, Admiral Ernest King, the Chief of US Naval Operations, and Hopkins were sent to Britain by Roosevelt with instructions to reach agreement with their opposite numbers on operational plans for 1942 and 1943. When the Americans found that the British were firmly of the opinion that the sole practicable option for 1942 was Gynmast, they only accepted it with the greatest reluctance and insisted that, if it were undertaken, there would be no question of mounting Round-Up in 1943. One of the crucial points made by Churchill during these considerations was that the assault on North Africa should *not* be regarded as predudicial to the invasion of Western Europe. Nor should it be seen as a defensive move, but as one which would yield new potential for attack. In a minute notable for the accuracy of its forecast as to how Allied strategy would develop in the next two years, Churchill wrote:

The flank attack may become the main attack, and the main attack a holding operation in the early stages. Our second front will in fact comprise both the Atlantic and Mediterranean coasts of Europe, and we can push either right-handed, left-handed, or both-handed, as our resources and circumstances permit. Meanwhile, we shall pin down the largest number possible of enemy troops opposite *Bolero* . . . In so vast and complex a scene above all it is specially desirable to have options open which allow of strategic manoeuvres according as events unfold.

Although, as was noted in Chapter 1, the Mediterranean strategy became one, not of manoeuvre, but of attrition, nevertheless in this minute Churchill put his finger on one of the key issues of strategic priorities which was to confront Allied military counsels during the coming years. When Roosevelt' advisers reported back to him about the British position and the reasoning behind it, Roosevelt gave instructions that Torch – the new codename for Gymnast – should be carried out as soon as possible. Thus it was decided that the second front to be opened by a joint Anglo-American effort was to be in North Africa.

It was to North Africa also that Churchill was shortly to go in order to see for himself how the battle against Rommel could be won – he was not satisfied with Auchinleck's apparent inability to finish the campaign off – and when he heard on 30 July that Sir Archibald Clark Kerr, the British Ambassador in Moscow,[1] recommended an early meeting between himself and Stalin, he determined to fly to Cairo as soon as possible and go on from there to meet the Soviet leader in Moscow. While, at this time, he still regarded the cross-Channel operation as the most important one, and was anxious that the bombing of Germany should be intensified in order to prepare for it, he was strengthened by the knowledge that when he met Stalin, he would not only be able to review the war situation as a whole, but also explain the plans he had made with Roosevelt for 'offensive action in 1942'. Churchill was greatly admired by all those close to him for his courage and determination in undertaking such a journey at such a time. Even the King wrote to him, stressing in particular that the Prime Minister's planned meetings with Stalin and Smuts[2] and the deliberations they would have 'may be the turning point of the war'. The King urged Churchill to take great care of himself, and added how delighted he would be when he was safely back home. Churchill replied with his customary dutiful courtesy, noting that Auchinleck's proposed delay in mounting another

[1] Cripps had been brought back from Moscow in February, and appointed Lord Privy Seal and Leader of the House of Commons.
[2] Smuts, Prime Minister of South Africa since 1939, made frequent visits to Europe and North Africa (in which theatre South African troops were engaged). Churchill consulted him frequently, and on this occasion had arranged a meeting while he was in Cairo.

offensive shocked him, and that the prospects for 'a joyous meeting' in Russia were 'meagre', but he hoped to smooth things over, and was in no doubt about the ultimate outcome.

Churchill, accompanied by Brooke, among others, arrived in Cairo on 4 August, and instantly set about the task of finding out for himself what was wrong and what needed to be done to put it right. Next day he visited the Alamein position. After touring the front, talking to troops and discussing the situation with Auchinleck and Lieutenant-General William ('Strafer') Gott, the commander of XIII Corps, he concluded that wherever the fault lay, it was not with the troops or their equipment. After further exchanges on the following day with Field Marshal Smuts, Richard Casey (the Minister of State in the Middle East), and the CIGS, he made up his mind. In a signal to the Deputy Prime Minister, Attlee, Churchill recommended 'drastic and immediate changes' in the Middle East Command, including a redrawing of boundaries so that the 'Middle East' included Egypt, Palestine and Syria, but not Persia or Iraq. Auchinleck was to go and Alexander would become Commander-in-Chief; Montgomery, by now a lieutenant-general, was to have succeeded Alexander in command of Operation Torch and Gott to have taken over Eighth Army, but the latter was tragically killed when his aircraft was shot down on 7 August. On General Brooke's strong advice, therefore, Churchill sent another message to Attlee:

CIGS decisively recommends Montgomery for Eighth Army. Smuts and I feel this post must be filled at once. Pray send him by special plane at the earliest moment. Advise me when he will arrive.

Before Montgomery did arrive Churchill found time to write to his wife, describing his tour of the Eighth Army, commenting on its being 'baffled and bewildered by its defeats' and suffering from 'a kind of apathy and exhaustion. . . which only new strong hands, and above all the gleam of victory can dispel'. He refers to Alexander's 'grand capacities for war' and to Montgomery as 'a highly competent, daring and energetic soldier, who if disagreeable to those about him was equally so to the enemy'. Auchinleck, he says, has made bad choices of subordinates and 'I am making a thorough clearance'.[1]

In appointing Alexander and Montgomery, Churchill not only got new

---

[1] It is pleasing to note that among the 'very fine fellows in the field' he includes those two great 12th Lancers, Major-General Lumsden and Major-General (later General Sir) Richard McCreery. He invites some of his son's friends to dinner, including the founder of the SAS, Major (later Colonel) David Stirling, Randolph having served for a time as an intelligence officer on the General Staff in Cairo.

strong hands, but a battle-winning team. Both men got on well with Churchill, and their relationship with him and with each other, together with their roles in planning and fighting battles, were important elements in the whole campaign that followed. Nigel Nicolson summed up the relationship between the two generals when he wrote that Alexander

> decided that his subordinate, Montgomery, must take first place not only in planning and fighting the coming battle, but in public esteem. He deliberately effaced himself. Montgomery had a flair for arousing adulation, and enjoyed it; Alexander was embarrassed by it, and was incapable of jealousy. Eighth Army, he felt, must identify with a single commander, and Montgomery's self-confidence and authority would grow with his success and fame. So Alexander gave him his chance, never countermanding his orders, rarely suggesting an element in his plan, and supported him by every possible means, political, administrative and psychological, to achieve their common object, the defeat of Rommel. It was a remarkable demonstration of his self-control.

Churchill was not to see the profound effect that Montgomery was to have on Eighth Army until after his return from Moscow, but before going there he gave Alexander a directive which emphasized in his own words how imperative were 'simplicity of task and singleness of aim'. The document, dated 10 August, read:

1. Your prime and main duty will be to take or destroy at the earliest opportunity the German-Italian Army commanded by Field-Marshal Rommel, together with all its supplies and establishments in Egypt and Libya.

2. You will discharge or cause to be discharged such other duties as pertain to your Command, without prejudice to the task described in paragraph 1, which must be considered paramount in His Majesty's interests.

At this stage in the war the Wehrmacht would have welcomed a directive from its Supreme Commander which represented both simplicity of task and singleness of aim. But on the Eastern Front Hitler was providing them with neither one nor the other; quite the contrary, in fact. The German offensive in the east had begun on 28 June, at the time when Eighth Army was withdrawing to Alamein. Army Group B under Bock was directed on Stalingrad with General Hermann Hoth's Fourth Panzer Army and Paulus's Sixth Army; Army Group A under List was headed south-east through the Caucasus with Baku as its final objective. Three weeks later, when Hitler confidently asserted – so well were the advances going – that the Russian was finished, General Halder, ever cautious, ever circumspect, was moved to concede that it looked uncommonly like it. In fact, Hitler had already made the tactical blunder which was to ensure that the Russian was *not* finished. It was the very success, initially, of this offensive that led him into the same sort of error of which he had been guilty a year earlier.

Instead of sticking to his plan, whereby the whole weight of Army Group B should concentrate on establishing the 'block' at Stalingrad before deciding what Hoth's Fourth Panzer Army would do next (and had he stuck to the plan it is probable that Stalingrad would have fallen, for the Russians would have had far less time to strengthen the city's defences), Hitler diverted Fourth Panzer Army before the Stalingrad battle was joined, diverted it, moreover, to help Army Group A which at that time did not need help, and then, as resistance at Stalingrad stiffened, redirected it there when it was already too late.[1] For Hitler it was the old story – no patient concentration, either of mind or material, on one objective at a time, but a wild dilettantism at its worst, dashing forward for all objectives at once, grossly exaggerating his own strength and the enemy's weakness, doubling the aim whilst halving the forces needed to achieve each, and by doing so, achieving neither. Churchill might have been impatient with his field commanders, but he did not countermand their orders.

By September the struggle for Stalingrad was raging and the thrust to the Caucasus had been halted by the Russians short of the main oilfields. The Wehrmacht's tide was as high as it had ever been or ever would be. Henceforth it would ebb. Yet Hitler, who in August had moved from his East Prussian headquarters to a new one, 'Werewolf', at Vinnitsa in the Ukraine, urged his armies on, sacked Halder and appointed General Kurt Zeitzler in his place. Halder had consistently protested against what he regarded as wastage of men in the battle for Stalingrad, and against its taking on a mystic importance for Hitler quite at odds with the price it was exacting. When Halder recommended that General Walther Model's Ninth Army in the centre should be withdrawn, Hitler lost control of himself. 'You always seem to make the same suggestion – retreat!' he furiously accused the Army Chief of Staff, adding that he demanded the same hardness from his commanders as from the troops. Halder was unwise enough to point out that fine soldiers were dying unnecessarily because the only sensible tactical decision was denied them by the Führer. At this Hitler resorted to shouting insults: 'What, Herr Halder – you who were as chairbound in the Great War as in this – what do you think you can teach me

---

[1] This chopping and changing brings to mind d'Erlon's Reserve Corps two days before Waterloo, which marched and counter-marched between Ligny and Quatre Bras, unable to influence either of those battles.

about the troops! You, who haven't even got a wound stripe on your uniform!' In his mould-breaking book, *The Face of Battle*, John Keegan commented on this sort of behaviour by the Supreme Commander: 'It is ironic to reflect that the taunt thrown into the faces of so many highly trained German Great General Staff officers, excluded by official policy from service in the trenches [during the Great War], by Hitler, ex-runner of the 16th Bavarian Reserve Regiment – that he knew more about the realities of war than they – had after all a coarse grain of truth to it.' Halder was not the only one to be sacked. List went, too, because of his failure to overcome the increasing enemy resistance in the Caucasus. Even the able Jodl, Chief of Operations at OKW, got the rough edge of Hitler's tongue when he pointed out that List had simply been carrying out the Supreme Commander's orders.

August 1942 was, on balance, a better month for Churchill than it was for Hitler. One of the latter's preoccupations at this time, quite apart from the main theatre, Russia, was Western Europe. 'What is the use of victories in Russia,' he had demanded of Halder, 'if I lose western Europe?' Not that he had any fear of losing it that year, but 1943 might be different, and after studying maps and photographs of the Channel and Atlantic coasts of France, his apprehension increased. Summoning his advisers to the Werewolf headquarters on 13 August, the Führer announced his decision to build the Atlantic Wall, which was to be ready by April 1943, and with no cost spared: 'Our most costly substance is the German man. The blood these fortifications will spare is worth the billions.' The Atlantic Wall would be based on thousands of bunkers, decoys, minefields, wire, gun-sites, heavy machine-guns, tanks and anti-tank guns. There was no denying Hitler's *Vorhersehung*, for even in August 1942 his depiction of what was to happen nearly two years later, was, as David Irving recorded, remarkable:

> The invasion proper would be preceded during the night by waves of parachute and glider sabotage troops with orders to disrupt the transport and signal systems and to disable headquarters units; next would come wave after wave of heavy bombers, saturation-bombing the invasion defences. The invasion would follow at dawn, with three or four thousand landing craft and total enemy air superiority . . .

But Hitler maintained that the Atlantic Wall would be a match for all this. He went on to say: 'If only the soldiers had the say in Britain, this operation they are peddling around as the Second Front would not take place. But as lunatics like that drunkard Churchill and Maccabeans and numskulls like that brilliantined dandy Eden are at the tiller, we have to be prepared for just about anything.'

The principal target of Hitler's invective, however, was having a more sympathetic reception to his ideas about the Second Front during his first meeting with Stalin in Moscow on 12 August. Churchill has explained how Stalin reacted when he outlined to him the Allied plans for landing in North-West Africa, Operation Torch:

> I described the military advantages of freeing the Mediterranean where still another front could be opened. In September we must win in Egypt, and in October in North Africa, all the time holding the enemy in Northern France [by the concentration of Allied forces in Britain]. If we could end the year in possession of North Africa we could threaten the belly of Hitler's Europe . . . I emphasized that we wanted to take the strain off the Russians. If we attempted that in Northern France we should meet with a rebuff. If we tried in North Africa we had a good chance of victory, and then we could help in Europe . . . Stalin seemed suddenly to grasp the strategic advantages of *Torch*. He recounted four main reasons for it. First, it would hit Rommel in the back; second, it would overawe Spain; third, it would produce fighting between Germans and Frenchmen in France, and fourth, it would expose Italy to the whole brunt of the war.

Churchill records that he was deeply impressed by Stalin's statement. Not all the exchanges between the two leaders were so agreeable, however. During their second meeting Stalin protested in strong terms about the Allied unwillingness to launch a cross-Channel operation in 1942, and even questioned the British determination to fight the Germans, referring in particular to the ill-fated PQ17 convoy, when, according to Stalin, the Royal Navy 'turned tail and fled from the enemy. You British are afraid of fighting. You should not think the Germans are supermen. You will have to fight sooner or later. You cannot win a war without fighting.' This was no language to use to a man like Churchill, who replied with such spirit and at such length that, as Averell Harriman remembered, 'the interpreter got so enthralled by Winston's speech' – which described amongst other things what the British had done in the year when they had fought on alone – 'that he put down his pencil,' and although Stalin had clearly not received a translation of all Churchill had wanted him to hear, the Soviet leader's mood changed, and with a laugh he conceded that it was the spirit, rather than the words, which mattered. Churchill had two more meetings with Stalin and was treated to some fairly lavish Russian hospitality. During their talks he was reassured by Stalin's confidence that the Russians would hold firm in the Causcasus, while Stalin appeared to warm to the idea of the Torch operation for North-West Africa. In commenting on these encounters, A.J.P. Taylor stresses that with their common aim of defeating Hitler, the two men, despite their differences, had too much common sense to quarrel seriously, although he casts doubt on Churchill's hope that he 'had established a genuine personal relationship with Stalin'. The real point was that by his undertaking such a broad spectrum of travels and consultations – America, the Middle East, Russia; Roosevelt, Smuts, Stalin – Churchill was uniquely placed to influence Allied strategic decisions and enable Britain (in a phrase dear to a recent Foreign Secretary, Douglas Hurd) to punch above her weight. He himself was satisfied with his Moscow visit, was convinced that it had been his duty personally to convey the disappointing news that there would be no second front in Europe in 1942 (although he did inform Stalin about an intended cross-Channel raid shortly to be executed), and in telegraphing to Attlee urged that Torch, whose strategic potential Stalin had instantly recognized, should be 'driven forward with superhuman energy on both sides of the ocean'.

In *Road to Victory*, Martin Gilbert explains that at this point Churchill was able to envisage how the war would now be waged against Germany and her European allies. A cross-Channel operation, (of which the timing would be fixed by himself, Roosevelt and their military advisers) would aim at Hitler's defeat, but before that the entire North African coast must come under Allied control – this was the 'focal point of Anglo-American efforts for the remaining four and a half months of 1942'. Meanwhile Russia must be supplied both by sea to the north and by land via Persia, and the bombing of Germany intensified. 'Churchill's task was to ensure that the Chiefs of Staff and the commanders in the field worked in harmony; that the essential war supplies flowed in the quantities needed to the areas which needed them; that all secondary operations agreed upon by the Chiefs of Staff were given the support they needed; and, above all, that in all matters of war policy, he and Roosevelt remained in the closest contact and accord.' It was a task which he was singularly well qualified to carry out.

Although on his return to Cairo on 17 August Churchill was to be greatly encouraged by the change in atmosphere brought about by Alexander and Montgomery, he was also to learn that one of the 'secondary operations' (the cross-Channel raid he had mentioned to Stalin) – in fact, the Dieppe raid – had gone badly awry. The Prime Minister received this information while visiting Montgomery at his headquarters on 19 August (the day of the raid) accompanied by Brooke and Alexander. For the time being he had to be content with Mountbatten's report that in spite of heavy losses – out of 5,000 troops which took part in the Dieppe raid, 'a reconnaissance in force', some 1,000 were killed and 2,000 taken prisoner – the morale of those returning was high and valuable lessons had been learned. Later, however, it became clear that planning, equipment, security and inter-service co-operation had been faulty, and would have to be put right before the great venture of invasion. Yet Churchill's two days with Montgomery, visiting the front line, talking to troops and senior officers, greatly cheered him, and he was able to send a confident report to Attlee and the War Cabinet. The new command arrangements had transformed the whole scene:

Alexander ordered Montgomery to prepare to take the offensive and meanwhile to hold all positions and Montgomery issued an invigorating directive to his commanders . . . The highest alacrity and activity prevails . . . I am satisfied that we have lively, confident, resolute men in command, working together as an admirable team under leaders of the highest military quality. Everything has been done and is being done that is possible, and it is now my duty to return home, as I have no part to play in the battle which must be left to those in whom we place our trust.

When it came to the Battle of El Alamein, however, and before the victory which Churchill so passionately longed and strove for had been won, he became so agitated over its tardiness in coming that he did *not* leave it to those in whom he had placed his trust. Indeed, so significant was this turning point in Great Britain's fortunes and so imminent was Rommel's attempt to pre-empt it – for when Churchill left Cairo on 23 August the Battle of Alam el Halfa was but a week away – that it is worth taking a closer look at the two principal actors on stage, Rommel, commanding the Panzerarmee, and Montgomery, commanding Eighth Army. They were, David Irving has maintained, in some ways alike. 'Both are lonely men,' he wrote, 'with more enemies than friends among their fellow generals; both are high-handed and arrogant professional soldiers devoid of all intellectual pursuits; both are awkward and insubordinate officers in harness but become magnificent and original battle commanders in their own right; neither smokes nor touches strong drink; both have a passion for winter sports and physical fitness.' They both excelled at public relations, employed a string of young, personable liaison officers, adopted idiosyncratic dress. Yet their differences were just as marked. Rommel's attitude to war is a chivalrous one, Montgomery simply wants to kill Germans; Rommel leads from the front, Montgomery retires to his caravan; Rommel is brilliant at the fast-flowing battle of manoeuvre, Montgomery's *chef d'oeuvre* is the set-piece battle of attrition; Rommel has an uncanny *Fingerspitzengefühl* (instinct, intuition), Montgomery finds out what is happening by dispatching relays of liaison officers round the battlefield – and has, of course, the priceless benefit of the Ultra signals telling him what Rommel is up to and what his difficulties are.

When the two men found themselves to be opponents, the fortunes of one were declining, those of the other about to ascend sharply. At one time Auchinleck and his subordinates had been so mesmerized by Rommel that the former had found it necessary to issue an order in which he required his commanders to make it plain to all that Rommel was nothing more than 'an ordinary German general'. Yet this was just what Rommel was not. Others, like Bock, Leeb, Fritsch, Rundstedt – these men were cast in the classic German General Staff mould, but not Rommel. Even Hitler observed of his commander in the Western Desert that 'the mere name suddenly begins to acquire the value of several divisions'. The truth was that he did have a magic that others did not have; beyond that, to the British soldiers he had come to represent the Axis forces in Africa as a whole. When these soldiers talked of 'Rommel' doing this or that, they meant the combined might of the enemy's armies ranged against them. Yet for Rommel the Alamein encounters with Montgomery were battles without hope, for in everything except courage and skill, the odds were heavily weighted against the Panzerarmee.

Of course, Montgomery had his own style, too. His various eccentricities – the two-badged beret, the bush hat with numerous regimental insignia, the handing-out of cigarettes to his troops, the photograph of Rommel in his caravan (in order to read his mind, presumably, whereas in fact Ultra was doing this) – all these public-relations gimmicks were mere window-dressing. What mattered about Montgomery was his clarity, his conviction, his confidence, together with his thoroughness and his determination to see an unromantic, slogging battle of attrition through to an inevitable conclusion – victory for *his* army. It was by mastering the mechanics of the set-piece battle that Montgomery set the seal of his authority on the Eighth Army, the Prime Minister and the country. His sense of certainty, his simple eloquence, the obvious grip he exerted over his subordinates and, through them, over the soldiers, his flamboyant press conferences and personal signals to Churchill – all these things illustrated the power of his leadership. Some disliked what they saw as vanity and showmanship, but on the whole people loved it, from the private soldier right up to the Prime Minister. It was just the sort of behaviour that Churchill admired and understood. It was the way in which he himself had behaved in 1915 at Antwerp. Long before, in the 1890s, he had been the most bumptious subaltern in the British Army and his sympathy now went out to the most bumptious general of that same army. The signals which Montgomery sent direct to the Prime Minister were in the same vein as Churchill's own telegrams during the Boer War – and what is more, Montgomery's messages made excellent copy for the Prime Minister's announcements in the House of Commons.

Yet even in Parliament Churchill paid tribute to the great qualities of Montgomery's adversary. As the days of August 1942 advanced, the shadows were lengthening for Rommel and the Panzerarmee. They still had not received the fuel and ammunition necessary for a successful operation, while

Montgomery's army was daily growing stronger and more confident. Nor, for Rommel, was the news from that other front in Russia, the front that would decide the fate of empires, reassuring. On the eve of his coming attack, he confided to his doctor that his decision to go ahead with the battle was the hardest he had yet taken. 'Either we manage to reach the Suez Canal, and the army in Russia succeeds in reaching the Caucasus, or . . .' He indicated with a gesture that the alternative could mean only – defeat. It is perhaps fitting, therefore, to finish off the Alamein battle here before turning to Torch and Hitler's reaction to it, and to what was happening on the Russian front.

As has been said, Montgomery enjoyed numerous advantages before the battle started – great superiority in weapons, men and supplies, a powerful Desert Air Force, the incalculably good fortune of Ultra intelligence, the total backing of his political and military chiefs, and plenty of *time* for preparation. It was hardly surprising, therefore, that when Rommel launched the Afrika Korps with a last, fine, careless rapture at the strong, deep, ready defences of Alam el Halfa on 31 August, Montgomery easily drove him off, commenting that next time it would be his service, with the score one-love in his favour. He loved sporting metaphors, and boasted that he would next hit the Germans for six out of Africa. It took him – aided by the Anglo-American invasion of French North Africa – about seven months to do so. Montgomery's 'service' began on the night of 23 October with the Battle of El Alamein. It lasted about twelve days, and although the course of the fighting was not without hiccups for the British, Rommel's Panzerarmee was simply crushed by its enemy's weight. Montgomery's master plan succeeded in the end because he had sufficient reserves to allow him to vary it. It was, however, during one of the Eighth Army Commander's pauses to think again that, on the morning of 29 October, Churchill, who suspected that the battle was losing momentum and petering out, summoned the CIGS and, as Brooke recalled, greeted him with a storm of reproach:

What, he asked, was *my* Monty doing now, allowing the battle to peter out? (Monty was always my Monty when he was out of favour.) He had done nothing now for the last three days, and now he was withdrawing troops from the front. Why had he told us he would be through in seven days if all he intended to do was to fight a half-hearted battle? Had we not got a single general who could win one single battle? etc, etc. When he stopped to regain his breath I asked him what had suddenly influenced him to arrive at these conclusions . . . The strain of the battle had had its effect on me, the anxiety was growing more and more intense every day and my temper was on edge . . . He flared up and asked whether he was not entitled to consult whomever he wished. To which I replied he certainly could provided he did not let those who knew little about military matters upset his equilibrium. He continued by stating that he was dissatisfied with the course of the battle and would hold a Chiefs of Staff meeting under his chairmanship at 12.30 to be attended by some of his colleagues.

Happily, at the meeting Brooke with unexpected but welcome support of Smuts, succeeded in convincing Churchill that the battle was proceeding satisfactorily, and that Montgomery was creating reserves for the next phase of the attack. Churchill thereupon sent Alexander a signal congratulating him and Montgomery on their achievement and urging them 'to shake the life out of Rommel's army and to make this a fight to the finish,' adding how timely a decisive success at Alamein would be in view of the forthcoming Allied landings in North-West Africa. As it turned out, it was not precisely a fight to the finish, but Eighth Army at length broke through Rommel's defences, and on 4 November Alexander was able to send a signal to Churchill saying that 'a severe defeat had been inflicted on the enemy's German and Italian forces under Rommel's command in Egypt'. The front had been broken, British armour was through, operating in the enemy's rear areas and harassing his retreating forces. Churchill was overjoyed, signalled the good news to Roosevelt – 'I feel sure you will regard this as a good prelude to *Torch*' – and sent his praises to Alexander and 'your brilliant lieutenant', proposing also 'to ring the bells all over Britian for the first time this war' at an appropriate moment, as recommended by Alexander. It is perhaps impossible to exaggerate the significance of the victory at El Alamein for Churchill. Although compared with the carnage of Stalingrad it was a relatively small affair, for the British it was all-important, a stepping stone to victory and an enormous boost to morale after so many previous disappointments. It was the turning point of Britain's fortunes, the redemption of all that Churchill had been striving for; and from this time forth, as he himself subsequently recorded, victory was to be the order of the day.

It was to be a turning point, too, in the fortunes of Rommel. When he realized on the evening of 2 November that the British preponderance in tanks and guns, together with their overwhelming air superiority, would mean that they were bound to break through, he decided that if he were to disengage successfully and withdraw to the Fuka position, he must get the retirement under way at once. His signal to Hitler's headquarters said as much, yet as he prepared for a general withdrawal, 'the greatest strategic genius of all time' took a hand in the affair. At about 1pm on 3 November, Rommel received the following message from Hitler:

With me the entire German people is watching your heroic defensive battle in Egypt, with rightful confidence in your leadership qualities and the courage of your German and Italian troops. In your situation there can be no thought but of persevering, of yielding not one yard, and of hurling every gun and every fighting man into the battle. Considerable air reinforcements are being transferred over the coming days to Commander-in-Chief South. The Duce and the commando supremo [Italian High Command] will also do their utmost to furnish you with the means to keep up the fight.

Despite his superiority the enemy must also be at the end of his strength. It would not be the first time in history that the stronger will has triumphed over the stronger battalions of an enemy. To your troops therefore you can offer no other path than that leading to Victory or Death.

During the next year or two Hitler was to become very prodigal with exhortations about not giving up a yard or an inch, about fighting with every gun and man available, about the alternative of victory or death – and it was all greatly to the benefit of the Allied cause. In this particular instance, however, Hitler's crass interference did not greatly affect the issue. Rommel, of course, unlike German generals on the Russian front, enjoyed the incalculable advantage of not having Führer headquarters just behind him. He was able to disobey orders by virtue of the huge distances which separated him from OKW. When the critical moment arrived he took full advantage of this separation. Yet Hitler was so angry at the delay between the arrival of Rommel's signal announcing his intention to withdraw – the latter had in fact already issued his orders for this move back – that he went through the familiar routine of bellowing at Keitel, sacked General Walter Warlimont, Jodl's deputy, and threatened the duty officer, whose fault it was that Hitler had not seen Rommel's signal as soon as it arrived, with instant death 'if you don't tell me the absolute truth'. Hitler also interrogated Rommel himself by radio, in particular asking when the withdrawal had begun. The Field-Marshal's reply – 'In the latter part of the night' – made it appear that had Hitler been shown the signal instantly, he could have intervened effectively to stop it. But Rommel's report had followed, not preceded, his decision to withdraw, so that Hitler's fury was unnecessary, as well as futile. That Rommel got away with such defiance showed the extent to which his name alone counted in public esteem, and caused Hitler to hesitate before taking the sort of disciplinary action – dismissal or even death – that other erring commanders had received. Although on receiving Hitler's 'Victory or Death' signal, some half-hearted attempts to hold existing positions were made, when both Field Marshal Albert Kesselring, the overall commander of German forces in the Mediterranean, and Rommel made it clear on the morning of 4 November that because there was no longer a battle front, there was no alternative but to revert to mobile warfare to contest the British advance until a defensive line at Fuka could be established, Hitler gave his reluctant and aggrieved consent.

Despite Churchill's instructions that Alexander and Montgomery were to 'take or destroy' Rommel's army 'at the earliest possible moment', and despite Hitler's interference, which if his orders had been followed, would have greatly assisted the British in carrying out these instructions, the hard core of Rommel's army got away. Quite apart from Montgomery's unwillingness to risk a pell-mell battle of manoeuvre with the Afrika Korps, a type of battle which had so disastrously puzzled his predecessors – for he preferred to plan certainties rather than take risks – both he and Alexander knew that the Anglo-American landings at the other end of the Mediterranean, which were to take place on 8 November, would, provided they were successful, seal Rommel's fate anyway. What no one could have foreseen, however, was Hitler's reaction to Torch.

Churchill's vision of Operation Torch was very different from that of his American allies; indeed, it was something even at odds with that of his own Chiefs of Staff. He looked upon it not simply as a kind of blocking operation in closing the ring, but as a prelude to the actual business of assaulting Hitler's *Festung Europa*. His hopes and plans were greatly stimulated by the fact that Torch itself went well – initially. Landings at Casablanca, Oran and Algiers were made on 8 November by Anglo-American troops under US General Dwight D. Eisenhower, – no small achievement for 110 cargo vessels and troopships with more than 200 warships to have run the gauntlet of enemy U-boats and within range of enemy aircraft. Resistance by the Vichy French forces was, at most, light: Algiers had been occupied the same day; Oran surrendered on 9 November and Casablanca two days later. The next task for Eisenhower's forces would be to drive on to Tunis, but any idea that this could be done quickly was put out of court by Hitler's violent and prompt reaction. His first comment, recorded Albert Speer, when the huge Allied fleet was reported moving eastward in the Mediterranean, was that this was the largest landing operation that had ever taken place in the history of the world, a remark spoken 'in a tone of respect, perhaps taking pride that he was the cause of enterprises of such magnitude'. Once he knew the expedition's destination, however, he acted swiftly. The occupation of southern France was rapidly effected – and led to the scuttling of the French fleet at Toulon – and Hitler dispatched troops in large numbers to Tunis. By the end of November 15,000 German soldiers were there, including highly experienced and skilled parachute, panzer and panzer grenadier regiments, together with the new, formidable Tiger tank, mounting the renowned 88mm gun. General Baron Jürgen von Arnim took command of the German and Italian divisions there on 8 December, and it was to be five months before the Allies captured Tunis and so made themselves masters of the North African shores.

Churchill's reactions to the success of Torch were more measured than

Hitler's. Having informed General de Gaulle, who took the news well, of the invasion of French territory, he then sent a telegram of congratulation to General Marshall, adding the shrewd comment that they would all of them find success 'not less puzzling though more agreeable' than what had gone before. Next day, 9 November, he composed a paper on strategy for 1943 in which he deprecated the Chiefs' of Staff idea that the next steps should be to occupy Sicily and Sardinia, proposing instead that apart from pinning down as many of the enemy as possible in northern France and the Low Countries by continuing with their preparations for an invasion, the Allies should attack Italy or southern France. When North Africa was securely in their hands, Churchill maintained, the Allies must undertake a 'large-scale offensive on the underbelly of the Axis in 1943'. They had to get on to the mainland of Europe and fight the enemy there.

On the following day, in a memorable speech at the Lord Mayor's Mansion House luncheon, Churchill reminded his audience that he had never promised anything but blood, tears, toil, and sweat, but went on to say that he was able to point to something new – victory. Referring to the Eighth Army's victory and the initial success of Torch, however, he warned: 'This is not the end. It is not even the beginning of the end. But it is, perhaps, the end of the beginning.' He added that whereas Britain's purpose in entering the war had been essentially one of duty and honour, yet 'We mean to hold our own. I have not become the King's First Minister in order to preside over the liquidation of the British Empire.' Next day in the House of Commons, Churchill was also able to remind Members that since the vote of censure four months earlier, much had been done in the way of planning and preparation so that effective action, first defensive, then offensive, against the enemy could be taken. He reminded them also that when it came to prodding people into action, he was the prodder. His speech was loudly cheered, and as John Martin, his Private Secretary since 1940, noted: 'Altogether it has been a triumphant and most cheering week for the PM.'

Meanwhile, the next moves in the execution of Anglo-American strategy still had to be agreed. During the second week of November Roosevelt and Churchill were frequently in touch by telegram and through their respective advisers. The main question was how to exploit Allied success in North Africa, though it was to some extent premature, for success in Tunis was still some months away. Nevertheless, certain options were put forward, and Churchill found himself very much in agreement with Roosevelt's ideas about moving forward to Sicily, Sardinia, Italy, Greece, and he most particularly welcomed the President's wish to obtain Turkey's support, something Churchill had long sought. (It was at this time, 15 November, that he at last authorized the ringing of church bells throughout Britain in celebration of the Egyptian victory.) He also sent a memorandum to the British Chiefs of Staff, with a copy to Roosevelt, in which he endorsed the latter's strategic concept. After clearing the North African shore of the Mediterranean, the Allies should strike at the underbelly of the Axis, with Sicily and Sardinia as 'obvious objectives'. Moreover, heavy bombing attacks could, he said, be launched against Italy 'to make her feel the weight of the war'; indeed, he regarded Sicily 'as by far the greatest prize'. As always the priorities of employing sea power cast their influence over all these considerations. Transatlantic convoys could, now that Torch's shipping requirements were reduced, be restored to their former volume, although this pointed to another vital need if Allied strategy were to prevail, for U-boat sinkings in November 1942 had risen to unprecedented heights – more than 700,000 tons. Fortunately the breaking of the new U-boat Enigma code in the following month eased the situation, but it was clear that the Battle of the Atlantic still had to be won. But in summing up his views on how to follow up the North African campaign, Churchill, in another memorable phrase, made it clear that the theatre was to be 'a spring-board and not a sofa'.

It would not, however, be either of those until its conquest was complete, and the troops that Hitler was pouring into Tunisia were imposing a considerable delay on that conquest. Elsewhere, Hitler was taking the very decisions that would ensure that countless more German soldiers – the same 'substance' which he himself had described as most costly – were sacrificed to his unwillingness to recognize military realities, for the Russians were preparing a shock for the German Army at Stalingrad from which it was never really to recover. This had its beginning on 19 November, and within two days the armies of General Vatutin and General Eremenko, advancing respectively from the north and south, had joined hands at Kalach, encircling the entire German Sixth Army of some 300,000 men. By 23 November Hitler was back at his East Prussian headquarters to hear the unwelcome advice from General Kurt Zeitzler, who had replaced Halder as Army Chief of Staff, and General von Weichs, the army group commander, that unless the Sixth Army was withdrawn, it was doomed. This appeal was echoed the same evening by the commander of Sixth Army himself, General von Paulus. Hitler would not hear of it, however: 'We are not budging from the Volga!' He had been right to stand firm in December 1941, and he would prove that he was right again a year later. It might just have happened this way had not the drive from the south to relieve Stalingrad by Field Marshal von Manstein, commanding the newly formed Army Group Don, been checked by General Rodion Malinovsky, and had not the Italian Eighth Army, responsible for the Don sector to the north-west of the city, simply collapsed. This event did not make things easier for Ciano, who visited Hitler at his headquarters on 18 December to suggest, at the Duce's behest, that if 1943 were to be the year in which the Allies would mount attacks in both Southern and Western Europe, a political 'accommodation' with Russia might be worth considering. The Führer brushed this suggestion aside, saying he would never agree to stripping the Eastern Front in order to prop up positions in the Mediterranean; later he instructed Admiral Wilhelm Canaris, head of the Abwehr, (the Intelligence Bureau of OKW), 'to keep an eye on Italy' for possible signs of defection.

Hitler was now playing a losing game. Although the war would still go on for two and a half years, he was about to throw away a quarter of a million soldiers at Stalingrad, and a similar number in Tunisia. On all fronts he had been stopped. The strategic initiative would never return, despite the launching of a few more desperate offensives.

> It had been a remarkable career [wrote Alan Bullock] while it lasted. At the moment when the tide turned in the autumn of 1942 Hitler was undisputed master of the greater part of continental Europe, with his armies threatening the Volga, the Caucasus, and the Nile. For the man who had begun by peddling third-rate sketches in the back-streets of Vienna this was no small achievement. But now the price had to be paid for the methods of treachery and violence by which it had been accomplished – and it was relentlessly exacted.

Hitler's War Directive No 47, dated 28 December 1942, so different in character from those which had gone before, shows at once that from 1943 onwards Germany was on the strategic defensive: 'The situation in the Mediterranean makes it possible that an attack may be made in the foreseeable future on Crete and on German and Italian bases in the Aegean Sea and the Balkan peninsula.' This sentence sets the tone. The directive is full of the word 'defence', and of phrases about preparing for 'defensive battles'. Thus Hitler was no longer in a position to ask himself where he would strike next. He was compelled to ask himself where the Allies would strike next.

It was a question which the Allies were constantly asking themselves. Although in early December Churchill was still hoping it would be possible to launch a cross-Channel operation by August 1943, slow Allied progress in Tunis, coupled with the view of the Chiefs of Staff that insufficient numbers of both troops and landing craft from the USA could be mustered in time, convinced him that what became known as the 'Mediterranean strategy' was the sounder alternative. The Joint Planning Staff paper, on which the Chiefs of Staff based their view, set out the choice with admirable brevity:

> The prizes open to the Allies in the Mediterranean in 1943 are very great. They include the severe reduction of German air-power, the reopening of

[367]

the short sea route [to India via the Suez Canal], the denial to Germany of oil, chrome and other minerals, the elimination of one of the Axis partners and the opening of the Balkans.

If we decide to exploit the position which we have gained, our first object should be to induce the Italians to lay down their arms everywhere; our next should be directed against the Balkans.

Unless Italy collapses far more quickly than we expect, this exploitation must, however, be at the expense of *Round-Up* in 1943.

We are therefore faced with the alternatives of:

(a) Concentrating resources in the United Kingdom for a *Round-Up* which may, in any event, be impracticable for 1943; and this at the cost of abandoning the great prizes open to us in the Mediterranean and of remaining inactive for many months during which Germany would recuperate;

or

(b) Pursuing the offensive in the Mediterranean with the knowledge that we shall only be able to assault Northern France next year if there is a pronounced decline in German fighting power. [This meant in effect that the cross-Channel operation would have to be postponed until 1944.]

We cannot have it both ways. In our view (b) is the correct strategy and will give the Russians more certain, and possibly even greater relief.

The controversy over this choice did not end even with the end of the war itself. Many years later John Grigg argued in *1943: The Victory That Never Was* that the cross-Channel invasion should have taken place in 1943, as the four prerequisites for landing successfully in France – air superiority, enough troops, shipping to carry them, and means to prevent the Germans concentrating against and eliminating an Allied beachhead – either existed or could have been created in 1943. But in making this highly questionable claim, Grigg overlooks the very commodity he believes the Allies could and should have saved – time. The choice between the two alternative operations was under discussion in December 1942; the troops needed for a 1943 invasion of France, together with their landing craft, could not have been released from Alexander's and Eisenhower's commands until after the conquest of North Africa, unless that conquest itself were to be jeopardized. Since victory in North Africa was not complete until May 1943, there would have been no time to move, train, equip and prepare for such an invasion in mid-1943 (launching the operation earlier or later in the year put it at risk from uncertain weather conditions). Moreover, with the Axis still powerful in the Mediterranean, one of the main purposes of conquering North Africa would have been forfeited. Even so distinguished a military historian as Michael Howard, never one to be uncritical of Allied strategy when such criticism was warranted, conceded that the strategy which was adopted was such that it still has to be shown that there was a better way of winning the war. In any event, the British Chiefs of Staff endorsed the Joint Planning Staff's views that the Mediterranean offensive should be pursued, and this paper became the brief for the next top-level round of Anglo-American consultations.

There still remained the matter of exactly *how* to pursue this offensive. An argument now sprang up as to whether to go for Sardinia or Sicily, once the North African coast had been cleared of Axis forces. This argument revolved around timings, ground forces required, the consequent demands on shipping and the question of air cover. It was also clear that the final clearing of Tunisia and the rest of North Africa was going to take much longer than had been hoped. Churchill was strongly in favour of an invasion of Sicily, codenamed Husky, as it alone 'gives a worthwhile prize, even if we have to wait till May. Moreover the PQ convoys [to Russia] can then be run regularly at least till the end of March.' It was agreed that these matters should be discussed by the two Allied leaders and their staffs at Casablanca in January 1943.

For security purposes, in any reference to the Casablanca Conference Roosevelt was to be known as Admiral Q. and Churchill as Mr P. Until they met, the policy of pursuing the offensive in the Mediterranean still had to receive a certificate of legitimacy. And since such a policy would have a profound effect on the future conduct of the war as a whole, it would be necessary, as Churchill put it, 'to mind their Ps and Qs'.

CHAPTER 8

1943 – Axeing the Axis

It's a thousand times easier to storm forward with an
army and gain victories, than to bring an army back in
an orderly condition after a reverse or a defeat.

ADOLF HITLER, December 1942

We start 1943 under conditions I would never have
dared hope for. Russia has held, Egypt for the present is
safe. There is hope of clearing North Africa of
Germans in the near future. The Mediterranean may be
partially opened up. Malta is safe for the present. We can
now work freely against Italy, and Russia is scoring
wonderful successes in Southern Russia.

GENERAL SIR ALAN BROOKE, 1 January 1943

Churchill flew to Casablanca on the evening of 12 January 1943. With him at
the conference were, among others, Brooke, Portal, Pound, Ismay and Dill, and
on the afternoon of 13 January work began to prepare the British position to
put to the Americans. Churchill's great purpose at Casablanca was to secure
agreement that Germany must be defeated first – that is, before Japan – and
that for the first part of 1943 the way to set about this was by a maximum effort
in the Mediterranean area, which would keep pressure on the Germans and
draw forces away from the Russian front. In addition, at this time Churchill was
still hoping that some kind of cross-Channel operation would be possible in
1943, as well as an offensive in Burma. The CIGS was more modest and more
realistic in his aims for the Casablanca Conference. He wanted three things –
endorsement of the 'Germany First' policy; agreement that for the present the
most effective way of attacking Germany would be through 'the medium of
Italy'; and that this last requirement would be best carried out by operations
against Sicily. In the event, Brooke got what he wanted.

In presenting the British position to the Combined Chiefs of Staff, one of the first points the CIGS made was about shipping. Unless the battle against the U-boats was won, he argued, the war itself could not be won. Only if the Allies could overcome the shortage of shipping would they be able to mount offensive operations. It was with their attacks on Allied shipping that the Germans still held the initiative; in other respects they were on the defensive. The soundness of Brooke's selection of the anti-U-boat campaign as being of the highest priority was endorsed by Hitler himself. As a result of Allied action to win the Atlantic battle by using aircraft carriers, long-range shore-based aircraft and radar-equipped surface escorts, the Germans lost eighty-seven U-boats between February and May 1943. So grave were these losses that the German Naval C-in-C, Doenitz, withdrew his submarines from the North Atlantic, although when Hitler heard of this he instantly ordered them back again. 'There can be no talk of let-up in submarine warfare,' he bellowed at Doenitz. 'The Atlantic is my first line of defence in the West.'

There was also the question of Germany's line of defence in the east, and it was clear that at Casablanca the Allies must decide how best to give Russia support. German pressure on the Soviet Union could to some extent be relieved by mounting amphibious operations in Europe, and in suggesting where, Brooke illustrated the extent to which military prudence dictated British strategic thinking, a prudence which the Americans frequently took to be unwillingness to launch a bold, concentrated and telling blow against the heart of the Third Reich. The CIGS argued that since east-west communications were so much easier and quicker for Germany than north-south routes, and since also the Mediterranean offered so many different and widely separated striking points, it was here rather than in France that the Germans would find it most difficult to counter an Allied incursion. His idea was not so much how to strike a *decisive* blow, but to strike one which the Germans could not instantly and effectively parry, and which at the same time, because the enemy would be obliged to react, would bring some relief to the Russians. The build-up of British and American divisions in the United Kingdom would in any event continue, so that operations in North-West Europe could be mounted when the Germans had been sufficiently weakened in France.

Another issue about which the British and Americans did not at first see eye to eye was what was to be done in the Pacific, for they could not allow the Japanese so to consolidate their gains in the South-West Pacific that it would be almost impossible to turn them out again. Furthermore, American supply lines to Australia would be permanently threatened. Pressure on the Japanese had to be kept up somehow, but whether it should be in Burma, the Dutch East Indies or towards the Philippines from the east was not certain. What was certain, though, was that the forces at present available in the Pacific were not adequate for the task. To allay American fears about Britain's position, Churchill gave the necessary assurances, and in a signal home to the War Cabinet, he explained: 'I thought it right to say in categorical terms that our interest and our honour were alike engaged and the determination of British Parliament and people to devote their whole resources to the defeat of Japan once Germany had been brought to her knees was not in doubt.' What did worry the British, however, was that if substantial resources were detached to the Far East too soon, there would be insufficient forces left in the west to fulfil the agreed strategy of defeating Germany first. These Allied differences were, however, largely reconciled at Casablanca, so that a blueprint for the conduct of the war in 1943 emerged from the conference.

After a second plenary meeting on 18 January, Churchill was able to send a report to the War Cabinet which indicated that his wish to exploit success in the Mediterranean area was to be fulfilled:

> Admiral Q. and I called a plenary conference this afternoon, at which the Combined Chiefs of Staff reported progress. It was a most satisfactory meeting. After five days' discussions and a good deal of apparent disagreement the Combined Chiefs of Staff are now, I think, unanimous in essentials about the conduct of the war in 1943 . . . The security of sea communications was agreed to be the first charge upon our combined resources, and the principle reaffirmed that we must concentrate first on the defeat of Germany. Full preparations for taking Sicily are to go ahead at once with a view to carrying out the operations at the earliest possible moment. In addition we hope to mount the Burma plan towards the end of this year . . . At home *Bolero* is to go ahead as far as our communications allow, with a view to a *Sledgehammer* of some sort this year or a return to the Continent with all available forces if Germany shows definite signs of collapse. In the Pacific, operations for the capture of Rabaul and the clearing of New Guinea are to continue in order to retain the initiative and hold Japan.

Although the final conference report differed somewhat, the essentials of what was to happen were there. Two other aspects of Churchill's meeting with Roosevelt deserve comment, however. The first concerned de Gaulle. Both Allied leaders were anxious that he should come to Casablanca to effect some reconciliation with General Henri Giraud, commanding the Free French forces in Algiers, and although de Gaulle only agreed to do so with some reluctance, he met Giraud and, on balance, made a good impression.[1] Churchill made a

---

[1] Giraud had been captured and imprisoned by the Germans in 1940, but had escaped from Germany and settled in the South of France. Just before the Torch landings he was picked up by a British submarine and taken to Gibraltar to confer with Eisenhower.

most telling comment with regard to de Gaulle's arrogant defiance and aloofness, although it was a comment full of emotional understanding for the Frenchman: 'England's grievous offence in de Gaulle's eyes is that she has helped France. He cannot bear to think that she needed help. He will not relax his vigilance in guarding her honour for a single instant.' Perhaps even Churchill could not have foreseen that in the end de Gaulle would give France back her honour.

The second aspect was the Allies' declaration about 'Unconditional Surrender'. The phrase had originated in a State Department document prepared for Roosevelt before the Casablanca Conference took place. This had contained a recommendation by the US Chiefs of Staff that their three principal enemies, Germany, Italy and Japan, must accept the unconditional surrender of their armed forces before any armistice could be agreed. In informing the War Cabinet of his and Roosevelt's intention to issue such a statement during their meeting with the press at the conference's conclusion, Churchill made the point that it 'should stimulate our friends in every country'. Roosevelt duly made the point at the press conference on 24 January. Too much has been made of the notion that this declaration stiffened German resistance, not least because, as Hugh Trevor-Roper has pointed out, there were probably few Germans who, choosing Nazi rule rather that unconditional surrender, 'would have been inspired to rebellion by an Allied assurance of moderation'.

Although agreement was reached at Casablanca that Churchill should make approaches to Turkey and that Operation Husky – the invasion of Sicily – should be mounted in July, no comprehensive long-term plans for a Mediterranean campaign were discussed or developed. It was, of course, the Americans' scepticism as to the likely dividends of such a campaign which explains the incompleteness of their plans for that theatre. Indeed, Marshall believed that Hitler would give up southern Italy when Sicily had been captured. What grounds he had for believing this is not clear, for there was nothing in either the Führer's character or his recent conduct of war to suggest that he would give up what he could hold on to. If Hitler were to be surprised at all, it would not be because the Allies were aiming to smash Italy's will to continue the struggle, but because having done so, they were so hesitant in wresting real advantage from it. Although there may have been doubts in Allied counsels as to the wisdom and potential benefits of attacking southern Europe, there was none in the German High Command as to the certainty or imminence of that attack – only the actual place was in question. Just, as earlier in the war, the Balkans had been a sensitive spot for Hitler, so much so that before launching Barbarossa he had been at great pains to seal the area off, now, with Barbarossa bogged down and the Allies nearing their possession of all North Africa, this southern flank must once again be made secure. Hence in his War Directive No

47 the Führer gave orders that in view of the North African situation, C-in-C South-East's responsibilities would include making fortress-like defences of the Dodecanese, Crete and the Peloponnese, together with preparations to meet any enemy attack in the Balkans, which might or might not be aided or condoned by Turkey.

It was, of course, just this last point that had long been exercising Churchill, who from the dark days of early 1941 had hoped to form some sort of Balkan alliance, to include Turkey, with which to take on the Germans. It was with a view to testing the Turkish water, as it were, that after the Casablanca Conference he flew via Cairo to Istanbul for talks with President Inönü and his advisers. Little was achieved except good will, but Brigadier (later Lieutenant-General Sir Ian) Jacob gave an amusing account of the way in which Churchill translated a paper on the war situation, which he had prepared in English while in Cairo, from English into French:

> This amounted to doing orally with no time for thought or preparation, a long Unseen into French, no small task. [An example of Churchill-French was *mouvay* meaning to move troops etc.]
>
> The P.M.'s French is fairly fluent, and he was rarely stuck for a word. But of course he could only make a perfectly literal translation, and his accent is almost pure English. The result was therefore completely intelligible to all the English present even if they had no knowledge of the language beyond what they learnt at school; but I feel sure the Turks could only have formed a very hazy idea of what the whole thing was about.
>
> The P.M. waded resolutely on, and came out at the far end bloody but unbowed. It was really quite a tour de force of an unusual kind! Peculiar though it all was, I do not think anyone felt like laughing. They couldn't help admiring his determination and self-possession. The Turks were much too polite to express any surprise or amusement.

At the end of his discussions, Churchill was able to telegraph Attlee that he had found Inönü very agreeable, in sympathy with Britain and longing for her victory; and while he himself had assured the Turks that he 'did not wish them to enter the war in any circumstances which would lead to Turkish disaster', he was sure that 'when the circumstances are favourable . . . it would be in the interests of Turkey to play her part'. On 31 January Churchill flew to Cyprus, and next day, to the great pride and joy of its officers and men, spent some time with his old regiment, the 4th Hussars, giving a stirring speech and finding them 'in fine fettle and up to full strength'. He then flew on to Cairo, where he exchanged telegrams with Stalin and Roosevelt about the Russian success at Stalingrad, where Paulus's Sixth Army was on the point of surrender, and

Allied plans agreed at Casablanca. Three days later he was at Eighth Army headquarters near Tripoli, congratulating the troops on their victories, telling them that 'after the war when a man is asked what he did it will be quite sufficient for him to say, "I marched and fought with the Desert Army",' and talking of clearing all North Africa of the enemy. In Tripoli itself, the 51st Highland Division, re-formed since its destruction at St Valéry in 1940, marched past Churchill – 'the tears rolled down the Prime Minister's cheeks as he took the salute' – and he also inspected the New Zealand Division, commanded by the renowned General Freyberg. He went next to Algiers, where he conferred with Eisenhower, Harold Macmillan (Minister Resident at Allied HQ, North-West Africa), and Giraud, among others, and received from Alexander his celebrated signal: 'Sir, the orders you gave me on August 15th 1942 have been fulfilled. His Majesty's enemies together with their impedimenta have been completely eliminated from Egypt, Cyrenaica, Libya, and Tripolitania. I now await your further instructions.' In fact Churchill's orders had *not* been fulfilled, for they had required Alexander 'to take or destroy' Rommel's forces, and this had not yet been done, although it soon would be. Churchill returned home on the morning of 7 February, and four days later told the House of Commons that agreed Anglo-American policy had produced 'a complete plan of action', which must now be executed, to make 'the enemy burn and bleed in every way that is physically and reasonably possible'.

The arch-enemy was meanwhile making some plans of his own. At his Wolfsschanze headquarters in East Prussia, Hitler was beginning to have new ideas about the war. A military decision continued to elude him – indeed, with his existing resources it seemed unattainable – yet the sheer space available on the Eastern Front gave him the opportunity for manoeuvre, which by itself could perhaps prolong the war, and give him more of that other vital commodity, time: time in which to develop new weapons, time to use them, and time with which to pluck victory from stalemate before he himself was checkmated. 'Space,' he declared to the long-suffering Jodl, 'is one of the most important military factors, you can conduct military operations only if you have space . . . in this huge space one can hold on and on. If we had a crisis like this last one [Paulus's surrender at Stalingrad on 2 February] on the old German border . . . Germany would have been finished. Here in the East we were able to cushion the blow. We have a battlefield here that has room for strategical operations.' For the time being, however, Hitler was content to leave control of operations in the southern wing of the Eastern Front to OKH and Manstein, who favoured flexible defence and was permitted to adjust the dispositions of his Army Group Don so that he could conduct that defence. The two met at Wolfsschanze on 5 February, and Hitler, no doubt to disarm Manstein, began with an admission of failure: 'I alone bear the responsibility for Stalingrad.' The

Field Marshal's first impression was that the Stalingrad tragedy had greatly affected Hitler, both because of the blow to his reputation and because of the soliders whose lives or liberty had been forfeited, although Manstein later revised this opinion, reflecting that all soldiers of the Reich, whether field marshals or lance-corporals, were 'mere tools of his war aims'. At this meeting Manstein sought concessions from the Führer, both on handling operations in southern Russia – in which he partially succeeded – and in the matter of Supreme Command, in which he was unsuccessful.

Recognizing that Hitler would never relinquish Supreme Command of the Wehrmacht or of the Army, Manstein tried to persuade him to appoint a 'Chief of Staff whom he must trust implicitly and vest with appropriate responsibility and authority'. By this means some sort of uniformity and continuity of command might be established. But Hitler, conscious of opposition from former subordinates and of the difficulty which might arise with Göring, Hitler's own nominated successor, declined to play. Besides, he wanted to preserve the final arbitration in matters of strategy for himself. Nevertheless, the mere fact of his willingness to discuss the matter and to give Manstein some freedom of decision about the deployment of the German Army's southern wing demonstrated that Hitler was in a concessionary mood. So he was, too, when he sent for Guderian, whom he had dismissed in December 1941, and who found the Führer much changed – greatly aged, less assured, hesitant in speech, and with a trembling left hand. But he also found him no less able to get his way: for Hitler regretted the 'misunderstandings' that had led to Guderian's dismissal, appealed for him to return to active service with the words 'I need you.' What soldier, knowing that things were going badly for his country, could have resisted such a request from his Commander-in-Chief? So Guderian became Inspector-General of Armoured Troops and was given wide powers with which to turn the panzer troops into a 'decisive weapon for winning the war'. He was authorized to deal direct with Speer, who was in charge of Armaments and Munitions, and to control armoured troops of both the Waffen-SS[1] and the Luftwaffe, as well as those of the army. Guderian served faithfully until the end. It was, however, ironical that not long after this new appointment, 'the greatest tank battle in the world' at Kursk dealt his armoured troops a blow from which they never really recovered. It was not until July that the German attack on the Kursk salient was launched and it was only made possible by Hitler's becoming impatient with Manstein's conduct of a mobile defensive battle, which simply led to more ground being lost. After visiting Manstein on 17 February at Zaporozhe (uncharacteristically close to the front

---

[1] The Waffen-SS consisted of combat troops, as distinct from the rest of the SS, which comprised security forces, concentration camp administration, and so on.

line for him), Hitler ordered him to stop withdrawing and retake Kharkov. He did, and by the second week of March the German Army had succeeded in re-establishing itself more or less on the line from which the 1942 offensive had been launched. This success made possible the very thing which Guderian was later to contemplate with incredulous aversion – even Hitler admitted that his stomach turned over at the thought of it – an offensive in the east in 1943. Why then did Hitler plan and order it? To which the answer, it seems, is that he could think of no alternative, that he had simply run out of ideas. We will look at this last German offensive in Russia shortly.

Meanwhile that other great protagonist of panzer warfare, Rommel, was making a near-final throw in North Africa, once more behaving like an eagle in a dovecote and fluttering the Allied armies in Tunisia at Kasserine Pass. After the Casablanca Conference, Allied operations to finish off Axis forces in North Africa were depressingly slow, despite new command arrangements, which made Eisenhower Supreme Allied Commander, Mediterranean, with Alexander as his deputy commanding a group of armies, Air Chief Marshal Sir Arthur Tedder Air C-in-C, and Cunningham commanding all naval forces. There was also a new German C-in-C South, the able and resolute Kesselring, who did not see eye to eye with Rommel. Yet the latter, after he had withdrawn from Tripoli and had established a defensive position at Mareth, was so confident that Montgomery's advance would, as usual, be deliberate rather than swift that he felt there was time for him to nip another danger in the bud, for an American advance from the west could cut off his withdrawal from Mareth. He therefore decided to attack the two Allied armies in turn, US First Army in the west first, then Eighth Army. Thus he might delay them both and keep the North African pot boiling for a little longer. On 14 February Rommel attacked the Americans with 10th and 21st Panzer Divisions, breaking through the Kasserine Pass on the 20th and turning towards Thala and Tebessa, initially causing confusion and even panic among some of the largely untested American units. But by 22 February Rommel had been halted – the British 6th Armoured Division playing an important part here – and with Eighth Army demonstrating against the Mareth Line, he withdrew. Hitler was in no doubt about the inevitable end in Tunisia, for Axis inability to protect supply ships meant that the bridgehead could not be held much longer; he hung on there, however, because of the effect the country's fall would have on Italy. Although he was beginning to suspect that Rommel's attitude was pessimistic, he appointed him to command Army Group Africa on 23 February in the hope that this would somehow induce him to strike one more decisive blow at the Allies. Yet Rommel knew that shortage of supplies made this impossible, and his appeal to Hitler for further withdrawals to shorten the front fell on deaf ears. The Desert Fox's final attack on the Eighth Army at Medenine on 6 March failed, as it was bound to fail given the depth and strength of Montgomery's defences, whereupon Hitler recalled him for consultation. He never returned to Africa, though he was still to be a thorn in the Allies' flesh, imposing a firm grip on Italy later that year, and in early 1944 doing great things in strengthening the Atlantic Wall.

General von Arnim took over command of the Panzerarmee, but resolute and skilful though he was, no general could prevent the inevitable end of the Axis position in Tunis, with Eighth Army advancing from the east and First Army from the west. On 12 May 1943 the campaign was over and some 250,000 German and Italian troops were in captivity. Alan Moorehead, one of the really great war correspondents, saw the surrender and described it as 'one of the most grotesque and awesome spectacles that can have occurred in this war – an entire German army laying down its arms'. On 13 May two signals were dispatched, among many others. One was from Alexander to Churchill and declared that the campaign was over and that the Allies were masters of the North African shores. The other was from Headquarters Afrikakorps to Army Group Africa and OKH, announcing that all its ammunition had been shot off, all arms and equipment destroyed. 'In accordance with orders received DAK [Deutsches Afrikakorps] has fought itself to the condition where it can fight no more. The German Afrika Korps must rise again.' Which it does, whenever the desert war is remembered, or written about, or talked of.

For Churchill, who had left for the United States on 4 May, victory in North Africa, of which he had been the architect, was the redemption of his strategy. It was, after all, the one place where British troops were engaging the German Army, so it is easy to understand his passionate concern with winning. Now that it had happened, he asked himself, what should be done with the victory? One thing was certain: in no circumstances would he allow 'the powerful British and British-controlled armies in the Mediterranean to stand idle'. The Prime Minister was impatient for action. Shortly after returning from his conferences in North Africa and Turkey, he had been disturbed to learn that General Eisenhower was proposing to postpone the invasion of Sicily from June to July. Churchill signalled to Hopkins saying how awful it would be if 'in April, May and June, not a single American or British soldier will be killing a single German or Italian soldier while the Russians are chasing 185 divisions around', and reminding the other that had they followed the advice of their professional military men, they would not even have landed in North Africa. He repeated his criticism of this proposed delay to the Chiefs of Staff, suggesting that if Allied soldiers were not engaging the enemy in the spring and early summer, 'we shall become a laughing stock'.

In the latter part of February Churchill had more things to worry him: an attack of pneumonia; Rommel's successes at Kasserine; 'that old humbug

Gandhi' and his hunger strike;[1] de Gaulle's intransigence (he wished to tour *mes fiefs*, his dominions, a move vetoed by Churchill); Stalin's pressing for a second front in Europe in 1943. But he convalesced at Chequers, was cheered by the growing weight of Britain's bombing raids on Germany, by news of the desperate supply state of Arnim's forces in Tunisia and by Montgomery's confident signals. On 21 March he was well enough to broadcast to the nation, telling them that everyone must continue to make every effort to prosecute the war. Britain might succeed in defeating Hitler next year, 'but it may well be the year after,' and he meant 'beat him and his powers of evil into death, dust and ashes'. After that, social change must come, so that proper systems of national health, national insurance, education would be available to all classes. He ended his broadcast by referring to Montgomery's advance and exhorting his audience to 'bend all our efforts to the war and to the ever more vigorous prosecution of our supreme task'.

Yet Churchill was by no means satisfied that some of the Allied military commanders were bending every effort vigorously to the prosecution of their tasks, and although he was at length reconciled to the idea that Husky should not take place until July, his exasperation and wrath knew no bounds when he learned on 8 April that Eisenhower was expressing doubts about the likelihood of successfully invading Sicily because of the presence of two German divisions there. His reaction was a sharp minute to the Chiefs of Staff:

> If the presence of two German divisions is held to be decisive against any operation of an offensive or amphibious character open to the million men now in North Africa, it is difficult to see how the war can be carried on. Months of preparation, sea power and air power in abundance, and yet two German divisions are sufficient to knock it all on the head ... We have told the Russians that they cannot have their supplies by the Northern convoy for the sake of *Husky*, and now *Husky* is to be abandoned if there are two German divisions in the neighbourhood. What Stalin would think of this, when he has 185 German divisions on his front I cannot imagine.

Churchill urged the British Chiefs of Staff to have nothing to do with such 'pusillanimous and defeatist doctrines'. They did not, nor did the US Chiefs of Staff. The operation would go ahead. Before it did, however, Allied leaders were to meet again, this time in Washington, for a conference codenamed Trident. On 29 April Churchill signalled to Roosevelt:

[1] The British authorities in India had imprisoned Gandhi, the leader of the Indian independence movement, in 1943 for 'concurring in civil disobedience action to obstruct the war effort'. While in prison he several times went on hunger strike as a further protest against Britain's failure to grant India independence. He was released in 1944.

It seems to me most necessary that we should all settle together, now, first Sicily and the exploitation thereof, and secondly the future of the Burma campaign in the light of our experiences and shipping stringency. There are also a number of other burning questions which you and I could with advantage bring up to date.

Before he left for America aboard the liner *Queen Mary* on 5 May, it had become clear that the Battle of the Atlantic was turning in the Allies' favour. Although U-boat packs were still attacking convoys and sinking merchant ships, their own losses were such that the combined efforts of Allied aircraft and surface escorts in locating and successfully attacking enemy submarines were beginning to gain the upper hand. Less welcome to Churchill, however, was the information that the Germans were developing long-range rockets, something which could influence strategy profoundly in 1944. While at sea, Churchill and the Chiefs of Staff were able to discuss, in the light of the excellent news from Alexander about victory in Tunisia, what to do after the conquest of Sicily. There was no shortage of options to consider: the invasion of Italy; the seizure of Sardinia and Corsica; operations in the eastern Mediterranean. Of these options, that of invading Italy was the one which appealed most to Churchill. He fully agreed with the view of the Chiefs of Staff that 'nothing should prevent us adhering to our main policy for the defeat of Germany first, and that the greatest step which we could take in 1943 towards this end would be the elimination of Italy.' This was easy enough to say, but led to many further questions. What would it take to eliminate Italy? Would a landing in the south of the country be enough? Would an Italian collapse oblige the Germans to withdraw, or would they reinforce their ally? These questions, and others, were discussed during the voyage to America by the planning staff, whose conclusion was that since Italy's collapse was highly probable, the real puzzle was not what Italy, but what Germany, would do. If the Germans reinforced Italy, the Russian front might be relieved; if they did not, the Allies would have a freer hand.

The one thing the joint planners seemed unable to grasp was that Hitler's conduct of war cared nothing for military logic and likelihoods. It was driven solely by his will, and this will was inexorably supported by the skill, dedication and fervour of the Wehrmacht. In stating their belief that the Germans would be unable to hold both northern Italy and the Balkans without hazarding the Russian front, the joint planners were wide of the mark. Their conclusion, however, highlighted one of the major strategic controversies of the war, even though it further misread the power of the Wehrmacht and its absolute subordination to the Führer's grip. The planners concluded that 'the Mediterranean offers us opportunities for action in the coming autumn and winter which may be decisive, and at the least will do far more to prepare the way for a cross-Channel operation in 1944 than we should achieve by attempting to transfer back to the United Kingdom any of the forces now in the Mediterranean.' [So much, it might be said, for John Grigg's theory, discussed earlier, that a cross-Channel operation should have been launched in 1943, when it is noted that the battle for Tunisia is just coming to an end and it is already the second week of May.] The planners' final point was that by seizing these opportunities, the Allies might break the Axis and successfully end the war *in 1944*.

Churchill's first meeting with Roosevelt for the Trident Conference took place on 12 May. He made it clear that after Sicily, the aim should be to knock Italy out of the war and take further weight off the Russians by threatening the Balkans. Since the cross-Channel assault could not take place before the spring of 1944, the victorious Allied armies in the Mediterranean area must not stand idle. Although Roosevelt agreed that there could be no cross-Channel venture in 1943, he was concerned that Allied involvement in Italy might set back the date of this venture in 1944. This, of course, had always been General Marshall's fear – that continued Mediterranean operations would jeopardize the invasion of North-West Europe in 1944. As there were by this time nearly 400,000 US servicemen in the Mediterranean area, and a mere 60,000 US soldiers in the United Kingdom,[1] his fear seemed justified. To Marshall the whole idea of a major exploitation of Allied progress in the Mediterranean was completely at odds with his longed-for cross-Channel operation. Thus the essential difference between the British and Americans was that whereas the former wanted to squeeze every possible dividend from the Mediterranean opportunity, while remaining firmly committed to an invasion of North-West Europe in 1944, the latter put the cross-Channel assault first and foremost and looked askance at any Mediterranean adventures which might interfere with it. The arguments in Washington went to and fro, but in the end broad agreement was reached, and on 25 May the recommendations of the Combined Chiefs of Staff were put to Churchill and Roosevelt. These specified the number of divisions to be made available in the United Kingdom for mounting a lodgement on the Continent, target date 1 May 1944, and also instructed the C-in-C in the Mediterranean theatre, Eisenhower, to mount operations in exploitation of Husky which would eliminate Italy from the war and contain as many German divisions as possible. This compromise between the differing Allied views was brought about not so much by either side giving up its cherished strategy, but by the limitation of landing craft available for Overlord, the final codename for

---

[1] By now, however, there were considerable numbers of American airmen in Britain, from the US Eight Air Force, which was committed to the combined bomber offensive against Germany with RAF Bomber Command.

the cross-Channel assault. To a large extent, therefore, the Trident Conference was most satisfactory from Churchill's point of view. Quite apart from getting his way about a continued Allied effort to exploit Husky, he obtained agreement that further research and development of an atomic weapon should be undertaken jointly by Britain and America. Moreover, he persuaded the President that General Marshall should accompany him, Churchill, to Algiers to discuss further with Allied commanders on the spot how to proceed with operations to knock Italy out of the war.

Churchill arrived in Algiers on 28 May and was met by Eisenhower, Alexander and Cunningham. He later recalled that his week or so there and in Tunis was one of the most 'pleasant memories of the war'. On the whole he had reason to be pleased. During his time there a reconciliation between de Gaulle and Giraud resulted in their agreement jointly to establish a Committee of National Liberation, of which they would be joint heads; Churchill had most satisfactory discussions with Eisenhower about what would happen after Sicily had been captured, for the American general expressed his willingness, if Sicily fell easily, 'to go straight to Italy' by crossing the Messina Straits and establishing a bridgehead on the mainland, while even Marshall somewhat reluctantly agreed to look at such plans with a favourable eye; on 1 June Churchill addressed assembled troops in the Roman amphitheatre at Carthage: Montgomery arrived and discussed his plans for Sicily; and in signalling to Roosevelt Churchill was able to express his confidence in Eisenhower and his satisfaction at their accord. At this time it seemed, as A.J.P. Taylor, observed, as if the British were still 'shaping the course of the war,' but in fact 'the sands were shifting under them. 1943 was the year when world leadership moved from Great Britain to the United States. British strength was running out. American strength was growing on a massive scale.' This trend did not prevent Churchill from announcing in the House of Commons on 8 June, three days after his return to England, that nations like Britain and the United States 'do not become exhausted by war. On the contrary they get stronger as it goes on,' and in reviewing the war situation he expressed his confidence in the 'ever-growing concert and unity' of their two countries, together with the 'personal friendship and regard' which he and Roosevelt shared. Nothing would separate them 'in comradeship and partnership of thought and action while we remain responsible for the conduct of affairs'.

Yet however pleased Churchill and Roosevelt might be with each other, Stalin was far from content when he heard that the invasion of Western Europe was not after all to take place in September 1943, but was to be postponed until the spring of 1944. He complained to the Western leaders that the Soviet Union had been taking on the bulk of the German Army and its allies for two years, that the Red Army was still fighting a powerful, dangerous enemy single-handed and making great sacrifices without 'serious support on the part of the Anglo-American forces'. Churchill replied robustly, telling Stalin that to throw away 'a hundred thousand men in a disastrous cross-Channel attack' would not help Russia. The best way to do this was to win battles, not lose them, and 'if Italy should be forced out of the war, the Germans will have to occupy the Riviera front, make a new front either on the Alps or the Po, and above all provide for the replacement of the numerous Italian divisions now in the Balkans'. He also expressed once again his willingness to meet Stalin at any place agreeable to the Soviet leader and to Roosevelt.

What Churchill was claiming – that an Italian collapse would cause huge problems for Germany – was endorsed by no less an authority than the Führer himself. Hitler's strategic dilemma as a result of defeat in North Africa was summed up by him in a speech made to his generals on 15 May at Wolfsschanze. The enemy had opened up the Mediterranean, and had powerful naval and air forces, as well as some twenty divisions, available to exploit the situation and persuade Germany's weaker allies to defect. Italy was a special danger. Only Mussolini himself could be trusted, and he might well be toppled from the leadership. Real power in Italy lay elsewhere. Nor could they expect a neutral Italy – she would defect to the enemy camp. This would mean a second front in Europe, and that was something to be prevented at all costs. Moreover, the western flank of the Balkans would be at risk. It was therefore just as well, Hitler told himself and his listeners, that the planned offensive in the east had been postponed, for forces available there could be rushed to Italy if there were a crisis. Eight panzer and four infantry divisions from the mobile reserve in the east would, he said, take a firm grip on Italy and defend her against any Anglo-American incursion (even Hitler could hardly have imagined how totally future events would confirm this forecast of his). No resistance could be expected from the Italians, and Hungary would have to be occupied. All this would have serious consequences on the Eastern Front. There would be risk in the Donetz region; the Orel bend might have to be evacuated; it might even be necessary to withdraw to the Luga Line in the north.

Had Churchill been permitted to hear all this, it would have vindicated absolutely his conviction that a Mediterranean strategy would bring relief to the Russians. David Irving has pointed out that this admission by the Führer 'destroys the myth that Hitler always refused to abandon territory in Russia, when it was strategically necessary'. Irving also drew attention to the fact that the dangers in Italy and neighbouring countries had a profound effect on Hitler's planned eastern offensive when it was eventually launched. Despite all the emphasis he had formerly been putting on this proposal to wipe out the Kursk salient, Operation Zitadelle, it was, Irving maintains, 'subordinated to the need to prop up a crumbling dictatorship in a country whose military value was nil'. A week after haranguing his generals, Hitler gave Rommel orders to deal with the situation which would arise in the event of Italy's collapse or defection. Half a dozen panzer or panzer grenadier divisions would quickly be moved from the eastern front and positioned on Italy's northern frontiers, ready to cross and take control of the country.

Thus immediately following the conquest of North Africa by the Allies, and before either Operation Husky to seize Sicily, or Operation Zitadelle were launched, we have the intriguing circumstance in which both the Germans and the Allies are making their plans for taking over Italy. The great difference between the two plans and how they might be executed was soon to become evident. The Germans would act *blitzartigschnell*, at lightning speed, at the whim of a single man, whose political instincts, and in this case strategic judgement, had in no way been blunted by four years of war. And once the orders were given, they would be carried out with all the ruthless efficiency and thoroughness of the German Army. On the other hand, however, any idea that the Allies would act with speed or boldness, or indeed would act at all without endless consultation, equivocation or taking counsel of fears – all the courage and imagination of Churchill notwithstanding – was soon to prove illusory. In any case the Allies had to take Sicily first. Before they did so, Hitler launched his Operation Citadel.

The operation was fatally flawed before it got under way. It had been delayed so long, partly because of indecision, partly because Hitler wanted the new Panther tanks to be employed, that by the time it came, the Russians were not merely ready for it; they were completely prepared to defeat it; indeed they might almost be said to have welcomed it, for having defeated it, they at once seized the initiative, never again to lose it. By July 5 when the last German offensive in Russia began, everything on the other side was ready. The Russian defensive zone had eight separate belts and extended to a depth of some two hundred miles. It bristled with every defensive device – mines, anti-tank guns, tank-killing teams, tanks themselves (including the excellent T-34 plus tank-destroyers mounting 122mm or 152mm guns), massed artillery and about a million soldiers. Against this formidable array was lined up the cream of the Wehrmacht, half a million men, with no less than seventeen panzer divisions. Model's Ninth Army had three panzer corps with two infantry corps in support, while Hoth's Fourth Panzer Army, advancing on a front of only thirty miles, contained the unprecedented total of nine panzer divisions, including such veterans as the SS Totenkopf, SS Leibstandarte, SS Das Reich and Grossdeutschland. The general feeling was that if a force as powerful and experienced as this could not smash the Russians, nothing could. Hitler believed that he would not just smash them, but that by driving them back to the Don – the Volga, even – he would at last be able to sweep up from the south-east behind Moscow and capture it. His Order of the Day of 5 July 1943 underlined the significance of the attack:

> Soldiers of the Reich! This day you are about to take part in an offensive of such importance that the whole future of the war may depend on its outcome. More than anything else, your victory will show the whole world that resistance to the power of the German Army is hopeless.

In the event, it was the German Army's defeat which showed the world that resistance to it was full of hope. Blitzkrieg tactics without the vital element of overwhelming air power could not prevail against a determined and well-prepared enemy whose depth, concentration and reserves seemed to be at once limitless and inexhaustible. The battle turned into one of senseless battering against defences which were too strong and numbers which were too great. Those taking part in the panzer drive found that the numbers of Russian tanks, which streamed 'like rats' all over the battlefield, seemed countless. The impression they had was one of overwhelming Russian power. The new Panther tank, of which so much had been expected, was disappointing, mechanically unreliable and most vulnerable to flanking fire. Neither Panthers nor Tigers could turn the scales. Hoth's formidable Fourth Panzer Army had simply indulged in what its veterans called a 'death ride', Guderian's panzers had been cut to pieces. Hitler called off the offensive.

Yet Hitler now had a concern far deeper than the fate of Guderian's panzers, which was that another attack had taken place, in an area, moreover, where space was at a premium. The Allies had landed in Sicily on 10 July. In spite of all the setbacks, there might still be plenty of room for manoeuvre in Russia, plenty of space for 'strategical operations', but the Allied descent on Sicily brought the war on land to the very gates of Festung Europa. This new development called for a further meeting between Hitler and Mussolini, and the two men duly conferred at Feltre, near Treviso, on 19 July. As usual, the talk was one-sided; its content was familiar, too, Hitler spoke for two hours about how to conduct war. There was nothing to be done but to go on fighting – in Russia, in Italy, on all fronts, everywhere. It was the will to resist that mattered. The poor Duce listened. He could not argue with 'the voice of History'. He did, however, try to make Hitler appreciate the danger of Italy being crushed by the combined weight of Britain and the United States, for her morale and power of resistance had been badly damaged. In reply, Hitler promised air and army reinforcements to defend Italy, a defence which was in Germany's interest, too. The crisis, he made plain, was one of leadership. He was right. Immediately after his meeting with Mussolini, back at the Berghof, he saw a report from Himmler which predicted a coup d'état to get rid of Mussolini and install as Prime

Minister a former Chief of the Italian General Staff, Marshal Pietro Badoglio, who would initiate peace talks as soon as the Allies had completed the conquest of Sicily. Himmler, too, was proved right on both counts. On 25 July King Victor Emmanuel III dismissed Mussolini and Badoglio formed a new government, although it would be a little longer before peace feelers were put out. Hitler, whose rage at Mussolini's fall reflected his concern that a dictator could so swiftly and easily be shorn of power, did not allow anger to cloud his judgement. Suspecting, as he did, that Badoglio would surrender all Italian forces sooner or later, he made his plans to prevent the military situation in Italy from getting out of hand. 'Undoubtedly in their treachery they will proclaim that they will remain loyal to us. Of course they won't remain loyal . . . We'll play the same game while preparing everything to take over the whole area with one stroke, and capture all the riffraff.' Even the Vatican could not embarrass Hitler – it could be taken over right away. So too could the entire rabble of a diplomatic corps as well, for he would get 'that bunch of swine' out. Later apologies could be made. Hitler had always been concerned that the Allies would take full advantage of Italy's 'treachery'. In this, however, he totally overestimated both their inclination and their ability to act quickly, as well as their strategic boldness when at last they did. Of course, had decisions been Churchill's alone, things might have been very different. It is time, therefore, to follow his doings and sayings from 10 July 1943, the day Sicily was invaded.

As soon as it was clear that the landings in Sicily were going well, Churchill began to urge upon the Chiefs of Staff that it was vital 'to use all our strength against Italy'. Moreover, he was anxious that an attack against the mainland should be made as far north as possible, and as early as 13 July, with his customary knack of producing some memorable phrases, minuted the Chiefs of Staff:

The question arises . . . why should we crawl up the leg like a harvest-bug from the ankle upwards? Let us rather strike at the knee . . .

Once we have established our Air power strongly in the Catanian plain and have occupied Messina, etc, why should we not use sea power and air power to land as high up in Italy as air fighter cover from the Catania area warrants?

Let the planners immediately prepare the best scheme possible for landing on the Italian west coast with the objective the port of Naples and the march on Rome, thus cut off and leave behind all the Axis forces in Western Sicily and all ditto in the toe, ball, heel and ankle. It would seem that two or three good divisions could take Naples and produce decisive results if not on the political attitude of Italy then upon the capital. Tell the planners to throw their hat over the fence; they need not be afraid there will not be plenty of dead weight to clog it.

It was just such bold and imaginative ideas that the Germans feared. They too need not have worried. Apart from the dead weight of which Churchill spoke, there were the realities of the Sicilian campaign, which was not going as quickly as had been hoped. However, he did at least succeed, while the campaign was still in progress, in getting Allied agreement to the invasion of the Italian mainland. His views were admirably expressed in a letter to Field Marshal Smuts, in which he used the phrase quoted earlier: 'I will in no circumstances allow the powerful British and British-controlled armies in the Mediterranean to stand idle . . . Not only must we take Rome and march as far north as possible in Italy, but our right hand must give succour to the Balkan patriots . . . I shall go to all lengths to procure the agreement of our Allies. If not, we have ample forces to act by ourselves.' His concern about the possibility of American reluctance was such that he sought yet another conference with Roosevelt, and it was agreed that this would take place in August at Quebec.

Meanwhile, although Eisenhower was clearly committed to carrying the war into Italy itself, Churchill was now beginning to have doubts as to whether continued success in the Mediterranean area was compatible with the withdrawal of seven Allied divisions from that theatre to take part in the cross-Channel operation in May of the following year. Nothing, however, would be more likely to arouse American suspicions – that the British were not wholly committed to the latter operation – than if he were to voice those doubts and seek reinforcements for the Italian campaign. When, therefore, the British Chiefs of Staff sought agreement that Allied resources in the Mediterranean should in no way be diminished until the situation was clearer, the Americans took it as further evidence of British reluctance to stick to agreed priorities with regard to the Far East and Overlord. Since this was something most unwelcome to them, they replied that Eisenhower would have to make do with what he had as far as a possible attack in the Naples area went. The US Chiefs of Staff most certainly did not intend to support any operations which would require an increase in forces over those agreed for post-Husky activities. In view of these diverging strategic priorities, together with the need to determine a strategy for the Far East, it was clear that the forthcoming Quebec Conference, codenamed Quadrant, would be both timely and controversial.

Before Churchill set off for Canada on 5 August, there had occurred, of course, the further promising event of Mussolini's dismissal and Badoglio's appointment. He had told the House of Commons on 27 July that if the Italians chose, they could initiate negotiations for peace, but that were they to allow the Germans 'to have their way' in Italy, the Allies would continue to wage war against them. The great irony of it all was, of course, that when the Italians did screw themselves to the point of negotiating peace terms, it was too late, and Hitler secured such a hold on Italy that it took the Allies the best part of two years to wrest the country from his grip. Churchill also made it plain that 'Britain's prime and capital foe is not Italy but Germany'. As he made preparations for his forthcoming meeting with Roosevelt, it was clear that he was encouraged by reports of progress being made in Sicily from Alexander who assured the Prime Minister that he regarded Sicily as a stepping stone to Italy. For his part, Churchill was determined not to allow American ideas about 'an early shock offensive across the Channel' to distract him from his insistence that every possible military and political advantage should be extracted from exploiting success in the Mediterranean. Oliver Harvey[1] made a telling point in this respect, noting how the Prime Minister 'on military matters is instinctively right ... As a war minister he is superb, driving our own Chiefs of Staff, guiding them like a coach and four, applying whip or brake as necessary, with the confidence and touch of genius.'

It was not only the Mediterranean theatre that was exercising Churchill at this time, although quite apart from Sicily, he was anxious to squeeze every advantage from the activities of the partisans in occupied Yuglosavia led by Tito; with unerring judgement, he chose the brilliant Fitzroy Maclean to join Tito 'as a daring Ambassador-Leader with these hardy and hunted guerrillas'. Maclean was to head the British Military Mission to Yugoslavia until the end of the war. The other theatre in which Churchill deplored the lack of progress was Burma, where 'commanders seem to be competing with one another to magnify their demands and the obstacles they have to overcome'; again captivated, as he always was, by the daring and unorthodox man of action, he had his eye on Major-General Orde Wingate and his long-range Chindit operations to penetrate behind Japanese lines, disrupt their communications and dominate the jungle. He instructed the Chiefs of Staff to have Wingate flown home for consultations. In Sicily itself things were going much more slowly than originally had been hoped, and in the end it was not until 16 August that troops of General George S. Patton's US Seventh Army entered Messina, the remaining Axis forces crossing over to the mainland early next morning. Thus the Sicilian campaign was over, but at the very same time Hitler gave orders to Rommel that he should move his divisions southwards across the Italian frontier. There would therefore be no easy options when the Allies began to plan the invasion of Italy. Conquering Sicily had taken 38 days (the Italian campaign was to last for over 600 days) and had cost the Allies some 20,000 men, while the Axis lost 164,000 killed, wounded and – by far the majority – made prisoner, of which 130,000 were Italians. General Sir William Jackson has shrewdly

---

[1] Harvey was Eden's Private Secretary until 1943, when he became Assistant Under-Secretary at the Foreign Office.

emphasized that the race for Messina was won, not by the competing British and Americans, respectively under Montgomery and Patton, but by the German commander, General Hans Hube, who succeeded in evacuating 60,000 of his troops, complete with weapons and vehicles, to reinforce the German Army's growing strength in southern Italy. Yet the Allies had achieved much. They had learned how to handle great armadas of warships and transports together with landing craft; they had been faced with the problems of mounting airborne operations and of lending air support to amphibious assaults; they had co-ordinated the direction of Anglo-American armies, aggravated by the prima-donna-like behaviour of men like Montgomery and Patton (between whom there was a strong rivalry and, often, friction) – all of which experience would be put to good use in the great enterprise of Overlord, still nearly a year away. What is more, Italy's dictator had been toppled, and his successor was about to break with the Axis altogether. In short, the Mediterranean strategy was paying off. The Allies *had* diverted German divisions from Russia and France, and *had* freed the Mediterranean Sea. Yet, as General Jackson noted: 'The main strategic lesson of Sicily remained unnoticed at the time' – namely, that the courage and skill of the Germans' defence, in which they showed themselves to be masters of delay and withdrawal even in the face of overwhelming military power, albeit greatly assisted by ideal defensive country, should have sounded a strong warning. And because of Hitler's foresight and decision, by the time the Allies actually invaded Italy, the Germans had *nineteen* divisions there, whose presence was to turn the Italian campaign into a slow, painful and costly slog. Furthermore, the way the Allies went about choosing where and how they applied their own divisions both amazed and delighted the Germans.

Churchill reached Canada on 9 August and in discussions with Roosevelt at Quebec and at the President's home in New York State, Hyde Park, they agreed the future command arrangements for South-East Asia – Mountbatten (with Wingate confirmed in command of the Long-Range Penetration Group and its operations in Burma) – and for Overlord – Marshall initially (to the great disappointment of Brooke), later Eisenhower. On 16 August Churchill received information from the British Ambassador to Spain, Sir Samuel Hoare, that General Castellano, Military Assistant to the Chief of the Italian General Staff, had presented himself to Hoare in Madrid to ask that secret arrangements be made for Italy to change sides. Clearly here was a chance not to be missed. Churchill, Roosevelt and their advisers agreed that Eisenhower was to communicate with Castellano by sending liaison officers to talk to him at Lisbon. The terms offered to the Italians were that hostilities should cease at a time to be determined by Eisenhower, shortly before the Allied forces set foot on the mainland; the Allies and the Italian Government would announce the armistice simultaneously; the Italians would instruct their armed forces and people to resist the Germans and collaborate with the Allies; Allied prisoners of war would be released; Italian shipping, naval and merchant, would move to Allied ports, and Italian aircraft to Allied airfields; and until the armistice was declared the Italians would resist passively. While this all sounded splendid in theory, the practice was somewhat different. General Castellano did not return to Rome until 27 August, and it had been agreed that the Italians must indicate their acceptance of the Allied terms by 30 August.

On 1 September Churchill, by this time in Washington, heard that Badoglio had accepted the Allied terms. The Quebec Conference had ended a week earlier, and despite differences of emphasis on the strategic priorities of Italy and Overlord, there had been general Allied agreement about both. Overlord would be mounted in the early summer of 1944, and the Italian campaign would be pursued as far as the general line Ancona-Pisa. The Allies also confirmed their previous accord about the development and manufacture of the atomic bomb, and formally recognized the (French) Committee of National Liberation under the joint leadership of de Gaulle and Giraud. Furthermore, Roosevelt and Churchill had declared their wishes to have a three-sided meeting with Stalin, and had issued an invitation to that effect. Churchill was still in Washington when the Italian surrender at last took place on 8 September. Five days earlier Montgomery's Eighth Army had crossed the Straits of Messina to land on the toe of Italy in what Ronald Lewin described as an 'unopposed crossing, supported by a cascade of fire from his own artillery, from naval guns and from the air . . . pure *opéra bouffe* in which it is said that the only casualty was a puma that had escaped from the zoo at Reggio'. On the following day, 9 September, General Mark Clark's US Fifth Army landed at Salerno, but the battle there became a desperate one, while the whole Allied handling of Italy's defection illustrated how slow and cautious they had been. Nothing could have been in greater contrast to the Germans' harnessing of those two decisive assets, speed and concentration. Six weeks had passed between the dismissal of Mussolini and the declaration of an armistice with Badoglio's government; six weeks in which Hitler had tightened his hold on Italy to the extent that he would be able to choose where and how to conduct defensive operations; six weeks during which the Allies had talked much and done little. By 10 September sixteen German divisions were in control of two-thirds of the Italian peninsula. The Italian Army was disarmed and immobilized. In a speech broadcast that day Hitler referred to the facility with which the Germans would now be able to carry on the struggle 'free of all burdensome encumbrances . . . Tactical necessity may compel us once and again to give up something on some front in this gigantic struggle, but it will never break the ring of steel that protects the Reich.' In fact, he would not be giving up much ground on this front for many months to come. Yet by holding fast here he was obliged to remove divisions from the Russian front; in short Hitler was conforming to Allied Mediterranean strategy – the southern front had become the very distraction which Churchill and his advisers had always hoped it would.

Kesselring, in overall command of the German forces in southern Italy, was a man after the Führer's heart; he believed in holding on to territory which could be properly defended, and he was not easily dismayed. When to his astonishment and delight – and in spite of Churchill having urged his military advisers not to crawl up the leg, but to strike at the knee – both Allied landings in 1943 were made south of Naples; when, further, by the end of the year he had successfully delayed their advance so that they were still some seventy miles from US Fifth Army's beachhead at Salerno, Hitler agreed that Kesselring should establish the Winter Line across the peninsula at a point only just to the north of Naples. More than six months would pass before the Allies captured Rome, and before they did, one more of those battles which would possess the world's imagination – Cassino – would have been fought by the Allies, lost, and finally won.

At the time of the Anschluss Hitler had promised that if Mussolini should ever need help or be in any danger, he could be certain that the Führer would stand by him, whatever happened, even if the whole world were against him. Now the Führer's promise was to be fulfilled again, for he determined to rescue Mussolini from the remote hotel in the Abruzzi Mountains to which Badoglio's regime had confined him. The rescue was carried out on 12 September in a daring airborne raid by an SS detachment under the command of Colonel Otto Skorzeny, and the Duce was taken to Hitler's Wolfsschanze headquarters at Rastenburg. Mussolini was no longer 'the greatest son of Italian soil since the collapse of the Roman Empire'. He was a broken old man who desired nothing more than to quit the political stage for ever and be permitted to go home to the Romagna. This, however, Hitler could not allow. The Duce must play his part. He was restored as Fascist leader and became nominal head of the new 'Italian Socialist Republic'. In his villa on Lake Garda he was a prisoner of the SS, held in hatred by his countrymen, contempt by his gaolers. He was even required to hand over his son-in-law, Count Ciano, to the Germans, who had the former Foreign Minister shot by a Fascist firing squad.[1]

Hitler might fulfil a promise made five and a half years earlier, but he could not alter the fact that the game seemed to be going wrong everywhere – on the

---

[1] Mussolini had dismissed Ciano as Foreign Minister in February, because he opposed Italian subservience to Germany; in July, the latter had led the group of Fascist leaders who had overthrown the Duce.

Eastern Front, in the Mediterranean, in the Atlantic (in September sixty-four U-boats were sunk, and two months later, Dönitz was despairing that 'the enemy holds every trump card, knows all our secrets and we know none of his'), in the ceaseless bombing of Germany. What then was Hitler to do? That dreaded circumstance, war on two fronts – east and west, leaving Italy out of the picture – was no longer a fanciful spectre, as his Directive No 51 of 3 November indicated, revealing as it did a final loss of the initiative and a surrendering of strategic control, as well as anticipating the deeds of dreadful note which the Allies were soon to perform:

The hard and costly struggle against Bolshevism during the last two and half years, which has involved the bulk of our military strength in the East, has demanded extreme exertions. The greatness of the danger and the general situation demanded it. But the situation has since changed. The danger in the East remains, but a greater danger now appears in the West: an Anglo-Saxon landing! In the East, the vast extent of the territory makes it possible for us to lose ground, even on a large scale, without a fatal blow being dealt to the nervous system of Germany.

It is very different in the West! Should the enemy succeed in breaching our defences on a wide front here, the immediate consequences would be unpredictable. Everything indicates that the enemy will launch an offensive against the Western front of Europe at the latest in the spring, perhaps even earlier.

Nevertheless, the Führer declares, action must be taken to strengthen the west. Panzer and panzer grenadier divisions are each to be equipped with nearly a hundred Mark IV PzKws; a Luftwaffe division will be converted to the mobile attack role; heavy anti-tank guns will be allocated to formations in the west; machine-gun emplacements will be sited here; reinforcements will be available there; coastal defences will be constructed; plans prepared; training undertaken. Furthermore, it was not long before Hitler appointed the one man likely to make a real difference to the defence of the so-called Atlantic Wall – early in 1944 Field Marshal Erwin Rommel took command of Army Group B, responsible for the very sector which the Allies were going to invade.

However concerned Hitler may have been with what *might* go wrong in the west, and in spite of 'the vast extent of territory', in the east things were going from bad to worse. After the failure of Citadel at Kursk, the Russians began to advance and went on advancing. Towns which the Germans had taken so easily now went down like ninepins in face of the sheer weight of Russian attack – Orel and Kharkov in August, Poltava and Smolensk in September, Kiev in November, Zhitomir at the end of the year. Objectives like the Donetz Basin and the Crimea, which Hitler had put so much store by, were either lost or cut off. His implacable refusal to conduct a mobile defence and his unwillingness to give up a yard of territory simply meant that hundreds of thousands of soldiers, many of them from the armies of satellite countries, were captured. Yet Hitler willingly paid the price in the hope that by hanging on in strength, he would not have to pay a higher political price – defection of allies or Turkey's abandonment of neutrality. He would give up nothing voluntarily: not Italy, nor Greece, nor Crete, nor the Crimea. He refused to recognize that the sacrifice was in vain. What might not his secret weapons do – jet aircraft, faster submarines, guided rockets? In his austere Wolfsschanze headquarters – 'a mixture of cloister and concentration camp,' as Jodl had it – where reports from military fronts were almost the sum of the news, the Führer sat in his bunker, held his military conferences, heard the reports from each front, announced his decisions, reflected on history and destiny, worried, went for short walks with his Alsatian bitch, Blondi, and brooded.

Churchill's programme was very different, both much more varied and much more agreeable. While he is still in Washington on 9 September a telegram arrives from Stalin proposing that the 'Big Three' meet in Tehran. Churchill accepts, and accepts also Roosevelt's suggestion that the Prime Minister and his family – his wife and one of his daughters are with him – make use of the White House as their home, while he, Roosevelt, is away. Then, on their way to Halifax, Nova Scotia, to embark for the return to England, the Churchills stay with the President at Hyde Park, and there celebrate their thirty-fifth wedding anniversary. It is a very happy occasion, and Mrs Churchill confides to her daughter, Mary, 'that my father had told her he loves her more and more every year'.

The Prime Minister was less happy about events in the Mediterranean, however, urging General Sir Henry ('Jumbo') Maitland Wilson, who had succeeded Alexander as C-in-C Middle East, to capture Rhodes (Churchill never ceased in his will-o'-the-wisp hankerings after Rhodes – all to no effect) and reminding him of the great deeds of such men as Clive, Peterborough and Rooke. He was also gravely concerned about the slow progress at Salerno, and was glad to hear that Alexander had himself visited the beachhead to sort things out; he was even more relieved to learn a few days later, while at sea in the battleship HMS *Renown*, that the latter considered the situation to be in hand. Before embarking in *Renown* on 14 September, Churchill had reproved the Chiefs of Staff for not exploiting the 'explosive' situation in the Balkans, and on a gentler note had sent a message to Roosevelt thanking the President for his hospitality, and adding, 'You know how I treasure the friendship with which you have honoured me and how profoundly I feel that we might together do something really fine and lasting for our two countries.' During the sea passage Churchill was able to prepare the speech outlining his recent doings and the state of the war which he delivered to the House of Commons on 21 September. In it, he explained the circumstances of the Salerno landings, making the point that the timings had been determined, not by delays arising from negotiations with the Italian government, but by the provision of landing craft. He spoke too of the Italian people's opportunity to 'take their rightful place among the democracies of the world' (they did, but at a terrible price, for war, and the aftermath of war, ravaged the country – such was the revenge taken on Italy for having permitted Mussolini to run the country for so long). Writing of this speech, Martin Gilbert reminds us of two incidents which bore further witness to Churchill's extraordinary qualities. Harold Nicolson noted once more the Prime Minister's mastery of the House: 'It is the combination of great flights of oratory with sudden swoops into the intimate and conversational. Of all his devices it is the one that never fails.' On a different note Churchill, whose compassion was infinite, took the opportunity to speak a sympathetic word to an old colleague, Sir Patrick Donner, about his wife's death; writing in reply, Donner expressed perfectly the feelings both of himself and countless others: 'It is in truth your greatness of heart that makes so many of us devoted to you.'

Churchill's restless energy and passionate desire for decisive action found their outlet in all sorts of ways during the coming weeks. A change in senior ministers was forced on him by the death of the Chancellor of the Exchequer, Sir Kingsley Wood. Sir John Anderson became Chancellor, Attlee Lord President of the Council, and Beaverbrook returned as Lord Privy Seal (and Churchill told Eden that, except for the two of them, this was the worst government the country had ever had!). He again returned to the matter of Rhodes, telling Eisenhower it should be seized; he tackled the problem of how to keep order in Greece, where rival Royalist and Communist resistance organizations were all too often at each other's throats, should Britain receive a request from the Greeks to do so; he signalled to Stalin about the difficulties of renewing convoys to Russia in the light of all the Allies' other shipping commitments in the Atlantic, the Mediterranean and the Far East, undertaking nevertheless that convoys would begin again in November; he wrestled with the Soviet request that Russia's post-war western frontiers should be recognized; he appalled the War Cabinet by speculating on the post-war condition of Germany – 'We mustn't weaken Germany too much – we may need her against Russia' (few other Western leaders saw the future so clearly in October 1943); he expressed to Mountbatten, before the latter's departure to take over as Supreme Allied Commander South-East Asia, his wishes for success in the task of engaging and wearing down the Japanese forces; he once more returned to the charge about Rhodes, greatly to the irritation of Brooke, who noted: 'He has worked himself into a frenzy of excitement about the Rhodes attack, has magnified its importance so that he can no longer see anything else and has set his heart on capturing this one island even at the expense of endangering his relations with the President and the Americans and the future of the Italian campaign.' This, it may be noted, is a further illustration of the different ways of conducting war pursued by the two leaders, British and German. Hitler would have overruled all opposition and simply ordered an operation he had set his heart on. Churchill might press for it with all his eloquence and spirit, but in the end would not overrule the views of Allied military commanders and Chiefs of Staff. Thus, when Eisenhower, after a meeting of Cs-in-C in Tunis on 9 October, reported that their Mediterranean resources were not sufficient to capture Rhodes and take objectives in Italy, that the choice was therefore between Rhodes and Rome, and that the Cs-in-C believed they must concentrate on the Italian campaign, Churchill gave way. By this time, too, 10 October, it was clear that the Germans meant to fight the Allies on the Winter Line south of Rome.

If Churchill did not get his way with regard to Rhodes, he was to find himself more successful in pursuing the Italian campaign itself. What was now to transpire was – in spite of all that had been agreed in the past – a resumption of the argument about the respective merits of a Mediterranean or a cross-Channel strategy. Controversy was renewed and given impetus by the Allies' slow progress in Italy, what Churchill was to call 'Deadlock on the Third Front'. Although in mid-September, with the Salerno beachheads secure and Eighth Army heading for Potenza, Alexander had been able to outline to his army commanders, Clark and Montgomery, the way in which he saw operations developing during the following month or so, there can rarely have been a grosser misappreciation either of what the Germans would do, or of what his own armies might be capable of. Even before receiving a very different review of the situation from Alexander, Churchill was having second thoughts about Overlord, and at a meeting with the Chiefs of Staff and others, including Smuts, on 19 October, he expressed the fear that 'by landing in Northwest Europe we might be giving the enemy the opportunity to concentrate, by reason of his excellent roads and rail communications, an overwhelming force against us and to inflict on us a military disaster greater than that of Dunkirk,' which would resuscitate Hitler and his regime. Smuts spoke in support of Churchill, recommending that what had happened in North Africa, Sicily and Italy 'now offered a clear run to victory provided we did not blunder,' whereas a cross-Channel operation was 'a very dangerous one'. Even the CIGS, Brooke, insisted that war should not be waged according to 'contracts' and that the question of where resources were to be applied should be reviewed in the light of the developing situation. But when Churchill set out some of these arguments in a telegram to Eden, who was in Moscow, in which he said that 'Neither the force built up in

Italy, nor that which will be ready in May to cross the Channel is adequate for what is required' and suggesting that Overlord might both spoil Italian and Balkan opportunities as well as itself being vulnerable, the Foreign Secretary rapidly made it clear in his reply that this would not do for the Russians, who were 'completely and blindly set on our invading Northern France and that there is absolutely *nothing* that we could suggest in any other part of the world which would reconcile them to a cancellation or even a postponement of *Overlord*'. All of which made it more and more necessary that the Big Three should meet.

Churchill did not give up his conviction that the battle for Italy must be vigorously pursued, and when Alexander signalled on 24 October that the Germans were at that time able to build up their strength more rapidly than the Allies, which would mean a stabilized front south of Rome, a surrender of the initiative and a long, costly, slogging advance to the capital, the Prime Minister returned to the charge, and on the same day signalled to Roosevelt, to whom Eisenhower had sent a copy of Alexander's report:

> You will have seen by now Eisenhower's report setting forth the condition into which we are sinking in Italy. We must not let this great Italian battle degenerate into a deadlock. At all costs we must win Rome and the airfields to the north of it. The fact that the enemy have diverted such powerful forces to this theatre vindicates our strategy. No one can doubt that by knocking out Italy we have enormously helped the Russian advance in the only way in which it could have been helped at this time. I feel that Eisenhower and Alexander must have what they need to win the battle in Italy, no matter what effect is produced on subsequent operations.

On this last point, however, the Americans would never agree with the British, and still less would the Russians. Next day Churchill signalled to Roosevelt again, expressing his concern that 'the year 1944 is loaded with danger. Great differences may develop between us and we may take the wrong turning. Or again we may make compromises and fall between two stools.' His greatest worry was that there might be serious differences over strategy between the British and Americans. There were – particularly with regard to landings in southern France – but in the end both the Italian campaign and Overlord were fought to successful conclusions. Whether these conclusions could have been brought about more rapidly may be doubted, given the remarkable power of the Wehrmacht and Hitler's inexorable grip on its employment. But in October 1943 the arguments between the Allies went on. From Washington General Marshall informed Churchill of the American view that Eisenhower had enough troops to fight the Italian campaign, and that the latter had himself declared that containing as many German divisions as possible in Italy was bound to help Overlord. Meanwhile, in Moscow Eden was reassuring Stalin about Churchill's commitment to the cross-Channel operation, provided there was no danger of defeat in Italy. Eden also reported that Stalin had shown great interest in the proposed Allied attack on southern France, as this should bring about even greater dispersion of Hitler's armies. At the same time, the Soviet leader was anxious to discover whether the Italian campaign would impose any delay in mounting Overlord, and in his reply Churchill assured Eden that Overlord would remain 'our principal operation for 1944', but that keeping some landing craft in the Mediterranean in order to win the battle for Rome might impose some delay.

Churchill was also worried that no definite date had yet been agreed for the Big Three meeting, and on 29 October he signalled to Roosevelt about it, also suggesting that the two of them should meet in Cairo on 20 November, before going to see Stalin. This was agreed on 30 October. The vexed question of landing craft for use in the Mediterranean, and of how long they might be retained, was still high on the agenda of the exchanges between Alexander and Churchill. Alexander required the craft in order to execute his plan for the capture of Rome, and when he heard that he would be allowed to keep them only until mid-December, he signalled to the Prime Minister that if this were so, he would be unable to 'carry out the whole of my plan', which included an amphibious landing on the coast south of Rome. Churchill replied on 6 November, telling him to proceed on the understanding that he would have the craft until mid-January 1944, confident that he would get the necessary agreement at the forthcoming conference with Roosevelt and others. He believed that the mere fact of there being more British divisions engaged in the Italian campaign than American made itself felt when such arguments about resources occurred, and it caused him to seek at least equality of British and British-controlled divisions with the Americans for Overlord too, simply on the grounds that such parity would strengthen British counsels. But next were to come the planned meetings – in Cairo discussions with senior British, American and Russian military men, and Churchill's talks with Roosevelt, then the Big Three conference at Tehran.

Churchill left Plymouth, again in *Renown*, on the evening of 12 November, bound at first for Gibraltar. There he talked with Macmillan, regretting that the Italian campaign 'has not been exploited with vigour and flexibility,' and expressing his apprehension about de Gaulle, who was clearly the dominant figure in France's Committee of National Liberation, and about the French leader's likely future attitude to Britain. From Gibraltar, Churchill sailed on to Algiers, where he made his celebrated comment about the Chiefs of Staff system, to the effect that with the three heads of the services round the table, no matter how notable their personal boldness and daring, what was displayed was the sum of their fears. Next to Malta, where he had an uncomfortable time in the Governor's Palace, unable to enjoy a hot bath, and received the bad news that Leros, which had been taken by British parachute troops two months earlier, had fallen. Then on again, arriving at Alexandria on 21 November, and immediately travelling straight on to Cairo by air. His first meeting with Roosevelt two days later dealt primarily with Far Eastern matters, and was followed next day by discussion of the most urgent problem before them – what was to be done about the conflicting demands of the Mediterranean and Overlord, both of which campaigns Stalin would expect to proceed. Churchill, although deploring the gloomy position in the Eastern Mediterranean, advocated an objective of the Pisa-Rimini line in Italy, and the continuation of Allied support for the Yugoslav patriots. Overlord must still be the top priority, but not so inflexibly as to rule out all Mediterranean initiatives, and it was for this reason that Alexander wanted to keep landing craft until mid-January. In sum, therefore, Churchill wanted to go for Rome in January and Rhodes in February, wanted to keep the Yugoslavs supplied, wanted to aim to get Turkey's support in controlling the Aegean, *and* wanted to prepare for Overlord. Meetings of the British Chiefs of Staff and the Combined Chiefs of Staff on 25 and 26 November – with Eisenhower very much to the fore in the latter discussion – confirmed the importance of pursuing the Italian campaign. Eisenhower wanted to go beyond the objective set by Churchill, and to aim for the Po Valley: 'in no other area could we so well threaten the whole German structure including France, the Balkans and the Reich itself. Here also our air would be closer to vital objectives in Germany.' (It is worth an ironic note here that Alexander's armies did not break into the Po Valley until 1945.) However inconclusive as to firm action these meetings (collectively known as the Cairo Conference) might have been – for nothing could really be finally decided until after the Big Three had met at Tehran – there was at least general agreement between the British and Americans that the Mediterranean theatre must be kept going. But Ismay told Churchill that although things could proceed in the Mediterranean as he, Churchill, wanted, as also could an operation against the Japanese, this would mean postponing Overlord until July 1944. The Far Eastern operation, Buccaneer, an amphibious assault across the Bay of Bengal, had been discussed by Churchill with General Chiang Kai-shek, the leader of the Nationalist Chinese, during the Cairo Conference, and it clearly had the support of Roosevelt.[1]

---

[1] Before leaving Cairo for Tehran Churchill had sent to Madame Chiang some small presents, including a 'sprightly and sagacious cat', observing that, like the ancient Egyptians, he was very fond of cats. He was very fond, too, of his regiment, the 4th Hussars, and as related at the beginning of this book, to their infinite satisfaction found time to spend a morning inspecting and talking to them.

On 27 November Churchill flew from Cairo to Tehran, and on the following afternoon the first meeting of the Big Three took place. In their opening statements, Roosevelt declared that their major task was to decide which of the various plans open to Anglo-American armies would most effectively assist Soviet forces; Stalin conceded that the Italian campaign had been valuable, but insisted that it was not the proper 'jumping-off ground' for invading Germany – the best place, he said was north or north-west France; Churchill's stance was equally familiar – the cross-Channel invasion came first, yet not only had the Mediterranean operations been the sole possible option for 1943, but they 'were of the first importance'. And since Overlord could not be mounted until spring or summer 1944, the question became what to do in the intervening months which would most help Russia without seriously postponing Overlord. The plan, Churchill said, would be to take Rome and destroy German divisions, as well as capturing airfields north of Rome from which to bomb southern Germany – 'and then to establish ourselves on a line towards Pisa-Rimini. After that the possibility of establishing a Third Front in conformity with, but not in substitution for, the cross-Channel operation would have to be planned.' He then mentioned two possible Allied moves, one into southern France, the other from 'the head of the Adriatic north-east towards the Danube', and it became clear from the subsequent discussion that Stalin greatly preferred the idea of landings in southern France. During this first session, much of the argument hinged on the timing and strength of Overlord and upon this option of invading southern France. There was also the question of what Turkish intentions might be, and of what the Allies should do about the Aegean. Three things were made clear. One was Stalin's view that Turkey would not agree to enter the war; another was that Roosevelt, despite what had been said at the Cairo Conference about possible postponement of Overlord, now talked of its launching at 'the prescribed time' as being a 'governing factor'; the third was Churchill's insistence that the capture of Rome could not be jeopardized for the sake of landings in southern France.

Churchill's continued concern with Italy was reflected in the second plenary session of the Big Three on 29 November. Brooke had pointed out the need to do something in the Mediterranean before Overlord was launched in order to prevent the Germans transferring divisions from Italy either to Russia or France. The alternatives were greater involvement in Yugoslavia, in order to help the partisans to hold down the Germans in the Balkans, or bringing Turkey into the war. Churchill seized on this need to reiterate his view that landing craft should be kept in the Mediterranean so that outflanking amphibious operations could assist the advance in Italy; these craft could also be used in the Aegean and, later, in southern France. Yet Churchill emphasized that all

Mediterranean operations would be designed to help both Russia and Overlord. Stalin, however, like the US Chiefs of Staff, turned the matter round: Overlord came first – all other operations were subsidiary. But on the following day it became clear during a meeting of the Combined Chiefs of Staff that if landing craft were to be retained in the Mediterranean until mid-January to assist with the Italian campaign, the earliest possible date for Overlord, in view of the moon period, would be between 5 and 10 June. Later that day Churchill again tried to persuade Stalin that the Italian campaign could yield huge dividends. Although the weather had been against them, and vital bridges had been blown by the retiring Germans, there would be a great push by Eighth Army in December, together with an amphibious operation, while Fifth Army held the enemy. 'It might,' Churchill said, 'turn into a miniature Stalingrad.'

Here he was wide of the mark. Progress in Italy was depressingly slow. Kesselring had decided to establish his winter line based on the Rivers Garigliano and Rapido in the west, then eastwards through Cassino and the central mountain range and on along the River Sangro to the opposite coast. Meanwhile he would delay the Allied advance and exact as many casualties as possible until this winter line was ready. So it turned out. In October and November Montgomery's Eighth Army made its way slowly and painfully up the eastern side of the country to the Sangro, while Fifth Army under Clark crossed the Volturno and edged towards the series of mountainous ridges which barred their way to Cassino. One of the campaign's participants, Fred Majdalany, described exactly what battles were like at this time:

> The Germans would hold a position for a time until it was seriously contested: then pull back a mile or two to the next defendable place, leaving behind a trail of blown bridges, minefields and road demolitions. There was always a new defendable place at hand. The Allied armies would begin with a night attack – ford the stream or river after dark, storm the heights on the far side, dig themselves in by dawn, and hope that by that time the Sappers, following on their heels, would have sufficiently repaired the demolitions and removed the obstacles to permit tanks to follow up and help consolidate the new positions. The Germans, watching these proceedings from their next vantage point, would attempt to frustrate them by raining down artillery and mortar fire on their own recently vacated positions.

These circumstances, together with the removal of seven divisions, three British and four American, from the Mediterranean theatre to the United Kingdom for Overlord, do much to explain why the advance in Italy was so ponderous. None the less, Churchill was still hoping for great things from the retention of landing craft, which he believed would enable the Allies to outflank the German defences and effect the early capture of Rome. He was to be sadly disappointed.

In Tehran on 30 November Roosevelt, presiding over the third plenary session, declared that 'agreement had been reached on the main military problems'. In essence this agreement was for Overlord to be launched in May, to be supported by a landing in southern France, and by a Russian offensive in the same month. At Churchill's suggestion a communiqué was drafted which referred to agreed plans to destroy the German forces by operations 'from the east, west and south'. That date, 30 November was, of course, Churchill's sixty-ninth birthday, and he was the host at a memorably jovial dinner party. On the following day, the last of the Tehran conference, the Big Three discussed political matters, including the future Soviet-Polish border, and also agreed the wording of five 'military conclusions': that Yugoslavia would be supported; that Turkey's participation was desirable; that if, in this event, Turkey were attacked by Bulgaria, Russia would intervene; that Overlord should take place 'during May 1944' together with a landing in southern France and a Soviet offensive to stop the Germans transferring troops to the west; and that there would be further military liaison between the three Powers. Churchill summed the conference up by signalling to Attlee that war plans were agreed and that relations between the three countries had 'never been so cordial and intimate'.

Churchill spent the last month of 1943 in North Africa. Having flown from Tehran back to Cairo on 2 December, he had further meetings with Roosevelt two days later, during which it became clear that Overlord and Anvil – the codename for the landings in southern France – would take priority over any offensive in the Far East. The two men also conferred with Ismet Inönü, the Turkish President, who again made it plain that he was not willing to bring Turkey into the war against Germany. (When Inönü bade farewell at the airfield outside Cairo, he actually embraced Churchill, who later told his daughter, Sarah, of the incident, adding: 'The truth is I'm irresistible. But don't tell Anthony [Eden], he's jealous.') Before Roosevelt left Cairo on 7 December, he told Churchill that the commander for Overlord would be Eisenhower, not Marshall, whom he needed in Washington. As usual Churchill was filling his days, meeting such people as Fitzroy Maclean and his old friend, Bill Deakin, both with the British Military Mission to Tito's partisans in Yugoslavia; King Farouk of Egypt and King George II of Greece; Generals Wilson and Brooke; Lord Jellicoe, a member of the Special Boat Section (part of the SAS), who had fought in Leros; Field Marshal Smuts; and many others. It was little wonder, therefore, that Brooke thought the Prime Minister was 'tired and flat', though in fact the reason lay elsewhere. After flying from Cairo to Tunisia on the night of 10 December, and arriving at Eisenhower's Carthage villa to sleep throughout the following day, it became obvious that Churchill was seriously unwell.

Even this did not prevent his discussing future command arrangments, although, sensibly, these were resolved later – Wilson to command in the Mediterranean, Alexander in Italy, and, supremely important, Montgomery to command the actual invasion force under Eisenhower. Churchill's pneumonia kept him in bed for about a week, but on 17 December he was joined at Carthage by his wife, Jock Colville and Grace Hamblin. Colville, expecting to find 'a recumbent invalid', saw instead 'a cheerful figure with a large cigar and a whisky and soda'. Irrepressible as ever, during the next days Churchill turned his attention again to the conflicting demands of Overlord, Anvil and Shingle, respectively the cross-Channel, southern France and Anzio operations, the latter being the proposed landing on the west coast of Italy, north of the German line, which had been mooted for so long.

Churchill was strongly in favour of the Anzio landing, even though it would delay the return of landing craft for Overlord. He therefore signalled to Roosevelt on Christmas Day, after conferring with his Commanders-in-Chief:

> What could be more dangerous than to let the Italian battle stagnate and fester on for another three months thus certainly gnawing into all preparation for . . . Overlord. We cannot afford to go forward leaving a half finished job behind us. It therefore seemed to those present that every effort should be made to bring off 'Shingle' on a two division basis around January 20th, and orders have been issued to General Alexander to prepare accordingly. If this opportunity is not grasped we must expect the ruin of Mediterranean campaign of 1944. I earnestly hope therefore that you may agree to the three weeks delay in return of the 56 landing craft and that all the authorities should be instructed to make sure that the May 'Overlord' is not prejudiced thereby.

Roosevelt's reply was received by Churchill on 28 December, by which time the Prime Minister was at Villa Taylor in Marrakesh. Roosevelt agreed in principle to the Anzio landings, subject to Stalin's approval to use of troops or equipment which might affect the timing or success of Overlord or Anvil. Quite independently of this consideration, however, there had been further thoughts on Overlord, which were to determine both its scope and timing. Eisenhower had clearly expressed his wish to delay the operation until the first week of June, which of course would give more time for landing craft used at Anzio to be returned; of even greater importance, General Montgomery, who had been shown a summary of the so-called COSSAC[1] plan for Overlord on 1 January

[1] Chief of Staff to Supreme Allied Commander – a secret staff under Lieutenant-General Sir Frederick Morgan which had been working on plans for the cross-Channel invasion since March 1943. It had a combined Anglo-American HQ, also known as COSSAC, in London.

1944 by Churchill himself during a picnic near Marrakesh, made it absolutely clear to the Prime Minister that: 'This will not do. I must have more in the initial punch.' Moreover, he added that 'the proposal to move so many divisions in over the same narrow strip of beaches would be quite impracticable and would lead to inextricable confusion.' In other words, Montgomery wanted a greater concentration of forces over a wider frontage. In signalling the General's 'very serious criticism' of the proposed plan to the Chiefs of Staff Committee, Churchill added the point that talk of 'invading' or 'assaulting' Europe was not the sort of language desirable for an operation whose object was 'the liberation of Europe from German tyranny . . . There is no need for us to make a present to Hitler of the idea that he is the defender of a Europe we are seeking to invade.' Thus as 1943 ended and 1944 began, Churchill, despite his serious illness, was buoyed up with Allied plans for taking the fight ever closer to the centre of Hitler's Festung Europa.

Hitler himself, although he had not succumbed to pneumonia, had little to comfort him as 1943 drew to a close. At the Führer Conference on 29 December, the questions being examined illustrated how completely the initiative had deserted him. Were all the Anglo-American invasion reports simply a colossal bluff 'to lure units away from the eastern front or prevent us from reinforcing that front at the crucial moment of the Soviet winter offensive?' Or did they represent a diversion from the real operation planned in the Balkans, or the Aegean, or Turkey? Or not there, or even in the west, but in Norway or Denmark? Could the Wehrmacht hold the Ukraine, vital for feeding Germany's people? What about the U-boat campaign – would it succeed or not? Such negative reflections augured ill for 1944. Yet Hitler, still living in a world created by his own desires and imagination, did not altogether dread the prospect of an Allied assault from the west. He might almost be said to have welcomed it, for he saw in it a possible solution to his strategic dilemma. Such a standpoint was not, in fact, mere self-delusion. What he knew at this time of Anglo-American amphibious operations did not alarm him; indeed, rather the reverse. The landings in North Africa had met with light or non-existent opposition; those in Sicily and Italy had been possible only, as he put it, with the help of traitors; at Dieppe in August 1942 the Canadians and British had suffered a bloody repulse; why, a year or two back even the forces of Vichy France had succeeded in defeating a joint Anglo-Free French attempt to seize Dakar. No – let them come. What might not be done when the much-heralded invasion of France had battered itself into a costly failure against the Atlantic defences. He would then be able to transfer such a weight of army and Luftwaffe units to the east that at last the decision which had so long eluded him would be realized. And then the Western Allies, beaten back and deprived of invasion as a strategic option, would be subdued by the new

V weapons,[1] by masses of jet aircraft, and by the latest submarines, which could remain submerged without the need to surface for battery charging, and could move below the surface as fast as they could on it.

That the Führer should pin his hopes on these new weapons is easily understood, for they offered the promise not just of stemming defeat, but of so dismaying the Allies that they might after all leave him alone with his conquests. What is less easy to understand is how he could be so confident of defeating the cross-Channel enterprise without guaranteeing the one military condition indispensable to such confidence – strong, fast-moving and sensibly placed reserves able to move at once to the point of landing or penetration and push the invaders back into the sea before reinforcement made them too strong. In making this point to Hitler, Jodl was insistent that any weakening of these reserves would result in a risk so acute that the entire Western situation might get out of hand. Yet in the event this is precisely what transpired. To understand the reason for this, it has to be remembered that just as space had been a barrier to Hitler's adventures in the east, so now space – in spite of its assets, providing him with an income of resources, of labour and of manoeuvre – was so ravenous in its demands for military security that his position began to resemble that of many another tyrant. His conquests were sticking on his hands. There were simply not enough forces to go round. Yet if the world required a demonstration of how to rob Peter in order to pay Paul, and of how to fight a war not on two fronts, but three, it was about to get it. There was perhaps no more remarkable contrast to the ignominious collapses of the French and Italian armies as soon as their homelands were seriously threatened than the way the German Army, deprived of most of that air support which had made panzer and Stuka so matchless a combination, could by sheer skill, courage and determination prolong a conflict whose result was no longer in doubt. Some people, Hitler was to tell General Thomale, give up if things go badly:

> One can't make world history that way. World history can only be made if, in addition to continual alertness, a man has fanatical determination and courage of his convictions which make him master of himself . . . No one can for ever. We can't, the other side can't. It's merely a question who can stand it longer.

A lot of things were to go badly for Hitler as 1944 blossomed into summer. But he was certainly not going to give up. There was still a good deal of world history for him to make.

---

[1] From *Vergeltungswaffe*, revenge weapon.

CHAPTER 9

1944 – The Third Reich at Bay

Under all circumstances we will continue this battle until, as Frederick the Great said, one of our damned enemies gets too tired to fight any more. We'll fight until we get a peace which secures the life of the German nation for the next fifty or hundred years, and which, above all, does not besmirch our honour a second time, as happened in 1918.

ADOLF HITLER, 1944

By undertaking two operations in the Mediterranean theatre, both would be doomed to failure. General Alexander would be forced on to the defensive, whilst the *Anvil* force struggled slowly forward up the Rhone Valley ... [splitting the Italian campaign into two operations] neither of which can do anything decisive [would be] in my humble and respectful opinion, the first major strategic and political error for which we two have to be responsible.

WINSTON CHURCHILL to FRANKLIN D. ROOSEVELT, July 1944

In November 1943 Churchill had asked the Chiefs of Staff whether they could assume victory over Germany in 1944, and the balance of opinion was that they could. They were wide of the mark, for – leaving aside the question of perfecting an atomic weapon and using it against Germany in that year – there was but one circumstance which could have yielded victory in Europe in 1944, the death of Hitler. Colonel Count Karl von Stauffenberg and his fellow conspirators tried and failed to assassinate the Führer in July of that year, and this failure simply hardened his conviction that Providence had marked him out to lead the German people to final victory; hardened, too, his purpose in continuing the struggle. Nevertheless, 1944 brought many victories, however hardly

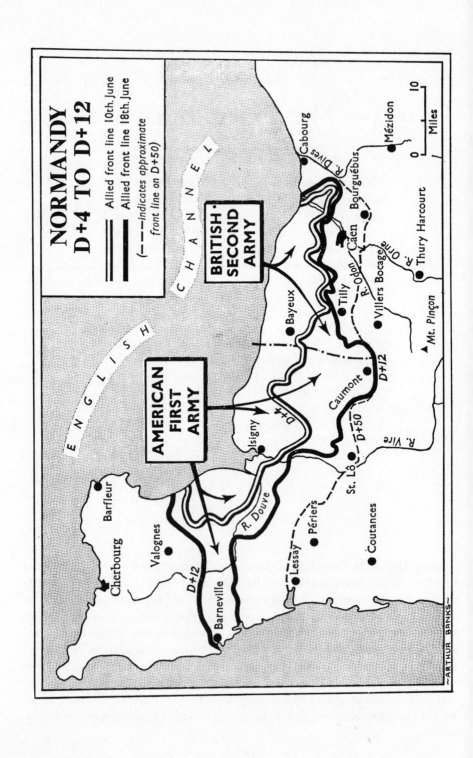

NORMANDY
D+4 TO D+12

Allied front line 10th June
Allied front line 18th June

(— — —) indicates approximate
front line on D+50

BRITISH·SECOND ARMY

AMERICAN FIRST ARMY

ENGLISH CHANNEL

Cabourg
R. Dives
Mézidon
Bourguébus
Caen
R. Odon
Villers Bocage
R. Orne
Thury Harcourt
Mt. Pinçon
Tilly
Bayeux
Caumont
D+12
D+50
R. Vire
Isigny
D+4
St. Lô
R. Douve
Périers
Coutances
Lessay
Barfleur
Valognes
Cherbourg
D+12
Barneville

0   10
Miles

~ARTHUR BANKS~

won, to the Allies – Cassino, Rome, the D-Day landings, Kohima and Imphal in Burma, the breakout in Normandy. And the year brought disappointments and setbacks too – Arnhem, the failure to crack the Gothic Line in Italy, the recovery of the German Army in the west, the Wehrmacht holding its enemies at bay – the Red Army short of East Prussia, the Western Allies in the Rhineland – and even, to the astonishment of all, launching a devastating counter-offensive in the Ardennes. It was a year of gigantic battles which, among other things, brought British troops into bitter conflict with the cream of Hitler's panzer, panzer grenadier, parachute and SS divisions.

The Battle of Cassino lasted for more than four months, from 15 January, when Allied shells first fell on Monastery Hill, until 18 May, when the Poles occupied the abbey itself. The battle began too soon and went on for too long. It started early in order to help bring about success at Anzio, a success which would have ended the Cassino battle much more quickly. But there was to be no victory at Anzio other than the gaining of a foothold. Opportunity and advantage were squandered. The Allies might afterwards congratulate themselves on dogged courage in the face of skilled and determined resistance and counter-attack, but the whole idea of the Anzio landings was to break the deadlock on the main front south of Rome. It did nothing of the sort. The attack had been planned for 20 January – later postponed to the 22nd – with one British and one American division under an American corps commander in the assault. Alexander also planned to launch an offensive against the Cassino line in order to draw enemy reserves away from areas where they might be well placed to interfere with the Anzio landings. There was, however, a snag to this admirable strategic idea. If the attack on Cassino were to precede the Anzio landings on 22 January by any proper interval, there was simply not the time to make the necessary preparations. The Cassino operation would merely be the continuation of an advance that had been going on for months in bad weather and with exhausted troops. As Fred Majdalany put it: 'The fact remains that the first assault on one of the most powerful defensive systems of the war was an *ad hoc* affair, hastily undertaken without anything like proper preparation.' It was hardly surprising, therefore, that the strategy failed.

It is notable that when Montgomery heard of the idea of a landing near Rome, he dismissed it as 'complete nonsense', pointing out the uncertainty of the weather, the ease with which German panzer divisions could concentrate against a landing, and the relatively few places suitable for such a venture, all of which would be watched by the enemy. This view was shared by US Fifth Army's Deputy Chief of Staff, who was in fact a British officer, the highly competent Brigadier Charles Richardson,[1] who echoed Montgomery and called

---

[1] Later General Sir Charles Richardson.

Anzio 'a complete nonsense from its inception'. It had always been clear, he maintained, that unless the Germans panicked – highly unlikely if they behaved in their customary way – any landing force would quickly be contained. What did surprise the Germans, though, was firstly how far south the blow fell, and secondly the utter lack of drive and initiative shown by the Allies after their landing had been effected. Yet for Churchill Anzio held out high hopes, so much so that as the time for its execution approached, he decided to return to London from Marrakesh. As he convalesced during the first two weeks of 1944, he had talks with the exiled Czech President, Eduard Beneš, and with de Gaulle, and examined further details of the Anzio operation before flying to Gibraltar on 14 January. There he was briefed by General Wilson and Admiral Sir John Cunningham[1] about final Anzio plans and embarked in the battleship *King George V* for the return passage to England. While he was still at sea on 17 Janaury, Fifth Army began its attacks across the Rivers Garigliano and Rapido to distract the Germans' attention from what was shortly to take place at Anzio. Churchill reached London on 18 January and that same day in the House of Commons received the most heartening welcome at Prime Minister's Question Time. Harold Nicolson recalled that his unexpected appearance caused the whole House to jump to its feet and break 'into cheer after cheer while Winston, very pink, rather shy, beaming with mischief, crept along the front bench and flung himself into his accustomed seat. He was flushed with pleasure and emotion, and hardly had he sat down when two large tears began to trickle down his cheeks. He mopped at them clumsily with a huge white handkerchief.'

Before the Anzio operation began, Churchill met members of the Polish Government-in-Exile, which was based in London, to discuss the vexed question of Poland's future frontiers, and he made it plain to the Polish Prime Minister, Stanislaw Mikolajcik, that whereas former German territory might be incorporated within Poland's western frontier, Britain would never take military action against the Soviet Union with regard to the country's eastern frontier. There he also made the point that military developments of the moment, with the Red Army advancing ever further westward, had to be recognized as determining factors. Moreover, he emphasized that the battle for Italy, while it might result in the establishment of a democratic government there, was designed to help the Russians' effort against the German Army. The Anzio landing would itself be part of this design, as well as being aimed at the liberation of Rome.

Yet it was much too soon to be talking of liberating Rome. In planning to

---

[1] The Naval C-in-C in the Mediterranean since 1943; no relation to Admiral Sir Andrew Cunningham.

facilitate an advance at Anzio by attacking south of Cassino, General Mark Clark had totally misappreciated the Germans' capacity and perseverance. The plan was that on 17 January Lieutenant-General Sir Richard McCreery's X Corps would cross the River Garigliano to the extreme west, then turn east towards the Liri valley; then three days later the US II Corps would cross the Rapido about five miles south of Cassino and break through to the Liri valley; while the Free French Corps would advance through the mountains north of Cassino and turn south-west; finally, on 22 January the Anzio ace would be played. The outcome was somewhat different. The British and French made some progress, but not enough to affect the crucial centre where the 36th (Texas) Division's two-day battle to cross the Rapido ended in disastrous, costly failure. Moreover at Anzio itself, despite gaining surprise, the American commander, Major-General John Lucas, far from exploiting initial success, pushing on inland and establishing a proper defensive zone, simply sat down by the sea and allowed Kesselring to seal off the beachhead. Churchill's comment was that a wildcat hurled ashore had become a stranded whale.

There was nothing unusual about the Allies underestimating the Germans' ability to react with speed and violence to an emergency, for the latter's capacity for improvisation was infinite. Kesselring's Chief of Staff, General Siegfried Westphal, later recorded that they had made numerous contingency plans against likely Allied amphibious assaults, so that if and when the Allies landed here or there in Italy, transmitting a codeword would instantly set in motion the necessary counter-action – troops, timings, routes all laid down and understood by those required to execute the plan. At Anzio there were at the time of the assault a mere two German battalions and some coastal batteries near by. 'The road to Rome,' wrote Westphal, 'was open. No one could have stopped a bold advance-guard entering the Holy City.' What would have happened then, of course, is another matter, but as it was, to the Germans' further surprise, their enemies simply contented themselves with building up their beachhead. Two days later German reinforcements under command of Colonel-General Eberhard von Mackensen's Fourteenth Army began to seal off the Allied intrusion. What is more, Hitler gave orders that the Cassino defences of the Gustav Line must be held at all costs, demanding 'the bitterest struggle for every yard'. He was not disappointed. On 28 January Churchill, already seriously concerned about the slow progress being made, signalled to General Alexander his satisfaction on learning that Clark was about to visit the Anzio beachhead: 'It would be unpleasant if your troops were sealed off there and the main army could not advance up from the south.' He could hardly have been more prophetic. On the same day Hitler sent a message to Kesselring, couched in the dramatic language which he employed to conceal the gravity of his strategic situation:

In the next few days the Battle for Rome will break out . . . It must be fought in holy wrath against an enemy who is waging a pitiless war of extermination against the German people, who shuns no means to that end, who is devoid of all higher ethical purpose, and who is intent only on the destruction of Germany and thereby of our European culture.

In fact, the battle for Rome had already broken out – but the Allies, to their misfortune, could not break out. Although at the end of the first day the best part of two divisions – 40,000 men and 3,000 vehicles – were safely ashore at Anzio, opportunity was not grasped. In reporting to Churchill, Alexander told him that mobile patrols were to be pushed forward to contact the enemy (to which the Prime Minister replied that he was glad to know that claims were being pegged out, rather than troops just digging in), but in fact nothing of the sort was happening. It had always been appreciated that the first two days would be crucial for moving inland, seizing important ground and giving *depth* to the invading forces' defence before the inevitable German counter-attack materialized. Yet General Lucas made no attempt to do so. He sat down, occupied the beachhead, and built up troops and supplies. A week after the landing four Allied divisions were holding an area some fifteen miles long and eight miles deep. Facing and containing them were elements of eight German divisions, *none* of which had been withdrawn from the Cassino front. The Anzio gamble had failed, and Churchill, principal architect of the venture, was bitterly disappointed that what he had regarded as so splendid an opportunity had been thrown away. (When he was informed that two weeks after the landing there were 18,000 vehicles, not counting tanks, in the beachhead to serve a total of some 70,000 troops, his comment was that the Allies must be enjoying a great superiority of chauffeurs.)

By 11 February Alexander was signalling to Churchill that with the first phase of the operation over, the next one, that of defeating enemy counter-attacks would begin. With that done, the offensive would be renewed to push forward and cut enemy communications between Rome and the Cassino position. When these counter-attacks came, as they did in the second half of February, they were defeated, but there was no advancing to cut German communications. In the end it was success at Cassino which relieved Anzio, not the other way round, although that had been the whole purpose of the landings. Major-General Lucian Truscott took over from Lucas and proved himself to be a competent commander, and although there was much to be said for his subsequent claim that the Anzio operation was not powerful enough to achieve its aim of cutting German communications and advancing to Rome, the fact remains that his predecessor had not even attempted to exploit opportunity during the first two days after the initial landings, when he had great freedom of manoeuvre. Furthermore, Ronald Lewin's *Ultra Goes to War* makes it clear that General Clark's claim about the need for US VI Corps to dig in at Anzio because Ultra had revealed German plans for reinforcement was both specious and absurd, since these reinforcements could not possibly have arrived until a week had passed. Clark was simply indulging in his customary practice of self-vindication.

In all this, we may sympathize with Churchill's frustration and disappointment. It was he who had pressed so hard for the war to be taken into Italy; it was he who had constantly urged bold strategic moves which would make maximum use of the Allies' great superiority in air and amphibious resources; it was he who had persuaded Roosevelt to keep landing craft in the Mediterranean area so that the Anzio operation could take place; and he had even telegraphed Stalin to tell him that a big attack would be launched against the German armies defending Rome, and gave a promise of good news before long. Yet Churchill was able to bear these disappointments, and the account he gave to the House of Commons on 22 February about the course of the Anzio battle did produce some justification of his strategy:

It was certainly no light matter to launch this considerable army upon the seas – forty or fifty thousand men . . . with all the uncertainty of winter weather . . . The landing was virtually unopposed. Subsequent events did not, however, take the course which had been hoped or planned. In the upshot we got a great army ashore . . .

The German reactions to this descent have been remarkable. Hitler has apparently resolved to defend Rome with the same obstinacy which he showed at Stalingrad, in Tunisia, and recently in the Dnieper bend. No fewer than seven extra German divisions were brought rapidly down from France, Northern Italy, and Yugoslavia, and a determined attempt has been made to destroy the bridgehead and drive us into the sea. Battles of prolonged and intense fierceness have been fought. At the same time the American and British Fifth[1] Army to the southward is pressing forward with all its strength.

On broad grounds of strategy, Hitler's decision to send into the south of Italy as many as eighteen divisions, involving something like half a million Germans, and to make a secondary front in Italy is not unwelcome to the Allies. We must fight the Germans somewhere, unless we are to stand still and watch the Russians. This wearing battle in Italy occupies troops who could not be employed in other greater operations, and it is an effective prelude to them.

[1] McCreery's British X Corps formed part of US Fifth Army.

In this way Churchill consoled himself that the Italian campaign was paying the right sort of dividend. Yet it was still not really of great concern to Hitler. Norman Stone's contention that 'Hitler was able to meet the Allied invasion of Italy almost without serious disruption of the war elsewhere' is a misleading overstatement, for the employment elsewhere of nearly twenty first-class German divisions could have had a profound impact – either in shoring up the crumbling Eastern Front, or in strengthening defences in the west. What it would be more accurate to say is that while Hitler had, of course, hoped that the Anzio beachhead would be eliminated – 'If we can wipe them out down there,' he observed, 'then there won't *be* an invasion anywhere else' – he was not willing to back this wishful thinking to the extent of denuding France of freshly formed panzer divisions. Indeed, when it became clear at the beginning of March that Mackensen's attempts to drive the Allies out of the Anzio beachhead had failed, he reconciled himself to a mere holding operation in the south, and when it is recalled that this holding operation was to last for more than another year, we must concede that it was an effective one. Yet for Hitler, what was happening in the east, and what he suspected was about to take place in the west, were in the early part of 1944 of far greater moment.

For Churchill too, even before the deadlock at Anzio became evident, the forthcoming invasion in the west was of great moment. Towards the end of January he ordered the setting-up of a committee 'to speed up and stimulate *Overlord* preparations in all aspects other than tactical and strategic'. This was to meet every week under his chairmanship, and as was customary in such cases it was his vigour and drive which informed and directed the committee's work. Ismay remembered that the Chairman would not brook any delay – 'the seemingly slothful or obstructive were tongue-lashed; competing differences were reconciled; priorities were settled; difficulties which at first appeared insuperable were overcome; and decisions were translated into immediate action.' Churchill's concern with Overlord was also made plain by his comments, in a telegram sent to Smuts on 27 February, about the lack of progress both at Anzio and Cassino:

Naturally I am very disappointed at what has appeared to be the frittering away of a brilliant opening in which both fortune and design had played their part. I do not in any way however repent of what has been done. As a result the Germans have now transferred into the south of Italy at least eight more divisions, so that in all there are eighteen south of Rome. It is vital to the success of *Overlord* that we keep away from that theatre and hold elsewhere as many German divisions as possible, and hard fighting in Italy throughout the spring will provide for the main operation a perfect prelude and accompaniment.

Two days later Churchill warned the Chiefs of Staff that sufficient resources must be provided to keep the Anzio battle going, for defeat there would 'jeopardize *Overlord* by enabling the Germans to send reinforcements from Italy to France, and by filling the Anglo-American Expeditionary Force with grave forebodings'. In his telegram to Smuts Churchill had expressed his continued confidence in Alexander, whom he had wanted to visit. His hope to have been at the latter's side had, however, been dashed by 'time, distance, illness and advancing years'.

Churchill was not the only one to be worried about ill health, Italy and the forthcoming invasion. On 23 February Hitler left his headquarters in East Prussia, Wolfsschanze, which was now well within range of the Allied bombing force, and went by train to the Berghof. He had said he wanted to be nearer the Italian front, but clearly the heavy bombing of Berlin had had its effect, and even as he arrived at Obersalzburg, 600 British bombers were attacking Schweinfurt, and the sounds of anti-aircraft fire could be heard. He was also suffering from serious eye trouble, and at the Führer Conference that evening those who had not recently seen him were shocked by his physical deterioration. David Irving comments that Hitler, in reply to Eva Braun's reproaches about his pronounced stoop when walking, put it down to 'the burden of worries I'm carrying all the time'. While at the Berghof he discussed the weapons industry with his armament experts, and was told that flying-bomb production was well under way, and that it was protected from attack by the underground factory in which the plant was housed. 'In fact, Hitler had not yet decided when to launch the V1 flying-bomb attack on Britain. But that he could still make crucial decisions was well illustrated when on 8 March – it having become quite clear that Hungary was not merely dragging her feet in supporting Germany, but was actually planning to sabotage communications with the Wehrmacht's forces in southern Russia – he gave orders that Hungary would be invaded by German battle groups on the 19th. David Irving called this last conquest of Hitler's 'an outstanding coup'. Although the German troops involved had been extracted from other fronts, the dividend of Hungary's industry and its contribution of twice the number of Hungarian divisions for the campaign against the Russians made it all worth while.

The Eastern Front was going to need everything it could get, and on 20 March Hitler treated his generals to a speech during which he explained how – once the Anglo-American invasion had been defeated – the situation in the east would be revolutionized by transferring there forty-five divisions now positioned elsewhere in Europe. Field Marshal Rommel, who was present, recalled later that Hitler talked about the new secret weapons, jet fighters and submarines, and told the assembled generals that the Allied invasion would be in Normandy and Brittany, not at the Pas de Calais. He also declared that the most suitable landing places were those offered by the 'west coast peninsulas of Cherbourg and Brest', for these areas were suited for creating bridgeheads which would then be enlarged. The Führer went on to lay down that the enemy must not be allowed to 'survive longer than hours or at most days', and he quoted the German success in repelling the raid on Dieppe as an example. Once the enemy had been defeated, they would not try again, since to organize a further attempt would take months, to say nothing of their losses. It would also be 'a crushing blow to British and American morale. For one thing, it will prevent Roosevelt from being re-elected in the United States . . . For another, war weariness will grip Britain even faster, and Churchill, already a sick old man with his influence waning, won't be able to carry through a new invasion operation.' Hitler concluded by showing how the invasion's defeat would mean final victory for Germany, as the transfer of strength to the east would transform the situation there. Thus 'the whole outcome of the war depends on each man fighting in the west, and that means the fate of the Reich as well.' At the end of this meeting, Hitler talked to Rommel in private, and appointed him to command Army Group B in the west with a degree of control over the Commander-in-Chief's mobile reserve. The C-in-C himself, Field Marshal von Rundstedt, was less than pleased with this turn of events, for, as we shall see, he and Rommel had wholly different ideas of how the invading forces should be defeated. First, however, it is necessary to look at how the 'sick old man' was faring.

As the preparations for Overlord continued, there was little sign of Churchill's influence waning. At the beginning of March he reacts to the resumption of German air raids on London, as he had done before, by donning a steel helmet to observe the proceedings from the roof, and then going out to inspect damage after the 'all clear' has sounded. He gives his mind to Overlord – an operation to which he is 'hardening' more and more as the deadlock in Italy continues – and in particular to the problems of the Mulberry floating harbour, the plans for airborne assault, the air and naval support arrangements. He contemplates another meeting with Roosevelt to discuss policy matters related to Italy, France, Poland and Ireland. He encourages Mountbatten in his endeavours in the Far East, but is deeply saddened to hear of Wingate's death in an air crash, noting 'how much I had counted upon this man of genius, who might well have been a man of destiny'. He visits American troops with Eisenhower, and congratulates Stalin on further Russian advances, although he is angered and depressed by failure to agree with him about Poland's future. He seeks improved relations with de Gaulle, whom he knews will welcome the participation of a Free French division in the forthcoming battles for France. He writes to his son, Randolph, who is with Tito's partisans in Yugoslavia, with news of the family, including his visits to the antiaircraft battery where his daughter, Mary, gives the fire orders. Yet all this activity notwithstanding, he is especially disappointed at the British lack of success at Monte Cassino. Sir Alexander Cadogan, the Deputy Permanent Under-Secretary to the Foreign Office, noted on 21 March that Churchill confessed how tired he felt, and in a signal to Alexander the Prime Minister admitted 'The war weighs very heavy on us all just now.' Out of the delay in Italy, however, came one decision which pleased him – a postponement of Anvil, the projected landing in southern France, in order that pressure could be kept up on the Italian front to pin down as many German divisions as possible when Overlord got under way. Brooke, the CIGS, recalled that on hearing about it on 22 March, Churchill was 'in a good mood, and all went well beyond wasting an hour with interruptions [by Churchill] of every description'. These interruptions included the Prime Minister's wanting to know what was happening in Hungary – a relevant question in view of Hitler's action there; criticism of the Chiefs' of Staff use of the English language and of General Maitland Wilson's intelligence; reflections on the strain of the last three years; and notice of his intention to broadcast to the nation four days later.

In this broadcast Churchill dealt with both the military situation and with plans for post-war improvements in such matters as housing, education and employment. He spoke in praise of Stalin's leadership and the Red Army's advances, and also of British successes against the Japanese in Burma. But he also warned of forthcoming events: 'The hour of our greatest effort and action is approaching,' and this would require the same coolness and toughness from everyone as had been shown during the days of the Blitz; indeed, 'We may also ourselves be the object of new forms of attack from the enemy' (the first flying-bomb attack on Britain was less than three months away). But the country had, he said, shown its resolution. 'She had never flinched or failed. And when the signal is given, the whole circle of avenging nations will hurl themselves upon the foe and batter out the life of the cruellist tyranny which has ever sought to bar the progress of mankind.' Although this broadcast was criticized by some, Harold Nicolson made the telling point that war weariness had much to do with such censure, and that 'the ill-success of Anzio and Cassino is . . . a sad augury of what will happen when the Second Front begins.'

In considering this lack of Allied success, it is important to understand the magnificent quality of the German Army. Whether we are talking about the defenders of Cassino or those who were shortly to be defending the bocage of Normandy and the city of Caen, all of us who actually argued the toss with the Germans know what brave, dedicated and skilful soldiers they were. Often their tactical improvisation in defence and counter-attack, their superb fieldcraft and skill in concealment, their brilliant use of mortars, above all their perfected practice of fighting with the all-arms team of tanks, guns and infantry – all in the face of Allied air supremacy – taught the Allies, who in the later stages of the war were too apt to rely on sheer ironmongery and weight of fire power rather than skill at arms, lesson after lesson. None had greater battle skills than the soldiers of the German 1st Parachute Division, whose fanatical bravery and unshakeable morale, together with their exceptional fighting ability, held together the whole foundation of the astonishing defence of Cassino. We may take as an example their resistance to the bombardment of the German defences in the town of Cassino itself, which began on 15 March. The idea was to obliterate the defenders by dropping 1,000 tons of bombs, and a rather greater weight of artillery shells, on the town. Yet despite this, soldiers of the 1st Parachute Division survived and went on with the fight. Alexander had expressed the view that it was inconceivable that troops should be left alive after eight hours' concentrated hammering. He was wrong, and later paid tribute to the German parachutists by saying that no other troops in the world could have stood up to such a battering and then gone on to fight with such fierceness and tenacity. It was to be another two months or so before the final, and this time conclusive, battle for Cassino would be fought. Hitler drew great comfort from the fact that in Italy enemy air superiority and bombing did not prevent German soldiers from fighting well, even though they had only slit trenches for protection. Therefore, the Führer argued the Atlantic Wall fortifications, which were protected by 20 feet of reinforced concrete, would render Allied air attacks impotent. Certainly his renowned lieutenant, Erwin Rommel, was doing his best to prepare for the assault he knew was coming.

In 1942 Hitler had recalled Field Marshal von Rundstedt, whom he had sacked as commander of Army Group South in Russia in November 1941, to be Commander-in-Chief West, and had ordered him to prepare for the expected invasion. Rundstedt had little faith in fixed linear fortifications; he had, after all, pushed through them himself often enough. Yet while it was true, as Jodl had said, that 'along a front of 2,600 kilometres it is impossible to reinforce the coastal front with a system of fortifications in depth at all points,' not to wrest every advantage from so formidable an obstacle as the English Channel would have been to misplay a strong hand. Such natural defences were not presented to military commanders every day. Rundstedt was fond of boasting that 'we Germans do not indulge in the tired Maginot Spirit,' and indeed the German Army had demonstrated on innumerable occasions with what aggressive spirit it could mount counter-attacks against even the most formidable offensives. Yet Time, as Shakespeare reminds us, has a wallet at his back in which he puts alms for oblivion. For Rundstedt not to seize with both hands the alms which Time offered him was to invite his own oblivion. His plan – to defend strongly those important areas which were most vulnerable, to deny ports through which the Allies could build up their strength, and to have powerful armoured reserves plus air support ready to move to enemy beachheads and eliminate them – made sense in theory. It made none in practice, for the conditions on which it depended – panzer troops and Luftwaffe units of sufficient power – simply did not exist. Rundstedt had some 60 divisions with which to defend his 2,000 miles of coastline, but half of these, against his will yet on the Führer's direct orders, were manning the Atlantic Wall. Many others were weak, worn-out formations from the Eastern Front. Although Rundstedt pressed repeatedly for more men and more weapons, and was as consistently denied them, he had received a not wholly welcome reinforcement in the form of another field marshal – Rommel.

As has been said, Rommel was to command Army Group B, responsible among others for the very sector which the Allies were going to invade. *His* ideas were very different from Rundstedt's, for he maintained that the invasion must be defeated on the beaches. Once ashore, he believed, Allied forces would be so powerfully supported by air forces that German mobile reserves designed to intervene would never get to the scene of action. Therefore the enemy had to be annihilated before he ever reached the main battlefield. The invading troops had to be stopped in the water. Rommel always matched his words with action, and in the relatively short time he had – from February 1944 – he deployed every kind of ingenious device for making the Allies' task more difficult: underwater explosives, millions of mines on the beaches, gun sites protected by steel and concrete, pillboxes, wire, machine-guns, 88mm anti-tank guns. To deter airborne landings he organized the flooding of low-lying ground and had booby-trapped posts driven into the earth where there were suitable dropping zones; areas where gliders might land were seeded with obstructions. His whole defensive strategy depended on having as much fire power in the shop window as possible, knowing as he did that obstacles, however fiendish or sophisticated, are not much use unless covered by fire. Being convinced that all would turn on the first twenty-four hours or so, for he believed that once the Allies were firmly ashore, it would be very difficult to dislodge them, he wanted to put as much panzer strength up in the front line as he could. In this, however, he was strongly opposed by the commander of Panzer Group West, General Geyr von Schweppenburg, who wanted to keep his main forces in reserve until the principal Allied landings had been located. The whole question was referred to Hitler, who backed neither view fully, so that Rommel did not get his panzers in sufficient strength forward, nor Geyr von Schweppenburg a powerful and properly supported reserve. Compromise proved fatal. There was, too, another area in which Hitler was to compromise, again greatly to the Allies' benefit. A great Allied deception operation was mounted to convince the Germans that the main landings would be made north of the Seine in the Pas de Calais area, and so convinced did the Germans become, that the entire Fifteenth Army was stationed well to the north-east of

Normandy. The one man to guess correctly where the landings would be effected was the Führer himself, with the result that certain reinforcements to the Normandy area were made, much to the consternation of Allied intelligence staffs. Happily, Hitler did not fully back his intuition, partly no doubt because he wished to protect the V weapon sites in the Pas de Calais sector.

While Hitler's worry was to keep his various enemies at bay until the new secret weapons should enable him to turn the tables on them, Churchill was finding that his grand strategic concept, of flexible manoeuvres and the ability to push right-handed in the Mediterranean, or left-handed in North-West Europe, or both-handed as circumstances and resources permitted, was undergoing some revision because of a lack of – resources. Although the American Chiefs of Staff had agreed to postpone Anvil, they had not agreed to cancel it. It was now to take place in July, a decision which both Brooke and Churchill deplored. The CIGS complained that it would mean calling a halt to operations in Italy in order to start new ones in southern France during the most crucial phase of Overlord. Churchill expressed his displeasure that decisive battles in Italy, having already been ruined by pulling out seven divisions for Overlord, were now to be compromised again by Anvil; he chafed, too, at the apparent incapability of Alexander's armies to renew the offensive at Cassino and Anzio. There was, however, some encouragement to be gleaned from a presentation of D-Day plans given at Montgomery's headquarters at St Paul's School in West London at which the General himself, Admiral Sir Bertram Ramsay and Air Chief Marshal Sir Trafford Leigh-Mallory[1] gave accounts of what was to happen. Churchill addressed the assembled commanders and later signalled to Roosevelt his confidence in the operation, dismissing fears that heavy casualties would be sustained; it was rather the Germans who would suffer in this way. But despite this hopeful note, the Prime Minister was beset with problems, and both Brooke and Colville observed how old and tired the Prime Minister seemed. Martin Gilbert has admirably summed up the innumerable difficulties with which, after four years at the head of affairs, Churchill was still faced:

> *Anvil* versus a vigorous follow-up campaign in Italy, the American refusal to transfer landing craft then lying unused in the Pacific in order to make sure of success in Italy, the Bay of Bengal versus the Pacific as the regions for Britain's Far Eastern offensive, the future of Poland, Yugoslavia and Greece demanding time and decisions, Anglo-American relations requiring a constant watch, Anglo-Soviet relations at a low ebb, de Gaulle clamant, *Overlord* looming, the German secret weapons imminent. No day passed without one or other, or several, of these issues demanding urgent discussion.

[1] Respectively the Allied forces' land, sea and air commanders for the invasion.

All of which would have broken any other man, so that it is little wonder that Churchill confided to Brooke on 7 May, having told him that 'Roosevelt was not well and that he was no longer the man he had been,' that 'this also applied to himself . . .' 'I have never yet heard him admit,' Brooke recorded, 'that he was beginning to fail.' Further encouragement was on the way, however.

On 11 May Alexander launched Operation Diadem, his great offensive in Italy whose object was to give the greatest possible assistance to Overlord by destroying or containing in the Mediterranean area as many German military formations as possible. Its purpose was not, it must be noted, to capture Rome – that was incidental to the plan. The operation certainly succeeded in containing some twenty-one operational German divisions. That it did not do more damage to General Heinrich von Viettinghoff's Tenth Army was the result of the Germans' skill in recovery and withdrawal, together with General Mark Clark's vanity, for he wanted his army to be the first to enter Rome. One of the most striking features of Alexander's offensive was the sheer international character of the armies which took part in it. Initial attacks were made by American, French, British and Polish divisions. Commonwealth participants included New Zealanders, Indians, Canadians and South Africans.[1] It was the Poles who eventually took Cassino; it was the French – the Goumiers from the Corps Expéditionnaire Français commanded by General Alphonse Juin – who outflanked the Gustav and Adolf Hitler Lines; it was the Americans who advanced so effectively from Anzio; and by 25 May, two weeks after the offensive began, it seemed that it was virtually all over for the Germans. The US Fifth and British Eighth Armies[2] had broken through the Gustav and Hitler lines from the south and caused Viettinghoff's Tenth Army to withdraw, while General Truscott's force from Anzio had broken out and was driving forward in order to trap the retiring Germans. It was then that General Clark gave his astonishing order to Truscott to change direction and head for Rome – in direct defiance of Alexander's instructions. Churchill, with unusual restraint, called this decision of Clark's 'unfortunate', but the fact was that much of Viettinghoff's Tenth Army got away to fight another day. For all Alexander's Order of the Day calling for the destruction of the German armies in Italy, almost another year was to pass before he finally achieved it and received their surrender. Yet

---

[1] Earlier that month, on 1 May, Churchill had opened a conference for the Dominion Prime Ministers, during which the war situation was reviewed, and the forthcoming great events in Italy and Normandy discussed. Colville noted 'the great tribute paid by the Dominion PMs to our own Prime Minister's leadership'.

[2] Eighth Army was now commanded by Lieutenant-General Sir Oliver Leese, Montgomery having returned to Britain early in January to take part in the planning for Overlord.

Rome fell on 4 June[1] and two days later Churchill announced the liberation of the Italian capital by Alexander's armies in a House of Commons statement. But however welcome this news, it was utterly overshadowed by a further piece of news – the Allies had that day landed in Normandy. 'Instantly, and irrevocably,' wrote Ronald Lewin, 'the Italian campaign had been reduced to a sideshow.' A.J.P. Taylor went so far as to claim that with the landings in France 'the taking of Rome, and indeed British strategy in the Mediterranean, lost all significance'. This view of things was not one held by Churchill at the time, however encouraged and stimulated he had been by the events of D-Day.

In predicting what would happen on D-Day, Montgomery, C-in-C of all ground forces – US, Canadian and British troops for Overlord, anticipated with great accuracy what would be the tactics of his old rival, Rommel. At his Final Presentation of Plans on 15 May, at which both HM King George VI and Churchill were present, Montgomery declared: 'He [Rommel] will do his best to Dunkirk us, not to fight the armoured battle on ground of his own choosing, but to avoid it altogether by preventing our tanks from landing by using his own tanks well forward. On D-Day he will try to force us from the beaches and secure Caen, Bayeux, Carentan.' Montgomery also anticipated that Rommel would try to contain what penetrations were made by holding tactically important positions commanding roads which led inland through the bocage.[2] What his own troops must do, therefore, was to thrust deeply in from the beaches and gain sufficient space to disrupt Rommel's plans, contain his reserves and build up more strength. Once they gained control of the main enemy lateral Granville-Vire-Argentan-Falaise-Caen and were firmly in possession of the area enclosed by it, they would have the lodgement area they wanted and could begin to expand.

In his book *The History of Warfare*, Montgomery explained that after obtaining his lodgement area – and it was to be many weeks after D-Day before he did – he would conduct the battle in such a way that the British[3] would draw and hold the main German, particularly armoured, strength against themselves on the left flank, allowing the Americans to push forward, gain more ground and break out on the right, the western, flank. 'So, more or less,' he wrote, 'the battle

---

[1] Harold Macmillan, who had been at Eton, sent a telegram to Alexander, a Harrovian, congratulating him on his victory and adding how thoughtful it was of Alexander to have won the city on the Fourth of June. To which Alexander replied: 'Thank you. What is the Fourth of June?'

[2] Wooded countryside, with many small irregular fields, copses, hedges and banks.

[3] As well as having command of all ground forces for the actual invasion (and for some time thereafter), Montgomery was also C-in-C Twenty-First Army Group, in which, besides British and Canadian troops, there were, or would be later, Polish and Free French formations.

developed.' 'More or less' was a necessary qualification, for like all Montgomery's so-called 'master plans', this one only worked because he had sufficient time, reserves and patience to vary it. This point is well illustrated by recalling that Caen – an objective that was to have been seized on D-Day, 6 June – was not actually taken until 10 July. But Montgomery was at his best in the hard-slogging, slow-moving, set-piece battle of attrition, and in the end his strategy prevailed. Indeed, Normandy was his *chef d'oeuvre*. He had made it clear at the outset that 'We shall have to send the soldiers into this party "seeing red". They must see red. We must get them completely on their toes, having absolute faith in the plan; and imbued with infectious optimism and offensive eagerness. Nothing must stop them. Nothing. If we send them into battle in this way – then we shall succeed.' One of Montgomery's greatest qualities as a commander was that he was able to win and keep the confidence of his soldiers. They thought of him as a battle winner, and they were right.

There had been a time when Hitler was thought of by his generals and soldiers as a battle winner. He had won Austria and Czechoslovakia without even fighting, then gone on to win battles for half of Poland, Denmark, Norway, Holland, Belgium, France and most of the Balkans, as well as Greece and Crete. But now things were going wrong everywhere. On the Eastern Front, quite apart from having to stomach the loss of the Ukraine, in April 1944 Hitler was obliged to witness débâcle in the Crimea where, in a five-week battle, the Wehrmacht lost over 75,000 soldiers. Furthermore, Germany's loss of the Crimea had an instant effect on Turkey, who now was persuaded to declare that she was no longer neutral – something Churchill had for so long been trying to bring about – but was on the side of the Allies, not in the sense of declaring war on Germany, but in ceasing to supply her with war material. After their success in the Crimea the Russians remained relatively quiet until June, and there was therefore between April and June no denuding of the Eastern Front. In Italy, before Alexander's Diadem offensive, Hitler took comfort from the fact that Kesselring was holding the Allies at bay – 'with his little finger' as the Führer put it. Even in late May, when Alexander's final offensive that would eventually lead to the capture of Rome was well under way, and Field Marshal Wolfgang von Richthofen, commanding the Luftwaffe in the south, had come to see him at the Berghof, what was happening in Italy was regarded by Hitler as a ruse to induce the German High Command to divert army and air force reserves away from France. Richthofen noted in his diary on 23 May:

3 pm with the Führer. He's grown older, good-looking,[1] very calm, very definite views on the military and political situation, no worries about any-

---

[1] Cf. Albert Speer: 'My God, how could I have never seen how ugly he is.'

thing. Again and again one can't help feeling this is a man blindly following his summons, walking unhesitatingly along the path prescribed to him without the slightest doubt as to its rightness and the final outcome . . . The unpleasant military occurrences at Cassino and since this morning at the Anzio beachhead are contemplated by him quite calmly: as he puts it, we can be thankful that we are fighting so far down. After all, last September [1943] we all thought, and he did too, that this summer would see us fighting in the Apennines or even in the Alps.

Even under the most difficult military circumstances, Hitler never forgot his position as a maker of world history, or what his place in that history would be. When the capture of Rome was clearly imminent, Kesselring wanted to destroy the bridges over the Tiber and so slow down the Allied advance, but Hitler would not hear of it. His enemies might destroy the Monte Cassino abbey, but he would not go down in history as the destroyer of Rome. In truth, however, this was irrelevant, for what was happening in Rome during the first week of June 1944 had little effect on the far more momentous activities in Normandy.

The days immediately preceding D-Day found Churchill enjoying himself in his special train at Portsmouth; visiting Eisenhower's headquarters, where on 3 June it was decided to postpone the launching of the invasion until the 6th, because of bad weather reports; going in a launch accompanied by Smuts and Ernest Bevin, the Minister of Labour and National Service, to look at landing craft; and watching the embarkation of troops at Southampton. Next day, 4 June, he received de Gaulle and told him how the landings would be effected and in what strength. Although the French leader hailed the planned invasion as 'an affair of momentous importance', he was notably aggrieved that no proper agreement had been reached about the future civil administration of France when liberated. Churchill did his best to smooth the meeting between them, and as Eden recalled: 'I arrived in time to walk down the railway line [to where Churchill's train was stopped] with de Gaulle. The Prime Minister, moved by his sense of history, was on the track to greet the General with arms outstretched. Unfortunately de Gaulle did not respond easily to such a mood.' The principal difficulty was that President Roosevelt was not willing to consent to conversations between Britain, the United States and France on *political* matters, although Roosevelt was perfectly content to receive de Gaulle himself. Churchill summed up the British Government's views like this: 'If General de Gaulle wanted to ask the President to agree to give him the title deeds of France, the answer was *No*. If he wanted to ask the President to agree that the Committee of National Liberation was the principal factor with whom we should deal in France, the answer was *Yes*.' De Gaulle's reaction was to say that he fully understood that if France and the United States were in disagreement, Britain would side with the United States. The meeting was not a success.

After returning to London, Churchill saw the Chiefs of Staff on the following day and was full of optimism both as to the outcome of the invasion and of Alexander's offensive, even going so far as to suggest that all the German forces in Italy would be accounted for, so that they could then 'decide how best to use our armies in Italy to support the main adventure'. Once more he was reverting to the idea of an alternative to Anvil; unfortunately, however, bitter fighting in Italy was to continue for the best part of another year. Churchill was also so optimistic about Overlord that Brooke felt it necessary 'to damp him down a bit'. In the event, the Prime Minister's optimism was justified, for when he received first reports of the invasion on waking in the 10 Downing Street Annexe on the morning of 6 June, it seemed that – except for the American landing at Omaha Beach – things had gone well. In telegraphing the news to Stalin Churchill explained that the airborne landings, which had been on a large scale, had been very successful; that for the sea assault, mines, obstructions and gun batteries had been dealt with; and that infantry, tanks and SP guns were making their way forward. That morning Churchill made a statement in the House of Commons, stressing how difficult and complicated had been 'this vast operation', and spoke there again in the evening about the satisfactory progress made. Next day it was clear that British troops had secured a 'substantial bridgehead', that Omaha Beach had been cleared of its defenders, that intense bombing of German positions had taken place and that the build-up was proceeding. Much would depend in the next few days upon which side could increase its strength more rapidly. 'By tonight,' Churchill signalled Stalin on the same day, 7 June, 'we hope to have the best part of a quarter of a million men ashore, including a considerable quantity of armour all landed from special ships or swimming ashore by themselves.' Another important advantage enjoyed by the Allies was that enemy opposition in the air and at sea was 'slight'. That same evening there was an easing of the British position with regard to de Gaulle. The War Cabinet agreed to seek à deux some basis of agreement in recognizing the French National Committee of Liberation as the 'authoritative government of France', and then 'commend it' to the United States.

Perhaps one of the most extraordinary circumstances surrounding the invasion of Normandy was that although during the night of 5–6 June it was clear to those Germans defending the Atlantic Wall that something was up – parachute and glider assaults, noises of landing craft and other vessels, including warships, offshore – and although reports to this effect were reaching Hitler's staff at the Berghof, the Supreme Commander of the Wehrmacht, who alone could authorize movement of reserves to counter the invasion, was not even woken up. In his incomparably valuable study, *Hitler's War*, David Irving explains that it was not until midday that the Führer learned, during his daily conference, of the situation, and therefore no decision on Rundstedt's requests to make use of OKW's panzer formations being kept in reserve could be taken; by then the Allies had seized a beachhead west of the River Orne which measured some two miles deep and fifteen miles wide. 'Thus,' Irving writes, 'by the time Hitler's war conference began, the Battle for France was already lost – if Rommel's dictum about defeating the enemy on the beaches had meant anything.' There were, however, two other reasons for the German failure to react quickly enough against the Normandy beachhead to drive the Allies back into the sea. One was that Allied air supremacy made it virtually impossible for the Germans to move their reserves forward by day. The other was that the Allied deception plan had been so effective that the German High Command still anticipated a further and *principal* landing by another invasion army elsewhere, so that Hitler felt unable to concentrate all available reserves against the Normandy incursion.

It soon became clear that the Allies were winning the battle of the build-up, for by 18 June Montgomery had twenty divisions ashore. Opposing him were only eighteen divisions, some so reduced in numbers that the actual fighting strength of these divisions was, in sum, perhaps only three-quarters of this total. Hitler had refused to acknowledge the realities of the situation when, on the day before, he had conferred with Rommel and Rundstedt at Margival – in the command post which, four years earlier, had been specially constructed for the Führer in order that he could supervise the invasion of England from it. General Hans Speidel, Rommel's Chief of Staff, who was present, reported that Hitler appeared 'worn and sleepless, playing nervously with his spectacles and an array of coloured pencils which he held between his fingers'. While Hitler sat on a stool, the two field marshals stood up and had to listen to a condemnation of the manner in which they had conducted the defence. He could not yet see that there was by now no question of throwing the invaders back into the sea, thereby allowing him once more to deploy all his strength to deal with the Red Army. He wanted nothing less than annihilation, and meanwhile every foot of territory was to be contested while the V weapons brought Britain to her senses.

When Rommel urged Hitler to end the war, he was sharply told to look to his own front and leave the war's future course to the Supreme Commander. Later that month both Rommel and Rundstedt renewed their efforts to persuade Hitler to end the war. But facts and reason held no interest for him, and certainly could not prevail upon him to the extent of making him change his mind. When the battle of the Odon removed any chance the Germans might have had to split Allied forces by striking at Bayeux, and Rundstedt warned OKW that the battle for Normandy was lost, Keitel was in despair. 'What shall we do?' he wailed. 'Make peace, you fools,' was Rundstedt's uncompromising reply. Once more he was relieved of his command, this time replaced by Kluge. Hitler could not admit that he was in the wrong; rather it was that one more of the 'gentlemen who write *von* in front of their names' had let him down. But not Kluge, nor any other soldier, could alter the realities of the situation, and Kluge was himself obliged to concede a few weeks later that 'in face of the enemy's complete command of the air, there is no possibility of our finding a strategy which will counterbalance its truly annihilating effect, unless we give up the field of battle'. He added that in spite of his determination to stand fast, as the Führer had ordered, the price to be paid was the destruction of his armies and the dissolution of the front.

So the Allied victory came about, although not as rapidly as Churchill had hoped. His own first visit to Normandy was much more agreeable than Hitler's. In his characteristic way, the Prime Minister had wanted to go to the beachhead on D-Day itself, and only the King's intervention, to the effect that if Churchill insisted on going, then he, the King, would come too, had deterred him. Now, on 12 June, accompanied by Smuts and Brooke, Churchill got his wish. He was never happier than when near the scene of military activity, and after being greeted on the beach by Montgomery, they all went to the General's headquarters, some five miles inland, for a briefing and lunch. Churchill's impressions of the countryside as they toured the bridgehead were admirably summed up by his comment that they were surrounded 'by fat cattle lying in luscious pastures with their paws crossed'. There seemed to be little actual fighting, except for air and naval activity. Back at the beaches Churchill watched more guns and tanks being unloaded, and then after embarking in a destroyer and observing naval bombardments of German positions, asked Admiral Vian, commanding the Eastern Task Force, whether their own destroyer could not join in.[1] Vian complied, and Churchill was later able to signal Roosevelt that 'we went and had a plug at the Hun from our destroyer, but although the range was 6,000 yards he did not honour us with a reply'. Nothing could have been better designed to cap so enjoyable a visit and allow the Prime Minister to return to London thoroughly content. But a grave and dangerous new phase of Hitler's war on Britain awaited him.

Next day, 13 June, came news of the first flying bombs. In this first attack only four of the twenty-seven V1s, as they were called, reached London, but many more were to do so before an effective defence against them was found.

---

[1] Vian's career had flourished since, in *Cossack*, he had captured the *Altmark*. Appointed to the DSO in 1940 (with Bars in the same year and 1941), he had been promoted rear admiral in 1941, and knighted in 1942.

In essentials, this involved the deployment of anti-aircraft guns at the coast to destroy them as they came in over the Channel, while fighter aircraft dealt with them inland. In all more than 6,000 people were killed by VIs, mostly in London, and their threat, together with the unnerving drone whose sudden cutting-off signified the bomb's imminent fall, were such that there was another evacuation of London by about 1½ million inhabitants. Churchill's reaction to the threat was, once more, characteristic of him. On the night of 15 June, during which some 150 flying bombs were launched against Britain, the Private Secretary on duty at the No 10 Annexe went outside to see what was happening, only to meet Churchill, who was already seeing for himself – 'exemplifying', as the Private Secretary put it, 'the PM's energy and (hair-raising) disregard for personal danger'. Churchill also signalled to Stalin that 'Hitler has started his secret weapon upon London', practically rejoiced in the idea that he and the people were once more in the front line, and agreed with the Crossbow Committee – which had been set up to deal with the VI problem – that sounding of sirens should be kept to a minimum for 'one must have sleep, and you either woke well rested [after a raid] or in a better land'. Although effective defensive action had virtually neutralized the VI attacks by early in September, they were followed by the even more destructive V2 rockets, against which no counter-measures were found.[1] More than 1,100 of them killed about 2,700 people, again mostly in London. Fortunately most of the rocket-launching sites were overrun relatively swiftly by the advancing Allied armies. It was, however, with the disappointingly slow advance of these armies in the latter part of June and the first three weeks or so of July that Churchill was now most concerned, together with the need to arm and supply the French Maquis in their guerrilla activities against the Germans, and with the American insistence that Anvil, the landings in southern France, should be launched by 15 August.

The question of pursuing the Italian campaign to bring off some great strategic success had long been dear to Churchill's heart, and in this he was supported by General Maitland Wilson, commanding in the Mediterranean. On 19 June Wilson signalled to Eisenhower, pointing out that to proceed with Anvil would mean halting Alexander's armies in Italy to the south of the Gothic [Pisa-Rimini] Line, thus disrupting the whole force and giving the Germans time to rest and regroup. He therefore argued for the rapid capture of Florence and an attack directed on Bologna, so that the Po could be forced early in August, the line Venice-Verona reached by the end of that month, after which there would be an advance on Trieste and the Ljubljana Gap. Fourteen divi-

---

[1] A true long-range ballistic missile, the V2 descended from beyond the earth's atmosphere at very high speed, and silently.

sions would be employed. Alexander went so far as to maintain that, given his present force of twenty-seven divisions – and making no deduction for Anvil (shortly to be renamed *Dragoon*) – once the Ljubljana Gap, through which ran the main communications from Italy into northern Yugoslavia, was in Allied hands, the road to Vienna, with all the political advantages thereby offered, would be open. Never mind all the difficult and mountainous country which barred the way, so Alexander's argument went, what his armies had done in Italy, they could do elsewhere. Not even the Alps would be an obstacle to his skilled and enthusiastic soldiers. It may be conceived how the prospect of an advance on Vienna fired Churchill's imagination. Brooke was more sceptical, however. They would be embarking on a campaign which would involve crossing the Alps in winter, and there would be three enemies – the Germans, the weather and the mountains. His mind was changed not by Churchill, nor by his American colleagues, but by the Germans. As soon as Ultra revealed that Kesselring, although intending to withdraw to the Gothic Line when forced to, was planning to delay that withdrawal as long as practicable by fighting south of that line from positions astride Lake Trasimene, the CIGS insisted that Alexander's strength must be maintained in order to harass and destroy as much as possible of the German Army in Italy *before* it sought refuge in the Gothic Line. A telegram from the British Chiefs of Staff to the Americans tried to make this clear:

> We are convinced that the Allied forces in the Mediterranean can best assist *Overlord* by completing the destruction of the German forces with which they are now in contact, and by continuing to engage, in maximum strength, all German reinforcements deployed to oppose their advance.

General Eisenhower's reply to Maitland Wilson made it clear that he was firmly of the opinion that Anvil should be undertaken at the expense of Allied armies in Italy. He saw the landing in southern France as part of his Normandy battle, and was certain that Allied resources would not permit two major campaigns to strive after two decisive objectives. The US Chiefs of Staff, of course, supported Eisenhower, and not even Churchill's eloquence with Roosevelt could move the Americans from this position. However much the Prime Minister might press the President that, while Overlord should be reinforced to the utmost, yet at the same time opportunities in the Mediterranean should not be missed, the latter continued to insist that five divisions must be withdrawn from Italy for Anvil/Dragoon (in the event six went). It was then that Churchill signalled to Roosevelt his opinion, quoted at the head of this chapter, that a 'major strategic and political error' was being made. He went further in making his disappointment and displeasure known:

[427]

What can I do Mr President, when your Chiefs of Staff insist on casting aside our Italian offensive campaign, with all its dazzling possibilities, relieving Hitler of all his anxieties in the Po basin, and when we are to see the integral life of this campaign drained off into the Rhone valley in the belief that it will in several months carry effective help to Eisenhower so far away in the North?

He added that if the US Chiefs of Staff insisted on these withdrawals from the Italian campaign, leaving 'all our hopes there dashed to the ground', HM Government 'must enter a solemn protest', though they would of course do everything possible 'to make a success of anything that is undertaken'. Churchill ended by expressing his sorrow to have to write in such a way, assuring Roosevelt that differences in how the war should be conducted would never diminish his personal gratitude to him. His suggestion in his telegram to Roosevelt that neither of the two operations into which the Italian campaign was being split would be decisive was borne out by events. Although Roosevelt had maintained that the twenty-one divisions left to Alexander would be sufficient 'to chase Kesselring north of Pisa-Rimini' the long-drawn-out and bloody battles for the Gothic Line were soon to prove him wrong. As for Anvil/Dragoon, which was eventually launched on 15 August, although it may have been what A.J.P. Taylor called 'a belated triumph for American views of strategy' in that it robbed Churchill of his Mediterranean adventure, 'postponement destroyed its purpose . . . [having been] planned in order to distract German strength from the north . . . it was now the landing in the north which distracted the Germans from the south'. To see how this came about, we must rejoin Montgomery in Normandy.

Churchill was, as always, impatient with the pace of battle. Although on 10 July he was able to send a congratulatory message to Montgomery on the capture of Caen, four days earlier at a conference with the Chiefs of Staff and ministers – held in the underground War Room as a protection against flying bombs (earlier that day he had addressed the House of Commons about the flying-bomb attacks and had reiterated his confidence in London's invincibility) – he had criticized Montgomery's slow progress and caution, greatly to Brooke's irritation. The CIGS, as usual, gave as good as he got, and suggested that Churchill should trust his generals and not belittle them; according to Brooke: 'He was furious with me, but I hope it may do some good in the future.' After the capture of Caen Churchill was able to send a favourable account of affairs in Normandy to Stalin, assuring him that the 'front will continue to broaden and the fighting will be unceasing'. He was also able to congratulate the Soviet leader on the Red Army's success in its summer offensive.

The second half of July 1944 was to usher in events of high drama on both the Eastern and Western Fronts. On 14 July Hitler had flown back to his Wolfsschanze headquarters at Rastenburg. He was convinced that only his presence there could put backbone into German resistance on the Eastern Front sufficiently to prevent collapse, and already the battle for Vilna, the last defensive stronghold before the Red Army reached East Prussia, had begun. Reichsminister Martin Bormann[1] commented on how timely it was that the Führer had returned personally 'to stiffen the often shamefully weak-kneed attitude of the Army's officers'. Hitler had ordered the establishment of a new defensive line based on the Rivers San and Vistula through the Warsaw bridgehead and northwards along the River Narev, then on forward of the East Prussian frontier to the Baltic. He had also given orders for the raising of fifteen more grenadier divisions in Germany, and on 15 July he summoned the commander of the Replacement Army, Colonel-General Friedrich Fromm, to Wolfsschanze. Fromm was accompanied by Colonel von Stauffenberg, his Chief of Staff, who was there to brief the Führer about the state of these new divisions. On the following day, as the Red Army continued its advance, seizing Grodno, crossing the River Bug and mounting an offensive towards Lvov, Churchill was investigating the possibility of a further Big Three meeting, signalling to Roosevelt that they must meet soon, and asking for the President's ideas. Roosevelt's reply suggested September.

In Normandy, Rommel was soldiering on, and was only stopped – as befitted such a man – by enemy action. His car was attacked by British aircraft on 17 July; gravely injured, he was finished with Normandy, indeed with any more generalship. Before he was wounded, however, he had made such dispositions that the progress of Operation Goodwood, Montgomery's great armoured attack to engage the German panzer divisions and 'write them down' to the extent that they could no longer prevent a break-out, was seriously hindered. The idea of Goodwood was for the three armoured divisions of British VIII Corps to advance, dominate the area Bourguébus-Vimont-Bretteville and destroy the enemy there. During its attempt to do so, VIII Corps contested the battlefield with SS General Sepp Dietrich's First Panzer Army; in particular, those old sparring partners from Western Desert days, 7th Armoured Division and 21st Panzer Division, were to argue the toss. The attack began on 18 July, after heavy bombing of the German positions, and although at first the British armour made some progress, they were – unbelievably at this stage of the war – not properly supported by infantry (the British were still not using armoured personnel carriers). The Germans, brilliant improvisers of defensive battle groups as they were, skilfully deployed tanks, anti-aircraft guns (in an anti-tank

---

[1] Hitler's Secretary since April 1943 and, since Hess's flight, effectively his deputy, Bormann wielded enormous influence with his master.

role) and SP guns to create a highly effective defence of the whole sector, making full use of defilade positions supplied by various villages, and successfully held up the British advance until 1st SS Panzer Division reinforced the Bourguébus Ridge. Some 600 British tanks were lost, about 7,000 yards of territory gained. By 19 July Goodwood had petered out. Richard Holmes compared it to a Great War 'push'. What it had achieved, however, was a further 'writing down' of German panzer strength, so that when Lieutenant-General Omar Bradley attempted to break out further west with his US Twelfth Army Group, as Montgomery had planned, he succeeded. On the following day, 20 July 1944, while Hitler was struggling with perhaps the worst crisis with which the Eastern Front had yet presented him, he was nearly assassinated.

Six months earlier, Guderian had tried in vain to convince Hitler of the need to appoint a Generalissimo with supreme responsibility for the East, just as Manstein had before him. Guderian had already addressed Goebbels and Himmler on the same point, but however much they might agree with him, they did nothing. Circumstances being as they were – with Guderian having lost all confidence in the Führer's military direction, and the latter unwilling to trust any individual or the army as a whole with independent power – it was no surprise that the running of the war stumbled along as before. Jodl perhaps put his finger on the real point when he asked Guderian: 'Do you know of a better supreme commander than Adolf Hitler?' It would not have been easy to name one, yet in the summer of 1944, when the war on two fronts – three if Italy is included – was bringing home to Hitler problems he had not previously encountered, his exercise of the supreme command had become calamitously bad; arguably as bad as he could possibly have made it. To insist that all important tactical decisions should be referred to him at the Berghof meant that on 6 June, when only immediate tactical response in Normandy could have been effective, he simply threw away any opportunity there might have been; as the days and weeks passed this same refusal to delegate simply made more certain than it already was both the Normandy bridgehead's inviolability, and the ease with which the Allies might break out from it. It was not just that Hitler could not bring himself to trust his commanders in the field; it was that his willpower had become a substitute for everything else.

On the Eastern Front things were even more serious. June had seen the Red Army begin its summer offensive. The German attempts to hold lines which were far too extended to defend properly and which Hitler would not agree to shorten led to the inevitable result. The front disintegrated. In July Minsk, Vilna, Pinsk, Grodno were all taken. East Prussia itself was threatened. It was little wonder, therefore, that there were those in the Wehrmacht and outside it who had begun once more to pluck up the courage to get rid of the man whose disastrous military policies were heading Germany for total defeat. But on 20

July Stauffenberg's bomb at Rastenburg failed to kill the Führer. Although badly shaken, but only slightly injured, he escaped with his life,[1] and his subsequent behaviour towards the conspirators, whether guilty or innocent, showed him at his most vindictive and most vile. Nothing seemed able, however, to shake his conviction that he had been chosen to shape the world's destiny. That same afternoon the puppet Mussolini arrived at Rastenburg to visit Hitler, who met him at the station, explained his remarkable escape, showed him the shambles of the conference room where the bomb had exploded, and led his guest off for tea. During the tea-party, an extraordinary scene took place. 'Quite suddenly,' wrote Hugh Trevor-Roper in *The Last Days of Hitler,*

> someone mentioned that other famous plot in Nazi history – the Roehm plot of June 30 1934, and the bloody purge which followed it. Immediately Hitler leapt up in a fit of frenzy, with foam on his lips, and shouted that he would be revenged on all traitors. Providence had just shown him once again, he screamed, that he had been chosen to make world history; and he ranted wildly about terrible punishments for women and children, – all of them would be thrown into concentration camps – an eye for an eye, and a tooth for a tooth – none should be spared who set himself against divine Providence. The court fell silent as the Führer raged for a full half-hour.

As far as revenge went, Hitler was as good as his word. His vengeance was appallingly comprehensive. In *The Nemesis of Power* John Wheeler-Bennett listed 160 of the victims – Admiral Canaris, Ulrich von Hassell (formerly the Ambassador in Rome), Witzleben, Beck and Rommel amongst them (the latter was allowed to take poison; then, to preserve the myth, he was given a state funeral with full military honours) – and noted that his list was not complete, that many more were executed. The 160 included 2 field marshals, 17 generals and more than 50 other officers. Those members of the *Offizierkorps* who did not know it already – and there could not have been many of them – thus had it brought home to them once and for all that the Führer was mad, bad, and dangerous to know. Churchill might have talked often enough about shooting generals; Hitler did so. 'I'm beginning to doubt,' he declared on the afternoon of 20 July, 'whether the German people are worthy of my great ideals. No one appreciates what I have done for them.' Yet however unworthy of him the leaders of the army might in his view have been, he could not in time of war do without them, particularly as the military situation was worse than it had ever been before. Nevertheless, first things had to come first, and what came now was the final subservience of the army to National Socialism. Guderian

---

[1] Of the others who had been in the room, one was killed instantly, four died from their injuries, and all the rest, including Jodl, were injured, some very severely.

became Chief of the Army General Staff on 21 July and two days later issued an Order of the Day in which he pledged to the Führer and the German people 'the unity of the Generals, of the Officer Corps and of the men of the Army'. Worse was to come. The Nazi salute became compulsory, and every General Staff officer was required to declare himself a 'National Socialist officer-leader'. But in spite of this capitulation Hitler continued to hold the army in open distrust. Germany's military position was hopeless enough already. That the commanders on all fronts should be distrusted and despised by their Supreme Commander was hardly a factor calculated to improve it. Just as the 20 July plot showed that the General Staff knew that Hitler had lost the war, so henceforth all military setbacks were classified by the Führer as acts of treachery.

On the day of the attempt on Hitler's life, Churchill was in France, since he wanted to visit both British and American troops on the eve of their break-out. He first went to Cherbourg, in the American sector, then on to inspect the beaches where US and British troops had landed. After spending the night aboard HMS *Enterprise*, he went the following day to Montgomery's headquarters, and spent the next two days touring the front, chatting to soldiers, watching guns in action, talking to generals, visiting Caen, touring RAF landing strips and generally enjoying himself. Moreover, his visit had, as such visits always did, a powerful effect on the men. 'I would like to tell you,' wrote Lieutenant-Colonel Stirling, Royal Artillery (subsequently a C-in-C British Army of the Rhine) 'how tremendously pleased, heartened and honoured every soldier was by your visit. It means very much to them that you should wish to come and see them at work in their gun pits.' On returning home, Churchill received news from Stalin that Lublin had been taken and that the Red Army's advance was continuing. In his reply, Churchill gave Stalin the latest information about Normandy and about plans for Italy and the Anvil/Dragoon landings; he also urged the Soviet leader to agree to a Big Three meeting in September – the place to be Scotland, which Roosevelt favoured.

On 25 July it became clear that Montgomery's strategy in Normandy had at last succeeded. A further attack by the British against the Germans positioned between Caen and Falaise had forced the latter to keep their panzer strength in the eastern sector, thereby enabling the Americans under Bradley and Patton (commanding US Third Army) to break through in the western part. Patton's armoured columns swept eastwards and the German armies were threatened with encirclement at Falaise. Now was the moment for Hitler to temper valour with discretion and withdraw his armies east of the Seine to fight again another day. In the event, however, he decided to do just the contrary, ordering Kluge[1]

---

[1] On 1 July Hitler had sacked Rundstedt – yet again – and replaced him with Kluge as C-in-C West.

to counter-attack the American corridor through Avranches and Mortain. What is more, from his East Prussian headquarters the Führer did not simply say what was to be done. Ignorant of the local situation, above all of the crippling influence of Allied air power, he laid down exactly how it was to be done. General Günther Blumentritt, Kluge's Chief of Staff, recorded that the plan, made from large-scale maps of France and without the benefit of any advice that Kluge and his subordinates might have had to offer, came to them in the greatest detail, showing which divisions were to be employed, which routes they were to advance along and which objectives were to be taken. That the attack failed was a matter of course. It was stopped and overwhelmed by Allied air power. When General Warlimont, Jodl's deputy on the OKW Operations Staff, explained to Hitler on 8 August what had happened and expatiated on the enormous difficulties of operating under the stifling effects of Allied air supremacy, adding that the counter-attack's failure certainly was not because of poor preparation, the Supreme Commander's reply revealed him at his most petulant, perverse and self-deluding – 'The attack failed because Field-Marshal von Kluge wanted it to fail.'

A week after Hitler's outburst, on 15 August, not only did the Allied landings in the south of France take place – far too late, as has already been observed, to influence affairs in Normandy – but Kluge, visiting the front, was out of touch with his headquarters for twelve hours. This led Hitler to believe that the Field Marshal was trying to make contact with the enemy in order to negotiate a surrender. Throughout his career, Hitler proved adept at finding good reasons for justifying a course on which he had already made up his mind. Having decided in this case that Kluge was bent on treachery, he was not slow to find reasons to fit in with all the other developments which might be related to his *idée toute faite*. It was only by chance, by accident he argued, that Kluge's plan of surrender had not succeeded: 'It's the only way you can explain everything the Army Group did; otherwise it would all be completely incomprehensible.'

So Kluge was dismissed and ordered back to Berlin, and Model was summoned to take over on the Western front. Each had something to report to the Führer. Kluge committed suicide on his way back to Germany. His farewell letter acknowledged the Führer's unparalleled leadership and applauded his iron will in conducting the gigantic battle, but urged him to concede that Providence might be more powerful still, and therefore to show his true greatness by putting an end to the hopeless struggle. Model's message, delivered after he had extracted what he could of the German Army in the West across the Seine, was more matter-of-fact. The best part of 20 infantry divisions, together with some 2,200 tanks and assault guns, had been the price of hanging on in Normandy. By anchoring the Seventh Army in a position where it could no longer react to the storm about to engulf it, Hitler had ensured that the

Falaise battle would devour two-thirds of its strength. Not Model nor anyone else could reverse the odds. Yet Hitler, even four months later, was talking of striving always to conduct a war of movement. In the summer of 1944 he had broken all the rules. He had forfeited both military strength and space without gaining enough of the commodity which in his view was most indispensable to him – time, time for the secret weapons, V rockets, jet aircraft, super submarines, to allow him to return to the charge and take a bond of fate. He had consistently contravened the very lesson which he himself had demonstrated so convincingly – that armoured forces could only operate with real success when complemented by air power. Worse still, he had continued with the dreadful process of putting the blame for his own mistakes on others. Above all, he had squandered, both in the east and the west, the Wehrmacht's power which he needed to fight the most important battle of his career, the battle for Germany. No wonder, as Speidel put it, the floodgates were creaking.

Yet like Macbeth, Hitler was determined to 'try the last'. On the very day of the Falaise battle, 19 August, he began to rattle the dice for a gambler's last throw; he began, in short, to plan for an offensive in the west. Jodl's diary for that day records the Führer's refusal to be dismayed and his intention to regain the initiative at the very first possible moment:

> August 19. The Führer discussed the equipment and manpower position in the West with Chief of *OKW*, Chief Army Staff and Speer. Prepare to *take the offensive in November* when the enemy's air forces can't operate. Main point: some *25 divisions must* be moved in the next one or two months.

On that same day Churchill was in Italy. The month so far had already given him a busy time of it. On 2 August he gave an account of the war situation to the House of Commons, reviewing the flying-bomb campaign against Britain, and assuring the House that every effort was being made to minimize the danger of further bombardment. At the same time the RAF was continuing to deliver an infinitely greater weight of bombs on Germany, although on military targets, rather than opting for the Germans' 'indiscriminate slaughter of the civilian population'. He spoke enthusiastically of the satisfactory end of Fascism in Italy, and of democratic progress in Greece. Meanwhile the 'German armies' were 'being beaten back on every front' and – referring to the 20 July plot – 'the highest personalities in the German Reich are murdering one another, or trying to, while the avenging Armies of the Allies close upon the doomed and ever-narrowing circle of their power.' His speech closed with some characteristically high-sounding phrases about battling on every front, intensifying the conflict, bearing whatever punishment might yet be in store – 'Drive on through the storm, now that it reaches its fury, with the same singleness of purpose and inflexibility of resolve as we showed to all the world when we were alone.'

Churchill had still not quite given up the idea of persuading Roosevelt and the American Chiefs of Staff to cancel Dragoon and employ its allotted forces – ten divisions in all – on the Atlantic coast instead and so speed up Eisenhower's advance across France. He signalled to Roosevelt about it; tried to convince Eisenhower at his headquarters on 5 August; sent a further plea to Harry Hopkins suggesting that the Dragoon divisions should be switched to St Nazaire as soon as it was captured, thus presenting Eisenhower 'with a new great port, as well as with a new army to operate on his right flank in the march'. On 7 August he flew to Normandy again, saw Montgomery and Bradley at their respective headquarters and then conferred again with Eisenhower, but on his return to London that day he found a reply from Hopkins warning him that a change of strategy from southern France to Brittany was most unlikely to be agreed. So it transpired, for in spite of another effort by the British Chiefs of Staff, on 8 August Churchill received a positive rejection from Roosevelt of any change. In his opinion, signalled the President, Dragoon should proceed as planned. He was supported by Eisenhower, and on 10 August the necessary orders for the execution of Dragoon were given.

It was not only in France that the question of how to exploit success was exercising British strategic planners. In Burma the British, Indian and Australian divisions from Fourteenth Army, under the brilliant and resolute General Slim, had decisively defeated the Japanese in the battles of Kohima and Imphal, which had followed the second Arakan campaign, and had lasted from March until July 1944. India had been saved, and the question which Mountbatten discussed with Churchill and the Chiefs of Staff on 8 August was how best to undertake the reconquest of Burma. Churchill was strongly in favour of Operation Vanguard, the recapture of Rangoon, and it was agreed next day that this operation should be given priority, while plans should also be made for the reconquest of Malaya. Should Germany collapse in the near future, it would be necessary to re-examine the strategic options, including that of taking Sumatra, from which the Japanese had ousted the Dutch. As far as assistance to the United States was concerned, it was decided that this would mainly be naval, for Britain would wish to participate in American action against Japan itself, and in Formosa.

Churchill was now bound for Italy, but before leaving on 10 August, he had agreed with Roosevelt that since the latter could not after all come to Scotland in view of the forthcoming presidential election, and because Stalin was unwilling to leave Russia, the two Western leaders should again meet at Quebec. They had to settle what the British should do in operations against Japan once Germany had surrendered, and also determine future policy for Alexander's armies in Italy – in his signal Churchill could not resist adding, referring to this last point, that there seemed to be a question of 'whether it [Alexander's Army] is to be bled white for *Dragoon* and thus stripped of all initiative'. As he was shortly to discover, however, although this army was bled, it was *not* stripped of all initiative. Churchill left England late on 10 August, flying first to Algiers, where he was able to talk to his son, Randolph, who was still recovering from injuries sustained in an air crash in Croatia. He was not, however, able to talk to de Gaulle, who had declined Churchill's invitation to meet him in Algiers, greatly to the Prime Minister's annoyance. Although Randolph advised his father to be more understanding towards de Gaulle, suggesting that from his position of victorious power, he could 'well afford to be magnanimous' to 'a frustrated man representing a defeated country', Churchill's later comment to his wife was that he feared a Gaullist France would be hostile to Britain. Churchill flew on to Naples, where he stayed with General Wilson at the Villa Rivalta. Next day, 12 August, on receiving news of the desperate struggle the Poles[1] were making against the Germans in Warsaw, Churchill signalled Stalin urging him to send aid in the form of arms and ammunition, as a Soviet army under Rokossovsky was a mere dozen miles from Warsaw. Stalin, whom Churchill had once described as 'a callous, a crafty, and an ill-informed giant', lived up to his callousness and craftiness by allowing the German Army to suppress the Polish rising in Warsaw with the utmost savagery and destruction, while the Red Army stood inactive at the gates of the city.

Churchill did not have much more success with Tito, whom he met at General Wilson's villa. He tried to persuade the Yugoslav leader to reaffirm his former statement that he would not impose a Communist regime on his country, and furthermore would undertake not to use armed strength to coerce the Yugoslav people in determining the country's future government. Tito was unwilling to go further than saying that it was not his intention to impose any regime on the people. More welcome to Churchill was a message from Roosevelt formally inviting him to a meeting at Quebec in September.

Eager as always to be near the scene of any military action, Churchill flew to Corsica on 14 August, and next day embarked in a destroyer, HMS *Kimberley*, to observe the landings in southern France, Operation Dragoon, which he had striven so hard and consistently to have cancelled. He was generous enough to signal Roosevelt that having witnessed the assault, all seemed to have gone well, with very few casualties. He also sent a message to the King describing the

---

[1] On 1 August, on the orders of the Polish Government-in-Exile, the 'Home Army', a large and powerful resistance organization, attempted to secure Warsaw before the Russians arrived. Under General Count Tadeusz Komorowski (who went under the codename 'Bor'), the Poles took the Germans by surprise, and it was not until 3 October that the rising was finally quelled. Polish casualties were about 15,000, German 10,000.

plan's perfect execution, assisted as it was by Eisenhower's operations in the north – in other words, it was 'the precise opposite of what was intended'. Churchill returned to Naples next day, but was soon on his way to further battlefields. On 17 August he met Alexander near Cassino and from high ground was given an account of how the battle had been fought. His longing to get to the front line was thwarted for several days by bad weather, but on 20 August he was able to visit the Canadians and observed the battle front near Florence. He still could not rid his mind of what he regarded as the wasted opportunity in Italy engendered by the removal of divisions from Alexander's command, continuing to hanker after a thrust into the Po Valley 'with all the gleaming possibilities and prizes which lay open towards Vienna'. Next Churchill was in Rome, where he discussed the problem of providing British troops for Greece, received good news from France where the Allied armies were making rapid progress (on 23 August the French Resistance rose up in Paris, and two days later General de Gaulle entered the city which was then cleared of Germans), talked to the Pope at the Vatican, and on the 23rd flew to Alexander's headquarters near Siena. Three days later he accompanied Alexander to watch the start of the latter's new offensive from an observation post. Churchill recalled later:

> The whole front of the Eighth Army offensive was visible. But apart from the smoke puffs of shells bursting seven or eight thousand yards away in a scattered fashion there was nothing to see.[1] Presently Alexander said that we had better not stay any longer, as the enemy would naturally be firing at observation posts like this and might begin again . . . [Churchill insisted on going further forward.]
>
> It was evident to me that only very loose fighting was in progress. In a few minutes the aide-de-camp came back and brought me to his chief who had found a very good place in the stone building, which was in fact an old château overlooking a rather sharp declivity. Here one certainly could see all that was possible. The Germans were firing with rifles and machine-guns from thick scrub on the farther side of the valley, about five hundred yards away. Our front line was beneath us. The firing was desultory and intermittent. But this was the nearest I got to the enemy and the time I heard most bullets in the Second World War.

Alexander commented that the Prime Minister loved being up in the front line, seeing British tanks and machine-guns in action, with shells flying over and

---

[1] Cf., again, Stendhal: 'From noon until three o'clock, we had an excellent view of all that can be seen of a battle – i.e., nothing at all.'

mines strewn about: 'It fascinated him – the real warrior at heart.' In responding to American pressure for a greater effort to be made on the Italian front in order to prevent the Germans withdrawing divisions from Italy to move them to the Western Front, however, Churchill pointed out that it was the weakening of Alexander's armies that had allowed this. Nevertheless, he told Roosevelt, Alexander had attacked on the Adriatic front, although he warned that although an advance of some nine miles had been made, 'the main position, the Gothic Line,[1] has still to be encountered'. Before leaving Italy, Churchill addressed a message to the Italian people, which was essentially one of reconciliation and of hope for the future. In commenting on this message in an editorial, *The Times* praised Churchill's strategic foresight in bending every effort to ensure that the Mediterranean was not lost to Britain during the war's earlier and most dangerous stages, and also spoke of the resultant defeat of the Axis in North Africa, Sicily and Italy, without which 'the launching of the invasion of Normandy would hardly have been imaginable'. It might be added here that the efforts and sacrifices of the Red Army had had something to do with it, too. None the less, to have the support of so influential a paper as *The Times* over such a fundamental feature of his strategy must have brought comfort. Having discussed further arrangements for a British landing in Greece, Churchill flew home via Malta, arriving on the evening of 29 August with a high temperature, having developed a chill during the flight. His wife noted that it was a slight attack, that in himself he was well. For a few days he remained in bed, but was as ever active, this time preparing for his forthcoming talks with Roosevelt in Quebec, codenamed Octagon.

As has been said, on 19 August Hitler was initiating plans for an offensive in the west. If this were to be launched, there would be two main requirements – stabilization of each front, and the creation of a strategic reserve. In the event, it proved much easier to halt the Western Allies than to slow down the Red Army. Hitler's War Directives for August and September 1944 are concerned with the construction of defensive positions in the south and west. Moreover, these directives dealt not only with military matters, nor were they addressed solely to military commanders. One of them reads:

> The system of positions for the defence of the Home theatre of war will be completed by a call-up of the civil population for total war. This is only possible by means of a political leadership conscious of its responsibilities. The great success which can be achieved by the employment of the masses in this way has already been shown in the East.

---

[1] Churchill found time to visit his old regiment, the 4th Hussars – as noted earlier – shortly before it took part in the Gothic Line battles.

In other words, foreign slave labour organized by Nazi Gauleiters (provincial governors) would build defensive walls for the German Reich. This was to be done in Northern Italy, the Apennine positions and the so-called Alpine Approaches; the West Wall would be rebuilt and put in a state of defence; the North Sea coast would be fortified and strengthened. In each of these directives clear distinction was drawn between the army and the party, and there is little doubt as to where Hitler places most reliance. The orders were given to the Führer's Secretary, Bormann, the 'Brown Eminence, sitting in the shadows', the man closest to Hitler for the longest period, although his power did not survive that of his master. Yet in the autumn of 1944 Bormann, as Reichsminister since May 1941, was still in control of the great Nazi Party machinery and through him went orders to his own chosen Gauleiters, 'new men, younger, more energetic, more fanatical men who owed everything not to the impersonal Party . . . but to Bormann himself'. In a directive dated 24 August 1944 overall responsibility for the West Wall, the so-called Siegfried Line, was given to the Gauleiters. Orders for its construction were complemented by instructions for its actual defence. Five years to the day after the declarations of war by Great Britain and France, Hitler's direction to Rundstedt, who had been reinstated as Commander-in-Chief West with effect from the following day, 4 September, began with an admission that the initiative had been forfeited:

Our own heavily tried forces, and the impossibility of bringing up adequate reinforcements quickly, do not allow us at the present moment to determine a line which must be held and which certainly can be held.

But the document hurried on to stress the need for gaining as much time as possible so that new formations could be raised and brought up to the west, ready for counter-attack. Therefore on the right (northern) flank and in the centre, the army would 'dispute every inch of ground'. On the left flank Army Group G was to assemble a mobile force, whose main task, after it had protected construction work on the Siegfried Line, would be 'to deliver a concentrated attack against the deep eastern flank and rear positions of the Americans'. In other words, Hitler's defence in the west would be designed to facilitate attack and so start again a war of movement.

Whether or not the Siegfried Line could be prepared, manned and held in sufficient strength depended on Rundstedt (whose reappointment dated from the day on which Antwerp fell to the Allies) and his ability to stop the movement of the Allied armies. His orders were to do this on the line of the Albert Canal, the Meuse and the Upper Moselle. Yet by 6 September, the day after he actually resumed command, the Allies had already established bridgeheads over the Albert Canal and the Meuse, and only by committing in a series of local attacks the very armoured forces which Model, who had reverted to command of Army Group B, had been assembling for a major counter-stroke was the line of the Upper Moselle being held. Six weeks would be needed, declared Rundstedt, to put the Siegfried Line in order, and while this was being done, he would require ten more infantry divisions and 2,000 tanks to conduct a successful defensive battle. Needless to say, he did not get them. Nevertheless, in spite of American forces crossing the Meuse on 8 September, actually reaching German soil four days later, and advancing across the frontier south of Aachen, and in spite also of Montgomery's bold but doomed airborne attempt to open the gap into northern Germany by seizing the road bridges over the Meuse, the Waal and the Lower Rhine at, respectively Grave, Nijmegen and Arnhem, the German defences held. This was not because of the tactical genius of Rundstedt or the courage and skill of the German soldiers – however great these were – but because the Allies failed to take this particular tide at the flood. They neglected those master rules for conducting war: absolute clarity of purpose, and ruthless concentration on that purpose. When we note that in September 1944, seventy-five miles of the Siegfried Line in Belgium were held by a mere eight battalions, it is clear enough that the Allies possessed the strength to break through it. What they would have done next is another matter, however, for Hitler still had some remarkable shocks for the Allies up his sleeve. Yet Speidel, Chief of Staff to Army Group B, commented:

> The halting of the Allied pursuit was a German variation of the 'miracle of the Marne' [for the French in 1914]. Had the Allies held on grimly to the retreating Germans they could have harried the breath out of every man and beast and ended the war half a year earlier. There were no German ground forces of any importance that could be thrown in and next to nothing in the air.

So much for the Western Front. But what was happening in the east? It may be doubted whether Hitler recalled the observation made by his historical hero, Frederick the Great, that there would always be more to lose than to gain by war with Russia, but by the autumn of 1944 there was little doubt about its truth. On the Eastern Front space was disappearing as fast as time. Although Model, before he had gone to France to replace Kluge, had pulled things together on the central Front in Poland, the Red Army had occupied Romania and had advanced into Yugoslavia and Hungary. The British had re-entered Greece after an absence of some three and a half years. East Prussia had for a time held firm, however. When, in August, Keitel had tried to persuade Hitler to take a short holiday at the Berghof, the latter had insisted: 'I am staying in Rastenburg. If I leave East Prussia, then East Prussia will fall. As long as I am here, it will be held.' Not until November did he return to Berlin. By then the Wehrmacht was doing its best to stem the Russian advance on the Danube. Meanwhile the pattern of building fortifications in west and south was being repeated in the east. Slovakia had been fortified and in December, while the Russians were besieging Budapest, Bratislava was declared to be a fortress. Formerly the whole of Europe had been declared a fortress; now its violation was almost complete. Except for Italy, where the skill and resolution of Kesselring held his armies firm on a winter line north of Rimini on the east coast to Pisa on the west, only the Reich was left. And Hitler, of course, required that all fortified positions protecting the Reich should be held at all costs. 'The war will decide,' read a November directive to the Wehrmacht, 'whether the German people shall continue to exist or perish. It demands selfless exertion from every individual. Situations which have seemed hopeless have been redeemed by the courage of soldiers contemptuous of death, by the steadfast perseverance of all ranks, and by inflexible, exalted leadership.'

It seemed that the Führer's own exalted leadership had produced the first requirement of his statement which Jodl had noted in his diary on 19 August – stabilization of the fronts. There was, however, still the question of the second one – could twenty-five divisions be moved to the west quickly enough to resume the offensive at a time when 'fog, night and snow' would furnish the Wehrmacht's Supreme Commander with a 'great opportunity'? 'As winter and the invading armies closed in upon them,' wrote Chester Wilmot, 'the German people and their armed forces rallied to uphold the rule of the very man who had led them to the brink of ruin.' Both men and machines would be needed if this rally were to be effective, both new divisions and the weapons to equip them. As for weapons, the remarkable efforts of Albert Speer, despite all the Allied strategic bombing, succeeded in rearming the Wehrmacht for one more offensive. In September 1944 alone, more single-engined fighter aircraft were produced than in any other month of the war, 3,031 in all; in that same month 170,000 rifles, 27,000 machine-guns, 1,000 anti-tank guns, over 2,000 mortars, 1,500 other artillery pieces, and 321,000 tons of ammunition left the factories. The output of tanks was equally impressive – some 2,500 Tigers, Panthers and Mark IVs were delivered during the three months up to September, and half that number again during the next three. Even the oil situation – bad weather which restricted Allied bombing, and harsh economy imposed on both military and civilian users, effected substantial savings – had improved to the extent that there was sufficient fuel to support both a defensive strategy, and an offensive one.

The tools were therefore available. As for soldiers, Reichsführer-SS Heinrich

Himmler,[1] whom Hitler had appointed C-in-C Home Army after the assassination attempt, raised no fewer than twenty-five Volksgrenadier divisions by using the last reserves of German manpower. Speer and Goebbels had long been trying to persuade the Führer of the absolute necessity for taking measures to mobilize the entire nation. At length, after the 20 July bomb plot, Goebbels was appointed Reich Commissioner for Total Mobilization of Resources for War, and between August and October raised more than half a million men for Hitler's new divisions. This was done by combing workers from factories, mustering soldiers from the Kriegsmarine and the Luftwaffe, and by reducing the call-up age to sixteen. Hitler was getting not only quantity, but quality, too, for many of these young men were precisely what he needed – young, fit, fanatical Nazis, whose training was carried out by battle-hardened experts. Brand-new weapons from Speer's factories also went to these freshly raised divisions. In addition to the twenty-five Volksgrenadier formations, a dozen panzer and panzer grenadier divisions were refitted for the west, while the Sixth Panzer Army had been re-formed, and now contained, amongst others, four SS panzer divisions. All in all, Germany managed to put together some forty divisions between September and December 1944. At last Hitler had a strategic reserve once more, and the power of the Wehrmacht – on paper, at least – was still awesome, totalling more than 10 million men, 75 per cent of them in the army and the Waffen-SS, with about 2 million in the Luftwaffe and 700,000 in the Kriegsmarine. Of the 7.5 million in the army, however, less than half that number were actually in the field. Roughly 2 million were on the Eastern Front and about 700,000 on the Western Front, the rest in Italy, the occupied territories, or Germany. The German Army's problem was that it was so widely committed. Halder accused Hitler of refusing to acknowledge any limit to possibility and of scattering formations of the German Army from the North Pole to the Libyan Desert. By late 1944 the Libyan Desert was far behind him, but the army still had large numbers of divisions in areas where they could no longer influence the decisive battles on the Central Fronts encircling Germany itself. Thus thirty divisions were cut off in Courland and Memel, on the Baltic,[2] a similar number in Hungary and Austria, rather fewer in Italy, seventeen in Scandinavia, ten in Yugoslavia. Napoleon had strung the Grande Armée out between Cadiz and Moscow, so breaking his own supreme rules of concentrating both purpose and force, and now Hitler was

---

[1] Himmler had long since ceased to be just the head of the SS. He now controlled the police, including the secret police, and since 1943 had been Minister of the Interior as well.

[2] The Courland was (and is now again) a province of Latvia; Memel (now Klaipeda) is a port in Lithuania.

repeating that catastrophic error. In the two most critical areas, the Wehrmacht deployed some 75 divisions in the west and 130 in the east.

The other side of the coin was very different. Whereas German strength represented the last scrapings of the barrel, Allied numbers in 1944 and 1945 went on growing. British and American fighting strength rose from about 14 million in mid-1943 to nearly 17 million a year later. The number of divisions at Eisenhower's disposal almost doubled between October 1944 and the end of the war in Europe. And the Red Army seemed to be inexhaustible. In Poland and East Prussia alone, while the Germans had deployed 75 divisions, the Russians, according to Stalin, had 180. What is more, at sea and in the air the Allies were virtually unchallengeable. Yet it was because of Hitler's determination to hang on to certain U-boat bases in the Western Baltic, so that he *would* be able to challenge the Allies at sea with the new submarines, that he tied up thirty to forty divisions in protecting the means of attacking western enemies from falling into the hands of the eastern enemy. To this desperate level had fallen the strategy of the man who had claimed that he would never fight a war on two fronts, and that his forces would be supreme in the air. Caught in the toils of his own wholly imagined picture of the situation, hanging on everywhere, refusing to give up space before time ran out, grasping at straws on the flanks while leaving the vital centre too weakly defended, having lost all strategic balance and almost all capability, in battle, of calling the tune, he yet held Wehrmacht, Party and people in thrall, and still talked of recapturing the initiative in the west. As was quoted at the head of this chapter, Hitler was determined to continue the battle 'until one of our damned enemies gets too tired to fight any more'. Yet while he was making plans for staving off defeat, Churchill, together with his fellow members of the Big Three, Roosevelt and Stalin, was putting together plans for Allied victory.

Shortly before embarking for his meeting with Roosevelt in Quebec, Churchill reverted to voicing his longed-for expectation of some great strategic triumph in Italy. His signal of 31 August to the President raised the point of what was to be done by the Fifth and Eighth Armies in that theatre 'once the German armies in Italy have been destroyed or unluckily have made their escape'. Once more he had glimpses of the Allies moving into Istria and Trieste, and so on to Vienna, and even spoke of the possibility of the war ending in a few months' time. Roosevelt's reply was equally sanguine in referring to what was to happen after the German forces in the Gothic Line had been broken, but he was more concerned with using forces in Italy to help Eisenhower advance into the heart of Germany, than to pursue what he and his advisers regarded as irrelevant strategic goals in Central Europe. Yet Churchill's *idée fixe* was not to be so easily dismissed, as was further illustrated by his signalling to Smuts that he still hoped 'to turn and break the Gothic Line, break into the Po valley, and ultimately advance by Trieste and the Ljubljana Gap to Vienna'. In the event, however, the Gothic Line proved to be a far harder nut to crack than he or the senior commanders in Italy had ever imagined, and as his own regiment, the 4th Hussars, was soon to discover.[1]

Alexander's original intention had been to attack with both his armies, Fifth and Eighth, in the centre of the Gothic Line, and, having thrust through the Apennines, to attempt to destroy Kesselring's forces *south* of the Po, then to cross that river north of Ferrara. But he was dissuaded from this plan by the Eighth Army commander, General Leese, who disliked both the prospect of mountain operations – he no longer had the French divisions under his command, and in any case wished to exploit his great strength in armour – and the idea of co-operating closely with the US Fifth Army. This change of plan was not without irony, for Alexander's deception measures relating to the central attack had been aimed at making the Germans believe that his main thrust would be on the Adriatic flank, which is precisely where Leese did in the end attack. Although Kesselring had temporarily taken his eye off the Adriatic, because he saw the Dragoon landings as a threat to his western flank, once he grasped where the real danger lay, his reinforcement of the key battleground was swift and effective.

Thus Eighth Army was to advance and break into the Gothic Line through the so-called Rimini Gap, then on to the Romagna – the Rimini-Bologna-Lake Comacchio triangle – and the Lombardy Plains. This part of the country was believed by some of Eighth Army's planning staff to be good going for tanks. They were to be swiftly disillusioned. Eighth Army's attack began on 25 August, while further west Fifth Army would break through the Futa and Il Giogo Passes and seize Bologna. Both armies fought gallantly and doggedly against the odds of rivers and ridges and rain, but the skilled defensive tactics and imaginative improvisions, which the Germans excelled at and so often displayed, were too much for them. The Allies came close to success (reinforcing the point that had Alexander not been robbed of so many divisions the story might have been different), but not close enough. Although Churchill had warned Alexander 'to be ready for a dash with armoured cars', there was to be no dash anywhere in Italy until May 1945, and even as early as October 1944, General Brooke, after visiting Alexander's headquarters, noted that 'Alex is getting stuck in the Apennines', his divisions 'pretty well whacked'. Whereas formerly the CIGS had been an ardent supporter of Churchill's hopes that the

---

[1] On 3 September 1944 1st Armoured Division was launched to break through the Gothic Line with the 4th Hussars leading – in the vanguard C Squadron, itself led by 3 Troop, commanded by the author. We met the enemy just south of Coriano and several days later we were still trying to fight our way forward, having lost five officers, thirty-five men and nine tanks. There was to be no breakthrough, but a bloody battle lasting months.

Mediterranean strategy could yield great strategic dividends, now he expressed his view that there was not 'much future left in this theatre'.

While Churchill's regiment and all the other fighting men of the Eighth Army were trying to break through the Gothic Line, he himself was making his way across the Atlantic in the *Queen Mary*, having sailed from Greenock on 5 September. Although what he continued to regard as the mistaken strategy of Dragoon was still on his mind, he told Colville that he would not 'beat up' the Americans about it. Rather, he would leave controversy 'to History', adding that 'he intended to be one of the historians'. In preparing for a meeting with the Chiefs of Staff, Churchill had read a highly optimistic report by the Joint Intelligence Committee which predicted advances against Germany from east and west, including the breaching of the Siegfried Line, before the end of 1944. Churchill was more circumspect. In spite of further advances in France and Belgium, he was aware of the serious logistic restraints on Eisenhower's armies, caused mainly by lack of ports, and was also conscious of Montgomery's apprehensions as to Eisenhower's intended strategy. Arguing that available resources would allow for only *one* major thrust into Germany – and that one, of course, to be his own – Montgomery was very critical of Eisenhower's intention to advance on a broad front. Churchill therefore made known both his doubts as to the JIC's confidence and his belief that the Germans would strongly resist attacks on their own Fatherland:

No one can tell what the future may bring forth. Will the Allies be able to advance in strength through the Siegfried Line into Germany during September, or will their Forces be so limited by supply conditions and the lack of ports as to enable the Germans to consolidate on the Siegfried Line?[1] Will they withdraw from Italy, in which case they will greatly strengthen their internal position? Will they be able to draw on their forces, at one time estimated at between 25 and 35 divisions, in the Baltic States? The fortifying and consolidating effect of a stand on the frontier of the native soil should not be underrated. It is at least likely that Hitler will be fighting on the 1st January as that he will collapse before then. If he does collapse before then, the reasons will be political rather than purely military.

It can thus be seen that Churchill's grasp of military realities was, even after five years of war, as acute as ever. Brooke, whose optimism as to an early end of the war with Germany was influenced by his desire to transfer British and Indian divisions to the Far East, was displeased by Churchill's disinclination to base

---

[1] Hitler succeeded not only in consolidating the Siegfried Line, but in delivering a devastating counter-attack which took the Allies by surprise.

plans on the probability of an early German collapse, yet it was the Prime Minister who was right. Two further points of disagreement between them were the latter's reluctance to contemplate sending forces from Italy to Burma for the Rangoon operation, and, equally, Brooke's impatience with Churchill's ideas for getting British forces to advance into Central Europe before the Russians got there. On board *Queen Mary* on 9 September, Churchill made known his views to the Chiefs of Staff, telling them, first, that for the Far East campaign, British troops 'should operate across the Indian Ocean [that is, from India] and not in the South-West Pacific'; second, that Britain should have 'powerful forces in Austria and from Trieste northwards at the close of the German war, and should not yield central and southern Europe entirely to Soviet ascendancy or domination'. (It is worth noting here that Churchill certainly got his wish, for British forces occupied parts of Austria and Venezia-Giulia, together with parts of Istria at the end of the war in Europe.) So strongly did he hold the view that the British should 'have a stake in central and southern Europe' that he even envisaged an amphibious operation to seize Istria, and was therefore opposed to any idea of there not being sufficient landing craft available for such a venture. He urged the Chiefs of Staff both to study the proposition and to ensure that there was no premature withdrawal of forces from Alexander's armies. Before reaching Canada, Churchill had a further meeting with the Chiefs of Staff at which he emphasized his disquiet at the latest demands being made by Mountbatten in order to undertake the capture of Rangoon, and although he conceded that forces from Europe might be required for this operation, it was too early to say when they might be made available. He also stated that Britain's aim in the war against Japan was both to 'engage Japanese forces with the maximum intensity, and at the same time to regain British territory'. On 10 September he and his entourage disembarked at Halifax; next morning Churchill was in Quebec, where President Roosevelt was already waiting for him.

It was Churchill who spoke first at the opening session of Octagon, and he was able to present an encouraging picture in reviewing recent events, in that the capture of Rome, the launching of Overlord and Dragoon, the progress being made both in Europe and the Far East, all pointed to 'the successful working of an extraordinarily efficient inter-Allied war machine'. He laid a special emphasis on the fact that the British Empire's effort in Europe was roughly equal in numbers of divisions to that of the United States, even though Britain 'had now entered the sixth year of the war', but he acknowledged that this effort, unlike America's, could not now increase. Once more he spoke of his concern that Alexander's forces in Italy should not be reduced before Kesselring's army had been either destroyed or obliged to withdraw, and on receiving assurance from General Marshall, went on to speak of 'giving Germany a stab in the Adriatic armpit,' with Vienna as the objective. He was therefore pleased to be told that it would be possible to mount an amphibious operation against Istria if necessary, and stressed the importance of forestalling the Russians, which such an operation would do much to achieve. As for the Far East, while forces for that theatre could not at present be withdrawn from Europe, plans for the capture of Rangoon should be pursued, while the British Fleet would assist in operations against Japan. Churchill was pleased with Roosevelt's reply, even though the President warned that 'the Germans could not yet be counted out', and as a result the Prime Minister signalled General Maitland Wilson that he could plan on 'no weakening' of Alexander's forces.

Not only military affairs were discussed at Quebec. There was also the question of the future of Lend-Lease after the war with Germany was over and while the war against Japan continued. This period, talked of as 'Stage II', was expected to last from early in 1945, the date by which it was thought Germany would be defeated, for perhaps as long as eighteen months, when it was thought that the Far Eastern war would be over. As A.J.P. Taylor pointed out, an arrangement for the continuation of US aid would be beneficial to Britain, particularly if the conditions of that aid were such that they complied with Churchill's request to Roosevelt that 'the United States should not attach any conditions to supplies delivered to Britain on Lend-Lease which would jeopardize the recovery of her export trade'. In other words, it would be a means of easing Britain's 'transition from war to peace'. In discussing Lend-Lease, Henry Morgenthau, the US Treasury Secretary, had proposed sums of 3,500 million dollars for Britain during Stage II and an [additional] credit of 3,000 million dollars for non-military purposes'. But Morgenthau also persuaded Roosevelt and Churchill to agree to and sign a programme for his proposal, known as the 'Morgenthau Plan', for Germany's future, in essence a scheme 'for eliminating the war-making industries in the Ruhr and in the Saar' and for turning Germany 'into a country primarily agricultural and pastoral in its character', and where rearmament would be impossible. That Churchill agreed to such a measure, which Eden insisted was one the War Cabinet would never assent to, was because his friend and principal scientific adviser, Lord Cherwell, persuaded him that the removal of German competition would be of great benefit to Britain's future exports. In the event Roosevelt later shelved the idea, and Churchill was content to acquiesce.[1]

[1] To a considerable extent, the Morgenthau Plan backfired on the Allies. Although it was shelved, details appeared in the American press, and Hitler and Goebbels used its terms to make propaganda to the effect that the Allies intended 'to exterminate us root and branch as a nation and a people'. Goebbels also made much of the fact that Morgenthau was Jewish, and the overall effect of this propaganda was a revival of enthusiasm for the Nazi Party in Germany and among her forces, something almost incredible in the light of the disasters on the Western and Eastern Fronts.

No major strategic decisions affecting current operations were taken at Quebec. While Churchill was reassured that Alexander could proceed with his plans to advance into the Po Valley (the Germans, however, decided otherwise), any landings in Istria would either have to be made soon, or not at all. Moreover, even though the Red Army's advance into Bulgaria gave rise to further British concern, there was nothing to spare for Allied adventures in the Balkans, except for two British brigades stationed in Egypt, which were available to occupy Athens. Churchill reiterated his view, and that of his military advisers, that the capture of Rangoon should be effected before the monsoon of 1945, and he also spoke of the possibility of Japan's succumbing to a programme of heavy bombing, thus bringing about an early end to the war there. After the conference was over (it ended on 16 September) Churchill and Roosevelt conferred at the latter's Hyde Park home, and agreed that the atomic bomb, which should be ready by August 1945, would if necessary be used against Japan, and re-used in order to induce the enemy to surrender. One matter which, although of crucial importance, was not resolved at Quebec, however, was that of future relations with Russia. This would have to wait for Churchill's Moscow meeting with Stalin, which followed hard upon Octagon.

During his passage back to England – he embarked in the *Queen Mary* at New York on 20 September and arrived in London six days later – Churchill prepared the speech he intended to deliver to the House of Commons, and played a lot of bezique with Colville. On his return he heard about the Arnhem operation and the grievous losses to the British 1st Airborne Division.[1] He took comfort, however, from the boldness of the Allied commanders in conceiving and executing such a plan. It must be remembered too that although the bridge at Arnhem was not held, the bridges south of it at Nijmegen and Grave were both taken and consolidated. Churchill therefore regarded the battle on the whole as 'a decided victory', although it did not, of course, hasten the end of the war in Europe in the way that had been hoped.

Before addressing the House of Commons on 28 September, Churchill signalled to Stalin, first telling him that in his speech he would pay tribute to the Russian Army's holding most of the enemy on its front, and then going on to refer to the need for the three Great Powers to co-ordinate plans, particularly with regard to Japan once the German Army had been defeated. He also expressed his willingness to come to Moscow in October. In the speech itself, Churchill spoke of the Normandy battle and how decisive it had been,

---

[1] Of the 10,000 or so officers and men of the division engaged at Arnhem (17–26 September), some 1,400 were killed and more than 6,000 captured, a great many of them wounded. Less than a quarter of the division got safely back to British lines.

although he exaggerated in suggesting that its exploitation had been perfect. As he had promised to Stalin, he reminded the House of 'the measureless services which Russia has rendered to the common cause, through long years of suffering, by tearing out the life of the German military monster,' adding that the Soviet Union was 'holding and beating far larger hostile forces than those which face the Allies in the West'. As for Italy, he was content simply to state that Alexander would aim at destroying Kesselring's army. He also praised the successful campaign of the Fourteenth Army in Burma, both in safeguarding American air communications to China and in repelling the attempted Japanese invasion of India. He rejected totally the idea that Mountbatten's Burma campaign had resulted in stalemate; on the contrary, it had been 'the largest and most important ground fighting that has yet taken place against the armies of Japan . . . [it] has resulted in the slaughter of between 50,000 and 60,000 Japanese and the capture of several hundred prisioners.[1] The Japanese Army has recoiled before our troops in deep depression and heavily mauled.' He then went on to assure the House that 'the war against the Japanese and other diseases of the jungle will be pressed forward with the utmost energy'. Churchill also mentioned his hopes of a Big Three meeting as soon as possible, emphasizing how much depended on 'the cordial, trustful and comprehending association of the British Empire, the United States and Soviet Russia, and no pains must be spared and no patience grudged which are necessary to bring that supreme hope to fruition'.

Churchill's next opportunity for making his own contribution to this desirable state of affairs was just round the corner, as he set off for Moscow on the evening of 7 October, Brooke and Eden travelling in a different aeroplane. His first stop was at Naples, where he conferred with Alexander and Wilson. It was clear from their gloomy survey of the situation 'that the withdrawals from the armies in Italy for the Riviera landings [Dragoon] had emasculated their campaign,' and Alexander listed the various difficulties facing him – inadequate strength, his armies strung across the mountains, poor lines of communication, bad weather, unsuitable country for tanks ahead, the Germans' defensive advantages. What it amounted to was that 'the Italian campaign had been wrecked by bad strategy'. If he were given three more divisions, he might do something. But in suggesting that three American divisions might be diverted from Eisenhower in France to himself in Italy, Alexander was nursing a vain hope, and when Churchill signalled to Roosevelt suggesting it, he received the most decided negative, based on a refusal to consider diverting forces to Italy when they were needed for the main battle against Germany itself. Churchill

---

[1] The contrast between the numbers of Japanese soldiers killed and those captured speaks loudly for their fanatical courage and contempt for death.

had to accept this, and while still exploring the idea of a further amphibious operation aimed at Istria or north-east Italy, concluded after his meeting with Wilson and Alexander that they 'can do nothing in the Italian theatre worth speaking of'. After this meeting he flew on to Cairo and thence to Moscow, arriving on the evening of 9 October. Before setting out for Russia he had signalled to Roosevelt to say that the main issue during his talks with Stalin would be Russia's territorial demands in Poland, and that since he knew the President's views on this subject, he would need no special guidance. Sure enough the first question to be tackled at Tolstoy – the codename for the meeting – was Poland. Stalin's position was broadly that a Soviet-Polish frontier in accordance with the Curzon Line of 1919[1] – which was similar to the one drawn in 1939 by Russia as the boundary between the German and Russian spheres of occupation – would assist discussion, and Churchill undertook to bring appropriate pressure to bear on the Polish Government-in-Exile.

Perhaps the most remarkable feature of this first meeting between Stalin and Churchill was what A.J.P. Taylor described as the way they 'shared out the political control of eastern Europe with odd statistical precision: Rumania 90 per cent Russian; Greece 90 per cent British; Hungary and Yugoslavia 50-50'. It was Churchill who made the proposal having first said as much, and then according to his own recollection, he wrote these percentages (which also included 'Bulgaria Russia 75% Others 25%') on a 'half-sheet of paper' and pushed it over the table to Stalin, who ticked it with a blue pencil and passed it back. Churchill's subsequent question as to whether such an offhand way of deciding the fate of millions might not be thought cynical, and had they better not burn the paper, prompted Stalin's reply 'No, you keep it'. The two men also discussed the future of Italy and Germany, Stalin making known his view that Germany 'should be deprived of the possibility of revenge' and that a long occupation of the country would be necessary. Next day Churchill sent Roosevelt a statement of his conversation with the Soviet leader, in both his name and Stalin's, having consulted Averell Harriman, Roosevelt's observer at Tolstoy. He remained in Moscow until 19 October, attending numerous meetings, luncheons, dinners, during which discussion ranged widely over such matters as Poland's frontiers, the Balkans, Soviet access to warm-water ports, the military situation on all fronts; he also enjoyed a performance of the Bolshoi Ballet, where he and Stalin were greeted with thunderous applause. On the 15th he was unwell with a fever and doctors in Cairo were ordered to fly to Moscow, only to have the order cancelled next day on his recovery. He also heard on this day that two British battalions had been welcomed by the Greeks

[1] In fact, the Poles rejected the Curzon Line, going on to secure nearly twice as much territory as the Allies had suggested, mainly from Lithuania and the Ukraine.

on their arrival in Athens. During the final day of negotiations, 17 October, Stalin and Churchill again discussed military developments, Germany's future, their two countries' economic problems, and the Polish frontier – on this last subject Stalin at last accepted Churchill's suggestion that the Curzon Line should be regarded as the 'basis for the frontier' rather than 'the frontier' *tout court*. On the day following, Churchill signalled Roosevelt about this, and also about 'the obvious resolve of the Soviet Government to attack Japan on the overthrow of Hitler'. Before leaving Moscow on the 19th Churchill attended a farewell dinner, during which it was made known that the Russian Army had reached Czechoslovakia. Next morning he received a gift of two vases for himself and his wife, and in his letter of thanks spoke of his pleasure at receiving a 'warm welcome' and at having had 'very pleasant talks together'. Stalin added to these courtesies by seeing him off at the airport, even boarding and inspecting the Prime Minister's aircraft, and absolutely waving his handkerchief as the aeroplane moved off. On the morning of 20 October Churchill, accompanied by Eden and Brooke, reached Cairo, from where he sent a message of thanks to Stalin, then flew on via Naples, reaching England in the late afternoon of the 22nd, and thence to Chequers.

Churchill had come home in a confident mood, and this was reflected in the speech he gave to the House of Commons on 27 October about his Moscow talks. Harold Nicolson was greatly impressed by the Prime Minister's appearance and performance. Far from his condition some months earlier, when he had appeared tired, unwell and hesitant, 'today he was superb. Cherubic, pink, solid and vociferous'. (Nicolson also noted that in the smoking-room afterwards, having at first ordered a single whisky and soda, the Prime Minister then told the barman, Collins, to delete the word 'single' and insert the word 'double', 'grinning like a schoolboy'.) Churchill had told the House that the war was still 'dour and hard', that fighting everywhere was likely 'to increase in scale and intensity' but that he believed they 'were in the last lap'. It was, though, necessary that the 'fullest effort' be made to ensure that the struggle was not unendurably prolonged. The unity of the Allies, which had for so long been his aim and in pursuit of which he had so often travelled, was something to be marvelled at. A good working arrangement had been reached with the Soviet Union with regard to Eastern European countries, which should augur well for post-war settlements. Churchill spoke again in the House of Commons on 31 October, saying that there could be no guarantee of an end to the war with Germany before the spring or summer of 1945, and then – here again he showed his remarkable ability to anticipate actual events – if there were to be a withdrawal from the Coalition by some parties, Parliament would be dissolved and elections held. Unless, therefore all parties decided to keep the Coalition in being until Japan too was defeated, 'we must look to the termination of the war against Nazism as a pointer which will fix the date of the General Election . . . I cannot think of anything more odious than for a Prime Minister to attempt to carry on with a Parliament so aged, and to try to grapple with the perplexing and tremendous problems of war and peace, and of the transition from war to peace, without being refreshed by contact with the people or without being relieved of any special burdens in that respect.' To have said such a thing at such a time weighs heavily in favour of judging him to have been not just a superb leader of the nation in war, but a true guardian of British democratic traditions.

In November Churchill was faced with more military command problems, for the wholly admirable Field Marshal Sir John Dill, who had done so much to smooth Anglo-American military co-operation, died in Washington. It was decided to replace him with Maitland Wilson, Alexander thereupon succeeding to the Mediterranean command, and Mark Clark taking Alexander's place as the army group commander in Italy. In that country itself, however, the appallingly wet weather had brought the Allied advance to a halt. Nor was the news from the Western Front encouraging. After a visit to France from 10 to 14 November – Churchill and General de Gaulle laid wreaths to honour the Unknown Soldier at the Arc de Triomphe, and took the salute at a parade in the Champs-Elysées, Churchill being rapturously greeted by the Paris crowd; in talks with de Gaulle he agreed that France should have a zone of occupation in Germany; there were lunches, at one of which he gave one of his splendid extempore speeches in French (Cadogan observing that he was not sure 'what it conveyed to the natives'); and there was a visit, again with de Gaulle, to the headquarters of General Jean-Marie de Lattre de Tassigny, commanding the French First Army, where after being frozen with cold, then thawed out with brandy, the Prime Minister made another 'of those indescribably funny French speeches which brought the house down' (this from Brooke, whose French was excellent) – after all this and before returning to England, Churchill visited Eisenhower at his headquarters near Rheims. There he was briefed about operations, although Brooke recorded that the Supreme Commander seemed to have little idea of what was going on. The fact was, of course, that not very much was going on, except that there was a good deal of discord between Eisenhower and Montgomery. As has been said, Montgomery had always favoured the idea of a concentrated thrust on a relatively narrow front – with himself in command; Eisenhower preferred the more cautious notion of advancing on a broad front, and he got his way.

The problem was essentially one of supplies, aggravated by Montgomery's failure to open up the port of Antwerp. So seriously did Eisenhower view the situation that on 9 October he signalled Montgomery that he considered Antwerp to be the most important of all their endeavours on the whole front, and that it was a matter requiring the Field Marshal's personal attention.[1] Less than a week later Eisenhower again urged Montgomery to get Antwerp into working order, informing him that both the CIGS and the US Army Chief of Staff regarded this operation as having absolute precedence over all others. This was enough for Montgomery, and he gave the necessary instructions (in a rare admission of error he subsequently recorded that he had been wrong about his Twenty-First Army Group's ability both to drive for the Ruhr *and* open up Antwerp). Following this exchange Eisenhower's directive of 28 October was in essence a continuation of the broad front strategy. Although the main effort was to be made in the north, in order to clear the enemy west of the Rhine, seize crossings over that river and advance into Germany, there would also be aggressive action in the south, again to destroy enemy forces west of the Rhine. When Eisenhower and Montgomery conferred a month later at Zonhoven, it was clear that few of the directive's aims had been realized. Indeed, such success as could be claimed had been in the south, rather than the north, the very reverse of what had been intended. Montgomery was not slow to convey his disappointment, and repeated it two days after meeting Eisenhower in a letter expressing his opinion that the plan had failed. A new plan, he said, which 'must not fail', must also observe the basic rule of concentration; moreover, since the theatre had two fronts, one north of the Ardennes, one south, there should be a *single* commander in *full* operational control in the north, and similarly a single commander in the south. Montgomery therefore suggested that either Bradley or himself should have this full operational control north of the Ardennes, and declared that it was the spring campaign which must now be planned. This apparently clear division of fronts, one north, one south of the Ardennes, overlooked a glaringly obvious fact – that there was a third front: *the Ardennes itself.*

It was a fact not overlooked by the Supreme Commander of the Wehrmacht, and while the Allied commanders were deliberating as to how to finish the war quickly, he was making plans to prolong it. On 16 September, the day before the launch of Operation Market Garden, the Allied airborne assault at Arnhem, Nijmegen and elsewhere, Hitler told Guderian, Keitel and Jodl that he had just made a momentous decision: 'I shall go over to the counter-attack,' he declared; 'that is to say here [pointing to a map] out of the Ardennes with the objective – Antwerp.' Nine days later, when the British 1st Airborne Division's withdrawal was under way, Hitler instructed Jodl to get on with the detailed planning. Jodl made a number of proposals to Hitler, two of which – a *Schwerpunkt* from Venlo to Antwerp, and a pincer movement from the areas of Luxembourg and Aachen – were seized upon by Hitler as the foundation for

---

[1] He had been promoted field marshal on 1 September.

his own plan, *Wacht am Rhein* (Watch on the Rhine), defensive in nomenclature, anything but that in concept. The Führer explained to Westphal, now Rundstedt's Chief of Staff, and Krebs, Model's Chief of Staff, on 24 October that the operation's purpose was to destroy all Allied forces north of the line Antwerp-Liège-Bastogne, in two phases – first, push to the Meuse and over it; second, capture Antwerp. Subsequent comments on the idea itself gave high marks to Hitler. Liddell Hart said it would have been a brilliant brainwave *if* Hitler had had sufficient military power; even Rundstedt called the *idea* a stroke of genius, even though the conditions necessary for its success were lacking; while OKW's diarist, Major Schramm, noted: 'Systematic re-examination confirmed that the area selected by the Führer actually was the most promising on the whole Western front.' When he wanted to make use of them, Hitler's *Fingerspitzengefühl*, his strategic grasp, his *Vorhersehung*, to say nothing of his continued and astonishing grasp of military detail, did not forsake him. His *concept* of an offensive was fundamentally sound. In spite of the errors made during and after the battle, the idea itself was in no way a mistake. Yet in the conduct of the battle, we see in the Führer the same refusal to face facts, the same stubborn insistence on reinforcing failure, the same substitution of willpower for adequate military resources, which had marred his handling of the campaigns in Africa, Russia and Normandy.

None the less, the forces to be assembled for his offensive were by no means contemptible. Model's Army Group B was to have three armies, Fifth Panzer and Sixth SS Panzer Armies for the main thrust and Seventh Army to guard the southern flank. There would be thirty divisions – eighteen infantry and twelve panzer or mechanized, although of this number Rundstedt would have to find three of the former and six of the latter. Fifteen hundred aircraft, including a hundred of the new Messerschmitt Me-262 jets,[1] and four million gallons of fuel would be provided. As for dates, Hitler had, on the advice of meteorologists, plucked two from the sky, as it were, – 20 and 25 November, irrespective of time needed to prepare for the operation, simply because bad weather then forecast for those dates would inhibit Allied air operations. In the event, however, the attack was not launched until mid-December. On 1 November Jodl sent Westphal the order, endorsed by Hitler in his own handwriting: 'Nicht abändern!' ('Not to be altered'). The plan was in essence no different from Hitler's original idea. The three armies were to attack between Montschau and Echternach. SS-General Dietrich's Sixth Panzer Army would

---

[1] Very fast and with an astonishing rate of climb, the Me-262 might have been a war-winning weapon had its numbers been greater, and had Hitler not insisted that it be used in a bombing/ground-strafing role, and not deployed far forward or in large numbers, for fear of losses or of one of the aircraft being captured.

strike the principal blow in the north, cross the Meuse at Huy and Andenne and then push on to capture Antwerp; General Hasso von Manteuffel's Fifth Panzer Army was to advance in the centre through Namur and Dinant to Brussels; Brandenberger's Seventh Army would cover the southern flank. Various objections to the plan were voiced by Rundstedt, Model – 'This plan hasn't got a damned leg to stand on' – and Manteuffel, but apart from Hitler's agreeing with the latter's suggestion that the attack should start early in the morning, in darkness, in order to make best use of daylight later, Jodl made plain the Führer's decision that the operation was 'unalterable in every detail'. Even Hitler had his misgivings, however, and had confided to Speer:

> If it does not succeed, I no longer see any possibility for ending the war well . . . But we will come through. A single breakthrough on the Western front! You'll see! It will lead to collapse and panic among the Americans. We'll drive straight through their middle and take Antwerp. Then they'll have lost their supply port. And a tremendous pocket will encircle the entire English army, with hundreds of thousands of prisoners. As we used to do in Russia.

One thing was certain: a German offensive would take the Allies by surprise. However divided they might have been as to the strategy to be adopted after Normandy, however furious or prolonged the argument about a single concentrated thrust or advance on a broad front, on one thing the Allies were agreed – the Germans would not, could not, attempt any large-scale counter-offensive. On 7 December Eisenhower discussed the situation with his two senior commanders, Bradley and Montgomery, at Maastricht. All were disturbed by the German recovery, by the enemy's revived morale and obvious ability to fight a co-ordinated defensive battle, particularly while the bad weather, which robbed the Allied air forces of their power to influence affairs, persisted. Of major concern to them was the question of what use Rundstedt would make of Sixth SS Panzer Army, the principal strategic reserve in the west. Montgomery's intelligence chief, Brigadier 'Bill' Williams, did not believe that Rundstedt would risk throwing away the most effective means he had of countering future Allied advances. He anticipated no surprises.

What may appear strange to us now is that Allied intelligence experts still seemed to expect the Wehrmacht to be manipulated in accordance with their ideas of military common sense. Even now they had not grasped, in spite of his frequent demonstrations of the fact, that Hitler did not conduct war in this way. Had it been as they thought, there might have been no Stalingrad, no Tunisia, no Kursk, no Avranches. Perhaps the stalemate of autumn 1944 and the change from Hitler's rash handling of the Normandy campaign to Rundstedt's more conventional behaviour once the Western Front had been stabilized, lulled them into a state of optimism quite at odds with the real position. General Bradley's intelligence chief had noted on 12 December that the Wehrmacht's breaking point might be reached at any moment, and even the circumspect Montgomery observed that the enemy was now unable to stage major offensive operations.

In fact, on 12 December, at his headquarters near Frankfurt, Hitler was haranguing all the senior commanders who were about to take part in the offensive, due to start four days later. These unfortunate generals had to endure a two-hour lecture during which he told them, without much originality, that war was a test of endurance. Endurance must continue as long as there was hope of victory. But endurance by defensive means alone was not enough. It was by offensive action that the enemy's confidence must be destroyed. 'From the outset of the war therefore I have striven to act offensively whenever possible, to conduct a war of movement and not to allow myself to be manoeuvred into a position comparable to that of the First World War.' It was necessary, he said, to choose the moment. Both politically and militarily the time was ripe. The Grand Alliance against Germany was fraught with incongruities – capitalists allied with Bolsheviks, imperialists in league with anti-imperialists, Russia and Britain so long antagonists in the Near and Middle East again at loggerheads over the Balkans and the Persian Gulf – the whole thing was ripe for disintegration. 'If we can now deliver a few more heavy blows, then at any moment this artificially bolstered common front may collapse with a mighty clap of thunder . . . Wars are finally decided by one side or the other recognizing that they cannot be won. We must allow no moment to pass without showing the enemy that, whatever he does, he can never reckon on a capitulation. Never! Never!'

If what Hitler had to say at his bunkered HQ, with its legendary Wagnerian title, Adlershorst – Eagle's Nest – did little to reassure those chosen to deliver these heavy blows, nor could the physical condition of the lecturer have done much to help. By December 1944 Hitler was a wreck. The years of living in underground bunkers, of subjecting himself to a routine of uninterrupted work, the strain of ceaseless responsibility and of maintaining his granite will intact, the eccentric hours he kept and diet he followed, his refusal to rest or take exercise – however strong his constitution might have been to start with, such maltreatment would not but take effect. Together with the various drugs administered by the sinister, repulsive Dr Morell, it had reduced Hitler to a state which Manteuffel described as that of an old, broken man. He stooped and shuffled, his face was pasty and puffy, his voice quavered, his hands trembled, one leg dragged behind him as he walked, a film of sheer exhaustion seemed at times to cover and cloud his eyes. Yet in spite of the game going wrong on all fronts, in spite of what perhaps had an even more powerful effect on his physical condition than mere bodily deterioration, namely the psychological effect of the frustration of his mission, of seeing all his hopes turned to disappointments, two things seemed to be unchanged. One was the strength of his will, the other his continued ability to impose this will on others. Only a few months before his harangue to the generals, he had in a rare moment of self-pity admitted that had the attempted assassination succeeded, it would have been a release from worry, from sleepless nights and great nervous suffering. He was nevertheless grateful to Destiny for having let him live. If there were not an iron will behind it, the battle could not be won. He lived only for the purpose of leading the fight.

Churchill too lived to lead the fight (although not for the fight alone), but his physical condition was infinitely superior to Hitler's, and he had moreover powerful allies and supremely competent, loyal and dedicated assistants who did not hesitate to tell him when they thought he was mistaken, and whose advice he wisely paid attention to. From time to time, therefore, he did not get his way. On returning from Paris he was disappointed to find that there would be no early meeting of the Big Three. Roosevelt had made it clear that they could not expect to persuade 'Uncle Joe' to meet them before late January or early February. Churchill was concerned not only by the consequent delay in settling such matters as Germany, France, Poland and the Balkans after the war's end, but also with Roosevelt's unwillingness to allow France to join in the Big Three discussions, particularly as the future position of France in relation to 'policing Germany' was so important. He was also disturbed by the American President's insistence that his country's troops should return home as quickly as they could be moved once Germany had been defeated, and he pointed out that when it came to holding down 'Western Germany beyond the present Russian occupation line' the British 'could not undertake the task without your aid and that of the French'. More encouraging, however, was the news from Greece, where it appeared that the presence of British troops, combined with Stalin's evident honouring of the formula for a 90 per cent British, 10 per cent Russian interest in Greece, was keeping the Greek Communists in check.[1]

Churchill had not abandoned the idea of some British move against Istria, especially in view of the evident impossibility of further significant advances

[1] During the German occupation of Greece, rival monarchist and communist resistance organizations had sprung as often as not at each other's throats as at the Germans'. After the British liberated Athens in October 1944 the two groups began openly to fight each other, each striving to dominate the country, until British forces had to be deployed to keep the two sides apart. As will be seen, Churchill was to be censured for using British troops to interfere in the domestic politics of a friendly nation, and one moreover that had resisted the Nazis.

on the main Italian front, and General Maitland Wilson had put forward proposals for capturing Trieste. The British Chiefs of Staff opposed the latter suggestion, however, on the grounds that Bologna was a far more important objective, while the Americans questioned whether Wilson would have the necessary resources for such an operation even in February 1945. Churchill at length accepted the joint British–US view that to transfer substantial forces to the Balkans would not 'be of assistance to the general war effort'. Towards the end of November Wilson left his Mediterranean command – Churchill sent his York aircraft (a 'civilianized' Avro Lancaster bomber) for him and entertained him to dinner at Chequers – in order to take up his new appointment as head of the British Joint Staff Mission in Washington. Lack of progress in Italy was matched by what was happening on the Western Front, and in a signal to Stalin of 23 November, Churchill referred to the severe weather there, saying that unless the Germans west of the Rhine could be defeated soon, there would be a winter lull, after which 'one more major onslaught should break the organized German resistance in the West'. There was to be anything but a 'lull' during the winter of 1944 on the Western Front, but Churchill was correct enough in predicting the result of a renewed assault thereafter.

There came at this time a further illustration of Churchill's sure grip of post-war realities, when he opposed Roosevelt's suggestion of issuing an Anglo-American statement to the effect that it was not their intention 'to devastate Germany or eliminate the German people', but simply to rid them of Nazism. The purpose of this declaration, according to Roosevelt, was to help 'break down German morale'. Churchill's response – that it was not the likely British and American treatment of them that the German people were afraid of, but Russian occupation and the probability that many of them would be taken off to 'toil to death in Russia . . . or Siberia', and that nothing the Allies themselves said now could 'eradicate this deep-seated fear' – was a model of common sense and reasonableness. Far from breaking down German morale, he argued, such a statement would signal Allied weakness and stimulate desperate German resistance. But while Churchill may have been able to influence Roosevelt in this respect, he had less success when it came to Stalin's insistence that the Polish National Committee established at Lublin, which had been liberated by the Red Army, should be recognized as the Provisional Government of Poland, as the Polish Government-in-Exile in London had 'lost touch with the national soil and have no contact with the Polish people'. Although Churchill did not accept Stalin's view – he was always conscious of the Polish forces, 100,000-strong, fighting with the utmost gallantry alongside the British in Italy and France – but he was powerless to prevent the Lublin Committee from declaring itself to be Poland's government.

On 30 November 1944 Churchill celebrated his seventieth birthday. On the previous day he had spoken in the debate on the Loyal Address, greatly impressing Harold Nicolson by his apparent fitness, by his speech, with its emphasis on the need for youth, and by his mastery of 'the Parliamentary art'. On his birthday itself he enjoyed a family party at the No 10 Annexe, and on the next day, having driven to Chequers – taking in the school concert at Harrow on his way – he signalled to Field Marshal Smuts, thanking him for his birthday greeting and including a review of the general war situation. In this message, which underlined how the broad front approach in the west had resulted in a 'strategic reverse', he spoke of a forthcoming spring offensive, but also admitted, in view of the American armies' preponderance, 'it is not so easy as it used to be for me to get things done'. In Italy too, although German divisions had been 'held' there, armoured superiority was inhibited by the bog-like nature of the Po Valley, and air power by bad weather – 'We cannot look for any very satisfactory events in Northern Italy at present.' Even in Burma 'we seem condemned to wallow at half-speed through these jungles'. In short, it was not a very 'jolly' picture, though all the troubles would, he said, be mastered.

There was certainly no shortage of troubles. In Yugoslavia Tito was making difficulties over the post-war political regime there. In Greece the Communists were refusing to demobilize their guerrilla forces, and when the Communists clashed with the Greek police in Athens, with casualties on both sides, Churchill ordered General Scobie, commanding British forces there, to restore and maintain order in Athens, and if necessary to neutralize or destroy the Greek partisan and Communist guerrilla bands. Scobie, who was reinforced and in the end had some 60,000 British troops under him, was told to hold and dominate Athens 'without bloodshed if possible, but also with bloodshed if necessary'. While the Greek crisis was still weighing heavily upon him, Churchill was further urging Roosevelt for action to resolve the cheerless situation that seemed to be facing the Allies on all fronts – in Europe and the Far East – by agreeing to a top-level meeting. Churchill was also immensely put out by the US State Department's criticism of British policy both in Greece and Italy. Moreover, when sorrows came, they certainly did not come single spies, but in battalions, for he even had to face sharp opposition to his further intervention in Greece both from the British press and in the House of Commons, where a motion of censure was debated on 7 and 8 December. Although defeated by 279 votes to 30, there were many Labour members who abstained; furthermore, as Macmillan observed next day, 'He has won the debate but not the battle of Athens.' He was, however, determined to win it, and after spending Christmas Eve with his family, flew to Athens on Christmas Day with Eden, and was met there by Alexander, Macmillan and Sir Rex Leeper, the British Ambassador to Greece. Aboard HMS *Ajax* that evening, Churchill conferred with George Papandreou, the Greek Prime Minister, and Archbishop

Dimitrios Damaskinos, and on the following evening there was a dramatic meeting at the Greek Foreign Office, presided over by the Archbishop, at which the three delegates of ELAS (the Greek Communist military wing), French and American observers, Colonel Popoff, the Russian representative, Papandreou, Churchill, Eden, Alexander and others were all present. After the Archbishop had spoken words of welcome, Churchill made his own statement:

> Mr Eden and I have come all this way, although great battles are raging in Belgium and on the German frontier, to make this effort to rescue Greece from a miserable fate and raise her to a point of great fame and repute.

Having made it clear that Britain would leave the Greeks to decide their own country's future, whether as a monarchy or a republic, Churchill expressed the hope that the conference would restore Greece to its former position and assured those present that 'we shall preserve that old friendship between Greece and Great Britain which played so notable a part in the establishment of Greek independence.' Throughout the time that he was speaking, there could be heard gunfire, mortar shells exploding and Beaufighters firing rockets at positions held by ELAS insurgents – so much so, Colville recorded, that the noise nearly drowned the Prime Minister's voice. As if to underline this conflict, at the end of Churchill's speech Alexander made the telling point that he deprecated the need for his soldiers to be fighting Greeks, adding that the Greeks should be fighting against the Germans with his own soldiers in Italy. After further speeches by Maximos, a Greek royalist, Papandreou and one of the ELAS leaders, Churchill told the assembled Greeks to finish the work that had been started, and took his leave. They were not very successful in finishing the work satisfactorily and, as Churchill later wrote, 'Bitter and animated discussions between the Greek parties occupied all the following day.' When Archbishop Damaskinos – whom Churchill described as 'a scheming medieval prelate' – reported that evening that the ELAS leaders had been thoroughly uncompromising,[1] Churchill agreed that on his return to London he would ask the King of Greece to appoint the Archbishop as Regent and to entrust him with the formation of a government which would exclude Communists. Meanwhile the British would continue with the fight either until ELAS agreed to a truce or until Athens had been cleared of them; moreover, British forces would remain in the country until Greece had formed its own National Army. Churchill and Eden left Athens by air on the next morning, 28 December.

---

[1] Since Greece was uncertain as to whether she wished to return to the rule of King George II, it had been suggested that Damaskinos, Archbishop of Athens, should be appointed Regent.

On that same day Hitler was treating his generals to a further lecture. By this time it was clear that his counter-offensive was losing momentum. It had begun well enough, and obtained all the surprise that Hitler could have wished for. Yet in spite of initial successes and advances when Model launched his two panzer armies forward in Operation *Herbstnebel* ('Autumn Mist'), as it was called, at 5.30 am on the morning of 16 December, with twenty German divisions on the move through the woods and mists of the Eifel, the noise of their movement drowned by the V1s which roared overhead and the bombardment of American positions by 2,000 German guns; in spite of Rundstedt's exhortation to his soldiers 'to achieve things beyond human possibilities for our Fatherland and Führer,' and Manteuffel's somewhat more practical message, 'Forward double time'; in spite of the fact that the battle was to last for three weeks; the operation was really decided in the first four days by the spontaneous defensive action of Bradley's armies, which succeeded in blocking, and later defeating, the advancing German divisions. As early as 23 December, a week after the attack had started, Model told Speer that the offensive had definitely failed, but that Hitler had ordered it to continue. The heroic defence of Bastogne by Brigadier-General Anthony McAuliffe and the US 101st Airborne Division (it was he who rejected the German commander's call for surrender with the celebrated answer 'Nuts!'); the grip established by Montgomery on the northern shoulders of the German penetration; the intervention of Patton's Third Army; the weather clearing on Christmas Eve allowing 5,000 Allied aircraft to fill the sky above the battlefield, swoop on the German columns and prevent supplies reaching them – all these combined to ensure that by 27 December the momentum of the German forces had been broken. The question now was whether they could be extricated.

Hitler, not surprisingly, spurned his generals' advice, which called for withdrawal. Yet there were doubly compelling grounds for following it. Not only was there the danger that his armies committed in the Ardennes would be destroyed, but the situation in the east, as Guderian had come all the way from that front to tell him, was such that if troops were not transferred there soon, the coming Russian winter offensive could not be held. Hitler's reply was the very embodiment of his refusal to look hard facts in the face, of his locking his mind away in a world where only his own wishes had any reality at all. He dismissed Russian preparations as bluff: 'It's the greatest imposture since Genghis Khan. Who's responsible for producing all this rubbish?' Nor was he prepared to accept correction from Guderian. 'There's no need for you to try to teach me. I've been commanding the German Army in the field for five years, and during that time I've had more practical experience than any "gentleman" of the General Staff could ever hope to have.' No, there would be no transfer of troops to the east and no withdrawal from the west. Quite the contrary, there would be a renewal of the western offensive, with both a new attempt to reach the Meuse and an attack into Northern Alsace.

So, on 28 December, his long-suffering commanders were again assembled, and again put through the mill. Not ready for an attack? Of course they were not ready! 'Gentlemen, I have been in this business for eleven years and during those eleven years I have never heard anybody report that everything was completely ready.' Then, in a characteristic display of self-deception, the Führer compared the German position in the west with that of the Russians two or three years earlier, able to take advantage of an enemy whose front was extended and whose offensive strength was dwindling. The question now was whether Germany had the will to remain in existence. Besides, the Ardennes offensive had achieved great things, thrown the enemy off balance, upset *his* offensive plans. Then Hitler was somehow moved to make a strange confession, to the effect that the enemy 'has had to admit that there is no chance of the war being decided before August, perhaps not before the end of next year'. But he was quick to deny the implications of this remark: there was no possibility of his envisaging, even remotely, the loss of the war. He had, he said, never learned to know the word 'capitulation'. He would fight on until at last the scales tipped in their favour. Then they would smash the Americans, destroy one half of the enemy's western front. 'We shall yet master fate'.

As 1944 ended Hitler, at his Eagle's Nest headquarters, was struggling with the problems of how to relieve Budapest, now invested by the Red Army, and with how to mount further attacks on Eisenhower's armies through Saarbrücken. It would not be long now before both the Eastern and Western Fronts collapsed. Meanwhile Churchill, back at home after his Greek adventure, was proposing to Roosevelt that the two of them should meet Stalin at Yalta. On Roosevelt's suggesting that he might come to Malta first by sea, Churchill replied on 1 January 1945 that he would be delighted and would be waiting on the quay, adding, in characteristically buoyant vein, 'No more let us falter! From Malta to Yalta! Let nobody alter!' The Big Three meeting at Yalta was to be the last one at which Churchill, Roosevelt and Stalin conferred together, and at it would be decided the fate of Germany.

CHAPTER 10

1945 – *ENDKAMPF*

I say quite frankly that Berlin remains of high strategic
importance . . . should [it] be in our grasp we should certainly take it.

WINSTON CHURCHILL to FRANKLIN D. ROOSEVELT,

1 April 1945

I expect the relief of Berlin. What is Heinrici's Army
doing? Where is Wenck? What is happening to the
Ninth Army? When will Wenck and Ninth Army join
us?

Signal from ADOLF HITLER to GENERAL KEITEL,

28 April 1945

At the beginning of 1945 the strategic situation of the Third Reich was without
hope. The initiative which Hitler had enjoyed for so long, and with such cruel
consequences, had gone for ever, and Germany's enemies by land, sea and air
were closing in for the kill. But as the leader of Germany had never learned to
know the word 'capitulation', the struggle for Europe went on. The hopelessness of this struggle from Germany's point of view was perhaps most strikingly illustrated by her absolute incapacity to meet on anything like tolerable
terms the threat she faced from Allied air forces, particularly in the west. Even
a great concentration of German air strength in the Fatherland did not alter her
condition of helplessness. On the last day of 1944 the Luftwaffe had deployed
the great bulk of its fighters in the west either in direct support of the armies or
for air defence. More than three-quarters of the total number of its day
fighters, some 2,300, and all but a few of the night fighters were there. In addition, nearly a million men of the Wehrmacht were needed to man anti-aircraft
defences. Yet on that same day, 31 December 1944, starting in the protective
darkness many hours before dawn, Albert Speer drove from Dietrich's headquarters in the Ardennes to Hitler's Eagle's Nest, some two hundred miles

ALLIED ADVANCES, JANUARY-MAY 1945

0   150
Miles

Allied thrusts.

Territory held by Allies, 27 January 1945.

Allied gains, 27 January-8 May 1945.

Neutral territory.

The front on 27 January 1945.

The front on 8 May 1945.

BRADLEY   Names of Allied commanders.

MODEL   Names of German commanders.

International frontiers (pre-war).

away. It took him twenty-two hours. The reason he was forced to proceed at an average speed of less than 10 miles an hour was because again and again he was obliged to stop and scurry for cover from enemy fighters, and this in the very sector where most of the Luftwaffe was positioned. Even before setting off, Speer's talk with Dietrich had been constantly interrupted by low-level bombing attacks from massed US Air Force formations, which were helping Eisenhower's armies to put paid to Hitler's Ardennes counter-offensive. 'Howling and exploding bombs, clouds illuminated in red and yellow hues, droning motors, and no defence anywhere –' wrote Speer, 'I was stunned by this scene of military impotence which Hitler's miscalculations had given such a grotesque setting.' Yet the Führer had claimed that in the air Germany would be supreme.

The contradictory claptrap with which Hitler regaled his generals on 28 December, on the eve of his offensive in Alsace, has already been noted. During this conference – if conference is the right word for what, on the one hand, was a monologue painting a picture of a fictional world, and making both a statement of intention and an exhortation to still greater effort, and what on the other was a response whose outward loyalty to a doomed cause concealed despair and disillusion – Hitler, in one more colossal fabrication of untruths, deceived himself on two counts, first as to the local situation on the Western Front, second in referring to the future conduct of the war. On the first count, the Ardennes offensive had, he said, transformed the situation (as indeed it had – although not in the way Hitler meant), a tremendous easing had taken place, the Allies were off balance, had eaten up their reserves, abandoned all their offensive plans, and all that was needed now was simply to knock away half the enemy's Western Front merely by annihilating the American divisions one by one. Once this had been done, Hitler claimed that a further forty-five German divisions would be ready and the enemy would be unable to resist these extra forces. Where these divisions were to come from was not made known, yet the absurdity of the whole strategic situation was that Hitler could have put his hands on more than forty-five divisions had he chosen to cut his losses, forget about irrelevant sideshows and concentrate his forces on the one thing that really mattered – the defence of Germany. In his own words to the generals he put his finger on the key point of his strategic dilemma: 'We should not forget that even today we are defending an area . . . which is essentially larger than Germany has ever been, and that there is at our disposal an armed force which even today is unquestionably the most powerful on earth.' It was precisely the first of these points – the size of the area being defended – which made even the most powerful armed force on earth (an insupportable claim, in fact, when the Red Army, plus Anglo-American air and naval forces, are considered) quite inadequate.

At this time Hitler had 260 divisions in the field. Their distribution reflected his claim about the size of the area to be defended, and at the same time illustrated how strategically frail and vulnerable Germany's whole position was. In the west were 76 divisions, in Italy 24, in Yugoslavia 10, in Scandinavia 17. In the east were 133 divisions. Of these 75 were in the vital areas of East Prussia and Poland; the rest were guarding strategic trifles in Courland, Memel and Hungary. Against this German deployment, Eisenhower's groups of armies numbered some 78 divisions, while the Russians had 180 divisions on the Polish part of the Eastern Front alone. If, instead of hanging on everywhere, Hitler had adopted a deployment to guard against Germany's greatest dangers – that is, to keep the Western Allies in check on the Rhine and the Apennines, to concentrate against the Red Army *and* to maintain a substantial reserve – positioning, say, 100 divisions to dispute the field with the Anglo-American armies, and the rest against the Russians, then arguably Guderian, when discussing the situation with Hitler on 9 January, would have had no need to describe the Eastern Front as a house of cards. Why was it then that Hitler rejected a deployment most likely to wrest advantage from the military probabilities? The answer lay in his last-minute hopes, not of staving off defeat, but of snatching victory at the twelfth hour, snatching it by means of his new air and sea weapons.

It must always remain a disagreeable reflection that had Hitler given the right people the right instructions at the right time, he might have been in possession of nuclear weapons – capable of delivery either by jet aircraft or by land- and submarine-launched rockets – well before the Western Allies. That he would not have hesitated to use them goes without saying. It is strange that Hitler showed so little interest in the possibility of an atomic bomb. If ever there were a weapon which epitomized the revolutionary and the violent, this was it. But, says Speer, 'the idea quite obviously strained his intellectual capacity; he was unable to grasp the revolutionary nature of nuclear physics.' Only once in all the conferences which Speer had with Hitler was nuclear fission mentioned, and then only briefly. Speer adds, however, that he was certain the Führer would have employed such weapons against Britain.

After Hitler's tirade of 28 December, Rundstedt had assured the Führer that absolutely everything would be done to make the new offensive a success. But despite this assurance, instead of Hitler's armies mastering fate, fate went on to master them. On New Year's Day 1945 eight German divisions attacked from the Saar to the south, both west and east of the Vosges. Hitler had predicted that in this New Year the German people would put behind them the miseries of 1944 and see what an excellent beginning 1945 was to have. In the event, however, there was no tactical surprise and very little progress. The main German attack towards the Saverne Gap was quickly halted, while east of the

Vosges the Germans were faced by a skilful and resolute withdrawal which ended at the Maginot Line. Eisenhower was not obliged to switch reserves from elsewhere. But Himmler, now commanding Army Group *Ober-Rhein*, did succeed in his attack from the Colmar Pocket in securing a small bridgehead over the Rhine north of Strasbourg. This threat to Strasbourg, the capital of Alsace, which had been captured by de Lattre de Tassigny's French First Army, caused Eisenhower to endorse US Sixth Army Group's orders to the effect that while efforts would be made to hold Strasbourg and Mulhouse, these efforts would not be allowed to 'jeopardize the integrity of forces in a withdrawal to a rearward position,' that is, back to the Vosges. The loss of Strasbourg would have been unthinkable for the French, and it was clear that General de Lattre de Tassigny, with the powerful support of Generals Juin and de Gaulle, had interpreted his instructions as meaning that the city's defence was to be 'unequivocal'. In such a situation it was fortunate that the greatest Allied expert at reconciling political and military contradictions – Churchill – should have been there to resolve the problem. When on the one hand Eisenhower's Chief of Staff, Lieutenant-General Walter Bedell Smith threatened to withhold supplies from the French First Army, and on the other Juin stated that he would deny American forces the use of French railways, it was clear that something had to be done.

It was arranged that de Gaulle and Eisenhower would meet at the latter's headquarters on 3 January. In order to strengthen his position de Gaulle signalled to Roosevelt and Churchill asking for support. Roosevelt's reply made it clear that he left the matter to Eisenhower. Churchill came in person, and his intervention was decisive – yet in his own account of the affair, he refers to his presence at Eisenhower's headquarters as having been due to chance. When, during their meeting, Eisenhower pointed to the need for withdrawal to a shorter line, de Gaulle declared that strategic considerations notwithstanding, Alsace was sacred French territory. To lose it again would be a national disaster. 'At the present moment we are concerned with Strasbourg. I have ordered the French First Army to defend the city. It will therefore do so, in any case.' Churchill weighed in with his view that the significance of Alsace to the French must be considered; after further exchanges, as he tells it, 'finally the Supreme Commander came round to my point of view'. General Jacob Devers, commanding Sixth Army Group, was told to hold Strasbourg, and he did. Such was the outcome of what Churchill referred to as an 'awkward situation' during the Ardennes battle.

The battle itself was drawing to a close now, and when it became clear that Montgomery's drive for Houffalize was going to succeed, even Hitler agreed that Model could withdraw his forces to the east, for he could not afford to lose his principal panzer reserves. By 14 January OKW Operation Staff's War Diary recorded that the initiative in the Ardennes area had passed to the enemy, and two days later, exactly a month since the onset of Hitler's last offensive, the Führer gave permission for a general withdrawal. By doing so he conceded that this offensive had failed. On the say day, 16 January, he moved from Adlershorst to Berlin. There was another battle for him to direct – the last one of all, the battle for Berlin itself. It would not be an easy battle to fight, for there was a limit even to the Wehrmacht's power. It had been no mean feat to scrape up twenty-eight divisions for the Ardennes offensive, with all the artillery and logistic support that were needed to back them. But in just one month, Hitler had lost 120,000 soldiers, 600 tanks and assault guns, more than 1,600 aircraft, and vast quantities of equipment and supplies. He had gambled away his last reserves. There were no more German armies to be raised.

This melancholy reflection made little difference to the Wehrmacht's Supreme Commander. Hitler had already consoled himself by quoting to General Thomale, Chief of Staff Panzer Forces, from the letters of Frederick the Great, who during the fifth year of the Seven Years' War, referred to his formerly wonderful army as 'a muck heap. I have no leaders any more, my generals are incompetent, the officers are no commanders, the troops are wretched.' Despite all its losses and Hitler's recent squandering of reserves, even at this late stage the Wehrmacht could not be described as a muck heap. It still contained a formidable number of divisions. There were leaders galore; German generals were as experienced, resolute and competent as those in any army; the officers commanded well; the troops still fought bravely and skilfully. In no respect did the Führer's position resemble that of Frederick the Great in 1760 – save one. His military condition was without hope, for the residual power of the Wehrmacht notwithstanding, its divisions were scattered so widely over so many fronts that the priceless military principles of concentration of force and singleness of purpose had gone for ever. Yet from the very paradox of his military impotence Hitler drew strength, and it was then that he told Thomale that a man could not make world history by giving up if things went badly. That history could only be made by the man whose fanatical determination, courage and conviction would enable him to hold out longer than the enemy. The Germans would do so, according to their leader, because they had everything at stake.

During his visit to Eisenhower's headquarters, it had been explained to Churchill that plans for a further offensive in the west were dependent upon knowing when the next Russian attack on the Eastern Front would take place. On 6 January, therefore, Churchill signalled to Stalin, asking whether 'we can count on a major Russian offensive on the Vistula front, or elsewhere, during January'. He undertook to keep any such information most secretly guarded, to be passed only to Brooke and Eisenhower, and pointed out the latter's need to know what Stalin's intentions were as it affected 'all his and our major decisions'. Churchill was thrilled to receive a swift and most encouraging reply saying that there was to be a major Russian offensive on the Central Front 'not later than the second half of January'. The information was passed to Eisenhower by the hand of Churchill's aide-de-camp, Lieutenant-Commander Tommy Thompson. Not everything went so well, however. Always anxious to smooth and cement Anglo-American military relations, Churchill was greatly distressed at this time by Montgomery's ill-advised press conference about the Ardennes battle, which had implied that he had been the principal influence in winning the battle, whereas in fact it had been the staunch fighting qualities of American soldiers. Churchill was sufficiently concerned to tell the Chiefs of Staff how deeply offended American generals had been by Montgomery's 'patronizing tone', which 'completely overlooked the fact that the United States have lost perhaps 80,000 men and we but 2,000 or 3,000'. In particular, Churchill was worried about the effect it all might have on future command arrangements, although Montgomery later acknowledged that the victory had been primarily an American one. There was now to be a pause in the west before Eisenhower launched his next major attack. In the East it was another story.

As has been shown, by January 1945 the Supreme Commander of the Wehrmacht had so disposed his armies that the most vulnerable front of all, both militarily and politically, the front in Poland and East Prussia, was, in comparative terms, the most weakly held, the one least likely to be capable of withstanding a violent and prolonged assault – which was precisely what it was about to receive. Not for nothing had Guderian described the Eastern Front as a house of cards, adding that if it were broken anywhere it would collapse everywhere. In that same month of January, no fewer than 300 divisions of the Red Army, including 25 tank armies, were getting ready to end the war. In the north two groups of armies under Chernyakhovsky and Rokossovsky were to converge on East Prussia; Zhukov's and Koniev's groups in the centre were to aim at Berlin and Upper Silesia; further south, two more groups would clear Slovakia and take both Vienna and Budapest; finally, Petrov was to reoccupy the Northern Carpathians. The Russians could afford to operate over such broad fronts, but the German divisions facing them were too reduced to be able to do so. Moreover, they were in no respect concentrated to meet what was coming in the critical central sector. So inept had Hitler's handling of the war become that on this 600-mile front the Russian forces likely to attack were twice as strong as those which the United States and Britain could bring to bear against a defensive strength comparable to that in the east. Such a curious juggling of resources, so distorted a reading of priorities, could not add up to military security. But Hitler was no longer concerned with military security. He was living in his own imagined world into which all facts had to be fitted. In the west the initiative would be maintained – even though it had been lost for ever; in the east there would be neither reinforcement nor withdrawal. 'I get an attack of the horrors,' he declared, 'whenever I hear that there must be a withdrawal somewhere or other in order to have room for manoeuvre, I've heard that sort of thing for the past two years and the results have always been appalling.'

They were about to be appalling again, for on 12 January Stalin launched his greatest offensive of the war. For the central stroke in Poland and East Prussia he employed 180 divisions with 4 tank armies, each of the latter containing 1,200 tanks. Koniev's army group rapidly broke out of its bridgehead on the Upper Vistula, and the first of a series of disasters which engulfed the Eastern Front was under way. Two weeks after starting their offensive the Russians were on German soil, in Silesia and Pomerania, whence Hitler's first blitzkrieg against Poland had been mounted. Guderian, never one to despair, set to work in forming a new Army Group Vistula to stem the Russian advance. Its front would stretch from Poznan to Graudenz, and Guderian intended to give this army group all the reserves he was mustering from the west, including Sepp Dietrich's Sixth SS Panzer Army. Hoping to be able to direct its operations himself – and it would have been difficult to find anyone better qualified or more likely to make telling use of it – Guderian proposed General von Weichs as a nominal army group commander. Hitler, who had been in the Führerbunker beneath the Chancellery in Berlin since 16 January, finally disillusioned with the professional soldiers, appointed – of all people – Himmler. Guderian was so appalled that in conversation with Ribbentrop on 26 January, he suggested that the two of them should go to the Führer and try 'to secure an armistice on at least one front'. Ribbentrop jibbed at this, but was himself aghast when Guderian asked him how he would feel when the Russians were at the gates of Berlin in three or four weeks' time. When the Foreign Minister asked if he really thought this was possible, Guderian replied that it was not merely possible, but, because of Hitler's leadership, certain. The conversation was duly reported to Hitler, who in Guderian's presence referred to it as treason. But the great panzer leader did not lack the courage of his convictions and flatly tried to argue the strategic issues with the Führer there and then. Hitler refused to discuss them.

Churchill's activities in London at this time, while he was preparing for the Yalta meeting, were as numerous and as wide-ranging as ever. On 18 January, as part of a speech on the war situation, he told the House of Commons:

Both in the West and in the East overwhelming forces are ranged on our side. Military victory may be distant, it will certainly be costly, but it is no longer in doubt. The physical and scientific force which our foes hurled upon us in the early years has changed sides and the British Commonwealth, the United States and the Soviet Union undoubtedly possess the power to beat down to the ground in dust and ashes the prodigious might of the war-making nations and the conspiracies which assailed us. But, as the sense of mortal peril has passed from our side to that of our cruel foes, they gain the stimulus of despair and we tend to lose the bond of combined self-preservation, or are in danger of losing it.

It was therefore necessary, he went on, for the Allies to unite in a joint purpose in order to achieve military victory as quickly as possible, and without 'jabber, babble and discord while victory is still unattained'. Whether they could do so, however, was 'the supreme question alike of the hour and of the age'.

In spite of the continuing dangers of enemy action, notably from the V2 rockets, jet aircraft, and U-boats, Churchill reiterated his confidence in the military might of the Allies, adding that whatever political differences might exist between them, the Big Three would shortly be meeting to discuss such matters. On the question of whether de Gaulle should be allowed to join the forthcoming Yalta Conference, he was clearly against the idea, not only because of the likelihood that the General would disrupt harmony by intrigue, but also because France's military effort hardly justified her being considered as a 'Fourth Power'. There were other considerations affecting Yalta, too, for the Red Army's further advances, while prompting Churchill to send a congratulatory signal to Stalin on 27 January, also compelled him to admit that except for Greece, it now looked as if all the Balkans would be 'bolshevized; and there is nothing I can do to prevent it. There is nothing I can do for Poland either.' Before leaving England, in response to a recommendation by the Joint Intelligence Committee that the Russian effort would be further assisted – and the war thereby shortened – by the use of the Anglo-American strategic bombing force against German cities such as Berlin, Leipzig and Dresden, he asked the Air Staff to examine the question and let him know what was proposed. On 29 January he left by air for Malta, accompanied by his daughter, Sarah, while Brooke, Eden and others flew there in another aeroplane. On the morning of 2 February Roosevelt arrived at Malta aboard the cruiser USS *Quincy*, so that what Churchill had wished for – discussions between the British and American Chiefs of Staff and between himself and Roosevelt *before* meeting the Russians at Yalta – could now take place. The principal point of disagreement between the British and Americans during their meetings from 30 January to 1 February had concerned how the Western Allies should deploy their armies in thrusting across and beyond the Rhine, and in particular what should be the respective strengths of the northern and southern thrusts.

The British view was that to have two thrusts against the expected opposition precluded the possibility of either one being decisive, while the Americans thought it unsound to stake everything on a single thrust, particularly on so narrow a front. In the end, however, the only thing that required changing was the wording of the document setting out Eisenhower's intentions. A new version removed reference to the possible need to use either or both of the two approaches, and also to the need to close the Rhine along its entire German-held length as a preliminary to further advance. Eisenhower accepted this revised plan and assured the Combined Chiefs of Staff that he would seize the Rhine crossings in the north immediately it was feasible, without waiting to close up to the river everywhere. Furthermore, he added, the northern crossing would be made in maximum strength as soon as possible. Both sides expressed themselves satisfied, and the Combined Chiefs of Staff reported accordingly to Churchill and Roosevelt.

On 3 February both Churchill and Roosevelt flew to the Crimea, and on the following day the first meeting of the Big Three took place at Yalta. Churchill had already explained to Stalin that in four days' time, Montgomery, with Twenty-First Army Group and the US Ninth Army, would launch his offensive directed at Düsseldorf and the Rhine. As the plenary session got under way, he asked the Soviet leader for advice on river crossing, as well as putting forward again an idea that he and Stalin had discussed before, that of an Allied thrust in northern Italy directed on the Ljubljana Gap in order to make contact with the southernmost Russian forces. Stalin explained what the Red Army was doing and agreed, in response to Churchill's request that the Russian offensive should continue, that it would do so until the end of March. It was clear that on the Western Front there was nothing like the same superiority of strength over the Germans as in the east, except with regard to air forces and armour. Churchill also asked Stalin 'to take Danzig' because many of the new U-boats, which by now were harassing shipping near the British Isles, were being constructed there. It was agreed that the respective military staffs should consult in order to co-ordinate their offensive plans. It was also clear at this first meeting that Roosevelt was a sick man, and, as Admiral Sir Andrew Cunningham[1] put it, did not 'appear to know what he is talking about'.

The Yalta talks lasted until 11 February and on that day the Big Three signed a statement which detailed what had been decided. The decisions taken were concerned less with how to end the war than with what to do when the war was over. Diplomacy rather than strategy called the tune, and the powerful strategic position of the Soviet Union enabled Stalin to stick to his principal objectives, although the British and Americans gave up only one thing – the future of

---

[1] Cunningham had been appointed First Sea Lord in 1943, and thus was one of the Chiefs of Staff.

Poland. By then, however, Poland was so firmly in Russian hands that it was plainly the Soviet Union which would dominate the country's future government. The agreed statement had eight sections which dealt with the defeat of Germany; her post-war control by the Three Powers (four in the end, as Churchill persuaded the other leaders that France should have an occupation zone); reparations; the establishment of the United Nations; Poland; liberated Europe; Yugoslavia; consultation between Foreign Secretaries. Chester Wilmot called Yalta Stalin's greatest victory, but he was thinking not so much of what was actually agreed by the Big Three as of the subsequent political consequences. It must be remembered that the other two, Roosevelt and Churchill, had widely different objectives. The American President was primarily concerned with the rapid conclusion of the European war and with the need to persuade the Soviet Union then to join the United States and Britain in finishing off the war against Japan; Stalin could obviously help in both these respects. For his part, Churchill was more concerned about the burgeoning Soviet threat to the Western position in post-war Europe, Poland's deteriorating prospects, the growing Russian claims over German territory and the reparations from Germany for which the Soviet Union was pressing. Furthermore, Churchill was self-evidently not in the same position to help Roosevelt as was Stalin, for Britain had shot her military bolt. Thus there developed the somewhat absurd situation in which Roosevelt, whose real interests and aims closely coincided with Churchill's, having gained the assurances he sought from Stalin, lent little or no support to Churchill as he tried to secure the undertakings that would remove his apprehensions.

The different attitudes of these three men reflected both their characters and their principles. President Roosevelt believed in the United Nations. Generalissimo Stalin believed in the power of the Red Army and all the associated instruments of terror to which countries occupied by that army would be subjected. Prime Minister Churchill believed in the lessons of the past, in his own strategic and historical instinct, in moderation and balance of power. It was not to be expected that they would agree about all the great issues which were discussed at Yalta. The tragedy which eroded so much of the triumph to come was that Churchill failed to convince Roosevelt that Stalin's sole concern, first and last, was the security of the Russian state, with which he identified himself. Concern for the Soviet Union's security led him to press for the dismemberment of Germany. Yet agreement in principle as to the need to break up the German state was more easily reached than agreement as to the practical methods of doing so, and in the end, of course, Germany was not dismembered; by the time the Allies conferred at Potsdam in July 1945 the policy had been dropped. While it had been agreed that no central German government was to be established, it was clear that dismemberment and reparations were incompatible. Not surprisingly, West and East chose reparations. But at Yalta, Churchill was especially anxious to gain agreement that the French should have a zone of occupation, not least because of Roosevelt's statement that United States troops would probably stay in Europe for no more than two years. In discussing this question, neither Stalin nor Roosevelt showed that magnanimity which Churchill had always advocated. The former, perhaps forgetting his own dealings with the Führer immediately before and during the first two years of the war, complained that the French had not stood firm against the enemy, had indeed opened the gates to them. Roosevelt was inclined to allow the French a zone, but no voice in the Control Commission – an absurd contradiction. He was later persuaded to concede that the French would probably be less trouble in the Control Commission than outside it. When the President withdrew his opposition, so did Stalin, and Churchill in this instance had his way. All in all, Churchill had reason to be satisfied with his efforts at Yalta. Colville referred to the Prime Minister's having won 'another great personal success. He was tireless in pressing for this Conference, in spite of Roosevelt's apathy, and deserves most of the credit for what has been achieved.' Beaverbrook went even further, writing to Churchill that 'you now appear to your countrymen to be the greatest statesman as well as the greatest warrior'. Hitler, predictably, was less enthusiastic:

> These warmongers at Yalta must be denounced – so insulted and attacked that they will have no chance to a make an offer to the German people. Under no circumstances must there be an offer. That gang only wants to separate the German people from their leadership. I've always said surrender is absolutely out of the question. History is not going to be repeated.

On 13 February, while Churchill was resting aboard the *Franconia* at Sevastopol[1] before his flight next day to Athens, the city of Dresden was subjected to the first of a series of terrible bombing attacks by British and American aircraft. In Berlin, meanwhile, Hitler conducted another Führer Conference in the Chancellery. Apart from Hitler, Keitel, Jodl and other members of the staff

---

[1] Once the conference had ended, Churchill was able to visit battlefields of the Crimean War, no great distance from Yalta, including 'the wonderful valley down which the Light Brigade charged and the ridge which the Highland Regiments defended' (the latter is a reference to the action, on the same day as the Charge, in which the 93rd Highlanders, not having time to form a defensive square, formed up in two ranks and drove off a vastly superior force of Russian cavalry, thereby earning the immortal sobriquet, 'the Thin Red Line'). The Charge of the Light Brigade at Balaclava in 1854 was of special interest to him, as his own regiment, then the 4th Light Dragoons, played a prominent and distinguished part in it.

who normally attended, those present were Himmler, still in command of Army Group Vistula, Sepp Dietrich and General Wenck, whom Guderian, Chief of the Army General Staff, had brought with him. The main issue was how and when the army group would conduct a counter-attack from Arnswalde against Zhukov's extended right flank. Guderian rightly insisted that it should be launched quickly, before Russian reserves came up, and that it should be directed by Wenck, not Himmler. Hitler was arguing every point with the Chief of the General Staff, and in turn being contradicted by him. Guderian recalled the disagreeable scene:

> And so it went on for two hours. His fists raised, his cheeks flushed with rage, his whole body trembling, the man stood there in front of me, beside himself with fury and having lost all self-control. After each outburst of rage, Hitler would stride up and down the carpet edge, then suddenly stop immediately before me and hurl his next accusation in my face. He was almost screaming, his eyes seemed about to pop out of his head and the veins stood out on his temples.

Military affairs conducted by conferences of this sort could hardly be expected to prosper. Even though Guderian gained his point – with his most charming smile Hitler told him that the General Staff had that day won a battle – it was, he wrote, the last battle he was to win, and it came too late. In the event Krebs (not Wenck, who had by then been injured) commanded the counter-attack – the last of all the offensives mounted by the German Army in the war. Flawed by intrigue, lack of both men and material, and bad leadership – all three symptoms of the disease from which the Third Reich was about to die – it petered out after a few days in failure. In short, the field was lost. Not everything was lost, however. The unconquerable will remained. Eleven years earlier Hitler had proclaimed that if Germany found herself at war with Russia, Britain and France, and found she could not conquer them, half the world would be dragged into destruction. No one would triumph over Germany. There would be no surrender. The time to draw on that courage never to submit or yield was now at hand. So was 'immortal hate and study of revenge'. And Hitler, like Satan in *Paradise Lost*, was determined to vent his hatred and revenge on those about him. He gave orders for the destruction of Germany:

> If the war is to be lost [he told Speer] the nation will also perish. This fate is inevitable. There is no need to consider the basis even of a most primitive existence any longer. On the contrary, it is better to destroy even that, and to destroy it ourselves. The nation has proved itself weak, and the future belongs solely to the stronger eastern nation.

[475]

Such nihilism reveals Adolf Hitler at his worst, confirming absolutely his former cry of 'Weltmacht oder Niedergang', world power or ruin, and endorsing all over again Churchill's sharp condemnation of the Führer as 'this evil man, this monstrous abortion of hatred and defeat'. That Hitler was thwarted in his intention to erase the German nation owed much to the courageous disobedience of Speer, who had so often told his master that the war was lost. What must still puzzle us is the extraordinary grip over these same German people that Hitler, even in the depths of adversity, still maintained. During one of Speer's visits to the Western Front on the Rhine in February 1945, he sat unrecognized among a group of miners, and found to his amazement that the ordinary soldier and worker still believed in their Führer. 'They believed that he, and only he, both understood the working class from which he had risen, and the mystery of politics which had been concealed from the rest of the German race, and that he would therefore be able, as no one else, to work the miracle of their salvation from this forlorn predicament.' It was understandable that, during his first triumphs from 1936 to 1940 and even 1941, the German people should look upon him as a genius, an almost superhuman ruler who found solutions to all problems no matter how intricate or profound, who struck down all enemies of the Reich no matter how numerous or powerfully armed. But when this same man, almost bereft of power, surrounded by military failure, his policies cracking in absolute ruin, and he himself in any event no longer visible or audible to the people, still held them spellbound, it may perhaps be conceded that his claim to be a maker of world history was no idle boast. When – living in a world of his own, secreted in his various Führer headquarters, formerly keeping himself remote from shattered cities, now in the heart of his capital, bunkered, wired-in, SS-guarded, with only an Alsatian bitch and his own henchmen for companions – he was able to prolong the struggle long beyond the time when its hopelessness was obvious to all, and yet still keep alive some spark of hope, then it becomes all too clear that Hitler's willpower was remarkable indeed. It is possible even to discern some faint resemblance between the man and his hero, Frederick the Great, for both – though in very different ways and with very different results – had 'given an example unrivalled in history of what capacity and resolution can effect against the greatest superiority of power, and the utmost spite of fortune'.

Fortune was certainly giving vent to her spite in the last months of the war. By February 1945 the Russians were threatening Vienna and even Berlin; in March the American and British armies crossed the Rhine, and the Red Army attacked at Küstrin, east of Berlin, and in Hungary; in April Model's army group in the Ruhr was surrounded, Alexander's armies broke into the Po Valley, the Americans reached the Elbe, Königsberg fell to the Russians, then

Vienna, and by breaching the Oder defences the road to Berlin was opened to them; by the middle of the month no further effective German resistance was possible. But the Wehrmacht's Supreme Commander had not yet abandoned hope. He once more shuffled his subordinates. Kesselring replaced Rundstedt in the west; Krebs relieved Guderian as Army Chief of Staff. The Führer himself, however, remained, as he had done for five and a half years, intimately concerned, as C-in-C of the Wehrmacht and of the German Army, with the war's direction. His difficulties arose from the fact that the German Army had been totally defeated in the field. What is more, he was cut off in Berlin. Yet still he sent out orders that could not be obeyed, and conducted futile conferences.

While Hitler stayed in Berlin until the end, Churchill undertook a more peripatetic programme. His journey home from the Crimea took him first to Athens, where he was greatly acclaimed, with the Acropolis floodlit in his honour; then to Egypt, where he took his last farewell (as it would turn out) of President Roosevelt, and had meetings with the kings of both Saudi Arabia and Egypt, the President of Syria, and the Emperor Haile Selassie of Ethiopia. Back in Britain on 20 February, he gave an account of the Yalta Conference to the House of Commons a week later. Although he assured the House that Stalin had given 'solemn declarations . . . that the sovereign independence of Poland is to be maintained,' adding that he believed the Soviet leader would stick to his obligations, he sounded a note of warning as to the dangers 'if some awful schism arose between the Western democracies and the Russian Soviet Union'. He believed, he said, that the three Great Powers' unity had been strengthened, as had their understanding of each other; together they had 'the unchallengeable power to lead the world to prosperity, freedom and happiness. The Great Powers must seek to serve and not to rule.' Yet Colville observed that the Prime Minister seemed to be trying to convince himself 'that all is well, but in his heart I think he is worried about Poland and not convinced of the strength of our moral position'. At the same time, Churchill was himself the first to recognize the realities of power. The Russians, he said, 'are on the spot; even the massed majesty of the British Empire would not avail to turn them off that spot'.

Next he set off again to do what he so liked doing – visiting troops in the battle area. On 3 March he looked at the Siegfried Line in company with Montgomery and Brooke, and as the latter recorded, was displeased because he was not allowed to go nearer to the actual fighting. He also visited the Canadian First Army, which, although so named, in fact contained more British soldiers than Canadians – Churchill was always anxious that it should be widely known whenever British formations were engaged with the enemy in order to strengthen his hand when it came to peace negotiations. After visiting Eisenhower at his headquarters he returned to London on 6 March. He was by now deeply worried about what was happening in Romania, Bulgaria and Poland, and signalled to Roosevelt expressing his concern that if 'the spirit of the Yalta declaration' were not carried out in establishing a new Polish government (Stalin had agreed to the holding of 'free elections' there), they would have failed. He also told Stalin that the Soviet Foreign Minister, Molotov, was conducting the discussions on Poland in Moscow in a way that differed significantly from what had been agreed at Yalta. But it was clear from Roosevelt's replies – written by the State Department – that there would be little American support for Churchill's attempts to overcome Russian obstruction to Allied observers of what the Soviet Union, regardless of the Yalta accords, regarded as its own business.

In addressing the Conservative Party Conference on 15 March, the Prime Minister delivered one of his straightforward statements about the sort of world that soldiers returning from the war would have to face. It was vital, he said, that the Conservative Party should tell the truth about it, 'acting in accordance with the verities of our position,' and not attempt to 'gain a span of shabbily-bought office by easy and fickle froth and chatter'. The British people, perhaps to a greater extent now than ever before, would want to face realities: 'This is no time for humbug and blandishments, but for grim, stark facts and figures, and for action to meet immediate needs.' As for the war itself, Churchill had noted the continued resistance of Kesselring's armies in Italy, something which, together with the fight the Germans were still putting up in Hungary, prompted him to ask the Chiefs of Staff to get the Joint Intelligence Committee to 'consider the possibility that Hitler, after losing Berlin and Northern Germany, will retire to the mountainous and wooded parts of Southern Germany and endeavour to prolong the fight there'. It was a pertinent question, and was later to exercise Eisenhower himself in considering whether or not the Western Allies should make a dash for Berlin itself. Churchill was also deeply concerned about the bombing of German cities (at least 100,000 civilians had been killed in the raids on Dresden), even though he and his ministers, together with the Chiefs of Staff, had authorized the policy. He was on happier ground when, on 23 March, he again visited Montgomery in order to witness the British crossing of the Rhine. That evening he signalled Stalin from Montgomery's headquarters to the effect that a major battle to force the Rhine was about to be launched which, in addition to the assault troops that would cross the river in boats, would employ an airborne corps, 2,000 guns and substantial armoured reserves to exploit the bridgeheads, which should be established next day. (While at Montgomery's headquarters, Churchill was able to continue with his reading and dispatching of telegrams, as he had been provided with a caravan as his office, and another one for sleeping.) It was already clear that the Russians were disturbed by their fear, as Churchill put it, 'of our doing a deal in the west to hold them well back in the east'. This fear had been prompted by the activities of General Wolff, the German liaison officer with Mussolini's Republican Government in northern Italy. Through agents in Switzerland, Wolff had made contact with Alexander's headquarters with a view to negotiating the surrender of Kesselring's army group in Italy. No such deal was in fact under way, but rumours of it resulted in some sharp exchanges between Stalin, Roosevelt and Churchill a dozen days or so later.

On 24 March Churchill was in his element as he watched Montgomery's attack across the Rhine, first from an observation post overlooking the river, from which he saw the 2,000 aircraft streaming overhead to release their parachute troops and gliders, but noted, too, 'with a sense of tragedy aircraft in twos and threes coming back askew, asmoke, or even in flames. Also at this time tiny specks came floating to earth. Imagination built on a good deal of experience told a hard and painful tale. It seemed however that nineteen out of every twenty of the aircraft that had started came back in good order, having discharged their mission.' Next Churchill and Brooke went in armoured cars to see where the 51st Highland Division had crossed the Rhine, and visited the 3rd Division's headquarters. Brooke recorded that he had some difficulty in persuading the Prime Minister not 'to go messing about on the Rhine crossings'. Next day Churchill enjoyed himself even more, first visiting Eisenhower, then going with the Supreme Commander to the Rhine, crossing to the other side with Montgomery and others, and finally coming under fire from German artillery at the Wesel railway bridge. At this Lieutenant-General William Simpson, commanding US Ninth Army, pointed out to the Prime Minister that with German snipers in front of them and shelling at both sides of the bridge, he could not accept responsibility for his visitor's safety, and asked him to come away. Brooke then remembered that 'The look on Winston's face was just like that of a small boy being called away from his sand-castles on the beach by his nurse! He put both his arms round one of the twisted girders of the bridge and looked over his shoulder at Simpson with pouting mouth and angry eyes. Thank heaven he came away quietly. It was a sad wrench for him; he was enjoying himself immensely.' Churchill had yet another good day on 26 March, crossing the Rhine with Montgomery, although he was upset by his sight of German civilians and the strained expression on their faces. He returned to England that evening.

Once Montgomery's Twenty-First Army Group was across the Rhine, the restraints imposed on his advance were more those engendered by bridges, routes and logistics rather than by enemy action. A week after his successful crossing, Montgomery had 20 divisions and 1,500 tanks under his hand for his advance, which was planned both to provide the northern claw of a pincer to encircle the Ruhr, and to initiate a gallop across the Westphalian Plain to the

Elbe. Meanwhile Eisenhower had instructed Bradley, reinforced with more American divisions, to complete the Ruhr encirclement and drive east to link up with the Red Army. Accordingly, on 28 March Lieutenant-General Courtney Hodges's (US First) Army broke out of the greatly extended Remagen bridgehead,[1] which now stretched from Bonn to Koblenz, in an easterly direction, while Patton's US Third Army advanced from the Mainz area. Three days later the armies of Patton and Hodges joined hands near Giessen and, breaking clear of Kesselring's delaying forces, thrust on to the Frankfurt-Kassel area in order to close the trap east of Model's Army Group B, which was defending the Ruhr. There was a major tank battle at Sennelager, the famous panzer training area, but the relatively few panzers and SP guns in German hands could not prevail against the numbers enjoyed by the Americans. Model was surrounded, and with him more than 300,000 men. The Field Marshal himself preferred suicide to capture; his men became prisoners of war.

It seemed that this was a choice facing another German commander – the Wehrmacht's Supreme Commander, Adolf Hitler himself. For as March 1945 came to a close, he was confronted with some disagreeable military realities, and it would require all his willpower and all his gift for reducing problems to their simplest terms, if any solutions were to be found. Since the turn of the year everything had gone wrong. Attack in the west had failed, at huge cost in the case of the Ardennes offensive. Now defence in the west had failed too; Eisenhower's armies were across the Rhine and there was little to stop them from motoring to the Elbe and beyond. Attack in the east had also failed with the abortive Danube offensive and the futile attempt to savage Zhukov's northern flank. Defence in the east had failed as well. The Red Army was across the Oder, on the Elbe and within a few days' march of Berlin. One place alone remained to the Führer, his headquarters in the bunker beneath the Reich Chancellery. And it was becoming clear that only the fall of Berlin, or rather the fall of one man besieged there, would bring it all to an end. Churchill was thoroughly alive to the strategic significance of the German capital, and was shortly to join the controversy about its capture. Before doing so, however, he paid a tribute to Lloyd George, who had died on 26 March. This eulogy to one who had been so close a political ally and personal friend was characteristic of Churchill's eloquence, generosity, compassion and recognition of greatness. On 28 March, he told the House of Commons:

[1] In the first week of March, as the Western Allies closed up to the Rhine, it was feared that the Germans had destroyed all the bridges and rendered impassable all other crossings over the river. On 7 March, however, advanced elements of US 9th Armoured Division 'bounced' the feebly defended bridge at Remagen, which, though damaged by a demolition charge, they captured intact. The Americans poured men and material across the bridge, and within days had a substantial bridgehead.

When I first became Lloyd George's friend and active associate, now more than forty years ago, this deep love of the people, the profound knowledge of their lives and of the undue and needless pressure under which they lived, impressed itself indelibly upon my mind ... [as Prime Minister] he imparted immediately a new surge of strength, of impulse, far stronger than anything that had been known up to that time, and extending over the whole field of wartime Government, every part of which was of equal interest to him. His long life was, from almost the beginning to almost the end, spent in political strife and controversy. He aroused intense and sometimes needless antagonisms. He had fierce and bitter quarrels at various times with all the parties. He faced undismayed the storms of criticism and hostility. In spite of all obstacles, including those he raised himself, he achieved his main purpose. As a man of action, resource and creative energy he stood, when at his zenith, without a rival.[1]

The controversy over Berlin arose from the fact that Eisenhower had done what is customary with military commanders – he had changed his mind. After the great victory in Normandy, he had told his two principal subordinates, Bradley and Montgomery, that he regarded Berlin as a primary objective. 'Clearly, Berlin is the main prize ... There is no doubt whatsoever, in my mind, that we should concentrate all our energies and resources on a rapid thrust to Berlin. Our strategy, however, will have to be coordinated with that of the Russians.' After the successful Rhine crossings, Montgomery had given his orders that when the Ruhr had been encircled and he had effected his junction with Bradley, British Second and US Ninth Armies (the latter still under command of Twenty-First Army Group) should advance with maximum speed and energy to the Elbe from Hamburg to Magdeburg, with the emphasis very much on 'getting the whips out' and leading the advance with fast-moving armoured spearheads, capturing airfields on the way to ensure their subsequent use for close air support. These orders had been issued on 27 March, but on the following day, when Montgomery's troops had already begun their advance, there came a bombshell. Eisenhower not only completely changed the plan, but communicated directly with Stalin in order to co-ordinate his operations with those of the Red Army. The Supreme Commander's signal to Montgomery endorsed the latter's plan only up to the point of his linking with Bradley east of the Ruhr. Thereafter, not only was the US Ninth Army to be removed from Montgomery's command, but the signal made it plain that the main Allied thrust would be, not to Berlin, but to Leipzig and Dresden. In

[1] As Martin Gilbert says, those listening felt that these latter words could be applied equally to Churchill himself.

countering the Field Marshal's objections, Eisenhower reiterated that it was his intention to destroy the enemy forces by advancing on the Kassel-Leipzig axis; and in acknowledging to Montgomery that he had made no mention of Berlin, he added: 'So far as I am concerned, that place has become nothing but a geographical location; I have never been interested in those. My purpose is to destroy the enemy forces and his power to resist.' While it may be understood that Eisenhower might have regarded the capture of Berlin by his armies as no longer feasible – after all, the Russians, already across the Oder, were less than 40 miles from the city, while Twenty-First Army Group was still 300 miles away – and while Eisenhower may also have been worried about the possibility of Hitler's retiring to the so-called 'National Redoubt' in the Bavarian and Austrian mountains and conducting there a last desperate stand which it might take much time and many lives to reduce, it is less easy to comprehend his sudden abandoning of the pursuit of political objectives, of which Berlin was, by his own previous reckoning, of supreme importance.

Churchill was in no doubt about it, and on 31 March expressed his concern to the Chiefs of Staff:

It seems to me that the chief criticism of the new Eisenhower plan is that it shifts the axis of the main advance upon Berlin to the direction through Leipzig to Dresden, and thus raises the question of whether the Twenty-first Army Group will not be so stretched as to lose its offensive power, especially after it has been deprived of the Ninth United States Army. Thus we might be condemned to an almost static role in the north and virtually prevented from crossing the Elbe until an altogether later stage in the operation has been reached. All prospect of the British entering Berlin with the Americans is ruled out . . . it also seems that General Eisenhower may be wrong in supposing Berlin to be largely devoid of military and political importance. Even though German Government departments have to a great extent moved to the south, the dominating fact on German minds of the fall of Berlin and leaving it to the Russians to take at a later stage does not appear to me correct. As long as Berlin holds out and withstands a siege in the ruins, as it may easily do, German resistance will be stimulated. The fall of Berlin might cause nearly all Germans to despair . . .

(Here it is worth commenting that it was Berlin's imminent fall that caused the last of Germany's war lords, not to despair, for despair was not in Hitler's make-up, but to opt for self-slaughter and so bring the war to an end.) Stalin's reaction to Eisenhower's plan, so different from Churchill's, simply redoubled the Prime Minister's instinctive disinclination to allow Berlin to fall into the hands of the Red Army. The Soviet leader positively embraced the new plan since it 'entirely coincides with the plan of the Soviet High Command'. Berlin, declared Stalin, had lost its former strategic importance and therefore only secondary Soviet forces would be directed against it – a statement which prompted Churchill to write that events hardly provided corroboration. In any case, it was not as if Churchill were trying to effect fundamental changes in what Eisenhower proposed to do. He was merely saying that the Western Allies should stick to the course of action already agreed upon. His message to the Supreme Commander of 31 March reads:

> I should greatly prefer persistence in the plan on which we crossed the Rhine, namely, that the Ninth US Army should march with the Twenty-first Army Group to the Elbe and beyond Berlin. This would not be in any way inconsistent with the great central thrust which you are now so rightly developing as a result of the brilliant operations of your armies south of the Ruhr. It only shifts the weight of one army to the northern flank.

Yet Eisenhower had his way. He too argued that he was doing no more than reverting to his original idea – to make one great drive to the east after the Ruhr had been taken in order to capture both the bulk of what was left of the enemy's industrial capacity, and the area to which Germany's administrative structure had moved or was moving. The fault in Eisenhower's reasoning was the oldest of military faults: he was pursuing the wrong objective. He was still thinking of how to remove Germany's capacity to wage war. His mind was still on the defeat of the Wehrmacht. It was no longer this that Churchill was concerned with, however. To his way of thinking this defeat had already been accomplished even though the act of surrender was still to come. It was the link-up with Russia *after* the war was finished that worried him.[1] What he wanted to know was who would get to the Baltic first, who would control Germany's North Sea ports. The pity of it was that a single objective – Berlin – held the key both to the final demise of the Führer and thus the war's end, *and* to a strong bargaining position for further dealings with Russia.

So that when Eisenhower finally opted for a single powerful thrust, he aimed at the wrong target. At last he had got the tactics right, but not the strategy. He was not alone, however, for Bradley, an excellent tactician but no strategist, spoke contemptuously of the British desire to 'complicate the war with political foresight and non-military objectives' – which brings to mind Hitler's refusal to go for Moscow in 1941. Yet as late as the first week of April, Eisenhower was still toying with the idea of changing his mind again, and in a

---

[1] 'There is only one thing worse than fighting with Allies,' Churchill told Brooke, 'and that is fighting without them.'

signal to Marshall, admitting that the purpose of the war was to realize political aims, offered to alter his plans and take Berlin if the Combined Chiefs of Staff thought it proper. Whether he could have done so before the Red Army must remain a matter of conjecture. But on 11 April the armoured spearheads of US Ninth Army were over the Elbe near Magdeburg, a mere seventy miles from Berlin, at a time when Zhukov's forces had not even resumed the offensive and would not do so for a further five days. The probability, therefore, is that British and American forces *could* have got to Berlin, if not before the Russians – Zhukov reached the city's eastern suburbs on 21 April – at least simultaneously, had the order to do so been given. What difference it would have made to subsequent arrangements is, of course, another matter. Churchill's signal to Eisenhower of 2 April, challenging the Soviet suggestion that Berlin had lost its former strategic significance, stressed that this point should be viewed from political aspects, and added: 'I deem it highly important that we should shake hands with the Russians as far to the East as possible.' He also pointed out to the Chiefs of Staff three days later that 'if we cross the Elbe and advance to Berlin, or on a line between Berlin and the Baltic which is well within the Russian zone, we should not give this up as a military matter. It is a matter of State to be considered between the three Governments, and in relation to what the Russians do in the south where they will soon have occupied, not only Vienna, but all Austria.' There was, he said, to be no question of withdrawing from such a line without consultation. Decisions could not be made by military staffs – 'They must be referred to the President and me.'

Here Churchill was already anticipating a further worsening of relations between the Western Allies and the Soviet Union, something that Hitler had long foreseen and even drawn comfort from. On 1 April the Führer painted a prophetic picture to the sinister Bormann, in which he admitted the imminent defeat of Germany:

> With the defeat of the Reich and pending the emergence of the Asiatic, the African and perhaps the South American nationalisms, there will remain in the world only two Great Powers capable of confronting each other – the United States and Soviet Russia. The laws of both history and geography will compel these two powers to a trial of strength, either military or in the fields of economics and ideology. These same laws make it inevitable that both Powers should become enemies of Europe. And it is equally certain that both these Powers will sooner or later find it desirable to seek the support of the sole surviving great nation in Europe, the German people.

'Those who dismiss Hitler's political gifts as negligible,' commented Alan Bullock, 'may well be asked how many in the spring of 1945, with the war not yet over, saw the future so clearly.' The Führer's *Vorhersehung* did not forsake him even at the end.

That end was not far off now, and would be brought about by the imminence of the Red Army's arrival at the Berlin Chancellery itself. For despite all Churchill's urging and Eisenhower's offer to send his armies to the German capital, General Marshall and his military men had become obsessed with the mythical National Redoubt and turned their faces aside from political realities. Eisenhower's final orders required the Western Allied forces to halt on the general line of the Rivers Elbe and Mulde, except for Montgomery's group of armies, which pressed on to the Baltic. With this single last exception the orders could not have better suited Stalin. The glittering prize, however tarnished it might have been by bombing and shellfire, this great political plum of Berlin was not for plucking by Eisenhower or Montgomery. It was into Zhukov's hand that it would fall.

Hitler's prediction of a breach between his Eastern and Western enemies had received ample confirmation when, on 3 April, Stalin accused Roosevelt of authorizing negotiations which would allow Anglo-American troops to advance unopposed into the heart of Germany, while German forces continued to fight against the Russians. This provoked a spirited reply from Roosevelt – or rather from his staff, for the President was by then far too ill to attend to official business – and caused Churchill to address Stalin thus:

> The President has sent me his correspondence with you about the contacts made in Switzerland between a British and American officer on Field-Marshal Alexander's Staff and a German general named Wolff relating to possible surrender of Kesselring's army in Northern Italy . . . There were no negotiations in Switzerland even for a military surrender of Kesselring's army. Still less did any political-military plot enter into our thoughts . . . We consider that Field-Marshal Alexander has full right to accept the surrender of the German army of twenty-five divisions on his front in Italy, and to discuss such matters with German envoys who have the power to settle the terms of capitulation . . . There is, however, a possibility that the whole of this request to parley was one of those attempts which are made by the enemy with the object of sowing distrust between Allies.

Five days later, Churchill received an assurance from Stalin that he had no intention of offending anyone, but merely wished to state his mind clearly and frankly. Churchill had no doubt that relations with Russia were deteriorating, having told the War Cabinet as much on 3 April. There had been difficulties over Poland, and might be more about the United Nations. They could not count 'on Russia as a beneficient influence in Europe, or as a willing partner in maintaining the peace of the world. Yet, at the end of the war, Russia would be left in a position of preponderant power and influence throughout the whole of Europe.' Churchill also referred to the end of the war in a letter to his wife, who was in Moscow, saying that he thought the Coalition Government would break up shortly and that he expected a general election to take place in June.

He had always hoped for great things in Italy, and soon after the last great battle there began on 9 April, when the Eighth Army attacked across the River Senio (Churchill's regiment, the 4th Hussars, playing a very active part), events justified his later claim that 'Gleaming successes marked the end of our campaigns in the Mediterranean.' For once, the fighting in Italy became fluid. Eighth Army rushed forward, with 6th Armoured Division leading, to Ferrara; the Poles captured Bologna; US Fifth Army broke through the mountains and reached the Po; the Allied air forces wreaked destruction on retiring enemy columns; thousands of Germans were cut off by the link-up of Fifth and Eighth Armies; the Po was crossed; the fleeing remnants of General Heinrich von Vietinghoff's forces (Vietinghoff had succeeded Kesselring when the latter became C-in-C West) were pursued to the Adige; then that river was crossed and Allied troops, unhindered by opposition, made for Padua, Treviso, Venice, Vicenza, Trento, Brescia and Alessandria. On 29 April Churchill was able to signal Stalin:

I have just received a telegram from Field-Marshal Alexander[1] that after a meeting at which your officers were present the Germans accepted the terms of unconditional surrender presented to them and are sending the material clauses of the instrument of surrender to General von Vietinghoff, with the request to name the date and hour at which conclusion of hostilities can be made effective. It looks as if the entire German forces south of the Alps will almost immediately surrender.

They did. On 2 May almost a million German soldiers became prisoners of war. The Italian campaign was at an end, and Churchill was able to signal to Alexander: 'I rejoice in the magnificently planned and executed operations of the Fifteenth Group of Armies, which are resulting in the complete destruction or capture of all the enemy forces south of the Alps . . . This great final battle in Italy will long stand out in history as one of the most famous epidodes in this Second World War.'

Much had happened between 9 April and the end of the war in Italy. On 12 April Roosevelt had died. Churchill sent telegrams to his widow, to Hopkins,

[1] He had been promoted field marshal after the capture of Rome in June 1944.

and to Roosevelt's successor, the Vice-President, Harry S. Truman; he received and replied to a sympathetic letter from the King; and determined at first to fly to the United States for Roosevelt's funeral (which would also enable him to meet and talk to Truman), but later decided duty must keep him at home. On 17 April he attended the memorial service for the late President in St Paul's Cathedral, and that afternoon spoke in the House of Commons. He and Roosevelt had met nine times during the war and exchanged more than 1,700 messages:

> I conceived an admiration for him as a statesman, a man of affairs, and a war leader. I felt the utmost confidence in his upright, inspiring character and outlook, and a personal regard – affection I must say – for him beyond my power to express today. His love of his own country, his respect for its constitution, his power of gauging the tides and currents of its mobile public opinion, were always evident, but added to these were the beatings of that generous heart which was always stirred to anger and to action by spectacles of aggression and oppression by the strong against the weak. It is, indeed, a bitter loss to humanity that those heart-beats are stilled for ever . . . he died in harness, and we may well say in battle harness, like his soldiers, sailors, and airmen, who side by side with ours are carrying on their task to the end all over the world. What an enviable death was his. He had brought his country through the worst of its perils and the heaviest of its toils. Victory had cast its sure and steady beam upon him.

Roosevelt, Churchill concluded, was 'the greatest American friend we have ever known, and the greatest champion of freedom who has ever brought help and comfort from the new world to the old'.

Hitler's reaction to the news was somewhat different. When Goebbels heard of Roosevelt's death on Friday 13 April as he entered the Ministry of Propaganda during a heavy air raid – he had just returned from visiting trops at Küstrin – he instantly ordered some of the best champagne and telephoned Hitler in the bunker: 'My Führer, I congratulate you! Roosevelt is dead. It is written in the stars that the second half of April will be the turning-point for us. This is Friday, April the 13th. It is the turning-point!' Hitler's reply, reported an onlooker, although no one other than Goebbels heard it, put the latter into a state of ecstasy. The two men exulted in the President's death, seeing in it a historical parallel with the death of Czarina Elizabeth in 1762 which had saved Frederick the Great. Their triumphant mood was not to last long.

Two days later, on 15 April, Hitler issued his last two directives. One dealt with command arrangements made necessary by the cutting of communications, for as the Red Army drew nearer, so Berlin became increasingly isolated.

In an area where the Führer was not present, a commander-in-chief appointed by him would take charge of military operations and command all forces on all fronts. If Hitler were cut off in the south, Dönitz would command in the north; if Hitler were in the north, Kesselring would take charge in the south. But still 'the unified control of operations by myself personally, as hitherto, will not be altered,' and 'the activity of the Commander-in-Chief of a separated area will be initiated only on special orders from me.' Even when in reality he had no control over operations, Hitler clung to the illusion of supreme command. The second directive was a defiant exhortation to his soldiers on the Eastern Front, referring to the latest Red Army attack, and to the Russian intention to reduce Germany to ruins. The Führer reminded his soldiers of the fate which threatened the German people: 'While the old men will be murdered, the women and girls will be reduced to barrack-room whores. The remainder will be marched off to Siberia.' But, he said, this enemy thrust had been foreseen, a strong front was being built, massive artillery fire would greet the Russians, new German infantry units had been formed. 'If every soldier on the Eastern front does his duty in the days and weeks which lie ahead, the last assault of Asia will crumple, just as the invasion by our enemies in the West will fail, in spite of everything . . . At this moment, when Fate has removed from the earth the greatest war criminal of all time [Roosevelt], the turning-point of this war will be decided.'

Although Hitler had now completely lost control of everything that was happening outside his immediate entourage (which included Eva Braun, who had joined him in the bunker, determined to stay until the end), although he had become *ein Feldherr ohne Truppen*, a war lord without the means of waging war, he still concerned himself with the disposition of imaginary forces, with the manipulation of great armies which no longer existed. Furthermore, although he had also toyed with the idea of leaving Berlin on 20 April, his fifty-sixth birthday, at the military conference that day, convened after his birthday celebrations, he delayed any decision to go to the south, and instead next day directed one last battle. By 21 April Zhukov had reached Berlin's eastern suburbs, while his fellow marshal, Koniev, was nearing Dresden; on that day, too, General Eisenhower, choosing a natural junction as a place for his armies to link up with Soviet forces and so avoid accidental clashes with them, gave orders for his leading formations to halt on the general line of the Elbe and Mulde. Yet Hitler was making, or thought he was making, his last stand in Berlin, and giving precise tactical instructions to General Karl Koller, a Luftwaffe officer and Göring's Chief of Staff, who had stayed behind with Hitler in the bunker when Göring had left the day before. In spite of the hopelessness of further resistance, Koller was not the man to stand up to Hitler. Few were. Elderly, scrupulous and a fusspot, much given to hand-wringing and soul-searching, he would endure the Führer's raving, his screamed insults and threats – 'the entire Luftwaffe staff should be hanged!' – with a tremble, but without a protest.

Hitler's orders on this occasion, indeed as on most occasions since his assumption of the Supreme Army Command, were couched in the greatest detail. These troops here would be withdrawn from the north of the city to counter-attack the Russians in the southern suburbs; those Luftwaffe ground units there would take part; every tank that could be mustered, every aircraft the Luftwaffe could put into the skies, every man of every battalion – everything and everybody would make an all-out, final, desperate attempt to throw back the enemy. An SS general, Obergruppenführer Felix Steiner, would command the attack. Hitler's orders were accompanied by his customary threats. Commanding officers who did not drive their attacks home would find their lives forfeit; Koller's own head would guarantee his vigilance, and ensure that the uttermost efforts were made.

It was all in vain. Hitler had long since, in the phrase used by Marmont about Napoleon, been making pictures, had long been living in a military world created by his own imagination, his own refusal to acknowledge unpalatable fact. Willpower had achieved much in the past. It could do nothing now. Battalions which did not exist could not influence a crisis which did. The attack never came off at all, never even got under way, while withdrawal of units from the north merely allowed the Russians to surge through that part of the front and occupy the centre of Berlin with their armoured forces. If it were possible for the military position to worsen, it was just such cold comfort that Hitler was obliged to stomach. He did not do so lightly. When, at the military conference next day, he discovered the true state of affairs, he completely lost control of himself. It seemed as if his nerve, which he had kept for so long in the face of so many reverses, had at last gone. A final shrieking, shouting match was duly played out before the long-suffering generals and staff. Three hours of denunciation followed. He had been deserted; the army had failed him; all was treason, lies, deceit, cowardly incompetence; it was the end; his great mission and the Third Reich itself had failed; nothing was left but for him to stay in Berlin and die.

If the conference rendered his staff bewildered, exhausted, distraught, the effect on Hitler himself was very different. Decision calmed him. He seemed able now serenely to face the future, albeit a limited future. Yet at the very moment of resigning himself to failure and death, he took the unwarranted and unforgivable step of resigning too from that great position which he had so long coveted, and so long enjoyed – command of the army. He would not delegate. He gave no instructions to his principal military assistants, Keitel and Jodl. When these two generals protested that after leading and directing for so long, he could not suddenly expect his staff to lead and direct themselves, he replied that he had no orders to give. He simply abdicated all responsibility. From the former position of directing the entire war machine, personally, continuously and arbitrarily, he swung fully about and would have nothing more to do with it. When Keitel and Jodl offered to withdraw troops from the west and divert them eastwards to save Berlin from the Russians, he pushed their suggestion aside. Nor would he have anything to do with the forces still intact in the south of the country. He had decided on *Götterdämmerung*.

It was here that Hitler failed as a military commander in a way that he had never failed before. In abrogating responsibility, he betrayed his command. He had talked enough of a soldier's duty, and of himself discharging his own duty merely as the first soldier of the Reich. Now, the first soldier, the Supreme Commander, C-in-C of the German Army, *der Oberste Feldherr, der Führer*, abandoned leadership and duty alike. Even the pliant Keitel and Jodl could not understand it. They left the bunker on that same day, 22 April, Keitel to join General Wenck, Jodl to Krampnitz on the western outskirts of Berlin. Next day Albert Speer paid his last visit to Hitler, and (as Trevor-Roper has so vividly described in an account of Hitler's last days which has never been equalled) found the Führer 'in a state of unnatural calm'. It was a most pronounced contrast to his explosive and violent outburst of the previous day. Speer believed that Hitler, having at last abandoned the illusion he had so long nursed about the possibility of winning the war, and having almost reconciled himself to defeat and failure, was able to look 'upon the world with more dispassionate, philosophical eyes, awaiting death as a release from a hard life full of difficulties'. This too, Trevor-Roper explains, makes comprehensible Hitler's apparent indifference to Speer's confessed disobedience to his master's own orders about the destruction of Germany's resources. Speer stayed in the bunker until the following morning, while Berlin suffered another Allied bombing raid. Hitler discussed with him his intention to stay in the bunker and shoot himself there, rather than risk capture by fighting alongside his troops defending Berlin. He told Speer also that he had made arrangements for his body to be burned, so that it could not be used by the enemy for propaganda purposes (Speer, unlike others who had urged the Führer to escape, approved of Hitler's decision to meet his death in Berlin). The Armaments Minister had a further conversation with the Führer about the telegram which Göring had despatched from Obersalzburg offering to take over the leadership. Hitler denounced it as 'A crass ultimatum. Nothing is spared me. No allegiances are kept, no honour lived up to, no betrayals that I have not experienced – and now this above all else. Nothing remains. Every wrong has already been done me.' There was, however, one wrong still to come. Before detailing what it was, it should be said that the malevolent Bormann, who was closer to the Führer's ear than anyone, turned Göring's move to his own advantage, and made sure, with Hitler's approval, that the threatening answer sent to Göring resulted in the Reich Marshal's resignation from all his posts.

Early on the morning of 24 April, Speer quitted the bunker. Here, before we leave him, it is worth recalling the verdict of 'Guilty' that Trevor-Roper recorded against him (long before Gitta Sereny wrote about Speer's 'battle with truth'): 'In a political sense, Speer is the real criminal of Nazi Germany; for he, more than any other, represented that fatal philosophy which has made havoc of Germany and nearly shipwrecked the world. For ten years he sat at the very centre of political power; his keen intelligence diagnosed the nature and observed the mutations of Nazi government and policy; he saw and despised the personalities around him; he heard their outrageous orders and understood their fantastic ambitions; but he did nothing.' It is apposite, too, to recall the same historian's memorable picture of Hitler's last days as a military commander;

Hitler had long been accustomed, from underground bunkers, to direct the operations of non-existent armies, to dictate their strategy and tactics, dispose their forces, calculate their gains, and then to denounce the treachery of their generals when the actual results failed to correspond with his private conclusions. So in these days he would expound the tactics whereby Wenck would relieve the city. Pacing up and down in the Bunker . . . he would wave a road-map, fast decomposing with the sweat of his hands, and explain to any casual visitor the complicated military operations whereby they would all be saved. Sometimes he would shout orders, as if himself directing the defences; sometimes he would spread the map on his table, and stooping over it, with trembling hands he would arrange and rearrange a set of buttons, as consolatory symbols of relieving armies.

But the truth was that Wenck's army, and Heinrici's, and Busse's – all those referred to in Hitler's agitated signal to Keitel, quoted at the head of this chapter – were phantoms. Yet such was the almost incomprehensible magic of the man that he could still imbue others with hope in the military situation, hope which he himself had thrown away. That he was still at this late stage able to exercise so persistent a fascination over his subordinates is dramatically illustrated by the result of Field Marshal Ritter Robert von Greim's visit to the bunker on April 27, the day before Hitler's almost hysterical appeal to Keitel. The end was but three days away, but somehow or other the customary spell was cast. There was no need for despair, Greim told the incredulous General Koller on the telephone. Victory was inevitable. 'Everything will be well. The presence of the Führer and his confidence have completely inspired me.'

Less inspiring, certainly for the Führer himself, was the news brought to him on the evening of 28 April that Himmler, who was hundreds of miles away on the Baltic coast – *Treuer Heinrich* – had conferred with Count Folke Bernadotte of Sweden in order to negotiate peace. This, the Führer raged, was the last great wrong done to him! He took what revenge he could. Himmler's SS liaison officer, General Hermann Fegelein, in spite of being the husband of Eva Braun's sister, was shot. Then, on 29 April, the day before his own death, Hitler married Eva Braun, dictated his will and political testament, and held his last military conference. After disclaiming responsibility for making war in 1939, Hitler's testament declares that the war 'will one day go down in history as the most glorious and heroic manifestation of a people's will to live,' and states that 'I cannot forsake the city which is the capital of this state'. He would stay in Berlin and choose death voluntarily. He could not resist heaping blame on the army. As Trevor-Roper commented, as a soldier in the Great War, Hitler had been able to hold politicians responsible for treachery. Now in his own war, he was as a politician able to attribute failure to the soldiers, and to blame 'all for betraying him'. Göring and Himmler were expelled from the Party for their treachery, and Dönitz was appointed Hitler's successor as Reich President and Supreme Commander of the Armed Forces. Having made other appointments for Germany's future government – Goebbels to be Reich Chancellor; Bormann Party Chancellor; the Austrian Nazi leader, Seyss-Inquart, Foreign Minister; Saur, Speer's deputy, to become Armaments Minister; Field Marshal Schörner to be Army C-in-C (all these appointments were no more than illusions, except perhaps that of Dönitz, who did in the end negotiate the final surrender terms) – Hitler not only gave orders that these men should continue the Nazi regime, but 'above all else, uphold the racial laws in all their severity, and mercilessly resist the universal poisoner of all nations, international Jewry'. Even with the hands of the clock almost at midnight, he could not hold back from one more attack on the Jews. Hitler's personal will explained his marriage to Eva Braun, her choice of sharing his fate, disposed of his possessions to the Party or state, and left his collection of paintings to a picture gallery to be established at Linz. Bormann was to execute the will, which ended with the wish that the bodies of the Führer and his wife should be burnt 'in the place where I have performed the greater part of my daily work during the course of my twelve years' service to my people'.

At ten o'clock on the evening of 29 April the Supreme Commander of the Wehrmacht held his final military conference. He had been holding such conferences, day in, day out, for years, and if there is but one among many military lessons which may be drawn from that prolonged series of meetings at which a war lord listened to situation reports and gave his orders as a result of, or despite, them, it is that in a war from which so much human error had been eliminated by technological advances alone, human error was nonetheless still the principal factor in determining the outcome. At this conference General Weidling, the Commandant of Berlin, described the ever-deteriorating situation and gave it as his opinion that the Russians would reach the Chancellery three days from that time at the latest. The defending troops should therefore seek to break out at once. In accordance with the pattern that had gone before Hitler pronounced against this course of action, and there the matter rested. One other participant of the conference was Colonel Nicolaus von Below, Hitler's Luftwaffe Adjutant, and to this long-standing member of his entourage the Führer entrusted a postscript to his testament. It was, as Trevor-Roper recorded, Hitler's valediction to the Wehrmacht, and once more does its Supreme Commander little credit:

> The people and the Armed Forces have given their all in this long and hard struggle. The sacrifice has been enormous. But my trust has been misused by many people. Disloyalty and betrayal have undermined resistance throughout the war. It was therefore not granted to me to lead the people to victory. The Army General Staff cannot be compared with the General Staff of the First World War. Its achievements were far behind those of the fighting front.

There was now but one thing for Hitler to do, for the Russians were, after all, only a few streets away. On the morning of 30 April, he had received the customary military reports from the Chancellery Commandant, Brigadier Mohnke, and appeared indifferent to the fact that Russian forces were more or less all round the Chancellery area, and some in Vossstrasse very close to the building itself. After quietly eating lunch at about two o'clock in the company of his secretaries, while Eva ate hers in her own room, Hitler and his wife came out of his suite, shook hands with the assembled company, including Bormann and Goebbels, Generals Wilhelm Burgdorf and Hans Krebs, his SS Adjutant, Colonel Guensche; his servant, Heinz Linge, and the secretaries, and then returned to their suite of rooms. Shortly afterwards there came a single shot. Those entering the rooms saw Hitler, who had shot himself through the mouth, lying on a blood-stained sofa. Beside him was Eva, dead from having swallowed poison. The grisly business of burning the bodies, as Hitler had ordered, then got under way. The word had already gone round the bunker: 'Der Chef ist tot.' Having killed untold millions of human beings, Adolf Hitler had killed one more. The last enemy was conquered. Treason had done his worst: nor steel, nor poison, malice domestic, foreign levy, nothing, could touch him further.

Churchill heard of Hitler's death on the evening of 1 May while dining with

Beaverbrook and others. Colville brought the news that Hamburg radio had announced Hitler's death, 'fighting with his last breath against Bolshevism,' and the Prime Minister was inclined to give that piece of propaganda the benefit of the doubt. It was characteristic of Churchill to comment that he thought Hitler 'was perfectly right to die like that'; what more proper death for a military leader in defeat, he must have reflected, than to die fighting? It took the more realistic Beaverbrook to observe that obviously Hitler had not died in this way.

Since, two days before Hitler's death, Mussolini, in company with his mistress, Clara Petacci, had been captured by Italian partisans and shot, Churchill was able to signal to his wife, who was still in Russia, that 'both our great enemies are dead,' while adding that several crises were 'coming to a head'. During the second half of April, when it was clear to Churchill that British and American troops would *not* make their way to Berlin, whereas the Russians would, he was especially anxious that Montgomery's armies should as quickly as possible push on to the Baltic port of Lübeck and so prevent the Red Army, already at Stettin, from occupying Denmark. He was therefore delighted to hear on 3 May that British troops had occupied Lübeck; indeed, it was a good day all round, for not only had Rangoon been taken, but United States forces had reached both Bavaria and Innsbruck. What is more, Montgomery had signalled to say that Admiral Dönitz, Hitler's nominated successor, had sent his representatives to Lüneburg Heath, where Montgomery's headquarters were, to negotiate terms for surrender. Churchill's grinned comment to Colville at the end of so momentous a day was that it was nice to be winning. He had, of course, already congratulated Alexander on his great Italian victory, and, having urged Truman to agree that this victory must be followed up by an advance to Trieste and Venezia Giulia, was gratified by the American President's reply to the effect that Alexander's establishment of control over Trieste and Pola, together with the securing of lines of communication to Austria, would not need Russian agreement beforehand. But while these matters were proceeding satisfactorily, Churchill was not able to influence Stalin with regard to Poland, nor did he succeed in persuading Eisenhower to advance to occupy Prague.

He had, however, established a good working relationship with President Truman, both by telegram exchanges and by telephone. Only a week after Roosevelt's death, Churchill had given his opinion to Eden that the new President was not going to be bullied by Russia, and that it was important that Anglo-American strength should be recognized by the Soviets if 'a lasting friendship with the Russian people' were to be made. During his exchanges with Stalin at the time of Himmler's peace offer, although Churchill was at pains to reassure the Soviet leader that there could be no question of German surrender other than to the three major Powers simultaneously, yet he found himself completely in accord with Truman's views, and his amicable discussions with the US President had ended with eager anticipation of their forthcoming meeting. It was a different matter when it came to Churchill's dealings with Stalin, however, and his signal to the latter of 29 April deprecated the growing misunderstanding between them:

> There is not much comfort in looking into a future where you and the countries you dominate, plus the Communist Parties in many other States, are all drawn up on one side, and those who rally to the English-speaking nations and their associates or Dominions are on the other. It is quite obvious that their quarrel would tear the world to pieces and that all of us leading men on either side who had anything to do with that would be shamed before history. Even embarking on a long period of suspicions, of abuse and counter-abuse and of opposing policies would be a disaster hampering the great developments of world prosperity for the masses which are attainable only by our trinity.

In spite of this appeal, the disputes with Stalin continued, as Churchill became increasingly worried by the dangers of Soviet influence and control in Austria, Yugoslavia, Poland and Czechoslovakia. Although he had signalled to Truman urging him to influence Eisenhower to seize any opportunity to advance into western Czechoslovakia and occupy Prague – a move which could greatly affect the post-war situation there and in nearby countries, for 'if the Western Allies play no significant part in Czechoslovakia's liberation, that country will go the same way as Yugoslavia' – Eisenhower had already decided not to go beyond the area of Linz in Austria, and there would be no American advance to Prague. Churchill's further concerns about Europe's future were aggravated by the

> proposed withdrawal of the United States Army to the occupational lines which were arranged with the Russians and Americans in Quebec . . . [which] would mean the tide of Russian domination sweeping forward 120 miles on a front of 300 or 400 miles. This would be an event which, it if occurred, would be one of the most melancholy in history . . . Thus the territories under Russian control would include the Baltic Provinces, all of Germany to the occupational line, all Czechoslovakia, a large part of Austria, the whole of Yugoslavia, Hungary, Roumania, Bulgaria, until Greece in her present tottering condition is reached. It would include all the great capitals of middle Europe including Berlin, Vienna, Budapest, Belgrade, Bucharest and Sofia . . . This constitutes an event in the history of Europe to which there has been no parallel . . .

Yet, Churchill told Eden on 4 May, provided the Allies made proper use of what 'bargaining counters' they had *before* there was any question of weakening the US armies in Europe, there were still hopes of a satisfactory solution.

It was also on 4 May that Montgomery telephoned Churchill in Downing Street to tell him that the German delegation at his headquarters had signed 'an instrument of surrender by which all German forces, naval, army and air in Denmark, Holland, Schleswig Holstein, the Frisian Islands and Heligoland would lay down their arms at 8am double British summer time, on the 5th May'. Churchill thereupon telephoned Eisenhower, who explained that German representatives were coming to his headquarters, and that he proposed to tell them that 'the German Armies opposite the Anglo-American Armies should surrender to them, and the German Armies opposite the Russian Armies should surrender to the Soviet'. It was then that Churchill received a note from General Ismay congratulating him as a man 'whose superb leadership has today been crowned with a triumph which only History will be able to measure'. He asked the Chiefs of Staff to come to the Cabinet Room, where he thanked them for all they had done – but he insisted, too, that where British and American troops had occupied parts of Germany in the allotted Russian zone, they should not move out and so give up a 'valuable bargaining counter' until the three heads of state had met. He was also able to signal the good news to his wife, who was still in Moscow, while sounding a note of warning as to the international political dangers underlying these triumphs. The actual instrument of unconditional surrender on all fronts was signed at Eisenhower's headquarters at 2.41am on 7 May, Jodl signing for Germany, Bedell Smith, Eisenhower's Chief of Staff, for the Allied Supreme Command, General François Sevez for France, and General Ivan Suslaparov for the Soviet Union. There was some disagreement and confusion about the actual announcement of victory, as Stalin wished it to be delayed until the morning of 9 May, whereas, in view of the public awareness in Britain that the war was over, Churchill insisted that Victory in Europe Day should be the 8th.

On the morning of 8 May 1945, Winston Churchill prepared his broadcast to the nation, which he gave from Downing Street that afternoon, after having had lunch with King George VI at Buckingham Palace. In his message to the people, Churchill told them of Jodl's signing of the instrument of surrender, an agreement which would be ratified in Berlin at Marshal Zhukov's headquarters that same day. 'The German war,' he declared, 'is therefore at an end':

After years of intense preparation, Germany hurled herself on Poland at the beginning of September, 1939; and, in pursuance of our guarantee to Poland and in agreement with the French Republic, Great Britain, the British

Empire and Commonwealth of Nations, declared war upon this foul aggressor. After gallant France had been struck down, we, from this Island and from our united Empire, maintained the struggle single-handed for a whole year until we were joined by the military might of Soviet Russia, and later by the overwhelming power and resources of the United States of America.

Having announced that the 'evil-doers' were 'now prostrate before us', the Prime Minister said that after 'a brief period of rejoicing' it would be necessary to turn their attention to Japan. 'We must now devote all our strength and resources to the completion of our task, both at home and abroad. Advance, Britannia! Long live the cause of freedom! God save the King.' His wife and son both sent their greetings on hearing his speech, which, after driving to the House of Commons through crowds of cheering people, he repeated in the Chamber, adding his profound gratitude to the House for its 'noble support'. Then, recalling that at the end of the Great War, rather than indulge in debate, the House had 'desired to offer thanks to Almighty God,' he moved 'That this House do now attend at the Church of St Margaret, Westminster, to give humble and reverent thanks to Almighty God for our deliverance from the threat of German domination.'

His day was still not over. After having driven back to Buckingham Palace, where the King received the War Cabinet and Chiefs of Staff, he went to Whitehall and spoke to the crowds massing there from the balcony of the Ministry of Health; his audience, on hearing Churchill say 'This is your victory,' roared back 'No – it is yours.' Having dined at Downing Street – his daughters, Diana and Sarah, with him – he returned to address the crowds in Whitehall again. Greeted by tumultuous cheering, he told the people:

My dear friends, this is your hour. This is not victory of a party or of any class. It's a victory of the great British nation as a whole. We were the first, in this ancient island, to draw the sword against tyranny. After a while we were left all alone against the most tremendous military power that has been seen. We were all alone for a whole year . . . So we came back after long months from the jaws of death, out of the mouth of hell, while all the world wondered . . .[1] We have emerged from one deadly struggle – a terrible foe has been cast on the ground and awaits our judgment and our mercy . . .

He then reminded the people that there was another foe to be dealt with, 'and we must turn ourselves to fulfil our duty to our own countrymen, and to our

---

[1] Here he was quoting, with great freedom, from Tennyson's 'The Charge of the Light Brigade'.

gallant allies of the United States who were so foully and treacherously attacked by Japan. We will go hand in hand with them. Even if it is a hard struggle we will not be the ones who will fail.' But first, he said, there would be a holiday to celebrate Victory in Europe.

It was almost exactly five years since Churchill had offered his people blood, toil, tears and sweat, and he had made good his offer, for there had been plenty of all four. On 13 May 1940 he had said that his government's policy was to wage war, and he had waged it. He had also said that their aim was victory, 'victory at all costs, victory in spite of all terror, victory, however long and hard the road may be'. The road had been long and hard for the British people; they had endured much terror; the cost to them had been incalculable. But he had given them victory. No one in Britain had equalled him in courage, example, effort, inspiration, confidence or perseverance. By these, Churchill had kept Britain's honour bright.

CHAPTER 11

Verdict

─────────

'But what will history say?'
'History, Sir, will lie.'
GEORGE BERNARD SHAW, *The Devil's Disciple*

We do not need to lie, however. And when it comes to judging the voice of history – of historians and biographers – when it speaks of the doings and sayings of great men, we must pay attention to the work of both those who knew the great men and those who did not. Thus while what Speer, Goebbels or Guderian have to say about what Hitler was really like is essential to our understanding of the man, so too are the writings of Joachim Fest, Hugh Trevor-Roper and David Irving, who did not. The difference, however, is that between the report of a man who took part in the making of history, and of one who read about it, sometimes years later. Equally, while we pay great heed to the recollections of Churchill's political colleagues like Lloyd George or Eden, his military men such as Brooke and Ismay, his own family, and close friends like Violet Bonham Carter, his private secretaries, Marsh, Colville or Montague Browne, at the same time no student of his life and achievements could be without Martin Gilbert's majestic biography or Robert Blake's collection of essays, nor should the revisionist comments of John Charmley or Alan Clark be ignored. However, the contrast between points of view held by men of action on the one hand, and academics on the other, may be illustrated by the celebrated answer given nearly a hundred years ago by Lord Macdonnell to Lord Morley during a debate in the House of Lords on reform of the administration of India: 'I have played,' he said, 'upon that stormy harp whose strings are the hearts of men; the noble lord opposite has spent his life writing books about books.'

Nelson always maintained that second to doing great deeds came writing about them. Churchill did both. Having made a great deal of history between 1940 and 1945, he made less afterwards, despite some speeches which were to have a powerful and lasting influence, yet he wrote a great deal, both about events and about himself. It might, in fact, be questioned whether Churchill really *needed* a biographer at all, for his astonishing range of autobiographical works covers almost every phase and aspect of his long life. There is no merit in questioning the *need*, however, for as Sir Isaiah Berlin wrote of Churchill's 'account of his stewardship' in the Second World War – an account in which 'he speaks his memorable lines with a large, unhurried and stately utterance in a blaze of light' – Churchill lived his life knowing 'that his work and his person will remain the object of scrutiny and judgement to many generations'. Thus no matter how warmly one might endorse Berlin's opinion that Churchill's own narrative 'is a great public performance and has the attribute of formal magnificence', and no matter how much one relishes Churchill's 'words, the splendid phrases, the sustained quality of feeling . . . which convey his vision of himself and of his world', yet still one eagerly devours the recollections of those who, by virtue of being at the centre of things, were influenced by and subject to his deliberations, decisions and actions. And one welcomes, too, the pronouncements of other writers who, while they were not there, still offer much in their assessments of the character and activities of the man who was called by his successor as Prime Minister in 1945, Clement Attlee, the 'greatest Englishman of our time'.

It could be said, perhaps, that just as Cathy tells Nelly in *Wuthering Heights*: 'I am Heathcliff', just as Louis XIV claimed: 'L'état, c'est moi!' just as de Gaulle was France's spirit, so in 1940 and the years following, Churchill was England. It is not by any means the first time this view has been stated. We have only to refer to Martin Gilbert's great biographical work to note that 'a cartoon in *Punch* on 21 May 1913 showed Churchill [then First Lord of the Admiralty] in a deckchair on the *Enchantress*, lying back smoking a cigar, asking Asquith, who was reading a newspaper: "Any home news?", to which Asquith replies: "How can there be with you here?"'

Of all the portraits of Churchill put together by those in the second category above – those, that is, who did not know him, but whose work and lives have been spent studying and writing about him – Martin Gilbert's undoubtedly comes first. While this book does not trace Churchill's life after 1945 – since his duel with Hitler ended then – Gilbert's last volume, *Never Despair*, does relate the story of his last twenty years. Gilbert reminds us that at a meeting of the Other Club, some three and a half weeks after Churchill's death, Lord Chandos (as Oliver Lyttelton had become) spoke of Churchill's powers as 'those of imagination, experience and magnanimity . . . he saw man as a noble and not as a mean creature.' That he himself was noble, supremely so, few have ever doubted.

Churchill was indeed a noble spirit, sustained in his long life by a faith in the capacity of man to live in peace, to seek prosperity, and to ward off threats and dangers by his own exertions. His love of country, his sense of fair play, his hopes for the human race, were matched by formidable powers of work and thought, vision and foresight. His path had often been dogged by controversy, disappointment and abuse, but these had never deflected him from his sense of duty and his faith in the British people.

Gilbert also reminds us at the very end of his monument to Churchill's life of the tribute to him paid by his son, Randolph, in a letter written soon after his father had given up his second premiership in 1955: 'Glory, which is achieved through a just exercise of power – which itself is accumulated by genius, toil, courage and self-sacrifice – alone remains. Your glory is enshrined for ever on the unperishable plinth of your achievements; and can never be destroyed or tarnished. It will flow with the centuries.'

So completely will most people agree with these sentiments that it must appear to be something of a puzzle that Dr Charmley should have subtitled his own biography of Churchill *The End of Glory*. Indeed, in the closing pages of his book, Charmley seems to be guilty of ambivalence. Having first stated that 'nothing could dim Churchill's glory', he goes on to say that since the three things Churchill stood for (according to Charmley, that is) – the British Empire, Britain's independence and an 'anti-Socialist' vision of the nation – were by July 1945, when Churchill relinquished the premiership, all in jeopardy, this signalled 'the end of glory'. It is not only the premise itself that may be challenged, for although the Empire diminished after 1945, as was inevitable on India's independence two years later, it lingered on for a good many years and the Commonwealth survives still; British independence – in the sense of the country earning most of its living, indulging in military action in the interests of moderation and justice, taking its own line in European matters – is still discernible; and who is to say today that Britain is socialist? – not even the Labour Party leadership, it seems. But leaving these points aside, Churchill's vision and ideals were far broader than Dr Charmley's concept of them. Sir Isaiah Berlin is the man to put him right on this score, when he writes that 'Mr Churchill . . . knows with unshakeable certainty what he considers to be big, handsome, noble, and worthy of pursuit by someone in high station, and what, on the contrary, he abhors as being dim, grey, thin, likely to lower or destroy the play of colour and movement in the universe.' Timidity, compromise, pessimism – anything which would 'diminish the forces of life' or lower the 'vital and vibrant energy' which he admired in others, and possessed so outstandingly himself – he rejected absolutely. This brings to mind one other thing that Lord Chandos said at the Other Club dinner just referred to: 'the only people he [Churchill] never forgave were those, who, in the words he so often used, "fell beneath the level of events".' Churchill himself always rose to and above the level of events. Berlin goes on to emphasize Churchill's belief in world order, in great states and civilization, in American democracy, in France and Anglo-French accord, even in Germany 'as a great, historically hallowed state'. And when it comes to Churchill's sense of and dependence on history itself, Berlin tells us: 'The clear, brightly coloured vision of history, in terms of which he conceives both the present and the future, is the inexhaustible source from which he draws the primary stuff out of which his universe is so solidly built, so richly and elaborately ornamented.'

It has to be allowed, however, that John Charmley's writings about Churchill created quite a stir. While no one would question his industry or his scholarship, when he suggested that Churchill should have negotiated some kind of peace terms with Hitler in 1941, he at once forfeited any reputation he might have had for military or political judgement. In supporting him, Alan Clark, who is after all a responsible historian (if a readably irresponsible diarist), should have known better, but he was presumably simply indulging his bent for being mischievously disputatious. The trouble with such suggestions, however, is that those making them seem to be unable or unwilling to follow them through to a credible conclusion. So that if we leave aside the sheeer impossibility of Churchill's abandoning his oft-repeated vow to overthrow the evil of Nazism and to fight on to the end for Europe's liberation from it, and if we ignore Hitler's cynical declaration that he was willing to sign any agreement one day and unhesitatingly break it the next – 'It would be sheer stupidity to refuse to make use of such measures merely because one might possibly be driven into a position where a solemn promise would have to be broken' – even if we push these points to one side, we are still faced with the small matter, not revealed by Dr Charmley or Mr Clark, of what the actual terms of such a peace agreement in 1941 would have been. A few questions illustrate how unrealistic are their suggestions.

Would Great Britain have been left in possession of both her Royal Naval and merchant fleets, with absolute freedom of the seas for trading and other purposes? Would Italy have abandoned her African colonies? Would Greece and Albania have been free? Would Rommel and the Afrika Korps have quit Libya? Would Britain have been at liberty to maintain her armed forces at their – by 1941 – not contemptible level, and to deploy them where she wanted other than in Hitler's domains? What would Britain have said to France, the Low Countries, Denmark, Norway, and to Poland? Would Hitler have agreed – the agreement to have been subject to rigid verification measures – to cease research into and development of V weapons, jet aircraft, new submarines – and nuclear weapons? Would he, after the subjection of all Eastern Europe including Russia, once more have declared that he had no further territorial claims? Would he have guaranteed the integrity of the British Empire? Or would the whole negotiated peace – on the bizarre assumption that it could ever have come off at all – simply have proved to be another Peace of Amiens, the truce between Great Britain and France of 1802–1803, during which Napoleon feverishly prepared for a resumption of hostilities? Certainly the prospect of a triumphant Führer, an enslaved Russia, a pliant Western Europe, an all-powerful Wehrmacht fully equipped with Hitler's so-called secret weapons, and a quiescent Britain, unsupported by the infinite resources of the United States, is not one calculated to inspire much confidence. It is more a recipe for Germany's realization of what Hitler had always spoken of as the alternative to the *Niedergang*, ruin, he finally accomplished – that is to say, *Weltmacht*, world power. But, as is clear from all that we have observed of Churchill's character and purpose, it was unthinkable that he would ever betray his country, his people or himself by contemplating such a peace. And just as the Charmley/Clark theory of peace between Britain and Germany in 1941 can be dismissed, in Michael Harrington's words, as a 'silly and distasteful war game', so too can be rejected their contention that Churchill's policy of alliance with America led to a more rapid end of empire and decline of Britain's ordered society – on the sole ground that given the actual conditions of December 1941, as well as of the months and years that followed, there was no alternative to such an alliance if Britain's national interests and the world's future order were to be safeguarded. Perhaps the most extraordinary of Charmley's assertions is that America entered the European war, not because of Churchill's persuasiveness, but to protect her own interests! He seems to have overlooked the point that it was Hitler who declared war on the United States.

It is time to turn from the guru historians who did not know Churchill to some of the public servants who did. Churchill's youngest daughter, Mary (Lady Soames), has expressed her displeasure caused by 'all the things that are written about my father by people who never knew him at all'. At the same time, however, she has acknowledged her gratification at some of the things written about her father by people who did know him well. One of the last to do so was Anthony Montague Browne, whose attractive account of his years as Churchill's Private Secretary shows how lovable the man was. His book, *Long Sunset*, is so full of gems that it is hard – short of very lengthy quotation – to do justice to them. Lady Soames herself pays tribute to Montague Browne's devoted service, both in the Foreword to his book – 'he guarded Winston's interests with a vigilant eye. And as a companion he was perfect: patient, seeking to stimulate or divert, or playing cards for long hours . . . [he] has faithfully recorded the shafts of late sunshine which quite often illuminated the fading landscape' – and in a letter she wrote to him on the evening of Churchill's funeral, 30 January 1965, in which she thanks him for, among many other things, his 'vigilance and determination in guarding my Father's fame and honour, when he could no longer fight his own battles'. Montague Browne's own recollections are crammed with the most entertaining anecdotes (indeed, he admits that he nearly called his book *Anecdotage*). A particularly endearing story concerns Churchill's dislike of being interrupted when working on one of his speeches. On one such occasion during his second premiership (1951–5), while he was still in bed at No 10 doing just such work, Montague Browne, on his way upstairs to see the great man, is ambushed by Eden and 'Rab' Butler who urgently wish to see the Prime Minister, and who accompany his private secretary upstairs. When he informs Churchill that the Foreign Secretary and the Chancellor of the Exchequer, who are waiting outside the bedroom door, wish to see him, however, the retort, perfectly audible to all, is: 'Tell them to go and bugger themselves.' As Montague Browne makes his way out to give the visitors some suitably softened message, another shout follows him: 'There is no need for them to carry out that instruction literally.' On hearing anecdotes like this, it is impossible not to warm still further to the Prime Minister. So too at Chequers after a row with his wife, Clemmie, culminating in her sweeping out of the room saying quietly, 'Winston, I have been married to you for 45 years for better' – and then at full volume – '*and for worse!*', Churchill 'looked at me silently for a moment and then observed solemnly: "I am the most unhappy of men." This was so manifestly absurd that I could not help bursting into an unseemly peal of laughter, which WSC did not seem to mind.' Montague Browne notes, too, that Churchill said to him quite early on in his service at No 10: 'I blub an awful lot, you know. You'll have to get used to it.' He saw what his employer meant when the great man looked, for example, at a Roll of Honour at Boodle's bearing the names of former friends killed in war. Some of Montague Browne's asides simply confirm all over again what we already knew: 'WSC was undoubtedly endowed with fiercely proud courage;' 'Anyone who knew him soon realized that WSC was a truly humane man;' or again, 'WSC had an almost unqualified respect for military prowess.'

Another of Churchill's Private Secretaries, Sir John (Jock) Colville, whom we have frequently met in these pages already, has described in his delightful *Footprints in Time* what life at No 10 was like in wartime. His book, too, is full of endearing anecdotes about the Prime Minister. It was, he writes, 'the most exhilarating of all experiences to serve, at close quarters and in war, that wayward, romantic, expansive and explosive genius . . .' For Colville, writing of the few men he encountered who had true greatness, Churchill 'towers above the rest . . . because he had independence of spirit, the courage of a lion, faith in himself and his cause, the capacity and imagination to inspire, an unwavering belief in the triumph of good over evil, a tireless determination to achieve victory at whatever cost, balanced by chivalry to the foe; and in his soul, the poetry which turned what he was trying to do into romance.' Colville, like Montague Browne, writes of the Prime Minister's respect for military commanders, notably Alexander, Montgomery and Brooke. Churchill admired Alexander for his cool, calm conduct of withdrawals in the early part of the war, for his gallantry, chivalry, patience and tactful co-operation with allies, his artistic bent and his sure handling of Montgomery. Monty, too, was a favourite. He was confident, thorough, a great trainer, a battle winner, and was adept at supplying the Prime Minister with just the sort of dispatches from his head-quarters in the field to lend weight and drama to Churchill's declarations in the House of Commons. Moreover, he always ensured that when the Prime Minister visited him there was a proper supply of good champagne. But perhaps the most interesting and important relationship between Churchill and one of his military men was that with his CIGS from December 1941, onwards, Field Marshal Sir Alan Brooke.

The two men were to have some stormy exchanges, but Brooke himself was never in any doubt about the Prime Minister's greatness or indispensability. Thus this entry in his diary in 1941: 'It is surprising how he maintains a light-hearted exterior in spite of the vast burdens he is bearing. He is quite the most wonderful man I have ever met, and is a source of never-ending interest to me, studying and getting to realize that occasionally such human beings make their appearance on this earth. Human beings who stand out head and shoulders above all others.' The best book about Field Marshal Lord Alanbrooke (as he became) is that by David Fraser who, in discussing his subject's relationship with Churchill, writes:

Alanbrooke profoundly admired Churchill yet found his ideas often unre-alistic, his habits of mind irrational and infuriating, his method of work frus-trating and exhausting, and his temper sometimes vile . . . Yet he loved him. He loved his courage, his humour, his readiness to bear huge burdens for England . . . For his part Churchill probably found Alanbrooke a trying sub-ordinate. The latter's uncompromising negatives, his bleak resistance to cajolery, his practical approach, his reliance on facts alone were often tedious to Churchill. Yet Churchill loved Alanbrooke and to others often said so. He had implicit trust in him . . . To Churchill the war was a great drama, often terrible, generally exhilarating, tragic and triumphant by turns, but never dull. He lived it to the full. To Alanbrooke, the soldier, it was a grim and dis-tasteful business, a matter for exact calculations, hard logical thought, lonely constancy and iron will . . . All in all, Churchill and Alanbrooke formed a remarkable combination. To be chief adviser to a genius demands a certain genius of its own sort, and Alanbrooke possessed it.

This narrative has talked much of Churchill's strategy, which while he still had any choice in the matter was largely determined by his conviction that in the Mediterranean, and more particularly in Allied possession of the whole of North Africa, lay great opportunity. In making this strategic choice, it must be said that he was wholly vindicated by events. It was largely because of Churchill's vision and initiative that the great Anglo-American invasion of French North Africa took place, while his earlier insistence on reinforcing the Middle East at a time when grave dangers threatened the United Kingdom itself was, in the end, to bring the Axis in North Africa to defeat. In September 1940, only three months after the British Expeditionary Force had been obliged to quit France via Dunkirk, we find Churchill declaring that he wanted 'to wage war on a great scale in the Middle East', and in spite of the possibility of invasion and the bombing of British towns, factories and ports, 'we have steadfastly reinforced the Middle East . . . have sent over 30,000 men, nearly half our best tanks, many anti-aircraft guns needed to protect our vital aircraft factories, two of the finest units in the Fleet, the *Illustrious* and *Valiant*, and a considerable number of Hurricane fighters and Wellington bombers.' It was, of course, Churchill's passionate concern with assuming the offensive, together with the opportunity created by Italy's entry into the war, which determined this strategy, and in the end the whole idea of a Mediterranean strategy, which would prove to be a distraction for the Wehrmacht and an opportune theatre of exploitation for the Allies, began to unfold. That there were setbacks during the time – almost three years – that it took to win the battle for North Africa does not diminish either the boldness of Churchill's policy or the strategic advantages which were at length gained from it. David Fraser makes a telling point when he argues that 'at its best Churchill's grand strategic vision was superior to that of his professional advisers', and John Keegan – of all today's military historians the most *simpatico* – confirms this judgement when he writes that 'Churchill's fixed belief that the northern shore of the Mediterranean was a theatre which offered wide strategic advantage was to be proved correct.' In his fine essay on this subject (which is in Lord Blake's splendid collection), Keegan also reminds us of the admirable answer Churchill made to the Russian Ambassador, Maisky, when asked by him in July 1940 what was his general strategy: 'My general strategy at present is to last out the next three months.'

By returning briefly to those darker days, we may perhaps note three more tributes to Churchill's greatness, before turning once more to the qualities and achievements of his arch-enemy. Violet Bonham Carter – Churchill's friend for so long, whose book, *Winston Churchill as I Knew Him*, is such a delight, who described him as 'a glow worm', and who wrote that *he* needed no blood transfusion, unlike some of his colleagues – had this to say in a letter to the newly appointed Prime Minister in May 1940:

My wish is now realized. I can face all that is to come with faith and confidence.

I know, as you do, that the wind has been sown, and that, for a time at least, we must *all* reap the whirlwind. But you will ride it – instead of being driven before it.

Thank heaven that you are there, and at the helm of our destiny – and may the nation's spirit be kindled by your own.

That spirit was so kindled, as a very different observer, Professor R.V. Jones, the scientific intelligence expert, noted:

> 1940 was dominated by Churchill . . . Pre-eminent in courage . . . he under-stood the essence of supreme decisions . . . 1940 was a time which eloquence could not exaggerate, and which demanded a man of more than life size. Throughout his life he had had a sense of history and a feeling of destiny . . . In speech after speech he helped the people of Britain to see where they stood in history . . . Everyone knew, in that mysterious way that tells true from false, that here was a man who would stand to the last; and in this confidence they could stand with him.

Whereas Jones was in a position to observe Churchill at close hand in counsel, A.J.P. Taylor viewed him with the more detached eye of the historian, but a historian who knew human worth when he saw it: 'Churchill carried the war on his shoulders. These shoulders were broad. But the burden was excessive. Churchill provided political inspiration and leadership. He determined strategy and settled the disputed questions in home policy . . . he never drew breath. In this turmoil of activity he made some great mistakes and many small ones. The wonder is that he did not make more. No other man could have done what he did, and with a zest which rarely flagged.'

It was just as well that Hitler too made mistakes. Indeed, it was especially fortunate that just as Hitler advocated that if lies were to be told, they should be colossal lies, so when it came to making mistakes, the Führer made some blunders of such colossal magnitude that they can only be explained as being the results of the megalomania of a man who had come to believe in his own strategic genius and infallibility to the exclusion of all reason, fact, logic or shrewd weighing of the odds. We have seen how time after time his political *Fingerspitzengefühl*, instinct, timing and opportunism, backed by the *threat* of force, won him bloodless victory after victory; we have seen too how his initial *use* of force won him some astonishing military victories, while he still stuck to broad strategic directives with adequate military resources to carry them out, leaving the actual execution to professional commanders. It was when he took on the business of commanding the German Army in the field that the game began to go badly wrong. Indeed, by the end of 1941 the game was already lost – short of having at his disposal either an abundance of new weapons, or even of atomic ones – for by then Germany was at war with the British Empire, the Soviet Union and the United States. Given that there was no stopping Hitler going to war with Russia – an ingredient of his *Weltanschauung* long since declared and never relinquished – to have added the United States to his list of opponents was simply to conform to what Churchill had for so long been striving to bring about. Yet despite all these errors, it was as a great military commander, as a man of historical greatness, that Hitler saw himself. Not so his military subordinates, for once the Supreme Commander of the Wehrmacht was dead, he became the repository for all the strategic mistakes, all the tactical faults of the German Army. A comment made on Halder's *Hitler als Feldherr* (*Hitler as War Lord*) was that it gives the impression that if the Führer had not interfered, his generals would have won the war. What Halder does not tell us, however, is exactly what might have been meant by winning the war. As we have seen, it might have been possible to have put the Russians at a greater disadvantage by waging the Barbarossa campaign differently, but whether even the capture of Moscow would have caused Stalin to compromise and call a halt to operations may be doubted.

Halder's book is little more than one unmitigated condemnation of the Führer's military faculty. While he concedes that Hitler, by virtue of his overpowering will, dominated the political and military leadership of the war, was in fact 'the dynamo of the war effort', he maintains that failure to balance political aims against the limitations of what the Wehrmacht could do is enough in itself to dismiss any idea of Hitler being called a great military leader. It might be noted here that if all those acknowledged to be great commanders are to be condemned for allowing ambition to outrun resources – Alexander and Napoleon among them – then who shall escape calumny? But in Hitler's case there were special reasons for his overestimating his capabilities. His whole career had shown him that nearly all problems could be resolved by force; indeed, the threat of it alone was often enough. In 1936 a mere three battalions had cowed the Western Powers during the reoccupation of the Rhineland; thus, provided the use of force went hand in hand with sound political calculation, its effect could be quite out of proportion to its extent. Only when Hitler ceased to weigh those political considerations accurately – he confidently predicted, for example, that kicking in Russia's door would bring the whole rotten structure crashing down – did he begin to rely on willpower and force by themselves, even though they were palpably insufficient to subdue the force and will which were set in opposition.

Halder also maintains that Hitler was incapable of inspiring his executive commanders and staffs with confidence in his guidance. Here the former Chief of Army Staff is on less sure ground, for after the triumphs of 1940 – triumphs achieved in spite of General Staff advice – there were few waverers. Later, when Hitler began to demand impossible performances from inadequate resources, the wavering began. Yet the evidence of Rommel, Guderian, Manstein, Speer, to say nothing of Keitel, Jodl and many lesser figures, is emphatically unanimous that Hitler seemed able, by the power of his personality and the ascendancy which he had over them, to inspire confidence in those around him even when the situation seemed hopeless. The truth was that whereas, in the earlier years of the war, he conducted his military conferences with moderate restraint, seeking opinion, feeling his way, success bred both confidence in his own strategic genius and contempt for others – and, worst of all, contempt for fact. We have seen where Hitler's talents lay and where they did not. He could plan a campaign brilliantly and say how a small-scale action should be conducted, demonstrating a sure grasp of weapons and tactics. But when it came to handling army groups and their components in battle, he faltered. Military campaigns could be compared with political ones, for intuition played a major role; low-level tactics, too, could be mastered by an amateur; but tactics on the grand scale, with all the problems of movement, fire support, air co-operation, logistics and the interdependent operations of many formations, both enemy and friendly, requires years of training and practice, which Hitler necessarily lacked. What must surprise us, in view of his instant comprehension of the blitzkrieg potential of panzer and Stuka and his insistence on being supreme in the air, is that he refused to see that the Wehrmacht, no matter how determined its commanders, excellent its equipment, brilliant its tactics or devotedly brave its soldiers, could not prevail against Allied air supremacy which was both absolute and omnipresent.

Hitler's political acumen, nerves of steel, infinite reserves of resolution and unshakeable will need no iteration here; they have been in evidence throughout the telling of this story. So has been his imagination – in the sense of his gift for grasping how to exploit situations to his own advantage, whether by propaganda, political or military means, and how to put these means, all of which contained a core of violence, to extreme use. Extreme use meant war, and war meant reliance of a sort on the generals. The evidence of Hitler's generals is varied, and is perhaps most revealing not during the battles of conquest, when most of them were more or less convinced, but during the beginnings of defeat. Their views are coloured, too, by the positions from which they were formed, whether from Hitler's OKW, where the plans were made, or in the field, where they were carried out. Jodl told an audience of Gauleiters in November 1943, when it was clear to most generals prepared to face facts that the war was lost: 'I must testify that he [Hitler] is the soul not only of the political but also of the military conduct of the war, and that the force of his will-power and the creative riches of his thought animate and hold together the whole of the *Wehrmacht*.'

Commanders in the field saw things differently. When Rommel heard Hitler announce that if the German people were incapable of winning the war, they could rot, he commented: 'Sometimes you feel he's no longer quite normal.' Rommel had no illusions about Hitler's shortcomings as a strategist. Although dazzled by the successes of Poland and France, and fortunate enough not to have commanded on the Eastern Front, he had been overruled too often in Africa and Normandy, had seen too many opportunities missed, too many mistakes made, to be in doubt. Yet until he became convinced that Hitler was out to destroy Germany, his loyalty did not waver. Guderian's loyalty never wavered at all, but it was to the army and to Germany that his loyalty was directed. Yet he was associated with Hitler from the very beginning until almost the end. Guderian judged Hitler's willpower to be his most outstanding quality; by it 'he compelled men to follow him'. His principal failing as Supreme Commander – and the criticism is fitting from so brilliant an exponent of blitzkrieg – in Guderian's opinion was that he did not match the boldness of his strategic vision with a comparable boldness in its execution. If he had planned more carefully and then acted with more single-minded speed, results might have been different. But when Guderian points out that Hitler turned upside-down Moltke's formula, namely to weigh the considerations first, then take the risks, he forgets Hitler's whole concept of blitzkrieg, which was that by taking huge risks and backing them with huge force, considerations would take care of themselves. This inverted formula worked in France; then, when Churchill's and Britain's defiance made it clear that only a very different strategy involving long preparations could wrest decision from stalemate there, the same formula was applied to Russia; there, however, his strategy, 'lacking in consistency and subject to continual vacillation in execution', crashed in ruins. To Guderian, the Führer was

> a man lacking wisdom and moderation . . . going in solitary haste from success to success and then pressing on from failure to failure, his head full of stupendous plans, clinging ever more frantically to the last vanishing prospects of victory . . . with a fanatic's intensity he grasped at every straw which he imagined might save himself and his work from destruction. His entire and very great will-power was devoted to this one idea which was now all that pre-occupied him – never to give in, never to surrender.'

Most of those entitled to an opinion worth heeding as to Hitler's conduct of affairs as Führer of the Third Reich – whether his contemporaries or not, whether acquainted with him or not, whether soldiers, politicians, historians, civil servants or academics, of whatever nationality – condemn this conduct root and branch. General Halder called him: 'This demoniac man was no soldier leader in the German sense. And above all he was not a great General.' 'A thousand years will pass' (the predicted era of the Third Reich itself) said Hans Frank, the Nazi Governor-General of Poland, not long before he was hanged at Nuremberg, 'and the guilt of Germany will not be erased.' Another general, Brauchitsch, in contemplating the Führer's evil genius, declared that 'Hitler was the fate of Germany and this fate could not be stayed.' Even Albert Speer, who had at one time thought of Hitler as his friend, and even though he recognized the dreadful finale to which Hitler's policies were leading, did nothing to hinder them until right at the end, tried to explain the Nazi phenomenon away by claiming that the German people were spellbound by Hitler, that he and he alone determined the nation's fate. Yet even the story of Hitler and the Third Reich has its revisionists.[1] More than thirty years ago Alan Clark wrote of Hitler that 'No truly objective historian could refrain from admiring this man. His capacity for mastering detail, his sense of History, his retentive memory, his strategic vision – all these had flaws, but they were brilliant nonetheless.' And more recently, as we have seen, Mr Clark has – for what reason is still unclear – been trying to persuade us that Britain should have made peace with Hitler in 1941, putting aside altogether his policy of exterminating the Jews and other 'sub-humans' (it may be noted here that David Irving still maintains that Hitler knew nothing of the Holocaust, and challenges all comers to produce written evidence that he did). Bernard Levin, in an article in *The Times* on 9 August 1996, tells of a wealthy Swiss banker, François Genoud, who made known before his death his opinion of Hitler: 'He was my hero. He still is. He will remain one of the greatest men of our time.' As might be expected, Levin's condemnation of Genoud is almost as total as general condemnation of the Nazi dictator himself, yet the point about Hitler's great-

[1] In 1986 Reinhard Spitzy, who served in the German Diplomatic Corps, was at one time one of Ribbentrop's personal assistants, and later joined the Intelligence Service, published a book called *So haben wir das Reich verspielt* (*Thus We Gambled Away the Reich*), which has had a great success in Germany, but has not, as far as I know, been translated into English, nor published here. Spitzy was often in Hitler's company, and shows how kind and considerate Hitler could be when he chose. After a long journey to see and report to the Führer, Spitzy finds Hitler asking whether he has had breakfast, and then ordering some for him. When he learns of Spitzy's engagement to an English girl, he is thoroughly sympathetic. When they go to Vienna after the Anschluss, Hitler tells Spitzy he must go and see his parents there. The fact is, of course, that Hitler could readily switch from being brutal and cynical to being charming and courteous. He was, as Alan Bullock put it, a consummate actor. Yet his political ruthlessness and lust for power and conquest have obscured his undoubted capacity for personal kindness to his staff and associates.

ness is one that even the most distinguished and authoritative of our historians have found themselves obliged to acknowledge.

Trevor-Roper confirms that Hitler believed in 'historical greatness', something which was to him 'more important than the happiness or survival of a people; and he conceived of himself as a great man, – in which he was surely not mistaken; for it is absurd to suggest that one who made such a stir in the world was of ordinary stature. The Germans accepted him as the Messiah for whom they were waiting, and in the hours of his apparent success they sacrificed their political institutions to him; for they believed not in them, but in the man.' Trevor-Roper also gives it as his view that Hitler's military talents were by no means contemptible. He emphasizes the width of Hitler's knowledge, his mastery of detail, and points once more to the results he achieved against the professionals' advice. Alan Bullock, too, points out that in 1940 Hitler had achieved in a matter of four weeks what the Kaiser and the Imperial German Army had failed to achieve in four years; that he alone had insisted on the French Army's rottenness and the certainty of rapid successes in the west; that he had seized on Manstein's plan and Guderian's tactics and forced their adoption against powerful professional doubts and fears; that he had built the Wehrmacht which made victory possible. 'If Hitler, therefore, is justly to be made responsible for the later disasters of the German Army, he is entitled to the major share of the credit for the victories of 1940; the German generals cannot have it both ways.' But, Bullock goes on, it was this very victory, the most startling of German arms, which was his undoing, for having ignored the professional soldiers' advice once and triumphed, he never again allowed himself to be swayed by them against his own inclination. His greater grasp of political matters had never been in doubt; after 1940 there seemed to be no doubt either about his superior judgement in strategy and tactics. We might almost observe that the German General Staff had only themselves to blame, for had they supported Hitler's strategic and tactical ideas more enthusiastically during the years of conquest, they might have been able to influence him more easily during the years of resistance; ironically enough, it was while Hitler was creating the image of his own infallibility that his strategic gambles came off, and it was once he began, despite much evidence to the contrary, wholly to believe in himself that he and the Wehrmacht began to falter. What must perhaps still puzzle us is that while winning, he seemed as able to combine brilliant discernment at one moment with crass stupidity at the next, as he did when he was losing. As war lord he brooks no rival.

In a somewhat gloomy, though nevertheless compelling, article which appeared in *The Times* in April 1995, William Rees-Mogg asks the question: 'Was Hitler the true shaper of our destiny?' He maintains that world history for the last fifty years is simply the result of the Second World War, and that 'the four men who framed our modern world were Hitler, Roosevelt, Stalin and Churchill'. While agreeing that Churchill's actions in 1940 were decisive, in that but for them, Hitler might have won, defeating Russia and coming to some accommodation with the United States, Lord Rees-Mogg suggests that the enduring significance of these four men will be in the order in which their names appear above. Thus he suggests that although 'Winston Churchill was probably the most admirable' of the four, he was the 'least important'. He gives his reasons thus: whereas 'Churchill has faded because the British Empire has vanished, Stalin has faded with the break-up of the Soviet Union, and even Roosevelt's memory is in decline because power is shifting away from the United States . . .' but in spite of Hitler's utter failure and his repudiation by the German people, yet 'I do not believe the influence of Hitler is finished'. Lord Rees-Mogg goes on to say: 'In the 21st century, there is a danger that the world will find that Roosevelt and Churchill are figures of purely historic significance, that the nihilism of Hitler's anger and hatred can still threaten the order of human society. More than the other leaders', his evil spirit may still prove to be a living force.' It is a melancholy reflection, and one that Hitler would have relished. He would have been equally gratified, while acknowledging it as no more than his right, to have seen his name coupled with that of Alexander the Great, of whom Cyril Connolly wrote that he had 'a Hitlerian gift of involving whole nations in his destiny, through their willing acceptance of his self-styled divinity. He heads all lists of conquerors.' Yet Hitler's name would not be far below. Was he perhaps last of the German conquerors? If so, if he helped to persuade his self-adopted country to renounce for ever the use of force as a means of national policy, then he may in spite of everything have done the state some service. This service will not compensate for his tyrannical exercise of power, the vicious acts of revenge, the blood lust which seemed insatiable, the nihilism as an end in itself. We must in any case most profoundly hope that Lord Rees-Mogg may prove to be mistaken.

This hope is powerfully reinforced when we note what Alan Bullock has to say near the end of his masterly study: 'The passions which ruled Hitler's mind were ignoble: hatred, resentment, the lust to dominate, and, where he could not dominate, destroy. His career did not exalt but debased the human condition.' How different, John Keegan tells us, was Churchill: 'Churchill was moved by a passion for liberty and moral grandeur which his own country, first, and then the alliance of the English-speaking democracies, epitomized. His moral sense and almost mystical patriotism shine forth from every passage of [Martin] Gilbert's books, illuminating every great decision he took.' Here I will borrow a phrase once employed by that great scholar of Arab history, Albert Hourani: 'I like people with simple hearts and complicated minds' – surely the best of all coalitions. Churchill had a simple heart and a complicated mind. Hitler had no heart and a demoniac mind – of all coalitions the worst.

Both men made world history. Dr Charmley has conceded that Churchill 'altered the history of the world and that can't be said of any Prime Minister since'. Churchill did so by opposing Hitler, who according to Donald Watt 'Willed, wanted, craved war and the desolation brought by war. He did not want the war he got.' But it was the war he got which also changed the history of the world. At the head of Chapter 2 I quoted Disraeli's judgement that 'Youth is a blunder; Manhood a struggle; Old Age a regret.' For Hitler youth *was* a blunder; for Churchill a glorious adventure. For both men manhood was a struggle. Hitler did not reach old age; Churchill did. It was emphatically not a regret. Macbeth, it will be remembered, declared that 'that which should accompany old age' was made up of 'honour, love, obedience, troops of friends'. How fitting, how agreeable, how rewarding it is to record that Churchill was accompanied by all of these inestimably precious things – to the very end.

30 January 1965

Just as Churchill's life, as we have seen from these pages, had been a pageant of achievement, so his funeral was a pageant of homage. As the commanding officer of his old regiment (originally the 4th Hussars, by this time renamed the Queen's Royal Irish Hussars – Churchill had been Colonel of both) I took part in the ceremony with my regimental comrades. We formed a Vigil Party for the Lying-in-State in Westminster Hall; we carried his insignia and standards in the funeral procession; the Trumpet-Major, Sergeant King, sounded Reveille in St Paul's Cathedral; and a Bearer Party took the Colonel of the Regiment on his last journey from Waterloo Station to Bladon in Oxfordshire, and in the churchyard there laid him to rest. Those of us who took part in that day will never forget it. There is no other army in the world (and never has been) that could, under the splendid guidance and direction of the Household Division, have produced the dignity, solemnity, drilled perfection and sheer emotion of the procession from Parliament Square to St Paul's, the Dead March from *Saul* played by innumerable bands, the servicemen with reversed arms lining the streets, and behind them Churchill's people, silent, grave, some weeping, all filled with pride and awe. For those of us slow-marching in the procession who had been members of his regiment and had been presented to him both during the war and at later regimental occasions, there was a very special participatory elation. Churchill had joined the 4th Hussars in 1895, had soldiered with them in India, played in the winning regimental polo team, charged at Omdurman (albeit with another regiment), become their Colonel in the dark days of 1941 after serious losses in Greece, visited them no fewer than four times in war, attended their dinners and parades in peace, stayed on as Colonel after amalgamation with the 8th Hussars, and symbolized their twin mottoes, *Pristinae Virtutis Memores* and *Mente et Manu* as no other man ever had or could. He had been, as one former commanding officer, Lieutenant-Colonel Sir George Kennard, had put it, the greatest Hussar of them all. Back in our barracks in Germany a few days later, we held our own simple and brief Drumhead Memorial Service, and during it I was able to remind the regiment of the words with which Sir Isaiah Berlin had completed his infinitely rich miniature, *Mr Churchill in 1940*:

A man larger than life, composed of bigger and simpler elements than ordinary men, a gigantic historical figure during his own lifetime, superhumanly bold, strong and imaginative, one of the two greatest men of action his nation has produced, an orator of prodigious powers, the saviour of his country, a mythical hero who belongs to legend as much as to reality, the largest human being of our time.

Select Bibliography

BERLIN, ISAIAH, *Mr Churchill in 1940*, London 1949

BLAKE, ROBERT and LOUIS, WM ROGER (eds), *Churchill* (essays), Oxford 1993

BONHAM CARTER, VIOLET, *Winston Churchill As I Knew Him* (1966 edition), London 1965

BRYANT, SIR ARTHUR, *The Lion and the Unicorn*, London 1969

BULLOCK, ALAN, *Hitler: A Study in Tyranny* (revised edition), London 1962

CHARMLEY, JOHN, *Churchill: The End of Glory*, London 1993

CHURCHILL, RANDOLPH S., *Winston S. Churchill*, Volume I *Youth 1874–1900*, London, 1966; Volume II *Young Statesman 1900–1914*, London 1967

CHURCHILL, WINSTON S., *The River War*, London 1899

—, *The World Crisis*, London 1923–31

—, *My Early Life*, London 1930

—, *Great Contemporaries*, London 1937

—, *The Second World War* (6 volumes), London 1949–54

CLARK, ALAN, *Barbarossa*, London 1965

COLVILLE, JOHN, *Footprints in Time*, London 1976

CRAIG, GORDON A., *Germany 1866–1945*, Oxford 1978

ENSOR, SIR ROBERT, *England 1870–1914*, Oxford 1936

FEST, JOACHIM, *The Face of the Third Reich*, London 1970

—, *Plotting Hitler's Death*, London 1996

FITZHERBERT, MARGARET, *The Man Who Was Greenmantle*, London

FRASER, DAVID, *Alanbrooke*, London 1982

GILBERT, MARTIN, *Winston S. Churchill*, Volume III *The Challenge of War, 1914–1916*; Volume IV *World in Torment, 1917–1922*; Volume V *Prophet of Truth, 1922–1939*; Volume VI *Finest Hour, 1939–1941*; Volume VII *Road to Victory, 1941–1945*; Volume VIII *'Never Despair', 1945–1965* – London 1971–88

GUDERIAN, GENERAL HEINZ, *Panzer Leader*, London 1952

HALDER, COLONEL-GENERAL FRANZ, *Hitler as War Lord*, London 1950

HITLER, ADOLF, *Mein Kampf*, London 1939

HOWARD, MICHAEL, *The Mediterranean Strategy in the Second World War* (*Grand Strategy*, vol. iv), London 1972

IRVING, DAVID, *Hitler's War* (revised edition), London 1991

JACKSON, GENERAL SIR WILLIAM, *The Battle for Italy*, London 1967

JONES, R.V., *Most Secret War*, London 1978

KEEGAN, JOHN, *The Face of Battle*, London 1976

—, *The Battle for History*, London 1995

MACDONALD, LYN, *They Called It Passchendaele*, London

MAJDALANY, FRED, *The Monastery*, London 1945

—, *Cassino: Portrait of a Battle*, London 1957

MONTAGUE BROWNE, ANTHONY, *Long Sunset*, London 1995

MORRIS, JAMES (JAN), *Farewell the Trumpets*, London 1978

NICOLSON, NIGEL (ed.), *Harold Nicolson: Diaries and Letters*, Volume I *1930–39*; Volume II *1939–45*; Volume III *1945–61*, London 1966–8

RANFURLY, HERMIONE, COUNTESS OF, *To the War with Whitaker*, London 1994

RAUSCHNING, HERMANN, *Hitler Speaks*, London 1939

ROBERTS, ANDREW, *Eminent Churchillians*, London 1994

SHIRER, WILLIAM L., *Berlin Diary*, London 1941

SPEER, ALBERT, *Erinnerungen*, Berlin 1969

—, *Inside the Third Reich*, London 1970

SPITZY, REINHARD, *So haben wir das Reich verspielt*, Munich 1986

STONE, NORMAN, *Hitler*, London 1980

TAYLOR, A.J.P., *English History 1914–1945*, Oxford 1965

Trevor-Roper, H.R. (ed.), *Hitler's War Directives 1939–1945*, London 1964

—, *The Last Days of Hitler* (4th edition), London 1971

VERCORS (JEAN BRULLER), *The Battle of Silence*, London 1968

WILMOT, CHESTER, *The Struggle for Europe*, London 1952

WOODRUFF, PHILIP, *The Men Who Ruled India*, Volume II *The Guardians*, London 1954

Index

Martin, John (Churchill's private secretary), 365
Mawdsley, James, 36
Maximos, Greek royalist, 460
Maxton, James, 339
Maze, Paul, 292
Mediterranean campaign/strategy, 11–12, 279, 285, 286, 287, 288, 289, 292, 294, 296, 298, 300, 301, 302, 303, 304–5, 306, 307, 310, 314, 329, 330–1, 344, 345–6, 352, 357, 364, 367–9, 370, 371, 372, 373, 378, 380–1, 383, 387–8, 389, 391, 392, 393, 398, 399–400, 418, 438, 506
Meinertzhagen, Colonel Richard, 159
Melbourne, Lord, 43, 48, 171
Memel, 224, 466; German annexation of, 226
merchant shipping, 244, 250, 289, 293, 304, 308, 311–12, 343, 366, 371; convoys, 116, 238, 246, 285, 310, 320, 323, 327, 351, 366, 369, 380, 394
Mesopotamia, 139 &n, 143, 146, 153, 154, 155, 156; see also Iraq
Methuen, General Lord, 42
Metternich, Count, 67
Meux, Admiral of the Fleet Sir Hedworth, 108–9
Middle East, 10–11, 13, 140, 153, 154–9, 160, 240, 276, 279, 283–6, 288, 289, 292, 293, 295, 296, 297, 298, 300, 305–12, 313, 314, 320, 321–2, 324, 327–9, 330–1, 338, 339, 340, 344, 345, 346–7, 350, 352–4, 359–64, 375, 506
Mikolajcik, Stanislaw, 408
Mildmay, Lord, 168
Military Service Act (1916), 104–5
Milne, General Sir George, 147
Milner, Sir Alfred (Lord), 37, 54n, 112, 114, 140
Milton, John, 14–15
Minney, R.J., 220
Model, Field Marshal Walther, 355, 433, 434, 440, 454, 455, 461, 467, 476, 480
Mohnke, Brigadier, 493
Molotov, Vyacheslav, 229–30, 299, 348, 349, 478
Monro, General Sir Charles, 91, 101–2
Montagu, Edwin, 94, 148
Monte Cassino, 412, 422; see also Cassino
Montgomery, Field Marshal Bernard, 305, 354–5, 358, 359, 360–2, 364, 377–8, 379, 382, 389, 390, 395, 400, 402–3, 407, 418, 420–1, 424, 425, 428, 429, 432, 435, 440, 445, 452–3, 455, 461, 467, 469, 472, 477, 478, 479, 481–2, 485, 494, 496, 505; *The History of Warfare*, 420–1
Morell, Dr Theodor, 225, 456
Morgan, Lieut-General Sir Frederick, 402n
Morgenthau, Henry, 447
Morgenthau Plan, 447 &n
Morley, John, 59
Morning Post, 37, 40, 41, 81–2, 114, 121, 170
Morocco, 62–3, 202, 298–9, 328
Morris, James (Jan), 39, 88, 91, 158, 340; *Farewell the Trumpets*, xi, 154
Morrison, Herbert, 272, 295
Morton, Major Desmond, 198
Moscow, 313, 317, 318, 319, 324, 325, 338
Moscow Conference (1942), 357–8
Moscow Conference 'Tolstoy' (1944), 448, 449–51
Mosley, Sir Oswald, 263 &n
Mountbatten, Vice-Admiral Lord Louis, 65, 72, 82, 344, 348, 358, 389, 394, 414, 435, 446, 449
Mulberry floating harbour, 414
Munich, 70, 123, 126–36, 178
Munich Agreement (1938), 193n, 215, 220, 222–4, 225
Munich Putsch (8–9 Nov., 1923), 131–2, 190
Mussolini, Benito, 200, 201, 217–18, 223, 257, 274–5, 284, 287, 288, 298–9, 346–7, 383, 394, 431; Hitler's relations with, 217–18, 274, 276, 298–9, 302, 304, 307, 337; Hitler's meeting at Feltre with (1943), 385; replaced as Prime Minister by Marshal Badoglio, 385–6, 387; rescued from Abruzzi mountains by Skorzeny, 391; nominal head of Italian Socialist Republic, 391, 479; shot by Italian partisans, 494

Napier, Sir William, 32
Napoleon I Bonaparte, 1, 10, 48, 82, 114, 175, 196, 207, 291, 298, 326, 337, 442, 489, 503
Narvik, 245 &n, 248–9, 250
Nazi Party (National Socialist German Workers' Party: NSDAP), 57, 69, 70, 74, 125, 126, 127, 128 &n, 130, 131, 133, 134, 135 &n, 178, 181, 190, 439
Nazi-Soviet Pact of Non-Aggression (1939), 229–30 &n
Nelson, Admiral Horatio, Lord, 1, 10, 114, 162, 499